Who's Who
IN EUROPE 1450–1750

THE ROUTLEDGE WHO'S WHO SERIES

Accessible, authoritative and enlightening, these are the definitive
biographical guides to a diverse range of subjects drawn from literature
and the arts, history and politics, religion and mythology.

Who's Who
IN EUROPE
1450–1750

Henry Kamen

London and New York

First published 2000
by Routledge
11 New Fetter Lane, London EC4P 4EE

Simultaneously published in the USA and Canada
by Routledge
29 West 35th Street, New York, NY 10001

First published in paperback 2002

Routledge is an imprint of the Taylor & Francis Group

Typeset in Sabon by Routledge
Printed and bound in Great Britain by
Biddles Ltd, Guildford and King's Lynn

British Library Cataloguing in Publication Data
A catalogue record for this book is available from the British Library

Library of Congress Cataloging in Publication Data
A catalogue record for this book has beeen requested

ISBN 0–415–14727–1 (Hbk)
ISBN 0–415–14728–X (Pbk)

Contents

Contributors

Dr Judith Etzion, Department of Musicology, Bar Ilan University, Ramat Gan, Israel [JE]

Gabrielle Greenwood, Hallward Library, University of Nottingham, England [GG]

Professor Jane Campbell Hutchison, Department of Art History, Elvehjem Museum of Art, University of Wisconsin-Madison, Madison, Wisconsin, USA [JH]

Professor John A. Marino, Department of History, University of California at San Diego, La Jolla, California, USA [JM]

Professor R.B. Tate, Department of Hispanic Studies, University of Nottingham, England [BT]

Dr Frances Willmoth, Department of History and Philosophy of Science, University of Cambridge, England [FW]

Preface

This book is intended to be a quick reference source for scholars, students and members of the wider reading public. It aims to cover a notable gap in early modern studies, where there already exist specialised biographical dictionaries for certain disciplines, but none exists for those wishing to look at all disciplines. The work is directed in the first instance to historians, and lesser emphasis is given, for example, to explanations of art or literature. On the other hand, students of art or literature will also find information on persons mentioned in their reading about the period.

Shortcomings in any such compilation are inevitable. Like the other contributors to the volume, I have spent much time mulling over the entries and hope that this gives me the privilege of being able to add a brief personal note. I have come to think of the entries affectionately as 'Kamen's One Thousand', but of course they are not mine by choice, since many are there because their claim was undeniable and others, possibly more deserving, are not there because I reluctantly edged them out. Many popes and queens and saints have been erased; and because it was a man's world the male gender dominates. Every now and then, however, as compiler I felt that in the midst of the terrible conflicts of the early modern world I had come across names with whom I would as lief have tarried awhile: I name, at random, John Evelyn diligent in his garden in Deptford, an unhurried Lady Mary Wortley Montagu relaxing in the sunshine of the Mediterranean, Richard Baxter preaching in Restoration England.

The choice of names was in some measure arbitrary. Persons from the Ottoman Empire, which occupied part of Europe at the time, have been excluded; but a Barbary corsair has been allowed in. Persons of European origin but whose careers were almost entirely spent outside Europe (such as Pedro de Valdivia or Cotton Mather) have not been included; on the other hand, those whose careers linked Europe with the outside world (such as Cortés and Hudson) have been accepted.

The major problem has been over whether to give names in their original or their English form, and how to reconcile the usage of different countries. As a rough rule, names have been given according to the most common use in scholarly English books. Apparent inconsistencies, such as using both 'Margaret' and 'Marguerite', follow from the established form employed for each person in scholarly studies. The family name Medici has different national forms, which have been respected. Non-English titles of books, paintings and other creative works are normally given in English translation only, except where the work is probably better known by its original title (as in some works of literature), or where it appears more informative to offer both the original and a translation (to show, for example, that the work was published only in Latin). Entries are normally given by family name or by first name or by title; some complex names (De La Court, for example) are given with the 'de' first. In a very few cases, the original form of the name is given in parentheses after the English form used in the entry. Cross-referenced items are indicated in small capitals.

The project could not have reached fruition without the very valuable expertise of my fellow contributors, who undertook a task that certainly occupied more time than they expected and who have, I trust, enjoyed as much as I did the company of our friends in the past.

Henry Kamen

A

Abravanel, Isaac (1437–1508) Jewish leader. A Jewish family that rose to prominence in fourteenth-century Spain, when some converted to Christianity, the Abravanels were also settled in Lisbon, where Isaac was born, son of the financier Judah. From a young age he showed great interest in philosophy and biblical studies, but followed his father's calling as a financier to the Portuguese crown. Political troubles in Portugal obliged him in 1483 to flee to Castile, where he determined to spend his life in study; but by 1484 he was attracted into the service of Ferdinand and Isabella, to whom he advanced considerable sums to help finance the wars against the Muslims of Granada. He was also given control of the important tax on sheep-herding. His rise to influence occurred at the very time that the Inquisition in Spain was conducting an anti-Semitic campaign against converted Jews, and demonstrates the resilience of religious attitudes at that time. When in 1492 a royal decree ordered the conversion or expulsion of Spain's Jews, he refused to convert and left the country with his family for Naples. Special permission was granted for him to take a quantity of gold and valuables with him. Though they entered the service of the crown of Naples, the stay of the Abravanels there was made difficult by sporadic persecution, mainly at the instigation of the invading French. Eventually they moved to settle in 1503 in Venice, where Isaac died. During these last years he devoted himself to his philosophic writings, in particular to messianic reflections (in a trilogy written from 1496 onwards) on the historic destiny of his persecuted people. Some of his biblical commentaries were published in Hebrew in the early 1500s in Venice.

Acarie, Barbe (Jeanne Avrillot), in religion Marie de l'Incarnation (1566–1618) founder of the Carmelite order in France. Born into a leading family of the Paris robe nobility, from an early age she showed a wish to enter religion, but her parents married her (1582) to a rich official, with whom she had six children. She continued her religious exercises within her married life, and also gave active political support to the Catholic League in Paris, but her family underwent travails as a result of the civil wars of those years. Immediately after the coming of peace, she made her residence the centre for reunions of like-minded adepts of religious mysticism, among them the English priest Benedict of Canfield, the future chancellor Michel de MARILLAC, the king's confessor father Coton and cardinal BÉRULLE. She arranged for the introduction into Paris of the reformed Carmelites from Spain (1604), an important step that initiated the Catholic reform movement in France; in total nineteen Carmelite convents were in existence when she died. Her support for

FRANCIS DE SALES and Jeanne de CHANTAL was also crucial in the establishment of several other religious orders. On her husband's death in 1613, she retired as a nun to the convent in Amiens. She was beatified in 1791.

Acontius, Jacob (Jacopo Aconcio) (*c.* 1500–*c.*66) engineer and writer. Born in Trent, he apparently studied law, then became a Protestant and in 1557–8 was in the Swiss lands; he went to England in about 1559, and became naturalised there (1561). He practised as an engineer, helping in land reclamation schemes, and was patronised by the earl of LEICESTER. A liberal thinker in religious matters, in 1565 he published at Basel in Latin his *Satanae Stratagemata*, which distinguished between essential and peripheral beliefs in Christianity, held that disputes among Christians over doctrine were the stratagems of Satan, and spoke against the use of the death penalty by the secular power for the religious offence of heresy. Freedom of belief was essential; it would lead to diversity of opinions, but 'truth will prevail, and falsehood will be vanquished', thus defeating the wiles of Satan. The first English translation, in 1648, with a preface addressed to Cromwell, was highly influential in promoting ideas favourable to religious toleration; other editions came out in French (1565), German (1647) and Dutch (1662).

Acosta, José de (1540–1600) Spanish missionary and writer. Of Jewish descent, he entered the Jesuits when young, studied at Salamanca, was ordained priest 1566 and taught in the colleges of the society. In 1571 he was sent to work in Peru, and stayed there fifteen years, becoming provincial of the Jesuits, and working both for Church reform and for the conversion of the Indians. He strongly opposed the policies of the colonial government towards the natives. In 1587 he went to Mexico and then returned to Spain, where he played an active part in Jesuit politics,

and in 1593 became rector of the college in Salamanca. An indefatigable writer, his major works dealt with aspects of Indian society and with the natural environment of the New World: *De procuranda Indorum salute* (On the Salvation of the Indians) (1588) argued for greater liberty for the native Indians, and the *Historia natural y moral de las Indias* (Natural and Moral History of the Indians) (1590) was a pioneering ethnological survey of the great Amerindian cultures and of the Incas in particular.

Acquaviva, Claudio (1543–1615) fifth and youngest general of the Society of Jesus. The youngest son of the duke of Atri, he joined the order in 1567, became provincial of Naples (his native land) and was elected general of the order in 1581. His term of office was marked by the rapid growth of the Jesuits from about 5,000 to more than 13,000 members and from 21 to 32 provinces. He initiated the drawing up of annual reports of all the provinces, and supervised the elaboration of a practical code of education for Jesuit schools, the *Ratio atque institutio studiorum* (Programme of Studies) (1586).

Adam, Robert (1728–92) Scots architect active in London. Son of the architect William Adam, he and his older brother James (1730–94) created the 'Adam style' of neo-classical architecture that replaced the Palladian in popularity *c.*1770. Robert, educated at Edinburgh University and later in Rome, where he became a member of the Academy of St Luke (1754), had also travelled in France, and visited Spalato, later publishing *Ruins of the Palace of the Emperor Diocletian at Spalato* (1764), an important contribution to the archaeology of the Roman Empire. Settling in London (1758) he was appointed one of the two Architects of the King's Works (1761). However, the Adam brothers are best remembered for their designs for country houses, including Luton Hoo, Croome Court, Kenwood House and

Osterley Park, distinguished by their convenient floor plans and delicately coloured ornament – this last being lost in transition to the United States, where Adam influence was spread by means of the black-and-white illustrations in their three-volume publication, *Works in Architecture of Robert and James Adam* (London, 1773–1822) and where Adam ornamentation was recreated in white plaster.

[JH]

Addison, Joseph (1672–1719) English essayist. The son of the dean of Lichfield, he studied at Queen's College, Oxford, then toured the continent (1699–1703), spending over a year each in France and Italy. From 1704 he occupied administrative posts, and in 1709 entered Parliament as MP for Malmesbury, a seat he held for life; that year he also went to Ireland as under-secretary. He was already deeply involved in controversial writing in defence of the Whigs. After the fall of the Whigs in 1710, he turned to journalism, and as a member of the Kit-Cat Club he renewed his friendship with an old schoolfellow Richard Steele and made a new one with Jonathan SWIFT. He collaborated with Richard Steele in the weekly *Tatler* (1709), and joined with him in 1711–12 to publish the yet more influential *Spectator*. Politically neutral, the journal gained success through its humour and literary criticism. Addison also turned his hand to the theatre: his musical play *Rosamund* was a moderate success, his tragedy *Cato* a great one and his prose comedy *The Drummer* a failure. It is his skill as a journalist that earns Addison his place in English literature. His essays, written in pure elegant prose and dealing with the manners, morals and concerns of the day, appealed to the emerging middle class and provided a model for contributors to periodicals up to the end of the eighteenth century. In 1715 he returned to political office with the Whigs, and in 1716 married the countess of Warwick.

[GG & HK]

Adrian VI (Adrian Dedel of Utrecht, 1459–1523) pope 1522–3. Born at Utrecht, he studied at Deventer and the university of Louvain, where he was ordained, taught theology, and served as chancellor and rector. He was a humanistically inclined scholar and reformer sympathetic to ERASMUS and VIVES, with a reputation for austerity and high moral character. Appointed tutor to the future CHARLES V in 1507, he subsequently served Charles in Spain as bishop of Tortosa in 1516, grand inquisitor, cardinal in 1517, and eventually the emperor's regent. His compromise election *in absentia* was probably influenced by the recent election of Charles as emperor and his own moral reputation. His attempts at curial reform and his approach to win the allegiance of ZWINGLI rather than condemning the Zürich reformer outright reflected his recognition of the need for clerical and episcopal reform. Both the curia and the Roman populace opposed his actions and his brief twenty-one month reign doomed Adrian's reformist intentions as he failed to negotiate peace between Charles V and FRANCIS I, to stop the Lutheran movement, to keep Zwingli within the Church and to reform the Roman curia. The reform of the Church from above could not be accomplished by the sincerity of a short-lived, foreign pope alone, but awaited almost two more decades of political and religious developments within and outside of the Church before the climate for reform could take hold.

[JM]

Agreda, María Jesús de (1602–65) Spanish nun. Born María Coronel, she spent all her life in the little town of Agreda (Aragon), by whose name she has become known. Her family, of lesser nobility in standing, was religious to a fault, and when she was sixteen her parents turned their household into a convent and all the children took religious vows. María quickly acquired fame for her supernatural revelations, became abbess of the family convent in 1627, and in 1633 transferred the community to a new convent outside the town. It was there that the king, PHILIP IV, visited her in 1643 during one of his journeys, thus initiating a life-long relationship of great importance and interest. The correspondence between the nun and the king (published in 1885) demonstrates that she came to exercise a profound influence over Philip, advising him on the very smallest concerns of state, while on his side he unburdened his personal concerns to her. Her principal published work, rewritten by her in 1655 after several problems with early manuscript versions, which were burnt in 1649, was the *Mística ciudad de Dios* (Mystical City of God). This was published posthumously in 1670 in Madrid, but immediately attracted adverse reactions among sections of the clergy, leading the Inquisition to ban the book for a period (1672–86). Thereafter the work achieved great popularity, with over 100 printings over the next century, but continued to be under suspicion by authorities in the Church (mainly in France and Rome) who feared possible Quietist overtones to Sor María's mysticism.

Agricola, Georg (1494–1555) humanist scholar, called the father of mineralogy for his empirical studies of mining and metallurgy. Born Georg Bauer in Saxony, he studied the humanist curriculum at the university of Leipzig from 1514–18 and taught Latin and Greek in Zwickau from 1518–22. In 1523 he moved to Italy, where he studied medicine, natural science and philosophy at Bologna and Padua, and completed clinical studies in Venice. At Venice he worked for the Aldine Press in preparing the 1525 edition of Galen and made acquaintance with ERASMUS and John Clement (Thomas MORE's former secretary). In 1526 he returned to Saxony

where he served as town physician in Joachimsthal (1527–33) and Chemnitz (1533–55), as burgomaster of Chemnitz in 1546 and briefly as diplomatic envoy between MAURICE of Saxony and CHARLES V, while he pursued his studies in the observation and classification of minerals. In 1530 he published his first treatise on metals, which contained an introduction by Erasmus. Later works culminating in his posthumous magnum opus, *De re metallica* (On Metallurgy) (1556), established his reputation as an innovator in the experimental approach to natural science willing to challenge ancient wisdom. His work surveyed a wide range of topics on metals and mining: classical allusions and ancient techniques, the geology of ore deposits and their origins from aqueous solution, the system of law, ownership and management of Saxon mines, assaying ores and smelting metals.

[JM]

Agrippa of Nettesheim, Cornelius (1486–1535) German humanist and occult philosopher who moved easily in Germany, Italy and France during the Reformation era as a moderate Erasmian with vague ideas on evangelical religious reform. Born in Cologne, he lectured on the Kabbalistic works of REUCHLIN at Dôle in 1509 and became both a doctor of law and medicine at Pavia in 1512. Agrippa was an orator and public defender at Metz, served as physician to the queen mother of France, Louise of Savoy, in 1524, became an imperial historiographer under CHARLES V in 1529, and worked in the court of the reformist archbishop of Cologne 1532–5. His major work, *De occulta philosophia* (On Occult Philosophy) (first complete edition, 1533) laid out his position that magic was the best way to know God and nature. It explored all aspects of the philosophical–magical tradition – Orphic hymns, hermetic learning, Kabbala, Pythagorean numerology, Platonic dialogues, and Neoplatonic writings – and was the principal source for the Faust legend. In the course of his studies, however, Agrippa began to have doubts concerning man's ability to attain truth and included in this final edition portions of his earlier 1530 treatise, 'On the uncertainty and vanity of the arts and sciences'. One of the early statements of Renaissance scepticism that later may have influenced MONTAIGNE, this sharply critical attack on learning got him in trouble with the Cologne inquisitor who banished him from Germany in 1535.

[JM]

Alba, Fernando Álvarez de Toledo, 3rd duke of (1507–82) Spanish general. Born into an illustrious family and orphaned at the age of three, he dedicated himself from the age of seventeen to a military career. In 1535 he accompanied CHARLES V on the expedition to Tunis, and from that time served in the emperor's armies. He entered the Spanish council of state (1545) and became the crown's principal adviser on politics and war. In 1547 he led the Imperial forces to victory over the Schmalkaldic league (battle of Mühlberg, 1547), but later failed to capture Metz (1552–3). The emperor recommended him, though with reservations, to PHILIP II who consulted him closely on all affairs; but Alba had to contend with the rival influence of the prince of EBOLI. Viceroy of Naples from 1556 to 1559, he invaded the Papal States and successfully browbeat the pope. His most difficult task was his appointment as governor of the Netherlands (1567), with orders to control heresy and rebellion there. Arriving in Brussels with 10,000 troops, he instituted a ruthless policy of repression, using as his judicial instrument a specially appointed council of Troubles, nicknamed the council of Blood. Among its executed victims were the counts of EGMONT and HORNES (1568). From 1572 the provinces, aided by the Sea Beggars, rose in rebellion and frustrated Alba's attempt to subdue through terror. He was withdrawn by Philip II in 1573. Shortly after his return,

he and his family had to withdraw from court because of an impolitic marriage by his son don Fadrique. He was called out of retirement in order to lead the Spanish invasion of Portugal in 1580, a task he completed successfully despite bad health and his advanced years. He died in the royal palace at Lisbon.

Alberoni, Giulio (1664–1752) chief miniter of Spain. Born in Piacenza of humble origins, he determined to advance himself by studying, and in 1690 was ordained priest, served first in a country parish then went to Rome, where he picked up and mastered the French language. He met the duke de Vendôme in Parma, entered his service and returned with him to France and then to Spain (1711), where he succeeded in being appointed agent of the duke of Parma in Madrid. He negotiated the marriage of the duke's daughter Elizabeth FARNESE, with PHILIP V, and profited from the new queen's favour to establish his own influence. He became chief minister of Spain (1716) and cardinal (1717), and promoted a policy of aggression by Spain in the western Mediterranean, with attacks on Sardinia (1717) and Sicily (1718). In 1719 he was abruptly dismissed from office by the king, and went to live in Italy, where he entered the papal service and directed the draining of the marshes in Romagna.

Albert of Austria, archduke (1559–1621) Sixth son of the emperor MAXIMILIAN II and of Maria, sister of PHILIP II of Spain, he went to Spain with his brother Wenzel in 1570, at a time when the son-less Philip was considering the boys as candidates for his throne. Albert stayed on to pass his formative years in Spain. Later Philip proposed making him archbishop of Toledo, and in 1577 obtained a cardinalate for him. From 1583 to 1593 Albert served as viceroy of Portugal, also taking on the role of Inquisitor General of that realm. In 1593 he was called to Madrid to take over some administrative responsibility from the ailing Philip, and was also nominated archbishop of Toledo (1594). He had barely accepted these tasks when it was decided to appoint him governor of the Spanish Netherlands, with the Infanta ISABEL as his wife (the marriage was celebrated just after Philip's death, in 1598). From 1596 Albert was in the Netherlands, carrying out with great skill a military and diplomatic role. He helped SPINOLA to besiege Antwerp, and in 1609 negotiated and signed the Twelve Years' Truce between Spain and the United Provinces, which he attempted in vain to extend. In the early years of the Thirty Years War he took charge of the campaign in the Netherlands, with Spinola as general.

Albert of Brandenburg (1490–1545) German cardinal. Son of the elector of Brandenburg, he was brought up for a career in the Church, ordained priest (1513) and then appointed by his brother, the current elector, as archbishop of Magdeburg, to which he added shortly afterwards the post of archbishop and elector of Mainz, crowning these elevations with the rank of cardinal in 1518. By dint of these appointments, he became one of the most powerful princes of the Holy Roman Empire, and used his influence to help secure the imperial crown for CHARLES V in 1519. Thereafter he remained a key figure in German politics. At the same time, he was a firm supporter of humanist figures such as Ulrich von HUTTEN and REUCHLIN, and favoured the policy of peaceful reform advocated by the Erasmians. These attitudes made him adopt a moderate stance in the controversy surrounding LUTHER; he disapproved of any action against Luther that might precipitate an ideological split, and continued through the early 1530s with an ambiguous posture towards the Reformation. Not until about 1540 did he favour firm moves against the Protestant party, but at the same time he continued to back liberal

reformers and the changes proposed by the council of Trent.

Albert, margrave of Brandenburg-Ansbach (1490–1568) Third son of the Hohenzollern Frederick of Brandenburg-Ansbach, he was elected grand master of the Teutonic order of knights in 1511, but refused to swear allegiance to the king of Poland, overlord of the lands of the Prussian order, and was obliged to use both war and diplomacy to further his aims. Finally, after a visit to LUTHER in 1523, he realised that the secularisation of his states would offer a favourable solution, and prepared the way for freeing his lands from Catholic jurisdiction by allowing the entry of Lutheran preachers. In 1525, by the terms of the peace of Cracow agreed with Poland, he became the 1st duke of Prussia (1525–68), under Polish suzerainty. The diet of Königsberg (December 1525) passed new legislation establishing the forms of government in Prussia, and adopting the Reformation.

Albuquerque, Affonso d' (1453–1515) founder of the Portuguese empire in Asia. Of high noble stock, most of his early years were spent fighting the Muslims in north Africa, and he took part in the conquest of Tangiers in 1471. In 1503 he was first sent out to India, in the wake of previous voyages by GAMA and Cabral; on his second voyage (1507) he reconnoitred the Arab territories of Africa, and briefly captured Ormuz. At the end of 1509 he succeeded Francisco da Almeida as viceroy of the Portuguese forts in India, where he conquered several territories including Cochin and eventually Goa (1510). He then extended Portuguese settlements through Ceylon to the Moluccas, and reinforced the foothold in India by taking Calicut. He died at sea while returning to Goa from an expedition to Ormuz.

Alciato (Alciati), Andrea (1492–1550) The most outstanding Italian jurist of the Renaissance, his most influential book may have been his introductory text on emblematics, *Emblemata* (1531). Born in Milan, he won wide fame in a distinguished legal career that took him to a law chair at Avignon in 1518, Bourges between 1529 and 1533, and on to Bologna, Ferrara and Pavia where he died. As a scholar of civil law, Alciato applied the humanist study of philology and late antique history and literature to source criticism of the Justinian code, the *Corpus iuris civilis*. He investigated the layers of commentary on the *Corpus* to establish their historical origins. His studies undercut the statutes' claims to a timeless natural law by showing how commentaries reflected their contemporary circumstances. Traditionalists did not object to his studies because Alciato strengthened the *Corpus* by demonstrating the practical value of the glossators and by emphasising the relationship between legal principles and applications. The *Emblemata*, important for its moral aphorisms and ethical concerns, went through 170 editions and was widely translated as the pioneering study of an important Renaissance mode of knowledge.

[JM]

Alemán, Mateo (1547–?1615) Spanish novelist, son of a doctor. Little is known of Mateo Alemán's life: he was a civil servant and one-time inspector of mines, who spent a short spell in prison and then emigrated to Mexico. After 1615 all traces of him are lost. He is remembered as the author of the archetypal picaresque novel *Guzmán de Alfarache*, subtitled *Atalaya de la vida humana* (*A Bird's Eye View of Human Life*), part I 1599, part II 1604. By this latter date twenty Spanish editions had appeared, thus rivalling the popularity of *Don Quixote*. It signals the opening of a new horizon in fiction, in the form of a rambling large-scale first-person narrative told by the fictional author, a vagabond scoundrel or *pícaro*. The fictional author explains how his parents' life of crime had determined his own career. Scenes of low life flicker across Spain and

Italy and everywhere in raw detail human failings are exposed by this anti-hero who flanks his pessimism with extensive moral comments, added after his supposed reform. Man is held to be deeply stained by original sin; but this is not to say that the narrative is deterministic, since that original sin was committed out of free will. Both concepts are clearly linked. Technically the most significant element is the manipulation of a first person narrator who is both actor and commentator. The purpose of the narrative is explicitly didactic and exemplary; there are no mysteries, no shadowy areas. This pessimistic colouring is characteristic of Spanish Counter-Reformation literature.

[BT]

Alembert, Jean Le Rond, known as d' (1717–83) French mathematician. He was born in Paris out of wedlock and abandoned, but his father later spent care and money on educating him well. He was trained in law (but never practised), then moved to medicine, and finally settled on mathematics, which he largely taught himself. In 1739 he read his first paper to the Academy of Sciences, of which he became a member two years later. At the age of twenty six he published his *Traité de dynamique*, containing 'd'Alembert's principle', which states that Newton third law of motion (for every action there is an equal and opposite reaction) is true for bodies that are free to move as well as for bodies rigidly fixed. Other mathematical works followed, notably his *Traité de l'équilibre et du mouvement des fluides* (Treatise on the Balance and Flow of Fluids) (1744). This was followed by the development of partial differential equations, in a paper that won him a prize at the Berlin Academy, to which he was elected (1747). From 1761 he also published eight volumes of *Opuscules mathematiques*. But he was also deeply interested in social ideas, and from 1746 became associated with the preparation of the *Encyclopédie*, edited by Diderot, and wrote the introduction for the first publish-ed volume. His collaboration brought him into close contact with the other leading French philosophers of the day, and in 1756 he stayed with VOLTAIRE at Geneva in order to write his controversial article on that city. He also wrote influential essays on literature, and on music (*Éléments de musique*, 1752). He was elected to the French Academy in 1754, and became its permanent secretary in 1772. His complete works were published in several volumes in the early nineteenth century.

Alexander VI (Roderigo Borgia, *c*.1431–1503) pope 1492–1503. This Catalan-born nobleman's education in canon law at Bologna and numerous ecclesiastical benefices were provided by his uncle Alonso Borgia (the bishop of Valenica, favourite of Alfonso I of Aragon, and future pope Calixtus III, 1455–8). Roderigo rose rapidly during his uncle's pontificate: cardinal (1456), vice-chancellor of the Church, the highest office in papal administration (1457), and archbishop of Valencia (1458). As vice-chancellor of the Church for thirty-five years until his election to the papacy in 1492, he amassed an enormous fortune, patronised the arts, fathered numerous children, and lived the life of a Renaissance prince. Elected pope over his rival, Giuliano della Rovere (the later JULIUS II), he presided over papal politics during the first decade of the Italian Wars and manœuvred to establish a dynastic legacy for his family in Italy. Using his considerable administrative skill and energy, he initially attempted to re-form papal finances, to press war against the Ottoman Turks, and rather unsuccess-fully to restore order to the Papal States. He negotiated the Treaty of Tordesillas (1494), which divided the New World between Spain and Portugal and granted them royal control over the Church in their colonial conquests. While he success-fully resisted recognising CHARLES VIII's Angevin claim to Naples in the 1494–5

French invasions by enlisting the aid of the Ottoman emperor Bayezid II and allying with Milan, Venice and the Holy Roman Empire, he later supported LOUIS XII's 1499 French invasion in the hope of gaining political advantage over the other Italian states. He sponsored his son Ce-sare BORGIA's military campaigns into the Romagna in 1499–1503 and only Cesare's own illness at the time of Alexander's death thwarted their dynastic ambitions. Despised and maligned in his own time, he remains the symbol of the decadence of the Renaissance papacy, mired in lasci-vious living and shameless nepotism.

[JM]

Alexander VII (Fabio Chigi, 1599–1667) pope 1655–67. A member of an old, impecunious Sienese family, he was a dilettante scholar who liked to surround himself with men of real learning. He had a humanist education and trained in law and theology for the papal diplomatic service. He was appointed vice-legate to Ferrara and later nuncio at Cologne (1639–51). He represented the papacy during the peace negotiations to end the Thirty Years War and argued unsuccess-fully for a hard line against accommoda-tion with France and the Protestants at the Peace of Westphalia (1648). In 1651 he became papal secretary of state and cardinal in 1652. Elected to the papacy in 1655, he continued to be haunted by the failures of papal policy in international affairs. He resisted the French assertions of LOUIS XIV and took action against the Jansenists. He also welcomed queen CHRISTINA VASA of Sweden's conversion and her transfer to Rome. His real claim to fame during his twelve-year pontificate was his architectural patronage as devel-oper of the city of Rome. In this age of BERNINI and the Baroque, he planned and commissioned a wide range of *teatri* or grand architectural designs that were stage sets for performing and observing the actions and spectacles of the city. Unencumbered streets with long views and spacious squares with dominant monumental structures, his works transformed Rome. Bernini's colonnade and redesign of St Peter's square may be the most famous, but the list is daunting: the church of Santa Maria della Pace, piazza and church; S. Andrea al Quirinale; Santa Maria del Popolo, its adjoining city gate and Piazza del Popolo; and among the unrealised projects, Piazza Colonna and S. Andrea della Valle. He is also memorialised in Bernini's sculpture: his tomb monument and the Cathedra Petri in St Peter's, the Constantine in the Scala Regia, and numerous portraits, busts, and reliefs.

[JM]

Alexander VIII (Pietro Vito Ottoboni, 1610–91) pope 1689–91. Born in Brescia, he was a Venetian nobleman whose father was chancellor of Venice. After receiving his law degree at Padua, he became governor of Terni, Rieti and Spoleto in 1630 and later moved to Rome as auditor of the Rota. In 1652 he was made a cardinal, appointed bishop of Brescia in 1654, and served as grand inquisitor of the Roman Inquisition and secretary of the Holy Office. As an octogenarian pope, his eighteen-month reign was marked by a lessening of tensions with LOUIS XIV's France and the reciprocal decreased friendship with the emperor LEOPOLD I.

[JM]

Alexei I (1629–76) tsar of Russia 1645–76. Son and successor of MICHAEL ROMANOV, his reign was one of the most decisive for the evolution of the Russian state, and also saw the penetration of western cultural influences. In his early years the government was controlled by the boyar MOROZOV. To achieve internal stability Alexei called the Duma, and conceded the Law Code (*Ulozhenie*) of 1649. War against the invading Poles and Swedes occupied the greater part of his reign and virtually all state finance. In the course of two wars against the Poles (1654–67), he extended the Russian frontier to Smolensk, and occupied the eastern Ukraine and Kiev (treaty of Andrusovo 1667). This was also the period when the Ukraine under the leadership of KHMELNITSKY sought Russian protection against the Poles. Alexei's attempts to gain a port on the Baltic through war against the Swedes failed (1656–8). Meanwhile, Russian settlers penetrated the interior of the continent, colonising Siberia and reaching the Pacific. Internally, Russian society was deeply affected by the schism (*raskol*) in the Church between Old and New Believers, provoked by the reforms of patriarch NIKON, who was chief minister for a period (1652–8). The impact of the famous revolt (1670) of Stenka RAZIN in the Cossack lands was less marked. Alexei's first wife (1648) was mother of tsars Fyodor and Ivan, and of the regent SOFIA; his second (1671) was mother of PETER THE GREAT.

Allen, William (1532–94) English cardinal. Lancashire-born, he was educated at Oriel College, Oxford. In 1556 he became principal of St Mary's Hall, Oxford, but left England in 1561 because of the unfavourable religious situation, and settled at Louvain, where he made contact with other Catholic exiles. In 1562 he returned secretly, visiting Lancashire and Oxford, and then left finally in 1565. Ordained priest at Mechelen (1567), he devoted himself to the foundation of a college at Douai to educate missionary priests for England; it began functioning from 1568, relying mainly on the exiles for financing. On the outbreak of the troubles in the Netherlands, the college was expelled from Douai but re-founded itself at Reims (1578); in 1579 an offshoot college was founded in Rome. The college eventually returned to Douai in 1593. Its most famous early enterprise was the 1580 mission to England of CAMPION and PERSONS. Allen was created cardinal in 1587. His writings, such as *A True ... Defence of English Catholics* (1584), aimed to demonstrate the loyalty of his co-religionists to the lawful government of England, but not to the new church established there. He was inevitably drawn into much political intrigue to further his cause, and his links with PHILIP II of Spain were much criticised, as was his support for the 1588 armada against England. He died at Rome, where he is buried. By its missionary work, the Douai college contributed significantly to the survival of English Catholicism. Allen also directed from Rome the publication of the new 'Douai' Bible in English, closely based on the Latin Vulgate.

Althusius (Althaus), Johannes (1557–1638) German political philosopher. Born in Diedenshausen, Westphalia, he studied in Cologne and at Basel, where in 1586 he obtained his doctorate in law. In the same year he published his first book, on Roman jurisprudence. He went on to teach law and philosophy at the Calvinist university of Herborn in Nassau till 1604, serving at the same time as a lawyer in Dillenburg. During these years he published his most famous book, the *Politica methodice digesta* (1603, with enlarged editions 1610 and 1614). In 1604 he became a city councillor of Emden, where he spent the rest of his life. In the *Politica* he attempted to summarise various contemporary views in law and theology that contributed to the development of a science of politics. An opponent of absolutism, he held that sovereignty belongs to the political community, not to its ruler. The community acts through its representative assembly, which itself is subject to divine and natural law. He was also one of the first systematic supporters of religious toleration: 'whoever wishes to have a peaceful realm should abstain from persecution'.

Amelot, Michel-Jean, marquis de Gournay (1655–1724) French diplomat. From a family of leading administrators originating in the Orléanais, several of them magistrates of the parlement of Paris, he

followed his father's footsteps, becoming a councillor of the parlement in 1674 and master of requests in 1677. He then entered upon a distinguished diplomatic career, serving as ambassador in Venice (1682–5), then in Portugal (1685–8) and in the Swiss cantons (1689–98). The French crown rewarded him by converting the family lordship of Gournay into a marquisate (1693) and appointing him councillor of state (1695). On returning from Switzerland he was appointed head of the newly created council of Commerce. In 1705 he was sent at a critical moment – the outbreak of the war of the Spanish Succession – as ambassador to the new French king of Spain, PHILIP V. During just over four years (1705–9) in the peninsula, he made his mark on the Bourbon monarchy, initiating important reforms in the army, the administration and politics. His next major assignment was as ambassador to Rome (1715), to settle differences with the papacy over Church affairs. In the subsequent regency of the duke d'ORLÉANS he was given a post little befitting his merits, as president of the council for Commerce (1716–21).

Amerbach, Bonifacius (1495–1562) Born in Basel, he was the youngest child of the famous printer Johann Amerbach (d.1513), a native of Franconia who settled from 1478 in Basel and built up a flourishing printing press. Bonifacius studied at the university there and developed an interest in humanist studies, but then went on to study law at Freiburg and in Avignon. He took his doctorate in Avignon, then returned to Basel where he took up the chair of Roman law, subsequently became rector of the university, and was appointed (1535) legal adviser to the city. He also became a close friend of ERASMUS, staying on in Basel when the latter was obliged to leave in 1529 because of the triumph of the Reformation there. A conservative in religion but also opposed to coercion, he disagreed with the intolerance of the reformers in his home city but managed to survive opposition, and in 1535 helped Erasmus to return to Basel and also became his chief legal heir. One of the most outstanding European opponents of intolerance, he befriended several famous refugees, including CASTELLION, in the city. He corresponded with the great humanists of his time, and exceptionally preserved all his letters, which form one of the most valuable collections of the century.

Amyraut, Moïse (1596–1664) French Protestant theologian. Born in Anjou, he was educated at the newly founded Calvinist college of Saumur, where his teacher was the Scots theologian Cameron. His subsequent career was spent in the service of the Huguenot churches. In 1631 he was a deputy for the churches in Anjou to the assembly at Charenton, and in 1632 returned to Saumur as a professor. In his principal work, *Traité de la prédestination* (Treatise on Predestination) (1634), he followed Cameron in presenting a moderate version of the doctrine, and was attacked by more traditional Calvinist thinkers. He continued to play a prominent part in the Huguenot assemblies, especially those of Loudun in 1647 and 1659. The most celebrated Calvinist theologian in France, he influenced the growth of a liberal school of theology that had an impact on thinkers both in his country and in Holland.

Andreä, Johann Valentin (1586–1654) Son of a Lutheran pastor from near Tübingen, he was educated at the university, graduating in 1603. He then travelled extensively through France and Italy, settling down as pastor in Vaihingen (Stuttgart) (1614–20), later moving to the nearby town of Calw. In 1639 he moved to Stuttgart as preacher, and was finally appointed pastor at former monasteries in the region. His most famous work, the *Christianopolis* (1619), was a sketch of a small Utopian society of 'about 400 citizens' who owned no property, used no money, and dedicated themselves to study and

work. At the same time he had an ardent interest in Hermetic writings (writings associated with the mythical personage Hermes Trismegistus), reflected in his *The Chemical Wedding* (1616), which sought to relate ancient knowledge with the Christian tradition and contemporary science. His works were widely read, and even imitated in practice by later sectarian groups. Perhaps the best known spin-off from his writings was the growth of Rosicrucianism. He seems to have been a co-author of the work *Fama Fraternitatis* (1614), describing a secret society founded by a fifteenth-century German nobleman, Christian Rosenkreuz, who had apparently been given access to the ancient lore of Persia and India. The work went through nine editions in three years, and inspired the foundation of societies using the name of the mythical founder.

Angelico, Frate Giovanni di Fiesole ('Il Beato') (*c*.1400–55) Italian painter. Born Guido di Pietro near Vicchio (Mugello Valley, Tuscany), he apparently was trained before 1417 while still a layman and was taking commissions in Florence by 1418. First mentioned as a member of the Dominican order in 1423, he was living in the Observant monastery of San Domenico at Fiesole, where he remained as Vicario and maintained his workshop until 1441. Later (from 1443), during his tenure as *sindico* of the Dominican convent of San Marco in Florence, Angelico and his workshop were responsible for the monastery's extensive programme of frescoes. Called to Rome by Eugenius IV (*c*.1445–7) to fresco the chapel of Nicholas V, he was also employed during the summer months at the cathedral of Orvieto to fresco the cappella di San Brizio. In 1449 or 1450 he returned to Tuscany, becoming prior at Fiesole (1450), and painting the high altar of the Franciscan church of San Buonaventura at Bosco ai Frati on commission from Cosimo de' MEDICI. When he died in Rome in 1455 he was the most influential Florentine painter of the day, and at the century's end the followers of SAVONAROLA were to revive interest in his art as paradigmatic for their own theories. He had successfully expressed the Dominican Observant reverence for divine immanence in nature in terms of Renaissance perspective and pristine colour. Lorenzo VALLA is said to have been the author of his two epitaphs, and the rumour persists that it was he who had been Eugenius IV's first choice to serve as archbishop of Florence when a vacancy occurred in 1445, but that it was the painter himself who nominated Fra Antonino Pierozzi, the future St Antoninus, who was duly appointed by the pope.

[JH]

Anguisciola (Anguissola), Sofonisba (c. 1530–1626) Italian painter and portraitist. Born of a noble father in Cremona as the eldest child with a brother and five sisters, she and her sister Elena were taught music and art, and studied painting with local artists Bernardino Campi and Bernardino Gatti (Il Sojaro). Her father encouraged this early training and even wrote to MICHELANGELO to obtain a drawing that she might copy. Her fame had spread so widely that in 1559 she was invited to the court of PHILIP II in Spain where she resided ten years painting portraits of the royal family and herself. By 1571 she had married Fabrizio Moncada, brother of the viceroy of Sicily, and settled in Palermo. After his death in 1578, she met Orazio Lomellini, the Genoese ship captain on her return voyage to Cremona, whom she married by 1584. By the end of her long life, she had returned to Palermo where VAN DYCK met her in 1624. She was the first Italian woman artist to gain an international reputation and her portraits and self-portraits are fine examples of the Northern Italian late Renaissance tradition.

[JM]

Anjou, François de Valois, duke d'Alençon, later (from 1576) duke d' (1554–84) The fourth son of HENRY II and CATHERINE DE MÉDICIS, brother to CHARLES IX and HENRY III, he was physically crippled and of short stature, but dedicated himself to an active political career that often differed from that of the French government. He emerged in 1574 as a leader of the *politiques*, who sought co-operation between Catholics and Protestants during a critical phase of the French civil wars, but the government bought peace (treaty of Monsieur, 1576) by conceding extensive liberty to Protestants and granting Alençon the title of duke d'Anjou. After failing in a project to marry ELIZABETH I of England, he was considered as a sovereign for the Netherlands, then in rebellion against PHILIP II, and in 1581 was accepted as their ruler but found conditions intolerable and abandoned the country (1583). He died of typhus the following year.

Anne of Austria (1601–66) queen of France 1615–66. Daughter of PHILIP III of Spain, she was married in 1615 (in a twin marriage ceremony on the French border, when her brother Philip married the princess of France) to LOUIS XIII, but the marriage was not a success. She was subsequently linked emotionally with the duke of BUCKINGHAM. An opponent of cardinal RICHELIEU, who suspected her of pro-Spanish leanings, she and the queen mother MARIE DE MÉDICIS failed to make the king sack him in 1630 (the Day of Dupes). After twenty five years of marriage she produced an heir (1638, the later LOUIS XIV), then two years later another son, Philippe. On her husband's death (1643) she became regent, placing all her confidence in cardinal MAZARIN, with whom she maintained very close personal relations. She played an important role in defending the survival of the throne and of the cardinal against her enemies during the Fronde (1648–52). Her regency officially ended in 1651 when she had the young Louis declared of age in order to disarm the opposition.

Anne of Denmark (1574–1619) queen of England 1589–1619. She was born in Jutland, daughter of FREDERIK II OF DENMARK, and as part of the continuing dynastic links between Denmark and Scotland, in August 1589 she was married by proxy to JAMES VI of Scotland, who went over personally and married her in November. By spring 1590 the couple were in residence in Holyrood palace; she eventually bore James six children, most of whom died young. When her husband became James I of England, she played an active part in the cultural life of the court, contributing significantly to royal expenditure. Though she showed an inclination to Catholicism from her early days in England, she never formally converted to it.

Anne Stuart (1665–1714) queen of Great Britain and Ireland 1702–14 and last Stuart ruler of the realms. The second daughter of JAMES II's first wife, Anne Hyde (who died 1671), in 1683 she was married to prince George of Denmark, brother of the king of Denmark. Her private preferences influenced her public attitude considerably. She developed an attachment to Sarah Churchill, who became one of the ladies of her bedchamber; she grew to dislike her stepmother, James' second wife Mary of Modena; and she disapproved of her father's politics, abandoning him during the invasion in 1688 of WILLIAM III of Orange. She was also greatly dissatisfied with the treatment accorded to her and her husband by the new rulers, William and Mary (her sister). The rejection by the court of Sarah's husband MARLBOROUGH in 1692 sealed the rift between Anne and her sister. Crowned queen in 1702 after the death of king William, she took an diligent part in the political life of her reign, and actively supported the interests of Marlborough and the Whigs. Her most notable political act was her assent to the act of union between England and Scotland (March 1707). In 1707 also the queen

began to distance herself from the Marlboroughs, and adopted as her confidant Abigail Hill, Mrs MASHAM. Her reliance on Masham was strengthened by the death of George of Denmark in 1708; in 1710 a final dramatic confrontation broke the friendship between Sarah Churchill and the queen. The queen's drift towards the Tories accorded with the general desire for peace (treaty of Utrecht 1713). Plagued by continuous bad health and grieved by the deaths of all the children to whom she gave birth (5 of her 18 pregnancies survived briefly), she was an embittered woman in her last years. Her decision to be succeeded by a member of the house of Hanover, rather than by her own Stuart family, then in exile, was of decisive importance for the monarchy.

Annese, Gennaro (d.1648) One of the leaders of the Naples revolt of 1647, he took over from the murdered MASANIELLO, and proclaimed a republic under the tutelage of France. The Spaniards sent a fleet to invest the city, and he finally surrendered Naples to them (April 1648), but was detained and executed.

Antoine de Bourbon (1518–62) king of Navarre 1555–62. As duke de Vendôme, he married in 1548 JEANNE D'ALBRET, heiress to Navarre, and thereby became also king of Navarre; he was the father of the future HENRY IV. Though declaring himself for the Protestant cause, he wavered between the two religions. On the death of the French king FRANCIS II (1560) he was appointed lieutenant general of France, and changed back to Catholicism in order to assume the post. He then led the royal forces against the Protestants commanded by his own brother Louis I de Bourbon, prince de CONDÉ. He was mortally wounded at the siege of Rouen.

Antonio, prior of Crato (1531–95) pretender to the throne of Portugal. Illegitimate son of the infante Luis (brother of king João III), he was brought up to be a priest, entered the order of Malta and obtained the priorate of Crato (Ocrato, in Portuguese). He took part as a soldier in the ill-fated expedition to Africa of king SEBASTIAN, who perished with most of his nobles at the battle of Alcazarquivir (1578). Captured in the battle, he was ransomed and on his return laid claim to the vacant throne, now contested by PHILIP II of Spain among other claimants. His claim was supported by a very small section of Portuguese opinion, backed by the English and French. The troops available to him were defeated by the duke of ALBA, who invaded Portugal in 1580, and he fled from the country in an English vessel. He participated, with foreign help, in later unsuccessful attempts on Portugal. He died in Paris.

Aretino, Pietro (1492–1556) poet, prose writer and dramatist. His bitingly satiric pen and penchant for gossip gained him great fame and wealth in Renaissance Italy. Son of an Arezzo shoemaker, he took the name of his native city. With doubtful formal education, he received the patronage of his mother's aristocratic 'protector' and dabbled in painting and poetry among cultivated gentlemen in Perugia. In 1517 he entered the household of the banker–patron Agostino Chigi in Rome and eventually supported the ambitions of Giulio de' Medici (the future CLEMENT VII). During his ten years in Rome, he exhibited great ability in pasquinades and lampoons by exploiting political and clerical gossip, and he turned the popular genre of news broadsheets (*avisi*) into political and personal commentary. His lewd poems (1524) for Giulio Romano's banned engravings of love-making positions only increased his notoriety. Aretino moved to Venice in 1527 where he resided in luxury as a literary lion, the friend of artists such as TITIAN, and scurrilous satirist of the rich and famous for the remaining thirty years of his life. In addition to his ephemeral scandal-mongering writing which provided

him a kind of blackmail income, his letters gained great renown and caused ARIOSTO to dub him 'the Scourge of Princes'. His collected letters (published 1537, 1542, 1544, 1550, and posthumously 1557) revel in the courtier mode – topics and style of wit, elegant simplicity and mannered ease. Other notable literary works continued to mine the deceit and decadence of Renaissance Rome: *La cortigiana* (written 1525, revised 1534) and *Il Marescalco* (The Stablemaster, written 1526–7, published 1533) are among the best of his five comedies, and *Ragionamenti* (1534–6) is a series of dialogues among Roman prostitutes on the ideal life of a woman – convent, marriage, or brothel. His tragedy *Orazio* (published 1546; 'The Horatii'), based on Livy's story of the conflict between the Horatii and Curiatii, is considered one of sixteenth-century Italy's best dramas.

[JM]

Argenson, Marc René, marquis de (1652–1721) Creator of the first French police system, in 1697 he became lieutenant-general of police, and in 1715 president of the conseil de l'intérieur, rising to become chancellor and president of the council of finance (1718), a post in which he opposed the financial proposals of LAW, but was obliged to resign. His son, René Louis (1694–1757), after a distinguished career in the administration became minister of foreign affairs (1744–7), and a patron of the Enlightenment.

Argyll, earls and dukes of
8th earl and 1st marquis, Archibald Campbell (1607–61) Scots noble. A passionate defender of the interests of his clan and of Scotland, he led the Presbyterian Covenanters (1638) in their struggle against the attempts of CHARLES I to impose Anglican forms of worship. Inheriting the earldom from his father in 1638, he was additionally created marquis in 1641 as part of the king's concessions to the Covenanters. He helped create a Scots alliance

with the Parliament of England during the early civil war, based on a Parliamentary promise to impose Presbyterianism on England. In Scotland he faced a serious military challenge from the royalists led by MONTROSE, who defeated his forces at Inverlochy (1645); but later that year he defeated Montrose at Philiphaugh. The execution of CHARLES I by the English made him change sides: he proclaimed CHARLES II in Scotland, but was subsequently defeated at Dunbar (1650) by the forces of CROMWELL, to whom he submitted. After the Restoration (1660) he was arrested as a traitor, and beheaded in Edinburgh.

9th earl, Archibald Campbell (1629–85) Son of the 8th earl of the same name, he fought principally for the royalists during the civil war and after the Restoration his father's title and lands were granted to him (1663). However, at the accession of JAMES II he supported MONMOUTH's rebellion (1685) and attempted to raise Scotland for him; he was captured and beheaded at Edinburgh.

10th earl and 1st duke, Archibald Campbell (1651–1703) Eldest son of the 9th earl of the same name, he gave support in Scotland to the 1688 revolution that dethroned JAMES II, and had his title and estates restored in 1690; but he used the occasion to eliminate his rivals the clan of the Macdonalds, in the notorious massacre of Glencoe (1692). In 1701 he was created duke.

2nd duke, John Campbell (1678–1743) Eldest son of the 1st duke, he actively supported the Union with England (1707), was rewarded with numerous English titles, and served with distinction on the continent in the war of the Spanish Succession. As commander of the military forces in north Britain he helped put down the Jacobite rising of 1715, was created duke of Greenwich in 1719 and field-marshal in 1736. He retired from government office in 1740.

Arias Montano, Benito (1527–98) Born in the province of Badajoz, he studied in Seville and then at Alcalá university, where he graduated in 1549 and continued with further studies. His passion for learning led him to study several different subjects; he also came to master thirteen languages, among them Hebrew and Arabic and, later during his travels, Dutch, French and Italian. From 1553 he was at Salamanca, then later took holy orders. In 1562–4 he assisted at the council of Trent. In 1567 PHILIP II summoned him to plan a new Bible based on the original languages, to be printed in Antwerp; and appointed him honorary royal chaplain. From 1568–75 he remained mostly in Flanders, where he made arrangements with the printer PLANTIN for the new Bible (published eventually in eight volumes). At the same time, he acted as adviser to the duke of ALBA on the policies to be adopted during the Dutch revolt, then in its crucial early stages. In Antwerp he became friendly with members of a sectarian tendency called the Family of Love, but never himself adopted their outlook. Recalled to Spain, in part because his advice conflicted with official policy on the revolt, he was appointed by the king as librarian (1577) to the Escorial, a task which occupied him at intervals over the next twenty years. Though he carried out subsequent missions for the king, his real wish was always to retire to a life of solitary reflection in his chosen retreat at Aracena, in Huelva province. The greatest Spanish scholar of his day, his energies were devoted entirely to philological duties, such as the royal Bible or the Index of prohibited books he drew up for the Netherlands Inquisition in 1570. No evidence has ever been produced to verify the theory that he was of Jewish origin.

Ariosto, Ludovico (1474–1533) author of the *Orlando Furioso*, Renaissance Italy's greatest epic poem. Son of a Ferrara nobleman who wanted to prepare him for a legal career, he unwillingly studied law at the university of Ferrara from 1489–94. Afterwards, five years of literary studies were interrupted by his father's death in 1500 as he was constrained to head his household and provide for his four brothers and five sisters. He entered service with the ESTE family as a courtier of cardinal Ippolito (1503–17) and later his brother, duke Alfonso I (1518–22), with numerous military and diplomatic missions during the Italian wars. His last posting was as governor of the Garfagnana in the remote Apennines before retiring back in Ferrara. His comedies were among the earliest Renaissance examples of borrowing from Roman drama – two prose comedies (later versified), *La cassaria* (1508) and *I suppositi* (1509), and two verse comedies, *Il negromante* and *La Lena* (1520s); and his *Satires* (1517–25) were modelled on Horace. His reputation rests on the *Orlando Furioso*, which he worked on from about 1505 for the rest of his life, and was published in three versions in 1516, 1521 and 1532. The first two versions are 40 cantos in ottavo rima and the third in 46 cantos, with the last two versions increasingly influenced by BEMBO's language and style. The *Cinque Canti*, five rejected cantos written to continue the first version, were published posthumously in 1545. The plot follows the story line in Boiardo's *Orlando innamorato* (1483; 1495), the maddening love of Orlando for Angelica, the Muslim–Christian wars of the Carolingian epic cycle, and the love between the pagan prince Ruggiero and the warrior maiden Brademante, putative founders of the Este dynasty. Its historical topicality and ethical dilemmas of love and war, madness and rationality, capture the concerns of a society transformed during the trauma of the long Italian wars.

[JM]

Arminius (Jacob Hermans) (1560–1609) Dutch Calvinist theologian. Born near Leiden, he experienced in 1575 the destruction of his home village by the Spaniards and the death of several members of his family. In 1576 he entered Leiden university as a student, and in 1582 went to study at Geneva, where he failed to be impressed by the prevailing outlook, preferring the views of reformers in Basel. In 1586 he made a tour of Italy and returned the next year to Amsterdam, where he became a Calvinist pastor, married (1590) and fathered twelve children. Subsequently professor of theology at the university of Leiden (1603), he redefined the traditional Calvinist doctrine of predestination by suggesting that all men might be included within God's scheme of salvation, and modifying the accepted views on free-will and grace. His doctrines caused serious splits among Dutch theologians, and provoked responses from his colleague at the university, GOMARUS. Supporters of Arminius were termed Remonstrants after 1610, when they 'remonstrated' to the government and asked for toleration. In 1618 an international conference of Calvinist divines (the Synod of Dort) expelled the Remonstrants from the official church. Political opponents of the Remonstrants in Holland used the opportunity to overthrow the pro-Remonstrant government led by OLDENBARNEVELT. Subsequently some Arminians converted to the Catholic faith. The ideas of Arminius had some vogue in England, where 'Arminian' became a term of political abuse, applied by Protestants to those Anglican clergy who emphasised the traditional elements of Christian theology.

Arnauld, Angélique (1591–1661) Jansenist leader. Born Jacqueline Arnauld, second daughter of Antoine, she was destined by her parents for a religious career, and at the age of eight took the habit, entering the family-owned convent of Port Royal (outside Paris) as abbess in 1602, where she took the religious name of Angélique. Indifferent at first to the religious calling, she was converted at the age of eighteen, and decided to reform her convent to the strict cloister, refusing even to let her father enter the premises but allowing him to speak to her through a grille ('day of the grille', September 1609). From that time she dedicated herself to the cause of reform, adopted as confessor of the convent the abbé SAINT-CYRAN (1635), and drifted into support of the tenets of Jansenism. In 1626 she founded another convent within Paris: this became the principal Port-Royal, while the previous convent became known as Port-Royal des Champs. A tremendously dynamic woman, she succeeded in converting Port-Royal into a centre of spiritual and cultural influence, but came into conflict with hostile religious interests, notably the Jesuits.

Arnauld, Antoine (1560–1619) Jansenist leader. Prominent lawyer, and father of twenty two children, among them Angélique ARNAULD. A firm supporter of Gallicanism (the autonomy of the French Church and crown from papal control), his attitude was rewarded by HENRY IV, who appointed him advocate-general and councillor of state. An opponent of the Jesuits, he delivered a famous speech against them (1594) and petitioned against their return to France (1602). His eldest son, Robert Arnauld d'Andilly (1589–1674), spent a distinguished career in the administration, ending as intendant of the army (1634). Retiring at fifty five to Port-Royal, he devoted himself to a life of piety and letters. Robert's daughter Angélique Arnauld d'Andilly (1624–84) entered Port-Royal as a novice at the age of twenty, and eventually became its abbess (1678).

Arnauld, Antoine (1612–94) 'the great Arnauld'. Twentieth child of Antoine ARNAULD, he became the most active of the Jansenist publicists. Converted by the views of SAINT-CYRAN, he studied at the Sorbonne, where he did his doctorate on the doctrine of grace. Shortly after he published *On Frequent Communion* (1643), which attacked Jesuit views on the subject; when these replied to the polemic, he published his *The Moral Theology of the Jesuits*, which aroused public controversy and ended in his suspension from the Sorbonne. He retired to Port-Royal (1656–68), devoting himself to further writing, some directed against the Calvinists. Finally he left France and settled in Brussels, where he continued to engage in controversy against other intellectuals, including DESCARTES and BAYLE.

Arnauld, Jeanne (1593–1671), known in religion as Agnes. Sister of Angélique ARNAULD, she was also directed towards a religious life by her parents, became abbess of St-Cyr at the age of seven, then entered Port-Royal des Champs in 1608, became its abbess (1636–42) and then moved to the new Port-Royal of Paris as its director. She played a prominent part in the resistance of the nuns to signing the Formulary (1661–5) drawn up by the Church authorities, which identified alleged errors in Jansenism.

Arnim, Hans Georg von (1583–1641) One of the great German mercenary commanders of the Thirty Years War and a firm Lutheran, he began his career in the forces of GUSTAV II ADOLF VASA of Sweden (1613–17), fought for Poland against the Turks, then served the emperor. He was recruited as a commander by WALLENSTEIN, playing a leading role in the campaigns in northern Germany in 1628, the year he was made field-marshal. In 1629, in protest against the emperor's Edict of Restitution, he left to become commander of the forces of Lutheran Saxony. As such, he allied with the invading forces of Gustav Adolf, helping the Swedes to secure victory at Breitenfeld (1631) and taking part in the occupation of Bohemia and Silesia. After the treaty of Prague (1635) signed between the elector of Saxony and the emperor, Arnim retired to his family estates at Boitzenburg. He was arrested there in 1637 by the Swedes on a charge of treason and taken prisoner to Sweden, but escaped a year later and re-joined the Saxon forces in an effort to dislodge foreign troops from German soil. He died at Dresden.

Aske, Robert (d.1537) English rebel leader. Of Yorkshire origin, at one time he practised as an attorney at Gray's Inn, and became one of the leaders of the 1536 uprising in Yorkshire during the Pilgrimage of Grace. To pacify the rising, HENRY VIII invited him to London at Christmas and promised concessions. Aske was satisfied to the extent of trying to assuage a further rising in January 1537, but in May he was arrested, confined in the Tower, and sentenced to death. In June he and other rebel leaders were taken north, and Aske was hanged in York.

Askew, Anne (1521–46) English Protestant martyr. Second daughter of a Lincolnshire gentleman, she showed a zeal for Bible study from an early age. Her father married her to Thomas Kyme of Kelsey, with whom she had two children; but differences with her husband caused her to leave home for London, where in 1545 she was examined on suspicion of heresy before bishop Bonner, who showed himself sympathetic to her intelligent discourse and released her after she signed a profession of belief. The next year she was examined again, but was more recalcitrant, and was sent to prison in Newgate and then the Tower, where torture was applied. In July 1546 she and three other accused were burnt at the stake in Smithfield. Her own account of her cross-examination was published immediately after her death, in Marburg (Germany), and contributed to her fame as the first woman Protestant martyr in England.

Atterbury, Francis (1662–1732) bishop of Rochester 1713–22. Born at Milton Keynes, where his father was rector, he went to Oxford, where he became a tutor at Christ Church, received holy orders (1687), married and then moved to London as a preacher and royal chaplain. At the accession of queen ANNE STUART he was made her chaplain, became known for his active public defence of Tory principles and the rights of the clergy, and was rapidly promoted to dean of Christ Church and then to the see of Rochester. After the accession of the house of Hanover, he made contact with the Jacobites, and for this was in 1722 arrested, sent to the Tower, tried by the House of Lords, and deprived of his posts and expelled from England. He lived in exile mainly in France; after his death his body was returned to England and buried privately in Westminster Abbey.

Aubigné, Théodore-Agrippa d' (1552–1630) French scholar, poet and soldier. Born in Saintonge, Poitou, of minor nobility, from infancy he showed a remarkable aptitude for learning, and was brought up as a convinced Calvinist. At thirteen he went to Geneva to study, and on returning to Saintonge enlisted in the Protestant army at sixteen. He devoted the rest of his life to three passions: his religion, his studies and his career as a soldier. During the campaigns of the French civil wars he fell deeply in love (1570) with a Catholic girl who later married another; the event launched him into his career as a poet. In 1572 he fled from Paris after killing his opponent in a duel; the flight saved him from the subsequent massacre of Protestants on the night of St Bartholomew. From 1573 he became the intimate companion of Henry of Navarre, in exploits both of love and of war. In 1583 he achieved a certain stability by marrying a Poitou heiress whom he had been courting for six years, and settled down as a country gentleman; but soon returned to the last campaigns of the war. Disgusted by the conversion of HENRY IV and by the unsatisfactory tolerance conceded by the edict of Nantes, he retired to his estates in 1600 (his wife had died in 1595), and devoted himself to letters, producing poems and commencing his *Histoire universelle*. Still restless, in 1620 he took part in the revolt of his fellow-Protestant ROHAN, and when it failed fled to Geneva, where he was greeted with open arms and resumed his Poitou lifestyle. He acquired a dwelling with estates, continued his poems and history, and (aged seventy one) married again. His *Histoire universelle*, in which he hoped to depict 'the folly of men and the power of God', came out in Geneva in a first edition in 1612–19 and a second, in three volumes, in 1626.

Augustus II (1670–1733) elector of Saxony as Frederick Augustus I (1694–1733), king of Poland as Augustus II (1697–1733). He succeeded his brother John George II as elector, then became a Catholic in order to obtain election, on the death of John SOBIESKI, as king of Poland. He allied with other northern powers against CHARLES XII VASA of Sweden, who dethroned him in favour of STANISLAS LESZCZYNSKI; but after the defeat of the Swedes was restored to his throne. Nicknamed 'the Strong' because of his sexual exploits, he was said to have had scores of mistresses and numberless children.

Avvakum (1620–82) a founder of the Old Believer sect in Russia. Son of a village priest, he became a priest, went to Moscow and while there (1646–7) became converted to a sect of zealots. In 1652, when he was priest of the cathedral of Kazan in Moscow, he attacked the reforms of patriarch NIKON, and was exiled from the city. In 1663 he had an interview with the tsar and accused Nikon of heresy. His following, based on opposition to Nikon's changes in the language and music of public worship, and indeed to all foreign influences, grew. In 1664 a church council in Moscow unfrocked him and condemned him to exile and imprisonment. Confined for fifteen years, he used the time to write his main works, as well as his *Life* (1672–5). As his companion in exile he had a little black hen, reputed to be the champion egg-layer of Siberia. Eventually he was condemned by an edict of the tsar to be burned at the stake. Possibly the most outstanding Russian writer of his day, notably in his *Life*, he began a protest against religious change that led to a schism (*raskol*) of dissidents, who were known as 'old believers' (*starovery*), from the official Orthodox Church. The schism has lasted down to today.

Azpilcueta, Martín de (1492–1586) Spanish moral theologian. From a noble family in Navarre, he studied at Alcalá and then at Toulouse, where he obtained his doctorate in canon law (1514), took holy orders and became professor (1518–21). From 1524 to 1537 he held chairs in Salamanca, then in 1537 was persuaded to move to the newly founded university of Coimbra, where he remained until 1555. Consulted occasionally by the Spanish crown, in 1567 he was charged by PHILIP II with the defence of the imprisoned archbishop of Toledo, CARRANZA, but seems to have displeased the king by his energetic defence of Carranza. His best-known work was his *Manual for Confessors*, published first in Coimbra in Latin (1552) and then translated by him into Spanish (1556). It went through several editions and became the standard reference work for Spanish clergy.

B

Ba'al Shem Tov (meaning 'master of the divine name') A term used in Kabbalistic and Hasidic (Jewish) literature since mediaeval times to refer to one with special secret knowledge, it became used with frequency in early modern central and eastern Europe to apply both to serious scholars and to mountebanks; about the latter, various legendary and humorous stories were created. The term was applied in particular to the founder of modern Hasidim, Israel ben Eliezer Ba'al Shem Tov (c.1700–60). Born of a poor family of Podolia (Poland), after years of eking out a living he went to live in the Carpathians, where he developed his ideas. From 1730, when he settled in Tluste, he began to disseminate his ideas and build up a following both as teacher and as worker of miracles of healing. Placing his emphasis on prayer and mystical exaltation, he travelled in the region talking to people and curing them. One of the major prophets of Jewish history, he drew his ideas less from orthodox tradition than from the Kabbala and other mystical influences, which placed personal salvation before communal salvation. But he left no authentic personal writings and no portraits of him exist; his teachings were transmitted only through the publications of his disciples, first printed in 1782. His ideas were given further prominence in the twentieth century through the writings of the great Jewish thinker Martin Buber.

Babington, Antony (1561–86) English conspirator. From a Derbyshire gentry family, he was brought up as a Catholic, and served as page to MARY STUART during her imprisonment in Sheffield. He made contact in 1580 with the newly arrived Jesuit missionaries CAMPION and PERSONS, and from about 1583, while in France, made contact with exiles who planned to liberate Mary and organise a rising. By 1585 the plans included the assassination of queen ELIZABETH I, a task entrusted to Babington himself. Mary approved the plans, with which the Spanish ambassador MENDOZA and PHILIP II were also familiar. The spies of secretary WALSINGHAM were aware of all moves made, and in August 1586 twelve conspirators, including Babington, were arrested; they were executed a month later by hanging and quartering. The written plans of the plotters were used by the government to justify the subsequent execution of Mary.

Bach, Carl Philipp Emanuel (1714–88) German composer and keyboard player. He was the most outstanding keyboard player (especially as a clavichordist) of the early Classical period and a composer of striking originality. His highly expressive style (*Empfindsamer stil*) exhibits proto-Romantic characteristics, which influenced the stylistic development of Haydn and Mozart. Following his initial musical education with his father, he studied law at the universities of Leipzig and Frankfurt an der Oder. He served as harpsichordist and music teacher at the court of Frederick the Great in Berlin (1740–68) and as music director in Hamburg (1768–88). His circle of friends included some of the leading German intellectuals of the period. His best known works for the keyboard are the *Prussian Sonatas* (1743, dedicated to Frederick), the *Württemberg Sonatas* (1744), six collections 'for connoisseurs and amateurs' (1779–87) and some piano concertos. He also composed symphonies, chamber works and sacred music. His *Essay on the True Art of Playing Keyboard Instruments* (1753) is an invaluable practical guide, which also sheds light on important aesthetic aspects of the early Classical style.

[JE]

Bach, Johann Christian (1735–82) German composer and keyboard player. From 1762 until his death he lived mainly in London; hence was dubbed the 'English Bach'. There he prospered as a composer of Italian operas for the King's Theatre, a music teacher to queen Charlotte and a co-director (with C.F. Abel) of public concerts. He also composed operas for the court at Mannheim and the Royal Academy of Music in Paris. His popularity declined in his last years and he ended his life in financial ruin. Although he was a highly versatile composer, he is remembered primarily for his harpsichord and/or piano sonatas and concertos, chamber works and symphonies. These exemplify the lyrical and 'natural' qualities of the galant style (*style galant*) of the early Classical period. Mozart, who visited him in London in 1764 (at the age of eight) was profoundly influenced by him.

[JE]

Bach, Johann Sebastian (1685–1750) German composer and organist. One of the greatest composers in European music history, he descended from a long family line of musicians, who had settled in Thuringia in the sixteenth century. Among his own sons, the most notable composers are Wilhelm Friedemann (1710–84), Carl Philipp Emanuel BACH (1714–88), Johann Christoph Friedrich (1732–95) and Johann Christian BACH (1735–82). Born in Eisenach, Johann Sebastian spent his early career as an organist in Arnstadt (1705–7) and Mühlhausen (1707–8), and as an organist and concertmaster at the court of Weimar (1708–17). Some remarkable cantatas and brilliant organ works (e.g. the famous *Toccata and Fugue in D minor*) already date from this period. During his subsequent employment as *Kapellmeister* at the court of Cöthen (1717–23) he composed solely instrumental music, such as the *Well-tempered Clavier I*, the six *Brandenburg Concerti*, the four orchestral suites, violin concertos, and numerous chamber ensembles and organ works. From 1723 until his death he lived in Leipzig as a kantor at St Thomas and music director of the city's main churches. During the first years there he composed and performed over 250 church cantatas and the monumental *St John Passion* and *St Matthew Passion*. Following his continuous altercation with the church authorities, he gradually neglected his official duties and devoted his energy to the collegium musicum. His best-known works of the 1730s and early 1740s are for the keyboard (e.g. the *Italian Concerto*, the harpsichord concertos, the *Goldberg Variations*, and the *Well-tempered Clavier II*). His late works exhibit astounding contrapuntal intricacy, as exemplified in *The Art of the Fugue*, *The Musical Offering* (dedicated to Frederick the Great) and various canons. He also completed the monumental B minor mass. Bach's towering stature is manifested in a wondrous and highly individual manner of assimilating the various musical styles of the Baroque. His thematic inventiveness, rhythmic vitality, contrapuntal mastery and harmonic wealth often merge into broad architectural designs of astounding expressive qualities.

Yet, following the change of musical taste in the 1730s (i.e. the early Classical style), he was criticised for his excessive complexity and was soon forgotten, except for a small circle of admirers (including Haydn, Mozart and Beethoven). The performance of the *St Matthew Passion*, conducted by Mendelssohn in Berlin (1829), inaugurated the 'Bach revival', which has not since waned.

[JE]

Bacon, Francis, baron Verulam, viscount St Alban (1561–1626) English lawyer, politician, writer and philosopher. The son of a Lord Keeper of the Great Seal to Elizabeth I, he pursued a career in the law, diplomacy and politics. Under James I he held a succession of offices, from Solicitor General (1607) to Lord Chancellor (1618), but was impeached by Parliament for corruption and expelled from public life in 1621. He had by then already published a great deal, most notably: *Essayes* (1597 and later editions); *The Advancement of Learning* (1614), a detailed analysis of the varieties and organisation of human knowledge; and, after much redrafting, the *Novum Organum* or *Instauratio Magna* (1620). In this last, instructions for the pursuit of knowledge through the 'inductive method' of reasoning were offered as the basis of the 'Great Instauration' that would restore man's control over the natural world. In his retirement Bacon produced *De Augmentis Scientiarum* (an expanded version of *The Advancement of Learning*); two of six planned 'natural histories'; and *The New Atlantis* (1627), drafted years before, describing a utopia in which collaborative investigation of nature played an important role. The early Royal Society included amongst its members many 'Baconians', who revered him as the principal creator of the conceptual foundations of their experimental methodology although few of them followed his prescriptions to the letter.

[FW]

Bancroft, Richard (1544–1610) English bishop. Educated at Cambridge, where he took his doctorate (1585), he became a firm opponent of Puritan tendencies in the Church. He was appointed canon of Westminster (1587), preached a noted sermon at Paul's Cross against the Puritans (1589), and played a key part in the uncovering of those who printed the Marprelate tracts. Chaplain to archbishop WHITGIFT from 1592, in 1597 he was made bishop of London. After JAMES I became king, Bancroft took a strongly anti-Puritan line at the Hampton Court conference (1604) between representatives of the different views in the Church. In 1604 he was made archbishop of Canterbury, and in 1608 chancellor of Oxford university.

Banér, Johan Gustafsson (1596–1641) Son of one of Sweden's leading nobles, he entered the army and participated in the early campaigns (1615) of king GUSTAV II ADOLF VASA in the Baltic territories, principally Poland and Livonia. He rose quickly to the rank of general, served with the Swedes during their intervention in Germany in the Thirty Years War, and in 1634 became field-marshal. After the defeat of the Swedes at Nördlingen (1634) he assumed command of their armies in Germany, securing a victory at Wittstock (1636). Subsequent successes, mainly in Bohemia, were small. Banér occupied himself negotiating the possibility of lands and position for himself in Germany, spent most of his time in bed with his newly acquired (1640) young wife, and drank heavily. He died of ill-health at Halberstadt.

Barbarossa, Khair ad-Din (*c.*1476–1546) By some accounts son of a Sicilian Christian who embraced Islam, he and his elder brother Aruj became pirate leaders in the western Mediterranean and harassed the Christian states. When Aruj was killed by the Spanish in 1518, Khair entered the service of the Ottoman empire, receiving in return considerable military help from Istanbul. He captured Algiers in 1529 and made it the seat of his power. Appointed admiral-in-chief of the empire in 1533, he went on to capture Tunisia. Though he lost Tunis and Goletta to the forces of CHARLES V in 1535, he confirmed Turkish naval supremacy over the greater part of the Mediterranean.

Baronio, Cesare (1538–1607) cardinal and Church historian. Born of nobility of ordinary means, he was educated at Veroli and Naples until 1557, when he transferred to Rome where he received his law degree in 1561 and was ordained in 1564. He joined St Philip NERI and the community that later became the Oratorians. In response to the Lutheran apologist history *Centuriae Magdeburgenses* (The Centuries of Magdeburg) (13 vols, 1559–74), he began a Catholic response that led to his equally biased, twelve-volume narrative Church history, *Annales ecclesiastici* (1588–1607) that traced ecclesiastical history from Innocent III in 1198 to 1565 with the continuation by Odorico Rinaldi. Despite its authoritative source references and transcriptions of documents, inscriptions and coins, it was received as a biased account by the Protestants and rebutted by the French humanist, Isaac Casaubon, in his *Exercitationes in Baronium* (Essays on Baronio). In 1593 he succeeded Philip Neri as head of the Oratory and was confessor to CLEMENT VII, who named him cardinal in 1596. As a priest he continued regular parochial duties in addition to his research and writing, and as a cardinal he continued his *Annals* and his enormous correspondence, sat on various commissions, went on diplomatic missions, revised the Roman martyrology and served as Vatican Librarian from 1597.

[JM]

Bart, Jean (1650–1702) Flemish naval captain. Of a well-known family among the Flemish corsairs of Dunkirk, his father and grandfather had followed the profession, and he enlisted when young in the fleet of admiral de RUYTER. He then entered the service of France, commanded his own ship and distinguished himself in the war against the Dutch (1672–8). Later he was in action in the Mediterranean (1680). During the war of the League of Augsburg he used Dunkirk as his base against the enemy; captured in an engagement (1689) by the English, he managed to escape. His subsequent exploits in French pay, against foreign fleets and occasionally transporting notable personages, gained him acclamation; the king in 1694 summoned him to Versailles to create him *chevalier.* In 1694 he broke the English naval blockade of Dunkirk, and in 1696 won a victory over the Dutch fleet. He died of illness in Dunkirk while preparing his ships to intervene in the war of the Spanish Succession.

Bassompierre, François de (1579–1646) French general and diplomat. Scion of a minor branch of the ruling house of Cleves, he came from a military family (his father served in the French forces as colonel of cavalry). He studied in Freiburg, travelled in Italy, and came in 1598 to Paris, where he decided to stay. He entered the service of France, served in wars against Savoy and in Hungary, and in 1609 was about to marry the daughter of the constable of France, Charlotte de Montmorency, when the fifty-six-year-old king HENRY IV forbade the marriage because he himself was infatuated with the young lady. During the regency he was appointed in 1614 colonel of the Swiss guard. Ambassador to Spain in 1621, he returned to play a leading part in the military campaigns of LOUIS XIII against the insurgent Protestant nobles. For these services he was created marshal of France in 1622. He served as ambassador to the Swiss (1622–6), and then went on a mission to England, and later to the Swiss again (1630). Suspected by RICHELIEU of complicity in the events leading to the 'Day of Dupes' (1630), he was imprisoned in the Bastille (1631–43) and released only on the cardinal's death. He spent the years of his confinement writing his memoirs (Cologne 1665) and an account of his diplomatic service.

Báthory, Elizabeth (1560–1614) Niece of Stephen BÁTHORY, she is famous as the historical origin of one of the most recurrent vampire myths. Married in 1575 to count Nádasdy, she was accused of attempting, from the age of 34, to preserve her beauty by bathing regularly in the blood of young girls who were lured to her castle. Over a period of six years, according to subsequent evidence, she tortured and murdered between thirty and seventy women. In 1610 an enquiry was begun in Bratislava into the rumours of murders; several of her accomplices were arrested and executed, and she was imprisoned for life in the fortress of Cachtice.

Báthory, Stephen (István) (1533–86) king of Poland as Stephen I (1575–86). The Báthory were a noble Catholic family of Hungary. Stephen, prince of Transylvania since 1571, and married to a daughter of the Polish king, was in 1575 chosen by the Polish magnates for the elective crown of Poland, thanks largely to the efforts of Jan ZAMOYSKI, who became the power behind the throne during this reign. A notable military commander, Stephen led successful campaigns against the Russia of IVAN IV ('the Terrible'), and annexed Livonia (1582). A strong Catholic, he invited the Jesuits into Poland and significantly advanced the cause of the Counter-Reformation there. He was succeeded as ruling prince of Transylvania by both his son, and his grandson Sigismund (1572–1613). The latter was elected prince in 1581 but had continuous conflicts with the emperor RUDOLF II and eventually abdicated and ceded his territory to the emperor in 1602.

Baxter, Richard (1615–91) English religious writer. A native of Shropshire, he was educated inadequately in a local school, and dedicated himself to studying to be a clergyman. In 1638 he took orders, and taught in a school at Dudley; he also began reading, and came to question the more traditional aspects of Anglican liturgical practice. In 1641 he was invited by a local congregation to go and preach in Kidderminster, where he first began to exercise his influence as an innovator in religious matters. The hazards of the civil war made him move to Coventry (1642), and he served as a military chaplain with CROMWELL. Speaking of the war, he felt that 'both parties were to blame', but that 'whoever was faulty, the people's liberties should not be forfeited'. After the war he returned to Kidderminster, which he left in 1660 for London, where he joined the Presbyterians in supporting the Restoration of CHARLES II. Appointed as one of the chaplains to the king, and offered a bishopric, he preferred to withdraw from active church life when measures were taken against nonconformist clergy, and from 1662 lived quietly in Middlesex. But he was occasionally persecuted, first under Charles II and then in 1685 under JAMES II, when he was tried by judge JEFFREYS and imprisoned (1685–6). One of the great spiritual men of all time, Baxter influenced contemporaries by his preaching and his gentleness, and through his voluminous writings he reached the minds of later generations. His extensive autobiographical materials were first published in 1696 as the *Reliquiae Baxterianae*.

Bayard, Pierre Terrail, seigneur of (1475–1524) French soldier. Born in the chateau Bayard, near Grenoble, of a noble family, he devoted his whole life to a military career. A page at the court of Savoy and then of France, he first served with the French in Italy in the 1490s, contributing to the capture of Milan (1499), and then went south to Naples to fight against the Spaniards, distinguishing himself in a historic feat at the Garigliano (1503), when he defended the bridge for an hour alone against two hundred men. After further campaigns in Italy, he went to Artois to fight against the English and was captured, but was released without ransom as a gesture to his bravery. Appointed (1515) as commander in Dauphiné, he alternated his role there with military actions in Italy and in France. His last action was with the French forces that attempted to recover Milan from CHARLES V in 1524. Grievously wounded during the French retreat, he was attended to on the field while the enemy commanders came to pay their last respects. His body was taken to Grenoble. Famous in his own lifetime as a model of knightly virtues, he was known as 'le chevalier sans peur et sans reproche', the fearless and blameless knight.

Bayle, Pierre (1647–1706) French philosopher. Born in the county of Foix, where his father was a Calvinist pastor, he was first educated in a Calvinist school and then by Jesuits in Toulouse, where he converted to Catholicism, returning later to his previous faith. He studied for a while in Geneva, then later (1670) took a job as professor at the Protestant college at Sedan, where he remained till 1681. In this year the increasing persecution of Protestants in France made him move to Rotterdam, where he taught philosophy. In 1682 he published there (anonymously) his *Letter on the Comet of 1680*. From 1684–7 he edited the journal *Nouvelles de la république des lettres*. He also crossed swords with DESCARTES in an essay published in 1684. The revocation of the Edict of Nantes in 1685 elicited from him one of his most seminal pieces, the *Philosophical Commentary on the Words of Jesus Christ: Make Them Come In* (1686), in which he argued against all religious persecution, on the grounds that absolute certainty is unattainable and that 'the conscience which is in error has the

same rights as that which is not'. He opposed armed rebellion against LOUIS XIV, the path proposed by another refugee, the pastor JURIEU. In 1690, at Jurieu's insistence, he was deprived of his teaching post. His most famous work, the *Dictionnaire historique et critique* (1695), resumed his religious and philosophical thought, subjecting persons and concepts to a dispassionate critique that often called into doubt widely accepted beliefs. Some have seen him as questioning religion and as a forerunner of the Enlightenment. He extended his scepticism to contemporary philosophers, whom he criticised in order to underscore their contradictions. Despite being prohibited in France, the *Dictionnaire* achieved instant success, was quickly banned by both Protestants and Catholics, and went through several editions. It inspired many later thinkers: Jefferson recommended it as one of the 100 major books with which to start the Library of Congress. Bayle as a sceptic emphasised that an atheist society could be moral and a Christian one immoral; he did not deny the role of faith, but doubted the reliability of reason.

Beaton, David (1494–1546) Scots cardinal. At sixteen he went to study in Paris, and when still young acted as Scots ambassador to France (1519–25). He became lord privy seal to the king, James V, from 1528; a cardinal in 1538, he became archbishop of St Andrews in 1539. A firm supporter of the alliance with France, he backed the marriage of the king to Margaret of France (1533) and then to MARY OF GUISE (1538). After James' death (1542), he led the pro-French party which supported the young queen MARY STUART: his success provoked a brief English invasion of Scotland in 1544. He led the battle against heresy, expelled John KNOX from the university and burnt the preacher George Wishart (1546), but was assassinated by noble friends of Wishart.

Beaufort, Lady Margaret (1443–1509) countess of Richmond and Derby. Daughter of the 1st duke of Somerset, she was married when very young (1455) to the earl of Richmond, Edmund Tudor, who died the year after but left her pregnant with a son, later to be HENRY VII, in January 1457. She subsequently married the son of the duke of Buckingham, lord Stanley, whose defection from the side of king Richard III at Bosworth helped Margaret's son to win the throne. In retirement after Henry's accession, she took a nun's vows and had John FISHER as confessor. An outstanding patron of the Church and of scholarship, she endowed the divinity professorships (1502) at Oxford and Cambridge which still bear her name, and founded Christ's and St John's Colleges at the latter university. She patronised Caxton, and translated books of devotion into English.

Bedford, earls of The Russells, a Dorset family, rose to significance in the fourteenth century and played an important role in the politics of early modern Europe.

1st earl, John Russell (1486–1555) He rose to favour under HENRY VIII, whom he served in military campaigns and diplomatic missions in Europe in the 1520s, entered Parliament in 1529, and helped to suppress the Pilgrimage of Grace; in 1540 he was created lord high admiral and in 1542 lord privy seal. He served on the regency council under EDWARD VI and put down the western rising, for which he was created earl (1550). He continued in favour under MARY I, and was one of those sent to Spain to arrange the marriage with PHILIP II, dying shortly after his return.

2nd earl, Francis Russell (1527–85) Only son of the 1st earl, he was an active Protestant and fled to the continent during the reign of MARY I. Under queen ELIZABETH I he entered the privy council and played an active role in government,

serving as governor of Berwick and (in 1576) president of the council of Wales.

4th earl, Francis Russell (1593–1641) He succeeded to the title in 1627 and was an active member of the opposition to CHARLES I STUART in Parliament. In 1640 he took part in negotiations with the Scots, and was seen as a principal leader of Parliament, but died suddenly.

5th earl and 1st duke, William Russell (1613–1700) Eldest son of the 4th earl, he was educated at Oxford, and sat in the Long Parliament for Devon. He sided with the Parliament, commanding a troop in 1642, but passed briefly to the royalists in 1643, then refused to take either side; after the Restoration he occupied several lesser posts, and spent much time draining the Fens. In 1694 he was created duke (partly in consideration of the fame of his son, Lord William RUSSELL, as a martyr), and marquis of Tavistock.

Behn, Aphra (1640–89) playwright, novelist and poet. Born in Kent, daughter of an innkeeper, she spent some time in Surinam, where a member of her family was an official and whose setting she later used for her best-known novel *Oronokoo or the History of the Royal Slave* (1688). On her return to England in 1664 she married Mr Behn, a merchant of Dutch origin (he apparently died in 1665 in the plague). In 1666, she was employed by the government as a secret agent in Antwerp on the outbreak of the Dutch war. The first Englishwoman to make her living by writing, from 1670 onwards she achieved literary celebrity with her complicated comedies of intrigues and low life. Her plays include *The Rover* (in two parts, 1677 and 1681) and *The Feigned Courtezans* (dedicated to Nell GWYNNE, 1678). She also published fifteen prose works, notably *Oronokoo*, as well as translations from French and classical languages. Noted for wit and generosity, she had a wide circle of literary and political friends including Dryden, Southerne and the earl of Rochester. She was attacked both for her outspokenness on political matters and for her audacity in writing with the freedom of a man. She is buried in Westminster Abbey.

[HK & GG]

Bellarmine, Robert (Bellarmino, Roberto) (1542–1621) Italian cardinal. A member of the Jesuit order from 1560, he studied in Rome, then taught at Louvain and returned to Rome (1576) to become professor at the Jesuit college and one of the most influential theorists of his time. His course lectures, published as the *Disputationes* (1586–93), were put briefly on the Roman Index because of the disapproval of pope SIXTUS V, but became fundamental to Catholic apologetics. He became rector of the college, served briefly on a diplomatic mission to France (1590) then became provincial of his order in Naples (1595) and eventually cardinal (1599). He served briefly as archbishop of Capua (1602–5) then returned to Rome to aid Paul V in the administration of the affairs of papacy. He was canonised in 1930. His *Tractatus de potestate summa pontificis* (Treatise on Papal Power) (1610), written against the theories of absolute royal power of the Franco-Scots writer William Barclay, reasserted the Catholic view of the pope's authority over kings in spiritual matters. The obligation to obey the prince, he argued, is modified in specific circumstances where the prince contravenes the law of God; in this event, the pope also has the right to depose the prince.

Bembo, Pietro (1470–1547) Italian poet, literary theorist and cardinal. Son of a noble Venetian envoy to various courts, he himself is portrayed as a poet-savant in the ideal court at Urbino in CASTIGLIONE's *The Courtier*. His first notable literary success, *Gli Asolani* (1505), dedicated to Lucrezia BORGIA with whom he exchanged Platonic love letters, is a dialogue on the nature of love set within a narrative and containing numerous lyrics. He served as secretary to LEO X during his pontificate (1513–21) and then retired to Padua. He completed his most important work, *Prose della volgar lingua*, in 1525. It codified Italian grammar and orthography, and engaged the current debate on language. He was an exponent of literary imitation, that is, Cicero for Latin, fourteenth-century Tuscan for the vernacular; Boccaccio in prose, and Petrarch in verse. By the end of the sixteenth century, his position on language had won out. He circulated in manuscript and later published his own lyric poetry in *Rime* (1530). In 1529 he became historiographer of Venice, librarian of St Mark's, and was back in Rome as cardinal in 1539 dedicated to theology and classical history.

[JM]

Benedict XIV (Prospero Lambertini, 1675–1758) pope 1740–58. Born of Bolognese nobility, he was educated by tutors and later studied in Rome where he received a doctorate in law and theology. He entered the papal bureaucracy under Innocent XII and held eleven offices under CLEMENT XI and Innocent XIII. Most notably his work in 1701 as advocate for two canonisations led to his appointment in 1708 as Promoter of the Faith responsible for all canonisations until 1727, and to an important book on the canonisation process. In 1728 he was made a cardinal and 1731 archbishop of Bologna, where he initiated numerous synods and episcopal visitations. As pope after 1740, he reigned during the war of the Austrian Succession (1740–8) and sought to curb absolute rulers in their attempts to establish national churches by signing concordats with Naples, Spain and Portugal. In the Papal States, he promoted economic and trade reform, founded learned societies, and supported the Vatican Museum, Vatican Library and university of Rome. He associated himself with Enlightenment reform, was a friend of VOLTAIRE and

MONTESQUIEU, and is remembered as an intelligent and moderate pope.

[JM]

Bering, Vitus Jonassen (1680–1741) A Danish naval officer in the service of the tsar, he fought against the Swedes and was in 1725 put in charge of a mission to explore Russian territory on the Pacific coast. He found that Asia was separated by sea from the New World, and in 1728 crossed over the straits that were given his name. He undertook a new expedition (1741), during which he reconnoitred Alaska and the Aleutians, but died during it.

Berkeley, George (1685–1753) Irish philosopher. Born into the English élite in Kilkenny and educated at Trinity College, Dublin, where he became a fellow, he early showed an interest in the new philosophy of his time, and did virtually all his creative philosophical writing before 1713. His *Essay Towards a New Theory of Vision* (1709) argued that one's perception of visual distance depends on our accumulated experience of objects, and that someone born blind and suddenly given sight could not depend on vision alone to judge distance. His major work, the *Principles of Human Knowledge* (1710), argued, on the premiss that objects are a sum of qualities accessible to the senses, that physical objects exist only if they are perceived, that is, *esse est percipi*. In 1713 he published his *Dialogues* on the same theme. After 1713 he lived in London, making extensive visits to the continent, mainly Italy, and returned to Ireland in 1721. He now became fascinated by the opportunities for settlement offered by America, and sailed with his newly acquired wife (1728) for Newport, Rhode Island, where he spent the next three years. He is author of the famous line: 'Westward the course of empire takes its way'. He returned home in 1732, was nominated bishop of Cloyne in 1734, and spent the next eighteen years in his diocese, retiring eventually to Eng-

land where he died at Oxford. Considered to be one of the three great empiricists of British philosophy, with LOCKE and HUME, his views never achieved much public success and were seldom taken seriously.

Bernard (Bernhard), duke of Saxe Weimar (1604–39) One of the most brilliant Protestant generals of the Thirty Years War, he was active fighting on the Protestant side from the earliest stages of the conflict, but rose to prominence when he became an ally of GUSTAV II ADOLF VASA during the latter's campaigns. When Gustav was killed at Lützen (1632), Bernard with French support took over command of the Swedish forces; but continual friction between German and Swedish generals impeded the war effort. The joint forces were defeated by the Spanish Imperial army at the battle of Nördlingen (1634). After the peace of Prague (1635) between Saxony and the emperor, he came to an agreement the same year with RICHELIEU, who guaranteed payment of his forces. The campaigns, conducted in the Rhineland, were highly successful, culminating in the capture of the key fortress of Breisach (1638). Shortly after, Bernard died suddenly of a fever. His disappearance was of capital importance, forcing France to intervene directly in the Thirty Years War where it had previously interfered only through mercenary armies.

Bernard, Samuel (1651–1739) French financier. He was possibly of Flemish origin, and his father was a minor painter and engraver in the French royal service. Brought up a Calvinist, he made his fortune in the textile trade, opportunely converting to Catholicism at the time of the Revocation of the Edict of Nantes (1685). He went on to become one of the leading government financiers of his time, lent extensively to the government of LOUIS XIV and founded the Guinea Company. He lost large sums in the financial crash of 1709, but recouped his fortune and continued as a financier to LOUIS XV and to the kings of Sweden and Poland; he also survived the crash provoked by LAW's financial schemes. He was ennobled in 1699, created count de Coubert in 1725 and councillor of state in 1730.

Bernini, Gianlorenzo (1598–1690) Italian sculptor, architect, painter and city planner, who served seven popes (Paul V to INNOCENT XI) and two kings (CHARLES I of England and LOUIS XIV) and was by far the most influential artist of the Italian Baroque style. Born in Naples, he was brought to Rome as a child when his father, the sculptor Pietro Bernini (1562–1629) was commissioned to work on the funerary chapel of pope Paul V. A child prodigy, Bernini made drawings from the Roman and Hellenistic sculpture in the papal collections and the frescoes of Raphael and Michelangelo in the Vatican. Cardinal Matteo Barberini – the future URBAN VIII – was assigned to be his tutor. His first important client was Paul V's nephew cardinal Scipione Borghese (c.1615–24), for whom the life-sized *Pluto and Proserpina* group, the dynamic *David*, and *Apollo and Daphne* (Rome, Galleria Borghese) were made. Works for Urban VIII included the colossal *St Longinus* (1629–38) and bronze baldacchino of St Peter's (1624–33), as well as the papal tomb. For the family of cardinal Federigo Cornaro, son of the doge of Venice, he designed a funerary chapel (Church of Sta. Maria Vittoria, Rome, 1645–52), in which the marble *Ecstasy of St Teresa of Avila* appears suspended on a marble cloud above the altar while portrait sculptures of the seven Cornaro cardinals and a doge are portrayed in two balconies on either side like spectators at a play. As architect of St Peter's and superintendent of Public Works in Rome he completed the basilica of St Peter's and its principal approach to the city – two gigantic, curving colonnades (1656–67). His illusionistic sculpture involved the exact imitation of flesh and fabric and the acute observation of facial expression and of

the human figure in action. He often controlled the lighting or mixed the media of sculpture, architecture and painting for theatrical effect, and was the single person most responsible for giving Rome its predominantly Baroque appearance.

[JH]

Bérulle, Pierre de (1575–1628) French cardinal. Of a noble family, he was educated by the Jesuits, showed a disposition to the religious life, and entered the priesthood (1599). In Paris he was in contact with other like-minded Catholics such as Madame ACARIE and father Benedict of Canfield, and dedicated himself to the cause of reform among the clergy. He went to Spain in 1604 on a diplomatic mission, and arranged for the Discalced Carmelite order to be introduced into France, and for the writings of St TERESA OF AVILA to be translated. In 1611 he founded in Paris a congregation of the Oratory based on that of Philip NERI in Rome, and directed the foundation of other religious institutions. In 1623 he published his principal work, *The Greatness of Jesus*, which emphasised a Christ-centred spirituality. In 1627 he was created cardinal at the king's request. One of the leaders of the so-called 'devout party', which supported an alliance with Spain to promote Catholic interests, Bérulle attracted the strong hostility of RICHELIEU, whose policy called for an alliance of all Frenchmen against Spain.

Berwick, James Fitz-James, 1st duke of (1670–1734) Natural son of JAMES II and of Arabella Churchill, sister of the duke of MARLBOROUGH, he was born and partly educated in France. Created duke by James II in 1687, after the revolution of 1688 he took part in military campaigns in Ireland, and served at the battle of the Boyne (1690). He entered French service in 1693, and was briefly made commander in 1704 of the French forces intervening in the Iberian peninsula during the war of the Spanish Succession. In 1705 he was sent to put down the rebellion of the Camisards (Huguenots) in southern France, and created marshal of France in 1706 after recovering Nice from the army of EUGÈNE OF SAVOY-CARIGNAN. From 1706 he became supreme commander of the Franco-Spanish troops in the war in the peninsula, and led them to victory at Almansa (1707), for which he was rewarded with the titles of duke of Liria and of Jérica. He also directed the siege of Barcelona, entering the city in 1714. In 1733 he was appointed commander of the French forces on the Rhine during the war of the Polish Succession, and was killed at the siege of Philippsburg. His *Memoirs* were published posthumously in 1778.

Bethlen Gábor (1580–1629) prince of Transylvania 1613–29. Born into a leading Hungarian Protestant family, he attended at the court of Transylvania under successive rulers, but his differences with a ruling prince of the Báthory family forced him to flee to the Turks, sovereigns of Transylvania, who gave him support and installed him as prince; the change was approved by the Diet at Kolozsvár in 1613. While the Habsburgs were busy with events in Bohemia in 1618–20 he used the opportunity to overrun most of northern Hungary, and captured Pozsony (now Bratislava) together with the famous crown of St Stephen; the exultant Diet elected him king of Hungary (1620). Bethlen promised to support his fellow-Protestant Frederick of Bohemia (FREDER-ICK V OF WITTELSBACH), but after the battle of the White Mountain (1620) the emperor FERDINAND II, with superior forces at his disposal, persuaded Bethlen to return the crown and transfer the kingship to the Habsburgs. In return for this agreement (1621), he was guaranteed toleration for Hungary's Protestants, extensive estates in Hungary and the title of prince of the empire. He renewed the anti-Habsburg struggle again in 1623 but was defeated and made to agree to the treaty of Vienna (1624). His subsequent military

career, fuelled by incessant intrigues with Poles and with Swedes in an effort to remove the Germanic Habsburgs from Hungary, was likewise unfruitful.

Beza (Bèze), Théodore de (1519–1605) French reformer. Son of lesser nobles of Vézelay, he studied law at Orléans and at Bourges. A serious illness made him rethink his life and he converted to the Reformation (1548). He went to Geneva, where he met CALVIN; shortly after he became professor of Greek at Lausanne (1549), where he composed his tragedy *Abraham Sacrificed*. In 1554 he published in Geneva perhaps his best-known work, the *De Hereticis*, a direct answer to CASTELLION's defence of religious toleration: in it he firmly asserted the right of the secular power to defend true religion, and approved use of the death penalty against heretics. In 1557 he was put in charge of a diplomatic mission to Germany, where he met MELANCHTHON. In 1558 he settled in Geneva as aide to Calvin, and helped in the spread of the Reformed doctrines among the French nobility. He went to France to take part in the colloquy of Poissy (1560), and at the beginning of the civil wars acted as pastor to the Huguenot forces. He returned to Geneva in 1563, and assumed leadership of its church after the death of Calvin; but continued his links with Protestant France, where he presided over the synods of La Rochelle (1571) and Nîmes (1572). He also continued an active career of controversy and learned publications, translating the psalms into French (1563) and the New Testament into Latin from Greek (1556).

Biron, Armand de Gontaut, baron de (1524–92) A leading Catholic commander during the French civil wars, he supported royal authority, and was appointed grand master of artillery and, in 1577, marshal of France. One of the first to rally to HENRY IV as king, he fought on his side in subsequent campaigns and died at the siege of Epernay.

Biron, Charles de Gontaut, duke de (1562–1602) Son of Armand de Gontaut, baron of BIRON, he became a favourite of the king, and was showered with honours by him, becoming admiral of France (1592), marshal (1594), governor of Burgundy (1595) and duke (1598). His success went to his head; he conspired against the king and entered into relations with Savoy and with Spain (1601). He was arrested, and decapitated in the Bastille.

Blake, Robert (1599–1657) English admiral. A Somerset country gentleman, he was educated at Oxford, entering Parliament in 1640 and again in 1645. From 1642 he was an active supporter of the Parliamentary cause and fought for it in the west country. Though he had no apparent experience of the sea, in 1649 he was given command of a naval squadron, pursued the royalist fleet of prince RUPERT into the Mediterranean and destroyed many of its ships off Cartagena (1650). Appointed to CROMWELL's council of state (1651–2) he was nominated to the Barebones Parliament (1653). During his period of command he undertook several important reforms, specially in naval tactics. In the Commonwealth's war of 1652–4 against the United Provinces he commanded the main English fleet in the Channel, facing the forces of TROMP and DE RUYTER. In 1654 he was sent to reconnoitre the Mediterranean, and fought the Barbary corsairs. His last great success was the destruction of the Spanish treasure fleet off Santa Cruz in Tenerife (April 1657), but he died before his vessel returned to Plymouth.

Boabdil, (Abu Abd-allah Mohammed XI), known by Spaniards as (d.1527) Last Muslim ruler of the kingdom of Granada, he acquired the throne (1482) by overthrowing his father, but was plunged into a war with the Christians, who released

him on his oath that he would become their vassal. Once released, he foreswore his oath, and led the resistance to the forces of FERDINAND II OF TRASTÁMARA and ISABELLA THE CATHOLIC. Granada finally surrendered to the Christians on 2 January 1492. Boabdil, like the rest of the Muslim élite, was confirmed in his rank and property, but found life under the Christians impossible, and emigrated to Fez in north Africa in 1493. A site overlooking Granada is known to this day as 'The Moor's Last Sigh', purporting to be the spot from which the departing Boabdil had his last view of the city.

Bocskai, Stephen (István) (1557–1606) prince of Transylvania (1605–6). As a leading noble, he at first favoured alliances with the dominant power of the Catholic Habsburgs, but later became leader of the Protestant resistance to emperor RUDOLF II. Elected prince of Transylvania and king of Hungary by the diet at Szerencs (1605), he joined forces with the Turks against the Habsburgs, forcing from the latter the peace of Vienna (1606), which recognised the liberties of Hungary. He died shortly after, allegedly poisoned.

Bodin, Jean (1529–96) French scholar and writer. In 1548 he went to pursue higher studies at Paris, where he learnt Greek and Hebrew. Though in minor orders, he gave up thoughts of a religious life, went to study law at Toulouse (1556–61) and came under the influence of Calvinism. He became an advocate of the parlement of Paris, and one of the advisers of the duke d'Alençon (later ANJOU); he also narrowly escaped being killed in the massacre of St Bartholomew's Eve (1572). He was later appointed an advocate of the king, and elected deputy to the Estates General of Blois (1576). He accompanied Anjou when the latter went to England seeking the hand of Elizabeth. During the subsequent phases of the civil wars in France, he veered to the side of the

Catholic League, but in 1593 declared himself for HENRY IV. One of the greatest scholars of his time, he combined extensive learning with active participation in military and political affairs. His chief written works concern law, politics and philosophy. They include the *Methodus ad facilem Historiarum cognitionem* (1566) (*Method for Easy Comprehension of History*); the *Réponse aux paradoxes de M. de Malestroit* (Reply to the Paradoxes of M. de Malestroit) (1566), which took issue over the causes of inflation and suggested a new explanation for the phenomenon; the *Six Books of the Republic* (1576); the *Démonomanie* (1580), which defended the reality of witchcraft; and the *Universale theatrum naturae* (1594) (*Theatre of Nature*). His *Heptaplomeres* (*Dialogue of Seven Wise Men*), written in about 1593, remained unpublished until 1857. In it he criticised all existing religions, concluding that truth is to be found in all beliefs. The *Republic*, re-edited almost annually during his lifetime and then translated into Latin, Italian, Spanish and German (but not English), was an analysis of contemporary politics that won him immediate notoriety. Confused and often contradictory in its exposition, it was more misunderstood than read. Bodin argued that in a well-ordered state the ruler must be absolute sovereign, supreme over all laws and parliaments, but subject to God and the natural law, and respectful of the constituent bodies in the state.

Bodley, Sir Thomas (1545–1613) English diplomat. Born in Exeter, his father was a Marian exile and he was educated in Geneva, returning after the accession of ELIZABETH I to be educated at Oxford, where he devoted himself to a study of languages, mastering Hebrew and then travelling on the continent, where he learned Italian, French and Spanish. He entered Parliament in 1584, and was then employed by queen Elizabeth on diplomatic missions to Denmark, Germany and France (1584–96), being knighted (1604)

for his services. After his diplomatic years, he devoted himself entirely to his chief care, the restoration of the great university library at Oxford, which was formally opened in 1602 and which thereafter bore his name.

Boehme, Jakob (1575–1624) German mystic. Born near Görlitz in Silesia of a Lutheran peasant family, he had little formal education but through reading picked up a taste for the culture of Luther's Bible, and for the writings of German mystics. Trained as a shoemaker, he settled in Görlitz, where he combined his profession with a dedication to godly living based on his own visionary experiences. The experiences impelled him to produce a book, *The Aurora* (1612), which had a devotional basis but extended into universal themes such as the struggle between good and evil. His writings, based on vague philosophy and theology, and influenced to an extent by the ideas of PARACELSUS, were treated with respect by those who had access to them. He then produced his more mature works, notably the *Great Mystery* (*Mysterium Magnum*) (1623), which explained the universe in terms of mysticism and of Biblical piety. He produced possibly thirty works in the last five years of his life. His writings had a widespread success in his own time (in England William LAW was influenced by him) and with later generations, and had a great influence on Romanticism. For Boehme our grasp of the universe is attained only through subordinating our will to God, who reveals himself through the visible world; the 'great mystery' is this revelation of God, available to those who have faith in him.

Boerhaave, Herman (1668–1738) Dutch physician and chemist, with wide-ranging scientific interests. As professor of medicine and botany at Leiden from 1709, later also professor of physics and of chemistry, he became a hugely influential teacher and author. He made few new medical discoveries, apart from being the first to describe the sweat glands, but is credited with founding the tradition of clinical teaching through his unusual practice of giving students direct contact with patients. He consequently earned the title of 'the Dutch Hippocrates' (plus a lot of money) and did a great deal to maintain Leiden's reputation as a European centre for medical studies. Textbooks on physiology and chemistry preceded *Elementae chemiae* (1732), his most important published work. A skilled experimentalist, he propounded a corpuscular view of matter, to be supported by experimentation and quantification; his understanding of the human body was also based upon mechanical principles, but not narrowly so. He was especially influential in acting as a channel through which English mechanical and experimental philosophy reached the continent. The Boerhaave Museum at Leiden is named in his honour.

[FW]

Boileau, Nicolas (1636–1711) (also called Despréaux) French poet and literary critic. Though he was early on destined for the Church, he did not take to theology and turned to the law. But he was enabled to indulge his abiding passion for literature when his father left him a small fortune. He became a friend of MOLIÈRE, LA FONTAINE, RACINE and other figures in the literary world. Against this background he sought to change traditional modes and install a new school of writers through the medium of his *Satires* (1680–98). His aesthetic principles were later set out in his *Art Poétique* (1674) and his *Epitres* (1663–95). As a result he gained the patronage of LOUIS XIV, who named him and Racine as his official historians. In 1684 at the king's express wish he entered the Académie Française. Boileau was no professional court flatterer. He attacked pomposity in well-established figures through burlesque, and was the guiding spirit behind the changing French

literary taste of the period, becoming known as the 'lawmaker of Parnassus'.

[BT]

Boisguilbert, Pierre le Pesant, sieur de (1646–1714) Born in Rouen of a leading family of officials, and cousin of VAUBAN, he held administrative office as lieutenant of the *bailliage* (bailiwick) of Rouen, using his expert knowledge to publish works on economic policy. His *Détail de la France* (1695) analysed, with some irony, the reasons for current economic problems, and proposed as a solution the radical reduction of taxes. His *Factum de la France* (1706) argued that lower taxes tended to increase productivity. Because both works proposed fundamental reforms in the system, they earned him the disfavour of the authorities; the *Factum* was banned for a while in 1707. He has generally been viewed as the earliest of the Physiocrats, who were to argue a generation later that the state should interfere as little as possible in productive economy.

Boleyn, Anne (1507–36) second wife of HENRY VIII of England and queen 1533–6. Daughter of Sir Thomas Boleyn, later earl of Wiltshire, she and her elder sister Mary were ladies-in-waiting of Henry's sister, and the king had a short affair with Mary. In the 1520s Henry's intentions moved to the younger sister, and by 1527 his attachment to her caused the first moves to obtain a divorce from his wife CATHERINE OF ARAGON; by 1528 Anne was set up in stately apartments at Greenwich. In 1533 Henry married the now pregnant Anne in secret, and shortly after she was crowned queen. After the birth of her daughter ELIZABETH I (1533), which disappointed the king's wish for a male heir, he began to tire of her; a subsequent miscarriage and a stillbirth failed to help her. Her fall from favour was precipitated by the struggle among political factions at court. She became an enemy of Thomas

CROMWELL, an opponent of her pro-French attitude, and was opposed by Catholics, hostile to her active support for the Reformation. Both groups combined to back sensational accusations against her. In 1536 she was arrested and accused of both adultery and incest (the latter, with her brother); historians consider the charges unproven. Tried by a select court of peers (among them her uncle and her father) in the Tower, she was condemned, and executed in May. Two days before, her marriage was pronounced invalid by the Church. Eleven days after her death, the king married Jane Seymour.

Bolingbroke, Henry St John, 1st viscount (1678–1751) English politician. Member of Parliament in 1701 for the Tory interest, despite a strong Whig family background, he attracted the attention of queen ANNE STUART. Appointed as secretary for War (1704–8) in the ministry run by Robert HARLEY, he was out of Parliament from 1708–10 but returned to become northern secretary of state (1710–14), and helped to conclude negotiations for the peace of Utrecht (1713), which earned him his noble title. After the death of Anne he was excluded from power by the Whig interest under GEORGE I, and exiled himself to France (1714), where he developed links with the Jacobites in favour of the Stuart succession. He soon dropped the Jacobite connection, married a French lady as his second wife, and dedicated himself to writing and reflection. Eventually in 1723 he obtained an official pardon for his Jacobite days and returned to England (1725), where he recovered his property and spent his time writing. He was, however, refused permission to resume his title or his seat in the Lords. Frustrated, and also disgusted by prevailing political corruption, he resumed his attacks (in the journal *The Craftsman*, which survived 1626–36) upon the Whigs and on the ministry of WALPOLE. From 1735 he made France his base, kept in touch with the opposition circle round the

prince of Wales, and wrote his best-known work, *The Idea of a Patriot King*, which circulated privately and was not formally published by him until 1749. In it he argued against the existence of parties, which he saw as selfish and destructive, and proposed the formation of an alliance of all opinions in defence of the crown. He returned home in 1744 and died in London.

Bolotnikov, Ivan Isaevich (d.1608) Russian rebel. A serf by origin, he fled from his estate to Cossack territory, where he was captured by Tatars and sold as a galley-slave to the Turks. Freed from the ships by German vessels, he went to Venice, then returned to Russia through Poland. In the summer of 1606 he became leader of a massive peasant rebellion in southern Russia, provoked by the famine of 1603 and by intensification of serfdom; his armies defeated the forces of tsar Vasilii SHUISKY and besieged Moscow (October 1606). After several conflicts with royal troops, his forces were finally defeated at Tula in October 1607. He was exiled and later executed.

Bonner, Edmund (*c*.1500–69) English ecclesiastic. As one of the clergy of HENRY VIII he ardently supported the king's plea for divorce from CATHERINE OF ARAGON, went to Rome (1532) to defend the plea, and carried out further missions in Germany and France (1538). While in France, he was appointed to the see of London (1539), and in 1542–3 was again on the continent as ambassador to the emperor. As a firm Catholic, he refused to accept the religious changes under EDWARD VI and spent a time in prison (1549–53). Freed on the accession of queen MARY I (1553), he took a leading part in the trials two years later of people suspected of heresy, and apparently earned among Protestants the epithet of 'bloody Bonner'. His malign reputation rests rather on the emotive testimony of the martyrologist John FOXE, than on any proven lust for persecution. When ELIZABETH I came to the throne (1558) he refused to conform to the new religion, and spent the last six years of his life in prison.

Bonneval, Claude, count de (1675–1747) French adventurer. From a noble family of Limousin and a relative of admiral Tourville, he dedicated his life to a military career. One of the most dramatic figures of his time, he served as an officer in Italy (1702–6) under CATINAT and VENDÔME, but was castigated by the war minister CHAMILLART for having given offence to Madame de MAINTENON. He then took service under the Austrians (1706), fighting with them against France at the battle of Malplaquet. Pardoned by the French, he returned to Paris in 1717 to get married, then served against the Turks at Belgrade. While in Brussels in 1724, he also quarrelled with prince EUGÈNE OF SAVOY-CARIGNAN, was imprisoned for insubordination but escaped to Venice and then to Bosnia (1729). There he turned Muslim (1730), went to Istanbul where he received the favour of the sultan, took the name of Achmed Pasha, and led the Turks to victory over the Austrians. In the 1740s he was in contact with the French during the war of the Austrian Succession. He died in Istanbul.

Borelli, Giovanni (or Gian) Alfonso (1608–79) Italian mathematician, medic and astronomer. As a lecturer in mathematics at Messina, later a professor there, and professor at Pisa from 1656, he published extensively: not only on mathematical topics but also on astronomy, especially the motions of Jupiter's satellites, and on physiology. In the last of these areas he studied respiration, circulation, digestion, the physical force involved in such processes, and the relation of brain and nerves to the action of muscles, which he was the first (in print, at least) to explain on mechanical principles. While at Messina he was a member of the Accademia della Fucina, and while at Pisa a

leading member of the Accademia del Cimento. In later life he returned to Messina, but was forced into exile as a rebel against the Spanish rulers of Sicily; he spent his last few years in Rome, participating in the Accademia Fisica-matematica sponsored by queen CHRISTINA VASA. His physiological theories were presented in a work dedicated to her: *De motu animalium* (2 vols, 1680–1). Meanwhile, his bravery was conspicuously demonstrated by expeditions to observe eruptions of Mount Etna at close quarters, which resulted in his publishing one of the earliest detailed accounts of volcanic activity.

[FW]

Borgia Family of Catalans who came to Italy with Alfonso the Magnanimous after his 1443 conquest of the kingdom of Naples. Vilified by its rivals, the family's foreign status and nepotism no doubt contributed to its nefarious reputation. As well as those that follow, see CALIXTUS III and ALEXANDER VI.

[JM]

Borgia, Cesare (*c*.1475/6–1507) captain general of papal forces under his father ALEXANDER VI and model for MACHIAVELLI's prince. As the younger son of Roderigo, he was originally groomed for an ecclesiastical career with studies at Perugia and Pisa, and appointment as archbishop of Valencia in 1492 and cardinal in 1493. Upon the death of his elder brother Juan, the duke of Gandía, in 1498, he renounced his clerical life to spearhead the reconquest of the Papal States. He married Charlotte d'Albret, sister of the king of Navarre and was made duke of Valentinois, called duke Valentino in Italy. His military efforts concentrated on carving out a dynastic base in the Romagna and it was there that he impressed the Florentine diplomat-historian Machiavelli so profoundly. In *The Prince* he is the epitome of the man of *fortuna*, whose brilliant ruthlessness wins him dubious praise. Ill himself at the time of his father's death, he was not able to seize the moment and found himself outmanœuvred by his chief rival, cardinal Giuliano della Rovere, who succeeded the brief interim pontificate of Paul III as JULIUS II in the same year 1503. Stripped of his power and strongholds, isolated and exiled, Cesare fled to Naples, Spain and eventually Navarre, where he was killed in local fighting in 1507.

[JM]

Borgia, Lucrezia (1480–1519) daughter of ALEXANDER VI and sister of Cesare BORGIA, and the central figure in their dynastic marriage strategies. There is no foundation to rumours of incest or poisonous intrigues; she was used as a pawn in three marriage plans. When her first marriage in 1492 to Giovanni Sforza of Pesaro was no longer politically expedient to papal policy, it was annulled. A second marriage in 1498 to Alfonso, duke of Bisceglie, illegitimate son of Alfonso II of Naples, ended with his murder by Cesare's agents in 1500, as another shift in papal alliances dictated. Her third marriage in 1502 to Alfonso d'ESTE, who became duke of Ferrara, produced seven children, four surviving infancy. At Ferrara, duchess after 1505, she became known as a patron of writers and artists, including a famous correspondence with BEMBO. In 1519 she died, of an infection following childbirth, as a reputed pious woman.

[JM]

Borja, Francisco de (1510–72) duke of Gandía. Eldest son of the second duke of Gandía (whose family name was rendered BORGIA in Italian), and great-nephew of pope ALEXANDER VI and of FERDINAND II OF TRASTÁMARA, he was educated in Saragossa and entered the service of the royal court. In 1529 he married a Portuguese lady-in-waiting of the empress Isabella, wife of CHARLES V. Charged with the funeral procession to Granada in 1539 of the empress, the sight of her wasted corpse shocked him profoundly with a conviction of the fragility of human life; the event began his spiritual conversion. He went on to serve as viceroy of Catalonia (1539–43), then retired to the family estates in Gandía (Valencia), to which title he succeeded on his father's death in 1542. After the death of his wife in 1546, he decided to retire from his possessions and entered the Society of Jesus (1548), then went to Rome. He returned to Spain in 1551, took holy orders and dedicated himself to missionary work and to the establishment of the Jesuits in Spain and Portugal. In 1559 an unauthorised edition of his book *Obras del Cristiano* (*The Works of a Christian*), was prohibited by the Inquisition and caused a stir that obliged him to leave Spain forever. He remained in Rome and in 1565 became general of the Jesuits, working effectively to organise the order in the foreign mission field.

Borromeo, Carlo (1538–84) cardinal archbishop of Milan who was the model of the post-Tridentine bishop. Born of a Milanese noble family, his clerical career advanced under his maternal uncle, pope PIUS IV. After his doctorate in civil and canon law from Pavia in 1559, Pius made him archbishop of Milan and Cardinal Nephew, resident in Rome as the leading figure in the papal court and Church curia. He was the pope's man at the third convocation of the council of Trent (1562–3), instrumental in executing its decrees, and steward of the Roman catechism of 1566. After the pope's death and election of his successor, Pius V, in 1566, Borromeo moved to his diocese in Milan where he established himself as the model pastor. His method of administration and his detailed regulations, along with the degree of autonomy granted to him as a former papal nephew to organise his diocese and its unique Ambrosian rite, made Milan and its Counter-Reformation practices the models of post-Tridentine reform in Italy and France. He was canonised in 1610, twenty-five years after his death.

[JM]

Bosch, Hieronymus (Jeroen van Aken) (*c*.1450–1516) Dutch painter active in 's-Hertogenbosch (Brabant). The descendant of a family of painters and joiners, he married a patrician wife (1481) twenty-five years older than himself, becoming one of the wealthiest 10 per cent of the city's citizens – a fact not without significance in light of his often bizarre imagery. He owned a house in the Schildersstraetken (Little Street of the Painters), and was the only artist privileged to belong to the Brotherhood of Our Lady, a religious confraternity dedicated to moral uplift and works of charity whose membership included the priests serving the parish of the church (now cathedral) of St John, as well as the city's most prominent citizens. Other members included count Henry III of Nassau, the first owner of the triptych known as *The Garden of Earthly Delights* (Madrid, Prado), and Diego de Guevara, whose collection of six of the artist's paintings was later acquired by PHILIP II. His activity as designer of a stained glass window, a chandelier and an altarpiece for the Brotherhood's chapel in St John's is recorded, as is the commission, for a Last Judgement (1504; now lost) for PHILIP THE FAIR of Burgundy. Other early collectors included queen ISABELLA, MARGARET OF AUSTRIA, the bishop of Utrecht Philip of Burgundy, and after Bosch's death cardinal GRANVELLE, the duke of ALBA and the emperor RUDOLF II. However, his liberal use of the fantastic and the grotesque have made him a great deal more famous in the twentieth century – since the advent of Freudian pyschology and Surrealist painting – than was the case in his own day. Some of the unusual features of his style are simply due to his provincial training, in the presence of illuminated manuscripts, German engravings, travel books, pharmaceutical equip-

ment, and popular hagiography (e.g. the *Golden Legend* and *Vitae Patrum*, both available in newly printed Dutch translations.) In other cases his imagery corresponds to archaic Dutch figures of speech – their moral values lost when his principal works were removed from the Netherlands to the Iberian peninsula in the sixteenth century.

[JH]

Bossuet, Jacques Bénigne (1627–1704) French bishop. The most illustrious prelate of his time, bishop of Condom (1669) then of Meaux (1681), he became distinguished as court orator at the funerals of the greatest personages of the day. Appointed tutor (1670–81) to the heir to the throne, Louis (who died before he could succeed), Bossuet devoted himself to the writing of political treatises that were intended to guide the future king in the paths of absolute kingship: the outstanding works of this genre were his *Discourse on World History* (1679) and the *Politique tirée de l'Ecriture sainte* (Politics Based on Holy Scripture). A firm supporter of the French crown against the pretensions of the papacy, he presided over the 1681 Assembly of the Clergy that drew up the Gallican Articles, affirming the privileges of the Gallican Church. An inveterate controversialist and stalwart conservative, he wrote against the Huguenots in France (and greeted with rapture the Revocation of the Edict of Nantes in 1685), argued against the new textual criticism of Richard SIMON and debated philosophy with LEIBNIZ. He was drawn into a famous conflict (1695–9) with FÉNELON over the case of madame GUYON. Bossuet epitomised the alliance between absolute monarchy and a conservative Church.

Botero, Giovanni (1544–1617) political theorist and historian. A native of Savoy, he studied in Jesuit schools in Palermo and Rome, where he was ordained in the order sometime between 1571–4. He continued his studies and served in various capacities in Rome, Paris, Milan, Padua and elsewhere before receiving an honourable discharge from the Jesuits in 1580 after twenty two years as a member. After two years of pastoral duties, he entered the reformist circle of cardinal Carlo BORROMEO in Milan as his secretary and member of his household. He stayed on as an intellectual guide and secretary to the saint's successor cardinal Federico Borromeo, with occasional diplomatic assignments for CARLO EMANUELE I of Savoy. In 1588 he published *Delle cause della grandezza e magnificenza della città* (The Causes of Greatness and Magnificence of Cities), quickly followed in 1589 by *Della ragion di stato* (On Reason of State). Both were anti-Machiavellian explorations of Reason of State political theory which accepted the hard-boiled realism in a Christian moral context and forwarded a demographic-geographic rationale underlying politics. His world history, *Relazioni universali*, which was continually added to and updated, first appeared in 1591. In 1599 he became the tutor of the Savoyard royal children at the court of Carlo Emanuele in Turin, where he lived the rest of his life as an honoured counsellor and secretary.

Bothwell, earls of

4th earl, James Hepburn (*c*.1536–78) Scots nobleman. He succeeded to his father's title in 1556 and, though a Protestant by persuasion, supported MARY STUART when she became queen and was appointed to her privy council (1561). From 1562–5 he was embroiled in political conflicts with other nobles, and was forced to flee to France. Recalled by Mary in 1565 to support her against the critics of her marriage with DARNLEY, he backed her in the controversy following the murder of RIZZIO (1566), and was rewarded with political power and the queen's affections. When Darnley was murdered he was accused of the crime, but was conveniently acquitted and subsequently married Mary (1567), according to Protestant rites. He was now created duke of Orkney and Shetland. The nobles, both Catholic and Protestant, rose against him and he fled to Denmark, where he ended his days in prison and insane.

5th earl, Francis Stuart Hepburn (d.1614) Created the 5th earl in 1581, he succeeded his uncle in the title, rising to high office under JAMES VI, but was involved in conspiracies, imprisoned on a charge of witchcraft, and eventually in 1591 outlawed by the Scots Parliament. He fled to France in about 1595 and died in poverty in Naples; the title became extinct.

Botticelli, Sandro

Botticelli, Sandro (Alessandro di Filipepi di Mariano di Vanni) (1445–1510) Florentine painter. Highly esteemed during the 1470s and 1480s – and again in the late nineteenth century when he was 'rediscovered' by Ruskin – his elegant, linear and shadowless style and liberal use of gold leaf were a visual counterpart to the Neoplatonic philosophy in vogue in the Medici circle – a deliberate snub to the scientific advances made in the uses of perspective and realistic human proportion by painters and sculptors of the Florentine mainstream. His paintings were made to seem old-fashioned by the more robust art of the young RAPHAEL, and his commissions became less frequent by 1490. According to VASARI he had been a student of Fra Filippo Lippi, becoming a master by 1470 and a member of the Company of St Luke in 1472, and was himself the teacher of Lippi's son Filippino. At his peak, his patrons included Lorenzo de' MEDICI and his son Piero; Ludovico SFORZA, Isabella d'ESTE, and Sixtus IV. His best works include the elaborate Neoplatonic allegories *Primavera* (*Birth of Spring*, 1478) and *Birth of Venus* (1484; both Florence, Uffizi), the *Madonna with Singing Angels* (Berlin), and frescoes depicting scenes from the life of Christ (1481; Rome, Sistine Chapel).

On the basis of the enigmatic inscription on his *Mystic Nativity* (1500; London, National Gallery) he is thought to have been a follower of SAVONAROLA in the 1490s. In January 1491 he was one of the judges for the design of the façade for the cathedral in Florence.

[JH]

Boufflers, Louis François, marquis then duke de (1644–1711) marshal of France. Born in the family chateau in Picardy, he dedicated himself to a military career, serving in north Africa (1664), Flanders (1667), Lorraine (1670) and in the war against Holland (1672). After further service in Germany, he was appointed lieutenant general in 1681, and governor of Lorraine in 1687. After campaigns against the Dutch in the 1690s, he was appointed marshal of France 1693. He was obliged to surrender Namur to WILLIAM III of Orange in 1695, but received recognition from the king, who created him duke that year. In the war of the Spanish Succession, he became famous for his four-month defence of Lille against prince EUGÈNE OF SAVOY-CARIGNAN in 1708, for which he was further honoured by LOUIS XIV. His last important command was with marshal VILLARS at the battle of Malplaquet, when he organised the retreat of the French armies.

Bouillon, Henri de la Tour d'Auvergne, viscount Turenne and 1st duke de (1555–1623) Born in the family chateau near Clermont, orphaned at three and brought up by his uncle the duke de Montmorency, he early became a Calvinist, and joined the Politique grouping of nobles who were opposed to HENRY III in the French civil wars. From about 1576 he gave his support to Henry of Navarre. In 1581 he took part in the duke d'ANJOU's invasion of the Netherlands, but was captured and remained prisoner until 1584; on his return he resumed his part in the civil wars. HENRY IV rewarded him

by supporting his marriage in 1591 to a rich heiress, from whom he derived that year the title of duke. He was created marshal by the king in 1592. He strongly disagreed with the king's conversion to Catholicism, and became involved in the BIRON conspiracy (1601–2) against Henry; when it was discovered he fled the country (1602–10). After Henry's death in 1610 he returned but continued to conspire with Calvinist nobles (ROHAN and the 3rd prince de CONDÉ) against the regency government led by SULLY. His second marriage (1595) was to a daughter of WILLIAM I of Orange, one of the sons of the marriage being the great TURENNE.

Bourbon This historic noble family eventually reigned over both France and Spain. Originating in the Bourbonnais, it wielded extensive local power from the thirteenth century, and from the fourteenth was participating in the government of France. In the process, it split into several branches: that of Vendôme (see ANTOINE DE BOURBON) gave seven kings to France; the Spanish branch has ruled Spain, with some gaps, since 1701.

Charles II, 8th duke de Bourbon, known as the constable of Bourbon (1490–1527) After a notable military career in the service of LOUIS XII, who appointed him constable of France (1514), he went on to achieve the victory of Marignano over Imperial forces in Italy (1515), and was appointed (1516) by FRANCIS I as viceroy of Milan. A conflict with the crown made him transfer his services (1523) to the emperor CHARLES V, who appointed him to command the Imperial armies, at whose head he defeated the French forces at the battle of Pavia (1525) and made the king of France prisoner. He died shortly after while leading the Imperial troops in the attack that led to the sack of Rome.

Charles, cardinal of Bourbon (1523–90) uncle of HENRY IV and holder of four bishoprics (including Rouen) and six abbeys (including Saint-Denis and Jumièges), and cardinal from 1548. As the principal male Catholic heir of the house he was in the 1580s selected as prospective heir to the throne by the Catholic League and supported by Spain. When HENRY III assassinated the Guise leaders in 1588, and imprisoned the cardinal, the League shifted their allegiance to the latter, whom they called 'Charles X'. Eventually he renounced his title in favour of his nephew Henry IV.

Louis Henri, duke de Bourbon, and 7th prince de Condé (1692–1740) As a leading member of his family rather than on his own merits, he was named head of the regency council during the minority of LOUIS XV, and became chief minister on the death of the regent ORLÉANS (1723) but retained power for only a short while and was supplanted in 1726 by cardinal FLEURY. He withdrew to his estates and devoted himself to the sciences.

Boyle, Robert (1627–91) English chemist and experimental scientist. A son of the first earl of Cork, he was associated with the HARTLIB group and with the scientific circle headed by John Wilkins at Oxford in the late 1650s. He employed Robert HOOKE and the instrument-maker Ralph Greatorex to design and construct England's first air-pump; in a 1662 study of air pressure he introduced what is now called 'Boyle's Law': that at constant temperature the volume of a gas varies inversely with the pressure. In 1668 he settled permanently in London, in the house of one of his learned elder sisters, Lady Ranelagh, where he set up a laboratory. He was an influential founder member of the Royal Society, though after some years he retreated from active involvement. This and his many publications earned him an unrivalled reputation as an experimenter and as a leading exponent of a 'mechanical philosophy' derived largely from DESCARTES. The combination proved especially fruitful in chemistry, where his belief that matter was composed of primary particles coales-

cing to form 'corpuscules' led to significant practical advances, and helped to distance the subject from its roots in medicine and alchemy. His promotion of a general experimental methodology was also of wider importance, especially amongst early Newtonians and thus to recent historians.

[FW]

Bradley, James (1693–1762) English astronomer. Encouraged to study and practice astronomy by his uncle, the Reverend James Pound (who had himself made observations in the Far East), he initially combined it with a career in the church. This altered when he was appointed Savilian professor of astronomy at Oxford, in 1721; he held that post until 1742, when he became third astronomer royal on the death of HALLEY. In a paper read to the Royal Society in 1729 he announced his discovery of the 'aberration of light' – the apparent displacement of stars produced by the combined effect of the finite speed of light and the earth's movement in its orbit, an effect which had been detected but misinterpreted by FLAMSTEED. It now provided the first observational confirmation of Copernicanism, as it could not have occurred unless the earth moved in an orbit. Bradley also discovered the nutation of the earth's axis, an uneven 'nodding' caused by the gravitational pull of the moon. He was not only highly regarded for these achievements but personally well-liked by all his contemporaries – an uncommon trait amongst the early astronomers royal.

[FW]

Brahe, Tycho (1546–1601) Danish astronomer. As a member of the highest nobility, he was able to indulge his taste for astronomy as a teenager, as a student at Copenhagen and at leading German universities. His early observations convinced him of the unreliability of existing astronomical tables; his own superior abilities were demonstrated in print by his analysis of the 'new star' (supernova) seen in Cassiopeia in 1572. Having secured the patronage of FREDERIK II OF DENMARK he was given the island of Hven, where from 1576 he established an observatory named 'Uraniborg'; it was lavishly equipped with large astronomical instruments, well-staffed with assistants, and had its own printing-press. This enabled him to make his work widely known, and to promote his own distinctive non-Copernican view of the solar system, in which the five known planets orbited the sun whilst the sun orbited the earth. After his patron's death he was forced to leave Denmark; in 1599 he settled in Prague, where he was supported by the emperor RUDOLF II until his death. His observations were then used by KEPLER (his former assistant) to deduce laws of planetary motion, and to publish the *Rudolphine Tables*, although the observations themselves were not published until later in the century.

[FW]

Bramante, Donato (Donato di Pascuccio d'Antonio) (*c*.1443–1514) Italian architect, painter and engineer, active in Milan and Rome. Considered 'the father of High Renaissance architecture', he was the son of a farmer in Monte Asdruvaldo, in the commune of Fermignano. He is first documented in 1477, as the creator of perspective decorations for the Palazzo del Podestà in Bergamo. His most important works include the Tempietto at the Roman church of S. Pietro in Montorio, commissioned (1502) by FERDINAND II OF TRASTÁMARA and ISABELLA THE CATHOLIC to mark the spot where St Peter was crucified; and his commissions for JULIUS II – the Vatican Belvedere and the original Greek cross plan for new St Peter's, which now forms the chancel area. He was a friend of LEONARDO DA VINCI's, and was also a poet, a gifted musician, and a favoured companion of Julius II, who liked Bramante to read Dante to him in the evening. The house he built for himself –

the Palazzo Caprini ('Raphael's House') – was acquired by RAPHAEL in 1517.

[JH]

Brant, Sebastian (1458–1521) Born in Strasbourg of a patrician family, he was educated at the university of Basel, where he completed a doctorate in law and taught in the law faculty, while also publishing his writings with several publishers in the city. An accomplished humanist, he enjoyed the friendship of REUCHLIN and was praised by ERASMUS. Though he wrote much in Latin (*Varia Carmina*, 1498), he became better known for his work in German. He is most famous for his 'Ship of Fools' (*Narrenschiff*) (Nürnberg 1494), a satirical poem depicting the follies and mistakes of mankind, which immediately achieved success in the German lands, becoming the most popular work in German literature before the epoch of Goethe. In 1500 he returned to Strasbourg, where he took up a career on the city council and identified himself with the humanists there, notably Jakob Wimpfeling.

Brantôme, Pierre de Bourdeille, abbé and lord of (1540–1614) French soldier and chronicler. Brought up at the court of the queen of Navarre, he was educated in Paris and in 1557 endowed with the abbey from which he derived his title. He travelled in Italy (1557–9), visited Scotland (1561, when MARY STUART returned), served with the Spanish forces at the capture of the African fortress of the Peñón de Vélez (1564), travelled through the peninsula, and was present at the meeting in Bayonne (1565) between CATHERINE DE MÉDICIS and the queen of Spain, then went on to Italy. From 1567 he was active on the royalist side in the French civil wars, and served the crown in several capacities. Injured after falling off his horse in 1581, he retired to write his memoirs from 1583. The multi-volume *Mémoires*, published for the first time in 1665–6, offer a superb commentary on the lives of the principal lords and ladies of his time.

Bravo, Juan (d.1521) From a noble family of Segovia, he served as a councillor of the city and leader of its militia, at a time when Segovia had joined the Comunero uprising of 1520 against the government of CHARLES V, who had just left for Germany. Leading the outnumbered Comunero forces into battle against the royalists at Villalar (23 April 1521), he and other leaders, notably Juan Padilla, were captured and on the following day executed. Bravo became one of the archetypal symbols of freedom for Castilians.

Brenz, Johannes (1499–1570) German religious reformer. Born near Stuttgart, the son of a judge, he graduated at Heidelberg university (1518) and lectured there. A contact with Luther in Heidelberg (1518) evoked his sympathy for the Reformation, but he continued his career, became a priest, and then began to introduce the Reformation during his tenure as parish priest of Schwäbisch Hall (1522–48). He advised the ruler of Württemberg on ways to introduce the Reformation in that state (1536), which he helped organise along Lutheran lines, culminating in ordinances of 1559. He also took part in the religious colloquies between Reformation leaders (Marburg 1529) and with Catholics (Regensburg 1541). In his early years he was known as an opponent of the use of force and as a favourer of toleration, but he changed his posture in later years. In the 1550s he held administrative posts in the cathedral of Stuttgart.

Browne, Sir Thomas (1605–82) English physician and writer. Graduating from Oxford in 1626, he practised medicine for a while, then after travelling through Europe settled in Norwich. He obtained his doctorate in medicine at Oxford (1637), and married (1641) a lady who bore him ten children. In 1643 he published a work which was written around 1635 and had circulated in manuscript till then: the *Religio Medici* (A Doctor's Faith). It was an immediate success, both in English and in the Latin translation published on the continent; subsequently, editions came out in all the major languages. Combining an appeal to orthodox belief, homely sentiment, informed reason and universal liberality, it brought faith and reason together and satisfied every type of reader. In later writings he explored various facets of philosophy and natural history, and became a national celebrity, knighted by CHARLES II in 1671.

Bruegel, Pieter the Elder (1525/30–69) Flemish painter and designer of engravings. First documented in the studio of Claudio Dorizi in Mechelen, he became a master in the Antwerp painters' guild in 1551, and travelled in Italy from 1551–*c*.4, where he was befriended by the papal miniaturist, Giulio Clovio. Returning to Antwerp by way of the Alps he was employed by the publisher Hieronymus Cock to supply drawings of wide-angled Alpine landscapes, and of grotesque and comic subject matter signed 'Hieronymus Bosch', as well as a series of Virtues and Vices, all for use as designs for engraving. His known paintings were all done 1557–69 – the majority after his marriage in 1563 to the daughter of Pieter Coecke van Aelst and his move to Brussels, where he lived in the parish of Notre Dame de la Chapelle in the Spanish quarter near the royal court. Sixteen of his paintings, apparently including the landscapes representing the labours of the months, were commissioned by the Antwerp financier Nicolas Jonghelinck, whose brother was the sculptor most favoured by cardinal GRANVELLE. Another patron was Abraham ORTELIUS. Posthumously the archduke Ernst and emperor RUDOLF II acquired the most important collection of the artist's work (now in the Kunsthistorisches Museum, Vienna.) The iconography of such paintings as the *Battle Between*

Carnival and Lent (1559, Vienna), or of
the engraving of *Faith* (1559/60) give
solid evidence of his Catholic faith, and
the fact that in January of 1568, shortly
before his death, a 'Pierre of Bruegel' was
exempted from the necessity to have
Spanish soldiers billeted in his house
suggests a high regard for him on the part
of the government in the south Netherlands. He died on 5 September 1569 and
was interred in the parish church of Notre
Dame de la Chapelle, leaving two infant
sons, Pieter the Younger (b. 1564), and
Jan (b. 1568), both of whom became
painters and founders of an artistic dynasty that endured well into the eighteenth century.

[JH]

Brulart, Nicolas, marquis de Sillery
(1544–1624) French politician. Son of a
noble member of the parlement of Paris,
he followed his father's career, becoming
master of requests (1574), member of the
parlement, and councillor of state (1587).
He carried out diplomatic functions for
the crown, mainly to the Swiss cantons.
Under HENRY IV he became a president of
the parlement (1595), was sent to negotiate the peace of Vervins (1598) with Spain,
and then went to Italy to settle the divorce
of the king from MARGUERITE OF VALOIS
and his marriage with MARIE DE MÉDICIS.
Chancellor and keeper of the seals from
1604, after the death of Henry IV he
acted as adviser to the queen regent in
the difficult political situation created by
the absence of a firm directing hand. He
retired from politics in 1616 to his estates
(made into a marquisate in 1619), but
returned again briefly to the regency
council in the last years of his life, though
without exercising significant influence.
His children married into associated noble
families in the government.

Brulart, Pierre (1583–1640) French politician. Heir to Nicholas BRULART, at the
age of seventeen he was already secretary
of state, thanks in part to his marriage to

the granddaughter of the minister Villeroy,
and was sent to Spain as special envoy to
negotiate the marriage of LOUIS XIII with
ANNE OF AUSTRIA. Thereafter he slowly
took charge of all foreign relations, combining control of diplomacy with that of
war. Opposed by RICHELIEU, he withdrew
from politics shortly after his father did.

Brunelleschi, Filippo (1377–1446) Florentine architect. The son of a notary, he was
first trained as a goldsmith, becoming a
master in 1404. However, he was destined
to become the creator of the first architectural monuments of the Italian Renaissance. Unlike Alberti, who was an
amateur most important as a theorist,
Brunelleschi successfully combined knowledge of the classical orders with the
brilliant and intuitive mind of an engineer.
His most monumental undertaking was
the construction of the dome of the
Florentine cathedral – one of the largest
surviving masonry domes, and the supreme engineering accomplishment of the
fifteenth century (1418–36). However,
still more important in their way were
the buildings in human scale that were his
own commissions, such as the Ospdale
degli Innocenti (orphanage, 1419); the
Medici family's parish church of San
Lorenzo (1434); the chapel for the Pazzi
banking family (after 1429) and church of
Sto. Spirito (begun 1442), where human
sight lines are taken into account. Brunelleschi is credited with the invention of
linear perspective, the standardised system
of foreshortening that was the single most
distinguishing characteristic of Italian fifteenth-century painting and relief sculpture.

[JH]

Bruno, Giordano (1548–1600) mercurial
natural philosopher whose strongly held
beliefs ran afoul of both Catholic and
Protestant establishments in the late sixteenth century. Born in Nola near Naples
and called the 'the Nolan', he studied
in Naples with the Dominicans from

1562–76 and was ordained as a Dominican priest in 1572. In 1576 he fled to Rome with a heresy charge against him, and only two months later fled again because of a false murder accusation. After rejecting his Dominican vows, he made his way to Geneva in 1578 where be became a Calvinist. But once again after a critical attack on a Calvinist professor, he found himself arrested, excommunicated, rehabilitated after retraction and allowed to leave for France. From Toulouse he made his way to Paris in 1581 where he published three mnemonic works and his comedy Il Candelaio (1582) (The Candlemaker). In 1583 he went on to England where confrontation with anti-Copernican professors at Oxford led to his composition of the Italian dialogues and The Ash Wednesday Supper (1584), both known for their cosmological and moral positions. He was in Paris again in 1585 lecturing against the Aristotelians and went on to Germany where his lectures at various universities through 1590 got him excommunicated by the Lutherans. In 1591 he accepted an invitation to Venice with the hope of winning the chair of mathematics at Padua, which was eventually offered to Galileo GALILEI in 1592. In 1592 he himself was denounced to the Inquisition and extradited to Rome where he spent seven years in prison on trial before his execution, by burning at the stake in 1600. He studied natural magic, memory systems and cosmology with his 'Nolan philosophy'. During the Risorgimento (the Italian movement for national unity), he became a symbol of truth resistant against the old order.

[JM]

Bucer (Butzer), Martin (1491–1551) religious reformer. Born in Sélestat (Schlettstadt), Alsace, he was educated locally and entered the Dominican order (1506), then went to Heidelberg university. He later fell under the influence of ERASMUS and then, more directly, of LUTHER; he obtained release from his religious vows (1521) and got married (1522). He then went to Germany for a while as a result of his friendship with Franz von SICKINGEN, whose chaplain he became. In 1523 he moved to Strasbourg, where he played a determining role in the process of the reform movement, which had already been initiated by Matthäus Zell. Thanks to his guidance, the city was inclined to Lutheran views, but Bucer subsequently shifted towards accepting ZWINGLI's views on the doctrine of the Eucharist. Adopting a moderate position, he brought Lutherans and Zwinglians together to discuss their differences at the colloquy of Marburg (1529), where the parties agreed to differ on the doctrine of the Eucharist, though Bucer made efforts in later years to achieve an agreement. The official doctrine of Strasbourg was regulated in a synod in 1533, and Bucer was appointed the city's chief religious minister. He helped with the extension of the Reformation to neighbouring territories, but also continued to work together with Catholics for a possible reunion of Christians (Regensburg colloquy 1541). When CHARLES V's Interim of 1548 was imposed in Strasbourg, Bucer was obliged to leave the city and went to England. He was appointed regius professor of divinity at the university of Cambridge (1549), where he wrote his principal work, De regno Christi, and died in that city. Under queen MARY I his body was exhumed and burnt at the stake.

Buchanan, George (1506–82) Scots writer. Educated at Paris and at St Andrews, he returned to Scotland in 1536 and was appointed tutor to the natural son of James V. Imprisoned in 1539 because of his satires against the religious orders, he fled to France, where he taught Latin first in Bordeaux then in Paris. Invited to Portugal to teach at the university of Coimbra (1547–52), he had further problems; he went to Paris, and was employed for five years as tutor to the son of marshal de Brissac. He returned to Scotland in about 1562, becoming an active supporter of the Reformation, and taking the side of the earl of MORAY in the events involving the imprisonment of MARY STUART. The Scots Parliament in 1570 appointed him tutor to the young JAMES VI, who always retained a favourable memory of Buchanan. His principal works were the *De jure regni* (On Government) (1579), an influential dialogue in favour of limited monarchy, in which he argued that the king is created by contract with the people, who always conserve their sovereign power and can depose him; and his highly successful *History of Scotland* (1582). Frequently the centre of controversy, he was a man of great culture, and corresponded with the chief intellectuals of his time. Samuel Johnson, a notorious critic of the Scots, later declared that Buchanan was the only man of genius Scotland had ever produced.

Buckingham, dukes of

1st duke, George Villiers (1592–1628) Son of a Leicestershire knight, he was presented to JAMES I in 1614 and soon replaced the king's favourite, Robert Carr, earl of SOMERSET, in the king's esteem. He was showered with unprecedented favours, becoming earl (1617) then duke (1623) of Buckingham, lord high admiral (1619), and the king's most powerful adviser. He also began to establish his influence over the prince of Wales, later king as Charles I from 1625. Buckingham's forays into foreign policy, however, were failures. In 1623 he accompanied the prince on a secret trip to Madrid with the purpose of achieving a marriage alliance with Spain, but succeeded only in provoking war. His intrigues in France (which included a presumed affair with the queen) ended with his unsuccessful attempt (1627) to capture the Ile de Ré and La Rochelle. The failures aroused bitter criticism in Parliament. While preparing a further expedition to France, he was assassinated by a naval officer, James Felton.

2nd duke, George Villiers (1628–87) He was brought up at court with the prince of Wales, the future CHARLES II, fought for him in the civil war, and returned from exile in 1657 to marry the daughter of lord FAIRFAX, but was imprisoned by the government. He was appointed to the privy council at the Restoration (1660), and from 1668 became a prominent member of the 'Cabal' ministry, but because of strong opposition in Parliament was dismissed from office in 1674. After further political activities, he retired to his estates in 1681. Strongheaded and restless, in 1668 he became notorious for killing the earl of Shrewsbury in a duel.

Budé, Guillaume (1467–1540) French humanist and founder of the Collège de France, he was also a diplomat and royal librarian. Educated in Paris and Orléans, he became especially proficient in Greek, learning philosophy, law, theology and medicine as well. In 1502 LOUIS XII sent him to Rome as ambassador to the coronation of pope JULIUS II. He later returned to Paris, served as a royal secretary until 1515, then travelled again to Rome as ambassador to Leo X. When the new king, FRANCIS I, appointed him royal librarian upon his return, Budé directed the assembling in the Palais de Fontainebleau of various royal manuscript collections; the library that he built formed the nucleus of today's French national library, the Bibliothèque Nationale. Budé also suggested to the king the creation of a college for the study of Greek, Latin and Hebrew. After some difficulties, this institution (the Collège de France) opened in 1530; it became a centre for higher studies in France and reawakened interest in classical languages and literature. Budé's *Commentarii linguae Graecae* (Commentaries on the Greek Language) (1529) was instrumental in the classical revival.

Buffon, Georges Louis Leclerc, count de (1707–88) French naturalist. After studying law and mathematics, he travelled through southern Europe and on his return succeeded to a large inheritance. His first published papers included one on probability theory which secured his admission to the Académie des Sciences; he also produced translations of Stephen Hales' *Vegetable Statics* and of John Colson's English version of Isaac NEWTON's work on 'fluxions'. In 1739 he was promoted to 'académicien-associé' in the botanical section and appointed director of the Jardin du Roi (now known as the Jardin des Plantes) in Paris. For the next half century he divided his time between Paris and his country estates, and through disciplined early rising sustained a prolific literary output. Besides numerous memoirs, he produced (with collaborators) a multi-volume *Histoire naturelle* (1749–67 and supplements) containing a theory of the earth, a history of man and an account of the quadrupeds; later sets of volumes were devoted to birds, minerals and a revised theory of the earth's development through 'epochs of nature'. The author's breadth of vision was remarkable by any standards, but his comparative lack of interest in making detailed observations or in developing any rigid system of classification meant that his writings came to be admired more for their literary style than their scientific content.

[FW]

Bugenhagen, Johannes (1485–1558) German religious reformer. Son of a city official in Pomerania, he studied at Greifswald (1502–4) and then taught at a local school. In 1509 he became a priest, and shortly after LUTHER began his activity came into contact with the latter's ideas. He began to correspond with the reformer, and visited him in 1521 at Wittenberg, staying on to study at the university, where he later (1533) gained a doctorate in theology and joined the teaching faculty. From 1525 he also became a pastor in the town. Thereafter as one of Luther's closest colleagues he began to extend the

influence of the new ideas in northern Germany, visiting Hamburg (1528–9), Pomerania (1534) and Schleswig-Holstein (1542), helping with the framing of rules for reformed churches in those areas. His most decisive role was in response to an invitation from Christian III of Denmark; he went to Copenhagen (1537–9), helped to reorganise the church and reform the university. After the victory of CHARLES V in the Schmalkaldic wars, Bugenhagen was criticised by other Lutherans for accepting the imperial Interim (1548). He wrote several tracts and commentaries, and helped Luther revise the German translation of the Bible.

Bullinger, Henry (1504–75) Swiss reformer. Born in Bremgarten (canton of Aargau), he was educated at the university of Cologne, graduating in 1520; he returned home a convinced supporter of the Reformation. In 1523 he became teacher in the school of the monastery at Kappel, where he introduced the new ideas and abolished the mass. He accepted ordination as a pastor in 1528 and the next year became pastor of Bremgarten, which he converted to the Reform. After the defeat and death of ZWINGLI at the battle of Kappel (1531), his position became insecure; he left with his family and went to Zürich, where he was offered Zwingli's post as leader of the community. For the rest of his life he was chief minister of the city. By his extensive contacts with other reformers and political figures (there is a voluminous surviving correspondence), his own substantial writings, and his authorship of the Second Helvetic Confession of faith, he became one of the great leaders of the European Reformation.

Bunyan, John (1628–88) English writer. Born in a Bedfordshire village, like his father before him he followed the trade of making and mending kettles; he had a rudimentary education, and at the age of sixteen enlisted in the forces raised by his county during the civil war. He married in about 1649, to a wife who influenced him to better his life. By 1657 he had become a preacher, and his fame spread. During the repression of nonconformists after the Restoration, he was arrested (1660) and spent the greater part of the next twelve years in gaol, where he spent the time reading and writing. Calvinist in outlook and a prolific writer, in 1666 he published *Grace Abounding*, his spiritual autobiography and one of the works by which he is chiefly known; and composed his masterpiece *Pilgrim's Progress*, which was first published in 1678. Pardoned and licensed to preach in 1672, he devoted his later years to incessant preaching and writing, both in Bedfordshire and in London. His later works included *The Holy War* (1682), and a second part to *Pilgrim's Progress* (1684). With a contagious literary style shaped by the Authorised Version of the Bible and Foxe's *Book of Martyrs*, *Pilgrim's Progress* became perhaps the most influential religious work produced in England in the century after the Reformation.

Burnet, Gilbert (1643–1715) Scots bishop. Born in Edinburgh of a Scots gentry family, he was educated in Aberdeen and entered the Anglican church; in 1665 he became minister at Saltoun, East Lothian, and in 1669 professor of divinity at Glasgow university (1669–73). He settled in England from 1674, where he became influential at court and won a reputation for his moderation in both religious and political matters. At the accession of JAMES II, he went to live on the continent. While in the Hague, he helped WILLIAM III of Orange with preparations for the invasion of England and landed with him at Torbay in 1688. He was made bishop of Salisbury, and subsequently played a prominent role in the House of Lords. His fame rests chiefly on his *History of My Own Time*, published after his death from 1723 onwards, an exceptionally lively, and occasionally tendentious, chronicle of the period.

Buxtehude, Dietrich (*c*.1637–1707) German composer and organist (born in Denmark). His entire career was spent in Lübeck. A brilliant organist and an outstanding composer, he exerted considerable influence on his younger contemporaries. His organ works (preludes and fugues, toccatas, chaconnes, various chorale compositions, suites, canzonas and variations) combine instrumental virtuosity and contrapuntal artistry. His numerous vocal works (cantatas, oratorios and chorales) are among the finest compositions for the Lutheran church before J.S. BACH. Many were performed in his annual series of *Abendmusiken* (public evening concerts given during the Advent season), which attracted to Lübeck numerous musicians, including J.S. Bach who supposedly walked some 200 miles to meet him in 1705.

[JE]

Byng, George, viscount Torrington (1663–1733) English admiral. He served in the navy from his youth, became an officer in 1683, and from 1702 served as rear-admiral in the war of the Spanish Succession, commanding the squadron that captured Gibraltar and won a naval victory off Málaga (1704). He was knighted (1704) for these services, elevated to admiral in 1707, and subsequently defeated the Spanish fleet off cape Passaro (1718). Ennobled in 1721, he became first lord of the admiralty in 1727.

Byrd, William (1543–1623) English composer. He was the most prolific, original and versatile composer of the Elizabethan period. His early career is recorded at the cathedral of Lincoln (1563–1670), probably his home town. He was subsequently appointed a gentleman of the chapel royal and served there as organist for two decades. From 1591 until his death he lived in Standon Massey (Essex). Although he was a Catholic, it did not seriously hamper his career. He composed hundreds of sacred works in Latin and

English, as well as instrumental works for keyboard and viol consorts. Among the best known collections for the Catholic Church are the two-volume *Gradualia* (1605 and 1607), and for the Anglican Church, *Psalmes, Sonnets and Songs* (1588), *Songs of Sundrie Natures* (1589), and *Psalmes, Songs, and Sonnets* (1611). His style draws upon the 'classical' Latin polyphony of the Counter-Reformation, the Anglican anthem, the Italian madrigal, the English part-song and various instrumental traditions. He is distinguished for his compositional mastery and highly individual, often audacious, musical expressiveness. Labelled '*Britannicae musicae parens*', he had a decisive impact on his younger English contemporaries.

[JE]

C

Cabot, John (Giovanni Caboto) (*c*.1450–*c*.99) Italian navigator. Born in Genoa, he became a Venetian citizen in 1476 and eventually settled in England around 1496. Commissioned by a group of Bristol merchants in 1496 to find a westward sea route to Asia, he seems to have made landfall in 1497 near Newfoundland. He made a second journey in 1498 but disappeared during it.

Cabot, Sebastian (*c*.1476–1557) The son of John Cabot, he was born in Venice. He apparently took part in the 1497 expedition, and on a subsequent voyage may have found the entrance to Hudson Bay (1508–9). He later entered the service of Spain (1512), and was appointed to various posts by king FERDINAND II OF TRASTÁMARA, but returned to England on the king's death. From 1519 he was again in Spain, contracted by CHARLES V, and in 1526–30 he led a Spanish expedition to south America, which was unsuccessful, leading to his imprisonment for a year on his return. From 1533, however, he was working again in Seville, where he served for the next eleven years in the Casa de Contratación (House of Trade) and drew up a famous map of the world (1544). In 1547 he returned to England. In 1551 the Company of Merchant Adventurers was formed, with the objective of discovering a north-east passage for trade to Asia; he was appointed governor for life. He was also first governor of the Muscovy Company (1555).

Cajetan (Gaetano), Tommaso de Vio, cardinal (1469–1534) Italian theologian. Born in Gaeta, he entered the Dominican order in 1484, taught theology at Rome (1501–8), and rose to become general of the order in 1508, cardinal in 1517 and bishop of Gaeta two years later. As papal legate to the diet of Augsburg in 1518, he tried in vain to win Luther over, and helped to draft the bull *Exsurge Domine*, condemning him (1520). From 1523–4 he was papal legate in Hungary, Poland and Bohemia, but retired to Gaeta in 1527. Cajetan's literary fame rests chiefly on his commentary on the *Summa* of Aquinas. He also wrote commentaries on Aristotle, and many lesser works.

Calderón de la Barca, Pedro (1600–81) The best known dramatist of the Spanish Golden Age after LOPE DE VEGA. In contrast to Lope he led a quiet life, a pupil of the Jesuits, a soldier then later on a priest (1651), dubbed by order of PHILIP IV a knight of the order of Santiago. Calderón stylised and heightened the tone of Lope's drama through tighter control, denser poetic texture, singing, dancing and scenic design. His approach to drama was significantly affected by the establishment of a permanent theatre for the Madrid court at the palace of the Buen

Retiro, where visiting Italian specialists produced spectacular stage effects. Calderón often reworked earlier dramas, but in his own work the protagonists are given to debate, monologue and analysis of current themes of the age, like free-will, grace and predestination. This is dramatic literature in the service of a Christian stoicism, often defined as *desengaño* and exemplified in his most famous play *La vida es sueño* (Life is a Dream), 1635. His output was not as great as Lope's, some 200 pieces, just as varied but more formally controlled. The sub-genre by which he is best known and of which he is the true perfector is the *Auto sacramental*, to which he dedicated himself exclusively in his final years. This species of liturgical drama is contrived to illustrate in allegorical form the meaning of the Eucharist, and was meant to be performed at church festivals on stages set up on carts in the streets. The meaning was enhanced and made more explicit by voice, song and visual effects for an audience of varying education. The *comedias* by which he is best known are *El alcalde de Zalamea* (The Mayor of Zalamea) (1642?), *El médico de su honra* (Doctor to his Own Honour) (1635), *El mágico prodigioso* (The Extraordinary Magician) (1635), and of the *autos*, *El gran teatro del mundo* (The Great Theatre of the World) and *La cena de Baltasar* (Belshazzar's Feast).

[BT]

Calixtus III (Alfonso Borgia, 1378–1458) pope 1455-8. He was a canon lawyer in the service of the House of Aragon who founded the family's fortunes in Italy. Made bishop of Valencia by Martin V in 1429, he reconciled Alfonso the Magnanimous and Martin. He was made cardinal by Eugenius IV in the year after Alfonso's conquest of Naples. He appointed his nephew Roderigo (1431–1503) vice-chancellor of the Church in 1457, a power base that eventually led to

the papacy thirty-five years later as ALEXANDER VI (1492–1503).

[JM]

Calvin, John (Cauvin, Jean) (1509–64) French religious reformer. Born at Noyon, on the Somme, son of a local official, from 1523 he was educated at the university of Paris under distinguished teachers, then studied at Orléans and Bourges. In 1533 he experienced a conversion to the cause of the Reformation, and after the 1534 'affair of the Placards' in Paris which induced the authorities to act against Protestants, felt it safer to leave the capital, settling eventually at Basel, where he published the first edition of his *Institutes* (1536) in Latin (translated by him into French, 1541). That same year he was invited by FAREL to help introduce the Reformation into Geneva, which he now (after a short exile in 1538–41 forced on him and Farel by political opponents in the city) made his home. Geneva under Calvin was transformed into a centre of reformed religion, with a carefully defined relationship between the ruling magistrates and the clergy. Some notoriety was caused in 1554 by the execution, at Calvin's instigation, of Servetus. There were also conflicts (1555) with a section of the magistracy, who were dubbed 'libertines'. By 1559, when Calvin founded his influential Academy, Geneva was wholly under his control. Calvin's religious views emphasised the majesty of God and the worthlessness of man; salvation by faith in Christ was a gift of God, granted through divine predestination. The influence of Calvinism spread rapidly; it became the dominant form of Protestantism in France, Scotland and the Netherlands. Its official tenets were soon modified by events: Calvin's emphasis on non-resistance to oppressors was overtaken by the active rebellion of Calvinist nobles against Catholic sovereigns, and his doctrine of predestination was later questioned by Calvinists in France and the Netherlands. In the twentieth century the

Calvinist ethic of self-discipline was seen by the sociologist Max Weber in 1905 as a formative influence in the growth of capitalism; but most later scholars have rejected the thesis.

Camoens, Luis Vaz de (?1524–80) The major versifier of Portuguese literature, a dramatist and a fine lyric poet in both Castilian and his own tongue, he is best known as the author of the national epic *Os Lusiads*, (1572) (The Sons of Lusus, i.e. of the demi-god who is associated with Portugal). Little is known of his early life, but it is possible that he was born into a modest noble family in Lisbon, studying later with a relative in Coimbra. It also seems possible that on his return to the capital he was involved in some stormy liaisons. He then appears as a soldier in Ceuta, north Africa, where he lost an eye. In 1553 he went off to India where he held several minor official posts in the Portuguese colonies including Macau. It is known that he was already engaged in writing and producing dramas, but his years there, he claims, were marked by deceptions and little reward. He was shipwrecked in the Mekong delta, losing all but his poetry. On his way back home in 1567 he was beached in Mozambique and robbed of some of his major literary works. Two years later he embarked for Lisbon where he lived in near poverty sustained by an irregularly paid royal pension. He lived to see the publication of his epic which, as he affirms, surpasses the classical epics because the central theme, the voyage of exploration by Vasco da Gama to India and the creation of the overseas Portuguese empire, was truth itself and not a fiction. The *Lusiads* is a long narrative poem in ten books embodying the pageant of Portuguese history pivoted on a single issue of the voyage, registering the birth of a nation, its mission and its possible future, all intertwined within a supernatural conflict between the rival powers of Juno and Bacchus, the deities of west and east, with Venus as a protecting power for the Portuguese crew. Camoens was determined to absorb Virgil as Virgil had absorbed Homer, and carry forward the panoply of Graeco-Roman culture into Christian Europe of the Renaissance, thereby creating out of a very idiosyncratic synthesis the only successful European literary epic dealing with a contemporary theme.

[BT]

Campanella, Tommaso (1568–1639) natural philosopher, theologian and political theorist. Son of an illiterate Calabrian shoemaker, he became a Dominican in 1583 with the religious name of Tommaso. He rejected the dominant Aristotelian tradition in favour of the teachings of his fellow Calabrian, Bernardino Telesio, whom he defended in *Philosophy Demonstrated by the Senses* (1591). Written in Naples where he studied at San Domenico Maggiore and frequented the scientific circle of Giambattista della Porta, it led to his first arrest and trial. In defiance of the sentence to return to Calabria, he made his way to Padua where in 1592 he was falsely accused of sodomy but had the charge dismissed, and conversed with Galileo GALILEI and Della Porta also in self-exile there. In 1594 the Venetian Inquisition arrested and detained him for almost two years for debating the faith with a Jew. Released in Rome, he was soon accused anew in 1597 for heresy, adjured, and returned to Calabria. In his home town of Stilo in 1599 he participated in an abortive millennial uprising, which caused his arrest and imprisonment in Naples for heresy and sedition from 1599 to 1626. He avoided execution by feigning madness, renewed his orthodoxy, and spent his imprisonment writing poetry, letters, and books – the most famous, a Platonic utopia, *The City of the Sun* (1602). His writing encompassed his polymath interests – anti-Aristotle, anti-MACHIAVELLI, magic and astrology, nature and natural phenomena, Galileo – and focused on the great themes for reform in a new, modern scientific age – a universal monarchy, an ecclesiastical state and naturalist religion. His work *The Spanish Monarchy* (1600), which argued that peace would be best achieved under a universal Spanish monarchy, albeit one subjected ultimately to control by the pope, was published from 1620 onwards, but with many passages inserted into it by the publisher, from the works of BOTERO. After release from prison, he worked in Rome from 1626 to 1634, but fled to France in 1634, where many of his unpublished works were printed as he continued his studies and writing until his death.

[JM]

Campillo, José del (1694–1744) Spanish politician. Asturian by origin, he was educated in Córdoba and entered the service of the intendant of Andalucia in Seville, through whose patronage he entered the administrative service of the crown, served briefly (1736) with the army in Italy and in 1738 became intendant general of Aragon. His outstanding work resulted in his being called to Madrid as secretary for finances; in 1741, he rose to become secretary of state for the marine, war and America, in effect the most important minister of the crown. An indefatigable proponent of reforms, he wrote many tracts on the theme, of which perhaps the best known is his *Lo que hay de más y de menos en España* (The Plus and Minus of Spain) (1741).

Campion, Edmund (1540–81) English Catholic martyr. After a brilliant career at Oxford, he abandoned the Anglican Church and England (1571), went to study at the English college at Douai, then travelled to Rome where he entered the Society of Jesus (1573). After a period of missionary work in Bohemia, he was ordained priest in Prague (1578), and sent back to England with Father PERSONS and others (1580). Constantly in hiding from government spies, he carried out his spiritual ministry to the Catholics, but was betrayed and arrested in 1581, judged on false evidence to be a traitor and executed at Tyburn. He was beatified in 1886.

Canaletto (Giovanni Antonio Canal) (1697–1768) Venetian painter and etcher. The son of a painter of theatrical scenery, he became the most important Italian artist specialising in *vedute* ('views'). He first painted sets for Venetian productions of VIVALDI operas, then accompanied his father to Rome in 1719 to create scenery for SCARLATTI's *Tito Sempronio Gracco* and *Turno Aricino*. According to his biographer, however, he 'couldn't work with theatre people', and consequently switched to easel pictures – fantasy views and landscapes at first, then (c.1720–40) actual cityscapes of Venice many of which were sold to English tourists, as were his etched *Capriccios* of the 1740s, which were largely marketed by his agent Joseph Smith, the future British consul. He worked for a decade in England (1746–55) painting views of the Thames. His many imitators and copyists included his nephew, Bernardo Bellotto, and the English painter Samuel Scott. The largest single collection of his early work was acquired in 1762 by George III. Due to the low esteem in which landscape painting was held, however, he was not elected to the Venetian Academy until 1763, when he was sixty six years old.

[JH]

Canisius, Peter (1521–97) Dutch-born Jesuit. Born Pierre de Hondt in Nijmegen, during his career he Latinised his name ('hound') to Canisius. He entered the new Company of Jesus as its first Germanic member in 1543, took orders in 1546, and was appointed a representative at the Council of Trent on behalf of the bishop of Augsburg. In 1549 he became professor of theology at the university of Ingolstadt. In 1555 he published his *Catechism*, which became throughout Europe the most popular of all catechisms of the century. Appointed provincial of the Jesuits for southern Germany and Austria (1556–69), he began a tireless campaign to win the area back for the Church, founding in the process Jesuit colleges in the major cities. After 1580 he retired to live in Switzerland. He was canonised in 1925.

Cano, Melchor (1509–60) Spanish theologian. He studied at Salamanca, where in 1533 he entered the Dominican order and first clashed, as a professor in the 1530s, with his life-long rival CARRANZA. A brilliant scholar and controversialist, he became professor of theology at Alcalá university (1543) and then at Salamanca (1547), attended the council of Trent on behalf of Spain, was nominated bishop of the Canary Islands in 1552 (a post from which he immediately resigned) and in 1558 became provincial of his order. A strong supporter of reform in the Church and a critic of papal pretensions, he was also an enemy of anti-semitism. But he was personally vindictive, was in large measure responsible for the persecution of his personal enemy archbishop CARRANZA, and violently opposed the Jesuits at every turn.

Capito (Köpfel), Wolfgang Faber (c.1478–1541) German religious reformer. Born in Haguenau in an artisan family, he was educated at Ingolstadt and Freiburg, then entered the Benedictine order. An enthusiast of humanist learning, he made contact while at Freiburg with Sebastian BRANT and others. In 1515 he was invited to Basel as cathedral preacher and professor at the university, and made the acquaintance of ERASMUS. He was one of the earliest supporters of Luther, persuading FROBEN to publish (1518) a Latin edition of Luther's early works, and visiting Luther in Wittenberg in 1522, which confirmed him in his views. He was in Strasbourg in 1523, and in collaboration with BUCER and the preacher Matthäus Zell, began the reform of that city, in close association with the ruling élite.

Caravaggio (Michelangelo Merisi) (1573–1610) Italian painter active mainly in Rome and Naples. Born in the north Italian town of Caravaggio, the son of an architect, he may have been apprenticed to Simone Peterzano (1584). Arriving in Rome at twenty, he was commissioned by Cardinal del Monte to paint such homoerotic works as the *Amor Victorious* (Berlin), the *Musical Party* (New York) and the *Bacchus* (Florence). Other important clients were Cardinal Scipione Borghese and Cardinal Matteo Barberini (the future pope URBAN VIII). Revolutionary religious commissions included the *Calling of St Matthew*, for the memorial chapel of cardinal Matteo Contarelli (San Luigi dei Francesi) in which dramatic lighting was used for the first time as a determining factor in the construction of figures, the choice of lower-class models and costumes tellingly evoking the low-rent world of early Christianity. Equally sensational were his paintings of the martyrdoms of Saints Peter and Paul (Cerasi chapel, S.Maria del Popolo) – like San Luigi a 'leftist', French-sympathising institution opposed to the conservative policies of the Spanish clergy. His religious paintings were considered lacking in 'decorum', and soon were removed from their altars to find their way into private hands, (e.g. the *Death of the Virgin*, with its too-realistic cadaver). The fastidious were also offended by his slovenly personal hygiene and sociopathic behaviour. He was arrested eleven times (1600–5), for carrying an unlicensed weapon, assaulting a waiter with a plate of artichokes, and other misdemeanours. He murdered a man over a tennis match in 1606 and fled to Naples, where again his art mesmerised other artists, who abandoned Mannerism to follow his example, but where the clergy were less appreciative. Jailed during a brief stay in Malta (1607–8) for insulting a knight, he escaped by sea to Syracuse, painting altarpieces there and in Messina and Palermo. He returned to Naples in October 1609, when he was savagely beaten by men hired by the Maltese knight whom he had insulted. Sailing to Port' Ercole, he was arrested by mistake, and died of fever in July 1610 while wandering on the beach in search of his belongings.

[JH]

Carissimi, Giacomo (1605–74) Italian composer and the leading exponent of the Baroque oratorio. From 1629 until his death he was a chapelmaster at the prestigious Collegio Germanico of the Jesuits in Rome. His dozen or so Latin oratorios are mainly based on texts adapted from the Old Testament; e.g. *Jephte*, *Jonas*, *Baltazar* and *Judicium salomonis*. They comprise a wide variety of recitatives, arias and choruses, whose dramatic poignancy and profound affectivity are conveyed through relatively simple musical means. They were admired throughout Europe and left a significant mark on the style of younger contemporaries, notably on Charpentier and Handel. He also composed numerous cantatas and other liturgical works.

[JE]

Carlo Emanuele I the Great (1562–1630) duke of Savoy (1580–1630). Son of duke EMANUELE FILIBERTO, he attempted to give security and character to his duchy by reconstructing the capital, Turin, and securing territorial gains. He intervened militarily in the French civil wars in order to secure possession of the marquisate of Saluzzo, eventually ceded to him in 1601 (Treaty of Lyon), but had to cede other frontier areas (Bresse, Bugey). In subsequent years his ambition emboldened him to attack, without success, Geneva (1602) and the Spanish-held fortress of Montferrato (1617). He married in 1585 the Infanta Catalina, daughter of PHILIP II of Spain.

Carlos, Don (1545–68) infante of Spain, son of PHILIP II by his first wife, the Portuguese princess Maria. From childhood he suffered clear physical incapacities and showed signs of mental instability, but since he was the only surviving heir to the throne his father was obliged to include him in policy plans. He was considered as a possible governor for the Netherlands, and also as husband for princess Elizabeth of Valois, of France, to whom Philip himself got married in 1560. Don Carlos' unstable conduct obliged his father to exclude him from consideration for any serious office of state. The prince's increasingly violent temperament and attempts to plot against Philip, led the king to decide on his imprisonment in a room in the palace in Madrid (January 1568), where he died seven months later. The dramatic events gave birth to absurd allegations by the king's enemies that he had murdered his son. The dramatist Schiller later drew on the story for a play (1787), and in his turn Verdi based his famous opera *Don Carlo* (1867) on Schiller's text.

Carranza, Bartolomé (1503–76) archbishop of Toledo. Born in Navarre, when young he became a member of the Dominican order, and was educated at Salamanca and Valladolid. In 1545 he first went as a Spanish delegate to the Council of Trent, was later selected by PHILIP II as chaplain and accompanied the king to England (1554–7), where he collaborated with Marian bishops in the repression of Protestants. Appointed by the king to the see of Toledo (1557) and consecrated in Brussels, he was, on returning to Spain the following year, accused of heresy and imprisoned by the Inquisition (1559), on the basis of chance conversations and of ambiguous passages in his *Commentaries on the Catechism* (Antwerp, 1558). He was placed under house arrest. His case, which dragged on for seventeen years, was rendered prejudicial to him by the personal hostility of Melchor Cano and of the Inquisitor General VALDÉS. The papacy succeeded in having him sent to Rome, where a compromise verdict was issued by the pope, two weeks before Carranza's death.

Carteret, John lord, 1st earl Granville (1690–1763) English politician. Eldest surviving son of the 1st baron Carteret, he succeeded to the title when only five years old, and was educated at Oxford. He participated actively in the House of Lords from 1711, was appointed ambassador to Sweden 1719, and successfully negotiated peace between Sweden and Denmark (1720). He took office in WALPOLE's administration (1721), but soon became his rival for power, and in 1724 Walpole sent him to Ireland as lord-lieutenant (1724–30). There Carteret relied greatly on the advice of SWIFT. On his return to England he helped to lead the opposition to Walpole, who resigned in 1742; Carteret entered the new government, and became secretary for foreign affairs, intervening actively in European politics and flattering the views of king GEORGE II, with whom he was present at the battle of Dettingen (1743). Ministerial quarrels obliged him to withdraw from office in 1744 (he inherited the title of earl on his mother's death that year), and despite subsequent negotiations he did not return to government.

Cartier, Jacques (1491–1557) French navigator. A native of the port of St Malo, he was commissioned by FRANCIS I to find a north-west passage to Asia, and in 1534 left St Malo with two ships and scouted Newfoundland; the next year he repeated the expedition with three vessels, scouted the estuary (August 1535) of the St Lawrence (which he named), penetrated into Indian territory to the site where Montreal was later built, and picked up from the natives the word for 'village' ('Canada'), by which the territory became known. He spent the winter in the region of what is now Quebec, returning to St Malo in the summer of 1536. A third expedition was undertaken in 1541, under the official direction of a governor appointed by the king. Apart from their contribution to seafaring knowledge, the voyages brought no practical advantage to France. Cartier was an accomplished sailor of little vision or acumen, and the accounts of his journeys published after his death were written not by him but by another hand. He spent his last years in his cups.

Cartwright, Thomas (1535–1603) English theologian and spokesman of English Presbyterianism. Educated at Cambridge, he became a fellow of St John's (1560) and then of Trinity College (1562); in both he became known for his strong tendency towards Calvinism. After a short stay in Ireland (1565–7), he was appointed Lady Margaret professor of divinity (1569) at Cambridge. The post gave him a public platform for his views, but stirred controversy in the university; the vice-chancellor, WHITGIFT, who was now also master of Trinity, deprived Cartwright of his professorship (1570) and his fellowship (1571). Cartwright went abroad to Geneva, returning to England in 1572, just as the first famous Puritan tract 'Admonition to the Parliament' appeared. His arrest was ordered, so he left the country again, living in Heidelberg then settling in Middelburg and Antwerp. He returned to England in 1585, was arrested and later released. The earl of Leicester then secured his appointment to a charity hospital in Warwick, where (despite a brief clash with the government in 1591, after which he went to Guernsey for a few years) he died rich and respected.

Casas, Bartolomé de las (1474–1566) Spanish defender of the rights of the American Indian. Son of a trader of Jewish origins from Segovia, he was born in Seville, where he went to school; in 1502 he went to America with his father, on the first of the many voyages he was to make. In 1512 he received a grant of Indians in America, and was also formally consecrated priest; but in 1514, after the visit of some Dominicans to Hispaniola, he began to have doubts about the treatment of the Indians: he gave up his Indians, and began his long fight to liberate them. He returned to Spain, where he spoke personally to FERDINAND II OF TRASTÁMARA, then to CISNEROS, then to CHARLES V, and in 1517 was given permission to try out his ideas and named 'protector of the Indians'. His main idea, which he tried to put into practice through small colonial settlements run by missionaries, was that the natives of America could be converted to Christianity and made to live like farmers, if they were ensured their personal freedom. His crowning achievement was to secure from the Spanish government the 'New Laws' of 1542, which guaranteed the eventual liberty of all Indians in America. In practice, he was bitterly opposed in America, where the laws provoked a major rebellion and were either suspended or modified; and in Spain he had to debate (1550) his ideas before the royal council. The firm support of both the emperor and later of PHILIP II failed, however, to achieve much. An indefatigable propagandist, Las Casas wrote several major works, among them his *History of the Indies* (published only in 1875), and the *Very Brief Relation of the Destruction of the Indies* (1552), an angry tract later much translated and employed as anti-Spanish propaganda. Symbol of the conscience of Europeans before the outrages committed in the colonies, his figure has been somewhat mythologised but he remains one of the outstanding historical figures of all time.

Castellion, Sébastien (*c.*1510–63) French writer. Son of a Savoyard farmer, he went to study in Lyon, where he obtained a post as tutor. Converted to the Reformation by reading the works of CALVIN, he visited his mentor in Geneva (1541) and taught there for a while. Differences of opinion between the two soon arose, over

interpretation of scripture and over its translation. In 1544, angered by the attitude of the ruling council, he left Geneva and moved to Basel, where he lived for the rest of his life, making a living from writing and by teaching Greek at the university. It was in Basel that he completed his Latin translation of the Bible, published in its entirety in 1551, with a dedication to EDWARD VI of England; it was translated into French in 1555. The execution of SERVET at Geneva in 1553 elicited from Castellion his most famous work, *De Haereticis, an sint persequendi* (On the Persecution of Heretics) (1554), published under the pseudonym Martin Bellius. An unflinching attack on all religious persecution, the work unleashed an international debate over toleration. From Geneva both Calvin and BEZA replied in outraged terms. Castellio replied to Calvin: 'To kill a man is not to defend a doctrine, but to kill a man. When the Genevans killed Servetus they did not defend a doctrine, they killed a man'. His *Contra libellum Calvini* was not published during his lifetime but came out in Holland in 1612.

Castiglione, Baldassare (1478–1529) Italian diplomat known for his widely influential book of noble manners and etiquette, *Il cortegiano* (*The Courtier*). Born to minor Mantuan nobility, his humanist education in Milan and his chivalric training at the court of Ludovico Sforza formed both his adult service and his literary production. He was a courtier and diplomat for the Gonzaga of Mantua (1500–4), the Montefeltro and della Rovere of Urbino (1504–16), and Mantua again (1516–24), before ending his career as papal nuncio to Spain (1524–9). His book *The Courtier* was one of the most important books of the sixteenth century. Revised from 1508 and published in 1528, it became the standard handbook for noble comportment across Europe. Its central ideas of grace and nonchalance (*sprezzatura*) set the noble's goal of behaviour as studied ease, 'that art is true art which does not seem to be art'. More than an etiquette book, it drew a nostalgic portrait of Urbino and its idyllic court with the utopian ideal of establishing the principles for the formation of the perfect courtier, his court lady, and his relationship to his prince as counsellor. Along the way, one is introduced to a wealth of knowledge about Renaissance courts and their gentlemen – soldiering, scholarship, music, dance, jokes, poetry and even Platonic love *alla* BEMBO. RAPHAEL painted his portrait in 1516.

[JM]

Catherine I (1684–1727) empress of Russia 1725–7. Of Polish peasant origin, Marta Skowronska was first married to a Swedish officer, then later became mistress to the Russian general Sheremetev, and after to the tsar's chief minister prince Menshikov. In 1705 she became mistress to PETER THE GREAT, changed her name to Catherine (Yekaterina) and turned Orthodox; they married officially in 1712. She played a distinguished part in Peter's reign. In 1724 he chose her as his successor and had her crowned empress. She succeeded him as ruler in 1725, but left policy in the hands of Menshikov, who governed through an instrument she had created, a supreme privy council of six members that replaced the institutions formerly used by Peter. She appointed as her successor Peter's grandson Peter II, but her own daughter by Peter, Elizabeth, ruled after Peter II, in a long reign (1741–62) that brought stability to the Russian monarchy.

Catherine of Aragon (1485–1536) queen of England. Daughter of FERDINAND II OF TRASTÁMARA and ISABELLA THE CATHOLIC of Spain, she married in 1501 Arthur prince of Wales, son of HENRY VII. The marriage was not consummated, and she was widowed four months later. She then married in 1509 Arthur's brother Henry (later HENRY VIII), by whom (1510–18)

she had five children, the only survivor being Mary. Her husband's attention wandered elsewhere, and in 1527 he demanded a divorce on the plea that his marriage did not accord with divine law because he had no right to marry his brother's wife. The consequent dispute involved high political interests, and was a major motive for Henry's decision to cut the nation's Church off from Rome. Eventually in 1533 a pro-Reformation archbishop of Canterbury, CRANMER, annulled the king's marriage. Catherine was moved in May 1534 to Kimbolton castle in Huntingdon, where she spent her last days.

Catherine of Braganza (1638–1705) queen of England. Daughter of JOHN IV of Portugal, in 1662 she married CHARLES II of England, to whom she brought as dowry the ports of Tangiers and Bombay, destined to become focal points for English commercial expansion. She led a difficult life at court, and was obliged by the king to include his mistresses among her ladies in waiting; her failure to produce an heir also weakened her position. But she stood firm against the accusations levelled at her during the anti-Catholic Popish Plot. After Charles' death she intended to return to Portugal, but did not do so until 1692, after the Revolution of 1688. In Portugal she exercised power for a while as regent (1704–5) during her brother the king's ill health.

Catherine of Genoa (Caterina Fieschi Adorno) (1447–1510) mystic known for her life of charity. Youngest of five children of high Genoese nobility, she was married to Giuliano Adorno at the age of sixteen, to ally the Fieschi and Adorno families, rival supporters of the Guelph and Ghibelline factions respectively. After ten years of unhappy marriage, she had the first of her mystic visions while confessing in 1473. With her husband's consent, they moved to a small house near the hospital of the Pammatone to serve the poor and sick. From 1479, they occupied two small rooms in the hospital. She served as an ordinary nurse (1479–90) and hospital administrator (1490–6), while he became a Franciscan tertiary until his death in 1497. In 1496 she developed an intimate friendship with a young Genoese lawyer, who along with her confessor was responsible for transcribing her mystical spiritual words and experiences in two books: *Trattato del Purgatorio* and *Dialogo*. She inspired the active apostolate and spiritual commitment of the Oratory of Divine Love and became the focus of a popular cult soon after her death. She was canonised in 1737.

[JM]

Catherine de Médicis (1519–89) queen of France. Daughter of Lorenzo II de' Medici and a French mother, she was married at the age of fourteen to the duke d'Orléans, later king HENRY II, whose affection however was directed rather to DIANE DE POITIERS. After the deaths of Henry and of his successor, Catherine's eldest son FRANCIS II, she became regent of France (1560). Faced with the task of protecting the Valois monarchy against powerful noble interests (the Guises and the Bourbons) and civil conflict based on Catholic–Calvinist divisions, she attempted to take a middle path, ably helped by chancellor L'HOSPITAL. She initiated the series of colloquies between Catholic and Calvinist theologians, by which she hoped to achieve peace; failing that, she made several important concessions of religious toleration. She was hostile to Spain, which she considered France's principal enemy; a meeting with her daughter the queen of Spain, Elizabeth of Valoise, at Bayonne (1565) did little to reassure her on this point. Events took a tragic turn with the massacre of Calvinists during the eve of St Bartholomew's (August 1572), for which she bears considerable responsibility. Dedicated above all to conserving the throne for her sons, three of whom became kings of France, she was over-

protective and may have contributed to the psychological problems all her children possessed.

Catinat, Nicolas (1637–1712) marshal of France. Trained as a lawyer, he quit his career on losing a case he considered just, and entered military service, where his part in the campaigns of 1667 in Flanders brought him to the personal attention of LOUIS XIV. In subsequent campaigns he distinguished himself as a serving officer under TURENNE, and played a key role both in Flanders and on the Italian frontier; he was appointed commander (1691–3) of the war against Savoy, and created marshal of France (1693). In the war of the Spanish Succession, he suffered reverses both in Italy and in Germany, and decided to retire from the army, despite appeals from Louis XIV in 1705. He spent his leisure years writing his memoirs, which were published only in 1819, in three volumes.

Cats, Jacob (1577–1660) Dutch politician and writer of verse. Born in Zeeland, Cats took his doctor's degree in law at Orléans, practiced at The Hague, and, after visits to Oxford and Cambridge, settled in Zeeland where he accumulated wealth by land reclamation. Becoming a magistrate, he was successively pensionary of Middelburg and Dordrecht and, from 1636 to 1651, grand pensionary of Holland. He took part in diplomatic missions to England: in 1627 to CHARLES I and in 1651–2, unsuccessfully, to CROMWELL. His background gave him an international outlook, and he was in sympathy with many of the English Puritan writers. Cats was primarily a writer of poetic emblem books, a type of literature popular in the seventeenth century that consisted of woodcuts or engravings accompanied by verses pointing to a moral. He used this form to express the major ethical concerns of early Dutch Calvinists, especially those dealing with love and marriage. His simple verses achieved enormous popularity, and remain a useful source of information about popular attitudes and customs.

Caxton, William (*c*.1422–91) the first professional English printer. Born in Kent, he was apprenticed in London, then left for Bruges (*c*.1442), where he stayed thirty years, working as governor of the Merchant Adventurers, which involved caring for trade and legal matters. By 1470 he had left business and joined the household of the new duchess of Burgundy, sister of the English king. In his spare time he did translating, and in order to produce more copies of his work decided to learn the art of printing. In Bruges he published in 1474 the first printed book in English, the *Recuyell of the Historyes of Troye*, which he himself translated. In 1476 he returned to England and set up a printing press at Westminster, where in 1477 he produced the first book printed in England, *The Dictes and Sayings of the Philosophers*. He devoted himself over the next fifteen years to printing and translating: his output in these years included Chaucer, Malory and Cicero.

Cecil, Robert, 1st earl of Salisbury (*c*.1563–1612) Younger son of William Cecil, he was educated at Cambridge, entered Parliament in 1584 and was knighted by queen ELIZABETH I in 1591, the year that he entered the privy council. In 1596 he became secretary of state and chief minister of the queen. Short and stooped (the queen called him 'my pygmy'), he was the perfect civil servant, managing both Parliament and foreign policy in the last years of the reign. Under king JAMES I he continued in office, his services earning him the title of earl (1605); he also accumulated considerable estates and offices, succeeding his father as master of the court of wards, and becoming lord high steward to the queen, and in 1608 lord treasurer. In February 1610 he proposed that Parliament accept a Great Contract to ensure the crown a regular income in exchange for the abandonment of feudal taxes; but both James and Parliament opposed the idea, which was dropped in November. His remarkable property of Hatfield Hall was acquired from the king in exchange for another (1607), but its reconstruction was not completed in his lifetime.

Cecil, William, lord Burghley (1520–98) English statesman. Of gentry origin, he was educated at Cambridge but without taking his degree; he then studied law at Gray's Inn. He entered Parliament in 1547, and in 1550, with his appointment as a secretary of state and member of the privy council, began his outstanding career as statesman. He was knighted in 1551. He played a low-profile role in the reign of queen MARY I, but when ELIZABETH I succeeded (1558) he was immediately appointed secretary of state, and entered Parliament in 1559. In 1561 he was appointed master of the court of wards. Architect of the principal political measures taken by Elizabeth at the beginning of her reign, he also managed state propaganda and intervened directly in all matters of foreign policy, maintaining a team of spies in England and on the continent to supply him with information. He brought about the fall and destruction of MARY STUART and supported the execution of alleged traitors such as NORFOLK. In 1571 the queen created him baron Burghley, and the next year lord treasurer. He lavished money on his residences, notably Burghley house, and established a powerful dynastic succession.

Cellini, Benvenuto (1500–71) Florentine goldsmith and sculptor whose *Autobiography* provides the best detailed characterisation of anyone of the age. Trained to be a musician at his father's insistence, he preferred the career of an artisan and was apprenticed as a goldsmith to learn the art of forging decorative table-sculpture and minting coins and medals. He worked predominantly in Rome from 1519 to 1540; the stay culminated in his imprisonment in the Castel Sant' Angelo (1537–9) on a charge of theft. He made a daring escape, was recaptured and pardoned by PAUL III, but emigrated to France (1540–5), where he was employed by FRANCIS I, residing in the Château de Nesle and serving the king in various capacities as goldsmith, sculptor, decorator and even designer of some architectural projects. The most famous works from these years are the elaborate golden salt cellar (Vienna, Kunsthistorisches Museum) and the bronze relief of a reclining Diana with a stag (Louvre), originally made for the Porte Dorée at Fontainebleau – his first works of sculpture. He was made a French citizen, but was forced to flee when accused of theft (1545). Back in Florence in 1545 until his death, he worked under the patronage of Cosimo I de' MEDICI and completed his most famous work, a bronze *Perseus* (1545–54) in the Loggia dei Lanzi outside the Palazzo Vecchio. After further charges of sodomy and assault (1557), he briefly considered entering the priesthood and actually took the first tonsure (1558), but thought better of it two years later and, at age sixty-two, married his housekeeper, the mother of some of his many children. Probably in response to the first edition of VASARI's *Lives of the Artists* (1550), he dictated his *Autobiography* between 1558–62, a work of extraordinary honesty on the life of the artist and the great personalities in the world he inhabited. He reveals himself in this often exaggerated and boastful work as petulant and irascible, a brawler and murderer, bisexually promiscuous, in and out of prison, sincerely religious and repentant and, above all, a man of artistic skill and passion, whose bravado and braggadocio with popes and princes (even claiming to have shot the constable of Bourbon and the prince of Orange while under siege in the Castel Sant' Angelo during the 1527 Sack of Rome) is matched by his frank and opinionated valuations of other ar-

tists and their works (from the divine MICHELANGELO to his disdained Florentine rivals Ammanati and Bandinelli). It was only first published in 1728 and later translated in the romantic period (1771 in English; 1796 in German; 1822 in French).

[JH & JM]

Cervantes Saavedra, Miguel de (1547–1616) Son of a doctor, Cervantes is the paramount figure in Spanish literature, comparable in influence with Shakespeare. Like him he lived through one of the most dramatic periods in European history. Born in Alcalá de Henares, educated at a private school in Madrid, he set out for Italy in 1569, joined the army, fought and was wounded in the victorious sea-battle of Lepanto against the Turks (1571). He took part in several other Mediterranean expeditions and on returning to Spain in 1575 he was captured at sea by Barbary pirates. As a result he spent five years in captivity in Algiers. Ransomed he returned to Spain and tried to break into the Madrid literary world with of all things a pastoral romance, *La Galatea* (1585), together with some theatre pieces. Unsuccessful, he quit Madrid, became a crown tax-collector for the Spanish Armada in Andalusia, travelling the roads and ending up in prison accused of faulty accounting. His subsequent years in Seville brought him into contact with the shadowy world of organised crime. Its argot seeped into his later works which are full of humour and irony rather than the pessimism of Mateo ALEMÁN. Most of his remaining life he spent becoming famous as a writer of comic fictions. Part I of *Don Quijote* appeared in 1605. In 1613 he published twelve short stories, *Novelas ejemplares* (Exemplary Short Stories) followed by a volume of plays, 1615. The appearance of a spurious sequel to *Don Quijote* stimulated him to produce Part II in 1615, and just before his death he completed what he considered to be his masterpiece, *Los trabajos* *de Persiles y Segismundo* (The Travails of Persiles and Segismundo) (1617). But posterity chose *Don Quijote*. Supposedly a parody of the popular genre of romances of chivalry, the story of a poverty-stricken knight deranged by his reading, and his simple-minded servant Sancho Panza, became the true forerunner of the modern European novel. Cervantes was a constant experimenter with all varieties of narrative strategies, and his own narrative as it advances from Part I to Part II shows an increasing mastery of the play between illusion and reality.

[BT]

Chamillart, Michel de (1652–1721) French minister of state. From a prominent family of robe nobility who made their careers in both Church and state, he was at first destined for holy orders but then entered the legal administration, became councillor of the parlement of Paris in 1676 and master of requests in 1686. He served briefly as intendant of Rouen (1689) then, with the powerful support of Madame de MAINTENON, went to Paris where he won favour with everyone, became controller general of finances (1699), minister of state (1700) and minister for war (1701). It was a time of increasing financial difficulty, and he did his best in the situation of economic crisis and continuous war faced by France. Dissatisfied with his work, the king replaced him with Desmarets for finances in 1708 and with Voysin for war in 1709. He retired to the solace of his estates in Maine.

Champaigne, Philippe de (1602–74) painter and academician, active in France. Born and trained in Brussels, he was a pupil of the landscape painter Jacques Fouquières (1620), whom he followed to Paris in 1621, becoming a naturalised citizen in 1629. His Paris patrons included LOUIS XIII; the queen mother, MARIE DE MÉDICIS, whose court painter he became; cardinal RICHELIEU; and later ANNE OF AUSTRIA, during the Regency,

and cardinal MAZARIN. One of the original founders of the French Academy of painting and sculpture (1648), he later held the positions of professor and then rector. Beginning in 1643 he came under the influence of Jansenist doctrine, and his two daughters entered the convent at Port-Royal. Although he was the decorator of Marie de Médicis' private chapel in the Palais du Luxembourg, and of the church of the Sorbonne, he is best remembered today as a portraitist.

[JH]

Champlain, Samuel de (*c*.1570–1635) discoverer. Son of a noble sea-captain from the Brie, he entered the navy and undertook sea voyages about which little information is available. He may have sailed to Spanish America; he certainly in 1603 visited Canada and the St Lawrence, visiting in subsequent years the New England coast. In 1608 he took part in a further expedition to explore the St Lawrence region, which he considered the most desirable area for French expansion, and in 1610 reached the present location of Montréal. Named lieutenant general of 'New France' in 1612, he explored the Ottawa area in 1613. A further expedition to the territories in 1615 was a failure, but in 1617–18 he went out again, this time with his wife, and commenced construction of a fort at Québec. A major problem was the state of warfare with the native Iroquois; the government sent out six Jesuits to help mediate in 1626. To back up Champlain's work, cardinal RICHELIEU in 1627 supported the establishment of a Company of New France. While preparing a further expedition with the help of the Jesuits, Champlain fell ill and died in the Jesuit mission.

Chantal, Jeanne Françoise de, baroness de Chantal (1572–1641) French co-founder of the Order of the Visitation. In 1592 she married the baron de Chantal, who was killed in a hunting accident (1601), leaving her with four children; she then took a vow of chastity and dedication to God. In 1604 she heard St FRANCIS DE SALES, bishop of Annecy-Geneva, preach the Lent at Dijon and placed herself under his direction. In 1610, with his help, she went to Annecy and founded the Order of the Visitation. She died in her convent at Moulins. Ten years after her death the order had 115 houses. She was canonised in 1767.

Chapuys, Eustache (c.1490–1556) Savoyard diplomat. Born at Annécy, Savoy, of lesser nobility, he studied at Turin (1507) and then later at Rome, where he got his doctorate in law. He entered the Church, and held office in the diocese of Geneva. From 1517 to 1519 he served the duke of Savoy on various diplomatic missions to the Swiss cities, then passed into the service of CHARLES V in the 1520s. In 1529 the emperor appointed him ambassador to England; it was to be his most famous posting, which he occupied with brief intervals from 1529 to 1545. His principal business was the divorce of HENRY VIII, on which he sent invaluable reports to Charles; he also effectively hindered the work of French diplomats in England.

Charles I Stuart (1600–49) king of England, Scotland and Ireland 1625–49. Second son of JAMES I, from 1618 he became a close friend of the duke of BUCKINGHAM: the two travelled to Spain in 1623 on the abortive enterprise to marry the Spanish infanta; in 1625, now king, he married HENRIETTA MARIA of France. A devout but unimaginative ruler, he relied for his first years on the services of BUCKINGHAM, whose mismanagement provoked constant conflicts with Parliament. Faced above all by a shortage of money, Charles was obliged to resort to tax measures that his critics denounced as illegal. He dissolved his fourth Parliament in 1629 and ruled without it (the 'Eleven Years Tyranny', 1629–40). During this crucial period, his most prominent ministers were STRAFFORD and LAUD, whose

policies aggravated opposition to the crown, particularly in religious matters. Pressed by the outbreak of rebellion in Scotland (1638–41), Charles was forced to call Parliament in order to ask for money; when it proved intractable (the Short Parliament) he dissolved it, but was then obliged to call another. The Long Parliament (1640–60) used the opportunity to bring about radical changes in government. The acts of the Long Parliament in their turn favoured the formation of a royalist party to support the king: the outcome was civil war, in which Charles' forces were finally defeated at the battle of Naseby (1645). In confinement, he negotiated an alliance with the Scots Presbyterians, and unleashed a second civil war (1648), which he again lost. His enemies blamed him for both wars and saw no option but to bring him to trial. Judged by a select court, whose legality he refused to accept, he was executed at Whitehall on 30 January 1649.

Charles II Habsburg (1661–1700) last Habsburg king of Spain (1665–1700). Sick and rickety from childhood, his constantly imminent death provoked disputes over the succession among European powers, who drew up a series of treaties (the first of them as early as 1668) partitioning the Spanish empire among themselves in case Charles died without an heir. He was married twice, each time without issue: in 1679 to Marie Louise of Orléans, daughter of the duke d'Orléans, and in 1689 to Mariana of Neuburg, daughter of the elector of the Palatinate. During his reign Spain lost several of its possessions to France in the wars of LOUIS XIV, notably Franche Comté, Artois and Netherlands frontier towns (treaty of Nijmegen 1678). In his last testament he left the throne to Louis XIV's grandson the duke d'Anjou; France's struggle to enforce this resulted in the war of the Spanish Succession. Though wholly dependent on his mother in his early years as king, Charles came in later years to display considerable initiative in government. His reputation as 'the bewitched king' rests entirely on one small episode during one of his recurrent illnesses (in 1699 an exorcist was called in to see if he could cure the king's impotence).

Charles II Stuart (1630–85) king of England, Scotland and Ireland 1660–85. Son of CHARLES I, after his father's defeat in the first civil war, he took refuge in France. On his father's execution he was proclaimed king of Scotland and crowned at Scone in 1651; his Scots army invaded England but was defeated at the battle of Worcester (September 1651), when he apparently escaped capture by hiding in an oak tree. He fled to the continent, where he was befriended by the Dutch and the French courts. Invited back to England by Parliament and the army in 1660, he was proclaimed in London in May. His restoration was engineered by the Anglican-royalist interest (Tories), who attempted under CLARENDON to retain control of the country; but his reign was notable for the emergence of active opposition groups (Whigs), led by SHAFTESBURY, dedicated to toleration for non-Anglicans. The king deliberately played a passive role in politics, giving the impression that he cared only for entertainment and his famous mistresses. But his dexterity in political crises (notably the years 1678–82 of the Exclusion Crisis, when his opponents failed to impose their demands over who should succeed Charles as king) reveal his great political ingenuity. A man of outstanding culture, under his rule Britain enjoyed unprecedented successes in political evolution, cultural achievement, naval expansion and commercial enterprise. His inglorious foreign policy in Europe, when he was for the most part a client of LOUIS XIV of France, had few negative consequences for Britain. Charles' marriage to CATHERINE OF BRAGANZA in 1662 also brought imperial benefits, but little connubial bliss. He died as a Catholic. Though he sired numerous

bastards, of whom the most prominent was MONMOUTH, he had no legitimate heir, and was succeeded by his brother, the Catholic duke of York (JAMES II).

Charles III (of Naples, later of Spain) (1716–88) Bourbon ruler of Naples (1734–59) and of Spain (1759–88) known for his 'enlightened' rule and reforms that spurred cultural and economic revival. Son of PHILIP V of Spain and Elizabeth FARNESE of Parma, he surrounded himself with competent ministers who facilitated the Enlightenment agenda. He ruled as duke of Parma in 1732–4 before assuming the crown of the kingdom of Naples as its first 'national' monarch in over 200 years. In his twenty-five year reign in Naples, he worked with his chief minister Bernardo Tanucci on reformist policies in relations with the Church, in feudal reform, on laws and judicial affairs, and above all on economic issues affecting finance, manufacturing, commerce and agriculture. On the death of his half-brother Ferdinand VI in 1759, he abdicated in favour of his third son, Ferdinand I, who remained subject to a regency under Tanucci, and as the new Spanish king, he continued to maintain close contacts in Naples. In Spain, he continued his reliance on strong ministers, the count of Aranda and the count of Floridablanca, to achieve an even broader reform agenda. He tried to subordinate the Church to the crown by curbing papal bulls in Spain without royal permission, by spearheading the attack on the Jesuits with their expulsion from Spain and its colonies in 1767, and by reforming the Inquisition. He reorganised ministries and royal councils, asserted more centralised administrative control through intendants, and supported national manufacturing and wider commercial activity. In addition to internal reform, the goal in Spain was to insure the survival of the Spanish colonial empire and the viability of Spain as a world power. Despite an unsuccessful foreign policy that was ineffective during the

Seven Years' War and American Revolution, the Bourbon reform's administrative reorganisation in the colonies achieved notable commercial growth.

[JM]

Charles V of Habsburg (1500–58) Holy Roman Emperor and king of Spain (as Charles I). Son of Philip the Fair (king Philip I of Castile) and JUANA THE MAD, grandson of the emperor MAXIMILIAN I, he was brought up in his native Netherlands by humanist tutors. He became duke of Burgundy (ruler of the Netherlands) on his father's death in 1506, and succeeded to the throne of Spain on the death of FERDINAND II OF TRASTÁMARA in 1516. He arrived in Spain in 1517 but was soon faced with hostility and a revolt of the principal Castilian cities (revolt of the Comuneros 1520–1). In 1519 he succeeded to the Holy Roman Empire on Maximilian's death, and left Spain to assume his German inheritance. His realms (which included Spain's territories in America and Italy) now constituted the biggest concentration of states ever ruled over by one person in all European history. But they brought problems. In northern Europe he faced two major threats: the spread of the Reformation, both among the German nobility and in his own Netherlands; and a military conflict with France. A notable victory over the French at Pavia (1525) gave the advantage to Charles in Italy, where in 1530 at Bologna the pope crowned him emperor. In Germany he was drawn into the Schmalkaldic War, which terminated with a victory at Mühlberg (1547) without solving the situation in Germany. The war against the Turks was not forgotten: in 1535 Charles headed a huge expedition that captured the city of Tunis. His untiring military travels and expeditions, together with his bad dietary regime, destroyed his health, and he abdicated in Brussels in 1556 from all his territories (except the Empire, which he retained

until 1558), retiring to live in Yuste in Spain, where he died. A notable scholar and general, and an outstanding patron of the arts, he was an unbending Catholic but also a man of liberal ideas, an admirer of ERASMUS and a profound opponent of the enslavement of the American Indians. Portraits by TITIAN capture him in all his grandeur.

Charles VI (1685–1740) emperor 1711–40. Second son of the emperor Leopold I, he married Elizabeth of Brunswick-Wolfenbüttel, whom he took with him to Spain in his first great intervention in politics, as pretender to the Spanish throne after the death of the last Habsburg there, CHARLES II. Based in Barcelona as 'Charles III' of Spain, he failed to win adequate support against majority Spanish loyalty to the French candidate, PHILIP V. In 1711 he became heir to the Imperial throne on the unexpected death of his elder brother Joseph, emperor from 1705 to 1711, and left for Vienna. His allies in the peninsula, England and the Dutch, refused to support him since they opposed a union of the Empire and Spain, and negotiated the peace of Utrecht (1713) with France, while the Empire negotiated the subsequent peace of Rastatt (1714). The rest of Charles' reign was spent in unravelling the territorial commitments of his extensive possessions. Wars provoked in the western Mediterranean by Spain ended with Spain recognising Austrian rule over the Netherlands and the Italian territories. In Austria he issued the Pragmatic Sanction (1713), affirming the identical rights of male and female heirs to the Habsburg territories, a law intended to protect the succession of his eldest daughter Maria Theresa. Austrian military successes were achieved largely by the generalship of prince EUGÈNE OF SAVOY-CARIGNAN, who scored important victories against the Turks. Unfortunately, the reign ended with a series of disastrous wars: that of the Polish

Succession (1733–5), in which Naples and Sicily were lost to Spain; and that against the Turks (1737–9).

Charles VIII of France (1470–98) king 1483–98. The only son of Louis XI, he succeeded to the throne at the age of 13, and the regency was controlled by his sister Anne and her husband Pierre de Bourbon, seigneur de Beaujeu. In 1491 he was married to Anne of Brittany, an historic event which united Brittany to the French crown. With ambitions to recuperate for France interests lost in preceding years, he launched his grand enterprise, an expedition to Italy to assert the right to the kingdom of Naples that he had inherited from the Angevins. He invaded Italy with his army in 1494 without much difficulty, entering Naples in triumph in February 1495, and was crowned king there. The enterprise set off nearly half a century of war both within Italy and between outside interests. The Holy League of Venice was formed between FERDINAND II OF TRASTÁMARA, the papacy, the emperor, Milan and Venice. Charles was forced to withdraw, succeeded in winning a victory at the battle of Fornovo (1495), but lost everything he had gained and retired to France. He died of a simple accident, hitting his head on a low doorway, while preparing for another expedition. He left no surviving issue, and was succeeded on the throne by his cousin the duke d'Orléans, with the title of LOUIS XII.

Charles IX (1550–74) king of France from 1560. Second son of HENRY II and CATHERINE DE MÉDICIS, he became king on the death of his brother FRANCIS II, but government remained in the hands of his mother as regent, until he was proclaimed of age in 1563. Dominated by Catherine, he attempted to assert his own will, and gave support in the royal council to the policies of the Huguenot leader COLIGNY, but pressed by the Catholic party and by his mother, he withdrew it. When in August 1572 an assassination attempt

was made on Coligny, he went further and sanctioned a general attack on the Huguenots, known as the massacre of St Bartholomew's day, August 23–4, 1572.

Charles IX Vasa (1550–1611) virtual ruler from 1599, king of Sweden 1604–11. Youngest son of GUSTAV I VASA and governor by his father's testament of the central provinces of Sweden, he used his power in 1568 to lead a rebellion against the ruling king, his half-brother ERIK XIV, that placed his brother John III on the throne. Supporter of the Lutheran Reformation, he opposed John III's attempts to reconcile the public practice of the new and the old faiths. The next king, supported by the council of nobles, was John's Catholic son Sigismund, then ruling Poland as SIGISMUND III VASA. Charles, playing on the fear of a Catholic restoration and the possibility of an absentee king, won noble support at the convention of Uppsala (1593) for the affirmation of Lutheranism as the state religion. Sigismund's opposition shortly led to a brief civil war and his deposition (1599). Charles took over virtual control, purged aristocratic opposition, and was declared king in 1604 (crowned 1607). The dynastic conflict with Poland ushered Sweden into a long period of war in the Baltic. Swedish forces invaded Poland and even Russia, but with little success. A parallel war with Denmark (the war of Kalmar, 1611–13) was likewise unfruitful. To back up the war effort, Karl introduced foreign technicians and sponsored the armament industries.

Charles X Gustav Vasa (1622–60) king of Sweden 1654–60. Grandson of CHARLES IX VASA through the latter's daughter Catherine, wife of John Casimir, count palatine of Zweibrücken, he dedicated his entire reign to war, becoming king on the abdication of queen CHRISTINA VASA. Dreaming of Swedish suzerainty over the Baltic region, he conducted the Great Northern War (1655–60) against Poland

and Denmark, occupying most of Poland in the summer of 1656. He then marched against Denmark, imposing on it the treaty of Roskilde (February 1658), by which the Danes ceded Skåne, Halland and Blekinge to Sweden, which thereby acquired its southern coastline. He died suddenly at Göteborg. Thanks to previous Swedish conquests, under him the Swedish empire attained its widest territorial extent.

Charles XI Vasa (1655–97) king of Sweden 1660–97. Aged five when he succeeded his father CHARLES X GUSTAV VASA, he did not govern directly until 1672. During his minority power was exercised by Magnus DE LA GARDIE and the regents; he took over direct control from about 1674. The regency period was one of difficulty in foreign affairs, culminating in the humiliating defeat of Swedish troops by Brandenburg at Fehrbellin (1675), a reverse that encouraged Denmark to invade Sweden. Charles led his troops to victory over the Danes, forcing them (treaty of Lund 1679) to abandon their claim to Skåne. He also married (1680) Ulrika Leonora, sister of Christian V of Denmark. In his reign the drive to reclaim alienated lands for the crown, thereby strengthening state finances and freeing the crown from the need to seek foreign subsidies, gathered force in both Sweden and Finland. Higher income enable him to budget for a regular national army and navy, and improve administration and education. After 1680 Sweden also kept free from alliances that implicated military obligations. Charles strengthened the absolutist nature of royal authority, with the help of the Diet, which was opposed to the power of the regents. In 1680 the Diet declared the king to be supreme over the regency council, in subsequent years affirmed the supremacy of the king over the Diet itself, and in 1693 declared Charles to be 'an absolute, sovereign king'. A dedicated, assiduous monarch with no dreams of military glory, Charles introduced various reforms but died unexpectedly at the age of 41.

Charles XII Vasa (1682–1718) king of Sweden 1697–1718. The most spectacular of the Vasa kings, his military adventures provoked the collapse of Sweden's imperial power. Aged only fifteen when he became king, his dedication to physical prowess gave his ministers an indication of his future evolution. He led his country into the Great Northern War (1700–21), against an aggressive alliance of Baltic states (Denmark, Saxony and Russia). He forced peace with Denmark; invaded Livonia and defeated the Russians at Narva (November 1700). He then invaded Poland, with the aim of making it a future base for operations, and expelled its king AUGUSTUS II, appointing STANISLAS LESZCZYNSKI in his place. The Polish campaign gave the Russians time to recover: at Poltava (July 1709) their forces crushed the Swedes, most of whom surrendered three days later to the Russians at Perevolochna. Charles took refuge in Turkish territory for five years, a dramatic period during which he had to fight his way out of a trap in 1713 at Bender (in modern Moldova). He managed to return to Swedish territory in 1714, and prepared for further campaigns against the Russians, but was killed by a stray bullet while directing the siege of Fredrikshald (Norway) against Danish forces. His campaigns brought little security to the Swedish possessions in northern Europe, which despite his real concern for them were dismembered at the treaty of Nystad (1721). He left no heir: 'I'll marry after the war is over' was one of his most repeated sayings. An archetypal military hero, his virtues were celebrated in Voltaire's *History of Charles XII* (1731).

Charles the Bold (1433–77) duke of Burgundy 1467–77. Son of duke Philip the Good and Isabella of Portugal, Charles was brought up in the French manner as a friend of the dauphin, afterward LOUIS XI of France. On becoming duke in 1467, he began his effort to make Burgundy independent of France, and his entire rule was occupied by wars against Louis XI, his liege lord. Already before his accession he became one of the principal leaders of the League of the Public Weal, an alliance of the leading French magnates against Louis. Charles was almost entirely successful until 1474. He created alliances with both England (in 1468 he married Margaret of York as his third wife) and the emperor against France. He aimed to unite his scattered possessions and organise them as a state. He freed them from French control, with the hope of extending his frontiers towards the Mediterranean. But his efforts to advance his borders towards Swiss territory were less successful; he was defeated by the Swiss in two notable battles, at Grandson and at Morat, in 1476. In 1477 he lost Nancy in a battle in which he was killed, his body being found some days later. The fragility of his achievement is proved by its rapid disintegration during the minority of MARY OF BURGUNDY, his daughter by Isabella of Bourbon.

Chevreuse, Marie de Rohan, duchess de (1600–79) Married first to the duke de LUYNES (1617), then in 1622 to Claude de Lorraine, duke de Chevreuse, she played a prominent part in the politics of her time, easing her way by continuous love affairs with gentlemen of importance. Associated with the noble groups opposed to RICHELIEU, she was a close friend of queen ANNE OF AUSTRIA, whom she initiated into a love affair with the duke of BUCKINGHAM. She seems also to have been one of the spirits behind the conspiracy in 1626 to remove the king, utilising for that purpose her lover, the prince de Chalais, who was executed for conspiring against the cardinal. Exiled for her role in the affair, she went to Lorraine, became the mistress of the duke and persuaded him to plot against France. Permitted back to Paris in 1628, she returned to plotting,

this time with the keeper of the seals, Châteauneuf (1633), and was exiled to the provinces. There she was involved in another plot against the government (1637), and fled to Spain and then to England (1638–40), returning to Paris shortly before the death of LOUIS XIII. She then participated in a movement of nobles, called the Cabale des Importants (1643), against the new government and the chief minister MAZARIN, and once again went into exile (1643–9). She returned (1649) to take an active part in the Fronde. She made her peace eventually with Mazarin's regime in 1652, and in her last years became very pious and the principal protector of the Jansenists of Port-Royal.

Child, Sir Josiah (1630–99) English politician and trader. Son of a London merchant, he worked in the administration of the navy, became mayor of Portsmouth, and served three times in Parliament. He made his career principally in the East India Company, rising to become its governor (1681) and making himself very wealthy in the process. His later fame rests chiefly on his tract *A New Discourse of Trade* (published 1665), which argued that lower interest rates and more freedom would benefit English trade in its competition with the Dutch. The work went into five editions before 1699, and came to have an important influence on the thinking of writers in Italy, France, Germany and Austria. The work's other main theme was the question of poverty and the employment of the poor. Child connected the two themes by arguing that high employment with good wages benefited trade: 'wherever wages are high, it is an infallible evidence of the riches of that country'.

Chippendale, Thomas (1718–79) English furniture-designer. Born in Yorkshire, he was in London from the 1740s, when he married (1748) and began to make his reputation as a furniture maker, in St

Martin's Lane. His success was such that he gave his name to a whole style of woodwork, both elaborate and delicate. In 1754 he published his celebrated *Gentleman and Cabinet-Maker's Director*, a book of designs for domestic furniture of the period, with drawings done by himself and his colleagues. The first and second (1755) editions contained 160 plates, the third edition (1762) 200. Different furniture-makers borrowed from and imitated his designs, with the result that a vast quantity of pieces from the period are known as 'Chippendale' but were not made by him or his associates. From the 1760s he was influenced in his style by the work of Robert ADAM, and his own designs had an extensive vogue in the American colonies.

Christian IV (1577–1648) king of Denmark and Norway 1588–1648. Son of king FREDERIK II OF DENMARK, he was well educated by tutors from Germany, succeeding to the throne when only eleven. A regency council administered affairs until he was crowned in 1596. His first entry into foreign policy was to direct a war (1611–13) against Sweden, against the wishes of the royal council (Rigsråd), with the aim of recovering lost territories. An active Lutheran, whose sister ANNE OF DENMARK was married to the king of England, he agreed to intervene in the Thirty Years War against the Catholic forces which had reached northern Germany, but was defeated by the forces of TILLY at Lutter (1626). When the forces of Tilly and WALLENSTEIN invaded Danish territory (Jutland) he made a defensive alliance with GUSTAV II ADOLF VASA, but later accepted a peace treaty with the emperor in 1629 (peace of Lübeck). The permanent conflict with Sweden broke out again in another war (1643–5), in which the Dutch, who sought freer trade in the Baltic, supported Sweden. Jutland was occupied and the Danish navy destroyed by a joint Dutch–Swedish fleet. Christian, who lost an eye in one of the battles, had to accept the peace of Brömsebro (1645), in which he had to cede Gotland, Ösel and Norwegian territory to Sweden. Though Denmark had failed as a great power, Christian in his long reign contributed much to the reform of mercantile policy, the improvement of public education, the foundation of new towns (among them Kristiania – later renamed Oslo – in Norway), and the beautification of Copenhagen.

Christian, prince of Anhalt-Bernburg (1568–1630) German prince and general. Born a Lutheran, he converted to Calvinism, and took service under the elector of Saxony 1586–92. As governor of the Upper Palatinate from 1595, he took a leading part in the organisation of the Evangelical Union (1608) against the Catholic princes, and encouraged the acceptance by the elector Palatine (FREDERICK V OF WITTELSBACH) of the Bohemian crown in 1618, an act that precipitated the Thirty Years War. General of Frederick's army, he was defeated at the battle of the White Mountain (1620).

Christina Vasa (1626–89) queen of Sweden 1632–54. Since she was aged only six at the death of her father GUSTAV II ADOLF VASA at Lützen (1632), government in Sweden was run by a regency council led by OXENSTIERNA. Christina entered council meetings from 1640, assumed power in 1644 and had herself crowned in 1650. The two main political challenges facing her were the war in Germany (in which she favoured a rapid peace), and the political role of the higher nobility in Sweden; in both respects her views did not coincide exactly with those of Oxenstierna. Energetic and independent, she had little patience with political conventions, and spent her crown finances profligately. She also showed a leaning to the old religion. A devotee of all aspects of learning, she invited leading scholars and musicians to Sweden, and was responsible for bringing DESCARTES to Stockholm to discuss philosophy with her. Policy differences with her advisers, and her distinctive personal habits, provoked a constitutional crisis that led finally to her startling abdication (1654). She travelled through Europe, was received into the Catholic Church in Brussels, and given a triumphant welcome in Rome (1655). Thereafter (financed in part by revenues from her Swedish estates) she took part in various abortive political activities both in Rome and elsewhere. She made two brief return visits to Sweden (1660, 1667). Above all, she became famous in Italy for her cultural role: her palace in Rome, the Palazzo Riario, became known as the meeting place for writers, artists (she befriended BERNINI) and musicians (she patronised SCARLATTI and CORELLI), and she founded the Arcadian Academy for scholarly discussion. Her tomb is in St Peter's.

Cinq-Mars, Henri Coiffier de Ruzé d'Effiat, marquis de (1620–42) Son of a marshal of France, his father died when he was twelve and he was befriended at court by RICHELIEU, who obtained for him the posts of captain in the royal guard (1635) and gentleman of the bedchamber (1638). The cardinal appears to have believed that Cinq-Mars would give him further control over the king, who became infatuated with the young man, would not be separated from him and bestowed further posts on him. Tensions arose between the cardinal and Cinq-Mars, who began to conspire against Richelieu. In 1642 evidence of Cinq-Mars' part in a conspiracy involving GASTON-JEAN-BAPTISTE, duke d'Orléans and the Spaniards, was brought to the king, who accepted the inevitable. The favourite was arrested, tried and decapitated at Lyon.

Cisneros, Francisco Jiménez de (1436–1517) archbishop of Toledo from 1495, cardinal and Inquisitor-General from 1507. Cisneros was without doubt the most powerful political figure appointed by FERDINAND II OF TRASTÁMARA and ISABELLA THE CATHOLIC to promote their policies. What he accomplished was in the main with their approval, whether it was in the reform of the religious orders, of ecclesiastical appointments, of the secular clergy and of education. As a Franciscan of Strict Observance, and Isabella's confessor from 1492, he became superior of all the Franciscan convents and pushed through his reforms despite the reserves of pope ALEXANDER VI. His aggressive approach to the Jewish and Muslim communities was in sharp contrast to the more charitable line of the first archbishop of Granada, Hernando de TALAVERA. Appointed as sole Inquisitor-General in 1507, he had always been a harsh prophet of Spain's messianic destiny. Those two faiths were faced with the stark choice of conversion or exile, a policy backed up, as always, by Isabella. As a consequence there were revolts in Andalusia, which might have provoked a riposte from north Africa. Ferdinand had plans to meet this threat, and Cisneros himself led an expedition to Oran in 1509. His approach to missionary work in the New World was less forceful, and not at all successful. He also played a key role in the difficult discussions over succession to the throne consequent on the mental health of the infanta JUANA THE MAD. He attempted to have her declared incapable, but Ferdinand opposed this, and Cisneros had to be satisfied with a cardinalate. In the field of educational reform his major achievement was the foundation of the university of Alcalá de Henares in 1508. It was to lead the way in theological studies, where Hebrew and Greek ranked equal with Latin. Cisneros made an interesting series of appointments at the university, including converted Jews (*conversos*). Out of this collaboration emerged the famous Complutensian Polyglot Bible, with texts in Hebrew, Greek and Latin, an event unique in Europe at that time.

[BT]

Clarendon, Edward Hyde, 1st earl of (1609–74) English statesman. Trained as a lawyer, he entered the House of Commons in the Short Parliament (1640), where he opposed the crown's policies while supporting royal authority and the state Church. In the Long Parliament he maintained his moderate position, but when the civil war broke out (1642) he rallied to CHARLES I. After the civil wars he accompanied CHARLES II into exile (1651), and at the Restoration (1660) was appointed Chancellor and effective head of the government, and created earl of Clarendon (1661). In the new royalist Parliament, his name was inappropiately given to the intolerant Church legislation (Clarendon Code) restricting dissenters. His aggressive foreign policy against the Dutch was a failure, and he was impeached by Parliament (1667). He retired to France, where he dedicated himself to defending his reputation through his writings. He took up again his great work, the *History of the Great Rebellion*, that he had begun in the 1640s. Written with remarkable detachment and in superb prose, it is one of the classics of English historical writing; it was published by his son in 1702. He also wrote his own *Life* (published 1759), from which much of the material of the History in its published version was drawn. His daughter Anne married in 1660 the duke of York (later JAMES II). A month after his death in France, he was brought home and buried in Westminster Abbey.

Claris, Pau (1586–1641) Catalan political leader. A canon of the bishopric of Urgell, from 1638 he presided over the Diputació of Catalonia (of which he was one of the ecclesiastical deputies) at a critical moment in relations between Catalonia and the government of OLIVARES in Madrid. When the conflict with Castile seemed irreparable, Claris led the group of Catalan leaders who favoured a total rupture with Spain and an alliance with France, and led the moves which in January 1641 recognised LOUIS XIII as king and accepted the French army into Barcelona. Always in poor health, he died suddenly even as the French troops entered Barcelona. Subsequent Catalan historiography idealised his role and presented him as a supporter of national independence from Spain.

Claude (le) Lorrain (Claudio Lorenese; Claude Gelée) (1600–82) French painter and etcher active in Rome. Born to a peasant couple in Lorraine, where (according to the art historian Joachim von Sandrart, who knew him personally) he first trained as a pastry-cook, he came to Rome quite early, perhaps at the age of twelve or thirteen. Sometime after 1618 in Naples he began to study landscape painting with the German-born Goffredo Wals, later returning to Rome to join the household of the Italian landscapist Agostino Tassi. Beginning in 1625 he spent two years as assistant to the court painter of the duke de Lorraine, before returning permanently to Rome in 1627, where he kept a modest bachelor household in the working-class parish of S.M. del Popolo. His earliest extant paintings date from 1629; by 1630 he was already much in demand – and being forged. His buyers included many members of the curia, as well as the French ambassador, URBAN VIII, and PHILIP IV of Spain. Although he is said to have been uneducated and semi-literate, he is credited with having perfected the art of idealised landscape, greatly influencing the second generation of Dutch Romanists, as well as English painters of the eighteenth and nineteenth centuries.

[JH]

Clement VII (Giulio de' Medici, 1478–1534) pope 1523. Born the illegitimate son of Giuliano de' Medici in the same year that his father was murdered during the Pazzi Conspiracy, he was raised by his uncle Lorenzo de' MEDICI in the humanist tradition. He had a sharp mind, had wide experience in political affairs, was a good financial administrator, a fine musician and a liberal patron of the arts and charitable enterprises – none of which prevented him from gaining the reputation of a weak and vacillating pope. With the Medici restoration in Florence in 1512 and the election of his cousin Giovanni as LEO X in 1513, he was made archbishop of Florence and cardinal to serve as Leo's vice-chancellor with chief responsibility in political affairs during a decade of growing rivalry between FRANCIS I and CHARLES V. He was particularly adept at keeping papal finances afloat and after 1519 he assumed responsibility for governing Florence. He commissioned RAPHAEL's *Transfiguration* altarpiece for his cathedral in Narbonne, France, and MICHELANGELO's Medici tombs for the New Sacristy in San Lorenzo in Florence. He was elected pope in the contested election after ADRIAN VI's short twenty-one month reign to face a number of daunting issues: weakened papal finances, the Protestants in Germany, HENRY VIII's demands for an annulment, Ottoman advances in Hungary, and the Habsburg–Valois war in Italy. Shifting sides from the emperor to France after the French defeat at Pavia (1525), his new alliance in the League of Cognac (1625) proved disastrous. Imperial troops sacked Rome in 1527 and he only managed to find tenuous sanctuary in the besieged Castel Sant' Angelo. He eventually made peace with Charles and crowned him at Bologna in 1530. He delayed a decision on Henry's English divorce until 1533 and took no initiatives for reform to resolve the Protestant schism, although his patronage promoted his hand-picked successor, Alessandro Farnese, as the reforming PAUL III. He is seen as the last of the Renaissance popes primarily interested in Italian politics, uninterested and intransigent on the questions of reform, indulgent patron of art and culture, and promoter of his family and city.

[JM]

Clement XI (Giovanni Francesco Albani, 1649–1721) pope 1700–21. Of noble birth, he spent his early career in political administration, becoming governor of the cities of Rieti and Orvieto. He then opted for a Church career, was made cardinal deacon in 1690, ordained as priest in 1700, and elected pope later the same year. Faced by the outbreak of the war of the Spanish Succession in 1702, he hesitated between supporting the French (who backed the new king of Spain, Philip V), and the Austrians (who backed the Habsburg claimant to Spain). Forced to recognise the Habsburg candidate when the Austrians invaded the Papal States in 1709, he failed to placate either side. Like his predecessors he was drawn into the French problems of Gallicanism and Jansenism. In 1713 he issued the bull *Unigenitus* against the Jansenists, but a section of the French bishops and clergy refused to accept it and went into virtual schism from Rome. Clement was also responsible for the controversial condemnation (in 1704, reinforced by his bull *Ex Illa Die* in 1715) of the Oriental Rites, by which he put an end to the tolerance by Jesuit missionaries in China of the mixture of Confucian ceremonies with Catholic rites.

Clément, Jacques (1567–89) Dominican friar and assassin. Born in the village of Sorbonne, near Sens, during the French civil wars he became obsessed with the harm being done to the Catholic cause by the king, HENRY III. After Henry had arranged for the assassination of the duke and cardinal of GUISE in 1588–9, he determined to act to defend the honour of God. He went to Paris, obtained an interview on 1 August at St-Cloud with the king, saying he wished to impart a secret if left alone with him, and then stabbed him. The guards rushed in and killed Clément, but the king died the next day.

Cobos, Francisco de los (1477–1547) Spanish statesman. From a noble family of Ubeda, he entered the bureaucracy of king Ferdinand in 1503, and on the king's death went to Flanders to seek the favour of the new king, Charles. Appointed as a secretary to Charles (later emperor as CHARLES V) in 1516, he returned to the peninsula with him and quickly rose in the royal service. During the king's frequent long absences from the peninsula, he took charge of the administration, initiated reforms and built up a new bureaucratic machinery. At the same time, he strengthened his hold on power and made himself rich. In 1529 he was appointed to the emperor's council of State. From this time he directed most of the affairs of the Mediterranean part of the empire, while cardinal GRANVELLE directed affairs in northern Europe. In that same year he was also granted the title of grand commander of León, a title by which he was thereafter always known. He continued to direct the affairs of the south when Philip began to act as regent in 1546. His importance as a bureaucrat cannot be exaggerated: he laid the foundations of Habsburg administration in Spain.

Coen, Jan Pieterszoon (1587–1629) founder of Dutch power in Asia. From a strict Calvinist family, he first sailed to Indonesia in 1607 in a fleet of the Dutch East India Company. On his return he submitted to the company in 1610 a report on trade possibilities in Asia, and was sent out again in 1612. From this period (in 1614 he was appointed director of the company's trade in the east) he began to build up Dutch commercial and strategic posts in the area around Java. Through links with native rulers, he cornered the spice trade from Asia, displaced Portuguese interests and attempted to keep the English out. In 1617 he was appointed governor of the Dutch East Indies. Ruthless in his treatment of the peoples of the region, he dreamed of building up for the company a great commercial empire that would stretch from the Indian ocean to Japan, and founded the Dutch city of Batavia (1619). While he was reporting back to his superiors in Holland in 1623, his plans were interrupted by the English, who complained of a so-called massacre of their citizens at Amboina. Coen was not allowed to return till 1627, and died shortly after in Batavia.

Coke, Sir Edward (1552–1634) English judge and constitutional authority. Born in Norfolk, educated at Cambridge and then at the Inner Temple, London, he was called to the bar 1578, married (1582) a daughter of the Paston family, and thanks to the patronage of lord Burghley made a rapid advance in public life. He entered Parliament in 1589, became speaker of the House of Commons (1592), attorney general (1593), chief justice of Common Pleas (1606) and chief justice of King's Bench (1613). In 1598, after his wife died, he married Burghley's granddaughter. Under JAMES I, Coke began to gain his reputation as defender of the common law against royal prerogative, and in 1616 as a result was removed from his post as chief justice. He returned to Parliament in 1620, and continued his differences with the government; in 1621 he was sent to the Tower for nine months. He continued his opposition in the Parliaments of 1624 and 1628; in the latter he made a speech in defence of the traditional laws, declaring that 'Magna Carta is such a fellow that he will have no sovereign'. Acknowledged as the greatest lawyer of his time, he is remembered chiefly for his legal writings: the *Reports* of current court cases, and the *Institutes*. He defended the superiority of English common law over both crown and Parliament, affirming in the case of proclamations (1610) that 'the king cannot create any offence which was not an offence before', and in Bonham's case that 'when an act of Parliament is against reason, the common law will adjudge such act to be void'. Such views, although directed against arbitrary government, were already anachronistic in the political situation of the time.

Colbert, Jean-Baptiste (1619–83) French minister of state. The Colbert family made their money in textiles in Reims in the sixteenth century, and by the seventeenth were ennobled officials. Jean-Baptiste, whose father had the rank of royal secretary, trained in Paris from the 1640s in the financial administration run by his relative LE TELLIER. In 1649 he became a councillor of state and administrative secretary to cardinal MAZARIN. In 1658 he purchased the barony of Seignelay (Burgundy) and entered the aristocracy. Appointed intendant of finances when LOUIS XIV began to rule directly, he accumulated the evidence that led to the downfall (1661) of the minister of finance, FOUQUET. Thereafter Colbert's rise was swift, culminating with his appointment as controller general of finance in 1665, to which he added other senior posts in the administration, making him supreme in all aspects of government other than war and diplomacy. He did not aim to innovate or reform, but rather to make more efficient the fiscal and bureaucratic machinery he took over. A protectionist in trade policy, he considered that the state should where necessary exercise an aggressive foreign policy in order to advance national wealth; he therefore supported the king's wars of aggression against Holland. Firmly backed by Louis XIV, he helped to mould France into the most powerful state in Europe: commerce and industry expanded, treasury income rose. He used his influence to place his family in the highest echelons: his three daughters became duchesses by marriage; his eldest son, later marquis de Seignelay, became minister of marine; his second son became

archbishop of Rouen; other family members occupied the highest offices of state.

Colet, John (1466/7–1519) English humanist and dean of St Paul's Cathedral, London. Son of a burgess knight who was twice lord mayor of London, he had already studied scholastic philosophy and rhetoric when he embarked on four years of formative travel and study in France and Italy. He studied Florentine Platonism under FICINO and PICO DELLA MIRANDOLA, which strongly influenced his Christian humanist practices upon his return to England c.1496. In 1498 he was ordained and lectured at Oxford where he invited ERASMUS, who was to share his passion for biblical scholarship and a 'simple' Christianity. There, he also befriended Thomas MORE and was one of the promoters of Renaissance humanist culture in England. His own lectures on St Paul's Epistle's are exemplary for their humanist method of biblical exegesis that emphasises the historical context, grammatical meaning, and personal message of the text. The goal of scholarship and piety marked both his teaching and his administrative career. He became dean of St Paul's Cathedral in 1504 and founded its humanist school c.1509 with the inheritance from his father's estate. In 1517 he was appointed to the royal council, but died soon after of a sweating sickness. Some of his financial reforms were directed towards the foundation of St Paul's School, for which a building was completed by 1512. He was the model of the engaged, reforming scholar-priest whose Christian humanism combined simple faith and scripture study.

[JM]

Coligny, Gaspard II, count de (1519–72) admiral of France. The Coligny family had their origins in mediaeval Burgundy, and rendered outstanding military service to the French crown. Son of the marshal de Châtillon, Gaspard was brought up at the royal court with the future HENRY II, and served in Flanders and Italy. King from 1547, Henry gave him posts of authority in the army, appointed him governor of Paris (1551) and admiral of France (1552). During campaigns in Picardy, Gaspard clashed with duke Francis of GUISE, creating an enmity with long-lasting consequences. He was made governor of Picardy (1555), where after the disastrous French defeat near St Quentin (1557) he defended the town against the enemy troops of PHILIP II, but was taken prisoner. During his imprisonment he read the Bible and became converted to the Reformation, declaring himself a Protestant in 1558. When the civil wars began in France he became one of the Calvinist military leaders, assuming leadership of the cause after the death of CONDÉ (1569); after the subsequent campaign he obtained from the government the advantageous peace of St Germain (1570). Called to participate in the government as a counterpoise to the Guises, he became chief councillor of state of CHARLES IX; but the Catholic nobles feared Protestant control of the crown. In August 1572, when both Catholic and Huguenot leaders were in Paris to celebrate the marriage of Henry of Navarre (the future HENRY IV) to MARGUERITE OF VALOIS, sister of the king, an attempt was made on Coligny's life. The next day, St Bartholomew's Eve, a general massacre of Huguenots took place in Paris (and in France); the admiral was one of the first victims, despatched by the young duke de Guise, who blamed him for the death of his father Francis of Guise during the civil wars.

Colonna, Vittoria (1490–1547) poet and follower of the *spirituali* movement in Italy. Daughter of Fabrizio Colonna (the leading Roman nobleman and strong pro-French partisan) and Agnese di Montefeltro (daughter of Federico, duke of Urbino), she was betrothed at the age of seven to Ferdinando d'Avalos, marquis of Pescara (a strongly pro-Spanish partisan), in a dynastic union to hedge the family's bets on

the outcome of the French–Spanish wars in Italy. With the destruction of family lands in war, she took up long residence in Ischia after 1501. At nineteen in 1509 she married d'Avalos, who soon distinguished himself in battle at Ravenna in 1512 (but was captured and imprisoned) and later after 1521 against the French, rising to become general of the Spanish forces at Pavia in 1525 (but was wounded and died a few months later). His absences inspired her great poetic theme of longing and far off love; and his death changed her life. Her poetry and thinking matured in the cultural orbit of Ischia/Naples and she associated herself with the literati around the court of LEO X, writers such as CASTIGLIONE, BEMBO, SADOLETO and Giovio, even offering hospitality in Ischia after the 1527 Sack of Rome. By 1530 she was back in Naples as a member of the religious circle around Juan de Valdés and after 1532 in Rome as one of the *spirituali*, the reform-minded Catholics in Italy. She was especially close to Cardinal Reginald POLE and it was in Rome in 1534 that she first met MICHELANGELO. In 1537 she resided in Ferrara and the first edition of 150 of her sonnets was published in Parma in 1538. By 1544 she was back in Rome and renewed and deepened her friendship with Michelangelo in the few years before her death. Death saved her from Inquisitorial investigation, but her poetry, culture, and spiritual ideals were widely praised by her contemporaries.

[JM]

Columbus, Christopher (1451–1506) discoverer of the 'New World'. A mystery surrounds his origins and early career, mainly because both he and his first biographer, his son Fernando, attempted to hide his plebeian origins. Born in the state of Genoa, he was probably of Spanish origin (he always wrote in Spanish), and went to sea at an early age, both in the Mediterranean and in the Atlantic; from the late 1470s he was based in

Portugal, where in 1479 he married. A man of daring and imagination, he aspired to sail to Asia by going westwards, but his plans for an expedition failed to find support, until in 1492 he was able to persuade FERDINAND II OF TRASTÁMARA and ISABELLA THE CATHOLIC of Spain to back him. His famous expedition (with three vessels) sailed from Palos (Andalusia) in Aug 1492 and made landfall on 12 October in the Bahamas; it returned to Lisbon in March 1493. The second fleet, with seventeen vessels, left Cadiz in September 1493, and began the first settlements; Columbus returned to Cadiz in June 1496. His third journey, with six vessels, left Sanlucar in May 1498, but faced conflicts among the settlers; a royal governor was sent out, and Columbus returned in chains to Spain in 1500. He eventually made a fourth expedition (1502–4). Though maintained in honour, he was neglected thereafter by the crown. To the end of his life he believed that he had made contact with Asia. After his death, his remains were transferred to Santo Domingo (1536), Havana (1795), and then back to Seville (1898). His family rose quickly into the highest Spanish aristocracy.

Comenius (Komenský), Jan Ámos (1592–1670) Czech intellectual. From a family who belonged to the religious group of Bohemian Brethren, educated at the university of Heidelberg (where he discovered the works of BACON), he was obliged to leave Bohemia in 1627 when the occupying Habsburg authorities decreed religious restrictions. He and other brethren went to settle in Leszno, Great Poland, in 1628, where he devoted himself to his ideas and also travelled through western Europe, where he met HARTLIB. In 1631 he published *Labyrinth of the World*, espousing a scheme for unity among Christians. In 1655, when the Swedes swept through Poland, the Brethren were expelled, and he spent the rest of his life in Amsterdam. He made himself

well-known in his lifetime as an educational reformer, through both his textbook publications (especially his *The Visible World in Pictures* of 1658, a manual for teaching languages with the help of illustrations) and his various writings on teaching methods. He expounded a system he called 'pansophy', whereby learning not only became simple and pleasurable, but also enabled men to understand the harmony of the universe and achieved moral reform through education. His aspirations were for universal peace, but he was also a passionate Czech patriot, concerned for the language and the liberty of his homeland. He was a major pioneer of modern pedagogical method.

Commynes, Philippe van den Clyte, seigneur de (1445–1509) French historian. Courtier and scholar (a good linguist, he curiously did not master Latin), he served in the Burgundian court and became chamberlain to CHARLES THE BOLD. In 1472 he entered the service of LOUIS XI of France, who heaped honours on him and used him in diplomatic missions to try and secure the unity of Burgundy and Flanders with France. After the king's death he was denounced by his enemies and imprisoned for eight months. He returned to favour and accompanied CHARLES VIII on his military expeditions to Italy; but had little role under the next king, LOUIS XII. He retired to his estates in Argenton and began writing his *Memoirs* (published 1523) on the two preceding reigns.

Concini, Concino, marshal d'Ancre (1575–1617) Of Florentine noble origin, he came to France in 1600 in the household of MARIE DE MÉDICIS, and rose to influence through the support of his wife, Leonora Galigai, lady-in-waiting of the queen. Occupying a minor post at court, during the queen's regency after the death of HENRY IV he obtained further advancement: he was made councillor of state

(1610), became marquis d'Ancre the same year, first gentleman of the royal bedchamber and governor of Amiens (1611) then later of Normandy (1616). In 1611 he replaced SULLY as chief minister, and in 1613 was created marshal of France, a step that excited the hostility of the nobility. He was particularly detested by the young king LOUIS XIII, who (influenced in part by his favourite Luynes) ordered his assassination, an act carried out by the royal guard when Concini arrived one day at the Louvre. His widow Leonora was accused of witchcraft, decapitated and burnt.

Condé, Henry II de Bourbon, 3rd prince de (1588–1646) known by courtesy as 'Monsieur le Prince'. Grandson of Louis I de Bourbon, prince de CONDÉ, and son of Henry I Bourbon, who was active in the civil wars on the Huguenot side, he was born after his father's death and brought up as a Catholic at the royal court. In 1609 he was married for convenience by HENRY IV to the young Charlotte de MONTMORENCY, with whom the king was infatuated; but Condé fled with her to Brussels to save her from his attentions. He returned after the king's assassination and was appointed to the regency council, but was dissatisfied with the honours accorded him and began to scheme with the duke de BOUILLON and other nobles who opposed the queen mother MARIE DE MÉDICIS. Arrested and imprisoned for three years in the chateau of Vincennes (1616–9), he emerged a changed man, absolutely faithful to the crown. After the disgrace of the queen mother's party in 1630, he gave his support to RICHELIEU, was appointed governor of Burgundy, became rich and powerful and served the monarchy in several military campaigns. He headed the regency council at the death of LOUIS XIII.

Condé, Louis I de Bourbon, 1st prince de (1530–69) Founder of the Condé title in the Bourbon family, Louis was a younger

son of the duke de Vendôme; his brother was ANTOINE DE BOURBON, king of Navarre and father of HENRY IV. In 1551 he married the Calvinist niece of the constable Montmorency, and was himself one of the first great nobles to become Protestant. He took part in the conspiracy of Amboise (1560), for which he was condemned to death but then reprieved. The massacre of Huguenots at Vassy (1562) angered him; he became the principal leader of the Huguenots in the civil wars, which for him were also a means to attack the Catholic GUISE family. Defeated in his principal battles, at Dreux (1562) and Jarnac (1569), he was taken prisoner in the latter and subsequently assassinated.

Condé, Louis II de Bourbon, 4th prince de (1621–86) ('the Great') A well-educated and gifted pupil of the Jesuits, duke d'Enghien until he succeeded to his father's title of Condé, he displayed from an early age a capacity for arms. He married the niece of cardinal RICHELIEU. His first service as soldier was in Picardy in 1640, whose military command was entrusted to him (he was only nineteen) by the king; it was there he led the French forces in a memorable victory over the army of Flanders at Rocroy (1643). Enghien participated successfully in other campaigns, notably against the Imperial army at Nördlingen (1645), and in Flanders where he captured the port of Dunkirk (1646, the year he began using the title Condé after his father's death). His most notable victory was over the Spanish army of Flanders at Lens (1648). In Paris, however, he had serious differences with MAZARIN and the regency government (in force since 1643) of ANNE OF AUSTRIA. Despite this, he supported the court in the first stage of the Fronde, obliging the rebel nobles to agree to the peace of Reuil (1649). Imprisoned together with his brother the prince of CONTI on Mazarin's orders in 1650, on his release a year later he headed a military Fronde of princes.

On the defeat of his forces by TURENNE, he went into exile to the Netherlands, where he commanded the army of Flanders against France. A condition of the peace of the Pyrenees (1659) between France and Spain was that Condé be pardoned. He continued his brilliant military career under LOUIS XIV, occupying Franche-Comté in 1668 and invading Holland in 1672, defeating the forces of the prince of Orange at Senef (1674). His last campaigns were in Alsace. Still young but plagued by gout, he retired in 1675 to his country estate at Chantilly, to which he invited the great literary figures of the day to talk with him and perform their theatrical works.

Condillac, Etienne Bonnot de (1714–80) French philosopher. Born in Grenoble of a family of senior officials, he was sent to study theology at the Sorbonne but gave his attention rather to philosophy and science. Ordained priest in 1740, he apparently never celebrated a mass; instead, he sought out the literary and philosophical salons where he could encounter the well-known philosophers. A follower of LOCKE, he published in 1746 his *Essai sur l'origine des connaissances humaines* (Essay on the Origin of Human Knowledge). In his *Traité des sensations* (Treatise on Feeling) (1754), which established him as one of France's leading philosophers, he suggested how perceptions are assimilated and produce understanding. Incorporating Locke and DESCARTES into his work, he differed from them in important detail. His concern was with the sources of knowledge and language, which he found rather in perception and reflection than in reason alone. His works after this date do not change the substance of his thought. In 1758 he was invited to Parma to become tutor to the duke's son Ferdinand, and on returning to France was elected to the French Academy in 1768. He achieved recognition throughout Europe, and shortly before his death declined the post of tutor to the dauphin.

Congreve, William (1670–1729) English dramatist. Born in Yorkshire but educated in Ireland where his father commanded a garrison, he was a contemporary of Swift at Trinity College, Dublin. Though he entered the Middle Temple, he left law for literature, and produced his first play in 1692. His comedy *The Old Bachelor* (1693) brought him instant fame. It was followed by *The Double Dealer* and *Love for Love. The Mourning Bride* (1697) is his only tragedy and contains the oft-quoted 'Music has charms to soothe a savage breast'. The same year he was engaged in a controversy with the Reverend William Collier who attacked the lewdness of the English stage. After a less favourable reception for *The Way of the World* in 1700, he gave up writing for the theatre, much to VOLTAIRE's disgust, to become a gentleman. Lord HALIFAX procured a government post for him and he was a close friend of Sarah, duchess of MARLBOROUGH. He continued to enjoy the esteem and company of prominent figures in the literary world, including POPE, STEELE and SWIFT. Despite somewhat feeble plots his comedies of manners show a subtle wit and keen observation of human foibles. He is regarded as the finest of the Restoration playwrights. He was buried in Westminster Abbey.

[GG]

Contarini, Gasparo (1483–1542) Venetian statesman and later cardinal, closely identified with Catholic Reform. Having studied philosophy and the humanist curriculum at Padua, he was one of the younger generation of Venetian patricians whose confidence in himself and the world was severely shaken by the complete Venetian defeat at Agnadello in 1509. In 1511 he experienced a spiritual crisis similar to Luther's recognition of the primacy of faith over works. In 1516 he composed a treatise 'On the Office of the Bishop' that outlined clerical abuses and correct episcopal behaviour. He remained interested in jurisdictional and administrative questions of good government. From 1520 to 1534 he held various offices within the Venetian state, especially diplomatic appointments to the imperial court of Charles V (1520–5) and the Vatican (1528–30). He wrote a treatise 'On the Offices of the Republic of Venice' (1523/4, revised 1531, published 1543), which had long-lasting influence on the debate over ideal government and mixed constitutions. During that period, he also wrote a theological response to LUTHER, whom he had seen at the Diet of Worms during his German embassy. In 1535 he was one of the new reform-minded cardinals created by PAUL III, and he chaired a papal commission to make recommendations for the Church's reform that concluded in 1537 that the root problem was papal pretension to the 'plenitude of power'. In 1541–2 he represented the Catholic party at the Colloquy of Regensburg, the last real attempt at reconciliation with the Protestants, and formulated the theory of 'double justification' to mediate the theological dispute. It was rejected by both sides.

[JM]

Conti, Armand de Bourbon, prince de (1629–66) Brother of the Great CONDÉ, he was trained for the Church and granted several abbeys (including St Denis and Cluny), but chose to enter a secular career and in 1646 was consigned the governorship of Champagne by his father. He took part in the Fronde against the government of MAZARIN, at first on the side of the parlement and then on that of his brother Condé, with whom he was imprisoned (1650–51). After his release he joined his family and other supporters in the 'Fronde of the princes' at Bordeaux. In 1653 he made his peace with the cardinal, married one of his nieces, was appointed governor of Guyenne and commanded the army in Catalonia (1654–5) and in Italy (1657). From 1660 he was governor of Languedoc. In his later years he became strongly attached to the Janse-

nists, along with his sister the duchess of LONGUEVILLE.

Conti, François Louis, prince de (1664–1709) Second son of Armaund de Bourbon, the 1st prince of CONTI, he had a distinguished military career in the armies of LOUIS XIV. In 1697 he was proposed as king of Poland by a section of the Polish Diet and sailed for Gdańsk, but discovered on arriving that the other candidate had already been crowned, and returned immediately to France.

Coornhert, Dirck Volckertszoon (1522–90) Dutch thinker and artist. Born in Amsterdam, son of a prosperous trader, he was educated well and then sent off on a grand tour that included Spain and Portugal. By profession an engraver, he first encountered the writings of the Reformation in 1544, but remained a nominal Catholic all his life; his favourite reading was Boethius' *Consolation of Philosophy*, which he translated into Dutch and used to read two or three times a year. Closely connected with WILLIAM I of Orange during the struggle for independence, he twice went into exile. Later he entered the Dutch administration, and became one of the secretaries of the States of Holland in 1572. His numerous works, many published only after his death, were brought together in three volumes in 1630. They include several defences of religious toleration (1591), and criticisms of Catholic as well as of Anabaptist doctrine.

Copernicus, Nicolaus (1473–1543) Polish astronomer. Educated at the expense of his uncle, a prince-bishop, he studied the then closely related subjects of astronomy, mathematics and medicine. Their pursuit took him to Italy, where he spent some time as assistant to an astronomer-astrologer and became acutely aware of the inadequacies of current knowledge. On his return he was employed as physician to his uncle and soon appointed canon of

Frauenburg (Frombork), a post which he retained until his death. His ideas for the radical improvement of astronomy were developed over many years, but he was cautious about revealing them; *De revolutionibus orbium coelestium* (*On the Revolutions of the Celestial Orbs*) was published very close to the time of his death. In it he argued that the sun rather than the earth is the centre of the solar system, that the earth performs a daily rotation upon its axis, and that it and the other planets revolve in orbits around the sun. As colleagues were equally concerned about the risks of provoking controversy, the volume appeared with a preface by Andreas Osiander (not approved by the author) suggesting it offered a mathematical device to ease calculation rather than a description of reality. The full acceptance of Copernican theory spread only slowly amongst other astronomers, over the following century or more.

[FW]

Copley, John Singleton (1738–1815) American painter active in Boston and London. The most gifted American-born artist of the eighteenth century, he was the son of an immigrant Irish tobacconist who died early. His mother's second husband was the engraver Peter Pelham, who gave his stepson his first art instruction, after which he also studied with the local artist John Smibert. Copley's most admired works today are still his portraits of Boston bourgeoisie, including the silversmith *Paul Revere* (1768; Boston Museum). After marrying the daughter of an agent for the British East India Company (1669) he became the next-door neighbour of John Hancock on Beacon Hill. Shortly before the American Revolution, in 1774, he left for London, where he was befriended by Benjamin WEST, and travelled to France and Italy to study ancient sculpture and Renaissance art before settling permanently in England and being elected to the Royal Academy as a history painter. His best-known history painting,

done in the new realistic style promoted by West, is *Watson and the Shark* (1778; London, Tate Gallery), commissioned privately by Brook Watson, who had been attacked by a shark thirty years earlier during his boyhood in Havana. Although it hardly qualified any longer as a current event, this painting is a precocious example of the atrocity pictures so beloved by the Romantics, which became admissible to the canon in the wake of Burke's *Essay on the Sublime*.

[JH]

Corelli, Arcangelo (1653–1713) Italian composer and violinist. Trained as a violinist from an early age, he went to Bologna in 1666 to further his musical education and subsequently joined the famous orchestra of the Academia Filharmonica. From 1674 until his death he lived in Rome. Distinguished as a virtuoso violinist, an outstanding composer and an excellent conductor, he was sought after by prominent Roman patrons. His instrumental works (violin sonatas, trio sonatas and *concerti grossi*) served as a paradigm for numerous composers of the late Baroque. His well-known *Christmas Concerto* (opus 6, no. 8) is so named because its concluding *Pastorale* is associated traditionally with the Bethlehem scene (similar *pastorale* movements appear in J.S. Bach's *Christmas Oratorio* and Handel's *Messiah*).

[JE]

Corneille, Pierre (1606–84) French dramatist. Born in Rouen of a noble family, he studied with the Jesuits and then served the crown in a minor legal capacity. He began his dramatic career with a comedy *Mélite* in 1629. Its instant success led to patronage by RICHELIEU, who formed a small group of authors who were to write under his direction. His first tragedy *Médée* (1635) was also a success, and was followed swiftly by his masterpiece *Le Cid* (1636), based on Spanish plays about the national hero of that name.

Fame provoked envy and ill-will amongst other writers and even in Richelieu himself. This led to the noisy academic debate known as *La Querelle du Cid* to which Corneille riposted by writing several other dramas which laid the basis for French classical drama, like *Horace* and *Cinna* (1640). The later plays are less important, and the lack of positive response led him to quit the theatre; he was eclipsed in due course by the brilliance of RACINE. His last years were full of misfortune and his death passed almost unnoticed. His tragedies are noted for the high-mindedness and sense of duty of both his heroes and heroines, but on the whole his characterisations lack the subtlety and passion which imbue the protagonists of Racine.

[BT]

Cortés, Hernán (1484–1547) Spanish conqueror of Mexico. Of a lesser noble family, he sought adventure in the New World, where he arrived (Santo Domingo) in 1504. He went to Cuba, working for governor Velázquez, who in 1518 put him in charge of an expedition to the mainland. He landed in the Yucatán peninsula, near Tabasco, in February 1519. After several months of difficult progress through the interior, they reached Tenochtitlán in November, and were favourably received by Montezuma. He left the city to return to the coast to deal with a hostile Spanish force, and on his return found that the Spaniards he had left in the city were in a state of war with the Aztecs. The city of Tenochtitlán was invested and fell after a year-long siege, in August 1521, a victory that would not have been possible but for the help of the very numerous enemies of the Aztecs. Cortés took part in further expeditions towards the south, to Honduras (1524–6). After a short return visit to Spain, when he was rewarded with rank, titles and lands by CHARLES V, and married the daughter of the count of Aguilar. He went to Mexico for a further period (1530–6), returning to Spain finally in 1539. He

took part in an unsuccessful expedition led by the emperor against Algiers in 1541, but was otherwise neglected by the government, and retired to his estate near Seville, where he died, almost forgotten. His remains were shortly after transferred to Mexico, where they disappeared during the revolutionary epoch. His famous *Letters* to the emperor, about the conquest of Mexico, were published shortly after they were written, in the 1520s.

Costa, Uriel da (1585–1640) Born Gabriel Acosta in Oporto in a devout Catholic family of New Christian (i.e. of Jewish ascendancy) origin, he studied at Coimbra and returned, with all his family, to the Jewish faith, emigrating to Amsterdam in order to practise it freely, and changing his name. Like some other returnee converts, he found that his views did not coincide with traditional Judaism. He attacked the rigidity of Jews in Amsterdam, and questioned the immortality of the soul. In 1633 he arrived at a reconciliation with the Amsterdam rabbis, but then had doubts about the Mosaic Law, and ceased to practice Judaism. After a further reconciliation with the synagogue, when he was subjected to the humiliation of having the congregation walk over him, he shot himself. He has been seen as a symbol of a free-thinker faced by intolerance, and as a predecessor of SPINOZA; but his views shocked Christians equally. His key work, *Examination of the Pharisean Traditions*, written in 1624, was suppressed at the time but has recently been rediscovered.

Couperin, François (*'le grand'*) (1668–1733) French composer and keyboard player. He descended from a family of notable Parisian musicians, among whom Louis Couperin (1626–61), his uncle, is the best known. He was an organist at St Gervais in Paris (from *c*.1683), and a harpsichordist and composer at the French court (from 1693). His music for the harpsichord (*clavecin*) is the most important corpus of its kind in eighteenth-century France. It comprises dance suites (*ordres*), whose exquisite, filigree-like qualities are analogous to the contemporaneous French rococo art. His chamber collections (e.g. trio sonatas and suites for viols) often 'reunite' the opposing French and Italian *goûts*, as represented by Lully and Corelli, respectively. He was highly esteemed during his lifetime and came to be known posthumously as the symbol of French national 'genuineness'. Debussy dedicated his *Preludes* to him, and Ravel paid him tribute in *Le tombeau de Couperin*.

[JE]

Coverdale, Miles (1488–1568) English translator of the Bible. He studied at Cambridge, became a priest and entered the city's Augustinian house where he was influenced by Robert Barnes and also made contact with Thomas CROMWELL. He apparently went to the continent after 1528; in 1535 a translation of the Bible into English, attributed to him, was in circulation, printed at Antwerp. A second edition, with a prologue by him, came out in 1550. His Bible is memorable as the first complete translation into English, but it did not use the original texts and relied only on other available translations, such as those by William TYNDALE (for the New Testament) and LUTHER. He also co-operated in other schemes for translating the Bible. He left England in 1540 when Cromwell was executed, but returned in 1548, benefited from CRANMER's influence and was appointed chaplain to the king. In 1551 he was appointed bishop of Exeter. At the accession of MARY I he was deprived of his see, and went to live on the continent. When ELIZABETH I came to the throne in 1559 he returned to England, and was given a London parish, where he continued producing translations and writing hymns.

Cranach, Lucas the Elder (1472–1553) Saxon court painter and printmaker,

apothecary, city councilman (1519–44/5), and mayor of Wittenberg (1537–43). Son of the Franconian painter Hans Maler, he is first documented as working at the ducal fortress at Coburg (1500). By early 1502 he had settled in Vienna, where he painted portraits of Johannes Cuspinian and other members of the university faculty, and design woodcut illustrations for the publisher Johannes Winterburger. By 1505 he had replaced Jacopo dei Barbari as court painter to the Saxon elector (FREDERICK III THE WISE) in Wittenberg, receiving (by 6 January 1508) a personal coat-of-arms and the commission for an illustrated catalogue of Frederick's collection of holy relics. After Frederick's death Cranach also served his successors, John the Steadfast and JOHN FREDERICK. In 1508 Frederick sent Cranach on a secret diplomatic mission to the Netherlands. He married the daughter of a Gotha city councilman (Barbara Brengbier, 1512), and fathered two son, Hans and Lucas the Younger, who were painters. When he married he had the grand house constructed, in which the exiled king CHRISTIAN of Denmark was a guest (1523). His friend LUTHER was godfather to Cranach's daughter Anna (b. 1520). Luther wrote to him from Frankfurt immediately after the Diet at Worms (1521), hinting at his planned disappearance; and Cranach was one of the few whom Luther visited in his disguise as 'Junker Jörg' on his surprise trip to Wittenberg from custody in the Wartburg (1522). Cranach was one of the three witnesses at Luther's wedding; was godfather to the couple's first child, Hans (1526); and loaned his printing equipment for Luther's early publications (1523–5). His close friendship with Luther may account for Luther's relatively moderate attitude towards religious works of art. However, Cranach also fulfilled commissions for Luther's foremost opponent, cardinal ALBERT OF BRANDENBURG, and made devotional works for Frederick the Wise. After the defeat by Charles V at Mühlberg (1547),

Cranach was ordered to join John Frederick in Augsburg as prisoner of war, because the emperor had imported his court painter, TITIAN. When John Frederick was moved to Weimar (1552) Cranach accompanied him. He died in Weimar in 1553.

[JH]

Cranfield, Lionel (1575–1645) earl of Middlesex. An English man of state, his successful early career as a merchant adventurer brought him the patronage of the duke of Buckingham; in 1613 he was knighted and made surveyor-general of the customs, and in 1614 entered Parliament for Hythe. In 1619 he was made master of the court of wards and chief commissioner of the navy, and in 1620 entered the privy council. In 1622 he became treasurer and was created earl. By now he was one of the chief ministers of the crown, dedicated principally to reforming the finances, a task which proved impossible. Opposition on all sides was strong, and in 1624 he was impeached before the House of Lords, stripped of his offices, fined and sent to the Tower. Released two weeks later, he lived thereafter in retirement, but was restored to his seat in the Lords in 1640.

Cranmer, Thomas (1489–1556) archbishop of Canterbury, chief author of the Anglican liturgy. Born in Nottinghamshire of local gentry, he was educated at Cambridge, where he graduated in 1511 and obtained his doctorate in 1526. In 1529 he publicly expressed the view that the question of the king's possible divorce did not fall within the rules of canon law, and promptly received the king's favour. In 1532 he was ambassador to the emperor's court at Regensburg, where he probably made the first steps towards Lutheranism (and also married, in secret, the niece of the reformer Osiander). He was consecrated archbishop of Canterbury in 1553. Despite misgivings, he also annulled Hen-

ry's marriage to Anne BOLEYN and later that of Anne of Cleves. Cranmer supported the reform of the church and was complicit in the execution of a number of famous heretics, but he opposed the Six Articles which gave Henry control over church dogma. After Henry's death, he did all in his power to further the cause of Protestantism. He promoted the translation of the Bible into English and helped in the formulation of the 42 (later 39) Articles of Religion. He was chiefly responsible for the final version of the book of Common Prayer (1st version 1549, 2nd version 1552). As the young king EDWARD VI lay dying, Cranmer was persuaded to agree that Lady Jane GREY should succeed to the throne. After her brief twelve-day reign, MARY I became queen and Cranmer was arrested for treason and then charged with heresy. He did recant, seven times, but finally had the courage to retract his recantations. He was burned at the stake at Oxford in March 1556.

[GG & HK]

Croissy, Charles Colbert, marquis de (1629–96) Younger brother of the great COLBERT, he also entered the service of MAZARIN, became intendant of Alsace (1656), judge of the parlement of Metz and then president of the high court of Alsace (1657). He then moved to the diplomatic service as envoy to Vienna and Rome (1660), exercising various other offices in France in the following years. From 1662 he enjoyed the title of marquis. Negotiator at the peace of Aix-la-Chapelle (1668), he was appointed ambassador (1670–4) to the England of CHARLES II, whom he won over to an anti-Dutch alliance; he went on to negotiate the treaty of Nijmegen (1678) with the Dutch. Secretary for foreign affairs from 1679 till his death, he collaborated actively in the aggressive policies of his king, but also had to contend with the rivalry of LOUVOIS. He took care to secure for his son TORCY the right of succession to his ministerial post.

Cromwell, Henry (1628–74) Oliver's fourth son served during the Protectorate as commander of the English forces in Ireland (1654–9), where he was harsh to the Irish but tolerant towards the Protestant settlers.

Cromwell, Oliver (1599–1658) English statesman of Welsh origin (the family name had been Williams), he was born in Huntingdon of gentry stock, and matriculated at Cambridge but without taking a degree. He married a city merchant's daughter (1620) and entered Parliament for Huntingdon (1628). By 1640 he was MP for Cambridge, playing an active part in the political events leading to the civil war. During the early war years he developed methods and discipline that enabled him to form in 1645 the New Model Army, a national force which he commanded under General FAIRFAX, and which brought victory at Naseby (June 1645). A deeply religious Puritan, he was an 'Independent' who opposed the domination of the major Christian groupings. He took a prominent part in the trial and condemnation of CHARLES I, and spent a short (1649–50) period in Ireland, where he treated native resistance with notable brutality. In June 1650 Parliament appointed him commander of the army, with which he invaded Scotland and defeated the Scots at Dunbar (3 September 1650). The next year he defeated the royalists again at Worcester (3 September 1651). Differences with the republican Long Parliament obliged him to suspend its sittings (April 1653), and assume power into his own hands. As Lord Protector (1653–8) he gave England a period of prosperity rarely known in its history: peace was made with the Dutch, trade and the economy flourished, religious liberty was guaranteed. His short rule was decisive in forming the character of British history. But his success was fatally flawed by the inability to find a constitutional alternative to military rule. A conservative moderate, fired by a wish to serve God and the nation, and a firm supporter of freedom of conscience, in his private life he was amiable and liberal. He had all the elements of greatness but died hated by all factions.

Cromwell, Richard (1626–1712) Third son of Oliver Cromwell, he succeeded his father as Protector in September 1658 but was unable to control the discontent in the army; he resigned in April 1659, thus preparing the way for a restoration of the monarchy. He went to France in 1660, but returned to England in 1680 and lived in obscurity under the name of Clarke.

Cromwell, Thomas (*c*.1485–1540) earl of Essex. Born in Putney of humble origins, he served in the army then entered the service of cardinal WOLSEY in 1514 and with his help entered Parliament in 1523. In 1525 he was entrusted with the dissolution of the lesser monasteries of England. After Wolsey's fall, he entered the service of HENRY VIII. He became architect of the policies of the king, piloting through Parliament the royal divorce and the break with Rome (Act of Supremacy 1534). In 1530 he was drafted onto the royal council, became privy councillor 1531, principal secretary to king 1534 and lord privy seal 1536. Protestant by inclination, he completed the dissolution of the monasteries, and attempted to direct foreign policy towards an alliance with the Lutheran princes; but the resulting marriage with Anne of Cleves (1539), for which he was rewarded with the title of earl (May 1540) and created lord high chamberlain, was not to Henry's liking, and Cromwell fell into sudden disfavour. Accused of treason by the conservative members of Henry's council, he was arrested by attainder (June) and executed on Tower Hill.

Croy, Charles de, 4th duke of Aerschot (1560–1612) Son of Philip III de CROY, he was the last duke of Aerschot of the house of Croy. He converted to Calvinism in 1582 after marrying a lady of that religion, and was well received by the prince of Orange in Antwerp; but became disillusioned with the policies of Orange and returned in 1585 to his former religion and adherence. He inherited the title and estates on his father's death, and was one of the principal ministers of the archdukes ALBERT and ISABEL.

Croy, Guillaume de (1458–1521) lord of Chièvres. From a distinguished noble family in the Netherlands, he made his early career in warfare, and served in Italy under the flag of France. In 1491 he was made a knight of the Golden Fleece, and some years later became councillor to duke PHILIP THE FAIR of Burgundy. He rose to become president of the council of finance (1504), then commander-in-chief and lieutenant-general of the Netherlands (1505). Appointed in 1509 tutor to the young Charles of Ghent, he rose even further in wealth and status, was granted extensive honours in Spain where he accompanied Charles as the new king (1517), and in 1518 was created marquis of Aerschot. A proponent of friendship between Burgundy and France, he also formulated policy and backed Charles' election as emperor CHARLES V in 1519. Childless in his own marriage, he directed his patronage towards his brother's son Guillaume (1498–1521), for whom he acquired vast honours (including the archbishopric of Toledo) but who disappointed him by dying in a hunting accident. He died later that same year.

Croy, Philip III de, duke of Aerschot (1526–95) Philip succeeded his childless elder brother, the second duke, in 1551. He was granted the Golden Fleece in 1556, playing a central role in the events of the revolt of the Netherlands. Unlike EGMONT and HORNES, he did not join the opposition to GRANVELLE; thereafter, he remained a faithful ally of Spain, remaining in the administration during the rule of the duke of ALBA. In later events, however, he tended to play a moderating role as the leading Catholic grandee. When the Estates General split with the regime of Don JUAN OF AUSTRIA in 1577, they appointed him governor of Flanders, but the Calvinists in the Estates protested and ordered the duke arrested. The differences on this occasion accelerated the division of the Netherlands into two separate states. Released after two weeks, he left the Netherlands and made his submission to PHILIP II (1580).

Cumberland, William Augustus, duke of (1721–65) Third son of GEORGE II, he adopted a military career that turned out to be less brilliant than his father hoped. He served in the war of the Austrian Succession (1740–8), and became commander of the allied forces, but was defeated by France's marshal de SAXE at the battle of Fontenoy (1745). Later that year he was recalled to England to repel the invasion of Jacobites under the Young Pretender Charles Edward. His forces defeated Charles at Culloden Moor in April 1746, and he continued mopping-up operations for three more months, during which he earned the nicknames of 'butcher Cumberland' and 'stinking Billy'. Returning to the continent to fight the French, in 1747 he was defeated again by Saxe; in the subsequent Seven Years' War (1756–63) he was no more successful, and was dismissed from his command by his father.

Cyrano de Bergerac, Savinien de (1619–55) French writer. Born in Paris of a bourgeois family, he led an informal student existence in Beauvais and in Paris, often in the company of freethinkers. In about 1638 he joined a troop of Gascon militia, built up a reputation for aggression, became known as a successful dueller, and went off to fight in the wars, but was wounded (Arras, 1640) and had to give up the idea of a military career. He returned to Paris to the more tranquil pursuit of writing, but lived up to his aggressive reputation by his quarrels with other writers, notably MOLIÈRE and Scarron. In 1653 he became a gentleman of the household of the duke of Arpajon, and shortly before his death seems to have experienced a profound conversion to religion. Persistently scorned as a writer until the late nineteenth century, and often remembered only for his prominent nose, Cyrano was a free-thinker with a wide-ranging interest in literature, philo-sophy and science. His play *The Death of Agrippina* was published in 1654, shortly before his death. His masterwork, unpublished when he died, was his *Autre Monde* (Other Worlds), a satire of imaginary society on the moon, on the sun, and among the stars, in which he criticised contemporary thinkers, rejected all orthodoxies, and pronounced in favour of a universal chain of being uniting all beings and things.

D

Dampier, William (1652–1715) English navigator. A farmer's son, he went to sea from the age of sixteen, fought against the Dutch in the 1572 war, toured the seas and from 1675 worked his way round the Caribbean and served as a buccaneer against the Spaniards in central America (1679–81). In the years after 1683 he served first among the pirates, sailing around the coasts of Africa and south America; then from 1686 took part in a daring trip to the Pacific, the Philippines, China and India, returning to England in 1691. His account of his *Voyage round the World* (1697) became an immediate success, and he was accordingly chosen to lead an expedition to the Pacific (1699–1701) for the British government. Subsequent trips to the Pacific (1703–7, 1708–11) took on the character of voyages of piracy rather than of discovery. He published accounts of his voyages (1697–9) and some hydrographic treatises.

Danby, Thomas Osborne, 1st earl of, and 1st duke of Leeds (1632–1712) English statesman. From Yorkshire gentry stock, he entered the Commons in 1665, became secretary of the navy in 1668 and rose quickly to become head of the government as lord treasurer in 1673, in the ministry that held power from 1674 to 1679. Created earl in 1674, he used the patronage system to build up a group of parliamentary supporters (the 'court' party) devoted to the crown but also united in support of Anglican supremacy and hostility to Catholicism and France. The upheaval created on the political scene by the Popish Plot and the Exclusion Crisis (1678 onwards) swept him from the scene: he was impeached, resigned from his posts (1679) and was sent to the Tower by the House of Lords (1679–84). After his release, he became in 1688 one of the signatories inviting WILLIAM III of Orange to invade England. Made chief minister again in 1690–9 under the new regime, he was created duke in 1694, but was impeached the following year for accepting bribes from the East India Company, and in 1699 deprived of his offices. He helped to create the conservative grouping that later came to be known as the Tories.

Darnley, Henry Stuart, lord (1545–67) husband of MARY STUART. Son of the 4th earl of Lennox, Matthew Stuart, and of Margaret, granddaughter of HENRY VII, his claims to the thrones of both England and Scotland played a major role in his short career. He had met his cousin Mary in France shortly after the death of her first husband, the French king, and his mother (then living with him in England) persuaded him to go to Scotland after Mary's arrival there. The young queen became infatuated with him, created him earl of Ross and duke of Albany, and in 1565 married him according to Catholic rites. The marriage was resented by Scots nobility and Protestant divines alike, and Mary herself had to put up with his boorish behaviour and drunkenness. He was also exceptionally jealous, and accused Mary of a liaison with her secretary RIZZIO, in whose subsequent murder (1566) he was directly involved. Three months after the murder, in June 1566, a son, James (later JAMES VI of Scotland), was born to Mary and Darnley. But the queen had not forgiven him. During her absence from one of their residences, Kirk O'Field, the building was blown up, with Darnley apparently inside it: his strangled body was found nearby. Three months later Mary married the presumed murderer, BOTHWELL.

Dathenus, Pieter (1531–90) Protestant theologian. Born in Flanders, he entered the Carmelite order when young, but around 1550 turned Protestant, left his order and went to London, where he worked as a printer. The succession of MARY I in 1553 made him leave for Denmark, but his dissatisfaction with the Lutheran regime made him leave first for Friesland and then for Frankfurt-on-Main, where he acted as pastor to Flemish refugees. Religious disputes among the reformed confessions led to an order by the city for the closure of non-Lutheran temples, so he and his community moved to Frankenthal, where the elector Palatine conceded them (1562) a place of worship. Here he published a tract detailing the sufferings of the refugees and defending religious toleration. He also translated the psalms into Flemish (1566). In 1566 he visited France in the company of the count Palatine Jean Casimir, to visit the Huguenot communities. At the end of the year and early 1567 he also visited and preached in Ghent and other cities. By this time he was a thorough and fiery Calvinist, in favour with the Palatinate and appointed by WILLIAM I of Orange in 1572 to liaise with the Protestants in Holland. From 1578 he spent most of his time in Ghent. He had serious differences with William of Orange, whom he did not consider a genuine believer. He also considered that the Netherlands must expel both Spaniards and French, extirpate Catholicism and establish Calvinism. Protesting against the acceptance of the duke d'ANJOU as ruler, he left first for Gdańsk and then settled in Elbing, where he gave up theology and acted only as a doctor, and where he died.

Davenant, Charles (1656–1714) English theorist on trade policy. Eldest son of the poet and dramatist Sir William D'Avenant, he was educated at Oxford (without graduating), entered Parliament as a member for Cornwall (1685), and served in public office as a commissioner of excise and eventually as inspector general of trade (1704). He made himself known principally through his tracts on political economy, such as the *Discourses on the Publick Revenues and Trade of England* (1698) and *Essays upon the Balance of Power* (1701). Numerous other writings dealt with trade balances, financial policy, and trade to Africa; they were published as his collected works in 1771.

De Bay (Baius), Michel (1513–89) Netherlands Catholic theologian. Born of a farming family in Hainault, he studied philosophy at the university of Louvain (1532–5), then went on to study theology for five more years. He was appointed professor in 1544, obtaining his doctorate in 1550. In 1551 he was appointed professor of holy scripture. Concerned to refute Protestant theologians through their own use of scripture, he applied himself to study the teachings of St Augustine on the role between God's saving grace and man's free will. He aroused controversy among other professors and members of religious orders. In order to calm the dispute, the authorities encouraged restraint on both sides, but Bay's opponents were unrelenting. A total of 76 phrases from his writings was sent to Rome and condemned by the papacy in 1567. Since Bay was never mentioned by name in the condemnation, he continued to hold office at the university, and even in 1575 appointed chancellor. He eventually accepted the official view on the subject in a formal meeting of the university (1580), but his ideas – known as Bayanism – continued to be in fashion in the Netherlands, and are historically important because they inspired the views of the Jansenist movement later.

De Geer, Louis (1587–1632) international financier of Netherlands origin. Born in Liége of minor nobility, and Protestant by religion, he emigrated to Dordrecht in the northern Netherlands, and then to Amsterdam, where he settled. His father had left him a substantial income, which he invested in trade and industry. His first negotiations with Sweden appear to have been in 1617, when he lent the crown money; he went there in 1619, and arranged to back the production of iron and copper. GUSTAV II ADOLF VASA conceded him various privileges, including that of chief supplier to the Swedish army, and granted him Swedish nationality in 1627. In 1644 he rendered a further service by supplying and arming a fleet to fight the Danes. He had fourteen children, who continued the family business. De Geer was an outstanding example of the aggressive achievements of merchant capitalism.

De la Court, Pieter (1618–85) Son of a Leiden merchant, he studied law and theology at the university, then entered his father's business, which inspired him to write his first book (1659), on the economic welfare of Leiden. His most famous and influential work was *The Interest of Holland, or Grounds of Holland's Welfare* (1662), published under the pseudonymous initials V.D.H. (the Dutch form – van den Hove – of his surname). Part of the text was in fact written by John de WITT, the Dutch leader, and the work was published with his name as author in the versions issued thirty years later in English and in French. Both then and in 1669, when it was republished, it provoked controversy because of its attack on the Calvinist clergy, and was banned by the States of Holland. De la Court's main concern was for freedom of trade and enterprise ('where there is liberty, there will be riches'), freedom and toleration in religion, reduction of taxation, maintenance of peace and defence of the republican oligarchy against the monarchist pretensions of the house of Orange and its Calvinist supporters. It was one of the most advanced political programmes of its time in Europe.

De la Gardie, Jacob, count (1583–1652) Swedish statesman. From a family of French origin, he was born in Reval (now Tallinn), trained as a soldier in Holland under Maurice of Nassau (1606–8), and as a magnate of Swedish Estonia was entrusted by CHARLES IX with the campaign against Russia (1608–13), during which the Swedes captured Moscow briefly but were later defeated at Klushino (1610). However, at the peace of Stolbova, he managed to secure from the Russians a territory that gave Sweden control of the Baltic coast and prevented Russian access to the sea. Appointed to the Swedish council of state 1613, governor of Livonia 1622–8, he was one of the regents (1633–44) ruling the state during the minority of queen CHRISTINA VASA, and had policy differences with OXENSTIERNA, who was directing the Swedish effort in Germany.

De la Gardie, Magnus Gabriel, count (1622–86) Son of Jacob DE LA GARDIE, and also born in Reval, he was educated at Uppsala and afterwards did the grand tour through the Netherlands and France. He was briefly ambassador to France (1646), and headed the Swedish delegation to the peace of Oliva (1660). He was the head of Sweden's administration from 1660 to 1680, becoming minister for war in 1672. The defeat by Brandenburg at the battle of Fehrbellin (1675), however, tainted his ministry and he was replaced and disgraced.

De Ruyter, Michiel Adriaanszoon (1607–76) Dutch admiral. He took to a seafaring career when very young, rose to be captain in 1635, and served in the first Anglo–Dutch war (1652–4). Employed to defend Denmark against the Swedes, in 1659 he won a notable victory over the Swedish fleet. The authorities sent him in 1664 on an expedition to the Guinea coast of South America to clear the seas of intruders. In the second Anglo–Dutch war (1665–7) he won the victory at Dunkirk (1666) over the forces under MONCK, then in the summer of 1667 carried out a raid on the Medway, when much of the English fleet was destroyed, making the treaty of Breda inevitable. In the Franco–Dutch war of 1672–8 his forces were sent to the Mediterranean as allies of the Spanish. With only twenty vessels under him, he was ill-equipped to deal with the larger French fleet of Duquesne. In January 1676 his detachment was forced to retreat; in April, in an action off Syracuse, he was killed and his ships were forced to retreat again.

Dee, John (1527–1608) English magus. Born in London, he was educated at Cambridge, where he was elected one of the original fellows (1546) of Trinity College, but his special knowledge of mathematics and astrology inclined him to an interest in exotic rather than traditional learning. In visits to the Netherlands and France (1548–50) he made contact with scientists from all over Europe; on returning to England, he became a parish rector (1553). Patronised by MARY I and PHILIP II when they were rulers, he was specially favoured by queen ELIZABETH I, who was anxious to learn about a 'great secret' that he promised to reveal to her. From 1562 he travelled extensively round the continent, and accumulated in his house in Mortlake, Surrey a large library of books on the sciences. Consulted by Elizabeth on everything from comets to geography, he recommended acceptance of the Gregorian calendar reform of 1582, but his views were rejected by the clergy. In 1582 he became influenced by the charlatan Edward Kelly, and devoted most of his time to occult practices, which the two publicised in their lengthy travels through Poland, Bohemia and Russia (1583–9). With a long white beard and dressed in the flowing robes of a magus, he apparently terrified the children when he went out of doors and, despite the queen's protection, was socially ostracised. He died poor.

Defoe, Daniel (1660–1731) English journalist, pamphleteer and novelist. The son of a London butcher, he was educated in a nonconformist school. He travelled widely in Europe before setting up in the hosiery business. A man of terrific energy and enormous versatility, he combined careers as merchant, government spy, pamphleteer and journalist. Despite his humble background, he read seven languages and displayed remarkable learning. Defoe took part in the MONMOUTH rebellion, though later he became a supporter of WILLIAM III of Orange. His satire *The Shortest Way with the Dissenters* offended the Tories and he was fined, pilloried and imprisoned (1703). On his release from Newgate gaol in 1704, he started *The Review*, a pioneer of English journalism that supported the Whig war policy and was patronised by the government; in subsequent years it covered not only commercial interests, but discussed political and domestic matters as well. He was also working as a government agent, transferring his allegiance to whichever party was in power and at the same time producing pamphlets, satires, a conduct book, histories and his first attempt at a novel. In 1716, with a new monthly paper called *Mercurius Politicus*, he began to defend the Tory government of the day.

He was nearly sixty before he began to write the works for which he is justly renowned. *Robinson Crusoe* was published 1719–20, *The Journal of the Plague Year* and *Moll Flanders* in 1722. His delightful guide book *A Tour through the whole Island of Great Britain* appeared in three volumes between 1724 and 1726. A prolific writer, by the time he died he had more than 500 published works. After 1726 he withdrew from journalism, and lived comfortably in his house in Stoke Newington. He is regarded as the founder of English journalism and the father of the English novel.

[GG & HK]

Del Cano (or, de Elcano), Sebastian (*c*.1470–1526) Spanish navigator, first sea captain to circumnavigate the globe. Born in Guipúzcoa, he was resident in Seville from the early years of the sixteenth century, and was chosen as one of the ship's officers who set out with MAGELLAN's expedition from Spain in 1519. After Magellan's death he took over command of the expedition, returning via Amboina, Timor and the Cape of Good Hope to Seville in 1522. Only eighteen men, in their vessel the *Victoria*, remained of the 237 who had set out in 1519. He was authorised by CHARLES V to accompany another expedition to the east. The seven vessels left La Coruña in July 1525, and sailed round Cape Horn into the Pacific, but Del Cano fell ill and died at sea. Neither he nor his family earned wealth or fame; only in the nineteenth century did his home town of Guetaria celebrate his exploits.

Del Río, Martín (1551–1608) Netherlands theologian. Born in Antwerp of Spanish origin, he very early showed his aptitude for learning and languages, mastering (it is said) the major classic ones as well as five contemporary ones. After his education in Antwerp he went to Paris, and continued to devour learning; he then went to Salamanca and obtained his doctorate there (1574). On his return he was appointed to legal posts in the government of Brabant, and was in Louvain just in time to save the library of Justus LIPSIUS from the advancing Spanish troops. Disappointed by the chaos in the Netherlands, he left all his posts, went to Spain, and at Valladolid entered the Jesuit order (1580). He was sent to teach at Liége, and after three years went to Louvain to teach. In this period he assembled the material of his work, *Disquisitiones magicae* (Essays on Magic), which he published long after (Mainz, 1593) and for which he is chiefly known. His movements thereafter are peregrinal: he was teaching at Graz in 1600, but shortly after was in Salamanca, returning in 1608 to Brussels, where he died shortly after his arrival. The *Disquisitiones* offered an authoritative summary of contemporary views about magic and witchcraft, and was meant in part to guide judicial tribunals. It achieved great success, and was reprinted twenty times. By asserting that witchcraft was real, it may have helped to stimulate the prosecution of so-called witches.

Descartes (Cartesius), René (1596–1650) French philosopher, mathematician and scientist. A native of Brittany, he was educated at the Jesuit college of La Flèche (1604–12), where he studied mathematics and astronomy, and then studied in Paris. In 1617 he enlisted in the Dutch army and later (1619) in that of Bavaria. He devoted his leisure time to examining problems in mathematics, mechanics and acoustics, and in 1619 (while in Bavaria) committed himself to establishing a new philosophical method for the pursuit of true knowledge. He left the army in 1621, and moved to Paris in 1625. During these unsettled years he met MERSENNE and joined in scientific discussions, but only began to bring his ideas to fruition in print after settling in the Netherlands in 1628. He abandoned a planned treatise on *Le monde* (*Traité de l'homme* plus *Traité* *de lumière*) after Galileo was condemned, but developed themes from it elsewhere. His *Discours de la méthode* (Discourse on Method) (1637), the first major philosophical work to be written in French, explained his use of doubt as a tool in the search for self-evident principles with standards of certainty comparable to those of mathematics. The source from which they could be derived was located in human reason itself (expressed in the phrase *cogito ergo sum* – I think therefore I am – and requiring the strict separation of mind and body); all other knowledge was to be arrived at through deduction from this, in contrast to BACON's data-gathering 'inductive method'. He did not, however, exclude experiment and hypothesis from playing a useful role, and personally undertook many experimental investigations. The *Discours* was accompanied by examples of practical results of his philosophical technique: *Météores*, on celestial and climatic phenomena; *La Dioptrique*, containing his theory of light as an instantaneously transmitted impulse, laws of reflection and refraction, and an analysis of vision; and *La Géométrie*, in which he introduced his algebraicised 'analytic geometry', an extremely important innovation. Thereafter he devoted his attention to philosophy, publishing the metaphysical *Meditationes de prima philosophia* (1641) and *Principia philosophiae* (Principles of Philosophy) (1644), which attempted to account for the whole of the natural world through a single system of mechanical principles. In *Les Passions de l'âme* (Principles of the Soul) (1649) he discussed human psychology in terms of direct reactions to external stimuli; his exploration of the physiological mechanisms of sensation and movement had a significant impact upon medicine and physiology. He then moved to Stockholm (1649), at the request of queen CHRISTINA VASA, but died soon afterwards. Despite criticism of their supposed atheistical tendencies, his writings were extremely influential.

[FW]

Desmarets, Nicolas, sieur de Maillebois (1648–1721) French minister of state. A nephew of COLBERT, he was educated by the Jesuits and at the age of fourteen began to work in his uncle's department. By 1672 he was a councillor of the parlement of Paris, then a member of the council of state (1673) and master of requests (1674). He became intendant of finance in 1678, but in 1683 was accused of malversation and obliged to retire from office. Recalled to the administration in 1690, he resumed his role in finances and then succeeded CHAMILLART as controller general (1708–15). He became responsible for the reforms needed to back up the wars of LOUIS XIV, carried out administrative restructuring and in 1710 suggested the idea of a tithe (*dixième*) on personal revenue. He retired from office during the regency government.

Diane de Poitiers (1499–1566) French noble lady and art patron. Of noble origin, in 1514 she married Louis de Brézé, count de Maulévrier and high seneschal of Normandy, twenty years her senior. Widowed in 1531, in about 1537 she became mistress of the duke d'Orléans, the future HENRY II, nineteen years younger than she and already married to CATHERINE DE MÉDICIS. Henry loved her passionately: when he was crowned, he bore the letters H and D on his robe. She exercised powerful influence at court, eclipsing the role of the queen. She was created duchess of Valentinois, became rich, and used her position to patronise culture but also to advance the interests of Catholicism and of the GUISE family. After Henry's unexpected death in 1559 she retired to the beautiful chateau that he had built for her at Anet. Her *Lettres* were published in 1866.

Dias, Bartolomeu (*c.*1450–1500) Portuguese navigator. Dias made an historic voyage from Lisbon in August 1487, to explore the African coastline previously explored by other sailors. A storm forced his ship round the cape of Good Hope (early 1488), which he did not at this time see. He sailed some way up the east coast of Africa; on his return voyage, he gave the cape its name 'for the hope it gave of the discovery of India', returning to Lisbon in December 1488. In 1497 he took part in the famous expedition commanded by da GAMA, which arrived in India the following year but which he accompanied only as far as Mina, on the west coast of Africa. In 1500 he joined the expedition commanded by Cabral which touched for the first time on the coast of Brazil, but on the journey from Brazil to India he disappeared during a storm near the cape of Good Hope.

Dmitri The false name given to at least three impostors who claimed to be prince Dmitri (1583–91), youngest son of IVAN IV of Russia and last representative of the Rurik dynasty. Dmitri was supposed to have succeeded his brother Fyodor as tsar, but died in mysterious circumstances (allegedly murdered by Boris GODUNOV). The subsequent period of dynastic instability, called the Time of Troubles (1598–1613), encouraged several interests to put forward pretenders to the throne. The first false Dmitri was Grisha Otrepiev (1580–1606), an unfrocked monk and puppet of the Polish intervention in Russia headed by SIGISMUND III VASA of Poland. He declared himself a Catholic in 1604, and invaded Muscovy with the help of Polish troops, defeated the forces of Boris Godunov, and had himself crowned tsar in Moscow in 1605. He was dethroned and murdered after a boyar revolt led by prince Vasilii SHUISKY, who became tsar. The second false Dmitri, commonly known as 'the bandit of Tushino', made his appearance in July 1607, and headed an intervention force that included Poles

and Cossacks, but got no further than Tushino, near Moscow (1608). A stalemate ensued between his troops and those of Shuisky until 1610, when the impostor was murdered by one of his followers. The third Dmitri surfaced in 1611 but was murdered in 1612.

Dolet, Etienne (1509–46) French printer. He was born in Orléans, but little is known of his origins; he studied in Paris then at Padua (1527–30), and spent a year in Venice as Latin secretary to the French ambassador. Around 1530 he settled in Toulouse but was expelled from the city four years later. During this period he became known for his radical attitude and unorthodoxy, and wrote several polemical works. He went on to become a printer in Lyon (1534), where he began to publish his writings, but in 1536 killed a man, fled to Paris where he received a royal pardon, and after a short spell in gaol was released in 1537. In 1538 he received a ten-year royal privilege to publish books, and with the proceeds married. From 1542 he began publishing books of doubtful orthodoxy, including unauthorised and heretical works. Imprisoned in 1542–3 for possessing the works of Calvin, he was released thanks to the intervention of highly placed persons including the queen of Navarre. In 1544 he was arrested again in Lyon for possessing heretical books, but fled to Piedmont; he returned, resumed publishing and was arrested at Troyes (1544). He was refused appeal and taken to Paris, where the parlement (1546) declared him guilty of aiding heretics and keeping heretical writings; he was tortured, hanged and then burnt in the Place Maubert.

Donatello (Donato di Niccolo di Betto Bardi) (?1386–1466) Florentine sculptor. The greatest and most versatile sculptor of the early Renaissance, he was the son of a wool-carder who had been briefly exiled from Florence for manslaughter. He made something of a fetish out of his working-class origins, could be difficult and deliberately rude, and may have been illiterate, but achieved unprecedented effects, both dramatic and technical, in all sculptural media. A member of the Arte di Pietra e Legname (workers in stone and wood), he nevertheless cast both the first free-standing, life-size nude bronze since late antiquity (*David*, Florence, Bargello), as well as the first Italian equestrian monument to be made in bronze since Roman times (*Gattamelatta*, 1449–53, Padua). Apprenticed to Lorenzo Ghiberti (1404–7), he was soon creating full-standing marble figures for both Florence cathedral and the guild church of Orsanmichele. The subtlety of his relief carvings, which manage to convey effects of aerial perspective, required the invention of a new Italian term, *relievo schiacciato* (flattened relief). He was the first since Roman times to capture accurately the proportions of young children, which differ drastically from those of the normal adult. Placed on retainer by Cosimo de' MEDICI, he lived rent-free in an old inn slated to be torn down; consequently there are no documents relating to his individual works for the Medici family, such as the bronze *David* or the late *Judith and Holofernes* group.

[JH]

Donne, John (1572–1631) English metaphysical poet. He was born into a staunchly Catholic family and educated at Oxford, Cambridge and the Inns of Court. He took part in Essex's expeditions to Cadiz (1596) and to the Azores (1597) and travelled extensively in Europe. He became secretary to Sir Thomas Egerton, Keeper of the Great Seal, and entered Parliament in 1601. However his secret marriage to the Keeper's niece, Anne More, led to his dismissal and a brief imprisonment. There followed a period of hardship and soul-searching. In 1615 he took Anglican orders and from 1621 until his death he was Dean of St Paul's. His best known works fall into two cate-

gories: the early ironic and erotic verse and the later religious poems. *Songs and Sonnets* and *Elegies*, written in early manhood, display remarkable realism and passion and are full of powerful and striking imagery. They mark a complete break with the convention of courtly love in Elizabethan verse. *La Coronna* and *The Holy Sonnets* belong to the latter period, but are full of the same intensity in their expression of the desire for union with God and their preoccupation with sin and death. He was the most influential preacher of his day and his sermons reveal the reasoning mind beneath a load of metaphysical conceit. Although widely distributed in manuscript, most of his work was not published until after his death. He fell out of favour in the eighteenth century. But interest revived in the late nineteenth and he is now recognised as one of England's finest poets.

[GG]

Doria The Doria were, since the thirteenth century, the leading aristocratic family of Genoa, devoting themselves to maritime enterprise.

Andrea Doria (1466–1560) Genoese admiral. The most distinguished admiral of his lineage and of his time. His early career as a soldier was spent away from Genoa, in the service of the papacy and Naples; in the latter realm he fought against the invading French troops and subsequently against the Spanish troops under Gonzalo FERNÁNDEZ DE CÓRDOBA. After these years he made his career as a naval captain, scoring victories against the Barbary corsairs of north Africa. When war broke out again in the Mediterranean between France and the emperor CHARLES V, he took service with the French, but in 1528 made the historic decision to put his privately financed fleet at the disposal of Charles V in exchange for political concessions in Genoa, where he strengthened his power and built the lavish palace of Fassolo. The alliance established Habsburg naval power in the Mediterranean, and the preponderance of the Doria in Genoa. He participated in all the important naval campaigns of the emperor, lived long but remained childless. His successor as admiral of the Genoese fleet was his great-nephew, Gian Andrea Doria.

Gian Andrea Doria (1540–1606) His mother was daughter of the great financier Adam Centurione. His successful term of service coincided with the reign of PHILIP II of Spain. Gian Andrea's debut as commander was a disaster: he led the naval forces on the Spanish expedition to the island of Djerba in 1560, when the Turks sank or seized half the vessels, and captured most of the army. In subsequent years, however, his forces took part with success in every significant expedition in the Mediterranean, and were largely responsible for the brilliant victory over the Turkish fleet at Lepanto (1571).

Dowland, John (1563–1626) English composer and lutenist. He was employed by distinguished patrons in England and the continent, and at the Elizabethan court from 1612 until his death. His works comprise secular airs with lute accompaniment (or alternately for four voices), psalms and religious songs, and compositions for solo lute and for instrumental consorts (e.g. the famous *Lachrimae or Seven Teares*, 1604). His airs circulated widely during his lifetime and are still regarded as the most attractive repertoire of this kind from the Elizabethan period. Their texts are often saturated with profound sentiments of despair, whose musical depiction reaches melodic and harmonic audaciousness unequalled by his English contemporaries (e.g. 'In darkness let me dwell').

[JE]

Drake, Sir Francis (1540–96) English naval captain. Born in Chatham, Kent, from the age of twenty five, when he captained his first ship, he dedicated himself to war at sea against the Spaniards. In 1568 he suffered with John Hawkins the reverse at San Juan de Ulúa in Mexico, and in 1572 made a notable capture of silver at Nombre de Dios, Panamá. In 1577 he sailed from Plymouth with a small escort (his own ship, the *Pelican* was shortly renamed *The Golden Hind*) that rounded Cape Horn, crossed the Pacific, and rounded the cape of Good Hope, arriving in England in September 1580. He was the first English captain to circumnavigate the globe, and was knighted by the queen on board *The Golden Hind* (April 1581). In 1584 he entered Parliament. From this time his naval expeditions were backed fully by the queen's ships and money, and he became the symbol of English heroism at sea. In 1585 he led a fleet of royal ships to the West Indies and carried out devastating attacks against Santo Domingo and Cartagena, returning home in July 1586. In April 1587 he led a squadron that descended on Cadiz, and burnt a good part of the Spanish fleet there. In 1588 he joined the English naval élite in the successful routing of the Spanish Armada. His final voyage to the West Indies was in August 1595, when he was taken ill with dysentery from which he died; he was buried at sea off the isthmus of Panama. Feared by the Spanish in both America and Spain, he was known as 'the Dragon' ('el Draco'), and the Spanish government even considered the possibility of having him assassinated.

Dryden, John (1631–1700) English dramatist, poet and critic. Born into a family with strong Parliamentarian and Anglican convictions, he was to change his own political and religious allegiances a number of times; his critics accused him of expediency. Much of his poetry was written to celebrate public occasions. In 1658 he wrote *The Heroic Stanzas* on the death of Cromwell and two years later he published *Astrea Redux* celebrating the restoration of Charles II. *Annus Mirabilis* (1667) deals with the Dutch naval wars and the fire of London. He was appointed Poet Laureate in 1668. Many of his early plays were written in rhyming couplets but he abandoned rhyme for blank verse in *All for Love*, an adaptation of 'Antony and Cleopatra'. It is his finest drama. In 1682 he published *Religio Laici*, his defence of the Church of England. His satirical poem *Absalom and Achitophel* which targeted lord SHAFTESBURY and the duke of MONMOUTH was immensely popular and helped turn the tide of feeling in favour of JAMES II. *The Hind and the Panther*, a much finer poem, was written after his conversion to Catholicism in 1687 and is an apology for his new faith. He stood firm in his final years by refusing to take the oath of allegiance to William and Mary and so lost his Laureateship. From then on he concentrated on translating the Greek and Roman classics including the whole of Virgil. He marks the beginning of the neoclassical, or Augustan, movement in English literature. His critical writings, which include the Prefaces to his plays, and his *Essay on Dramatic Poesy*, were extremely influential and are of lasting value.

[GG]

Du Bellay, Joachim (1522–60) French poet and leader with Pierre de RONSARD of the literary group, the Pléiade. A nobleman of Anjou, he was cousin to Cardinal Jean du Bellay, bishop of Paris, a literary patron and diplomat for FRANCIS I. Ronsard was his closest friend and associate among the informal group of seven French writers who took their name Pléiade from the seven tragic poets of Alexandria. He wrote the proto-academy's manifesto in 1549, 'The Defense and Illustration of the French Language', as a call to a national literary tradition against the cultural dominance of Italy. In 1549/50 he published his first collection of love sonnets, 'The Olive', in Petrarchan style. After serving on a diplomatic mission to Rome with his cousin Jean, he returned to Paris in 1558 to publish two collections of poems, *The Antiquities of Rome* and *Yearnings*, which expressed his nostalgia for home and his

disillusionment with Rome in a more personal style freed from Petrarchan influence. His life-long ill health and intermittent deafness led to his death soon thereafter at the age of thirty seven.

[JM]

Du Plessis-Mornay, Philippe (1549–1623) French soldier and scholar. Brought up as a Calvinist by his widowed mother, he studied in Paris and then, after a brief military period, travelled abroad and made contact with WILLIAM I of Orange. In France again, he escaped the night of the massacre of St Bartholomew (1572), fled to England and on his return (1573) took an active part in the civil wars. He is usually taken to be the author (under the pseudonym Junius Brutus) of the influential tract *Vindiciae contra tyrannos* (Defence Against Tyrants) (1579), which argued that government was based on a political contract between the people and the ruler, thereby limiting the authority of kings and justifying resistance to tyranny. From 1582 he was regularly in the service of Henry of Navarre, for whom he wrote several tracts against the Catholic party. In 1589, after helping to arrange an agreement on the succession to the crown from HENRY III to Navarre (HENRY IV), he accepted from the latter the governorship of Saumur, which he thereafter made the base for his activities as (a phrase applied to him at the time) 'pope of the Huguenots'. He took a leading part in the national assemblies of the Calvinists, and attempted (without much success) to bring about intercommunion between Lutherans and Calvinists. A man of great culture and author of learned treatises, he founded at Saumur a distinguished college which flourished until the revocation of the Edict of Nantes (1685).

Dudley, John, earl of Warwick and duke of Northumberland (1502–53) Son of Edmund Dudley, the minister of HENRY VII executed for treason in 1510, he managed to win favour with HENRY VIII, and rose to become lord high admiral (1543), taking a notable part in the naval war against France. A Protestant, at the king's death he succeeded in displacing the conservative Norfolk grouping in the royal council. In the reign of EDWARD VI he was created earl of Warwick (1547) and high chamberlain; that year he accompanied the army which invaded Scotland and won the battle of Pinkie (September). In 1549 he helped to put down KET's rising in Norfolk; in October he and his supporters in council engineered the fall of the duke of SOMERSET. He was now in command of the government, and in October 1550 became duke of Northumberland (a title that he held exceptionally, since it was normally held by the Percy family). The Reformation made great advances under him, in terms both of the seizure of Church property and the reforms in worship carried through by CRANMER. In the hope of bringing the crown into his own family, he persuaded Edward VI to exclude his sisters from the succession and name as heir Lady Jane GREY, who was opportunely married to his fourth son Guildford Dudley. He failed to rally support for Lady Jane on Edward's death, and in July 1553 was sent to the Tower by MARY I's government, then tried and executed.

Dufay, Guillaume (*c*.1400–74) Burgundian composer. He was the leading composer of the early Renaissance. Much of his career was spent between the Netherlands and various centres in Italy and France. In the last fifteen years he held prestigious administrative responsibilities at the cathedral of Cambrai (his home town). His compositional output comprises polyphonic settings of the Mass and Offices, motets and *chansons*. Among the best known are the mass *L'homme armé* and the mass *Se la face ay pale* (the former based on a popular song and the latter, on his own *chanson*), which served as a model for succeeding composers. His motet *Nuper rosarum flores* was composed

for the dedication of the cathedral of Florence (1436) and performed with great pomp. His numerous *chansons* are emblematic of the refined, chivalric-like character of the Burgundian court.

[JE]

Dumoulin, Charles (1500–66) French jurist. Son of a member of the parlement of Paris, he studied law in various French universities then followed his father in the legal profession in Paris, where he soon began to publish commentaries on aspects of the customary law of northern France, and became convinced of the need to unify the different legal uses of the country into one. The theme dominated his writings, notably his greatest and last work, *Le grand coutumier* (2 vols, 1567). In 1542 he became a Calvinist, but the decision did not interrupt his literary production. In 1551 one of his works provoked a lawsuit against him by the university of Paris, and for prudence he went abroad (1551–7), where he taught at the universities of Tübingen and later Besançon. Granted a royal pardon in 1557, he returned to produce further legal studies, notably his work on the French monarchy, published first in French and then in Latin as *De monarchia Francorum* (1564). Though these works were accepted without problems, he produced further tracts which, in the midst of the civil wars and in view of his conversion at this time to Lutheranism, provoked religious controversy among both Catholics and Calvinists and led to him being imprisoned (1564). One of his works was publicly burnt in Geneva. Despite his turbulent life, he died quietly in Paris.

Dürer, Albrecht (1471–1528) German painter, printmaker, mathematician and theorist. Widely travelled, he introduced Renaissance style north of the Alps. Born in Nuremberg the son of a Hungarian goldsmith, his godfather was the publisher Anton Koberger. He revolutionised the graphic arts by combining Italian one-point perspective, classical proportion theory, and the close study of nature with an unprecedented refinement of draftsmanship. The humanist Willibald Pirckheimer was his lifelong friend and mentor in classical literature, and his most important patrons included the Saxon elector (FREDERICK III THE WISE), cardinal ALBERT OF BRANDENBURG, Conrad Celtis, ERASMUS and MELANCHTHON. For the popular market he illustrated and published a luxury *Apocalypse* in both Latin and German editions (1498), as well as a *Life of the Virgin* and three sets of illustrations for the Passion of Christ. His prints were marketed internationally by two sales agents, whose contracts have survived. In 1509 he bought the house previously owned by the mathematician/astronomer Bernhard Walther, which still contained both its observatory and scientific library. Beginning in 1512 he became art director for several projects for the emperor MAXIMILIAN I. In 1517 he joined the study group led by LUTHER's confessor Johann von Staupitz, and sent LUTHER a

present of some art works – presumably prints – through Georg Spalatin, asking to receive copies of any new pamphlets written by the Reformer. Lazarus Spengler was his neighbour and confidante. In 1520, soon after Pirckheimer and Spengler had been named in the papal bull threatening Luther with excommunication, Dürer set off on a year-long trip to the Netherlands, attending the coronation of CHARLES V in Aachen. He kept a travel diary describing his experiences, including meetings with MARGARET OF AUSTRIA, ERASMUS and Christian II of Denmark, and in which he recorded a lament for Luther on hearing the false news of the reformer's arrest. Dismayed by the violence of the Peasants' War (1525) he painted the *Four Holy Men* (1526, Munich) for the Nuremberg city hall, inscribing it with biblical quotations regarding the danger of belief in false prophets. He died, aged fifty seven, in 1528, having spent his last years in preparing his theoretical manuscripts for publication.

[JH]

E

Eboli, Ana de Mendoza y Guzmán, princess of (1540–92) Spanish court lady. Daughter of a powerful grandee of the Mendoza family, she was married at the early age of thirteen to Ruy Gómez de Silva, prince of EBOLI, confidant of prince Philip (later PHILIP II) of Spain. Because of Ruy Gómez's long absence abroad at Philip's side, the marriage was not consummated until his return to Spain in 1557. Thereafter she bore her husband ten children. She became apparently (according to some of her portraits) blind in one eye, which she covered with a patch; but this is not supported by any documents, which speak only of her beauty. Ana de Mendoza was an ambitious woman. After her husband's death, she continued active at court, and developed a close friendship, based on political interest rather than on amorous motives, with one of the king's private secretaries, Antonio PÉREZ. Deeply religious, she also founded a convent in her town of Pastrana. Accused of complicity with Pérez in the murder of another secretary, Escobedo (1578), she and Pérez were arrested the year after. Confined first in a castle at Santorcaz, she was moved later to the family palace at Pastrana, and confined to a suite of rooms, where she died of an illness. Like Pérez, she plays a key role in Verdi's opera *Don Carlo*; but most of the literature written about her is, like the opera, fantasy.

Eboli, Ruy Gómez de Silva, prince of (1516–73) Son of Portuguese nobility, he went to Spain at the age of nine in the court of the empress Isabel, wife of CHARLES V, and was brought up in the household of prince Philip, eleven years his junior. Thereafter he became a close confidant of the prince, accompanied him to England in 1554, and on Philip's return to Spain in 1559 became effective chief minister, exercising key posts in the royal household and the treasury. Philip created him prince of Eboli (an estate in Italy), then duke of Pastrana when Eboli gave up his Italian holdings and acquired estates in Pastrana. Influential with Philip because of friendship and also because he always deferred to the king, Eboli built up a powerful network of patronage that came into conflict with the interests of the duke of ALBA. The rivalry between Alba and Eboli was however based not on differences of ideology, but on simple political interest. He was married in 1552 to Ana de Mendoza, the famous princess of Eboli. His children became rich and powerful grandees of Spain.

Eck, Johann Maier of (1486–1543) Son of a farmer from the Swabian village of Egg, he was educated at Heidelberg and Tübingen. From 1502 he was studying at Freiburg, took orders in 1508, and received his doctorate in theology (1510). From 1510 he was appointed professor of theology at Ingolstadt where, with brief absences, he remained the rest of his life. In 1518 he attacked LUTHER's 95 theses, and propelled himself into the centre of the Reformation debate. In 1519 he and Luther faced each other at a famous, though inconclusive, public debate in Leipzig. Eck, in his turn, was entrusted with the publication of the papal bull *Exsurge Domine* (1520) against Luther, and soon became identified as the chief spokesman for the Catholic cause, which he defended publicly in a debate with ZWINGLI (1526), and at the Diet of Augsburg (1530) and at successive colloquies with Protestant leaders. He was a noted preacher and a prolific writer; his *Enchiridion adversus Lutheranos* (1525), written against MELANCHTHON, was reprinted ninety times and became a basic pamphlet of the Catholic party. He published in 1537 a German translation of the Bible for Catholics.

Edward IV (1422–83) king of England 1461–83. Son of Richard, duke of York and leader of the Yorkist party (the white rose) in the Wars of the Roses, he led the opposition to king Henry VI. In 1461 he proclaimed himself king, subsequently defeating the Lancastrian forces in victories at Towton (1461) and Hexham (1464). However his main supporter the earl of Warwick changed sides and in 1470 brought Henry VI back to power, forcing Edward to flee into exile in the Netherlands. The following year he returned with a powerful force, defeated Warwick (who perished in the battle) at Barnet (April 1471) and then defeated the Lancastrian army at Tewkesbury (May). Henry VI was imprisoned in the Tower of London and subsequently murdered there. For the rest of the reign there was no serious threat to Edward's throne, though in 1478 he personally prosecuted the case against his brother the earl of Clarence, who was confined in the Tower and subsequently found drowned in a butt of malmsey wine.

Edward V (1470–83) king of England 1483. Succeeding his father Edward IV at the age of thirteen, his short reign marked the struggle for power between his mother's family, the Woodvilles, and his uncle Richard duke of Gloucester. A month after his succession, his uncle confined him in the Tower for his protection; four weeks later, the council prevailed on the queen mother to leave her second son, Richard the duke of York, to keep company with Edward in the Tower. Various dignitaries then declared in favour of Richard, who was crowned king as RICHARD III. According to the sources consulted by Thomas MORE, the princes were at some time thereafter smothered to death in the Tower and their bodies secretly disposed of.

Edward VI (1537–53) king of England 1547–53. Son of HENRY VIII and Jane Seymour, he was given a good humanist education, and inexplicably brought up as a Protestant at a time when his father and the court were still Catholic. He succeeded to the throne under the control of a regency council dominated by the Seymour family, headed by his uncle SOMERSET as lord protector. The reign was significant for a substantial advance of the Reformation, helped by suspension of the heresy laws. In 1549 Somerset was overthrown by John DUDLEY, duke of Northumberland, who persuaded the king to name as his heir Lady Jane GREY. A solitary person who committed his thoughts to a journal, he suffered poor health, became seriously ill in January 1553 and died in July.

Egmont, Lamoral, 4th count of (1522–68) Netherlands grandee and symbol of resistance to Spain. Born in Hainault, son of Jean IV, the 2nd count, who died serving CHARLES V in Milan, he succeeded to the title on the death of his elder brother Charles of wounds received in the disastrous attack on Algiers in 1541. In 1544 he married Sabine, countess Palatine. An inveterate man of warfare, he distinguished himself repeatedly in battle, crowning his reputation by winning for the House of Habsburg against the French the military victories of San Quentin (1557) and Gravelines (1558). After the departure of PHILIP II from the Netherlands in 1559, Egmont led the opposition to cardinal GRANVELLE and the pro-Spanish group in the Brussels government. When the duke of ALBA was sent to Brussels to put down the discontent, he commenced his harsh measures by arresting Egmont (September 1567), HORNES and other nobles. Nine months later Egmont and Hornes were publicly executed in Brussels, despite universal efforts in Europe to stop the executions. Egmont's tragedy was made the subject of a drama by Goethe (1788) and of an overture by Beethoven.

Eliot, Sir John (1592–1632) English politician. Born in Cornwall, he was educated at Oxford and the Inns, entered Parliament in 1614 and was knighted in 1618. He was a friend and client of the duke of BUCKINGHAM, who appointed him vice-admiral of Devon. In the 1624 Parliament he began to express his dissent with court policy, broke his link with the duke and in 1626 led impeachment proceedings against him, in a famous speech comparing the duke to the Roman tyrant Sejanus. He was imprisoned for a week in the Tower. In 1628 he took a leading part in promoting the Petition of Right. In March 1629 he drew up the famous three resolutions against popery and taxation, passed while the speaker of the Commons was held down in his chair. The next day he was sent to the Tower with eight other members of the Commons. He refused to give guarantees of good behaviour, and died in the Tower of consumption; as a consequence he was considered a martyr for the Parliamentary cause.

Elizabeth I Tudor (1533–1603) queen of England 1558–1603. Daughter of HENRY VIII and Anne BOLEYN, she had a difficult childhood: her mother was executed when she was only three, and she was declared illegitimate. In 1544, however, her right to the succession was reaffirmed. During the reigns of her brother EDWARD VI and sister MARY I she remained carefully aloof from politics and religious controversy. She dedicated herself rather to learning, and became an accomplished scholar and linguist: her political skill and decisive yet moderate character turned her into one of the most successful rulers of all time. On becoming queen, she immediately affirmed the Protestant nature of the national Church, but was more cautious in her approach to internal and international politics. The wish to avoid extremes became typical of her policies, though she was capable of brutal firmness when it appeared necessary: against sectarians, Puritans and papists, and against threats to security from rebellion and conspiracy. On all such occasions, her government made ample use of the death penalty, notably with the execution of the duke of NORFOLK in 1572 and of MARY STUART, queen of Scots, in 1587. Her alleged liberality in religion was accompanied by the execution of some two hundred Catholics during the reign; and she presided over the ruthless English occupation of Ireland. Astonishingly successful as a woman in a man's world, she never took the option of marrying, despite many pressures in favour of establishing a dynastic succession; but she cultivated several favourites, notably LEICESTER and ESSEX, who later disappointed her. By the end of the reign, her genuine popularity as well as an active campaign of propaganda in her favour overshadowed the growing political conflicts in Parliament and economic difficulties in the country. Her foreign policy was directed towards England's survival, and was marked by unsuccessful military action on the continent (in France in 1562 and in the Netherlands in 1585), and a hesitant attitude towards Spain. But her support for DRAKE, and her finally decisive stand against PHILIP II, culminating in the victory over the Spanish Armada (1588), did more than anything to consolidate her fame among the English and in Europe. With good reason, her reign may be viewed as an unprecedented era of cultural, political and economic successes.

Elizabeth Romanov (1709–61) empress of Russia 1741–61. Daughter of PETER THE GREAT and his second wife Catherine, she kept a low profile during the reign of the empress Anna (1730–40), niece of Peter the Great, but her supporters resented the dominance of foreign and German advisers and in 1741 staged a coup against Anna's infant successor Ivan. Power now returned to the Russian nobles, notably the members of the Shuvalov family. Elizabeth was a warm-hearted lady who enjoyed the good life and lovers, but disdained culture and left government to her nobles. The preferred language began to become French, and some cultural improvements took place (foundation of the university of Moscow, 1755). The foreign policy was directed mainly against Sweden (1741–3), with some territorial gains in Finland, and against Prussia in the Seven Years War (1756 onwards), when Russian forces scored major victories, occupied East Prussia and captured Königsberg (1758).

Elizabeth Stuart (1596–1662) queen of Bohemia 1619–20. Daughter of JAMES I of England, in 1613 she was married to FREDERICK V OF WITTELSBACH, elector of the Palatinate, and accompanied him into exile after he was deprived first of Bohemia and then of the Palatinate. They lived principally in The Hague, and then at Rhenen on the Rhine; after her husband's death in 1632 she continued to live at The Hague, returning to England in 1661. She had twenty children, among them Karl Ludwig, who in 1648 was restored as ruler of the Rhine Palatinate. Thanks to the succession through her youngest daughter Sophia, the crown of England

came back into her family in the eighteenth century. Another daughter, Elizabeth, known as the princess Palatine (1618–80), became well known for her dedication to learning in the Netherlands, where she knew Descartes and became an active proponent of Cartesian philosophy, and ended her career as abbess (from 1667) of a Lutheran foundation in Herford, Westphalia.

Elsevier, Louis (c.1546–1617) Netherlands printer. He was born in Louvain and became a bookbinder by profession, working in Antwerp and Douai, then converted to the Reformation and moved to Leiden with his family and his printing house in 1580. In 1594 he entered into a contract with Jean Paets to print and distribute books to his outlets, which included Cologne, Paris and Frankfurt. Fourteen years after he came to the city, in 1594 he was admitted to be a citizen of Leiden. Of his seven sons, five carried on the family business, notably Bonaventure (1583–1652) and Abraham (1592–1652). The main Leiden shop closed in 1659, but family branches continued to flourish in the seventeenth century, at The Hague (from 1601), Utrecht and Amsterdam.

Emanuele Filiberto, duke of Savoy (1528–80) Known as 'Iron Head', for much of his life he was a leader without a state, since France had expelled his father Carlo III from the dukedom in 1544. He built up a reputation as military leader in the service of France's enemy the emperor CHARLES V, whom he served in the German wars against the Schmalkadic League. Appointed commander of the forces in the Netherlands, he led the troops against the French in the resounding victory of St Quentin (1557). At the subsequent peace of Cateau-Cambrésis (1559), he agreed to marry the French king's sister, Marguerite, and was restored to the dukedom of Savoy, whose extent he consolidated by the acquisition of territories from neighbouring Italy and

Switzerland; in 1562 he fixed his capital in Turin.

Ensenada, Zenón de Somodevilla, marquis of (1702–81) Spanish politician. Born in Navarre (near Logroño), he rose through the state administrative apparatus in the reign of PHILIP V and obtained his first important post as naval intendant at El Ferrol. He accompanied the successful expedition against Oran in 1732. Some years later he organised the expedition to Naples that put Philip's son Charles on the Neapolitan throne and was rewarded with the title of marquis (1736). He was appointed secretary of state and of war in 1741, went to Italy as commander of the forces there, and in 1743 was appointed to the further responsibility of finances. He continued in office under the new king, Ferdinand VI, as chief minister of the crown, while foreign affairs were controlled by José de Carvajal. Among Ensenada's most important reforms was the re-introduction of the system of French-style administrative intendants (1749), first established in 1718 but with limited success. He also stimulated the development of the army and especially the navy, building up the Atlantic and Mediterranean fleets. His pro-French leanings in foreign policy provoked opposition that brought about his downfall (1754) and his banishment to Granada. At the accession of CHARLES III he was admitted back into the administration, but when the popular riots of 1766 (the Esquilache riots) brought about the expulsion of the Jesuits, he too was sacked, and retired to Medina del Campo, where he died.

Epernon, Jean-Louis de Nogaret de La Valette, duke d' (1554–1642) French grandee. Born of lesser country nobility, he was educated in Paris, supported the royalist party during the civil wars, and took service with many of the great nobles. From about 1578 he joined the household of the king, HENRY III, whom he served both in campaigns and on diplomatic missions, and was amply rewarded. The king purchased for him the castle of Epernon, which he erected into a dukedom (1581), made him first gentleman of the bedchamber, and granted him several provincial governorships. In the following years he played a leading role in the civil wars as general of the king, and received further honours: he was made admiral of France (1587), then appointed to various key governorships, including Provence and Normandy. Opposed bitterly by both sides in the civil war, and never secure of the king's support, he remained solid in his loyalty to the crown and accompanied the body of the assassinated Henry III. A strict Catholic, he opposed the succession of HENRY IV but after long hesitation recognised him eventually as king (1596); thereafter he served the monarchy faithfully. He was at Henry's side when the king was assassinated (1610), and gave his support to the subsequent regency, during which he opposed the schemes of the favourite CONCINI. When RICHELIEU came to power he was distanced from the court and appointed to the governorship of Guyenne (1622).

Episcopius, Simon (Simon Bisschop) (1583–1643) Dutch theologian. After studying theology at Leiden he became a pastor in 1610 then returned to the university in 1612 in the chair of theology, succeeding the anti-Arminian professor GOMARUS. Together with Uytenbogaert, a counsellor of the Dutch leader OLDENBARNEVELT, he was one of the spokesmen of the Arminian-inspired Remonstrant party in the republic. After the eventful Calvinist Synod of Dort (1618–19), he and several other Remonstrant leaders were banished from the Netherlands. He lived in Paris, Antwerp and Rouen until 1626, when he returned, becoming in 1634 head of the Remonstrant seminary in Amsterdam. In 1629 he published an *Apologia pro confessione Remonstrantium*; and his *Institutiones* *theologicae* (1650–1) offered a systematic basis for Remonstrant doctrine, based on tolerance and man's free will.

Erasmus, Desiderius (*c*.1466–1536) Dutch Christian humanist, the most important scholar of his age. His early humanist education was provided by the Brethren of the Common Life. An Augustinian canon, he was ordained a priest in 1492, but soon turned to the life of an independent scholar and was later dispensed from the monastic life and dress. At Oxford in 1499, John COLET encouraged his study of Greek that led to his biblical and religious scholarship. He journeyed across Europe producing a range and wealth of textual editions, handbooks, letters and religious essays that profoundly influenced humanistic learning and the coming Reformation. The *Adages* (1500; 1508), a collection of classical proverbs; the *Enchiridion* (Handbook of the Christian Soldier) (1503), an introduction to his self-styled 'philosophy of Christ'; and a critical edition of Lorenzo VALLA's *Annotations on the New Testament* (1505) were among his early works. In Italy 1506 to 1509, he studied in Turin and Bologna, and worked for Aldus MANUTIUS in Venice. In 1509 in the house of his friend Thomas MORE, he composed *Praise of Folly*, typical of his sharp satire of human actions and careers with his theological message to become a fool for Christ. Back in Basel in 1514, he published his most important work, a Greek edition of the New Testament with a facing Latin translation and appended notes (1516) and an edition of Jerome. In 1517 he worked in Louvain where he prepared his *Colloquies* (1518), a Latin primer of satirical and edifying stories, before settling again in Basel in 1521. After long refusing to become involved in the Reformation debate, he responded to LUTHER's theology in his ineffective essay *On Free Will* (1524). Erasmus was no match for the polemical theological controversialists and sought a middle road of peace, mild humour and reconciliation,

rejected and vilified by both sides. As the Reformation crisis turned into war, he moved to Freiburg in 1529 and returned to Basel in 1535.

[JM]

Erastus, Thomas (1524–83) Protestant theologian. Born Thomas Lüber in Baden, Switzerland, he studied medicine at university and in 1557 was invited to be professor of therapeutics at the university of Heidelberg. During his stay he supported the introduction of the Reformation (in its Zwinglian form) into the Palatinate, but opposed attempts by Calvinists to impose their particular discipline. In 1568 the English Calvinist Withers published in the city a set of theses propounding Calvinist order, to which he replied with a hundred counter-theses (the *Explicatio*, published posthumously in 1589 as seventy five theses), in which he firmly denied that church officials could excommunicate and punish, arguing that in a Christian society only the civil magistrate can impose discipline in religious matters. He backed, for example, the use by the state of the death penalty against witches (in a work of 1578). The Palatinate became officially Calvinist in 1570, and he was forced to leave his post a few years later on suspicion of heresy. In 1580 he was appointed professor of medicine and then of ethics in the university of Basel. His stand for the authority of the civil power in religion became a relevant issue in mid-seventeenth-century England, where the term 'Erastianism' came into existence to signify the doctrine that the state is supreme over the Church in matters of religion, a doctrine which he never explicitly held. His *Explicatio* was translated several times into English, and Erastianism became an official tenet of the established Anglican Church.

Erik XIV Vasa (1533–77) king of Sweden 1560–8. Son of GUSTAV I VASA, he attempted to strengthen royal authority against the nobility and members of the royal family. The major obstacle to Swedish power was Danish control of the territory and trade of the western Baltic; he therefore acquired a foothold in the eastern Baltic with the sovereignty of Reval (1561) and adjacent territories. Denmark in response allied with Poland and attacked Sweden in a lengthy war (1563–70). During this period Erik had a mental breakdown (1567), ordered some dissident nobles executed, and alienated his support. His half-brother John (who became king later as John III) led a conspiracy that deposed him in 1568. He ended his days in prison; his life inspired a play by Strindberg (1899).

Ernst Augustus (1629–98) duke of Brunswick, and first elector of Hanover 1692–8. Holder of the Lutheran bishopric of Osnabrück from 1660, in 1679 he became duke of Kalenberg-Göttingen, and finally in 1692 was created elector of Hanover by the emperor LEOPOLD I in recognition of his military services against France and the Turks. His son George became GEORGE I of England, and his daughter Sophia Charlotte became first queen of Prussia.

Espinosa, Diego de (1502–72) Spanish cardinal and minister. He studied law at Salamanca, then served as judge in the Castilian high courts in Seville and in Valladolid, before being appointed to the council of Castile and then, to the surprise of all, named president of the council in 1565 by PHILIP II. The following year he was appointed bishop of Siguenza and inquisitor general, obtaining a cardinalate in 1568. His rapid rise to supreme power was due to Philip's confidence in his efficiency. Espinosa supported a hard-line policy towards the Dutch rebels as well as towards the Moriscos who rebelled in 1569. Formal and arrogant, his personality was resented by the grandees and soon clashed with that of Philip. He died of a stroke shortly after being dismissed from office by the king.

Essex, Arthur Capel, 1st earl of (new creation) (1631–83) English peer. Son of Arthur, lord Capel, he was created earl at the Restoration in 1660, as compensation for the execution of his father in the royalist cause in 1649. He was employed by CHARLES II as ambassador to Denmark (1670), and served as lord lieutenant of Ireland from 1672 to 1677, a period he spent largely in that country. From 1677, inspired by personal grievances, he came out against Charles' minister DANBY, and during the Exclusion crisis vigorously opposed the government. A friend of Algernon SIDNEY and lord William RUSSELL, he supported the claims of the duke of MONMOUTH, and in 1683 was arrested on suspicion of being implicated in the Rye House plot to murder the king. Sent to the Tower, he committed suicide by cutting his throat in his cell. 'My lord Essex might have tried my mercy', Charles II commented, 'I owe a life to his family'.

Essex, Robert Devereux, 2nd earl of (1566–1601) English peer. Eldest son of the 1st earl (d.1576), who made his name by his savage colonisation of Ireland, he was promoted at court by his stepfather LEICESTER. Last of the leading court nobles of ELIZABETH I of England, he succeeded to Elizabeth's favour after the death of Leicester. Cultured and charming at court, he attempted to accumulate power through political influence and direct contact with European rulers. An adventurer by nature, he showed little acumen in the world of politics. In 1596 he commanded the large naval expedition that seized Cadiz and brought him popularity in London; but a subsequent expedition the year after failed miserably. The mismanagement of an expedition to Ireland in his new capacity as lord lieutenant (April–September 1599) precipitated his disgrace: he was tried before the council in June 1600 and stripped of all his offices. Hoping to recoup his fortunes, he plotted with his supporters to seize power.

Arrested in February 1601, he was tried in Westminster Hall and condemned to death. The queen hesitated, but signed the warrant.

Essex, Robert Devereux, 3rd earl of (1591–1646) Son of the 2nd earl of ESSEX, he had served in the war in Bohemia in 1620 and in the 'bishops war' against the Scots in 1639, and was a Presbyterian by conviction, factors that led to his appointment by the Long Parliament in July 1642 as commander-in-chief of the army on the outbreak of the civil war in England. After several indecisive campaigns, he resigned his command early in 1645.

Este A family of northern Italy who played an important role in politics and culture from the thirteenth century to the Napoleonic period. Dating from Carolingian times in Tuscany, the noble family took its name from an imperial land grant at Este, near Padua, and came to dominate the eastern half of the Po Valley. From 1267 they became lords of Ferrara and expanded their state westwards to Modena and Reggio and north to Rovigo. Their unusually long and uninterrupted reign owed much to their strategies of succession for illegitimate heirs and their dynastic marriages as well as their administrative abilities, attention to social and economic issues, and the suppression of dissent. The Renaissance dukes, prelates and patrons made the court of Ferrara famous for its men-of-arms and its cultural florescence.

Alfonso I Este (1476–34, duke from 1505) Son of Ercole I, he married Lucrezia BORGIA, who oversaw their brilliant court while he applied himself to military and diplomatic questions.

Alfonso II Este (1533–97, duke from 1559) Elder son of Ercole II and Renée (daughter of Louis XII of France), he was the last duke of Ferrara when the pope refused to acknowledge his illegitimate half-brother as successor, but the line continued in Modena and Reggio.

Beatrice Este (1475–97) Daughter of Ercole I, she married Ludovico SFORZA, the duke of Milan, and carried the humanist and artistic flowering of the court of Ferrara to Milan.

Borso Este (b. 1413–71, duke from 1450) Second of the three half-brothers, he was made duke of Modena and Reggio by emperor Frederick III and duke of Ferrara by pope Paul II.

Ercole I Este (b. 1431–1505, duke from 1471) He was the third of three half-brothers to succeed as duke of Ferrara. He maintained a pro-French policy during the Italian Wars after 1494, oversaw the expansion and rebuilding of the city, was a great patron of the arts, and fathered four children.

Ippolito Este (1479–1520) One of Ercole I's sons, he was a cardinal and noted patron of the arts.

Isabella Este (1474–1569) Eldest daughter of Ercole I, she married Francesco Gonzaga, marquis of Mantua. She brought her humanist learning and artistic patronage from Ferrara to establish an equally brilliant court at Mantua.

Leonello Este (b. 1407–50, duke 1441) Eldest of the three half-brothers who established the cultural importance of Ferrara, he was educated by the humanist Guarino; he befriended and acted as patron for a wide circle of poets, scholars, and painters.

[JM]

Estienne, Henri (1531–98) French printer. Eldest son of Robert ESTIENNE, he followed his father's tradition as a scholar. As a young man he toured Italy, and settled with his father in Geneva, becoming a Calvinist, but continued his travels and contacts. His printing output, including the works of CALVIN and BEZA, made him in effect the official printer of Geneva, but he had continuous difficulties with the authorities. In 1578 he left the city and returned for a period to France, where religious toleration was now accepted and the king, HENRY III, offered his patronage. From 1585 he divided his time between France, Switzerland and Germany, continuing to produce Greek and Latin editions. He died in a hospital in Lyon.

Estienne, Robert (1503–59) French printer. Originally from Provence, the Estienne family was based in Paris and later in Geneva. Robert was the most outstanding printer of France, and produced remarkable editions of works in Latin, Hebrew and Greek. He was also a well-known humanist, printing the Latin works of MELANCHTHON, HUTTEN, VALLA and ERASMUS; and as a lexicographer published a Latin *Thesaurus* (1543). Though enjoying royal protection, he was attacked by the Sorbonne for his sympathy to the Reformation and fled to Geneva in 1550; there he published the French works of CALVIN.

Eugène of Savoy-Carignan, prince of Savoy (1663–1736) military commander. Son of the duke of Savoy-Carignan and of Olympia MANCINI, niece of cardinal MAZARIN, he was destined for the Church but decided instead on a military career. Finding no chance of a career at the court of LOUIS XIV, he entered the service instead of the Austrian Habsburgs (1683), where he revealed his outstanding talents as a commander against the Turks and aided in the relief of Vienna (1683), the capture of Budapest (1686), and siege of Belgrade (1688). He rose to become field-marshal. During the war of the League of Augsburg he served the emperor both on the Rhine and in Italy. His decisive victory at Zenta (1697), when he annihilated a Turkish army three times larger, was instrumental in gaining most of Hungary for Austria at the subsequent treaty of Karlowitz, and so establishing the frontiers of the new Habsburg empire. He served as commander-in-chief in Italy during the war of the Spanish Succession,

scoring notable victories over the French armies. His victory at Turin (1706) assured all Milan and Lombardy for Austria. He then moved to Flanders, where he joined MARLBOROUGH (with whom he had recently served against the Franco-Bavarian forces in Germany), and took part in the famous victories over the French at Oudenarde (1708) and Malplaquet (1709). In 1712, however, his forces were defeated by marshal VILLARS at Denain. In 1714 he led the negotiators at the peace of Rastatt. Returning home to Austria, he continued the campaigns against the Turks, recovering Belgrade in 1717 (confirmed by the treaty of Passarowitz 1718). After a further brief spell as commander in the war of the Polish Succession, he retired to devote himself to a life of leisure and learning, and to the construction of his magnificent Baroque residence, the Belvedere, in Vienna. The greatest of all the generals to have served the Habsburgs, he was exceptional for his qualities both in war and in peace.

Evelyn, John (1620–1706) English diarist and scholar. Son of a man who had made his fortune producing gunpowder, he was fleetingly educated at Oxford and the Temple, but profitably spent the years 1643–7, which were highly conflictive in England, travelling on the continent, mainly in Italy. After a further short stay abroad (1649–52) he returned to settle in England, where he became one of the first members of the Royal Society, of which he acted as secretary in the year 1672–3; he twice refused to be president. Appointed to administrative posts after the Restoration, he was an active patron of music and the arts, devoting his special care to landscape gardening, at his residences in Deptford and Wooton. At Sayes Court, Deptford, the gardens were much visited and admired, but he was also constantly in London. A man of universal learning, his interests covered gardening, books, architecture and chemistry. Among his many writings, *Fumifugium* (1661) attacked London's smoke problem, and *Sylva* (1664) was a study on trees. His diaries, published as the *Memoirs* (2 vols 1818–19), are a valuable source for the history and culture of his time.

F

Fairfax, Thomas, 3rd baron Fairfax (1612–71) English general. Yorkshire-born, and son of the 2nd lord, he was educated at Cambridge, then went to the continent to study warfare and travel (1629–32). He served in the war against the Scots (1639) and was knighted (1640). On the outbreak of the civil war he joined other Yorkshire notables in supporting Parliament, and commanded with distinction in the northern campaigns of 1643–4. He led a section of the army that defeated CHARLES I on Marston Moor (1644), and in 1645 was appointed commander in chief of the Parliamentary forces. Under him the New Model Army, which he created and trained, obtained convincing victories (Naseby in 1645, and several sieges) that won the war. A staunch Presbyterian but also a conservative, he was reluctantly carried along by events, refused to approve of the trial and execution of the king, and resigned his post in 1650 rather than fight against the Scots. In retirement at his estate in Nunappleton, Yorkshire, under the Protectorate, he disagreed with aspects of the rule of CROMWELL. He worked for the Restoration of CHARLES II and entered the Convention Parliament (1660) but was, unsurprisingly, given little recognition by the new government.

Farel, Guillaume (1489–1565) French religious reformer. Born in the Dauphiné, he studied at Paris, with LEFÈVRE D'ÉTAPLES among his teachers, and graduated in 1517. In 1521 he joined the group of humanists at the court of the bishop of Meaux, and became a supporter of the Reformation. Facing difficulties in France, he went in 1523 to Basel, and in subsequent years moved among the reformed cities, particularly Strasbourg. He was a virulent polemicist, earning the bitter opposition of ERASMUS for slurs against the latter during a disputation in Basel which caused him to be expelled from that city. In 1526 he accepted a post in Bern, staying on to become reformer of that city and of Neuchâtel. He helped in the early stages of the reform movement in Geneva, to which city he recruited CALVIN in 1538. He became chief minister of Neuchâtel, where he died.

Farinelli (Broschi, Carlos) (1705–82) Italian castrato singer. He was the foremost eighteenth-century singer, whose dazzling appearances throughout Europe and brilliant vocal techniques affected the operatic style of the period. As the anecdote goes, upon his arrival at the court of Madrid in 1737 he won king PHILIP V's heart by singing to him the same arias every evening, thereby alleviating his chronic melancholia. In return he supervised lavish productions of Italian operas and was granted important administrative and political positions. After the death of king Ferdinand VI (1759) he retired comfortably to Bologna, where he often hosted dignitaries and famous musicians, such as Gluck and Mozart.

[JE]

Farnese, Alessandro (1545–92) duke of Parma 1586–92. Son of duke Ottavio and of MARGARET OF AUSTRIA, sister of CHARLES V, he was by birth cousin to PHILIP II, at whose court in Spain he spent his entire early life. In 1565 he married princess Maria of Portugal. One of the most prominent military commanders of his time, he took part in the battle of Lepanto and subsequently went to serve with the Spanish troops in the Netherlands, where in 1578 he was appointed commander and governor (1578) on the premature death of Don JUAN OF AUSTRIA. He achieved remarkable success on the battlefield, displaying a capacity for political negotiation, and a studied moderation in religious matters. Thanks to his efforts, the southern provinces agreed by the Union of Arras (1579) to remain loyal to the crown and the greater part of the Netherlands was recovered for Spain. The high point of his success was the capture of Antwerp (1585). After these years other military involvements, to which he expressed his opposition, made his task difficult: he was asked to help in the invasion of England (which never took place, after the defeat of the Armada in 1588), and he was ordered to invade France three times in the 1590s (each time with diminishing results). Wounded in one of these invasions, he died before news could arrive of Philip II's decision to remove him from his command.

Farnese, Elizabeth (1692–1766) queen of Spain 1714–46. Daughter of the duke of Parma, she was chosen in 1714 as the second wife of PHILIP V of Spain, whom she dominated personally and whose political policies she influenced in favour of her family's interests in Italy. She began

her period as queen by expelling the crown's French advisers, and placed her confidence first in the Italian priest ALBERONI and then in the Dutch adviser RIPPERDA. Her influence could be seen most clearly in the diversion of Spain's military energy towards the Mediterranean, directed against English and Austrian interests. One of her lifelong concerns was to win territorial possessions in Italy for her sons Charles and Philip: subsequent wars succeeded in gaining the kingdoms of Sicily and Naples for the former (1734) and the duchies of Milan, Parma and Piacenza for the latter (1743).

Fawkes, Guy (1570–1606) English conspirator. A native of York, he converted to Catholicism in his teens, and later went to Flanders to serve in the Spanish army (1593–5). In 1604 he and four others (one of them Robert Catesby), in protest against the reinforced penal laws against Catholics, devised a plot to blow up Parliament while the king, JAMES I, was there. In December they began digging a tunnel to connect a cellar of the Parliament building with a neighbouring house; by May the cellar was filled with explosives. In October the conspirators sent an anonymous note warning a Catholic lord, Monteagle, not to attend on the day Parliament was opened; he showed it to Robert CECIL (Lord Salisbury), and the plot was exposed. Fawkes was discovered in the cellar, arrested and tortured; he and his accomplices were executed in January 1606 in front of the Parliament building. The date of his arrest, 5 November, was subsequently cultivated by the Puritans as a day of national liberation from the Catholic menace, and has passed into English folklore as the annual festivity of fireworks.

Feijoo, Benito (1676–1764) Spanish monk and scholar. A native of Ourense (Galicia, Spain), at the age of fourteen he entered the Benedictine order, was educated at

Salamanca and returned to teach in Oviedo, where he spent the rest of his life. He had a deep interest in all types of learning, particularly in science and medicine. From 1726 to 1740 he published the eight volumes of his *Teatro Crítico*, which quickly established him with the Spanish public as the leading intellectual of the day. His reputation was further enhanced by the publication of five volumes (the last one in 1760) of *Cartas eruditas*. In 1750 the king, Ferdinand VI, extended to him the extraordinary favour of declaring his views officially protected. His works were translated during his lifetime into French and Italian, and after his death into English and German. Accepted today as the forerunner of the Enlightenment in Spain, his views were inspired in part by his reading of foreign writers (whom he studied in French translation), but he also drew on a reserve of rational Spanish thought.

Fénelon, François de Salignac de La Mothe (1651–1715) French ecclesiastic. Born in the family chateau in the Dordogne, he was educated by the Jesuits and ordained priest in 1675 in Paris, where he carried out his ministry and also had contacts with the court, notably the circle associated with SAINT-SIMON and the dukes of Beauvilliers and Chevreuse. During this period he wrote a tract on *L'éducation des filles*, which gained him the support of Madame de MAINTENON, founder of the college at St-Cyr. In 1688 he was introduced to madame GUYON by madame Maintenon. Appointed tutor (1689–95) to the heir to the throne, LOUIS XIV's grandson the duke of Burgundy, he wrote treatises that were meant to be a programme for the duke (who unfortunately died young). Together with a group of other conservative thinkers who wished to modify aspects of Louis XIV's regime, he proposed a return to the old constitution, based on the Estates General and the power of the noble class. His most celebrated writings are the highly critical

Letter to Louis XIV (unpublished in the king's lifetime) and the Utopian fable *Télémaque* (1699, soon withdrawn from circulation). Appointed archbishop of Cambrai (1695), he defended Guyon against her detractors and by publishing his *Maxims of the Saints* (1697) became involved in a controversy with BOSSUET over Guyon and the subject of Quietism. The case was taken to Rome and in 1699 a number of propositions in the *Maxims* were condemned. He accepted the condemnation publicly from his pulpit, and retired into silence on the question, but never changed his views.

Ferdinand I (1503–64) emperor 1558–64. Younger brother of the emperor CHARLES V, he was born in Spain and brought up as a Spaniard; but after the Comunero rebellion was encouraged to leave the country and was granted the hereditary Habsburg lands (1521–2). He was elected king of Bohemia and Hungary in 1526, and king of the Romans in 1531. After Charles V gradually withdrew from German affairs in the wake of the Schmalkaldic war, Ferdinand took over control as effective leader of the house of Habsburg, devoting himself to reorganisation of the imperial government, leading the struggle against the Turks (who besieged Vienna in 1529), and attempting to resolve religious differences through a policy of compromise. His reign marked a decisive step in the formation of the Austro-Hungarian monarchy, though the tendency to unity was arrested somewhat by the division of his territories among his heirs: MAXIMILIAN II received Austria, Bohemia and Hungary, but Ferdinand received the Tyrol and Charles received Inner Austria. Ferdinand logically came to differ with Charles V over policies, and was mainly responsible for the peace of Augsburg (1555) that settled the Reformation wars in Germany. Some three years after the emperor had abdicated from all his other realms he formally abdicated the empire (1558) in favour of Ferdinand. Though a firm Catholic, Ferdinand approached the religious conflicts in his dominions with caution, and backed the colloquy of Worms (1557), in which Catholic and Protestant humanists attempted to reach an understanding based on disagreeing over nonessentials.

Ferdinand II (1578–1637) emperor 1619–37. Born in Graz, grandson of FERDINAND I and son of the archduke Charles of Inner Austria, he was educated at the Jesuit university of Ingolstadt and became an active promoter of the Counter-Reformation in his estates of Styria and Carinthia. Elected to succeed his cousin MATTHIAS as king of Bohemia (1617), and then elected king of Hungary (1618), he succeeded to the empire in 1619, at the very time that a rebellion against his policies was breaking out in Bohemia, where the rebel leaders (Defenestration of Prague 1618) dethroned him and elected in his place the Calvinist elector Palatine (FREDERICK V OF WITTELSBACH). During the subsequent Thirty Years War, Ferdinand pursued a hard line (1629 Edict of Restitution) against the Protestant princes who opposed him. Allying with Catholic Bavaria against Protestants and Swedes, he had the good fortune to be served by a capable general, WALLENSTEIN, with whom he later quarrelled and had assassinated (1634). After the Catholic victory at Nördlingen (1634), he attempted to impose, in the Peace of Prague (1635), a policy of German unity against Swedish and French intervention.

Ferdinand II of Trastámara ('the Catholic') (1452–1516) king of Aragon and Sicily 1479–1516, ruler of Castile 1474–1504, and king of Naples 1504–16. Son of Juan II of Aragon, in 1469 he travelled to Castile during the civil wars there and secretly married princess ISABELLA. In 1474 the latter succeeded to the throne of Castile and Ferdinand in 1479 to that of Aragon: the two kingdoms were associated in a relationship that created 'Spain'. In political terms each realm remained totally separate, the union being one of the rulers only; but Ferdinand and Isabella achieved an almost total identity of purpose. Authoritarian in outlook and policy, Ferdinand had the capacity and imagination to pursue a policy of conciliation in the war-torn states of the peninsula. In Aragon he reformed municipal government and stabilised politics; in Castile he backed the queen in restoring order. He pursued an aggressive military policy against the Muslims of Granada (1482–92) and the French in Naples (1504) and Navarre (1512), with the result that all three realms were integrated into the Spanish crown by the end of his reign. He also systematically established the new Inquisition (from 1480) in his territories, riding roughshod over opposition to it. His foreign policy was active and pioneering: he pursued alliances abroad through marriages (such as that of his daughter CATHERINE OF ARAGON with prince Arthur of England), and developed a novel system of resident ambassadors. Perhaps the most memorable event of his reign was the announcement made to him and his wife in Barcelona in 1492 by COLUMBUS, of the discovery of new lands overseas. On Isabella's death in 1504, his rule over Castile lapsed, and he handed over power in Castile to his daughter. In 1506 he married Germaine de Foix, daughter of LOUIS XII of France, by whom he had a son who died in infancy; Germaine died in 1509. In 1510, after his daughter JUANA THE MAD retired from government, he was invited back to Castile to become regent. With no available heirs, he was obliged to accept the succession in both realms of Spain of his grandson, Charles of Ghent. MACHIAVELLI in his *Prince* admired Ferdinand as the ideal ruler for his astuteness and guile, thereby doing no small disservice to the king's reputation. In reality, Ferdinand governed Spain brilliantly in war and peace during its most formative phase, establishing it as a power in Europe and laying the foundations for its colonial expansion in the New World. PHILIP II is said to have observed later that 'we owe everything to him'.

Ferdinand VI (1713–59) king of Spain 1746–59. The second son of PHILIP V and Marie-Louise of Orléans, in 1729 he married the Portuguese princess Barbara of Braganza; his reign was one of uninterrupted peace for Spain, maintaining a strict neutrality between the conflicting interests of England and France, and of important economic advance, in which he was well served by his ministers José de Carvajal and the marquis of ENSENADA. He suffered from chronic depression and attendant illnesses, which became extreme after the death of his wife in 1758.

Ferdinand of Austria, the cardinal infante (1609–41) Third son of PHILIP III of Spain, and brother to PHILIP IV, as a youth he was destined for the Church, and created archbishop of Toledo and cardinal in 1619. He later became viceroy of Catalonia (1632) and then governor of Milan (1633), and finally in 1634 was appointed governor of the Netherlands. He had by then developed an innate interest in the art of war; he went to take up his post at the head of an army of 18,000 that entered Germany from Italy and won an unexpected victory against the Swedes at Nördlingen (1634). As governor of the Netherlands, he pursued a brilliant campaign against the Franco-Dutch forces, culminating in the spectacular routing of the French army a few miles north of Paris at Corbie (1636). He had scant interest in religion, devoting himself to politics, war and women.

Fermat, Pierre de (1610–65) French mathematician. Whilst pursuing a career as a lawyer and official of the parlement of Toulouse, he devoted his spare time to the study of mathematics, especially algebra. His contributions to its advance included deducing much of the mathematical theory of probability and principles of per-

mutations and combinations, and work on a form of calculus which anticipated DESCARTES' analytical geometry and influenced NEWTON. A marginal note amongst his papers states that he had proved the assertion that the equation $x^n + y^n = z^n$ has no solution in positive whole numbers when n is more than 2; later mathematicians' attempts to establish such a proof have recently been rewarded with success, though it cannot be claimed that 'Fermat's Last Theorem' has truly been recovered since the method employed is not one that would have been recognisable to Fermat. He published little in his lifetime, but circulated papers in manuscript; his *Varia opera mathematica* (1679) appeared posthumously.

[FW]

Fernández de Córdoba, Gonzalo (1453–1515) known as 'the Great Captain'. He rose to fame as a commander in the wars of Granada, and was sent by FERDINAND II OF TRASTÁMARA in 1495 to lead the Spanish troops against the French invading Naples. His decisive victories at Cerignola (April 1503) and the Garigliano (December 1503) confirmed him as one of the outstanding infantry generals of his time. Ferdinand came to Naples in 1507 to be confirmed as king, and returned to Spain with the general, who spent the rest of his days in retirement in Granada, disappointed at the king's failure to make further use of his services. He founded the important dynasty of nobles that bore his name.

Ferrante (Ferdinand) I of Naples (1423–94) king of Naples from 1458. Illegitimate son of Alfonso V of Aragon who had conquered Naples in 1443, he was groomed at an early age in administrative, military and diplomatic skills to succeed his father and was one of the most powerful political minds of the Italian Renaissance. Despite marriage to the daughter of the prince of Taranto, the most powerful of the Neapolitan barons, he met constant resistance from them, from the pro-French faction in the kingdom, and from the pope, who refused to confirm his investiture. Unsuccessful revolts in 1458–65 and again in 1485–7 dominated his domestic, anti-feudal policies. In international politics, he made Naples an important participant in the 1454 Peace of Lodi, the Italian states' defensive alliance against French and Ottoman invasion. He forged a personal alliance with Lorenzo de' MEDICI to limit Venetian and papal expansion. His daughter Eleonora was married to Ercole I d'ESTE of Ferrara in 1474 and the Florentines joined Naples against Venice and the papacy in the War of Ferrara (1482–4). He expelled the Ottomans from an eleven-month seizure of Otranto in 1481, and his daughter Beatrice was married to Matthias Corvinus, king of Hungary, to strengthen the alliance against the Turks in the Balkans. Cross marriages with the SFORZA in Milan linked their two dynasties, despite their rivalry for influence within Italy. He continued his father's court patronage and enjoyed the services of the humanists Panormita, Pontano and Diomede Carafa. His long-standing negative reputation for duplicity and cruelty result more from the victory of his enemies, the loss of Naples and the destruction of the Aragonese dynasty with the French invasions and the Italian Wars soon after his death in 1494.

[JM]

Feuquières, Isaac Manassès de Pas, marquis de (1590–1640) French general and diplomat. From a noble family of Picardy, he made the army his career, played a part in the siege of La Rochelle (1628–9) and received due promotion. During the Thirty Years War he received from RICHELIEU a diplomatic assignment in Germany, and succeeded in forming an alliance between France, Sweden and Protestant princes (League of Heilbronn 1633). During the siege of Thionville (1639) he was

wounded and died shortly after of his injuries.

Ficino, Marsilio (1433–99) Florentine humanist and philosopher whose translations and commentaries on Plato and his school influenced European thought into the eighteenth century. He studied the humanist curriculum and medicine in Florence. With the influx of Greek scholars and manuscripts after the fall of Constantinople, he began to study Greek in the 1450s. Cosimo de' MEDICI and his successors provided extraordinary patronage and established a Platonic Academy under him in 1462 at their villa at Careggi near Florence. There he began the Latin translation of Plato's dialogues (1463–9), with the publication of the corpus in 1484, the first western language translation of the complete works. In 1473 he was ordained a priest and held a minor benefice in the cathedral of Florence. He published his own thought on Plato, *Theologia Platonica* (1482), an influential neo-Platonic schema emphasising the hierarchy of being, the assent of the immortal soul to God, and Platonic love as spiritual love. He worked on translations of the later neo-Platonic writers, Plotinus, Proclus and others from 1484–92. He remained the leading figure within the Medicean intellectual circle, confidant, tutor and adviser until their overthrow in 1494. Retired to the Tuscan countryside for the rest of his life, he fell under Church suspicion (albeit ultimately exonerated) for his hermetic beliefs and interest in magic and astrology. His legacy of Platonic translations lasted into the eighteenth century and he remains the epitome of Renaissance attempts to synthesise classical learning and Christian thought.

[JM]

Fielding, Henry (1707–54) English novelist and playwright. He was born in Somerset, educated at Eton and started his career in London. After the failure of his two early plays he went in 1728 to study law in

Leiden but within a year he was back in London. Over the next twenty-five years he wrote many plays satirising the contemporary scene. *Tom Thumb, a Tragedy* (1730), a burlesque of the then popular heroic drama, is his best play and *The Miser*, his version of MOLIÈRE's *L'Avare*, was very successful. In 1737 the Theatrical Licensing Act forced the closure of his theatre. He went back to the law and took up journalism. He became editor of *The Champion* and in 1749 he was appointed Justice of the Peace for Westminster and Middlesex. His essays and pamphlets exposed the squalor and brutality of London life and his proposals, as well as his involvement with the organisation of the Bow Street Runners, were the origins of the modern police force. Meanwhile the publication of RICHARDSON's *Pamela* spurred him into parody, and *Joseph Andrews* (1742) evolved into a fine picaresque novel. He wrote three more novels including *The History of Tom Jones* (1749), with its charming anti-hero, an undisputed masterpiece. In 1754 he set out for Lisbon in the hope of recovering his health, but died there at the early age of forty five. The delightful *Journey of a Voyage to Lisbon* was published posthumously. He was an honest, generous man who poured contempt on the evils and hypocrisy of his times, and a major figure in the development of the English novel.

[GG]

Filaret, patriarch (Fyodor Nikitich Romanov) (1553–1633) Russian noble who played a key role in Muscovy during the Time of Troubles. Cousin of Fyodor I, last tsar of the Rurik dynasty to rule over Muscovy, he was an active soldier-diplomat, and at Fyodor's death (1598) there was a move to put him on the throne. However, Boris GODUNOV forced him to stand aside and made him enter the religious life in a monastery, from which he was liberated by the pseudo-DMITRI in 1606 and appointed metropolitan of Ros-

tov. On a diplomatic mission for Muscovy in Poland he was held captive 1611 to 1619. In his absence the boyars elected his son MICHAEL ROMANOV as tsar (1613). On his return to Russia he was appointed patriarch of Moscow and shared in the government with his son. Titled 'great governor', he made most of the important decisions.

Filmer, Sir Robert (*c*.1588–1653) English political theorist. Educated at Cambridge and Lincoln's Inn, and knighted by CHARLES I, he was a firm royalist supporter in the civil war, during which his property at East Sutton was plundered and he was imprisoned. Some of his writings, first published between 1648 and 1653, were reissued in 1679. He is best known for his treatise *Patriarcha*, which remained in manuscript until 1680, and enjoyed posthumous fame mainly because it was disputed by Algernon SIDNEY (in his *Discourses*) and by LOCKE, who derided it as 'nonsense' but devoted his first *Treatise of Civil Government* to attacking it. In it he argued in favour of absolute royal power, which he based not on scripture but on the natural authority of the king as head of the 'family', namely his subjects. Patriarchal authority, he argued, was the key to political obligation. The king's divine right as ruler could be traced back to Adam as the first father and king. His subsequent critics found little difficulty in refuting his ideas.

Fisher, John (1459–1535) bishop of Rochester 1504–35. Educated at Cambridge, he rapidly rose to become master of his college, in 1497 was appointed confessor to the king's mother, lady Margaret BEAUFORT, countess of Richmond, and in 1501 made vice-chancellor of the university. In 1503 he became the first holder of the Lady Margaret chair of divinity founded by her; and in 1504 became chancellor for life of the university. In that year he was appointed to his bishopric. A notable scholar and humanist, he helped to found St John's College (1511), for which Margaret had made a bequest. He entered the lists against LUTHER, and from the first opposed HENRY VIII's divorce (he was confessor to CATHERINE OF ARAGON) and the proposals for royal supremacy over the Church. In 1534 he refused to take the oath to the Act of Succession, and was (despite his poor health and advanced age) sent to the Tower (April) along with MORE. In prison, he refused (May 1535) to swear to the Act of Supremacy; at the same time the pope created him a cardinal. He was tried in June and executed at Tower Hill. He was canonised in 1935.

Flamsteed, John (1646–1719) English astronomer. The son of a Derby businessman, he first achieved recognition through correspondence with the Royal Society. In 1675 he was appointed as the king's 'astronomical observator', in effect the first astronomer royal, and director of the Royal Observatory about to be built at Greenwich. He retained the post until his death, despite friction with contemporaries who wanted speedy access to the Observatory's results. After initially cooperating with NEWTON and the other 'referees' administering a grant for publication of his works, he disapproved strongly of the *Historia coelestis* (1712) produced by them under HALLEY's editorship; he thus embarked upon producing his own three-volume edition, posthumously published (1725) and complemented by the *Atlas coelestis* (1729). Ironically it was Halley's edition, not Flamsteed's, that introduced the 'Flamsteed numbers' used ever since for the identification of stars. Geographers, meanwhile, are familiar with the 'Flamsteed projection' of the globe on the plane of the equator. During the nineteenth-century opprobrium was heaped upon him as an adversary of Newton's, and historians have only recently begun to give him the credit due to one of England's foremost practical astronomers. A complete edition of his correspondence (eds E.G. Forbes, L. Murdin and F. Willmoth, 3 vols, 1995, 1997 and forthcoming) is now in progress.

[FW]

Fleury, Hercule de, cardinal (1653–1743) French statesman. Son of a state administrator, he was educated in Paris, entered the Church (1676) and through his patrons was active at court, and became one of the chaplains to the queen (1677), then to the king (1678). He was appointed bishop of Fréjus (1698–1715) and was then summoned to court, where the dying king named him tutor to the future LOUIS XV. The death in 1723 of the regent and of cardinal Dubois, and the accession as king of Louis that year, seemed to promise great things for Fleury, but he waited. Eventually in 1726 the king replaced his chief minister the duke de BOURBON, appointed the ageing Fleury as chief minister, and obtained for him the rank of cardinal. For seventeen years, until his death, he exercised absolute power over the government and over foreign policy. His tenure of office was marked by a notable economic stability and by successes in overseas ventures. An efficient and conscientious minister, he neither enriched himself nor created a system of clients; in this he was possibly unique in his day.

Fludd, Robert (1574–1637) Of Welsh origin but born in Kent, he was educated at Oxford, and then spent nearly six years (1598–1605) travelling on the continent and studying medical science, returning to take his doctorate at Oxford in 1605. In 1609 he was elected a fellow of the College of Physicians, and practised medicine in London while devoting himself to writing treatises. He became a public adept of the Rosicrucian philosophy, publishing several tracts on the subject in Latin on the continent, which contributed to his fame among European scholars. He was influenced by PARACELSUS, Hermeticism and the Kabbala, and his works combine theology with the occult. Creation for him was an extension of divine light into matter, evil came from a darkness inside God. Only God exists, matter does not exist.

Fontenelle, Bernard le Bovier, sieur (1657–1757) French man of letters. Son of a high court lawyer from Rouen, and of the sister of CORNEILLE, he was educated in the legal profession, but lost the first and only case that he took up. Disillusioned, he turned to writing, and was soon producing a flood of mediocre poems and plays. When his first tragedy was hissed off the stage he moved to Paris (1685), where he plunged into literary circles and intellectual life. A versatile freethinker with sceptical inclinations, he entered a then current debate in defending the superiority of the 'moderns' over the 'ancients' in his *Digression on Ancients and Moderns* (1688). He then went on to philosophical writing, producing in 1686 his *Entretiens sur la pluralité des mondes* (*Conversations on the Plurality of Worlds*), a work famous for being the first to suggest that other planets could be inhabited. In 1691 he was elected to the French Academy and in 1697 to the Academy of Sciences, of which he became the permanent secretary, producing as part of his work editions of the learned speeches made at the election of members. He also defended the ideas of DESCARTES, and wrote *Elements of Infinitesimal Calculus* (1727) in the wake of NEWTON and LEIBNIZ. He lived long enough to bridge the period between the early scientific revolution and the Enlightenment, and his writings reflect the transition. He continued to publish works of both a literary and a philosophical nature, a man with a truly universal perspective on human achievement.

Fouquet, Nicolas (1615–80) French minister of state. Born in Paris, son of a prominent and wealthy judge and coun-

cillor of State, he was destined for the Church but was persuaded to take up law, and in 1633 was appointed a judge of the parlement of Metz. In 1636 his father obtained further posts for him; he subsequently served as intendant with the army in Spain and Flanders. During the Fronde he advanced his position by purchasing in 1650 the post of prosecutor of the parlement of Paris. A close colleague of MAZARIN since 1649, he was appointed in 1653 joint superintendant general of finance (from 1659 he was sole holder of the post). His success in helping to stabilise state finance was attended by his success in enriching himself and placing members of his family in posts of influence; he amassed a huge fortune which enabled him to build the chateau of Vaux (1656–9), where he held court to luminaries of the arts. When LOUIS XIV took over control of the state, he entrusted to Colbert the task of enquiring into Fouquet's handling of finances; the king was not pleased, either, with a sumptuously regal reception laid on for him at Vaux, which appeared to dwarf his own royal resources. Fouquet was arrested in 1661, and in 1664 was condemned to forfeit all his property and to perpetual prison. The fallen minister was confined in several places, last of all (1664) in the fortress at distant Pinerolo, where he apparently died in mysterious circumstances. The legend of a masked prisoner, deriving possibly from him or one of his incarcerated servants, later took the form of the story of a man in an iron mask.

Fox, George (1624–91) English founder of the Quakers. He had no formal schooling, became apprenticed to a shoemaker, and in 1643 underwent a mystical experience that changed his life. He then spent three indecisive years wandering round the Midlands, and from about 1647 began to preach. A visionary who emphasised spiritual truth and the triviality of formal religion, he offended by his direct manner and peculiarities of dress (he insisted on always wearing his hat). The first of his eight imprisonments was in 1649. The year after, he and his numerous followers became popularly known as 'Friends', a name that stuck. They came mainly from the lower middle class, and in the first years were known for their hysterical fervour in their meetings (hence 'shakers' or 'quakers'). Fox dedicated himself to a career of preaching, travelling incessantly throughout Great Britain, to Holland (1677, 1684) and to north America and the West Indies (1671-2), converting many to his beliefs and bringing into existence the community of Quakers. He married (1669) Margaret Fell, a gentlewoman who helped greatly to consolidate the movement. His *Journal*, published in 1694, remains a classic testimony of religious experience.

Foxe, John (1516-87) English martyrologist. He was educated at Oxford, where he became fellow of Magdalen (1539), a post he resigned six years later when he refused to conform to the official religious provisions. He moved to London, was ordained deacon, and left the country (1554) after the accession of queen MARY I, living mainly in Frankfurt and Basel in the company of other English emigrés and dedicating himself to writing and publishing. He had already become an opponent of religious intolerance (by whatever church) and division, and began to collect material on the persecutions in England. In 1559 he published in Latin, with the printer Oporin of Basel, a volume on the persecution to that date. He returned to England that year, was ordained by GRINDAL in London, and was befriended by the duke of NORFOLK. After collecting new materials, he published in 1563 his *Actes and Monuments*, an English version of his martyrology; it had great success, was re-issued in 1570 in an expanded edition of two large volumes, recommended by the bishops for use in all churches, and ran to two more editions in his lifetime (1576, 1583). The book

became an enduring classic, and shaped for centuries the religious mentality of English Protestants.

Francis I of Valois (1494-1547) king of France 1515-47. Son of Charles of Valois and Louise of Savoy, in 1514 he married the daughter of his cousin LOUIS XII. The latter had no male heir when he died in 1515, and was therefore succeeded by Francis, an accomplished Renaissance prince with outstanding capacities in both war and peace. As patron of the arts, he imported Italian tastes, employed CELLINI, LEONARDO DA VINCI and others on royal palaces at Fontainebleau and Blois, and encouraged humanist scholars in France. The formation of modern French administration dates from his reign. He reformed the royal councils, restructured the fiscal system, regulated the judicial spheres of the royal courts and the parlements, and passed the first decree making French the official language of the courts (1539). He also absorbed into the royal jurisdiction many of the great noble fiefs. In Church matters, he obtained through the concordat of Bologna (1516) confirmation of powers of patronage that the crown in theory possessed since the pragmatic sanction of Bourges (1438). In external matters he affirmed French territorial identity by an aggressive foreign policy; and gave his support to French explorers in the New World. French ambitions in Italy were boosted by the notable victory of Marignan (1515) against the Swiss; and friendship with England was affirmed at the meeting with HENRY VIII at the Field of the Cloth of Gold (1520). From this period, however, France was faced by the energetic hostility of the Habsburgs in the form of CHARLES V, whose forces at the battle of Pavia (1525) scored a notable victory and captured Francis, who was taken prisoner to Madrid. On his release, he did not cease his struggle, both diplomatic and military, to affirm France's position in Flanders and in the Mediterranean, for which he relied also on alliances (1536) with the Turks. A firm Catholic, in his early years he showed moderation to French Reformers and even allied actively with German Lutherans (1531). But after the affair of the Placards in Paris (1534) he began a harsh repression of Protestants. The sect of Waldensians also became victims of repression in a campaign against them in Provence in 1545.

Francis II of Brittany (1435–88) Duke from 1458, he succeeded his uncle Arthur III, and became the last great defender against France of his country's independence, which was severely threatened by the fact that he had no sons and therefore had to regulate the marriages of his daughters carefully. Francis joined a league against France in 1465, and allied himself with England in 1468 and 1475, agreeing also in 1481 to marry his eldest daughter Anne to the prince of Wales. Despite these moves, eventually in 1488 he was forced by France to sign the treaty of Le Verger, in which he undertook to contract marriages for his daughters Anne and Isabelle only with the French king's permission. Francis died that year, leaving the duchy to Anne. Of her many suitors the king of France, CHARLES VIII, demonstrated that he had the strongest claim on her by sending in an army (1491) and agreeing to withdraw only on condition that she married him. Brittany thereupon became a part of France.

Francis II of Valois (1544–60) king of France 1559–60. Eldest son of HENRY II and CATHERINE DE MÉDICIS, in 1558 he was married to the young MARY STUART, queen of Scots. Too young and incapable to be an active ruler when he succeeded his father, his short rule initiated the period of noble strife in France that led to the Civil Wars.

Francis III of Lorraine, emperor as Francis (Franz) I (1708–65) emperor 1745–65. Born in Nancy, son of the duke de

Lorraine, he succeeded as duke (1729) under the name Francis Stephen, and in 1736 married Maria Theresa, daughter of the emperor CHARLES VI. After the treaty of Vienna (1738), which ended the war of the Polish Succession, he exchanged his duchy for the grand duchy of Tuscany (1737–65). On the death of Charles VI in 1740, he laid claim to the Imperial throne, to which he eventually succeeded in 1745, though the real force in government was Maria Theresa. He had sixteen children by her, among them Joseph II, who became emperor, and Marie Antoinette, who married Louis XVI.

Francis de Sales (1567–1617) Savoyard bishop. Born in Savoy of a noble family, he was educated locally (to 1578) and at Paris (1578–88), with a view to entering the religious life. He then went to study in Padua and Venice before returning to Savoy in 1592. In 1593 he was ordained priest at Annecy, declaring in his first sermon that 'Geneva must be won back, through charity'. From 1594 he undertook missionary work in parts of Savoy where Calvinism had penetrated, and in 1597 had three interviews with BEZA in Geneva. In 1598 he went to Rome, was created bishop and granted revenues to help his missionary work. In Paris in 1601 he made contact with the group of Catholic reformers associated with Madame ACARIE, and in 1602 was appointed bishop of Annecy-Geneva, and from this date travelled incessantly, became an active collaborator of the Catholic reformers in the west of France, and introduced the reforms of Trent in his diocese. In 1604 he first met the baroness CHANTAL, whose spiritual life he profoundly affected. He died of an illness in Lyon. Perhaps the most respected cleric in all French history, demands for his canonisation were made very soon after his death; he was declared a saint in 1665. Of his writings the best known is his *Introduction to the Devout Life* (1609), which was reprinted forty times in his lifetime and translated into several languages.

Franck, Sebastian (1499–1543) German spiritual thinker. Born at Donauwörth, he studied in Ingolstadt and Heidelberg and became a priest in the diocese of Augsburg. After the spread of the Reformation, he became a Lutheran pastor, but within a few months shifted his allegiance to the Anabaptists in Nürnberg. He then left them, and moved to Strasbourg in 1529. In contact with other independent radicals such as Hans Denck, he began to reject established religious organisation and to favour a more spiritual outlook. This made his existence more difficult: he was expelled from Strasbourg in 1531 and from Ulm in 1532 (where wrote most of his books, including the *Weltbuch* of 1534), eventually settling down anonymously with his wife and six children in 1541 in Basel. His ideas are scattered through a variety of writings, which covered a surprising range of themes, religious, historical (the *Chronica, Zeytbuch und geschycht*, Strasbourg 1531, and *Germaniae Chronicon*, Augsburg 1538) and cosmographic. He is best known as one of the earliest consistent supporters of pacifism, a firm opponent of all persecution. His ideas have been viewed as pantheistic; they were certainly universal, making him almost unique in his day, and a major forerunner of subsequent philosophical ideas. He believed that there is no true Church, but that all churches have some of the truth: 'anyone who wishes me well and can bear with me is my brother, whether Papist, Lutheran, Zwinglian, Anabaptist or Turk'. LUTHER called him 'the mouth of the devil'. He is also outstanding as a radical who never sought followers nor founded a sect. His writings had some influence on the evolution of German prose.

Frederick I Hohenzollern (1657–1713) elector of Brandenburg 1688–1713 (as Frederick III), king of Prussia 1701–13 (as Frederick I). Born in Königsberg, third son of the Great Elector and of Louise of Orange, his most memorable achievement was securing the consent of the emperor LEOPOLD I, in exchange for military aid, to him adopting the title of 'king' in his territory of Prussia. He was crowned king in Königsberg (1701) with Lutheran and Calvinist clergy officiating; from this date, the name 'Prussia' was given officially to all the state of Brandenburg-Prussia. His second wife Sophia Charlotte, whom he married in 1684, was daughter of ERNST AUGUSTUS of Hanover, and gave him valuable support in his ambitious but expensive cultural enterprises. The great cultural advances of his reign included the founding of the university of Halle (1694), of the Academy of Arts (1696), and of the Academy of Sciences, founded in 1700 by Sophia Charlotte with the help of Leibniz. Despite Frederick's support for Germanisation, the official language of the court was French. The king was also a supporter of religious union among Protestants. His shifting military alliances, based on the extensive territorial interests of Prussia, involved him deeply in both western and eastern politics. He aimed to separate Prussia from its dependence on the Empire: in 1701 he prohibited appeals beyond Brandenburg's courts, and in 1702 set up a supreme court in Berlin. He joined the Grand Alliance of European powers against France in 1702 during the war of the Spanish Succession; and in 1709 proposed to Russia a partition of Poland.

Frederick III of Habsburg (1415–93) emperor 1440–93. From 1424 he had been duke of Styria with the title of Frederick V; elected to succeed his cousin Albert II as emperor in 1440, he journeyed to Rome to receive the Imperial crown (1452). Under him the Habsburg lands began their extension, with his inheritance of Upper and Lower Austria in 1457; and the marriage of his son MAXIMILIAN I OF HABSBURG into the house of Burgundy.

Frederick III the Wise (1463–1525) elector of Saxony 1486–1525. The eldest son of elector Ernst of Saxony, he succeeded to the title on his father's death; Ernst's will had stipulated that he should rule jointly with his brother Johann, which he did, though as dominant partner. He played a key role in agreeing to the election of CHARLES V as emperor in 1519. The emergence of LUTHER in Saxon territory was fated to give Frederick a major role in the evolution of the Reformation. Though a firm Catholic (with one of the most famous collection of saints' relics in his castle church at Wittenberg), he was concerned to protect the rights of his Saxon subjects and of his new university at Wittenberg (1502). He was also a patron of humanism, and stepped carefully between the conflicting religious tendencies. He therefore assured Luther protection to the Diet of Worms (1521) as well as after it, in his castle at Wartburg. Beyond protection, however, he extended no favours to the reformer, and never spoke to him personally. On the other hand, he connived at the introduction of Reformed practices in some of his territories, and took communion in both kinds on his deathbed.

Frederick V of Wittelsbach (1596–1632) elector Palatine 1610–23, king of Bohemia 1619–20. Son of the elector Frederick IV, he was educated as a Calvinist at the Huguenot academy in Sedan, then lived in the household of the duke de Bouillon (1605–12) in France. In 1613 he married ELIZABETH STUART, daughter of JAMES I of England; she brought a new elegance to the electoral court in Heidelberg, the active centre of German Calvinism. Nominal ruler since the death of his father, he was proclaimed of age in 1614 and began to rule personally. But he had poor political judgement, and was easily led by his advisers, notably prince CHRISTIAN, prince of Anhalt-Bernburg. In 1619 he accepted the crown of Bohemia from the Czech rebel nobility, the first act in the evolution of the Thirty Years War. His Bohemian forces were defeated by Imperial and Spanish troops at the battle of the White Mountain a year later (1620). Put to the ban of Empire by Imperial decree, he was deprived of his title, which was passed to Bavaria (1623), ruled by another branch of the Wittelsbach family. One part of his lands (the Rhine Palatinate) was occupied by Spanish troops and the other (the Upper Palatinate) was granted permanently to Bavaria (1628). Forced to live the rest of his life with his family in exile, mainly in The Hague, he died of fever while passing incognito through the Palatinate; his burial site has never been found.

Frederick Henry, prince of Orange and count of Nassau (1584–1647) stadtholder of the United Provinces 1625–47. The youngest son of WILLIAM I and successor to his half-brother MAURICE of Nassau, he was first the first stadholder to assume semi-monarchic powers. Educated at the university of Leiden and made a member of the council of state at the age of seventeen, he began to take part in most of Maurice's military expeditions and was sent on various foreign missions. During the serious politico-religious conflict between Remonstrants and Counter-Remonstrants in the years of the Synod of Dort 1618–19, he did not get involved, and continued his tolerant policies after coming to power. A woman-loving bachelor, he promised the dying Maurice to marry for dynastic reasons, and did so; his marriage to the attractive Amalia of Solms helped to create at The Hague a lively semi-royal court that enhanced the cultural and social standing of the republic. In politics he tended to promote his direct control, through the council of state and the States General, over the administration and foreign policy of each of the provinces, which in theory were autonomous republics but soon came to form passive components of a semi-monarchic regime. In 1631 his offices were made hereditary, and in 1637 the States gave him the title 'Highness'. He vigorously pursued the war against Spain, with a spectacular capture of 's Hertogenbosch (1629); in 1637 Breda was recovered. But the period after 1640 was less successful. His last diplomatic success was the marriage in 1641 between his heir, WILLIAM II, and Mary, the eldest daughter of CHARLES I of Great Britain. Thereafter the pressure for peace with Spain became irresistible, but he died shortly before the signing of the peace agreements (treaty of Westphalia 1648) that recognised the independence of the United provinces.

Frederick Louis, prince of Wales (1707–51) eldest son of GEORGE II of Great Britain and of queen Caroline. Born in Hanover, he was later created duke of Gloucester and duke of Edinburgh. He arrived in England for the first time in 1728 and was created prince of Wales, but the open hostility shown to him by the other members of his family, especially his father, marked his entire career. As the prospective heir, he operated an alternative court, and with Bubb Dodington as his chief adviser opposed the ministerial policies of WALPOLE. He especially resented his father's frustration of his marriage plans, and refusal to give him what he considered an adequate income. In 1737 the king announced an open split with his son, whose home thereafter became the focus of opposition politicians. A gambler and profligate, he also patronised the arts. He died suddenly after the bursting of an abscess caused by a blow from a tennis ball.

Frederick William of Hohenzollern (1620–88) 'the Great Elector', margrave and elector of Brandenburg 1640–88. Born in Berlin, eldest son of the elector GEORGE WILLIAM OF HOLLENZOLLORN, he spent his most formative years in Holland (1634–8) where he studied briefly at Leiden and was trained at the court of FREDERICK HENRY (whose daughter he

married) to appreciate the art, commercial expertise and military science of the Dutch. On succeeding his father as elector, out of the ruins of the Thirty Years War he created the orderly state of Brandenburg–Prussia based on firm regional control, and regular taxation. His key instrument was a new standing army, which he based on Dutch models, and which was given both an administrative and a military role. He established his political power in each of his regions by firm agreements with the ruling nobility and towns: the Recess of 1653 confirmed his authority in Brandenburg, and in the 1670s Prussia also gave in after strong pressure on the city of Königsberg. At the peace of Westphalia (1648) he obtained control of most of the southern coast of the Baltic; with his other extensive lands, this made him into the greatest territorial lord in Germany after the Habsburgs. At the peace of Oliva (1660) he freed his duchy of Prussia from Polish control, but with the treaty of St Germain (1679) he retained only a part of Swedish Pomerania (which he had won from the Swedes after a small but significant victory over them at Fehrbellin in 1675). During these wars, he managed to change sides repeatedly, while drawing subsidies from the major European states, particularly France. An active Calvinist, he welcomed Huguenot refugees expelled from France in 1685 (Edict of Potsdam); but he also tolerated the other Christian faiths in territories where they were the majority. By his support for culture, economic enterprise and commerce, he laid the foundations for Prussian power.

Frederick William I of Hohenzollern (1688–1740) 'the soldier king' of Prussia 1713–40. Son of FREDERICK I HOHENZOLLERN (1657–1713), who was the first elector of Brandenburg to become king of Prussia (1701), he grew up quick-tempered, spartan and with a passion for the military. He had firm authoritarian ideas and an enthusiasm for order. These traits were put into action when he took over the government on his father's death in 1713. Setting aside any concern for arts and letters, he devoted his entire energy and that of the state to administrative and military organisation. The army was professionalised, officered by nobles, and standardised in uniform, discipline and armament; to support it, a substantial war chest was created, and a Prussian spirit inculcated. By the end of his reign the army had doubled in size to become perhaps the third largest in Europe, but curiously the king was deeply committed to a peaceful foreign policy, participating only in the last stages of the Great Northern War against Sweden, as a result of which Prussia gained part of Pomerania (1720). In 1722 he restructured the state administration, and put the major communal services (post, customs) of the various territories under centralised financial control. A professional civil service was created. Decisions were made by the king rather than by regional bodies. It was the first step taken in the German lands towards an efficient, absolutist state. Brutish in his personal habits, and much given to drink and the company of soldiers, in religion he became an adept of the Pietist tendency, which originated in his university of Halle. He inevitably had severe problems in his domestic life, with his wife Sophia Dorothea of Hanover, daughter of GEORGE I of Great Britain, whom he married 1706, and with his eldest son and heir Frederick (later 'the Great') whom he considered effeminate.

Frederik I of Denmark (1471–1533) king of Denmark and Norway 1523–33. Younger son of Christian I, he became king in 1523 after a revolt of the nobles of Jutland and the consequent deposition of Christian II, his nephew; he also in 1524 accepted the throne of Norway. His reign is significant for the introduction of the Lutheran Reformation from 1526.

Frederik I of Sweden (1676–1751) king 1720–51. Son of the landgrave of Hesse-Kassel, in 1715 he married ULRIKE LEONORA, sister of CHARLES XII VASA, and acceded to the throne when she resigned her rights in his favour. After a generation of war, he brought peace to Sweden by treaties with Denmark and Russia (Nystad 1721), but had to surrender the Baltic provinces of Livonia and Estonia to the latter.

Frederik II of Denmark (1534–88) king of Denmark and Norway 1559–88. Son of Christian III (ruled 1534–59), he provoked the northern war against Sweden (1563–70), in which he hoped to recover lost territories, but failed to make any gains (peace of Stettin 1570). He devoted the rest of the reign to a peaceful consolidation of the Danish state and Danish commercial control through the revenues from the Sound.

Frescobaldi, Girolamo (1583–1643) Italian composer and organist. He was the foremost organ virtuoso of the early Baroque, whose works exerted profound influence throughout Europe, including on J.S. BACH. Following his musical training at the court of Ferrara, he gained the post of organist at St Peter's in Rome (1608) and was supported by the most prominent Roman ecclesiastical patrons. His organ works (toccatas, canzonas, ricercars, variations, dances and settings for the Catholic service) exhibit unprecedented instrumental virtuosity, yet elaborate compositional mastery and a highly expressive approach. He also composed outstanding vocal works.

[JE]

Froben, Hieronymus (1501–63) German printer. Eldest son of Johann FROBEN, he was educated at the university of Basel, and travelled widely in Europe. Under him the firm consolidated its position, achieving great success with its sales at the Frankfurt fair, and specialising in the collected works of selected authors. Notable among its products were the edition

(1538–40) of the collected works of Erasmus, whom he had persuaded to return to Basel and who lived in his house until his death.

Froben, Johann (*c*.1460–1527) German printer. He came from north of Würzburg but settled in Basel in 1490 and founded there one of the greatest printing presses of northern Europe. Beginning with publication of a Latin Bible in 1491, the press moved on to publish editions of interest to Renaissance learning, including works by ERASMUS (*Adagia*, 1513). His editions were notable for their clear layout and use of engravings. Though he published LUTHER in 1518, Johann was soon persuaded by Erasmus to desist from printing works by the reformers.

Frobisher, Sir Martin (1535–94) English sea captain. He went to sea at nineteen, then took part during the next ten years in regular voyages round the Mediterranean. When the Muscovy Company showed interest in exploring the possibility of a north-west passage, he led three expeditions (1576, 1577, 1578) towards the Arctic, with little positive result. He took part in DRAKE's expedition to the West Indies in 1585, and commanded the *Triumph* against the Spaniards in the 1588 Armada campaign, when he was knighted. Promoted to vice-admiral, he helped in the campaigns of HENRY IV of France against the Spaniards, and died of wounds near Brest.

Fugger A family of bankers based in Augsburg, whose fortunes were founded by Hans Fugger (d.1408). The family was divided into two main branches: the 'vom Reh' (of the deer), founded by the eldest son of Hans, Andreas (d.1457), and the 'von der Lilie' (of the lily), founded by the second son of Hans, Jakob (d.1469, father of Jakob II).

Jakob II Fugger (1459–1525) German banker who went to Italy to study finance methods, he took charge of the Fuggers in Innsbruck in 1485, and became chief financier to the Habsburg emperors, aiding crucially in the election of CHARLES V to the imperial title in 1519; in return, the Habsburgs rewarded the family with titles and land, on the basis of which the Fuggers became feudal lords with vast possessions and palaces, their economic interests centring on mining and trade. In 1514 Jakob was created a count of the empire. To keep the various branches of the Fugger empire informed about news that might affect their interests, the family patronised the famous Fugger Newsletters.

Anton Fugger (1493–1560) Nephew of Jakob II, he succeeded his childless uncle at the head of the business, maintaining the investments in landed wealth that protected the family against the major losses contracted through loans to Charles V and PHILIP II. A firm Catholic, he tried to maintain good relations with Protestant interests, but also had close links with the new Jesuit order and supported the preaching of Peter CANISIUS in Augsburg.

G

Gabrieli, Giovanni (*c.*1553–1612) Italian composer and organist. He was the foremost Venetian composer of the late Renaissance and the nephew of Andrea Gabrieli (1515–86), a celebrated Venetian composer and organist. After several years at the Bavarian court, under the musical direction of Orlando di Lasso, he returned to Venice in the early 1680s. There he held the posts of organist at St Mark's and at the confraternity of Scuola Grande di S. Rocco. His numerous vocal and instrumental works were largely written for the sumptuous religious ceremonies in Venice. These include Latin polychoral motets (for voices and instruments) and purely instrumental ensembles of immense diversity of contrasting, stereophonic-like sonorities. Apart from his reputation as an outstanding teacher (Heinrich SCHÜTZ was among his students), he exerted enormous influence in Italy and abroad throughout the seventeenth century.

[JE]

Gabrielle d'Estrées (1573–99) French court lady. Daughter of a leading military administrator and governor of the Ile-de-France, she got to know HENRY IV during a visit by the king to Picardy. Henry made her his mistress, giving her the titles of marquise de Montceaux (1595) and subsequently duchess de Beaufort (1597). For appearance's sake he married her off to a court noble, but then conceived the desire to marry her himself; she died shortly after, rumour averring that it was by poison. Her three sons by Henry were legitimised by him; one, César, founded the Vendôme family. Gabrielle's brother François had a distinguished career in both Church and state, and was created duke d'Estrées in 1648.

Gainsborough, Thomas (1722–88) English painter of portraits, landscapes and 'fancy pictures'. A founding member of the Royal Academy (1768), he was the son of a clothier and crêpe-maker who, having gone bankrupt (1733), had become a postmaster. After some preliminary training in his native Suffolk, he went to London (1740), and studied under the French engraver Gravelot, from whom he received the indirect influence of WATTEAU. He was then active as portrait painter of the country gentry in East Anglia (1748–50) and Ipswich (1752–9), also receiving a commission from the duke of Bedford for a pair of landscapes for Woburn Abbey. After moving to Bath (1759), he was privileged to see the Van Dycks at Wilton House (Wiltshire), an experience that changed his manner almost entirely. His direct copy of Van Dyck's double portrait of *Lords John and Bernard Stuart* (St Louis Art Museum) shows the depth of his admiration, while his own brilliant portraits of *The Hon. Mrs. Graham* (1777; Edinburgh) *Johann*

Christian Bach (1766) and the so-called *Blue Boy* (San Marino) are illustrative of his new manner, continued after his return to London in 1774. Despite his rivalry with his fellow Academician, Sir Joshua REYNOLDS, it was Reynolds who wrote a moving eulogy when Gainsborough died in 1788.

[JH]

Galilei, Galileo (1564–1642) Italian astronomer and physicist. Born at Pisa, he became professor of mathematics there from 1589; after a brief stay in Florence he moved to a chair at Padua, and then, in 1610, back to Florence as philosopher and mathematician to the Grand Duke. Even before his appointment at Pisa he discovered the isochronicity of the swings of pendulums, later applied to clock-making; devices he designed included the first thermometer. In the academic sphere he was embroiled in controversy from an early stage because of his criticisms of Aristotle. He responded to the invention of the telescope by constructing one of the first that was powerful enough to show features of the Moon's surface, the phases of the planets Venus and Mars, sunspots, previously unknown fixed stars, and four satellites of Jupiter. In 1610 he described these observations in *Siderius nuncius* (The Starry Messenger) and interpreted them as favouring the ideas of Copernicus; in reaction to another treatise claiming that sunspots revealed the Sun's rotation, he was warned by the church authorities that to hold or defend Copernican beliefs would henceforth be regarded as heretical. When his *Dialogo sopra i due massime sistemi del mondo* (Dialogue on the Two Chief Systems of the World) appeared in 1632, it was clear that he had paid little heed to the warning; a trial before the Inquisition concluded with his recantation. He spent his last years under house arrest, and his last major work (on 'the two new sciences') was printed in Holland.

[FW]

Gallas, Matthias (1584–1647) count of Campo, duke of Lucera. He became prominent as an officer in the Thirty Years War, and attached himself to WALLENSTEIN, under whom he served with distinction. Later he turned against his commander and helped to bring about his fall, in reward for which he received from the emperor FERDINAND II Wallenstein's estates of Friedland and a generalship in the Imperial army. He played a principal part in the victory at Nördlingen (1634), but subsequent campaigns were less successful. An Imperial invasion he led into Burgundy in 1636 turned into a disastrous retreat. Another invasion, this time of Denmark in 1644, also ended in withdrawal and the loss of many men, as a result of which Gallas was dismissed as commander.

Galway, Henri de Massue, marquis de Ruvigny, 1st earl of (1648–1720) A notable Huguenot soldier who served in the group of officers under marshal TURENNE, 1672–5, and took part in a diplomatic mission to England, at the time of the Revocation of the Edict of Nantes (1685), he chose to emigrate with his family to England, and was eventually settled with lands in Ireland. He served in the English army as major general of horse, took part in the Irish campaign against the forces of the former king JAMES II, and was in 1692 created viscount Galway. He served in campaigns against the French in Savoy in 1694, and was created earl in 1697. Appointed to lead the allied forces in the peninsula during the war of the Spanish Succession, he was decisively defeated by BERWICK at the battle of Almansa (1707), and retired to Ireland, where he served as a lord justice.

Gama, Vasco da, 1st count da Gama (1469–1524) Portuguese navigator. Son of a nobleman, he was active in naval matters from at least 1492. In 1497 he led a naval expedition of four vessels to seek a sea route to India, rounded the cape of

Good Hope (discovered shortly before by Bartholomeu DIAS), touching at various points of the east African coast, and reached Calicut (India) in May 1498, making him the first European captain to reach Asia by sea. Showered by honours on his return and appointed admiral, in 1502 he led a new expedition of twenty one ships, made landfall in Mozambique, and arrived in India. The expedition this time was explicitly aggressive: Gama's instructions were to secure Portuguese control of sea-routes, expel the Arabs, and subject native kingdoms in Africa and India; he carried out these instructions with notable brutality. After his return to Portugal he received no further commissions. Appointed viceroy of Portuguese India in 1524, he arrived at his post only to die shortly after, in Cochin; in 1538 his body was taken back to Portugal. Gama's exploits are the central theme of CAMOENS' literary classic Os Lusiads.

Gardiner, Stephen (c.1483–1555) English ecclesiastic. Educated at Cambridge, where he became a fellow and obtained doctorates in civil and canon law, from 1524 he became tutor to the duke of Norfolk's son, and then private secretary to WOLSEY. In 1528 he was chosen by HENRY VIII to go to Rome and seek annulment of the king's marriage to CATHERINE OF ARAGON. As a reward for his work he was appointed bishop of Winchester (1531), serving thereafter as ambassador to France and to Germany. A supporter of the royal supremacy (defended in his De vera obedientia of 1535), he remained always a firm Catholic, opposing the policies of Thomas CROMWELL and the drift towards Protestantism. He and the Norfolk grouping maintained the Catholic complexion of the royal council under Henry VIII. Under EDWARD VI he was imprisoned for most of the reign in the Tower, and deprived of his see (1551), but was reinstated by MARY I and created lord chancellor. Though disagreeing with the queen's marriage to Philip of Spain, he

directed the legal measures that restored the old religion. He was subsequently reviled by Protestant writers for presiding over the courts which condemned heretics, but claimed that he was simply carrying out orders and that 'it was not my doing'.

Garrick, David (1717–79) English actor. From a family of Huguenot stock, he went to school in Lichfield and in 1737 travelled to London with his school-teacher, Samuel JOHNSON. In the city he took part as an actor in amateur theatre performances to the detriment of his business as a wine merchant. From 1741 he achieved popularity for his interpretation of Richard III and other roles, principally from Shakespeare, in theatres at Drury Lane and Covent Garden. In 1763, rich and famous, he made a long trip to the continent, mainly Italy, for a year and a half. His death, aggravated by gout and herpes, was claimed by Dr Johnson to have 'eclipsed the gaiety of nations'. His pall was borne by the chief men of his day, and he was buried in Westminster Abbey, the first actor to be so honoured.

Gassendi (Gassend), Pierre (1592–1655) French philosopher and scientist. Having taken holy orders, he became a canon and from 1634 Provost of Digne; for a brief period, 1645–48, he was professor of mathematics at the Collège Royal, Paris. He studied natural philosophy from an early age, adhered to the cause of the 'Moderns' and publicly criticised many aspects of Aristotelianism in Exercitationum paradoxicarum adversus Aristoteleos libri septem (1624 and later editions under variant titles). After closely examining the ideas of Epicurus, he came to support atomism and the associated mechanical view of the behaviour of matter; he argued that Nature should be explained in terms of directly measurable properties and actions and that, properly conducted, such studies were fully compatible with Christianity. His few significant practical contributions to knowledge included a fairly accurate estimate of the speed of sound and observations of a solar transit of the planet Mercury. His literary contribution was probably more important, with biographies of ancient and modern colleagues – including Epicurus, COPERNICUS and Tycho BRAHE – amongst his best known works.

[FW]

Gaston-Jean-Baptiste, duke d'Orléans (1608–60) The third son of HENRY IV and brother of LOUIS XIII, he enjoyed several ducal titles before becoming duke d'Orléans in 1621 and distinguished himself by participating in virtually all the plots organised by nobles against the chief ministers of the crown. He took part in the Chalais conspiracy (1626), the MONTMORENCY rebellion (1632), the Cinq-Mars plot (1642) and the intrigues of MARIE DE MÉDICIS in her exile. In each case his royal blood saved him from punishment. On the death of Louis XIII he became a member of the regency government and lieutenant-general of the armies of the crown, serving well in the Flanders campaigns. But he continued to plot against cardinal MAZARIN and the regency, and during the Fronde (1648–51) was also implicated in rebellion. After the Fronde he was exiled from the court to his castle in Blois, where he died. His daughter Anne-Marie-Louise, later known as 'la Grande Mademoiselle', played an active part in the events of the Fronde.

Gattinara, Mercurino Arborio di (1465–1530) Savoyard statesman. Eldest son of a noble family of Piedmont, he was educated in law and obtained his doctorate from the university of Turin in 1493. When the duke of Savoy married the Habsburg MARGARET OF AUSTRIA in 1501, he was retained as a legal adviser to the duchess, and rose subsequently in the service of the Habsburg family. Margaret was appointed governor of the Netherlands on the death of her brother

PHILIP THE FAIR, and in reward for his services Gattinara was in 1508 appointed president of the parlement of Dôle (Franche-Comté). At the same time he acted for Margaret in arranging the conditions under which the future CHARLES V would succeed to the Spanish inheritance. When Charles later went to Spain, Gattinara was in 1518 appointed as his chancellor on the death of the previous holder of the office, Jean Le Sauvage. From this time, he played a crucial role in the policies of Charles' dominions, travelling with his master and guiding the administration. He promoted an actively anti-French stance, preferring rather the interests of the Mediterranean states, Italy and Spain. Meanwhile he accumulated estates and honours, and even acquired a cardinalate (1529). Travelling from Italy to be present at the Diet of Augsburg, he fell ill and died at Innsbruck. He was an enthusiastic supporter of ERASMUS, expressing to the latter in 1526 the belief that Erasmians – and not Lutherans or papists – were the true orthodox party. He also supported Dante's view of a Christian monarchy, and was the main inspirer of Charles V's ideas on the concept of imperial power.

Gentileschi, Artemesia (1593–1652/3) Italian painter. Daughter of the painter Orazio Gentileschi, who was a well-known follower of CARAVAGGIO, she learned her art from her father. In 1611, he apprenticed her to Agostino Tassi, a fellow painter associated with him in a number of commissions. Tassi raped her and then promised marriage, but when it never materialised, her father took him to court. After a five month trial in which her testimony was verified by means of torture with thumbscrews, he was finally acquitted although he had spent eight months in prison. One month after the trial, she married Pietro Antonio di Vincenzo Stiattesi and moved to Florence where she remained until 1620. There she joined the Accademia del Disegno in

1616 and was among the artists who decorated the Casa Buonarroti in 1617. She spent most of the 1620s in Rome and by August 1630 she had transferred to Naples, where she worked for the next two decades – with a visit to London to assist her father and then arrange affairs after his death in 1639. Her important and distinctive work is distinguished by her dramatic subjects, especially the biblical and mythological heroines who dominate her canvasses, such as Judith, Susanna, Lucretia, Bathsheba, Cleopatra, Esther and Diana.

George I (Georg I Ludwig) (1660–1727) elector of Hanover 1698–1727, king of Great Britain and Ireland 1714–27. Son of ERNST AUGUSTUS, first elector of Hanover, and of SOPHIA, grand-daughter of JAMES I of England, in 1682 he married his cousin Sophia Dorothea, whom he divorced in 1694 on the grounds of her infidelity (with the adventurous count Philip von Königsmark, who disappeared mysteriously) and had locked up till her death. Elector since 1698, he inherited further territories including the duchies of Bremen and Verden (1715–19), and in 1714 was called to the English throne on the death of queen ANNE STUART, as the most direct heir laid down by the Act of Settlement of 1701. A capable general, he served throughout his career in several campaigns. He went to England in 1714, entrusting political affairs exclusively to the Whig party under STANHOPE and WALPOLE. He did not like England, never learnt the language properly, and spent as much time as possible in Germany; he also detested his son George, prince of Wales, who was expelled from the palace in 1717. His reign was a period of important developments that, despite the scandal of the South Sea Bubble in 1720, established Whig supremacy and began Britain's role as a world power.

George II (Georg II Augustus) (1683–1760) elector of Hanover and king of Great Britain and Ireland 1727–60. Son of GEORGE I and of Sophia Dorothea, unlike his father (whom he detested) he displayed his affection for England, but in his turn he had serious disagreements with his son, Frederick the prince of Wales, in the period 1737–42. In his father's reign he and his comely wife Caroline of Ansbach (married 1705) set up a rival court at Leicester House. As king, he actively supported the Whigs under WALPOLE and under the PELHAMS, while participating closely in the politics of Hanover. The last English king to lead his troops personally into battle, he helped them to rout the French at Dettingen (1743), but his armies were defeated at Fontenoy (1745) and Lauffeld (1747) and he was obliged to agree to the treaty of Aix-la-Chapelle (1748). In the subsequent Seven Years War his forces under his son CUMBERLAND did even worse. However, in Britain the threat from the Scots Jacobites, who had penetrated well into England as a result of their advance in 1745, was demolished by the royal forces under Cumberland, which scored a victory at Culloden (1746). In America and in India during his reign significant gains were made at French expense, which consolidated British supremacy in those territories.

George William of Hohenzollern (1595–1640) margrave and elector of Brandenburg 1619–40. He was son of elector John Sigismund I, who had converted to Calvinism in 1613. His sister was married to GUSTAV II ADOLF VASA of Sweden, and he married the sister of the elector Palatine (FREDERICK V OF WITTELSBACH), dynastic links that governed the direction of the Thirty Years War, a conflict in which the scattered territories of Brandenburg were particularly vulnerable. He was also advised, however, by the Catholic noble Adam zu Schwarzenberg, who persuaded him, from 1627 onwards, to ally with the emperor. During the period of Swedish predominance (from 1631 up to the battle of Nördlingen, 1634) he was obliged to side with the Protestants, but immediately after he agreed with the emperor the peace of Prague (1635), which aimed to create a common German front against foreign forces. In 1638 he went to reside in Königsberg, where he died.

Gérard, Balthasar (1558–84) assassin. A native of Vuillafans (Franche-Comté), he was in Delft in the Netherlands shortly after 1578, and apparently on his own account decided to avail himself of the reward offered by the Spanish government for the assassination of WILLIAM I of Orange. He obtained an audience with the prince in July 1584 and fired two pistol shots at point-blank range, mortally wounding him. Tried for his crime, he was executed two weeks later. PHILIP II rewarded his family and gave them perpetual exemption from taxes, but the privilege was revoked when Franche-Comté passed under French sovereignty a century later.

Gesualdo, Carlo (*c*.1561–1613) prince of Venosa, Italian composer. The tempestuous events of his life have been romanticised in numerous literary works. Shortly after inheriting the principality of Venosa (1586) he assassinated his wife and her lover upon discovering them '*in flagrante delicto*'. His subsequent marriage to Leonora d'Este of Ferrara (1593) also proved to be luckless. Suffering from long spans of melancholia, he ended his life in seclusion at his estate in Gesualdo. As a nobleman, his choice of a musical career was certainly exceptional. He was actively involved in the renowned musical establishment at Ferrara and acquainted with outstanding musicians in Naples, Rome, Florence and Venice. Although he composed numerous sacred vocal works, he is known particularly for his six books of madrigals, whose highly individual qualities are thought to have reflected his melancholic personality. They have often been characterised as 'manneristic', due to

their morbid texts, excessive chromaticism and erratic changes of mood.

[JE]

Gibbons, Orlando (1583–1625) English composer and organist. Born in Cambridge, he began his career as a chorister at King's College (1596–8). Later on he was awarded the degrees of Mus.B. at Cambridge and D.Mus. at Oxford. He was appointed Gentleman and organist of the Chapel Royal (*c*.1602), as well as organist at Westminster Abbey and the King's Private Musick. A monument in his memory was erected in Canterbury cathedral, where his untimely death occurred during the welcome ceremonies of CHARLES I to queen Henrietta Maria. His works for the Anglican Church rank among the finest of the period. They include anthems and verses for multiple voices, which display remarkable originality in overall design and dramatic quality. His music for the keyboard and viol consorts ranges from the most intricate contrapuntal works to delightful dances (e.g. the famous pavan and galliard 'Lord Salisbury').

[JE]

Gilbert, Sir Humphrey (*c*.1539–83) English explorer. Devon-born, he was educated at Oxford. His widowed mother remarried (1547) and became the mother of Walter RALEIGH. He served in the French civil wars (1562), then 1566–70 played an important part in the brutal English military settlement of Ireland, and was knighted (1570) for his work. An MP in 1571, he served briefly in Flanders in 1572, but his thoughts were chiefly on his scheme for seeking a north-west passage to Asia, for which he received a charter in 1578. After a first disastrous expedition in 1578 (accompanied by Raleigh), he undertook another in 1583, during which he successfully planted the first English colony in north America, at St John, Newfoundland. The ships on this occasion lost contact with each other, and

Gilbert in his *Squirrel* disappeared some-where north of the Azores.

Gilbert, William (1540–1603) English physician and student of magnetism. Born in Colchester (Essex), which still cele-brates him as one of its most famous sons, he proceeded M.D. in 1569, whilst a fellow of St John's College, Cambridge. He became president of the College of Physicians in 1599, and served as physi-cian to Elizabeth I and her successor James I. His *De magnete* (1600) was to prove one of the most influential natural-philosophical works of the new century; it systematically examined the properties of magnets, set out the theory that the globe itself behaves as a large magnet, and des-cribed the electricity created by rubbing substances such as amber. The methods by which these investigations were carried out and presented were hailed by later proponents of experimental method, such as those of the early Royal Society, as a model for their own activities.

[FW]

Glanvill, Joseph (1636–80) English thin-ker. Born in Plymouth, he was educated at Oxford, then became rector in Frome and later (1666) in the abbey at Bath. He was appointed chaplain to CHARLES II from 1672. He is best known for his *The Vanity of Dogmatizing* (1661), which defended the experimental method for pursuing knowledge and attacked scholas-tic dogmatism. In his other writings he insisted on the validity of all methods of observation, and by extension he affirmed the reality of witchcraft because it was an observed phenomenon.

Godolphin, Sidney, 1st earl of (1645–1712) Brought up in the royal household of CHARLES II, he held various household posts, entered Parliament (1668), and served in the last government of Charles, when he was created baron. Under JAMES II he remained a supporter of the king to the last. He participated in the govern-ment of WILLIAM III and was responsible for important financial measures such as the foundation of the Bank of England (1694). From 1691 he was also in contact with the Jacobites abroad. In 1700 he headed a Tory ministry when the Whigs fell, and in 1702 headed the first govern-ment under queen ANNE STUART, in close alliance with MARLBOROUGH (to whose daughter his only son was married). He was created earl in 1706. In 1710, after trying vainly to work with a mixed Tory–Whig ministry at the height of the war of the Spanish Succession, he resigned.

Godunov, Boris Fyodorovich (1551–1605) tsar of Russia 1598–1605. He rose to prominence as one of the supporters of IVAN IV in the 1560s. The heir to the throne married his sister (1574), and shortly after Boris was made a boyar (1580). When the heir became tsar as Fyodor I, Boris occupied a prominent place in the government, and in 1587 became supreme in the state. Rumours then and later accused him of murdering the then heir to the throne, Fyodor's half-brother DMITRI, which left the tsar without an heir. On Fyodor's death, Boris became tsar (1598). Historians have usually con-sidered him an efficient ruler. He regu-lated the social structure of Muscovy by increasing the privileges of landowners and strengthening the bonds of serfdom, which he extended also into the urban areas. He attempted to secure the fron-tiers of Russian territory beyond the Urals and in the Caucasus. His rule was threa-tened persistently by the rise of the pseudo-DMITRIS, who were supported by dissident nobles. The conflicts and foreign intervention of the next few years are known in Russian history as the Time of Troubles (1598–1613). A few weeks after his death, an uprising in Moscow put an end to the rule of his son Fyodor, who had succeeded him as tsar.

Goes, Damião de (1502–74) Portuguese humanist. Born in Alenquer of lower nobility, he entered the court of king Manoel I as a page and was profoundly influenced by the rich cultural experiences there. In 1523 he was sent to Antwerp as secretary of the India house, which controlled outlets for Portugal's trade with Asia. At the same time he was employed all over Europe on diplomatic missions, during which he met LUTHER and MEL-ANCHTHON. Contact with scholars in the Netherlands inclined him to change his career for that of a humanist. In 1531 he entered the university of Louvain as a student, and travelled to Freiburg to meet ERASMUS, with whom he developed a friendship. In 1534 he went to Padua to study, and published there in 1538 a translation into Portuguese of Cicero. After a further long stay in the Netherlands he returned to Lisbon in 1545, and was appointed royal archivist and chronicler; his history of king Manoel's reign remains a fundamental source. In 1572 he was denounced by enemies for his old contacts with the German reformers, and imprisoned for a while.

Golitsyn, prince Vasily (1643–1714) Russian politician and reformer. Minister to tsar Fyodor III, under the subsequent regime of the regent SOFIA (1682–9) he exercised the reins of power. A cultivated and enlightened nobleman, he was one of the first Russians actively to encourage western influences, and had in mind a reform programme that included educational changes and full toleration of all religious beliefs. When supporters of PE-TER THE GREAT assumed power (1689) Golitsyn was dismissed and exiled to Arkhangelsk, where he died.

Gomarus (Goemaere), François (1563–1641) Dutch Protestant theologian. He was born in Bruges, but his parents were so attached to Calvinism that they preferred to live in the Palatinate, where they went in 1578. He was therefore educated in Neustadt, Heidelberg and Oxford, taking his doctorate in Heidelberg in 1584.

In 1594 he was invited to Leiden as professor of theology, where a few years later his differences of opinion with his colleague ARMINIUS unleashed a controversy that shook the Dutch state to its roots.

Gondomar, Diego Sarmiento de Acuña, count of (1567–1626) Spanish diplomat. Of Galician noble origin, he served both as soldier and as a senior administrator of finance, before being appointed in 1613 to his most famous role, that of Spanish ambassador to London. In England the suave diplomat surprisingly gained an ascendancy over JAMES I, influenced royal policies, and secured the execution of RALEIGH (1618). Gondomar left his mission that year, but was re-appointed in 1620, when Spain needed to assuage English hostility at the outbreak of the Thirty Years War. He also cultivated support for James' scheme of a marriage alliance between prince Charles and the infanta of Spain, and went back home in 1622 to further the arrangements; the failure of the talks during the secret visit of the prince to Spain in 1623 was in no way his fault. Aesthete and intellectual, he was the author of several proposals to introduce political and economic reforms into Spain.

Gonzaga, Charles I (1580–1637) first of the line of the house of Gonzaga-Nevers. The Gonzaga family were, from the fourteenth century, lords of Mantua. Federico II (1500–40) obtained from the emperor CHARLES V the erection of the marquisate of Mantua into a duchy (1530) and secured possession of the marquisate of Montferrat (1536). In 1627 a failure to produce male heirs led to the extinction of the senior Gonzaga line, and a dispute over the succession of Charles, Federico's grandson and duke of Nevers (a title inherited from his father in 1595). His claim, supported by France, was contested by that of the duke of Guastalla, Cesare Gonzaga, grandson of Federico's brother and client of the Habsburgs. The dispute over the strategically important duchy ended in the war for the Mantuan succession (1628–31), a dispute between France and Spain that ended in the peace of Cherasco (1631), which granted the duchy to Charles of Nevers, and obtained the key fortress of Pinerolo for France. On Charles' death the title passed to his grandson, Charles II, whose sister Anne Gonzaga (1616–84), known as the Princess Palatine through her marriage in 1645 to the count Palatine Edward, played an active role in the Fronde and in the French society of her day.

Gracián, Baltasar (1601–58) Spanish priest and man of letters. Born in Belmonte (Cuenca) he entered the Jesuit order at eighteen, studied in various Jesuit colleges and was ordained in 1627. He did not enjoy much of a reputation within the Aragonese province of the order, but he flourished under the tutelage and patronage of a highly educated nobleman, Vincencio Juan de Lastanosa, resident in Huesca. Gracián had a brilliant mind which he used to analyse contemporary patterns of social conduct. He worked on topics close to those cultivated by MA-CHIAVELLI, but with whom he did not agree. His advice to the social élite in power was, broadly, to remain aloof, watchful and distrustful. His hero was FERDINAND II OF TRASTÁMARA whom he commemorated in *El político don Fernando el Católico* (1640), while his general advice on social conduct is contained in *El discreto* (1646) and *El oráculo manual* (1647). His major and most abstruse work is *El criticón* (1651–7), a protracted and often dense allegorical narrative. It consists of a pilgrimage of two characters through contemporary scenery, learning, criticising, satirising. The lessons to be learnt are again aimed at those in power. They are not necessarily based on Christian doctrine, but are certainly coloured by the characteristic pessimism of the Counter-Reformation.

The book is written in an idiosyncratic, clipped style which he outlined in his *Agudeza y arte de ingenio* (1648), a handbook on the rhetoric of wit, a wit which relies on cerebral metaphors, neologisms, antitheses, subtle juxtapositions and double meanings. It is by this style, rather than content, that he is best known.

[BT]

Grandier, Urbain (1590–1634) French ecclesiastic. As parish priest of Loudun in France, he became notorious for his part in the affair of the Ursuline nuns of the convent at Loudun, who appointed him their spiritual supervisor. When arrested in 1633, he was accused of contributing to the alleged diabolic 'possession' of the nuns, and of having had carnal relations with some of them. The affair took on important dimensions because of RICHE-LIEU's intervention. The gravest charge finally levelled against Grandier was of diabolism: he was tortured and burnt alive at the stake.

Granvelle, Antoine Perrenot, lord of (1517–86) Franche-Comtois statesman. Son of Nicolas PERRENOT DE GRANVELLE, he was appointed bishop of Arras in 1538 and took holy orders two years later. From 1538 he was initiated into Imperial affairs by his father, whom he succeeded as effective head of the administration of CHARLES V. His efficiency appealed to PHILIP II, who employed him in the Netherlands as chief minister at the side of the governor, MARGARET OF PARMA, and obtained for him the archbishopric of Malines (1560) and a cardinal's hat (1561). His conflicts with the Netherlands nobility obliged Philip to let him retire to Franche-Comté in 1564. Shortly after, the king recalled him to service as minister in Rome and then as viceroy of Naples (1571–5), and finally as chief minister of Spain (1579), where Granvelle found himself frustrated in his attempts to pursue the policies he wished. Though an opponent of the Dutch rebels and of heresy, he supported preserving the constitution of the Netherlands. He also attempted, without success, to convince Philip II that French power must be destroyed. In 1584 he was appointed archbishop of Besançon, but remained in Spain, where he died shortly after. His legacy was an impressive palace he had built in Besançon, and a priceless collection of the state papers of his years as administrator.

Greco, El (Dominikos Theotocopoulos) (1541–1614) Cretan painter active in Spain. One of the last painters to work in the Mannerist style, El Greco ('the Greek') was born in Candia (modern Herakleion), where the Byzantine style was still current. In his late twenties (before 1570) he travelled to the Venetian Republic, where he was impressed by the work of Tintoretto. He next appeared in Rome, where his generous offer to repaint MICHELANGELO's *Last Judgement* was refused. Moving on to Spain (1577) he managed to alienate PHILIP II, who thoroughly disliked his *St Maurice and the Theban Legion*. He found his niche, however, in the smaller city of Toledo, which became his permanent home, and where his masterwork, the mural painting of *The Burial of Count Orgaz* (1588) can still be seen in the narthex of the church of Santo Tomas. Other major works from this period are the *Portrait of Cardinal Fernando Nino de Guevara*, head of the Inquisition (1600; New York); the *View of Toledo* (c.1610; New York); and the *Adoration of the Trinity*, based on a 1511 woodcut by DÜRER. His art soon seemed both provincial and superannuated beside that of young VELÁZQUEZ, whose activity began five years after El Greco's death. There was a spurt of interest in him on the part of the Romantic generation, who interpreted both his strangely elongated figures and reports of his difficult personality to mean that he must have been insane, and every few years brings an article from yet another twentieth-century ophthalmologist who has 'discovered' the artist's supposed astigmatism and grinds a pair of corrective spectacles capable of turning his wraith-like Madonnas into Rubenses. Comparison of his portraits with his holy figures, however, as can easily be done in the *Burial of Count Orgaz* where both are found together, reveals that his distortions were invariably purposeful, and are used in conjunction with the depiction of celestial space.

[JH]

Gregory XIII (Ugo Buoncampagni, 1502–85) pope 1572–85. The best known of his achievements was the reform of the old Julian calendar in 1582. Born and educated in Bologna, where he became professor of canon law (1531–9), he was employed by the papacy at the council of Trent (1561–3), created cardinal in 1565 and elected pope in 1572 to succeed PIUS V. A zealous promoter of reform in the Church, he particularly advanced the establishment of seminaries as urged by the council of Trent, and founded the Gregorian University in Rome. He helped the development of missions in the east, approved the constitutions of the new order of the Oratory (1614) and the reformed Carmelites (1580) and published a revised edition (1582) of the body of canon law. With the help of experts, in 1582 he decreed reforms in the previous calendar, drawn up by Julius Caesar in 46 BC. The new calendar, which came into force in October 1582, omitted ten days in order to bring the calendar into line with the solar year; the year was also to begin now on 1 January. The changes were accepted by Catholic states but not by Protestant ones, which adopted the new style only in the 1750s.

Gresham, Sir Thomas (c.1519–79) Educated at Cambridge, he was apprenticed under his uncle in the world of London finance and from 1543 was actively in business in the Netherlands. He was subsequently appointed the crown's agent in

Antwerp (1551–74), alternating his residence between that city and London, and combining his duties with that of diplomat, a role that earned him a knighthood (1559). His work, in the course of which he made himself rich, was directed to raising finance for the government, and promoting trade. In London he helped found a financial centre that in 1571 received the name Royal Exchange; he also founded a college in London. He did not personally formulate 'Gresham's Law', which holds that 'bad money drives out good', namely that when coins of equal face value but differing metal content are in circulation people will use the bad coin and hoard the good. Though based on Gresham's own writings, the 'law' was first stated by a British economist in the nineteenth century.

Grey, Lady Jane (1537–54) queen of England for nine days in 1553. Great-granddaughter of HENRY VII through her mother, and daughter of Henry Grey, marquis of Dorset and later duke of Suffolk, she was married (1553) by her father to lord Guildford Dudley, fourth son of EDWARD VI's chief minister John DUDLEY, the duke of Northumberland. The latter, wishing to avoid the succession of the Catholic Mary Tudor, persuaded the boy king to name Lady Jane as his heir. When Edward died, Jane was proclaimed queen by Northumberland; but Mary rallied her supporters successfully, and Jane (who was made to abdicate), her husband and her father were sent to the Tower. She and her family might have received mercy from MARY I's government, but Suffolk's implication in the rebellion led by Sir Thomas WYATT the Younger sealed their fate: Jane and her husband were executed. A young lady of talent and learning, she mastered Latin and Greek, and knew French, Italian and Hebrew; a strong Protestant, on the scaffold she denied ever wanting the crown and claimed that she died 'a true Christian woman'.

Griffenfeld, Peter Schumacher, count (1635–99) Son of a rich Danish merchant, he did the grand tour through Europe (1653–61) and on his return entered the administration, first as royal librarian (1663) then as secretary of the bedchamber (1665–70), rising to become member of the council of state. His great contribution was the drafting of the 1665 *Kongelov* (royal law), based on the theories of BODIN and GROTIUS, which established crown absolutism in Denmark. The substance of this law was reaffirmed in a later Danish law of 1683. Under king Christian V, Schumacher was ennobled as count (1670) and named chancellor (1674). When war broke out between Prussia and Sweden in 1675, Griffenfeld was blamed for the Swedish military reverses, forced to resign, then tried and sentenced to death (1676), a verdict commuted to life imprisonment; he died in prison in Norway.

Grimmelshausen, Hans Jakob von (c. 1621–76) German writer. When young, he was pressed into military service with the Imperial army during the Thirty Years War, but worked mainly as a clerk rather than a soldier. Born Lutheran, he became a Catholic during the war. After the war he continued in service as a clerk, then bought himself an inn and set up as a publican; thereafter he supplemented his income from beer with that from his writings about the war, and became mayor of the village of Renchen near Strasbourg. From 1666 to 1675 he published about twenty literary works, most of them with a didactic content. His *The Adventures of Simplicissimus* (1669), which described the hero's experiences during the Thirty Years' War, went through five editions by 1672, and was widely copied. Modelled on the Spanish picaresque novel, partly autobiographical and partly imaginary, it used satire and laughter to comment on human folly, attacking both cruelty and fanaticism. Of his other works, the best known is his

Landstörtzerin Courasche (*The Vagabond Courage*) (1670). Though often based on other literary sources rather than his own direct reporting, his writings have become the classic source for commentaries about the impact of war, and have directly influenced works such as Bertolt Brecht's play *Mother Courage*.

Grindal, Edmund (*c*.1519–83) Educated at Cambridge, he pursued a career at the university, and became an outstanding proponent of Protestant opinions; but left the country under queen MARY I and went to live in Germany. He returned at the accession of ELIZABETH I, and was appointed bishop of London (1559). As an avowed Calvinist, he disagreed with the use by clergy of Catholic vestments. Because of his refusal to act strongly against radicals in the church, he was translated to the see of York (1570), where he acted mainly against Catholic sympathisers. In 1575 he was appointed archbishop of Canterbury, but refused to collaborate with official moves against meetings ('prophesyings') of radical clergy, and in 1577 was suspended from his functions by Elizabeth.

Grotius, Hugo (Huigh de Groot) (1583–1645) Dutch jurist. From a leading Calvinist family of Delft, he was educated at Leiden (where he graduated at the age of fourteen) then went to France to obtain his doctorate in law at the university of Orléans. Asked to comment on a point of law by the East India Company in 1604, he produced a report of which a part was later published as his *Mare Liberum* (the Free Sea) (1609), arguing that the sea was free to all nations. In 1607 he was appointed advocate general of Holland and Zeeland, and in 1613 pensionary of Rotterdam. During the struggle by MAURICE OF NASSAU against OLDENBARNEVELT and the Counter-Remonstrants in 1618, he was condemned to prison in the castle of Loevestein, but in 1621 escaped in a crate of books and settled in Paris (1621),

where he was granted a pension by the king and wrote his classic *De jure belli ac pacis* (The Laws of War and of Peace) (1625). He returned briefly to Holland in 1631 after the death of Maurice, but left for Hamburg in 1631 and shortly after was honoured by Sweden in being appointed their ambassador to France (1634–44). Returning from a visit to Sweden in 1644, he died at Rostock. An opponent of religious persecution, he believed in the necessity for Christian unity and possible reunion with the Catholic Church. His works constitute the first major texts of international law, and are still relevant. He based human society on the concepts of natural law and social contract, thereby finally freeing political theory from its traditional dependence on divine authority. Just as natural law governs men within societies, so it governs relations between societies, binding nations to observe undertakings ('treaties') in the same way that individuals must observe obligations. Exceptional conduct between nations ('war') also has its obligations, which must be clearly defined in order to decide whether a war is just or not. His plea for liberty of the seas in *Mare Liberum* was responded to many years later by the English writer John SELDEN, on behalf of his government, with *Mare Clausum* (The Closed Sea) (1635).

Guevara, Fray Antonio de (*c*.1480–1545) A popular Spanish man of letters and commentator on a wide variety of topics, he offered opinions and moral advice to the average reader on practically everything. Brought up at court, he entered the Franciscan Order in 1504, returning to court as official preacher and historian of the crown. He did not really fulfil the current image of the Franciscan friar, writing as he did for the instruction of princes at the level of a fairly facile morality. His *Libro aureo del emperador Marco Aurelio* (Golden Book of the Emperor Marcus Aurelius) (1529), absorbed later into a larger version called *Reloj de* *príncipes* (A Timepiece for Princes) (1539), was a miscellany of stories and fictions associated with the Roman emperor. A runaway success, it was edited frequently in Spanish, French, Italian, English, German and Latin. His *Epístolas familiares* (1539–41) covered in the same manner a multiplicity of topics. They were fictions supposedly written to important individuals, and once again, widely read. But his reputation did not outlive the century.

[BT]

Guicciardini, Francesco (1483–1540) Florentine lawyer, diplomat, and historian of Italy during the Italian Wars. A member of one of Florence's most important patrician families, he studied civil law at Florence, Ferrara and Padua from 1498 to 1505 before setting up a legal practice in Florence that he was to maintain throughout his whole public career. In 1511 he was sent as ambassador to Spain and his presence there allowed him to maintain his position when Spanish help restored the MEDICI in 1512. Upon his return in 1514 he held local civic offices until entering papal service in 1516 under the Medici pope LEO X. He continued serving the papacy until the death of CLEMENT VII in 1534 as one of the important actors in the tumultuous affairs of the Italian Wars – governor of Modena, 1516; governor of Reggio, 1517; governor of Parma, 1519; president of the Romagna, 1524; advisor and lieutenant-general of papal forces after the Battle of Pavia advising the alliance with France against CHARLES V, which led to the 1527 Sack of Rome; governor of Bologna, 1531; advisor to the restored Medici duke, Alessandro, 1531; and promoter of Cosimo I de' MEDICI in 1537. During this involved public career in law and politics, he wrote extensively on his native city and the contemporary wars in Italy: *History of Florence* (1508–9), *Dialogue on the Government of Florence* (1524–5), *Florentine Affairs* (1528–30),

Considerations on the 'Discourses' of Machiavelli (c.1530), and unpublished 'Maxims'. His political thought was similar to, but distinct from his friend and compatriot MACHIAVELLI; he was less subservient to classical models, more pessimistic, and openly sympathetic to an oligarchic republic like Venice. After being frozen out of Cosimo I's inner circle, he spent his last years writing his chief work, the *History of Italy* (published posthumously 1561), which chronicled the Italian Wars from 1494 to 1534 in portraits of individual passions and ambition, constructed speeches on important issues, and pithy maxims.

[JM]

Guise, dukes de A younger son of the duke de Lorraine in the early sixteenth century inherited the county of Guise in France, together with its associated estates of Aumale, Joinville, Mayenne and others; in 1528 the county was made into a duchy by king Francis I.

1st duke, Claude of Lorraine (1496–1550) He distinguished himself during the French wars in Italy, and was an ardent supporter of the Catholic cause in France. He had thirteen children, among them MARY OF GUISE, mother of MARY STUART.

2nd duke, Francis I of Lorraine (1519–63) Son of Claude and a leading soldier of his time, he married (1549) Anna d'ESTE of Ferrara. In 1552 he captured Metz and successfully resisted a siege by CHARLES V. In 1557 he led the French troops into Italy against the Spaniards; then returned home after hearing of the humiliating French defeat at St Quentin, and captured Calais (January 1558) from the English, Spain's allies. After the death of king HENRY II, the Guises, led by Francis and his brother Charles, cardinal of Lorraine, played a dominating role in politics. The duke contributed to the outbreak of civil war by permitting the killing of Protestants at Vassy (1562). Shortly after he was murdered by a Calvinist, probably at the instigation of COLIGNY.

3rd duke, Henry I of Lorraine (1550–88) Eldest son of Francis I of Lorraine, he was determined to avenge his father's murder. He returned to France from Austria where he had been serving against the Turks, and led the Catholic forces against the Calvinist nobility. When the massacre of Protestants on St Bartholomew's Eve took place (August 1572), he personally helped to finish off the wounded Coligny. From 1576 he headed the Catholic League which relied on Spanish help; and he opposed the tendency of king HENRY III to ally with the heir to the throne, the Calvinist Henry of Navarre. In spring 1588 Guise's supporters in Paris took over the capital and imposed their will on the king; but the king retaliated by ordering the assassination of the duke and of his brother Louis II of Guise, cardinal of Lorraine.

Gustav I Vasa (1495–1560) king of Sweden 1523–60 and founder of the Vasa dynasty. Son of a Swedish noble, he dedicated himself to freeing his country from Danish rule. After two years of revolt (1521–3) he succeeded in expelling the Danes and dissolving the union of Kalmar, which had till then united Sweden, Denmark and Norway under one crown. He was elected king by the Diet, and proclaimed Swedish independence, secured with the aid of the ships and money of the city of Lübeck. He also persuaded the Diet at Västerås (1527) to accept the Lutheran Reformation; the property of the old Church was taken over by the nobles and the state. Because the change was imposed from above, real changes in religion were slow to mature.

Gustav II Adolf Vasa (1594–1632) king of Sweden 1611–32. Succeeding his father, Charles II, he was ably advised by his chancellor, OXENSTIERNA, at a time when the country was faced by dynastic and territorial threats in the Baltic. Opting for military solutions, he began his reign with military manœuvres, first against Russia (from whom, in the 1617 treaty of Stolbovo, he gained Ingria, Estonia and Karelia) and then against Poland (from whom he seized Riga and the Baltic ports, and then Livonia, conceded in the 1629 treaty of Altmark). Invited by RICHELIEU's France to intervene in the German lands (by the treaty of Bärwalde 1631), he took his army into the Thirty Years' War in the hope of territorial concessions on the south Baltic coast. Soon he was diverted from this aim by highly successful campaigns in Germany, crushing the Imperial army at Breitenfeld (1631); his success, however, confused his objectives. He achieved a final victory at Lützen (1632) against the army of WALLENSTEIN, but died of wounds received in the battle. His reign initiated the half-century of Swedish supremacy in northern Europe and the Baltic, but also began the depletion of the country's limited resources.

Guyon, Jeanne-Marie Bouvier de La Motte, madame (1648–1717) French mystic. Her father was a noble and judge in Montargis, where she was born. Brought up in a religious environment, in 1664 she married an engineer Jacques Guyon, twenty two years older, who died in 1676 and by whom she had five children. From 1681 to 1686 she resided mainly in the region of the French–Swiss border near Geneva, where she devoted herself to pious works. She published at Grenoble in 1685 her *Short Course in Prayer*, and became known for her mystical inclinations, which aroused the opposition of several leading clergy. Moving to Paris in 1686, she received the support of Madame de MAINTENON, who received her at her school at St-Cyr and in 1688 introduced her to FÉNELON. So began a friendship between the archbishop and the lady, based on a common interest in mystical spirituality, that had unfortunate consequences for them both. Attacks by other clergy on Guyon's 'Quietist' spirituality influenced Madame de Maintenon to withdraw her support from 1691, and in 1695 a high-level committee set up by agreement with Guyon and including bishop BOSSUET, condemned some of her doctrines; she submitted to the verdict, but later that year was detained. Fénelon reacted by publishing his *Maxims of the Saints* (1697), in implicit support of her position; the work provoked an immediate reply from Bossuet and set off a major controversy between the two bishops over the issue of Quietism. In 1698 Guyon was transferred to the Bastille, where she remained till her release in 1702, when she withdrew to spend her remaining years near Blois. A deeply religious woman, after her release she produced numerous writings, all published at Cologne. Her collected works were published in forty volumes later in the century.

Gwyn, Nell (Eleanor) (1650–87) English actress. She started her career selling oranges outside the Theatre Royal in Covent Garden, and through her actor lovers was introduced to the stage, where from 1665 she played accomplished parts in plays by DRYDEN and others, a profession that she continued with success to 1682. PEPYS commented approvingly on her roles. After one performance CHARLES II invited her home to supper, and made her his mistress. She owed her popularity with the people to their aversion for the king's Catholic mistress Louise de Kérouaille, duchess of Portsmouth. Her eldest son by Charles II was created duke of St Albans in 1684. The king always loved her; his last request to his brother JAMES II was 'Let not poor Nelly starve'. She did not starve, and became very rich. Her portrait was painted by Sir Peter Lely.

Gyllenstierna, Johan, count (1636–80) Swedish statesman. After doing the grand tour, he joined the household of the young CHARLES X GUSTAV VASA, and in 1668 was elected president of the parliament and member of the council of state. In 1574 he was named count. He advocated strong royal control of the administration with a lesser role for the royal council of nobility. His principal rival was DE LA GARDIE, who was however discredited after the defeats of the war of 1672–5. Appointed governor of Skåne, he built up an important power-base there and negotiated peace with Denmark. His plans for royal absolutism were fulfilled by the decree of the parliament in 1680 which subjected the powers of the council to those of the king.

H

Hakluyt, Richard (*c*.1552–1616) English writer. He studied at Oxford (1570–7), where he also gave lectures on maps and geography. He then took holy orders and from 1583 to 1588 served in Paris as chaplain to the English ambassador. From the first the accounts of geographical discoveries fascinated him; in Paris he collected information about French and Spanish voyages, writing his account 'A Discourse Concerning Western Planting' (1584), which was presented to the queen but remained unpublished. Returning to England, he published in one volume (1589) his *The Principall Navigations, Voiages and Discoveries*, subsequently much amplified and published in three volumes with the same title (1598–1600), and containing translations of foreign works as well as accounts of English voyages. In 1606 he was one of the chief backers of the colonisation of Virginia.

Hales, Stephen (1677–1761) English cleric and experimental scientist. Relying on the church for his livelihood, he obtained the curacy of Teddington, Middlesex, in 1709 (along with another benefice) and was based there for the rest of his life. But he also benefited from contact with the court, becoming clerk of the closet to the princess-dowager and chaplain to her son (later George III). He devoted much of his time to scientific research and was a fellow of the Royal Society from 1718; as a Newtonian, he preferred mechanistic explanations for natural phenomena. A skilful and accurate experimenter, he investigated plant physiology, the movement of sap and the process of transpiration, with unprecedented care; the impressive results of this work were published in his *Vegetable Statics* (1727). He also contributed to the study of animal physiology, especially in his *Statical Essays* (1733); in particular he studied the pressure of circulating blood. His experiments on air to study the products of combustion led him to devise the pneumatic trough for collecting gases; other practical inventions included ventilating-systems to counteract the dangerous effects of bad air on health.

[FW]

Halifax, Charles Montagu, 1st earl of (1661–1715) English statesman. Educated at Oxford, where he became the friend of NEWTON, he entered Parliament after the 1688 revolution, serving the Whig administration from 1692 in financial matters, for which he was appointed chancellor of the exchequer and member of the privy council in 1694. In 1695 he established important regulations for the issue of currency by the bank of England. First lord of the treasury 1697–9, he resigned on being defeated in the Commons, was created baron and passed to the Lords, where he defended himself against an impeachment (1701) and other moves made against him by the Tory majority in the Commons. Out of power under queen ANNE STUART, he became first lord of the treasury again (1714) under GEORGE I, and was created earl. Of great intellectual ability, he was president of the Royal Society (1695–8), a patron of literary men, and a (lesser) poet in his own right.

Halifax, George Savile, 1st marquis of (1633–95) English statesman. A member of Parliament at the Restoration of CHARLES II, he was appointed a member of the privy council (1672), but was ousted from it in 1676 after disagreements with the chief minister, DANBY. A firm supporter of moderation in politics, he opposed the pro-Catholic policies of the crown but also opposed the attempt (1673 Test Act) to exclude Catholics from public life. Created earl by the king in 1679, he helped Charles defeat in the House of Lords the Exclusion Bill (1680) that intended to bar the Catholic duke of York from succeeding to the throne; in 1682 he was created marquis. He was appointed lord privy seal in 1682 in Charles' last administration. Appointed lord president of the council on the accession to the throne (1685) of the duke, now JAMES II, he was dismissed soon after for opposing the king's pro-Catholic policies. In retirement over the next three years, he produced several writings that reveal his disillusion. An intellectual in politics, he was able to distance himself from politicking and analyse empirically the reality of power in several short works, of which the best known is *The Character of a Trimmer* (written 1684, published 1688). For Savile there are no fundamental principles of state; good government depends entirely upon the quality of those who govern. Of several existing types of government, the most preferable is 'mixed monarchy', combining king and Parliament. Political parties he regarded as a conspiracy against the well-being of the nation. When WILLIAM III of Orange invaded in 1688, James appealed to Hali-

fax to mediate between the two sides, but Halifax supported a settlement in favour of William and Mary. He was appointed lord privy seal (1689), but left office after pressure on him in 1690.

Halley, Edmond (1656–1742) English astronomer and natural philosopher. The son of a wealthy City businessman, he took up astronomy in his youth and when only twenty sailed for St Helena to compile the first substantial catalogue of the southern stars. Soon afterwards he visited Hevelius' observatory at Danzig on behalf of the Royal Society. He served as Clerk to the Society from 1686 and later as its Secretary, participated fully in the informal intellectual life of the London coffee-houses, edited and contributed papers to the *Philosophical Transactions*, and was especially closely linked with Sir Isaac NEWTON, whose *Principia* (1687) was printed with his help and financial backing. Later he undertook two voyages to study terrestrial magnetism and another to survey the English Channel; the maps published as a result included the first to show isogonal lines (lines of equal magnetic variation). In 1703 he obtained the Savilian chair of Geometry at Oxford; two years later he published an analysis of the motion of comets. He assisted the committee supervising expenditure of a royal grant for the publication of John FLAMSTEED's works and, to Flamsteed's fury, edited the volume published as *Historia coelestis* in 1712; his preface to it claimed that the content wholly supported Newton's theories. In 1720 he succeeded Flamsteed as Astronomer Royal; he devoted much of his time at Greenwich to work on lunar theory, but the results were never published.

[FW]

Hamilton, James, 3rd marquis then 1st duke of (1606–49) Son of the 2nd marquis, he was educated at Oxford, became marquis on his father's death in 1625, and took up the post of master of the horse in the household of CHARLES I (1628), becoming the king's chief adviser on Scottish questions. In 1638 he was sent to Scotland to pacify the country after the disturbances caused by the new prayer-book, but failed to satisfy the Covenanters, and was sent with an army into Scotland early in 1639. After the treaty of Berwick with the Scots (June 1639), he attempted again to reconcile differences between the English and the Scots, but only succeeded in alienating the Presbyterian leader the duke of ARGYLL (1642). Imprisoned briefly by the English royalists (1644–6) because of his failure in Scotland, but liberated by the troops of FAIRFAX, after the civil war he urged the now imprisoned Charles to accept the terms offered by the Scots for their support. On this basis, Hamilton entered England from the north with his Scottish army, but was defeated by CROMWELL at Preston (1648), surrendered and was later executed.

Hampden, John (1594–1643) English politician. Son of a Buckinghamshire gentleman (and related by family to Oliver CROMWELL), he was educated at Oxford and studied law at the Inner Temple. He entered Parliament in 1621, soon identifying himself with the opposition to CHARLES I and was imprisoned (1627) for refusing to pay a forced loan. He made himself prominent by his opposition to the levy of the ship-money tax on his estates in 1635; his case was tried 1637–8, and judgement given narrowly for the crown. He played an important part in the parliaments from 1640 onwards, supporting all the radical measures; was one of the five members of the Commons the king tried to arrest in 1642; and on the outbreak of civil war raised a regiment and served under ESSEX. He was mortally wounded during one of the skirmishes in Oxfordshire. A man of moderation, he commanded great respect from friend and foe alike.

Handel, George Frederick (1685–1759) German composer, naturalised in England. One of the greatest composers of the Baroque period, his reputation as a composer of oratorios and some instrumental works (notably *Water Music* and the *concerti grossi*) often overshadows his tremendous versatility and competence in other genres (e.g. Italian operas, cantatas and keyboard music). He received his initial musical education in Halle (his home town), where he also studied law and held the post of cathedral organist. His subsequent sojourns to Hamburg (1703–6) and Italy (1706–10) were decisive for the crystallisation of his musical style. Shortly after his appointment as music director to the elector of Hanover (1710), he took two leaves of absence to stage his operas in London. According to the well-known anecdote, the elector, who had meanwhile ascended to the English throne as king GEORGE I (1714), was angered at the composer's delayed return from his second leave. In order to regain the monarch's favour, the composer surprised him with the *Water Music* suite during his boating party on the Thames. He was also a music director to the duke of Chandos in Cannon (1717–20), before settling permanently in London. As music director of the newly founded Royal Academy of Music, he staged many of his own, highly successful Italian operas (e.g. *Radamisto, Floridante, Ottone, Giulio Cesare, Rodelinda* and *Admeto*). His operatic enterprises, however, sustained continuous difficulties due to financial loss, rival opera companies and the public's growing preference for lighter comic operas (e.g. *The Beggar's Opera*, 1828). In the late 1730s he began to channel his energy to oratorios, which eventually established his long-lasting fame. The oratorios are not sacred works (except for the *Messiah*) although they are based on Biblical stories (e.g. *Esther, Deborah, Israel in Egypt, Saul, Joseph and his*

Brethern, Belshazzar, Judas Maccabaeus, Joshua, Solomon and *Jephte*). Stylistically, they assimilate elements of the Italian opera, the English choral tradition and the German oratorio; yet they institute a novel, genuinely English genre. Their attractive melodic and harmonic features, majestic choruses of multifarious contrasts of sonorities, architectural magnitude and superb musical depiction of the text create altogether brilliant dramatic effects.

[JE]

Hardwicke, Philip Yorke, 1st earl of (1690–1764) English lord chancellor. One of the most distinguished lawyers of his time, he was educated at the Inns, where he held office, and later sat in Parliament (1719, 1722–34) and became solicitor general (1720), attorney general (1724) and lord chief justice. He was created baron in 1733 and lord chancellor in 1737. He was also powerful in politics, and for many years from 1740 onwards held the controlling power in government. During GEORGE II's absences on the continent he was on the regency council and had to cope with the Jacobite rising of 1745. After the Battle of Culloden he presided at the trial of the Scots Jacobite peers. He carried out the reform of 1746 which abolished the private heritable jurisdictions of the Scots landed gentry. Perhaps his best-known achievement in government was the reform of the English marriage laws (1753) which stipulated that no marriage could be solemnised (in the Anglican church) unless banns were read for three successive Sundays. Hardwicke, who was created earl in 1754, retired from politics in 1756. One of the most notable judges in British history, he laid the foundations for the important role played by 'equity', or discretionary judgements, in the British legal system.

Harley, Robert, 1st earl of Oxford (1661–1724) From a Puritan gentry family, privately educated and a student at the Inner Temple, he entered the House of Commons in 1689, and became Speaker of the House 1701–4; starting his political career as a Whig, he ended it as leader of the Tories. Brought into the Tory administration of GODOLPHIN as secretary of state (1704–8), he became a great manager of the Commons, employed a network of informers (among them, DEFOE), steered through the Act of Union of England and Scotland (1707), and rallied support for the British involvement in the war of the Spanish Succession. In opposition after 1708, he retained influence through the role of his cousin Lady Abigail MASHAM on queen ANNE STUART. He returned as chancellor of the Exchequer and leader of a completely Tory government (1710–14); in 1711 he was created earl. Dismissed from office five days before the queen's death, on the accession of GEORGE I he was impeached because of his handling of the treaty of Utrecht, and sent to the Tower (1715–17). He played little part in politics after this. A great bibliophile, at his death his rich manuscript collection, now the Harleian Collection in the British Library, consisted of over 6,000 volumes.

Haro, Luis Méndez de (1598–1661) Son of the marquis of Carpio and of his wife, the sister of OLIVARES, he led the court opposition in the 1640s to his uncle Olivares and succeeded him in 1643 as chief minister to PHILIP IV of Spain, but was unable to take effective action to confront the grave problems of the country. In effect, he was asked to take responsibility for peace treaties that confirmed Spain's decaying military role, notably the peace of Westphalia (1648) which ended the Thirty Years War. The war with France continued after 1648, though further reverses for Spain were in some measure a consequence of CROMWELL's military adventures, including the capture of Jamaica (1655) and English participation in the battle of the Dunes (1658) in the Netherlands. Haro personally negotiated the subsequent treaty of the Pyrenees (1659) with France, by which Catalonia north of the Pyrenees was ceded to France.

Harrington, James (1611–77) one of the most influential political theorists of mid-seventeenth century England. He was an intimate friend of CHARLES I, whom he accompanied to the scaffold; but his *The Commonwealth of Oceana* (1656) was dedicated to CROMWELL and attacked the views of HOBBES (whom he also reluctantly admired). Civil society, he believed, was sustained by a 'balance of property' among the population, that guaranteed political stability. Instability and the recent civil war had been caused by a disequilibrium of property. The state should be governed by a property-owning aristocracy supported by parliamentary government and universal suffrage; it should also concede liberty of conscience. 'Oceana', the imaginary state for which Harrington devised a constitution based on these principles, was a thinly disguised outline of England; Cromwell, however, was not attracted by the proposal.

Hartlib, Samuel (*c.*1600–62) Born in Elbing, son of a Polish merchant and his third wife, an Englishwoman, he emigrated to England in about 1628, studied at Cambridge and made contact with other intellectuals, notably John Dury and others, who were interested in social and educational ideas. He corresponded voluminously with intellectuals both in England and on the continent, and it was thanks to him that the educational reformer COMENIUS visited England. Among his many writings, *Considerations Tending to the Happy Accomplishment of England's Reformation* (1647) proposed reforms in education, and *Advancement of Husbandry* (1651) proposed founding of agricultural colleges. The work most attributed to him, *Macaria* (1641), a blueprint for a Utopia, was in fact written by one of his collaborators.

Harvey, William (1578–1657) English physician; discoverer of the circulation of the blood. Having studied at Cambridge and Padua, he was awarded the M.D. degree in 1602 and became a Fellow of the Royal College of Physicians five years later; he went on to be appointed physician to St Bartholomew's Hospital and to JAMES I. From 1616 he was Lumleian lecturer, and used this platform to announce his theory of the circulation of the blood, eventually set out in print in *Exercitatio anatomica de motu cordis et sanguinis in animalibus* (An Anatomical Exercise on the Motion of the Heart and Blood in Animals) (1628) and defended in *Exercitatio anatomica de circulatione sanguinis* (1649). As a result of serving CHARLES I during the Civil War, he was made Warden of Merton College, Oxford. In later life he produced a work on embryology and built a library for the Royal College of Physicians, which erected a statue of him.

[FW]

Hawkins, Sir John (1532–95) English sea captain. Son of the mayor and MP for Plymouth, he took to the sea from youth, participating in the family business of trading with Africa, mainly in slaves. From 1562, based in London, he traded on his own account. In 1562, with three vessels, he made his first slaving voyage, picking up blacks from Sierra Leone whom he sold to the Spaniards in Hispaniola. His second voyage, in 1564–5, won him a reputation for daring, but on his third voyage, in 1568, his ships were caught by the Spanish galleons in Vera Cruz harbour and only two (one with DRAKE aboard) returned to England. Unable to traffic further, he dabbled in other shady enterprises, entered Parliament in 1571, and succeeded his father-in-law as treasurer of the navy. He was third in command in the actions against the Spanish Armada in 1588, for which he was knighted on board the *Victory*. His last voyage was in the fleet sent under him and Drake to the West Indies in 1595; he died at sea off Puerto Rico.

Heinsius, Antonie (1641–1720) Dutch statesman. Born into the urban élite of Delft, he practised law there and was in 1679 appointed pensionary of the city. At first in disagreement with the anti-French policies of the stadholder WILLIAM III of Orange, he later accepted the need for an aggressive posture towards France, and was supported by William in 1689 for nomination as pensionary of Holland. During William's absences as king of England, he guided the foreign policy of the republic, particularly during the war of 1687–97 against France, and the war of the Spanish Succession (1701–14). After William's death (1702), he found little support in the States General, which criticised the advantages that England had apparently gained at the expense of Holland in the treaty of Utrecht (1713) that ended the war of the Succession.

Henrietta Maria (1609–69) queen of England 1625–49. Youngest daughter of HENRY IV of France and MARIE DE MÉDICIS, in 1625 she married CHARLES I of England, and gave him seven children, of whom six survived. An attractive and sociable personality, when her husband began to have political problems she gave him unflinching support, and on the outbreak of civil war in 1642 she personally made efforts (partly successful and therefore fiercely criticised in Parliament) to raise money and troops for him on the continent. In 1644 she left England and continued her efforts from abroad; she was in Paris when she received the news of her husband's execution. At the Restoration she returned for a time to London, then left in 1665 and lived her remaining days near Paris.

Henry I of Portugal (1512–80) king of Portugal 1578–80. He became king, most reluctantly, on the unexpected death of his nephew king SEBASTIAN. Until then, he had been Inquisitor General, then archbishop of Braga and later of Evora, and cardinal (1565). He was gouty, toothless and moribund at the time of his accession; many Portuguese looked to ANTONIO, prior of Crato, as a successor, but the upper classes tended to prefer the claims of PHILIP II of Spain, who eventually secured the throne by conquest in 1580–1.

Henry II of Valois (1519–59) king of France 1547–59. Son of FRANCIS I, he continued the long struggle of the Valois against the Habsburgs, a struggle that, after indecisive results in Italy and Flanders but gains in Germany, ended with him. A firm Catholic, he acted vigorously against Lutherans and put into action the Chambre Ardente, a special court (1547–50) to try heresy cases. He married in 1533 CATHERINE DE MÉDICIS, who gave him ten children; but at the same time he had as mistress DIANE DE POITIERS, twenty years his junior. By the peace of Cateau-Cambrésis (1559), which he agreed with the Habsburgs, France abandoned its claims in Italy but retained the bishoprics (Metz, Toul and Verdun) on the German frontier as well as Calais, taken from the English. At a joust held to celebrate the peace, he was fatally wounded when the lance of a Scots officer pierced his eye; he died ten days later. Three of his four sons by Catherine became kings of France.

Henry III of Valois (1551–89) king of Poland 1573–4 and of France 1574–89. Third son of HENRY II and CATHERINE DE MÉDICIS, he held the title of duke d'Anjou, and in 1573 was chosen by the Polish nobility as king of Poland; but on his brother CHARLES IX's death in 1574 returned to France and succeeded him as king. Like his mother, he tried to alternate between the noble factions in an attempt to stabilise the throne during the civil wars, and showed a preference for the 'politique' grouping, conceding in the Peace of Monsieur 1576 a generous degree of toleration to the Protestants. The subsequent formation of the Catholic League under Henry of GUISE put pressure on the king to change his policy, particularly after the death of his younger brother ANJOU (1584) converted the Calvinist Henry of Navarre into heir to the throne. To free himself of the League, the king in December 1588 ordered the assassination of the duke de GUISE and his brother the cardinal. In August 1589 he himself was assassinated by a Leaguer monk, Jacques CLÉMENT. Henry was the last king of the Valois dynasty.

Henry IV Bourbon (1553–1610) king of Navarre 1572–1610 and of France 1589–1610, first king of the Bourbon dynasty. Son of ANTOINE DE BOURBON and of JEANNE III D'ALBRET, queen of Navarre, brought up in Béarn and raised in the Calvinist faith by his mother, he proved his military prowess during the early civil wars, and after his father's death in 1565 emerged as leader of the Protestant cause. After the peace of St Germain (1570) it was arranged, as a sign of religious reconciliation, that he marry CHARLES IX's sister MARGUERITE OF VALOIS. The marriage celebrations in Paris were interrupted by the massacre of St Bartholomew's Eve (August 1572): Henry (who on his mother's death two months before had just succeeded to the title of Navarre) saved his life only by converting to Catholicism. Four years later he reverted publicly to Calvinism, and participated with energy in the wars against the Guises. The death of Henry III's brother ANJOU in 1584 made him next in line for the throne. When he succeeded in 1589, however, his support in France was limited mainly to the Protestants; and he was faced with Spanish military intervention and powerful opposition from the Catholic League under MAYENNE. In 1593, accordingly, he announced his conversion to Catholicism (his alleged statement that 'Paris is worth a mass' seems to be apocryphal), and in 1594, after obtaining

papal recognition, was crowned at Chartres. In March 1594 Paris, defended by a Spanish garrison, opened its gates to him; and in 1595 he declared war against Spain, a conflict resolved by the peace of Vervins in 1598. The pacification of France was Henry's greatest achievement: in religious terms, by the imposition of the Edict of Nantes (1598), which granted extensive toleration to Calvinists; in political terms, by reaching agreement with the great Catholic nobility and firmly repressing rebellions (e.g. in the execution of BIRON, 1602). He continued to maintain an active anti-Spanish foreign policy: it was on the eve of a possible military adventure abroad that he was assassinated in Paris by RAVAILLAC. In 1599 the king obtained an annulment of his marriage to Marguerite, and the next year married MARIE DE MÉDICIS; but he continued to indulge in his many mistresses, notably GABRIELLE D'ESTRÉES.

Henry IV of Castile, known as 'the Impotent' (1423–74) king of Castile and Leon 1454–74. Son of Juan II of Castile, he was born in Valladolid. In 1440 he married Blanche of Navarre, but because no children appeared he divorced her in 1453; in 1455, after succeeding to the throne, he married Juana of Portugal, sister to the young king Affonso V of that realm. No children to this union appeared until 1462, when princess Juana was born. By this time the king had gained his reputation for impotence, and the child became (perhaps unjustly) widely known as '*la Beltraneja*', implying that she was the daughter not of the king but of his minister Beltrán de la Cueva. The country was largely under the control of powerful nobles, who expressed their discontent by rebelling against Henry. In a notable ceremony at Avila in 1465, they deposed an effigy of the king and proclaimed as king in his place the king of Portugal. This began a long period of civil war, that continued even after Henry's sister ISABELLA was recognised by the king as heir (1468) after the unexpected death of Affonso that year. Henry made some later attempts to insist on the rights of his daughter, but without success, and the nobles, after prolonging a struggle from which they notably benefited, recognised Isabella as queen after an illness ended the king's life.

Henry VII Tudor (1457–1509) king of England 1485–1509, first ruler of the Tudor dynasty. Born in Wales, only (and posthumous) son of the earl of Richmond and of Margaret BEAUFORT (then aged fourteen), he became automatically, on the death of Henry VI in 1471, head of the house of Lancaster; and for his own safety he took refuge in Brittany during the reign of EDWARD IV of York. He landed with a small force in Wales in 1485, hoping to profit from the unpopularity of RICHARD III, and won a decisive victory over the royal troops three weeks later at Bosworth (August 1485). He ascended the throne as the first of the Tudors; his marriage to Elizabeth of York (1486) buried the dynastic conflict. In 1487 he put down a rising that supported the claims of the pretender Lambert SIMNEL, and had to face other opposition, but succeeded in establishing his power, strengthened by changes in the administration of government and above all by reforms in the method of collecting and accounting for revenue. In 1492 he made a short military expedition to besiege Boulogne against the forces of CHARLES VIII of France. The most serious threat to the throne came from the claims of Perkin WARBECK, who from 1492 until his capture in 1497 received the support of opponents of Henry in France, the Netherlands and Scotland. Warbeck was hanged in 1499; the young earl of Warwick, last male scion of the house of York, was accused of complicity with him and beheaded. To strengthen his dynasty Henry made several marriage alliances, notably that of his heir Arthur (d.1502) with CATHERINE OF ARAGON; he also actively pursued alliances with Burgundy and Spain.

Henry VIII Tudor (1491–1547) king of England 1509–47. The second son of HENRY VII, he succeeded to the throne because of the premature death (1502) of Arthur, who had married CATHERINE OF ARAGON. A highly gifted and erudite Renaissance prince, he was accomplished in warfare, the arts and music. The year 1513 was noted for his expedition with an army into France, and the defeat of the Scots (battle of Flodden). Peace was made with FRANCIS I of France at the celebrated Field of the Cloth of Gold (1520), but subsequently Henry identified himself with CHARLES V. His chief minister in the early part of his reign was cardinal WOLSEY (1514–29). An ardent Catholic all his life, in 1521 Henry published an attack against LUTHER, earning himself the papal title of 'Defender of the Faith'. The lack of a male heir from Catherine of Aragon, whom he married in 1509, induced him to take seriously his affair with Anne BOLEYN, and in 1527 he sought papal sanction for a divorce from the former. The struggle over the divorce precipitated a major political eruption, and was a direct cause of the schism (1533–4) of the English Church from Rome. Though he placed men of Protestant sympathies in power (e.g. CROMWELL and CRANMER) and even allowed his son EDWARD VI to be educated as a Protestant, Henry made sure that his Church (of which he became head through the Act of Supremacy 1534) stayed Catholic in belief. His dominant and tyrannical character has tended to eclipse recognition of the important contribution made by others, notably Cromwell, to the politics of the reign. After his divorce from Catherine (1533), managed by Cranmer, he married five more times: to Anne Boleyn (married 1533 and mother of ELIZABETH I, she was executed in 1536), Jane Seymour (married 1536, died 1537 giving birth to Edward VI), Anne of Cleves (divorced in 1540, seven months after the marriage), Catherine Howard (married 1540, executed 1542) and Catherine Parr (married 1543; she survived him).

Herrera, Juan de (*c*.1530–97) mathematician, urban planner and principal architect to PHILIP II of Spain. He was the creator of Spanish classicism, introducing ALBERTI's principles and the use of the Doric order (*estilo desornamentado*). He came from a patrician family in Santander, was educated at the university in Valladolid (to 1548), and was one of the courtiers who accompanied prince Philip on his tour of Italy, Germany and the Netherlands (1549). Enlisting in the army in 1553, he served the ageing CHARLES V in his retirement at Yuste, acquired experience in the science of fortification, and entered the service of Philip II when his father died in 1558. He was chosen to assist the court architect, Juan Bautista de Toledo, in the construction of Philip's colossal palace/monastery at El Escorial (1563–84), a gigantic and starkly impressive structure built – in honour of St Lawrence – on a gridiron-shaped plan. Herrera became principal architect when Juan Bautista died (1567), and was also responsible for the design of the palace at Aranjuez, and the Alcázar in Toledo, as well as the nucleus of the City Hall in Toledo – a structure later to be completed by El GRECO's son Jorge. Beginning in 1582 he was also head of the royal Academy of Mathematics.

[JH]

Heyn, Piet (1577–1629) Dutch admiral. Dedicated to life at sea, he was captured by the Spaniards in 1597 and spent four years rowing for them, then went home, became a merchant shipper and rose in fortune until in 1621 he became a director of the East India Company. His claim to fame in history is unique. Vice-admiral of the navy from 1624, in the summer of 1628 his vessels (31 ships, with over 600 guns and 4,000 men) surprised the annual silver fleet from the Spanish colonies in America, as it left harbour in Cuba on its way back to Spain. It was the first and last time that any naval commander was able to capture so large a treasure. The booty, worth several millions, yielded a dividend of 50 per cent to the East India Company's shareholders. The coup also ruined Spain's financial credit in Europe at a difficult period. Heyn did not live to spend his share; he was killed the year after in a naval action against the pirates who operated from the Spanish-held port of Dunkirk.

Hobbes, Thomas (1588–1679) English philosopher. Born in Malmesbury, son of a clergyman, he was educated locally then went to Oxford, where he graduated 1608. From 1608 to 1628 he became tutor to William Cavendish, later 2nd earl of Devonshire, and accompanied him on the grand tour (1610) of Europe, which opened to him intellectual horizons undreamt of in Oxford. From 1629–30 he acted once again as tutor to gentry, based in Paris; and subsequently, from 1631, became tutor to the 3rd earl, going with him on another grand tour. During his stays abroad he obtained some of the insights that made him review the current state of philosophy; he met Galileo GALILEI, MERSENNE and GASSENDI. Returning to England with Devonshire in 1537, he began to write his philosophical treatises. But the revolutionary events of 1640 made him seek refuge abroad in Paris, where he wrote his *De cive* (published 1642 in Latin, in English in 1651) and his *Leviathan* (published in London 1651) and other works; he personally donated a copy of the *Leviathan* to CHARLES II in Paris. Criticised for his views in France, he returned to England at the end of 1651, and spent the rest of his life peaceably (protected by the Devonshires) but in constant controversy with his detractors. One of the towering intellectuals of his time, he made wholly original contributions to philosophical thought. A philosophical materialist, he argued in *Leviathan* that men originally lived in a state of savage nature; they entered civil society by banding together to bestow on one sovereign the power to rule over them. Such a power resided absolutely in the hands of the sovereign, the 'Leviathan', and could not be revoked.

Hoffman, Melchior (*c*.1495–1543) German visionary prophet. Born in Swabia, he converted early to the Lutheran Reformation, for which he worked zealously in Livonia and northern Germany. His views brought hostility from other Lutheran clergy, who caused him to be expelled from Wolmar and Dorpat (1526), after which he moved to Stockholm and then to Kiel (Denmark). A perpetually wandering prophet, in 1529 he was in Strasbourg where he not only rejected Lutheran teaching, but explicitly adopted extreme Anabaptist views. He now believed that the Millennium (the second coming of Christ) would begin, after a period of signs and travails, in the year 1533. He had great success with preaching his new faith in the northern Netherlands (1530), where his numerous followers became known as Melchiorites. Hoffman returned to Strasbourg in the year of the Millennium, 1533, but was arrested as a fanatic and spent the rest of his life inside a cage in a tower. His prophetic (but non-violent) views had an immediate impact through their influence on other radical Anabaptists, such as JOHN OF LEIDEN, who set up an extremist regime in the city of Münster in 1534.

Hogarth, William (1697–1768) English painter, engraver and author. The son of a London schoolmaster imprisoned for debt (1708–12), Hogarth became the first English-born artist to attain the rank of Sergeant-painter to the king (1757). Apprenticed first to an engraver of silver tableware, Ellis G. Gamble, he later studied life drawing at the St Martin's Lane Academy (1720), and was one of the

founders of the second Academy in 1735. Largely self-taught as a painter and despairing of making a successful career as a history painter, he began publishing and marketing sets of satirical and moralising prints based on scenarios of his own invention (from 1721) which, after his promotion of the parliamentary legislation of 1735 known as 'Hogarth's Act', were protected by copyright. These lampooned modern morals, Italian opera, censorship of the theatre, the French, the clergy, the medical profession, the judiciary and English politics. He married the daughter of Sir James Thornhill, Sergeant-painter to the king (1729), and became a governor of St Bartholomew's hospital, as well as of the Foundling hospital. His most notable works are the engraved series *The Harlot's Progress* (1732); *A Rake's Progress* (1735); and *Marriage á la Mode* (1743); and his 1753 treatise, *The Analysis of Beauty*.

[JH]

Holbein, Hans the Younger (1497–1543) German painter, illustrator and designer of stained glass and jewellery, born in Augsburg and active in Basel and London. Leaving home as a teenager to settle in Basel, he was discovered by ERASMUS who helped him to receive portrait commissions from the publisher Johannes FROBEN, as well as from burgomaster Jakob Meyer; and from Erasmus' heir, AMERBACH, whose collection is preserved in the Basel Museum. Holbein was admitted to the Basel painters' guild on 25 September 1519, and at about the same time married Elsbeth Schmidt, the widow of a tanner. His commissions for religious works, include the *Dead Christ* (Basel) that later fascinated Dostoyevsky; the *Solothurn Madonna* for the Municipal Clerk, Johannes Gerster (Solothurn, Museum) and *Meyer Madonna* (Darmstadt, Prinz von Hessen und bei Rhein). After 1524 he adopted the three-colour chalk technique favoured by the Clouets for his portrait drawings. The Protestant iconoclasm in

Basel impelled him to travel to England (1526–8) with letters of introduction from Erasmus to Thomas MORE, whose family he portrayed. Other sitters included Sir Henry and Lady Guildford; HENRY VIII's German astronomer, Niclas Kratzer; and William WARHAM, archbishop of Canterbury. Returning to Basel he found conditions for religious commissions had not improved, and after painting the portrait of his wife and two children (Basel) abandoned his family to settle permanently in England (1532). This time he found German patrons in the London Steelyard – Thomas More now being out of favour. In addition to portraits of young Hanseatic merchants, he designed festival decorations for the coronation of Anne BOLEYN. The double portrait known, inaccurately, as *The Ambassadors* followed (1533; London), as did his appointment as Henry VIII's court painter. He portrayed Jane Seymour, Anne of Cleves, prince Edward, princess Christina of Denmark, assorted courtiers including the poet Thomas WYATT (the Elder) and finally the king's physician, Sir John Chambers. When he died in 1543, his will provided for an unnamed mistress and two young children, 'still at nurse'.

[JH]

Hooke, Robert (1635–1702) English experimental scientist. While studying at Oxford, he was recruited as an assistant by Robert BOYLE, for whom he helped to construct the first English air-pump. Soon after the foundation of the Royal Society he became its principal Curator of Experiments, was swiftly made a Fellow and served as Secretary to the Society from 1677 to 1682. At the same time he was Gresham Professor of Geometry from 1665 and Surveyor to the City of London from 1667. In the period of rebuilding after the Great Fire; he worked as an architect in association with Sir Christopher WREN, and was closely involved in the design and construction of the Royal Observatory. A prolific creator of experi-

ments and mechanical devices, he often claimed too much for them or insisted too vigorously upon his priority of invention, and was condemned as 'boastful' by contemporaries. He engaged in particularly bitter disputes with Oldenburg, HUYGENS, Hevelius, and NEWTON, the last of whom he claimed to have anticipated in perceiving an inverse square relationship associated with gravity. His few publications included *Micrographia* (1665), containing the first thorough account of observations with the microscope, and various *Lectures*. In discussing the behaviour of springs he propounded what is still known as 'Hooke's Law': the extension of an elastic body is proportional to the force exerted upon it.

[FW]

Hooker, Richard (1554–1600) English theologian. Educated at Oxford, he graduated there and became a fellow (1577) of Corpus Christi, taking holy orders in 1581; he subsequently occupied different livings in London and in country parishes, his last rectorship being near Canterbury. In 1592 he published the first volume of his chief work, *The Lawes of Ecclesiasticall Politie*, of which five volumes were published in his lifetime; other volumes were later published as part of the work, but were drawn from his notes on other subjects. The aim of the work, which achieved considerable success, was to reply to Puritan criticism of the nature of the national Church set up under ELIZABETH I, and to supply the Church with a sound philosophical and logical basis. Since all members of English society also belong to the English Church, he argued, then Church and society have the same purpose and constitution: 'with us one society is both Church and commonwealth', and Church and state in England were inseparable.

Hopkins, Matthew (d.1647) English witchfinder. Of obscure origin, he emerged into prominence in 1644, when he announced the discovery of witches living near his home at Manningtree, and succeeded in obtaining their trial and execution. He then proclaimed himself to be a 'Witch-Finder Generall', and began his travels on horseback through several towns, identifying witches for a fee. Some judicial authorities collaborated with him, and formalised the trial and execution of witches in the areas of Suffolk, Norfolk and Essex. Eventually he himself was condemned as a witch, and hanged.

Horn, Gustaf, count of Björneborg (1592–1657) Swedish general. Famous as one of the best generals of GUSTAV II ADOLF VASA during the Thirty Years War, he served under MAURICE OF NASSAU in the Netherlands (1614–18), and then in the 1620s in the Polish campaigns of the Swedish army. Under Gustav Adolf's command he served in the major battles of the German campaign, at Breitenfeld (1631) and with distinction at Lützen (1632). Captured at Nördlingen (1634), he was released eight years later. Back once more in Sweden, he led his forces in the wars against the war with Denmark (1644–5), forcing them into the peace of Brömsebro (1645). He was appointed governor of Livland in 1652, and field-marshal 1653. He rose to become commander-in-chief of the army.

Hornes, Philip of Montmorency, count of (1524–68) Related through his father to the powerful MONTMORENCY family of France, and through his mother to the EGMONT family of the Netherlands, he served CHARLES V as stadholder of Gelderland (from 1555), became captain of prince Philip's bodyguard, and served with distinction at St Quentin and the Gravelines. In 1556 he became a knight of the Golden Fleece. He returned to Spain with Philip, and spent two years there. Back home in the Netherlands, where he was a member of the council of State, he joined the opposition to GRANVELLE and

later to PHILIP II's policies. When the duke of ALBA arrived in Brussels with a Spanish army (1567), Hornes was taken into custody, together with Egmont and other opposition leaders. A year later, he was condemned to death and executed in Brussels, together with the earl of Egmont.

Hotman, François (1524–90) French jurist and noble, and professor of law at Paris in 1546, in 1547 he converted to the Reformation and built up a reputation as professor in Lausanne, Valence and then at Bourges, where he narrowly escaped the massacre of St Bartholomew (1572). He spent the rest of his life in Switzerland, teaching law at Geneva (1573) and later at Basel (1579), where he died. His most famous work was the *Franco-Gallia* (1573, translated the year after into French), which argued that the monarchy in France was originally elective and not hereditary. Written as a protest against the crown's implication in the 1572 massacre, it stressed that sovereignty in France resided in the people (or, more precisely, in 'men of wealth and honour representing the people'), rather than in the crown. Hotman's work was typical of the literature of resistance produced by many Huguenot writers in the years after the massacre.

Howard, Charles, lord of Effingham and earl of Nottingham (1536–1624) English admiral. As a cousin of queen ELIZABETH I, he advanced rapidly at her court, serving as ambassador to France (1559) and entering Parliament in 1562. He made the navy his career, became lord admiral in 1585 and was appointed commander of the forces that checked the Spanish Armada in 1588. Together with the earl of ESSEX, he led the naval force that descended on Cadiz in 1596, an exploit that earned him his earldom (1597). He played a key role in the transition to the reign of JAMES I.

Hubmaier, Balthasar (d.1528) German religious leader. Born near Augsburg, he studied under ECK at the university of Freiburg, and followed him to Ingolstadt, obtaining his doctorate there. He served first as priest in the cathedral at Regensburg, then as parish priest in Waldshut in the Breisgau. Here he began to read LUTHER, and showed particular interest in Zwingli; he reformed his congregation, and married. During the Peasants Revolt, he showed some sympathy for the insurgents. His radicalism extended itself to religion as well, and he identified himself with the Anabaptists. Allying with the Zürich Anabaptists Conrad Grebel and Felix Manz, he formed a group of 'Swiss Brethren', but repressive measures forced him to flee from the area. In Augsburg in 1526 he met the Anabaptist leader Hans Denck, and from there went to Moravia, where he became leader of a community of Anabaptists. His views were fairly moderate; unlike some radicals, he did not entirely reject the idea of collaboration with the state. His *Concerning Heretics and Those Who Burn Them* (1524) was the earliest plea for full toleration penned in Europe; persecution is against the law of Christ, and 'God's truth is immortal'. He was eventually seized, imprisoned and taken to Vienna where he was burnt at the stake; his wife was thrown into the Danube with a stone round her neck.

Hudson, Henry (1550–1611) In 1607 and 1608 he led expeditions, financed by the Muscovy Company, to the Arctic in search of a north-west sea passage to Asia. He led another expedition in 1609, financed this time by the Dutch East India Company and sailing from Amsterdam, which skirted Nova Scotia and entered into the river mouth that bears his name. On a fourth expedition, in 1610, he reached the great bay that also bears his name; but on the return trip the sailors mutinied against their hardships, and set Hudson, with eight others including his son, out on a raft on which they presumably perished since nothing more was heard of them.

Hume, David (1711–76) Scots philosopher. Born in Edinburgh of gentry stock, he was educated at the university and quickly abandoned the study of law in favour of reading literature and philosophy. From 1734 to 1737 he was in France, spending two years with the Jesuits at La Flèche, where DESCARTES had been educated, and where he wrote most of his chief philosophical work *A Treatise of Human Nature*, published in three volumes in 1739–40 in London without raising much interest. He returned to live in Berwickshire, where he published his *Essays*. After travelling across Europe (1748–9) as a military attaché, he published further writings, of which the most important was his *An Enquiry concerning Human Understanding* (1748). He thus completed all his philosophical work by 1751. In that year he moved to live in Edinburgh, turned his pen to writing historical works, and frequented intellectual clubs. His most significant work of this period was *The Natural History of Religion* (1757). In 1763 he accompanied the British ambassador to Paris, where he was fêted as an eminence. He also brought Rousseau back to England for a year, and himself returned finally to Edinburgh in 1769, now rich and successful. The leading neo-sceptic of the early modern period, he resumed previous empiricist and sceptical approaches into a constructive system, and argued that philosophy 'cannot go beyond experience'. He therefore rejected metaphysics, since it lay beyond reason. But he also denied the possibility of inductive reasoning, and with it rejected the possibility of attaining any certainty about anything. His influence on subsequent thinkers, whether for or against, was great; Kant claimed that reading Hume had wakened him from his dogmatic slumbers.

Hut, Hans (*c*.1495–1527) German religious sectarian. A bookseller from Bibra in Franconia, he made contact with the peasant leader MÜNTZER, who in 1525 entrusted him with the distribution of leaflets in Nürnberg. Hut was in Frankenhausen during the last crucial days of the peasant revolt, making radical speeches. He appeared again in Augsburg in 1527, where Hans Denck re-baptised him; from that time, he became known as the most radical of all the Anabaptist activists. His fiercely aggressive and chiliastic doctrines, which inevitably led to conflict with the civil authorities, alarmed other Anabaptists, who preferred more peaceful methods. A debate was held between him and HUBMAIER, leader of the peaceful south German Anabaptists, at Nikolsburg in Moravia, in the summer of 1526. In 1527 another similar meeting was held in Augsburg to try to settle differences within the communities, but many participants were arrested by the authorities and Hut was apparently killed trying to escape.

Hutten, Ulrich von (1488–1523) Born into a clan of Franconian knights in the family castle near Fulda, he was destined for a Church career and entered the monastery at Fulda but left after five years. He then wandered through various universities, including Cologne and Frankfurt an der Oder, making acquaintance with groups of humanist scholars, and publishing his first works. He went to Italy in 1512, intending to study law, but returned a year later, dedicating himself to publishing polemics in favour of the free knights of the empire. He returned to Italy for a further visit (1515–17) which stimulated his literary creativity and during which he prepared his contributions to the *Letters from Obscure Men* (Cologne 1517). He also returned with a strong feeling in favour of the duty of Germans to resist the tax demands of Rome. He entered the service of archbishop ALBERT OF BRANDENBURG (1517–19), and began to develop a radical hostility to the Catholic Church;

threatened with arrest, he fled for protection to the castle of Franz von SICKINGEN. Sickingen staged a rising against Imperial authority in 1522 but his forces were crushed; Hutten played no part in the rebellion, but had supported it and fled to Basel, from which he was quickly expelled. He died the year after, of syphilis, on an island in Lake Zürich.

Hutter, Jakob (d.1536) He came to prominence among the Anabaptists of Carinthia and then as head of the radicals in the Tirol (1529). By 1533 he had moved to Moravia as head of the communities there (1533). He was seized by the authorities in 1535, and burnt in 1536 in Innsbruck. His followers, known as the Hutterite Brethren, continued after his death to grow in Moravia as a Christian communist community; by the sixteenth century there were over eighty groups, which were however scattered by the authorities after the battle of the White Mountain. Tolerated in eighteenth century Russia, in the nineteenth large numbers emigrated to the Americas. They are today a flourishing worldwide community.

Huygens, Christiaan (1629–95) Dutch mathematician, physicist and astronomer. His father, Constantijn Huygens, was a diplomat and scholar in touch with DESCARTES and many other leading intellectual figures. Cartesianism had a strong influence on the young Christiaan, leading him to rely exclusively on mechanical and mathematical explanations of natural phenomena. At a practical level, he improved the design of telescope eyepieces and the grinding and polishing of their lenses; he was consequently the first to discover a satellite of Saturn, in 1656, publishing it with a theory of Saturn's ring in *Systema Saturnium* (1659). At the same time he worked on the idea of regulating a clock by a pendulum, in which he was the first to employ a compound pendulum and a balance wheel. He visited London in 1663, was then offered a post by the

Académie Royale des Sciences and remained in Paris until 1681. Ill-health having prompted a trip to the Hague, personal and political circumstances made it inadvisable for him to return to France. His publications included *Horologium oscillatorium* (1673), a highly sophisticated piece containing a mathematical theory of curvatures and analyses of the dynamics of oscillation and of circular motion (with laws of centrifugal force); and *Traité de la lumière* (1690), which expounded a wave theory of light. His *Oeuvres complètes* have been collected in 22 volumes (1888–1950).

[FW]

I

Ignatius of Loyola (1491–1556) Basque founder of the Jesuits. Youngest of the children of a noble of Guipúzcoa, he entered on a military career; in 1521, while helping to defend Pamplona against the French, he was wounded in the right leg and confined to bed, where reading and reflection made him decide to change his life. He made a pilgrimage to Montserrat in Catalonia (1522), and went on to Manresa, where during a year-long stay he experienced a spiritual conversion and began writing an early version of his *Spiritual Exercises*. After a visit to the Holy Land (1524) he returned to devote himself to study: first at the universities of Alcalá and Salamanca and then (1528–35) at Paris, where his chosen companions were mostly Spanish. He and six of these met in a chapel in Montmartre in 1534, and took vows to observe poverty and chastity and dedicate themselves to the conversion of the heathen. In 1537 in Rome Ignatius formally organised the group into the Society of Jesus; pope PAUL III, after some doubts, approved the society's constitution by a bull of 1540. The new grouping, which observed a special vow of obedience to the papacy, elected Ignatius as its first general in 1541, and rapidly increased its membership. Ignatius was canonised in 1622.

Innocent VIII (Giovanni Battista Cibo, 1432–92) pope 1484–92. Cardinal bishop in 1473, and governor of Rome in 1476, he was elected pope through the intrigues of Roderigo BORGIA. Like other popes of his time, once in power he furthered his family's interests, but he was also hostile to the Spanish presence in Italy, and invited the French to take over Naples from FERDINAND II OF TRASTÁMARA.

Innocent XI (Benedetto Odescalchi, 1611–89) pope 1676–89. Descended from an old Lombard family, he first studied with the Jesuits at Como, at fifteen he was apprenticed in the family bank in Genoa, and he completed his education with a doctorate in law at Naples in 1639. Tonsured one year later, he entered papal service under URBAN VIII as an apostolic protonotary and financial commissary to the Marches, later governor of Macerata. In 1645 he was named cardinal and in 1648 cardinal legate to Ferrara. In 1650 he was ordained and made bishop of Novara, but in 1652 returned to Rome to work in the curia. Upon papal election in 1676, he had the college of cardinals approve a 'Summary Agreement' of twelve articles of ecclesiastical reform whose three main objectives were to complete the work of Trent, to defend the freedom and rights of the Church, and to fight against the Ottoman Turks. He fought against LOUIS XIV's claims to ecclesiastical privileges (attempts to appoint and gain revenues from vacant sees and pretensions to excessive diplomatic immunity) in the Gallican crisis, aided in the relief of Vienna against the Turks in 1683, opposed the Quietism of Miguel de MOLINOS who was condemned in 1687, and gained renown for his personal piety. His canonisation process was opposed by the French court, and he was only beatified in 1956, with 13 August as his feast day.

[JM]

Ireton, Henry (1611–51) English general. From a Puritan gentry family, he was educated at Oxford and the Middle Temple. He is first noted as active for Parliament in the civil war in Nottingham, and thereafter served as an officer in several campaigns, including Naseby (1645). As a result of his friendship with CROMWELL, he married (1646) his daughter Bridget; the bond confirmed their close co-operation in following years, Ireton contributing the intellectual power and Cromwell the guiding hand. He entered the Long Parliament in 1645, took a leading part in the negotiations after 1647 between the army and Parliament, drew up 'The Heads of the Proposals', and at Putney in October 1647 debated against the radicals. More decisive than Cromwell, he dissolved Parliament (Pride's Purge 1648). He approved and signed the death-warrant of the king; and in 1649–51 as lord deputy of Ireland ruthlessly pursued the military conquest of the country, dying there of fever.

Isabel Clara Eugenia (1566–1633) ruler of the Spanish Netherlands 1598–1621. Eldest daughter of PHILIP II of Spain and Elizabeth Valois, after the deaths of her mother (1568) and her foster-mother queen Anna (1580) she became her father's closest solace, particularly after the departure (1585) of her sister Catalina as duchess of Savoy. Philip encouraged her to collaborate in his administrative work, and put forward her name in the 1590s as possible successor to the throne of France. When a peace settlement for

the Spanish Netherlands was being arranged, Philip accepted the proposal whereby she should marry the archduke ALBERT OF AUSTRIA and become co-ruler of the provinces. The marriage, solemnised after Philip's death, was celebrated in Valencia. She became a competent governor, ruling alone after Albert's death in 1621. The lack of an heir meant that the Netherlands reverted to Spanish control after her death.

Isabella the Catholic (1451–1504) queen of Castile and Aragon 1474–1504. After a stormy childhood in a Castile torn by civil war, she managed to rally enough support to maintain her claim to the throne, against that of Juana la Beltraneja, the purported daughter of king HENRY IV. Her marriage in 1469 to the heir of Aragon, FERDINAND, strengthened her party. Proclaimed queen in 1474, she and Ferdinand laid the foundations of Spain's imperial expansion and cultural identity. The acquisition of the Muslim kingdom of Granada in 1492, after ten years of campaigning, moved the pope in 1494 to grant her and her husband the title of 'Catholic monarchs'. Patron of COLUMBUS, her imagination made possible the new discoveries. She also actively encouraged the cultural Renaissance symbolised by the presentation to her in 1492 of NEBRIJA's new Castilian grammar. Her acts and policies were identical with those of her husband the king.

Ivan III Vasilievich (1440–1505) grand prince of Muscovy and Russia 1462–1505, known as 'the Great'. He succeeded his father Ivan II. The first 'national' ruler of Russia, he helped to bring the territory into being by uniting to the princedom of Moscow the regions of Yaroslavl (1463), Novgorod (1471–8), Tver and Kazan (1481), and areas bordering northern Russia. After a period of war against Lithuania (1487–94, 1500–03) several other territories were added to the Russian lands, and he finally freed Muscovy from Tatar domination. By marrying as his second wife (1472) Sofia Paleologus, niece of the last Byzantine emperor, he claimed for Russia the heritage of the eastern empire and established Moscow's claim to be the 'third Rome' (after Rome and Constantinople). Important departments of state administration were created for the first time, and he drew up a code of laws (the *Sudebnik* of 1497). He built the main structure of the Kremlin.

Ivan IV (1530–84) tsar of Russia 1533–84, known as 'the Terrible' (in Russian 'the Thunderer'). His father the grandduke Vasili III died when he was three, and his mother acted as regent until her death in 1538; thereafter the boyar nobles took power. Ivan decided to take control and in 1547 was crowned 'tsar' ('Caesar'), a title derived from the Byzantine emperors. In his early years he dedicated himself to consolidating the frontiers of Russia by the annexation of Kazan (1552) and Astrakhan (1556), but his efforts in the west failed against the superior power of the Swedes and the Poles (wars of Livonia 1558–82). In order to strengthen his position as ruler, from 1565 to 1575 – a period in which he appears to have become seriously deranged – he declared the central part of his domains an '*oprichnina*' or feudal reserve subject to his absolute rule; imposition of the system was accompanied by brutalities that earned him his nickname of 'Terrible'. Married seven times, he killed his son and heir Ivan (1581) during one of his drunken excesses. The image of a wholly cruel Ivan was modified during the Stalinist period in the twentieth century, particularly through the film on Ivan made by the director Eisenstein (1943, 1946).

J

James II Stuart (1633–1701) king of Great Britain and Ireland 1685–8 (in Scotland as James VII). Son of CHARLES I and younger brother of CHARLES II, he was duke of York from birth. He spent the period 1648–60 on the continent, mainly at The Hague and Paris; served against the Spaniards in the French army under TURENNE (1652–5); then briefly (1657) took service under the Spaniards. At the Restoration in 1660 he was appointed lord admiral, built up the fleet and prepared it for significant victories against the Dutch, including the capture of New Amsterdam in 1664, re-named New York in his honour. In 1660 he married Anne Hyde, by whom he had eight children, two of them subsequently queens: MARY II, who married WILLIAM III of Orange, and ANNE STUART. Among his illegitimate children was the duke of BERWICK. He declared himself a Catholic in 1672, and the year after married Mary of Modena, who gave him seven children, including James STUART, 'the Old Pretender'. Heir to his brother's throne, his religion provoked all the major anti-Catholic political crises of the last years of Charles II: the Test Acts, the Popish Plot, and the Exclusion Crisis. He succeeded to the crown with little opposition (the 1685 MONMOUTH rebellion was easily crushed). But he lost support subsequently because of his promotion of Catholics to sensitive posts (by using his power to 'dispense'

individuals from the operation of laws that excluded them from office), and his backing for religious toleration (Declarations of Indulgence 1687–8). The governing élite felt threatened in their control of power. The birth of a male heir in 1688 and the prospect of a Catholic dynasty persuaded some leading figures to invite the Protestant William of Orange to invade England. James fled the country (December 1688) for France. He made an unsuccessful effort to return via Ireland (battle of the Boyne, 1690), then retired to exile in St Germain, where his court became the focus for Jacobite (Latin 'Jacobus' = 'James') sympathisers.

James IV Stuart (1473–1513) king of Scots 1488–1513. In 1502 he married Margaret Tudor, daughter of HENRY VII, a link that gave the Stuarts their claim to the English throne. As part of his military alliance with France, he tried to invade England but he and his army were destroyed on Flodden field (September 1513).

James V Stuart (1512–42) king of Scots 1513–42. Succeeding his father as an infant, he did not take charge of affairs until 1528, when he broke up the pro-English grouping led by the regent Albany, and reaffirmed the alliance with France: he was married briefly to the daughter of FRANCIS I (1537) and then in

1538 married MARY OF GUISE, daughter of the duke de Guise, by whom he had as daughter MARY STUART. With the help of cardinal BEATON, he blocked the advance of the Reformation in Scotland. His anti-English military policy suffered a fatal reverse at the battle of Solway Moss (November 1542); he was seriously ill at the time, and the news hastened his end.

James VI and I Stuart (1566–1625) king James VI of Scots 1567–1625, and James I of England 1603–25, first monarch of the Stuart line in England. Son of MARY STUART and lord DARNLEY, he was proclaimed king when Scotland was torn apart by opposition to his mother, and by conflict between pro-French Catholics and pro-English Protestants. Accepted on all sides as heir to England, he soon antagonised all shades of opinion there by his political initiatives and lack of tact. Firm believer in the divine right of kings (expressed in his book on *The Trew Law of Free Monarchies*, published in 1598 when he was king of Scotland), and in the established Church (he resumed harrying of Puritans, and provoked frustrated Catholics into a Gunpowder Plot in 1605), he nonetheless respected Parliament and married a wife who sympathised with Catholicism (ANNE OF DENMARK). He felt he was gratifying the élite by distributing numerous favours and titles, but also antagonised them by putting power in the hands of his homosexual favourites, first Robert Carr, earl of SOMERSET, then George Villiers, duke of BUCKINGHAM. His neutralist foreign policy was seen by critics as damaging the interests of Protestantism; they pressed him without success to intervene militarily in favour of his daughter ELIZABETH STUART, wife of the ex-king of Bohemia. Protestants particularly denounced the influence of the Spanish ambassador GONDOMAR, and the attempt in 1623 to marry the prince of Wales to the king of Spain's daughter. Constitutional, financial and religious grievances combined to create a crisis over the relative roles of the crown and of the governing classes represented in Parliament. Apart from his *Trew Law*, James' other published works included an attack on witches (1597), and a vigorous *Counterblast to Tobacco* (1604).

Jansen, Cornelis Otto (1585–1638) Netherlands theologian. A native of Guelders, he was educated at Louvain university, then studied in France where he made contact with the future abbé de SAINT-CYRAN. He returned to Flanders in 1617, became bishop of Ypres in 1636 and died two years later in an epidemic. His fame rests on his posthumous work the *Augustinus* (1640), which became the centrepiece for a generation of theological battle. The theory of 'Jansenism' was not connected with Jansen in any way, but elaborated in subsequent years by French thinkers, notably SAINT-CYRAN and Antoine ARNAULD, who claimed to find their inspiration in the *Augustinus*. This work consequently bore the brunt of attack by Jesuits and other anti-Jansenists, and phrases from it were condemned by popes in 1642 (URBAN VIII's '*In eminenti*') and 1653 (Innocent X's '*Cum occasione*'). 'Jansenism' became a powerful and international ideological movement, representing very diverse ideas. Before the mid-eighteenth century it identified itself largely with opposition to the Jesuits and to papal authority. In the Netherlands it inspired the secession (1723) of a group of 'Old Catholics' from the official Church.

Jeanne III d'Albret (1528–72) queen of Navarre 1555–72. Daughter of king Henry II of Navarre and MARGUERITE OF NAVARRE, sister of FRANCIS I of France, she was first married (1541) to the duke de Cleves, but the marriage was annulled and in 1548 she married ANTOINE DE BOURBON, duke de Vendôme; in 1553 she gave birth to the future HENRY IV. When her father died (1555) she became queen of Navarre, and converted to Calvinism (1556), which she introduced into her territory. She died when visiting Paris for the marriage of her son Henry to MARGUERITE OF VALOIS.

Jeannin, Pierre (1540–1623) French administrator. Of humble origin, he studied law, entered the profession and rose to be councillor of the court of parlement at Dijon (1579) and subsequently its president (1581). A firm Catholic, he supported the Catholic League during the civil wars and became adviser to MAYENNE. He eventually accepted the succession of HENRY IV and became one of his most trusted ministers, playing an important role in diplomatic negotiations with Savoy and Spain.

Jeffreys, George (1645–89) 1st lord Jeffreys of Wem. Educated at Cambridge and the Inner Temple, he entered the service of the duke of York in 1677, was appointed recorder of London in 1678, and chief justice of Chester in 1680. Appointed chief justice of England in 1683, in 1685 at the accession of JAMES II he was created a baron. Though criticised even at the time for his harsh judgements, his ill fame rests largely on his severity during the repression in the western counties after MONMOUTH's rebellion (1685); after the events he was appointed lord chancellor. At the Revolution of 1688 he attempted to flee but was captured and sent to the Tower, where he died within months.

Jenatsch, Jörg (1596–1639) Swiss leader. He was son of the Protestant minister of Samaden, in the Swiss territory known an the Grey Leagues (Grisons in French, Graubünden in German), which were of great strategic importance because they controlled access to the Valtelline pass through eastern Switzerland. The Spanish armies based in Milan relied exclusively on the Valtelline for access to the Habsburg lands in the Empire, but had to contend with the rivalry within the Grey Leagues between the Protestant minority,

led by Jenatsch, and the Catholics, led by the related Planta family. Pastor from 1617 of the village of Scharans, in 1621 he fled from the territory after a conflict in which the Catholic leader Planta was murdered. He allied with France (1624), which sent troops in to occupy the valleys; they returned however to Spanish control after the treaty of Monzón (1626). In 1635 he became a Catholic and supported the Spaniards, but was assassinated by his nephew Pompeius Planta in a vendetta by the Planta family.

Jewel, John (1522–71) English theologian. He was educated at and made his career at Oxford, taking holy orders in *c.*1550, but during the repression under queen MARY I went to live in Frankfurt and especially Zürich (1555–9). Returning under ELIZABETH I, he was appointed bishop of Salisbury (1560), and began to publish defences of the theological position of the new Church of England, notably the *Apologia pro Ecclesia Anglicana* (1562), and other tracts written in response to attacks by the Catholic writer Thomas Harding. He was the first systematic defender of the 'middle way' of the Church of England.

John II (João II) (1455–95) king of Portugal 1481–95. Son of Affonso V, while prince he intervened actively in the Castilian civil wars of the 1470s, in support of the claims of La Beltraneja. Twice regent of the realm during his father's absences, he proved to be an outstanding patron of the overseas explorations being undertaken by the Portuguese in Africa and the Indian ocean. A notable scholar, he welcomed into Portugal the majority of Jews expelled from Spain in 1492.

John III Vasa (1537–92) king of Sweden 1569–92. Second son of GUSTAV I VASA and markedly sympathetic to Catholicism, he was suspected of plotting against the throne by his elder brother ERIK XIV, who had him imprisoned 1563–7. In 1568 he successfully ousted Erik and succeeded him as king. He made peace with Denmark (peace of Stettin 1570) and allied with Poland against Russia, from whom he wrested the Baltic territories of Karelia and Ingria (1583). In 1587 he secured the election of his son, the Catholic SIGISMUND III VASA, to the Polish throne.

John IV (João IV) (1604–56) 8th duke of Braganza and (1640–56), 1st king of Portugal of the Braganza dynasty. A descendant of the kings of the house of Avis, eldest son of the 7th duke and of the Castilian Anna de Velasco, daughter of the duke of Frias, he became the logical choice for Portuguese nobles who in 1640 sought a leader for their rebellion against Spain, which had occupied the country since 1580. Backed actively by France, he was crowned in 1641, and defeated the Spanish troops at Montijo, near Badajoz (1644). A notable lover of music, he wrote tracts on the subject and also composed.

John (Johann) Casimir (1543–92) count of the Rhine Palatinate 1576–92. A Calvinist and fourth son of the elector of the Palatinate, Frederick III, he intervened militarily on the side of the French Calvinists (1567–75) during the civil wars. In 1583 he became regent of the Palatinate for his nephew the elector Frederick IV.

John Casimir Vasa (Jan II Kazimierz) (1609–72) king of Poland 1648–68. The last male descendant of the Polish branch of the Vasa dynasty, and son of king SIGISMUND III VASA of Poland, after a short military career in western Europe he entered the Jesuit order in Italy in 1640, but in 1648 was dispensed of his vows by the pope in order to accept the throne of Poland after the death of his brother WŁADYSŁAW IV. It was a disastrous moment: Poland was threatened by the Swedes in the west, by the Russians and by the Cossacks in revolt under KHMELNITSKY. By the peace of Oliva (1660) he

had to grant Prussia to Brandenburg and Livonia to Sweden, by that of Andrusovo (1667) he surrendered the Ukraine to Russia. Faced in addition by internal rebellion (1665–6) and unable to manage, he abdicated in 1668 and retired to live in a monastery in France.

John of the Cross, St (1542–91) Spanish mystic and poet. Friend and disciple of TERESA OF AVILA, he was christened Juan de Yepes and was born in Avila. Graduating from Salamanca university, he entered the Carmelite Order in 1563; from 1567 he helped Teresa in her reforms. As a consequence he was imprisoned by an unreformed institution of his own Order in 1577 and treated very harshly. The following year he escaped into a convent of Discalced or reformed Carmelites. And it was during those eight months of prison that he wrote most of the mystical poetry for which he became famous. Like Teresa, in his prose commentaries to his poems, he used his own personal experience to express his visions, but as a trained theologian and scholastic thinker, his imagery takes on a more literary cast than hers. But where his personal experience and his reading combine to maximum effect is in his verse. Here he uses the age-old conventions of spiritual love, the search of the soul to immolate itself in the flame of divine ecstasy. The ostensibly erotic theme in his poem *Noche oscura del alma* (*Dark Night of the Soul*) is transmuted into spiritual longing, also evident in *Llama de amor viva* (*Living Flame of Love*), where the elements of a love poem end in explosive exclamations of mystical transports. The most sustained and elaborate lyric *Cántico espiritual* (*Spiritual Canticle*) is much more complex than any of his other poems. As before, the soul, or beloved, goes in search of the divine lover. One can often use his prose commentaries as a key to unlock the often impenetrable but evocative symbolism of the poetry. Teresa and John of the Cross may be located chronologically in the

Spanish Counter-Reformation, but the prose of one and the poetry of the other transcend these purely temporal boundaries.

[BT]

John Frederick (1503–54) elector of Saxony 1532–47. Head with PHILIP OF HESSE of the German Lutherans in the League of Schmalkalden, and captured by CHARLES v at Mühlberg (1547), by the peace terms he gave up the title of elector, and half his estates were passed to the Albertine line of the family, thus creating two Saxonies, an electoral and a ducal. He was held prisoner until 1552.

John Frederick II (1529–95) duke of Ernestine Saxony 1554–95. Son of JOHN FREDERICK, he founded the university of Jena, made an unsuccessful attempt to reconquer the territories of electoral Saxony (1567) and was imprisoned for life in the castle of Steyr, in Wiener Neustadt.

John George I (1585–1656) elector of Saxony 1611–56. Born in Dresden, second son of the elector Christian I, he succeeded his brother Christian II. The leading Lutheran prince of the empire, he was an affable and politically astute ruler, guided in part by the advice of his chaplain Hoë von Hoënegg. During the Thirty Years War he pursued a policy of survival, allying with the dominant Imperial party after the defeat of the Bohemian rebels (1620), then accepting alliance with the Swedes (1631) when they invaded northern Germany. Concerned to secure a Germany free of foreign invaders, he reverted to alliance with the Catholics after their victory at the battle of Nördlingen (1634), backed the emperor's peace of Prague (1635) and in return was assured the province of Lusatia (eventually confirmed at the peace of Westphalia in 1648). The imperial alliance did not bring immediate benefits, for the Swedish army overran Saxony, inflicting crushing defeats on the Saxon forces at Wittstock (1636) and Chemnitz (1639).

John of Leiden (Jan Beuckelszoon) (1509–36) Dutch Anabaptist leader. By profession a tailor, he acquired an elementary education and travelled a bit in search of his fortune, then returned to his native Leiden, where he married and settled down as an inn-keeper. He then fell under the influence of the radical Anabaptist leader Jan Mathijszoon of Haarlem, who sent him to preach the gospel in the city of Münster. The mission was startlingly successful. By 1534 the Anabaptists, headed by Jan, took over the government of the city and established a religious dictatorship. The city was invested by troops of the prince-bishop of Münster and other leaders; it fell in June 1535 and many of the besiegers were massacred. The episode served to discredit permanently the methods of the extreme Anabaptists.

Johnson, Samuel (1709–84) English lexicographer. Son of a Lichfield bookseller, he studied at Oxford for three years, but left out of poverty; after some while in Lichfield with no steady income, he set out for London (1737) together with David GARRICK to seek his fortune. He took up casual writing for the *Gentleman's Magazine*, but continued with economic difficulties until in 1747 he agreed to draw up a dictionary of the language and in 1750 began writing for the *Rambler*. Thereafter he won fame in literary circles, and in 1762 received an annual pension from the government. His lasting fame rests less on his literary work and the dictionary to which he devoted so much of his life, than on the account of his life and sayings recorded by his biographer James Boswell.

Jones, Inigo (1573–1652) English architect and scenographer to the Stuart courts. Born in London the son of a clothworker, he is first documented as 'picture-maker' to the earl of Rutland (1603), the newly appointed ambassador to the Danish court. According to his pupil, James Webb, he had visited Italy early on, and was called from Venice to work for king CHRISTIAN IV. He designed a masque for Christian's sister ANNE OF DENMARK, JAMES I's queen, which was staged in January, 1605 – a function that he continued to perform at the Stuart courts until such entertainments were halted by the English Civil Wars in the 1640s. Among the creators of the masques were the poets George Chapman and Ben JONSON (whose services were finally terminated when he disagreed with Jones as to whether the visual arts or literature were the more important). Jones also created nine masques (1605–13) which were performed at Christ Church College, Oxford, and one for Robert CECIL, earl of Salisbury, in celebration of the opening of the New Exchange in the Strand (London). He also redesigned the south front of the earl's new residence at Hatfield (1609–10), and a note in Jones' copy of Vitruvius' *De architectura* (Chatsworth) reveals that he visited Paris in 1609. Shortly afterward he was appointed architect to Henry, prince of Wales, becoming surveyor to the crown in 1615, after a second trip to Italy as a tour guide for Thomas Howard, 2nd earl Arundel (1613). During this trip he met the Italian architect Vincenzo Scamozzi (1552–1616) and made a concentrated study of Roman ruins, acquiring a copy of Palladio's *I Quattro Libri dell'Architettura*. His most important buildings were the Banqueting House at Whitehall (1619–22); the Queen's House at Greenwich (begun 1616); the Queen's Chapel at Marlborough Gate (1623–7); and the reconstruction of Wilton House after the fire in 1647.

[JH]

Jonson, Ben (1572–1637) English dramatist and poet. Born in London of a Scots family, he was educated at Westminster School, and spent some time working as a

bricklayer and serving as a soldier in Flanders before entering the world of the theatre as actor and playwright. In 1598 he killed a fellow actor in a duel, was imprisoned and only escaped execution by claiming benefit of clergy. The same year his play *Every Man in His Humour* was produced. It included SHAKESPEARE in the cast and met with immediate success. There followed a number of satirical comedies and tragedies in the classical mode. His finest plays were written between 1606 and 1614: *Volpone* (1605/6), *The Silent Woman*, *The Alchemist* (1612) and *Bartholomew Fayre* (1614). He wrote a number of masques for the court of James II and was given a pension by the king. No official title was bestowed but essentially he is regarded as the first Poet Laureate. He was at the centre of a group of writers, which included SHAKESPEARE, DONNE, Beaumont and Fletcher, who met at the Mermaid Tavern. Regarded as the greatest author of his age, he was admired by younger men such as Suckling, Herrick and Carew, who became known as 'the sons of Ben'. His poems and lyrics, many of which come from his plays including the famous *To Celia*, were collected in *Epigrams* and *The Forrest* (1616), and *Underwoods* (1640). The unfinished pastoral poem *The Sad Shepherd* displays his lyrical genius at its best.

[GG]

Joseph, father (François Joseph Le Clerc du Tremblay) (1577–1638) French ecclesiastic. Of noble origin, he commenced on a military career and had connections at court, but suddenly changed his life and entered the Capuchin order (1599). Fired by religious zeal, he preached first among the Huguenots, then went to Italy intending to go on crusade and preach to the Turks. He was appointed adviser to MARIE DE MÉDICIS, then to RICHELIEU, whose closest adviser he became from 1624, earning the title of being Richelieu's 'grey eminence'. He served the cardinal on diplomatic missions, built up for him a network of information throughout Europe based on the Capuchin friars, and probably influenced the political ideas of Richelieu.

Josquin des Prez (des Prés; or Despres) (*c*.1440–1521) Franco-Flemish composer. He was the foremost composer of the High Renaissance. Born in the vicinity of Hainault, he spent much of his career abroad (*c*.1459–*c*.1504), in prestigious posts in Milan, Rome (the Papal Chapel), Ferrara and LOUIS XII's court. After returning to his homeland he acted as a provost at Notre Dame of Condé-sur-l'Escaut. His compositional output consists of vocal polyphonic settings of the Ordinary of the Mass, numerous other liturgical works, and a wide variety of French *chansons*, Italian songs and instrumental pieces. His ingenuity lies in perfectly balanced sections of diverse polyphonic techniques, harmonious sonorities, unifying motivic ideas and a novel compositional approach to expressive depiction of the text. His works were regarded indeed as a paradigm of the 'perfect art' of the Renaissance and were widely diffused during and after his lifetime.

[JE]

Joyeuse
Anne, duke de Joyeuse (1561–87) French noble. He had a short but brilliant career as favourite of king HENRY III, was given the queen's sister in marriage, and was created duke then admiral of France (1582) and governor of Normandy (1586). He was killed while fighting against the Huguenots in Guyenne.
Francis Joyeuse (1562–1615) Brother of Anne, duke de Joyeuse, he entered the Church, became archbishop of Narbonne (1582), then of Toulouse (1583) and eventually of Rouen (1605) and cardinal (1583). He negotiated the reconciliation of HENRY IV to the Catholic faith, and played a leading role in subsequent political events, crowned LOUIS XIII king and in 1614

presided over the Estates General, the last before the Revolution of 1789.
Henry, duke de Joyeuse (1567–1608) Another brother of Anne, he served in the civil wars against the Huguenots, then on the death of his wife entered the Capuchin order (1587) with the name of *père Ange*, but returned to the world to lead the armies of the Catholic League in Languedoc. One of the last to accept Henry IV as king, he was rewarded with the rank of marshal and appointed governor of Languedoc (1596). Three years later he returned to his monastery and died while going barefoot on pilgrimage to Italy.

Juan of Austria (Don John of Austria) (1547–78) Natural son of CHARLES V and of his German mistress Barbara Blomberg (who later married an official in Brussels), he was raised secretly (1551–4) in Leganés (Castile), then in 1554 entrusted to a noble courtier to be brought up. In 1559 he was introduced to PHILIP II, who accepted him into his court. From an early age he was entrusted with posts of authority, but his independent disposition and refusal to accept advice caused problems with the king. In 1568 he was made captain-general of the Mediterranean fleet, and in 1569 was entrusted with putting down the revolt of the Granada Moriscos, which he completed successfully. In 1571 he commanded the Spanish–Italian fleet that won a spectacular victory over the Ottomans at Lepanto. In 1573 he recaptured Tunis briefly for Spain. Ambitious to rule over a kingdom of his own, he evolved a scheme to invade England and overthrow ELIZABETH I, marry MARY STUART and thereby rule England and also bring peace to western Europe. In 1576 he was appointed governor of the rebellious Netherlands; peace efforts failed, encouraging him to revert to a successful military attack against the rebels at Gembloux (1578). He died that year, of typhus, at Namur. His body was dismembered for ease of transport, taken back to Spain, reconstituted and then buried among the royal tombs in the Escorial.

Juan José of Austria (1629–79) Natural son of PHILIP IV and the actress María Calderón, by his success in putting down the MASANIELLO revolt (1647) in Naples, recovering Barcelona from the French (1652) and governing Spanish Flanders (1656–9) (where, however, he was defeated at the battle of the Dunes, 1658), he established a claim to be the leading general of the monarchy. The new regency government in 1665 under CHARLES II HABSBURG's German mother Mariana of Neuburg, however, had no place for him. He therefore devoted his efforts to removing Mariana's chief adviser, the German Jesuit Nithard, from power (1669). Appointed viceroy of Catalonia in order to remove him from Madrid, in 1676 he raised an army and marched on the capital, where he was immediately conceded full powers. He controlled the government for only a brief period (1677–9), dying prematurely. An innovator and reformer, with a deep interest in culture and science, he attempted various reforms but did not enjoy the time to implement his policies.

Juana 'the Mad' (Juana 'la Loca') (1479–1555) queen of Castile 1504–55 and of Aragon 1516–55. Daughter of FERDINAND II OF TRASTÁMARA and ISABELLA THE CATHOLIC, in 1496 she went to the Netherlands to marry Philip the Fair, archduke of Austria, and gave birth there to the future CHARLES V. In 1504 she and her husband succeeded Isabella as rulers of Castile, but her husband died shortly after (1506) and she broke down into insanity, a condition to which she had been tending for some time. Her father Ferdinand was declared regent of Castile though she continued to be recognised as queen. At his death (1516) Charles was declared king of the two realms of Castile and Aragon, but Juana was considered coruler with him. She lived until her death

in retirement in Tordesillas, emerging briefly only to be acclaimed by the Comunero rebels in 1520.

Julius II (Giuliano della Rovere, 1443–1513) pope 1503–13, the quintessential Renaissance prince, known for restoring papal grandeur and for his patronage of the arts. Nephew of Sixtus IV (1471–84), he became a cardinal in 1471 and accumulated numerous benefices – eight bishoprics, an archbishopric and numerous abbeys. He exerted great influence in the election of his uncle's successor, Innocent VIII (1484–92), but proved incapable of preventing his chief rival, Cardinal Roderigo Borgia, nephew of CALIXTUS III (1455–8), from being elected ALEXANDER VI (1492–1503). He spent most of the next decade in exile in France. He encouraged and accompanied the French king CHARLES VIII to invade Italy in 1494 and later LOUIS XII in 1502. He succeeded the brief pontificate of Pius III in 1503 and embarked on a strenuous policy of regaining lost papal territory in the Romagna and the cities of Perugia, Bologna, Rimini, Faenza and Mirandola. He made and broke alliances during this volatile decade of the Italian Wars, most notably leading the League of Cambrai in the defeat of Venice in 1509 and supporting the Spanish restoration of the Medici in Florence in 1512. He convened the Fifth Lateran Council in response to the French in 1512 and sponsored a self-serving church reform against simony and nepotism. His administrative ability and financial reforms placed the Church bureaucracy on a sounder footing. He set the foundation for the High Renaissance in Rome and employed BRAMANTE, RAPHAEL and MICHELANGELO. He began the building of the new St Peter's, commissioned Michelangelo to paint the Sistine Chapel ceiling, and Raphael the papal apartments. MACHIAVELLI praised him effusively for his political acumen and actions to recover the Papal States, but others like ERASMUS in his savage satire *Julius Exclusus* criticised him for his secular disregard for the spiritual mission of the Church.

[JM]

Julius III (Giovanni Maria Ciocchi del Monte, 1487–1555) pope 1550–5. Cardinal in 1536 and elected pope in February 1550, he was responsible for reconvening the council of Trent in 1551. He confirmed the constitutions of the Society of Jesus, for whom he founded the German College (1552) in Rome. An important patron of the arts, he appointed PALESTRINA as director of music at St Peter's and MICHELANGELO as chief architect.

Junius (Du Jon), François (1589–1677) Son of a French Calvinist theologian of the same name, he became a pastor in the Netherlands (1617) then from 1620 spent thirty years in England as tutor and librarian to the family of Thomas Howard, 4th earl of Arundel. During this period he built up a rich collection of old manuscripts, which he later bequeathed to the Bodleian Library at Oxford. He returned for a period (1651–74) to the Netherlands, then settled in England. He published important philological studies on Anglo-Saxon literature.

Jurieu, Pierre (1637–1713) Huguenot leader. Son of a Calvinist pastor, he studied at the Huguenot colleges of Saumur and Sedan, then in 1658 went to England where he took Anglican orders and on returning to France (1660) succeeded his father as pastor in Loir-et-Cher after being re-ordained as a Calvinist minister. A learned scholar and controversialist, he published erudite works on theology, philology and history, but after the appearance of his *The Policy of the French Clergy* (1681) he felt it safer to seek refuge in Holland, where he was given a post as pastor and as professor of theology. After the Revocation of the Edict of Nantes (1685) by LOUIS XIV, he dedicated himself to publishing fierce attacks on the French government and on French intellectuals for supporting the measure. The principal voice of Huguenot protest in exile, he felt it his duty to be intolerant towards the persecutors, and called for the overthrow of both state and Church in France. His *Les soupirs de la France esclave* (*The Groans of Enslaved France*) (1689) became a classic of polemic.

K

Karlstadt, Andreas Bodenstein von (c.1480–1541) German religious radical. Born in Karlstadt (Bavaria), he studied theology at Erfurt and Cologne; from 1505 to 1522, he was professor of philosophy and dean at the university of Wittenberg, where he was one of LUTHER's earliest supporters. He backed Luther against ECK at the disputation at Leipzig in 1519, and was accordingly condemned along with him in the papal bull of 1520. While Luther was in the Wartburg, Karlstadt took a leading part in pressing for reformation in Wittenberg: he served communion in both kinds in church, and also married. The appearance of the prophets of Zwickau in the town caused further disruption to the old order, which Luther stabilised when he came back in 1522. Karlstadt, however, was becoming more radical in his views, and left. He began to question virtually all the precepts of the traditional Church, and favoured social equality of believers; he was accordingly banished from Saxony. He then spent several years as a sort of wandering prophet in the German lands. In 1534, he finally settled in Basel, where he accepted a post in theology at the university, and where he died of the plague.

Karo (or Caro), Joseph (1488–1575) Talmudic and rabbinic scholar whose authoritative code of Jewish law is still important for Orthodox Jewry throughout the world. Born in Toledo, Castile, he fled with his family in the expulsion of 1492 to find residence in Ottoman Turkey, where he lived for forty years. He studied the Talmud under his father and his uncle, and was influenced by the martyr Solomon Molcho. In 1522 he began work on the *Beit Yosef* ('House of Joseph'), which was completed twenty years later in 1542 in Safed (upper Galilee), where he had gone to study and had emerged as the leader of a community of scholars with a large yeshivah of as many as 200 pupils. The *Beit Yosef*, published in Venice in 1550–1, was a codification of Jewish law that investigated divergent rulings back to the Talmud to find a consensus response or interpretation. His one volume digest of conclusions from the *Beit Yosef*, the *Shulhan Arukh* (Prepared Table), was published in Venice in 1565 and remains a standard reference on Jewish law for Orthodox Jews. He also wrote a commentary on the chief works of Maimonides and a mystical work on the Kabbala.

[JM]

Kepler, Johannes (1571–1630) German astronomer. After studying at Tübingen, where he became a Copernican, he taught mathematics at Graz; in 1600 he visited Prague and worked briefly as an assistant to Tycho BRAHE. In 1601 he inherited the records of Tycho's astronomical work and succeeded him as (unpaid) Imperial Mathematician; serving RUDOLF II and then MATTHIAS, he retained the title until his death. In order to earn money he taught at Linz from 1612 to 1626, and in the following year became astrologer to WALLENSTEIN. Alongside a continuing interest in astrology and mystical aspects of cosmology, he was responsible for important developments in astronomy: on the practical side he produced a volume on optics and devised a form of telescope; during his unsettled final years he produced the *Tabulae Rudolphinae* (1627) from Tycho's data. Analysis of some of this material had already led him to propose three fundamental laws of planetary motion based upon elliptical orbits and to explain the tides as the result of gravitational attraction by the Moon. These ideas were only slowly accepted by other astronomers, but came to prominence later in the century through their incorporation into the work of NEWTON.

[FW]

Ket, Robert (d.1549) English popular leader. A man of social standing as landowner in Norfolk, in July 1549 he led a rising of country-people protesting against the enclosure of common lands. The number of participants in the rising rose to 16,000; camped outside Norwich, they negotiated moderate demands with the authorities, but were treated as rebels after they occupied Norwich. The earl of Warwick, John DUDLEY, suppressed the rising bloodily with the help of German mercenaries; Ket and his brother were captured and hanged.

Khmelnitsky, Bohdan (1595–1657) Cossack national leader. A member of the lesser nobility of the Ukraine, he was educated by Jesuits and in 1620 took part in his first military action, when his father was killed and he was taken prisoner by the Turks for two years, which he spent in Istanbul. He was ransomed and returned home to his family estates. In the late 1620s he joined the Cossacks, rising to become military leader of the Zaporozhian host on the lower Dniepr, who were then under Polish control. His differences with the Warsaw government and local Polish nobility induced him in 1648 to lead the Cossacks in a national uprising against Poland. Broadening his support to include Orthodox peasants and clergy, and relying on aid from the Tatars of the Crimea, he defeated successive Polish forces and constructed a large Cossack confederation with its own finances and administration. When Poland refused to recognise his autonomy, he turned for help to Moscow and in the treaty of Pereyaslav (1654) recognised Russian sovereignty while retaining complete independence. Dissatisfied with the conditions of the treaty, he looked further for help from the Swedes (treaty of 1657), but died before any agreements were made. Forerunner of the Ukrainian state, his achievement was the creation of a Cossack-dominated entity uniting all sections of the population; he himself referred to the entity as 'Rus', thereby claiming an identity to which Muscovy also laid claim.

King, Gregory (1648–1712) Noted in his day as a genealogist and herald in the service of the nobility, and as an accomplished map-maker and engraver, he became (1684) registrar of the College of Arms, and adviser to the crown on ceremonial. His best-known work, the *Observations Upon the State and Condition of England, 1696*, remains a basic statistical source for population.

Knox, John (1505–72) Scots Calvinist reformer. After spending a brief time at Glasgow university, he took minor orders and became tutor to children of a family in Lothian, where he met (*c*.1545) the reformer George Wishart, contact with whom confirmed him as a supporter of the Reformation, and he began his career as a preacher in 1547. Taken prisoner that year by invading French galleys, he was retained on board ship and released only in 1549, when he went to England (1549–54) and with CRANMER's support preached the Reformation at court. At the accession of MARY I, he joined other Marian exiles on the continent, and had a historic meeting with CALVIN in Geneva (1554). After visiting Scotland in 1555–6, preaching there and building up political support among the nobles, he returned to Geneva, where in 1558 he published several tracts including *The First Blast of the Trumpet against the Monstrous Regiment of Women*, directed against Mary of England and the regent MARY OF GUISE in Scotland. Returning home definitively in 1559, he led the armed struggle which ended in the Scots Parliament (August 1560) establishing the Reformation by law. Knox became minister of St Giles, Edinburgh. The return of MARY STUART in 1561 provoked a fierce struggle, both personal and religious, between the queen and the reformer; but the new religion, to his disappointment, made little further advance. He left a manuscript 'History of the Reformation within Scotland', published first in London in 1584.

Königsmark, Aurora, countess von (1662–1728) Granddaughter of Hans Christopher, count von KÖNIGSMARK, she was one of the gifted literary women of her age, spoke several languages, wrote poetry and composed a comedy in French and an opera in German. She became the mistress of AUGUSTUS II, elector of Saxony, by whom she had a son, the future marshal de SAXE.

Königsmark, Hans Christopher, count von (1600–63) A general from north Germany, he took service under the Swedes in the last stages of the Thirty Years War, shared with TURENNE the honours of the victory of Zusmarshausen (1648), and captured the city of Prague, which he looted of some of its treasures.

Kurbsky, Andrei Mikhailovich, prince (1528–83) Russian statesman. The leading adviser of tsar IVAN IV, in 1547 he was appointed to the tsar's government, and also began his military career in the campaign (from 1549) against the Tartars of Kazan, which was annexed to Muscovy (1553). In 1556 he was promoted to the rank of boyar, and named in 1557 to lead the campaign against Livonia. After 1563, he lost Ivan's favour and fled in 1564 to Poland, where he was given a command in the forces fighting against Russia. Deeply religious and a gifted intellectual, he published an important (and hostile) history of the reign of Ivan; his correspondence, valuable for several aspects of Russian history, has been published.

L

La Bruyère, Jean de (1645–96) French essayist, moralist and author of prose portraits. Born in Paris, like many he was destined for the law, but like CORNEILLE he was able to give it up due to a small legacy with which he bought an office of the crown. He spent most of his life attached to the CONDÉ family in their chateau at Chantilly. This afforded him the opportunity of observing closely the fashions and failings of high society. In 1688 appeared *Les Caractères de Theophraste, traduits du grec avec les Caracères ou les Moeurs de ce siècle* (*The Characters of Theophrastus, Translated From the Greek with Other Characters, or, the Fashions of Our Times*). With the fourth edition Theophrastus nearly disappears and the volume renews itself constantly with additional sharp observations on contemporary life. That La Bruyère was received into the Académie Française in 1693 shows that his readers relished his wit. These prose portraits had sufficiently transparent allusions to known figures to create an avid readership. His popularity was also due to a fluid style and an ingenuity of expression that did not rely on convoluted rhetoric, but often fell into a neat aphoristic frame.

[BT]

La Chaise, François d'Aix de (père La Chaise) (1624–1709) French ecclesiastic. He entered the Society of Jesus in 1649, and in 1675 was selected to be confessor to LOUIS XIV, a position he held till his death. Although he was very influential with the king, there is no direct evidence to prove that he had any influence on the great policy decisions of the reign. The king built for him a small country house just outside Paris; in 1804 the lands attached to the house were converted into a cemetery, which was given the name of the confessor.

La Fayette, Madame Marie Madeleine de (1634–93) French authoress of sentimental romances. As Mademoiselle de la Vergne, a well-educated young girl, she married the Comte de La Fayette in 1655. While he looked after his estates in the countryside, she settled herself happily in Paris, attending the famous salon at the Hotel de Rambouillet. Later she created her own literary gathering where she received noteworthy writers of the day, like LA ROCHEFOUCAULD and Madame de SÉVIGNÉ. Her greatest literary success was the prose romance *La princesse de Clèves* (1678). Its success does not derive from exotic settings or adventures but from the drama of sentiment, not extravagantly expressed, but clothed in all that taut reserve attributed to the so-called 'honnêtes gens', those sensitive beings whose preoccupation lies in the close analysis of their intimate feelings.

[BT]

La Fontaine, Jean de (1621–95) French poet, dramatist and composer of short stories and verse fables. Like many of his contemporaries, he was intended for the church or a religious order, but changed to law and eventually achieved financial independence which allowed him to devote his life to letters. He enjoyed sympathetic patronage and the fellowship of writers from high society, like LA ROCHEFOUCAULD, Madame de LA FAYETTE and Madame de SÉVIGNÉ. His first collection of *Contes* (*Stories*) dated from 1664 and ran to 1675. His *Fables* appeared in 1664 and continued to 1683; he was admitted to the Académie Française in 1683. He had the reputation of being a dilettante, but his fame derives from patiently recreating and reworking the genre invented by Aesop and Phaedrus. The tedium of the moral was always enlivened with a mask of humour and burlesque.

[BT]

La Noue, François de (1531–91) French soldier and writer. After serving in the Italian wars and in the Netherlands, he became a Calvinist and fought in the French civil wars with distinction, but was wounded at the siege of Fontenay-le-Comte (1570) where his left arm had to be amputated and he was fitted with an artificial substitute that earned him the nickname thereafter of 'bras de fer' (iron arm). On an expedition against the Spaniards in the Netherlands he was captured and held prisoner for five years (1580–5), a period he spent reading the classical historians and writing his *Discours politiques et militaires* (1587), an impressively impartial account of the years of civil war in France. In the last stages of the civil wars, he served HENRY IV against the Catholic League, and died fighting against the duke de MERCOEUR in Brittany.

La Rochefoucauld, François VI, prince de Marcillac and (from 1650) 2nd duke de (1613–80) Scion of a distinguished noble family from Anjou, his Calvinist grandfather died fighting in the civil wars and his father, a Catholic, was the first duke. He served in the French forces in Italy and on his return participated in court intrigues against RICHELIEU, which earned him a brief exile to his estates; after Richelieu's death, he took part in intrigues against MAZARIN, and participated actively in the military campaigns in the Frondes (1648–52) against the cardinal. Temporarily blinded in action, he retired to his estates and gave up his adventurous activities. He returned to Paris in 1656 to take part in the literary life of the salons, wrote an account of the Frondes (*Mémoires sur les brigues*, 1662) and from 1665 onwards published various editions (the final and fifth was in 1678) of his *Réflexions et Maximes morales*. These latter, reflections on life around him, betoken a man inclined more to meditation than to action. They are crafted with a deliberate, perhaps excessive degree of fastidiousness, betraying a world motivated by *amour propre*, by pettiness and hypocrisy, a world remote from the dramatic universe of his contemporary CORNEILLE.

[HK & BT]

La Salle, Jean-Baptiste de (1651–1719) French priest and educator. Heir to a rich aristocratic family of Reims, he became canon of the cathedral (1667), and studied to be a priest in Paris, where he took orders (1678); but then became concerned for the education of the poor, gave his fortune to charity (1684) and founded the Institute for Brothers of the Christian schools (the Salesian Brothers). In 1690 he took the unusual decision that no brother of the Institute should be a priest. His scheme for education, *The Conduct of Schools* (1695), was complemented by a spiritual treatise *The Duties of a Christian* (1703). Canonised in 1900, La Salle was accepted in Catholic circles as the patron of the teaching profession.

La Salle, Robert Cavelier, sieur de (1643–87) French explorer. Son of a Rouen merchant, he entered the Jesuit order in 1658 but abandoned it eight years later, and left to seek his fortune in Canada (1667), where his best-known achievement was his journey down the Mississippi (January–April 1682) from the Great Lakes to the Gulf of Mexico, at the end of which he formally took possession of all the territory he had covered for France, naming it Louisiana in honour of LOUIS XIV. He returned to France and obtained government support for colonisation, returning to Louisiana with a small military force. He died during this abortive expedition, killed by mutineers in his force.

La Tour, Georges Dumësnil de (1593–1652) Born at Vic-sur-Seille, near Metz (Lorraine), he was the son of the owner of the local bakery. A Georges de La Tour – perhaps this painter – was active in the artists' guild in Paris in 1613. Nothing further is known until 1616 when, at the age of twenty-three, he was recorded at Vic as godfather of a child. In 1617 at Vic he married Diane Le Nerf, daughter of the duke de Lorraine's goldsmith, who had been ennobled and was one of the wealthiest citizens of Lunéville. When his father-in-law died in 1618, he became head of the Le Nerf family, and moved his own household to Lunéville (1620) where he lived until the city was burned during the conquest of Lorraine by France (1638), when he moved temporarily to Nancy, where he is documented as 'painter in ordinary to the king' (LOUIS XIII). Other patrons included duke Henry II of Lorraine, and cardinal RICHELIEU, whose inventory (1643) shows a painting of St Jerome by La Tour, probably the large picture now in Stockholm. When peace was restored he moved back to Lunéville (1643) where he remained until his death in 1652. A specialist in nocturnal subjects, both religious and secular, it has often been assumed that he spent some of the 'missing' years before 1616 in Italy absorbing the influence of CARAVAGGIO; however, there is no evidence of this.

Paintings of night scenes were an old speciality in Lorraine long before La Tour, and Caravaggio's stylistic influence is minimal at best, although La Tour shared themes of card-sharping with such French Caravaggisti as Valentin de Boulogne. His major source of inspiration was rather the spirit of Catholic reform in Lorraine.

[JH]

La Vallière, Louise Françoise de La Baume Le Blanc, duchess de (1644–1710) French court lady. Daughter of provincial nobility, on her parents' death she was placed in the care of the duchess d'Orléans, Henriette of England, sister-in-law of LOUIS XIV. She became the king's mistress in 1661, a relationship made public in 1663 when Louis gave her extensive property and formed her lands into a duchy (1667). Of her four children by him only two survived (a daughter married the prince of CONTI). Though genuinely in love with the king, her religious sentiments rebelled against the relationship: she twice fled the court and had to be sought in person by the king. At the age of only thirty, she decided to retire to a convent and in 1675 entered the Carmelite order for life, as sister Louise of Mercy. In retirement she wrote her *Reflections on the Mercy of God* (1680).

Laffemas, Barthélemy de (1545–1612) French minister of state. Born in Dauphiné of lesser nobility, he served with HENRY IV in the wars and in peace became a master of the king's household, a post in which he came to know how royal finances operated. In 1602 he was appointed controller general of commerce and played a key part in the economic policies of the period. He is best known for his writings on economic reform, notably *The Trade of a Merchant* (1606). He believed that favouring luxury industries would stop the importation of expensive luxury goods, and promoted the culture of mulberries for silkworms. His most lasting achievement was the establishment of the factory at Gobelins (1603). His son Isaac de Laffemas (1584–1657) followed a career in the parlement of Paris, became councillor of state, and was a much hated official of RICHELIEU for the severity with which he dealt with enemies of the state.

Laínez, Diego (1512–65) Spanish ecclesiastic. A fellow-student of IGNATIUS OF LOYOLA at the university of Alcalá, he furthered his studies at Paris, where he formed one of the group of six students who joined Ignatius in Montmartre in 1534 and took vows in common. In 1538 he was teaching at the university in Rome, and became one of the founders of the Society of Jesus, approved by the papacy in 1540. In 1556, on the death of Ignatius, he became the second general of the society. His missionary work in these years took him to Germany and, in particular, to the colloquy of Poissy in France; he subsequently acted as a papal theologian at the council of Trent. In his native Spain he was opposed by many, both at court and among the clergy, because of his Jewish ancestry.

Lassus, Orlande (Orlando di Lasso) (1532–94) Franco-Flemish composer. He was the most prolific, versatile and 'cosmopolitan' composer of the late Renaissance. Born in Hainaut, his career led him to numerous centres in France, Italy, Germany and the Low Countries, prior to and during his long service as singer and subsequently *kapellmeister* at the prestigious Bavarian Court in Munich (1556–94). His enormous compositional output (above 1,000 works) comprises every musical genre cultivated in the continent; i.e. Italian madrigals and lighter songs, French *chansons*, German *Lieder* and an immense variety of Latin polyphonic works, including more than 500 liturgical and ceremonial motets. His stylistic diversity, superb contrapuntal artistry, clarity of musical projection and exquisite depiction of textual images are

astonishing. The numerous publications of his works throughout Europe (more than those of any other composer), as well as the titles of nobility conferred on him, reflect his eminent stature at the time.

[JE]

Latimer, Hugh (1485–1555) English bishop and martyr. Educated at Cambridge, where he became a fellow, he later took up a post in a country parish and was prosecuted for his opinions (1532). In favour at the court of HENRY VIII, he was appointed bishop of Worcester in 1535; in this role, he gave his support to the execution of dissenters both Protestant and Catholic. He refused to support the pro-Catholic Six Articles (1539), resigned his see and was imprisoned for a while. Under MARY I he was arrested (1553), and burnt alive at Oxford together with his colleague RIDLEY, whom he comforted with the words, 'We shall this day light such a candle in England as I trust shall never be put out'.

Laud, William (1573–1645) archbishop of Canterbury. Son of a clothier, he studied at Oxford, where he became a fellow, took orders and became noted for his theological views, opposed to the Puritans and in favour of traditional ceremonial and piety; in 1611 he was elected president of St John's college. Dean of Gloucester in 1616, he was appointed bishop of St David's in 1621. His concern for the rites and rights of the Church appealed to CHARLES I, who furthered his career: he became a privy councillor in 1627, bishop of London in 1628, chancellor of Oxford in 1630 and archbishop of Canterbury in 1633. He used his position to combat Puritanism and emphasise 'the beauty of holiness', the exterior forms of worship; he repaired cathedrals, imposed visitations on the clergy and reclaimed rights for the Church. His reforms were imposed with the help of the royal prerogative courts of

Star Chamber and High Commission, thereby provoking bitter opposition. The extension of his measures to Scotland provoked (1639) the Bishops' Wars. He collaborated closely with the policies of STRAFFORD; both men were therefore marked as enemies by the Puritans. Impeached by the Long Parliament in 1640, he was confined in the Tower but tried only in 1644. The accusation of high treason against him could not be substantiated, so recourse was had to a bill of attainder, which required no proof; he was executed on Tower Hill.

Lauderdale, John Maitland, 2nd earl of and (from 1672) 1st duke of (1616–82) Scots political leader. A leading Scots supporter of the Presbyterian party and the Covenant in the early 1640s, in 1647 he began to negotiate with CHARLES I, at the time under custody of the Parliament, offering the king an 'Engagement' by which Charles would impose Presbyterianism on England in exchange for Scots support. After the king's execution he supported CHARLES II and his forces invaded England, but he was captured at the battle of Worcester (1651) and imprisoned for nine years. At the Restoration he played a prominent part in politics, was one of the ministers of the Cabal, and secretary for Scotland (1669). He resigned from office on grounds of ill-health in 1680.

Law, John (1671–1729) Scots financier. Son of a rich Edinburgh goldsmith who bought the estates of Lauriston (the lands gave Law's descendants their noble title) he went to London as a young man to work in the trade there. Seeking the safety of exile after having killed his opponent in a duel (1694), he travelled on the continent and broadened his knowledge of monetary systems. Back in Scotland in 1700, he proposed to the parliament the founding of a bank that would issue paper money; the plan was rejected, but Law took it with him on his subsequent

European travels, when he settled in Paris in 1710. When his friend the duke d'OR-LÉANS became regent, he authorised Law to found a private bank (1716), issuing paper money backed by the state. The immediate success of the bank encouraged Law to found a trading company for Louisiana (1717–18). In 1718 the bank was proclaimed a state bank, and encouraged widespread confidence and speculation, pushing the value of its assets upwards. This encouraged Law to issue further money, beyond the real value of available assets; in January 1720 he was appointed controller general of finance. In February 1720, however, the bubble burst, and Law was forced to flee the country. After wandering through northern Europe, he went to England (1721), where he spent several years; he eventually died, poor, in Italy.

Law, William (1686–1761) English religious writer. He studied at Cambridge, where he became a fellow and took orders. Of independent spirit, he retained a lifelong sympathy for the Jacobite cause, and expressed himself forcefully in published controversy. From 1727 he became tutor to the Gibbon family and particularly their son Edward (father of the historian) at Putney, where he published his *Serious Call to the Devout Life*, and was visited by John and Charles WESLEY. Law's famous book was probably the most influential religious book of modern times in England, with the exception of BUNYAN's *Pilgrim's Progress*. It was inspired by his reading of Tauler, a Kempis and other mystics; from *c*.1737 he also became an adept of the works of BOEHME. A mystic who laid stress on the exercise of moral virtues, charity, simple country living and the importance of education, rather than on external aspects such as churchgoing, he was one of the key influences on the English evangelical mind of his age. His collected works were published in nine volumes in 1762.

Le Nôtre, André (1613–1700) French architect. Son of the supervisor of the Tuileries gardens, he was first directed towards a career as painter, and was instructed in architecture by Mansart; but he preferred to study gardening, and followed his father at the Tuileries in 1637, becoming in 1638 director of gardens at the palais du Luxemburg. His first masterpiece was the park for the chateau of Vaux (1656–61). Subsequently entrusted by LOUIS XIV with the parks of the principal royal palaces, he was ennobled by the king in 1675 and made controller general of the royal residences.

Le Tellier, Michel (1603–85) French statesman. Son of a government official, he made the law his profession, in 1638 became a judge ('master of requests') of the council of state, and in 1640 intendant of the army on the Piedmont border. He was favoured by MAZARIN, who made him in 1643 secretary for affairs of war. Under LOUIS XIV he formed part of a triumvirate with LIONNE and COLBERT, with special responsibility for war. He introduced the first changes directed towards reform of the military apparatus, a task he handed over to his eldest son LOUVOIS, informally from 1666 and officially from 1677 when he himself was appointed chancellor. He made himself rich in office, and founded a powerful family dynasty.

Lebrun, Charles (1619–90) French classicist painter, tapestry designer, decorator and lecturer; one of the founders of the Académie Royale de Peinture et de Sculpture (1648; Director, 1683) The precocious son of the sculptor Nicolas Lebrun, and brother of a painter and an engraver, he studied under Simon Vouet, and was later influenced by POUSSIN, whom he met in Rome (1642–6), and by the study of antique statues and the paintings of RAPHAEL, as well as by contemporary Italian painting. His most important clients were cardinal RICHELIEU; the unfortunate financier FOUQUET, whose elaborate chateau at Vaux-le-Comte he decorated; and LOUIS XIV, for whom he worked at Fontainebleau, in the Galerie d'Apollon at the Louvre, and the royal apartments and Galerie des Glaces (Hall of Mirrors, 1679), Salon de Paix, Salon de Guerre, and on much of the garden sculpture at Versailles after the fall of Fouquet. In 1662 he was also made director of the new Gobelins factory (Manufacture Royale des Meubles de la Couronne), which provided complete furnishings for all of the royal residences, including the famous silver furniture for Versailles which was melted down during the French Revolution. As chancellor and director of the Académie, he championed the cause of drawing over colour as the proper basis of painting, and strove to standardise French art by means of rational rules for such things as depicting human emotion ('the passions') – a policy paralleling the establishment of grammatical and literary rules for the French language being undertaken by the Académie Française. Lebrun was less important as a painter than as the virtual art dictator of France from 1661 until Colbert's death in 1683.

[JH]

Leeuwenhoek, Antony van (1632–1723) Dutch naturalist and instrument-maker. He developed methods of grinding optical lenses in order to make 'simple' (single-lens) microscopes, achieving a magnification, at best, of nearly two hundred times. This was much greater than was then possible by any other means, although it was the compound rather than the simple microscope that was to produce advances in the longer term. Leeuwenhoek used his instruments to study and display human and animal anatomical structures (e.g. muscle, hair, skin, teeth, eyes). He consequently provided the first accurate description of blood corpuscles and of circulation of the blood through the capillaries, discovered the single-celled animals now known as protozoa, and came closer to seeing bacteria than anyone else was to for a further century. His observations disproved the idea of spontaneous generation. As a result of his comparatively humble origins and because he wrote only in Dutch, his claims at first seemed suspect to more learned contemporaries; but his findings were soon replicated and both the Royal Society and Académie des Sciences elected him to membership in 1680.

[FW]

Lefèvre d'Étaples, Jacques (c.1460–1536) Born in Étaples, Picardy, he was educated in Paris, graduating in 1479, and joined the university faculty as a teacher. In 1491–2 he made the first of three visits to Italy (the others were in 1500 and 1507), during which he met leading humanists, such as FICINO and PICO DELLA MIRANDOLA, and renewed his vision of the approach to learning. From 1492 he began publishing commentaries on Aristotle, followed by editions of Aristotle's major works. His intention was to break from scholastic exposition and present Aristotle in a new but still fundamentally Christian light, deriving from a study of the Church fathers. His Italian journey had introduced him also to Hermetic philosophy, and in 1499 he published in Paris the writings of the Pseudo-Areopagite. He next moved on to commentaries of Biblical texts, which he published from 1509 onwards. The issue of textual scholarship raised some differences between Lefèvre's outlook and that of ERASMUS. From 1521 he moved to take up posts in Meaux, where his patron Guillaume Briçonnet was bishop since 1516 and where he formed part of the group known as the 'Meaux circle'. In this period he began to read the early works of the German reformers, and to change his own spiritual position radically; he now looked critically at fundamental questions such as the Eucharist and the priesthood. Facing hostility, he fled to Strasbourg in 1525, but was recalled by FRANCIS I and appointed

tutor to the royal children (1526). This gave him peace to finish translating the Bible into French; it was published in 1530 in Antwerp. From this year he transferred to the court of MARGUERITE OF NAVARRE at Nérac, where he lived till his death.

Leibniz, Gottfried Wilhelm (1646–1716) German philosopher and mathematician. Born in Leipzig, where his father was a professor of philosophy, he studied law at the university and obtained his doctorate at Altdorf. In 1667 he entered the service of the elector of Mainz, and quickly established a network of learned correspondents, which he extended through visiting Paris and London on diplomatic missions; conversations with SPINOZA (1676) were especially influential in the development of his philosophical ideas. In 1676 he returned to Germany as librarian to the house of Hanover, but a further reason to travel was provided by the task of writing a history of the duke's family (which he never completed). Over the next two decades one of his favourite obsessions was a scheme to unite all Christians, to which end he patronised meetings in Hanover and pursued a correspondence with BOSSUET. He was invited to Berlin by Sophia Charlotte, electress of Brandenburg, prompted the foundation of the Berlin Academy in 1700 and was chosen as its life president. After a brief interlude as Imperial privy councillor at Vienna, he returned to Hanover and died there. His most important works were left unpublished. Throughout his career he pursued a broad range of scholarly interests with the overriding aim of creating a unified system of knowledge. Work on devising a universal language was linked to an attempt to turn logic into a symbolic system, which was in turn related to mathematical achievements. During the 1670s he was responsible for significant advances in algebra, the use of infinitesimals, and exploration of early forms of differential and integral calculus. Because he did not immediately publish his results, he was later unfairly accused of plagiarism from NEWTON. He was critical of Newton's cosmological theories, especially because of the lack of a physical explanation for gravity, and tried to reconcile their mathematical content with a theory based on vortices. He was influenced by but not wholly in agreement with DESCARTES, offering his own concept of physical substance as made up of 'monads', moved by the ether and an inherent '*vis viva*' in accordance with a divine plan.

[FW]

Leicester, Robert Dudley, earl of (1532–88) Fifth son of John DUDLEY, duke of Northumberland, in 1550 he married Amy Robsart, daughter of a gentleman of Norfolk, where Dudley was also prominent, becoming MP for the county in 1553. Sentenced to death with the other Dudleys for their support of Lady Jane GREY, he was pardoned in 1554, returned to active political life and in 1559 was a member of the privy council of ELIZABETH I. The young queen, who had grown up with Dudley, was possibly his lover at this period. In September 1560 Lady Amy was found dead at the foot of the staircase at Cumnor Place, near Abingdon, where she was then residing. Rumour instantly pointed the finger at Dudley, who insisted on a thorough investigation of the case by jury; a verdict of accidental death was returned. Thereafter Elizabeth discounted the possibility of marriage with Dudley, who however advanced in favour, being granted lands at Kenilworth (1563) and other places, and created earl (September 1564). The most powerful noble in the realm, he entertained the queen at Kenilworth for three weeks in July 1575. The complex relationship between the two developed in intensity; but in 1578 he secretly married Lettice Knollys, widow of the earl of Essex. He became a leader of the Puritan, anti-Spanish party at court. In 1585–7 he led the expeditionary force sent to aid the Dutch rebels against Spain,

but it was not a success. Shortly after the Armada campaign, for which the queen appointed him lieutenant-general of the army, he died suddenly; rumour hinted at poison.

Leo X (Giovanni de' Medici, 1475–1521) pope 1513–21. Second son of Lorenzo de' MEDICI, he was destined for the Church by his family and made a cardinal when aged thirteen. Subsequently he travelled through the Empire and France, settled in Rome (1500) and cultivated links with artists. He became head of the Medici family in 1503, returned to Florence in 1512 and ruled the city jointly with his brother. In 1513, however, he was elected pope to succeed JULIUS II; since he was not yet in holy orders he was hurriedly ordained four days later then made bishop. His pontificate was historic for two main reasons: it coincided with a key phase of the Italian wars (France had claims to Milan, while the Spaniards defended Naples), and with the outbreak of the Lutheran crisis in Germany. French military success at Marignano (1515) obliged him to agree to the treaty of Viterbo, by which he ceded Parma and Plasencia, and granted FRANCIS I the concordat of Bologna (1516). He responded to LUTHER's challenge by condemning his doctrines (bull *Exsurge Domine*, 1520) and then by excommunicating him (1521). Open to criticism for his practice of favouring members of his family; for his failure to implement any of the reforms proposed by the Lateran council (which ended in 1517); and for his military involvements; he is to be remembered primarily for his work as a patron of the arts.

León, Fray Luis de (1528–91) Spanish friar, university professor, Biblical translator and commentator. Born in Belmonte (Cuenca), of a well-off family, he entered the Augustinian order at fifteen, then attended Salamanca university, and spent the rest of his life in that area. He studied scripture, theology and classics: at the age of thirty he was made a Master in Theology. Not without certain opposition, he occupied various university chairs in Salamanca, eventually becoming one of its most famous teachers. It is well-known that the Spanish Inquisition wished to impose a rigid orthodoxy on university personnel, a rigidity which Leon, not a compliant individual, came up against. His translation of the *Song of Songs* into the vernacular brought him into conflict with that body and he was sentenced to nearly five years in prison. There he elaborated a great deal of his work, the best known of which are *La perfecta casada* (The Perfect Wife) (1583) and his Odes, published by Quevedo in 1631. His biblical translations and commentaries were not published until 1779. The importance of his work in the vernacular lies in showing the capacity of the Spanish language to deal simply with complex topics, inspired throughout by his Renaissance Platonism. This is also evident in his poetry, written in imitation of Horatian odes. The central theme is the search for serenity of mind in a world full of emotional stress. He was not a radical thinker, nor a rebel, but a scholar who showed how one could use the common tongue to express difficult ideas for the average intelligent reader.

[BT]

Leonardo da Vinci (1452–1519) Italian High Renaissance painter, sculptor, architect, engineer, natural scientist and theorist. Born in the Tuscan hill town of Vinci, he was the illegitimate son of a young peasant or servant woman. His father, who later became a Florentine notary, took a bride of his own social class, and adopted Leonardo, apprenticing him at fifteen to Andrea del Verrocchio. Leonardo was admitted to the painters' guild in 1472. Handicapped by his 'commercial' education (arithmetic, plane geometry and algebra but little Latin, still the language of scholarly discourse) Leonardo

nevertheless considered himself a scientist, and is best known today through the 6,500 sheets of raw data taken in his characteristic left-handed 'mirror writing', detailing his knowledge of aerodynamics, comparative and human anatomy, botany, civil engineering, geography, geology, hydraulics, military science and optics, as well as his memoranda on the art of painting, which he evidently had intended for later publication. He left Florence in 1481, abandoning an unfinished *Adoration of the Magi* commissioned by the monastery of S. Donato a Scopeto, and entered the service of Ludovico SFORZA in Milan, where he remained for eighteen years as a civil engineer and designer of armaments, as well as painter and musician. He later served Cesare BORGIA as cartographer and master of armaments on the latter's military campaigns with the papal forces in central Italy. Only seventeen of his paintings survive: four unfinished and several in poor condition because of his use of experimental methods or materials. Two, however, are arguably the most famous paintings in the world: the *Last Supper* (Milan, Sta. Maria delle Grazie), a mural commissioned by Ludovico SFORZA for the refectory of the Dominican monks, and the *Mona Lisa* (Louvre; begun *c*.1503), which has been the subject of more lavish praise, speculation and undignified parody than any other single work of art. According to Vasari (who had never seen the painting), the sitter was the wife of Francesco del Giocondo. However, the portrait was never delivered, but remained in the artist's possession throughout his life, even as an exile in France. Its unprecedented format and chiaroscuro technique, as well as the woman's unprecedented smile suggest that it probably was kept as a demonstration piece. About 1503 Leonardo was commissioned by the Florentine Signoria to paint a mural depicting *The Battle of Anghiari* in the large audience hall of the Palazzo Vecchio, still unfinished when he left the city in 1506 to return to Milan at the invitation of the French governor Charles II d'Amboise, for whom he worked as architect until 1513. In 1517, now sixty four years old, he accepted FRANCIS I's invitation to settle in France as 'First Royal Painter, Architect and Engineer'. Little remains of this last period but a disturbing series of drawings, the *Deluges*, for he had lost the use of one hand, probably due to a stroke. He died in France in 1519, aged sixty seven.

[JH]

Leopold I (1640–1705) emperor 1658–1705. Second son and successor of Ferdinand III, he became heir when his elder brother died of smallpox. King of Hungary in 1655 and of Bohemia in 1656, he was elected emperor in 1658. He concentrated on building up his dynasty's power in the hereditary lands of the east rather than in Germany. The greatest challenge he faced was that from the Turks, who were pushed back by the army under MONTECUCCOLI at the St Gotthard pass (1664), but returned in 1683 to mount a dramatic siege of Vienna, relieved by the forces under John SOBIESKI. Now on the offensive, Imperial forces captured Belgrade and obtained the treaty of Karlowitz (1699) by which the emperor received all Hungary and Transylvania. In western Europe, Leopold attempted to limit the ambitions of LOUIS XIV and took part in all the wars against France; but he also collaborated in the several secret treaties partitioning the possessions of the Spanish monarchy in the event of the death of CHARLES II HABSBURG of Spain, and played an active military part in the opening stages of the war of the Spanish Succession. A firm Catholic and an advocate of strong economic policies, he made substantial contributions to the building programme in Baroque Vienna, and patronised Baroque music. His first wife was daughter of PHILIP IV of Spain; his third, Eleanora of Pfalz-Neuburg, was mother to the emperors Joseph I and CHARLES VI.

Lerma, Francisco Gómez de Sandoval y Rojas, marquis of Denia then duke of (1553–1625) Son of the marquis of Denia and 3rd count of Lerma, under PHILIP II he was a page in the palace, later becoming head of the household of the future PHILIP III and briefly viceroy of his native Valencia. When Philip became king he was created duke (1599), given lands and favours and confirmed as chief minister; he placed his family in lucrative posts, married his children well and accumulated an enormous fortune. The king took little part in government, which he left in Lerma's hands; the duke moved the court temporarily from Madrid to Valladolid (1600–6) in order to retain his influence over Philip. Though Lerma's period of power signalled the rise of the *valido* (favourite) as minister, it also restored authority to the constitutional bodies (the Cortes and the councils), encouraged the development of political thought (Juan de MARIANA), and fostered ideas for reform among treatise-writers (*arbitristas*). In foreign affairs the duke favoured peace, resulting in the end of conflicts with England (1604) and the Dutch rebels (Twelve Years Truce 1609), and a marriage alliance with France in 1615, when the king's sister Anna married LOUIS XIII and his son Philip married Louis' sister Elizabeth. The most notable national event was the expulsion of the Moriscos of Spain (1609–14), approved of by Lerma after initial opposition. In 1618 the duke achieved a bizarre wish, to be created cardinal. Opposition to his rule focused around his son, the duke of UCEDA, who succeeded him as *valido* when in 1619 Philip III dismissed the duke from power. Lerma retired to his estates and was made to disgorge much of his fortune.

Lesdiguières, François de Bonne, duke de (1543–1626) French military leader. Beginning his career as a lawyer in the parlement of Grenoble, he became an active Calvinist, changed his profession and entered the ranks of the Calvinist forces in the civil war, where he soon displayed his abilities: by 1577 he was put in command of the Huguenot forces in Dauphiné. His achievements made HENRY IV appoint him general of the armies in the Savoy-Dauphiné area, a task he fulfilled with such success that in 1591 the king made him governor of Dauphiné. He was created marshal in 1608 and duke in 1611, serving LOUIS XIII faithfully against the Huguenot rebels of 1620–1. In 1622 he converted to Catholicism and was rewarded with the post of Constable of France.

Leslie, Alexander, 1st earl of Leven (1580–1661) Scots general. Born in Angus, the illegitimate son of gentry, he received no formal education and from about 1604 was serving on the continent as a soldier. In 1605 he was fighting under the crown of Sweden, which he served for the next thirty years, becoming one of its most distinguished generals. In 1628 he successfully defended Stralsund for GUS-TAV II ADOLF VASA, against the forces of WALLENSTEIN; and was at the king's side at Lützen (1632). He came back at intervals to Scotland to visit his family; in 1638 he returned to lead the Covenanter troops against the English, crossing with them into England in 1640 and seizing Newcastle. When peace was made (treaty of Ripon), CHARLES I accompanied Leslie's army into Scotland and created him earl (1641). The outbreak of civil war in England saw Leven back in England with his army, on the side of Parliament (1644–7); he later refused to take part in the unsuccessful Scots expedition to support Charles (1648). In 1650, however, he led the Scots forces supporting CHARLES II, and was routed by CROMWELL at Dunbar. In 1651 he was captured by the English and taken prisoner to London; released in 1654, he retired to spend his remaining years in Fife.

Lessing, Gotthold Ephraim (1729–81) German dramatist and literary critic, educated at Leipzig university. His early plays show the influence of French and English dramatists, both in comedy and tragedy. His finest achievement was *Minna von Barnhelm* (1767), the first German 'comedy of manners'. His last play *Nathan der Weise* (1779), became famous as a convincing plea for religious tolerance. But it is as a dramatic critic that Lessing was known throughout Europe, and he figures as one of the principle forces in the German *Aufklärung* (Enlightenment). He was seen as freeing German literature from the counterfeiting of French classicism, and he introduced Shakespeare as an alternative path to follow. His collection of letters on dramatic topics reached a climax with *Laocoon* (1776), a seminal analysis of the differences and limitations of the different creative arts. It set a new standard for critical discussion in the future.

[BT]

L'Estoile, Pierre de (1546–1611) French diarist. An official of the French chancellery from 1569 to 1601, he used his intimate knowledge of the great persons of his day to write, from 1574 onwards, a unique account of their private lives and public activities. Never intended for publication, the so-called 'Memoirs' have the appearance of a gossip column, but their information is invariably reliable and a valuable source of information for the politics of the time. They were published in part shortly after his death; modern editions include all the sections censored by previous editors.

L'Hospital, Michel de (1505–73) French minister of state. He studied law at Padua, returning to Paris in 1534 with his protector the cardinal of Grammont, married and obtained as part of his wife's dowry a post in the parlement of Paris. Ambassador to the council of Trent in

1547, in 1550 he entered the household administration of Marguerite of Valois, sister of Henry II, joined the royal privy council in 1553 and took charge of a section of finances in 1555. In 1560 CATHERINE DE MÉDICIS appointed him chancellor of France, at a moment when civil and religious war threatened. Over the next few years he expressed his ideas in a series of public speeches and writings that conserve his reputation as one of the most remarkable statesmen of his day. He strongly supported royal authority as the only solution to the conflicts in France; of all evils, he declared, civil war is the worst. The use of force against a dissenting opinion, he maintained, is self-defeating, for it destroys liberty, 'and liberty and life go together'. In his discourse to the Estates General at Orléans in 1560 he appealed for mutual toleration between the faiths, and made later efforts to appease the Huguenots, without success. He resigned his post in 1568, disappointed by the failure of his moderate policies and suspected by all parties; his solution, nevertheless, was that eventually adopted by the crown under HENRY IV.

Lilburne, John (1614–57) English radical leader. Apprenticed to a clothier in London (1630–6), he helped in illegal printing and had to flee to Holland; on his return (1637) he was arrested, whipped and pilloried, but continued to publish his tracts. In the civil war he served as a captain for Parliament and was taken prisoner for a while, ending the campaign with the rank of lieutenant-colonel. He then left the army (1645) because an oath to the (Presbyterian) Covenant was made obligatory. Assertive and quarrelsome, in the following period he fell out with all opinions, and was several times ordered imprisoned by Parliament; but he appealed to his rights as a 'freeborn Englishman' (1647) and with his friend Richard Overton published pamphlets appealing beyond the House of Commons to the 'people'. He and his friends were conse-

quently dubbed 'Levellers' and accused of wishing to 'level' all social classes to one. In 1647 he issued his radical *Agreement of the People*, whose ideas he attempted to spread among the officers and soldiers of the army, following it up with a flood of other pamphlets. Parliament brought him to trial (October 1649), but he was triumphantly acquitted by the jury. Banished from the realm by Parliament in 1652, he went to Holland. On his return he was arrested and tried, was again acquitted by jury, but rearrested and kept in confinement in the Channel Islands. Released to go home (1655), he declared himself a Quaker, and spent his last days peaceably.

Limborch, Philip van (1633–1712) Dutch pastor and publicist. Son of a merchant and lawyer of Amsterdam, he was educated locally and at Utrecht, entered the ministry, and became one of the most prominent defenders of the Remonstrant (or Arminian) party in the Netherlands. He held posts as pastor in Gouda (1657) and in Amsterdam (1667). He wrote copiously, mainly on the Remonstrant question, and was the earliest scholar to give serious attention to the phenomenon of persecution represented by the Inquisition, in his famous *Historia Inquisitionis* (1692).

Linnaeus, Carolus (Carl von Linné) (1707–78) Swedish naturalist. He studied medicine at Lund and at Uppsala, where financial troubles were eased by his living in the household of the astronomer Anders Celsius. He soon turned to the study of natural history, lecturing on botany and undertaking a long journey through the north of Scandinavia in order to discover and classify new plants (as he later did elsewhere in Europe). At an early stage of his career he decided that the sexual organs of plants would provide the best basis for a new system of classification, a plan realised in his *Systema naturae* (1735 and many later expanded editions).

This set out a system for classifying plants by generic and specific names, offered precise definitions of the various species, and grouped genera in classes and orders; the same system was applied to animals and minerals, and the human body (strictly distinguished from the soul) was identified as *homo sapiens*. Though the details of arrangement were later subject to alteration, the orderly method adopted proved highly influential. The value of his work was recognised in his appointment as assistant professor and then, in 1742, professor of botany at Lund. After his death his library and collection of plants were bought by an English botanist, James Edward Smith, and came into the custody of the 'Linnaean Society' founded by Smith in 1788.

[FW]

Lionne, Hugues de (1611–71) French minister of state. From a noble family of Grenoble, he was nephew of the leading diplomat Abel Servien. Employed from 1643 by MAZARIN on diplomatic missions, he played a leading part in negotiating the peace of the Pyrenees (1659) with Spain. Under LOUIS XIV he became a member of the king's council and in 1663 was made secretary of state for foreign affairs. He was largely responsible for the diplomatic moves that prepared Louis' earlier wars of aggression, notably the War of Devolution. In 1668 he also negotiated the first of the secret treaties partitioning the Spanish empire in the event of there being no heir to the king of Spain, CHARLES II HABSBURG. One of the great ministers of the early part of Louis' reign, he established a notable dynasty of nobles and servants of the crown.

Lipsius, Justus (Joost Lips) (1547–1606) Flemish humanist. Born in Overijse near Brussels, he became one of the leading humanists of the age. In 1572 he accepted a post at the university of Jena, after changing from his Catholic religion to Lutheranism, and then at Cologne. But he spent most of his active life at Leiden (1579–92), for which he became a Calvinist. Finally, persuaded by his friend the Jesuit Martin DEL RÍO, he became a Catholic again, moving to the university of Louvain (1592) in the last years of his life. Known mainly for his commentaries on Latin authors such as Tacitus (1574) and Seneca (1605), he was a universal scholar who maintained an active correspondence (published in 1727 in 5 volumes) with the leading intellectuals of his day, from all nations and all faiths. A proponent of Stoicism both as philosophy and as moral discipline, he was also one of the leading publicists of the vogue, then gaining currency, for the writings of Tacitus.

Lisola, Franz Paul, Freiherr von (1613–74) Austrian diplomat. Born in the Franche-Comté of a family of Franco-Italian origin, he studied law in Dôle, and in 1638 was invited into the service of the emperor Ferdinand III by TRAUTT-MANSDORF. He served as ambassador to England (1643), and on several other diplomatic missions to Warsaw, Berlin, Madrid and Brussels; he also took part in the Westphalia negotiations. In the international situation of the 1670s, all his work was aimed at building up alliances between the European powers against the France of LOUIS XIV; he is justly famous as the most outstanding anti-French diplomat and publicist of his day. He was created baron of the Empire in 1659. His *Le bouclier d'État et de justice* (Shield of the State and of Justice) was an attack on Louis' aggressions. On behalf of the emperor, he helped to bring about the coalition between Austria, the United Provinces, Spain and Brandenburg (1673) against France, which had invaded the United Provinces. His great work was the agreement that in 1673 united the Spanish Netherlands, which the Spaniards were unable to defend adequately, with the emperor. He died in The Hague.

Locke, John (1632–1704) English philosopher. Educated at Oxford, where he taught for a while, he made friends with scientists who later formed the Royal Society, of which he was elected a fellow in 1668; and himself studied medicine for a possible career. He was chosen as tutor to the future earl of SHAFTESBURY, to whom he became secretary (1672); in this period he also made a lengthy visit (1675–77) to France. Closely associated with the earl's political fortunes, he accompanied him as secretary into exile (1683) after the defeat of the Whigs during the Popish Plot, and lived in Holland, where he made the acquaintance of literary figures. Returning after the 1688 Revolution, he settled in Essex. His best-known works germinated over a period of years: the *Essay Concerning Human Understanding* appeared in 1690; a *Letter Concerning Toleration*, begun in the 1660s, came out in Latin and English in 1689, and was followed by two more tracts on the same theme (1690, 1692); and his *Two Treatises of Government*, written in the 1680s, were published in 1690. The *Second Treatise* contains the fundamentals of his political philosophy; in it he argues that 'the chief end of men putting themselves under government, is the preservation of their property', and that all government is based on contract or 'consent'. Active as an adviser on trade to the government from 1696, Locke continued to write. His stature as a philosopher and political thinker is unequalled in western history. The treatises on *Government* and *Toleration* were the foundation of English liberalism for over a century, and were seen as defences of the political system established in Britain after the revolution of 1688; they also profoundly inspired the fathers of the American Revolution. In general his ideas were much admired by VOLTAIRE and other Enlightenment figures. In philosophy he may be seen as the founder of empiricism, the view that all our knowledge is derived from experience rather than from innate ideas.

Lomonosov, Mikhail Vasilievich (1711–65) Russian scientist with encyclopaedic interests. He studied at the Academy of St Petersburg, then from 1736 at the universities of Marburg and Freiburg before returning to St Petersburg in 1741. Beginning as a linguist and philosopher, he turned to chemistry and mathematics and ultimately to the physical sciences, especially mineralogy; as a result he became the first person to offer lectures on scientific subjects in Russian. At a theoretical level, he tried to establish explanations of heat, gravity and weight, within a corpuscularian framework; he also proposed a theory of electricity. His mineralogical experiments were matched by a practical interest in Russia's mineral resources. Elected a member of scientific academies of Sweden and Bologna, he also wrote about his country's geography, history and antiquities, and recorded its weather. His pioneering volume on Russian grammar (1757) was a landmark in philology. He is best known as the founder of the university of Moscow, named after him, plans for which he elaborated from 1755 onwards. His complete works have been published in 11 volumes (1950–83).

[FW]

Longueville, Anne-Geneviève de Bourbon-Condé, duchess of (1619–79) Daughter of Henry II, 3rd prince de CONDÉ, and Charlotte de Montmorency (sister of Henry duke of MONTMORENCY), and sister to the Great CONDÉ and the prince of CONTI, she grew up in an atmosphere of intrigue and conspiracy. Strikingly attractive, she was married in 1642 to Henry duke de Longueville as his second wife; he was twenty four years older, and she resorted to several lovers, among them the duke de LA ROCHEFOUCAULD, who influenced her to participate in the Fronde against MAZARIN. She involved herself directly in military events. When her husband and two brothers were arrested in the second Fronde (1650) she tried to raise Normandy against the king, and in

1652 she helped to rally Bordeaux and the south for Condé. After the Fronde, she turned to religion, joined the Jansenists of Port-Royal and became their greatest protector.

Lope de Vega Carpio, Felix (1562–1635) Spanish dramatist. The most prolific figure of the so-called Spanish Golden Age, Lope was known as a 'monster of Nature' because of his stormy personal relationships and his extraordinary literary productivity. A succession of women run through his social life and figure in his writings. On the other hand he became a familiar of the Spanish Inquisition in 1608 and was ordained a priest in 1614. His writings cover almost all the known literary genres, from the pastoral romance in both its secular and religious guises, to the short story. His poetic output is astonishing – some three thousand sonnets for example – ranging from ballads, verse epistles, odes, epics both national and religious, to mythological and burlesque narratives. He could also write highly mannered poetry full of conceits. Through all his poetry runs his fascination for the popular lyric, which is embedded in his dramatic exposition, a practice much imitated by his posterity. Indeed it is through the theatre that Lope is best known. He has been called the creator of the national drama, and is the author or part-author of some five hundred plays at least. The formula which he devised lasted on the Spanish stage until late in the eighteenth century, and is enshrined in his *Arte nuevo de hacer comedias en este tiempo* (*The Art of Writing Plays in Our Time*) (*c*.1607). It will be noted that the term *comedia* covers plays which have either happy or tragic endings. This formula involved abandoning the classical unities and contriving a close relationship between author and public. Lope gave them what they wanted, without ever breaking any established social or moral codes. His plays were unashamedly 'escapist' and remote from what later became known as literary realism. The famous code of honour which defined marital relationships between men and women gave rise to provoking situations involving vengeance by the husband, but this did not stimulate debate. Lope's aim was above all to entertain through rapid movement, brilliant versification and constant inventiveness. Character development had little to do with his theatrical art, and his success in subsequent generations is confirmed by the manner in which his plays were pillaged by his followers. Characteristic of his plays are *El caballero de Olmedo, Fuenteovejuna* and *El castigo sin venganza*.

[BT]

Louis XI (1423–83) king of France 1461–83. Son and successor of Charles VII, of the house of Valois, he made fundamental advances in creating the territorial integrity of France, till then divided into independent princedoms and dominated by the presence of the English. Commonly known as 'the universal spider' because of his political intrigues, he claimed to identify the interests of France with his crown. Married (1436) to the daughter of the king of Scotland, he grew up politically restless, and after an abortive rebellion against his father (1440) was pardoned and installed as ruler of Dauphiné; but after a subsequent plot (1445) was exiled to his province, where he initiated a historic reform of Dauphiné's institutions. Ruler from 1461, his principal concern was the threat to France from its powerful external enemies, principally the English and Burgundians, and from ambitious French nobles. The death of CHARLES THE BOLD of Burgundy in battle (1477) made it possible for Louis, after a campaign against MARY OF BURGUNDY, to secure by the treaty of Arras (1482) full sovereignty over the duchy of Burgundy as well as Picardy, together with possession of the Franche-Comté as a dowry for Mary's daughter Margaret, who was now pledged to marry Louis' heir, the future

CHARLES VIII. Louis' inheritance the year before (1481) of Maine and Provence consolidated the rise of the modern French state.

Louis XII (1462–1515) king of France 1498–1515. Duke d'Orléans from 1465, in 1476 he was forced by LOUIS XI to marry his sterile second daughter Jeanne. During the minority of CHARLES VIII he led the noble opposition to the crown, for which he was imprisoned for three years (1488–91). Reconciled with the king, he led one of the French armies that invaded Italy (1494), with a personal interest since he had a claim to the duchy of Milan through his Visconti grandmother. When Charles died heirless Louis was proclaimed king (1498), immediately obtained papal nullity of his marriage to Jeanne, and married Charles' widow Anne of Brittany. He then devoted himself wholeheartedly to the Italian wars, seizing Milan (1500) and Naples (1501), but was unable to hold on to the gains. He was driven out of Naples by the Spanish forces under FERNÁNDEZ DE CÓRDOBA (battle at Garigliano 1503) and had to give up Milan. In 1509 he descended again on Italy, and was faced by the Holy League (1511). His troops won a notable victory at Ravenna (1512) but in 1513 were defeated at Novara and forced to withdraw. In 1514, after the death of Anne, he married a third time, with the English HENRY VIII's sister Mary. He had two surviving daughters and no male heir, so was succeeded by his cousin FRANCIS I.

Louis XIII (1601–43) king of France 1610–43. Eldest son of HENRY IV and MARIE DE MÉDICIS, during his early years as king the regency (1610–14) was exercised by his mother, who left affairs in the hands of CONCINI. In 1615 he was married to the Spanish infanta, ANNE OF AUSTRIA, an unhappy marriage that produced no live heirs till 1638. In 1617 Louis had Concini assassinated, but in his turn left affairs in the hands of his

favourite LUYNES, after whose death and a short period of conflict with Marie de Médicis he began the long collaboration with RICHELIEU (1624–42). Weak and effeminate, Louis was certainly capable of firm enterprise (as in his military campaigns around 1620); but was notoriously bisexual (he was reputed to have a homosexual relationship with Luynes, and also had women lovers). A pious Catholic, the king supported the cardinal in all his policies and decisions, and therefore in some way contributed to the strengthening of the monarchy during his rule. The birth of his sons Louis (1638) and Philippe (1642) guaranteed the succession.

Louis XIV (1638–1715) king of France 1643–1715. Son of LOUIS XIII and ANNE OF AUSTRIA, he grew up during a turbulent regency directed by his mother, and was not declared king until 1651 during the Fronde. In those years he learned to oppose political instability, and from 1652 was ably guided in the principles of government by MAZARIN, who taught him to be his own master and bequeathed him a reliable group of ministers. From 1661, when Mazarin died, he took personal control of government: among his first acts was the disgrace of FOUQUET (September 1661), for corruption. Thereafter he collaborated closely with his ministers, who in his early years were COLBERT, LIONNE and LE TELLIER. The earlier part of his reign, to about 1683 (the year Colbert died), has normally been considered a period of great success in the consolidation of government, the launching of reforms, and the patronage of culture. The later years, by contrast, when the militarist policies of LOUVOIS were predominant, have been considered more problematic; and also experienced the great oppression of the Protestants that ended with the Revocation (1685) of the Edict of Nantes. This division ignores the fact that already from the 1660s Louis was committed to the policy of military aggression that eventually bankrupted his regime. On the positive side, as VOLTAIRE took pains to emphasise in his *Century of Louis XIV*, the France of Louis XIV made an unprecedented contribution to western civilisation in every branch of science and the arts, even when it frowned on disapproved ideas. The great palace at Versailles was a monument to royal 'absolutism'. Louis married, as a corollary of peace with Spain in 1659, Maria Teresa the daughter of PHILIP IV (she died in 1683); but had numerous love affairs, both before the marriage (with Mazarin's niece) and during the greater part of his reign (LA VALLIÈRE, Montespan, among others). His last mistress was madame de MAINTENON, whom he married secretly after the queen's death. His long life prejudiced the succession: his heir the dauphin died in 1711, and the dauphin's eldest son the duke of Burgundy died in 1712. Louis was consequently succeeded by Burgundy's son Louis. Around 1670 Louis began to compose his so-called *Mémoires*, which he dictated to secretaries; written for the education of the future dauphin, they shed interesting light on his own character.

Louis XV (1710–74) king of France 1715–74. During his infancy the government was directed by the regent ORLÉANS and after Orléans' death in 1723 by Louis Henri, duke de BOURBON (1723–6). Crowned in Reims in 1722, Louis was married at Bourbon's instance in 1725 to Marie Leszczynska, seven years his senior and daughter of STANISLAS LESZCZYNSKI. One of his first independent acts was to retire Bourbon in 1726 and replace him with his former tutor, cardinal FLEURY, who remained chief minister for seventeen years. On Fleury's death in 1743, the king became his own chief minister, but the period coincided unfortunately with diplomatic and military reverses. At the disastrous treaty of Paris (1763) which ended the Seven Years War, France lost Canada, Louisiana, much of the Carib-

bean and effective power in India. From the 1730s court life was profoundly influenced by Louis' successive mistresses, of whom the most significant were POMPADOUR (1744–64) and Du Barry. His reign has always been viewed unfavourably, in part because the period coincided with the eclipse of French power by that of England, in part because it has been seen as a prelude to the French Revolution.

Louis of Nassau (1538–74) Younger brother of WILLIAM I of Orange, he was born in Dillenburg, and became in his own right a leader of the lesser nobility of the Netherlands, particularly those who, like him, were Protestants. He led the moves to demand religious toleration from the government of MARGARET OF PARMA, and went into exile on the arrival of the duke of ALBA in 1567. From 1568 he led various military expeditions against the Spanish troops, most of them unsuccessful. He consequently relied for help on the French and on admiral COLIGNY, but this became unavailable after the massacre of St Bartholomew eliminated Protestant power in France. He and his younger brother Henry were killed near Nijmegen, in an attempted invasion across the Meuse from Germany.

Louvois, François Michel Le Tellier, marquis de (1639–91) French minister of state. Son of the leading minister of war Michel LE TELLIER, he was educated at the Jesuit college of Clermont and groomed to follow directly in his father's footsteps, taking over his posts when they were vacated. From 1672 he was minister of war and member of the council of state, acting jointly with his father; on his father's promotion to chancellor of France in 1677 he took over the direction of military affairs. From this period his capital role in reforming French administration and the military machine made him, after COLBERT, the country's chief minister; after Colbert's death in 1683 his authority was supreme. He is associated with the creation of a modernised army, equipped with up-to-date weapons and techniques and backed up by the appropriate administration (notably the intendants) and services (hospitals). He has also been seen as the inspirer of LOUIS XIV's aggressive wars against the rest of Europe, and has been particularly criticised for his order to lay waste the Palatinate in 1688. He supported the billetting of soldiers (the so-called 'dragonnades') on Protestant households in the period leading up to the Revocation of the Edict of Nantes. No other minister contributed more to the military preponderance of France in the seventeenth century.

Lully, Jean-Baptiste (1632–87) French composer, violinist and dancer. Born in Florence, he arrived in France at the age of fourteen, as a valet and music teacher to Madamoiselle de Montpensier at the Tuileries. His extraordinary talent led him to the court of LOUIS XIV in 1653. Through the most unscrupulous stratagem he gradually gained there the sole monopoly of the major musical activities. His authoritarian position may be regarded, indeed, as a small-scale reflection of Louis XIV's absolutism. His first task entailed writing and directing *ballets de cour* (court spectacles with dance and music). He also joined, and later trained, the king's string orchestra (*Les vingt-quatre Violons du Roi*) and established his own, smaller string ensemble (*Les Petits Violons*). Both became the most celebrated orchestral ensembles in Europe. In 1664 he began to collaborate with Molière on comedy-ballets, such as the well-known *Le bourgeois gentilhomme* (1670). From 1773 onward he composed fifteen operas (*tragédies lyriques*), which constitute the most sumptuous musical manifestation of Louis XIV's court. His last years were devoted primarily to church music. After his death his operas continued to be revered as an emblem of French classical 'purity'. Their overtures, dances and choruses left

a strong stylistic mark on eighteenth-century composers throughout Europe.

[JE]

Luther, Martin (1483–1546) Born in Eisleben, Saxony, eldest son of Hans Luther, who was of peasant origin but made some money in the local mining industry, he studied law at the university of Erfurt but then decided to enter religion in the Augustinian friars. In 1510 he went to Rome on business of his order, and on his return obtained his doctorate in theology (1512) and succeeded his mentor Johann von Staupitz as professor of scripture in the new university of Wittenberg, where his future career was to be based. Publication of his ninety five theses (1517) on the question of indulgences, is commonly taken to be the event that provoked the many debates and conflicts of the German Reformation. In the same period he also experienced the spiritual relief that convinced him that salvation (through faith) came from God and not through man's efforts. Condemned by a papal bull (1520), and summoned to defend himself at the Diet of Worms (1521), he began to publish rousing tracts and retired for security to the Wartburg castle of the elector of Saxony (FREDERICK III THE WISE). His key tracts *To the Christian Nobility of the German Nation*, *The Babylonian Captivity of the Church* and *The Freedom of a Christian Man* all belong to 1520. From this period he moved to develop his other views, helped in subsequent years by controversy with his other reforming colleagues, notably MELANCHTHON. No formal 'Lutheran' doctrine was formulated until the Augsburg Confession of 1530, but different theological views were prevalent long after. One of Luther's greatest personal achievements was his translation of the New Testament during his stay at the Wartburg. Published in 1522, in Saxon German, it became a major medium for the reforming message. The Reformation as a revolutionary movement had deep roots and complex causes, but Luther created it in the sense that he identified it with himself, and gave it an unequivocal voice. In 1525 he married an ex-nun, Katherina von Bora, and had three sons and three daughters.

Luxembourg, François Henri de Montmorency-Bouteville, duke de (1628–95) marshal of France. Posthumous son of the Montmorency-Bouteville executed in 1627 on RICHELIEU's orders for duelling, he began his military career in the army of CONDÉ in Flanders and took part in the victory at Lens (1648). He followed Condé into the Fronde, and with him entered the service of the Spaniards in Flanders after it; but made his peace with the court after the treaty of the Pyrenees (1659). He married in 1661, thanks to Condé's influence, the heiress to the house of Luxembourg and took over the title of duke. He became one of LOUIS XIV's great generals, as commander-in-chief of the armies invading Holland in 1672. In 1675 he was created marshal. He gained signal victories in the Netherlands in 1677–8, but in 1679 spent a year in the Bastille because of implication in an intrigue. He later returned to the Netherlands front to win the outstanding victories at Fleurus (1690), Steinkerk (1692) and Neerwinden (1693).

Luynes, Charles d'Albert, duke de (1578–1621) French royal favourite. From a French noble family of Italian origin, he was brought up at court as page to HENRY IV and then as court falconer, in which role he attracted the attention of LOUIS XIII, whose close favourite he became after the removal by assassination of CONCINI. Appointed governor of Picardy, then constable of France and Keeper of the Seals (1621), he accumulated riches and became duke (1619). At the same time he did much to fortify the king's position. He reconciled Louis with his estranged mother, and personally led the royal forces against rebellious nobles and Huguenots in the south of France (1619–20). He also encouraged the king to unify his kingdom of Béarn with France (1620). Luynes died suddenly of fever during the military campaign in Guyenne. Unjustly maligned by posterity, he put into practice much of the programme that cardinal RICHELIEU was later to adopt.

M

Mabillon, Jean (1632–1707) French scholar and one of the founders of critical historiography. He became a monk of the Benedictine order in Reims in 1652, taking orders eight years later; in 1664 he settled in the abbey at Saint-Germain-des-Prés, with the Congregation of St Maur, an offshoot of the Benedictine order. Over the next twenty years he prepared several learned editions of works, establishing as he did so new rules for the examination of historical texts. His most important work was the *De Re Diplomatica* (1681, with a supplement later), which pioneered Latin paleography and developed principles for determining the authenticity of medieval documents. He and his students published monumental histories of their Benedictine order.

Macanaz, Melchor de (1670–1760) Born in Albacete, Hellín, and educated in Valencia and then at Salamanca, where he studied law (1689–93), he went to Madrid, where he obtained a post as secretary to a noble who became viceroy of Aragon. He then passed into the service of the king, PHILIP V, and was appointed secretary to the council of Castile, for which he drew up several learned papers demonstrating the need to abolish the laws (*fueros*) of the autonomous provinces of the crown of Aragon, then in rebellion against the crown. He was sent to Valencia in 1707 to implement the abolition, which was decreed as a permanent law (June 1707) applicable to the provinces of Valencia and Aragon. In 1711 he was sent to Aragon to implement similar measures. Appointed attorney-general of the crown in 1713, he came into conflict with the Inquisition, which secured his banishment from Spain. He lived the next stage of his life in France, where he continued to perform services for the Spanish government, which in 1748 tricked him into returning to Spain. He was at once arrested, and imprisoned (in La Coruña) for the next twelve years, being released only in 1760, four months before his death. He was one of the best-known spokesmen for Spanish 'regalism' (or royal absolutism).

Machiavelli, Niccolò (1469–1527) Florentine man of politics considered the most important political theorist of the Renaissance. Of an old line Florentine family, he grew up in relative poverty. He entered the newly formed republican government in 1498 closely associated with its leader, Piero Soderini, and served as head of the second chancery and secretary of the Ten of War in charge of foreign affairs and defence. He himself went on diplomatic missions to LOUIS XII, MAXIMILIAN I OF HABSBURG, JULIUS II, and Cesare BORGIA, who became the model for his ideal prince, a man of decisive action. With the Medici restoration in 1512 and his suspected involvement in an anti-Medici plot in 1513 – despite denial under torture – he was exiled to his small farm outside the city where he unsuccessfully petitioned to win Medici favour from LEO X to re-enter government. There he wrote a number of enduring classics of political theory. *The Prince* (1513, published posthumously 1532), which examines how a newly acquired territory could be maintained, became the touchstone of a new realism in political affairs that placed what would be called 'reason of state' above individual morality. The *Discourses on the First Decades of Livy* (1516–19), a treatise on his preference for republican government, is wound around a commentary on Livy's founding of Rome. *The Art of War* (1519–20) defends his erroneous position that a citizen army is more effective than mercenaries and *The Florentine Histories* (1520–5) was written for Cardinal Giulio de' Medici, who as CLEMENT VII received the completed work. He also wrote two noteworthy comedies, *La Mandragola* (1518) with its convoluted plot of deception in seduction and *Clizia* (1524–5). A Medici commission led to his meeting with Francesco GUICCIARDINI in 1521 and their strong friendship produced an important literary exchange, but his slight Medici patronage caused the Florentine republic of 1527 to refuse to recall him shortly before his death.

[JM]

Magellan, Ferdinand (Fernão de Magalhaes) (1480–1521) Son of a noble, he went to India (1505–12) with ALBUQUERQUE, then to Morocco, then entered the service of Spain and obtained the support of CHARLES V for an expedition to find a route to Asia sailing westwards. He set out in September 1519 from Sanlucar on the *Trinidad*, with four other vessels, and made his voyage round the southern tip of the American continent, struggling for five weeks through the straits that later bore his name. Only three ships remained when they entered the Pacific. In the Philippines, Magellan and several of his men were killed in a conflict with natives (March 1521). Finally only one vessel, the *Victoria*, returned to Spain in September 1522, under DEL CANO.

Maine, Louis Auguste de Bourbon, duke de (1670–1736) Son of LOUIS XIV and Madame de MAINTENON, and greatly loved by his father, he was legitimised in 1673, received the title of duke, appointed master of artillery and lieutenant general, and given the right to succeed to the throne in default of princes of the blood (July 1714). On the death of Louis XIV, the regent ORLÉANS persuaded the parlement (1717) to deprive the duke of his rights of succession; the regent also deprived him of the post of tutor to LOUIS XV. Maine then got involved (1718) in a conspiracy against the regent organised by the prince of Cellamare, Spain's ambassador to France. He, his wife and the ambassador were arrested. Maine was imprisoned for just over a year, then retired from public life to his chateau at Sceaux, but his wife continued her social life there.

Maintenon, Françoise d'Aubigné, marquise de (1635–1719) She was born in prison where her father, son of the poet Agrippa d'AUBIGNÉ, and mother were confined for espionage. On obtaining their liberty, the family went to live in Martinique; after her father's death there, the family returned to France (1647). In 1652 she married the poet Scarron, paralytic and twenty five years her senior, and began to take part in cultural activities, making the acquaintance of Madames de SÉVIGNÉ and de LA FAYETTE. After Scarron's death (1660) she was introduced to Louis XIV's mistress Madame de Montespan, helped to bring up secretly the children Montespan had by the king and when they were legitimised (1673) she appeared openly at court in her own right and was rewarded with the title of marquise de Maintenon. After

Montespan's fall from favour she succeeded to the affections of the king, and was married to him secretly (no documentary evidence of the marriage survives) in about 1683. Though she appears to have influenced the king's personal and religious behaviour profoundly, she did not intrude into policy-making. She disagreed with several aspects of royal policy (including the revocation of the Edict of Nantes 1685), and was hostile to LOUVOIS's war policies. She sympathised with the conservative reformers associated with FÉNELON. She had an interest in education, and in 1686 founded the college at St-Cyr for the education of poor noble girls.

Maitland of Lethington, Sir William (c.1528–73) Scots nobleman. Of aristocratic origin, son of the poet and lawyer Sir Richard Maitland, as an official of the Scots crown but an opponent of French influence he strongly supported an alliance with England, and under MARY STUART acted as emissary to queen ELIZABETH I. Concerned to keep the country tranquil, if possible by marrying Mary to an English noble, he took part in the plots at court to murder Mary's lover DARNLEY and remove BOTHWELL. He fell foul both of the Scots nobles under Morton and of the invading English army, to whom he surrendered Edinburgh castle, where he died in prison shortly after.

Malebranche, Nicolas (1638–1715) French philosopher. Born in Paris, he studied philosophy and theology at the Sorbonne, entered the congregation of the Oratory and was ordained priest 1664, the year that he discovered DESCARTES' philosophy and decided to use it in his own enquiries, which also took in mathematics and science. His principal work was *The Search After Truth* (2 volumes, 1674–5), in which he explained his two main innovations. The first, namely the vision in God, accepted Descartes view that ideas are the basis of knowledge, but

argued that ideas are essentially in God and are known to us through God, so that man has access not just to simple ideas but to universal principles. The second, known as 'occasionalism', argued that finite created beings, because they are passive, have no causal efficacy but are 'occasional' causes, and only God is a true causal agent. His *Treatise on Nature and on Grace* (1680, condemned by Rome 1690) and subsequent works, elaborated his views, which provoked polemics with other philosophers, especially with Antoine ARNAULD. The official Church suspected the drift of his thought and put his principal works on the Roman Index in 1709.

Malherbe, François de (1555–1628) French lyric poet, commemorated by BOILEAU's famous line 'enfin Malherbe vint' (and then came Malherbe), heralding the literary reformer of the French classical period. Born at Caen of professional parents, he sought in his youth a patron who could offer him financial independence to pursue a poetic career. He became secretary to the duke d'Angoulême (1576–86); on the latter's death he lived in straitened circumstances until he was able to achieve a comfortable position at court from 1605 onwards. During this period most of his poetry was written (odes, sonnets etc.). His own poetry was unexciting and short on wit and sentiment. But he is best remembered as one who attempted successfully to block the effusive affectations of the current imported taste, and substitute a more sober, restrained and impersonal expression.

[BT]

Manasseh ben Israel (1604–57) Jewish scholar. Born in Madeira of a family of Portuguese New Christians (that is, of Jewish origin), his original name was Manoel Dias Soeiro. It was changed to Manasseh by his father, who emigrated to Amsterdam with his family after appearing in an *auto da fé* in Lisbon, accused of practising the Jewish religion. Intellectually precocious when young, Manasseh in 1626 founded the first Hebrew printing press in Amsterdam, specialising in works in Hebrew, Latin, Spanish and Portuguese. Many of his own writings, in Latin, were published by himself and address a Christian readership. Regarded at the time as the leading Jewish scholar in western Europe, he had close links with GROTIUS and with REMBRANDT; the latter painted his portrait and did the engravings for his book *Piedra Gloriosa* (The Glorious Stone) (1655). Manasseh took a leading part in negotiating the return of the Jews to England (they had been expelled in 1290). His *Hope of Israel* (1650) looked on the return as a key step in the millennarian hope of reuniting all the peoples of Israel. He went to England in 1655 and submitted a petition to Cromwell; in 1656 the council of state assented to the Jewish presence and allowed Jews the use of a synagogue and cemetery, though no formal permission to return was issued. Manasseh returned to Holland in 1657 and died the same year.

Mancini sisters   The five nieces of MAZARIN, daughters of a Roman noble who married the cardinal's sister, were famed for their beauty and elegance.

Hortense Mancini (1646–99) In 1661 she married a noble who took the title of duke de Mazarin; she also inherited the cardinal's fortune. Tiring of her husband, she left him in 1666 and travelled abroad, living first in Savoy and then in London, where she opened an intellectual salon and reputedly became a mistress of CHARLES II.

Laura Mancini (1636–57) In 1651 she married Louis de Vendôme, duke de Mercoeur, and was to die while in labour.

Marie Mancini (1640–c.1706) A childhood friend of Louis XIV, she became the great love of the young king, who wished to marry her. However, Mazarin prohibited the marriage and removed Marie from the court, marrying her in 1661 in Italy to the prince Colonna. She soon separated from him and returned to Paris, hoping to be welcomed by Louis, who however refused to see her and ordered her to a convent. Marie escaped and spent the rest of her life wandering from country to country, living for a while as a nun in Spain.

Marie-Anne Mancini (1649–1714) In 1662 she married the duke de Bouillon, and unlike her errant sisters devoted her life to society and culture in the Paris of her day.

Olympia Mancini (1639–1708) She married the count of Soissons in 1657, and was the mother of prince EUGÈNE OF SAVOY-CARIGNAN. For a while mistress of LOUIS XIV, she occupied a post in the royal household but had to leave (1665) because of the hostility of court ladies including Louise de LA VALLIÈRE.

Mandeville, Bernard de (c.1670–1733) Dutch thinker. Born in Rotterdam, he studied medicine at Leiden university and in 1692 qualified as a physician. He made a tour of Europe in the mid-1690s, found England very congenial, married there and settled permanently in London. Irritated by the movements for suppression of vice and prostitution in the capital, he began to publish essays arguing that vice was an integral aspect of virtue, and that human actions were based on logical self-interest; in this humans were, he said, like animals. He became known, and was vigorously attacked, for his essay *The Fable of the Bees* (first published 1705, revised 1714), a satire which argued that human vices were the principal mechanism of social advance, and that expenditure rather than saving helped to create wealth. In 1724 he published a defence of brothels, arguing that vice could not be prohibited and should be regulated. Though widely denounced, his ideas were subsequently borrowed by many thinkers.

Mansfeld, Ernst, count von (1580–1626) German general. Born in Luxemburg but of Saxon origin, son of the former governor Peter von Mansfeld, he made the army his career and served the emperor in Hungary and Germany but after a quarrel over reward for his services joined the Protestant nobles in Germany during the Thirty Years War, and was a commander of the rebel forces in Bohemia supporting the elector (FREDERICK V OF WITTELSBACH) in 1618. After the defeat at the White Mountain (1620) he moved to the Rhineland and carried out a war of attrition against the Catholic forces, together with Christian of Brunswick. An impenitent mercenary, from 1624 he entered into the pay of both England and France, but his forces were severely defeated by WALLENSTEIN at the bridge of Dessau (1626). He then went to Transylvania, where he failed to recruit the support of BETHLEN GÁBOR. On his way to Venice to seek subsidies for his army, he died in Bosnia near Sarajevo.

Mantegna, Andrea (1430/1–1506) north Italian painter and engraver. The son of a carpenter in Isola del Carturo, near Vicenza, he was legally adopted in 1442 by his teacher, Francesco Squarcione, and was enrolled in the Paduan painters' guild in the early 1440s. Feeling himself exploited, he left Squarcione's studio in 1448, and in 1455 successfully sued him for damages. At the age of eighteen he was employed as one of four artists to fresco the Ovetari Chapel in the Church of the Eremitani (Padua; 1449–57; bombed in 1944). While in Padua he also painted an altarpiece for the church of San Zeno in Verona (1457–59). In 1452–3 he married Jacopo Bellini's daughter Nicolosia, and in 1457 accepted an appointment as court painter to Ludovico II Gonzaga, 2nd Marchese of Mantua. He worked for half a century at this court, becoming one of the first princely painters of the Renaissance. The most important surviving works from his first decade in Mantua are the wall and ceiling frescoes in the Camera degli Sposi (Bridal Chamber) of

the ducal palace (completed 1474) commemorating the marriage of Ludovico to Barbara of Brandenburg, which demonstrate both his skill in portraiture as well as his fascination with linear perspective. During a two-year digression to Rome, he made a careful study of classical antiquities, and decorated the private chapel of INNOCENT VIII (destroyed 1730, to make way for a new wing of the Vatican Museum). Returning to Mantua late in 1490, where he was to remain until his death, he completed the *Triumphs of Caesar* (Hampton Court), as well as two mythologies for Isabella d'ESTE (the so-called *Parnassus*, 1497, and *Minerva Expelling the Vices from the Garden of Virtue*, 1502, both now in the Louvre). It seems to have been in this period that the daringly foreshortened *Dead Christ* (Milan) and the beautiful monochrome canvases, including the *Samson and Delilah* (London), as well as the elegant drawing of *Judith* (Uffizi) were done. A number of engravings in Mantegna's manner were made; recently, however, the actual extent of the artist's own involvement in printmaking has been questioned. Although very beautiful, and very important as influences on DÜRER, Jan Gossaert and others, it is possible that only the original drawings may have been done by Mantegna.

[JH]

Manuel I 'the Fortunate' (1469–1521) king of Portugal 1495–1521. He succeeded his heirless cousin JOHN II as king, and continued the crown's interest in seafaring; the voyages of Vasco da GAMA and Cabral were undertaken in his reign. He developed his links with Spain by marrying his son to a Spanish princess; he also expelled (in 1497) the Spanish Jews who had immigrated after the expulsions from Spain in 1492.

Manutius, Aldus (1449–1515) humanist scholar and tutor who turned printer to establish the Aldine Press in Venice. Born in Bassiano near Rome and studying in Rome and Ferrara, he came to Venice in 1490. He published his first book, his own Latin grammar, in 1493 and his first dated book, the *Erotemata* or *Constantine Lascaris*, in 1495. The Aldine press printed Greek and Latin classics as well as vernacular titles in excellently edited octavo format, inexpensive editions. Greek first editions of classical and post-classical writers numbered thirty; his five-volume Aristotle (1495–8) was probably his most famous edition. Latin editions usually were printed in press runs of 1,000 copies in an italic type face invented by his type cutter, Francesco Griffo. His distinctive device, the Aldine anchor and dolphin, first appeared in a 1502 Dante. A 1502 Sophocles first mentions the Aldine academy, the group of scholars engaged in editing and proof-reading. Notable scholars such as ERAS-MUS, who worked for him in 1508, participated in the high quality produc-tion of Aldine books. In 1505 he married, and his in-laws, the Asolani, entered the business. The press was the busiest in Venice and published about 130 editions between 1495 and his death in 1515. His in-law heirs abandoned the use of scho-larly editors and quality degenerated until his third son, Paulus, took over the press in 1533. In turn, Aldus Manutius the Younger, a son of Paulus, succeeded his father in 1561 and continued until 1585. The Aldine Press printed as many as 1,000 editions between 1495 and 1595.

[JM]

Mar, earls of A name shared by succes-sive distinguished members of a Scots noble family based in Stirling castle.
1st earl, John Erskine (d.1572) Son of Lord Erskine, he was guardian for MARY STUART during her minority, and as a Protestant worked to hold the balance between Catholic and Protestant nobles. A member of the privy council under Mary, he was created earl and in 1566 was appointed guardian of her heir James.

In 1567, however, he joined with other nobles to depose Mary and declare as king the young James, for whom he was appointed regent in 1571.
2nd earl, John Erskine (1558–1634) Son of the 1st earl, he was involved in the turbulent politics of the nobles during the minority of JAMES VI, and fled to England in 1584 but returned the year after and became one of the leading ministers of the king, particularly after James' accession to the English throne.
6th earl, John Erskine (1675–1732) He became earl in 1689 and secretary of state for Scotland under queen ANNE STUART, but was dismissed on the accession of George I (1714), and gave his support to the Jacobites. In 1715 he went to Scot-land, rallied support among the clans and proclaimed James STUART, the Old Pre-tender, as king. His forces were defeated by the duke of ARGYLL, and in 1716 he fled Scotland in the company of the pretender, whom he accompanied to Rome.

Marenzio, Luca (*c*.1553–99) Italian com-poser and singer. He was the most famous and prolific madrigalist of the Renaiss-ance. Most of his career was spent under the patronage of powerful ecclesiastical figures in Rome. He also stayed for a while at the opulent court of the Medici family in Florence, where he composed two *intermedi* for the grandiose theatrical spectacle, *La Pellegrina* (1589). He died in Rome shortly after returning from a two-year visit to the Polish court. Although he composed numerous sacred works, his fame rests on his seventeen madrigal books and three publications of villanellas and canzonettas (lighter art songs). Many were set to the texts of famous poets such as Petrarch, Sannazaro and Guarini. His mature madrigals, in particular, display a vivid and bold compositional approach to the depiction of the various images and moods suggested by the poetry. Their multiple republication and wide diffusion abroad (especially in England) testify to the composer's high esteem at the time.

[JE]

Margaret of Austria (1480–1530) duchess of Savoy, governor of the Netherlands. Daughter of the emperor MAXIMILIAN I and of MARY OF BURGUNDY, at the age of three she was promised to the future CHARLES VIII of France and went to live in the French court. When Charles married Anne of Brittany in 1491, she returned to live with her father and married in 1497 the infante Juan of Spain, who died shortly after. She then married in 1501 Filiberto the Fair, duke of Savoy, who died four years later. After this unhappy sequence, she decided never to marry again, and from 1506 acted for her father and then for her nephew Charles as governor of the Netherlands, whose destinies she directed in war and peace until her death. Her continent-wide family links also gave her a crucial voice in the politics of other nations, and she was valued as a diplomatic negotiator. She resided in Mechelen, from were she directed her considerable patronage in the arts.

Margaret of Parma (1522–86) Illegitimate daughter of the emperor CHARLES V and a girl from Oudenaarde, she was brought up by MARGARET OF AUSTRIA as a member of the family. In 1536 she was married to the Medici duke of Florence, who died shortly after; and in 1538 married Ottavio Farnese, duke of Parma. Her stay in Italy completely Italianised her; she thereafter had problems expressing herself in her native language. In 1559 she accepted the post of governor of the Netherlands for PHILIP II of Spain, but soon faced problems with the dissident nobility, and had to contend with the outbreak of religious contention. She was replaced in 1567 by the duke of ALBA and returned to Italy. In 1580 she returned to the Netherlands for a second term as governor, on the invitation of Philip II, and attempted unsuccessfully to collaborate with her son

Alessandro FARNESE, who commanded the army there; she relinquished the post in 1582 and returned to Italy. Her correspondence with Philip II in Italian and in French has been published.

Marguerite of Navarre (or, of Angoulême) (1492–1549) queen of Navarre (1492–1549) French humanist. Daughter of the duke d'Angoulême and sister to the future FRANCIS I, in 1509 she was married to Charles, duke d'Alençon (who died, childless, in 1525). When her brother became king in 1515, she was able to use court patronage to indulge her profound intellectual and religious interests, attracting writers and humanists. In 1521 she began to extend her patronage to the humanist group centred on Briçonnet, bishop of Meaux, and on LEFÈVRE D'ÉTAPLES. In 1527 she married Henry d'Albret, king of Navarre; of their children only one, JEANNE D'ALBRET, survived infancy. Marguerite had already started publishing her writings, and in 1531 her *Mirror of the Sinful Soul* provoked criticism from orthodox theologians. After the beginning of persecution of reformers in the 'affair of the Placards' (1534) she withdrew to her estates in Nérac, Béarn, and made her court into a centre of Renaissance scholarship, corresponded with some of the leading figures of the reform movement, such as CALVIN, and invited writers to Navarre. RABELAIS dedicated one of his works to her. A highly gifted personality, she knew several languages including Greek and Hebrew. Her fame rests principally on the *Heptameron*, a collection of travellers' tales modelled on the *Decameron* of Boccaccio, written in the 1540s and published after her death in Paris, in 1558-9.

Marguerite of Valois (Margot) (1553–1615) queen of Navarre 1572–99 and of France 1593–9. Daughter of HENRY II of France and CATHERINE DE MEDICIS, she was married to Henry of Navarre (later HENRY IV) in Paris in the week before the massacre of St Bartholomew, 1572. This political marriage was not to the personal liking of either of the spouses. Already at nineteen a veteran of several love affairs, she continued to complicate her life with lovers, and in Nérac (Navarre) ran a lively and dissolute court. Intolerant of her infidelities, Henry ordered her confined in the chateau of Usson, in Auvergne (from 1587 to 1605). After he became king of France, Henry secured from the pope a decree annulling the marriage, but in 1605 the ex-queen was allowed to come to Paris. Margot was the author of a book of poems, and also wrote her own *Mémoires* (published 1628), which cover the years up to 1582.

Mariana, Juan de (1536–1624) Spanish theologian. Natural son of a priest of Talavera (Toledo), he studied at Alcalá and entered the Society of Jesus in 1554; he was ordained (1562) in Rome, where he took a doctorate in theology. He taught in Messina (1567–9) and in Paris (1569–74), then returned to spend the rest of his life in the Jesuit college at Toledo. He played a prominent part in the Church, participated in the Toledo provincial council of 1582 and helped the Inquisition to draw up the 1583 Index of prohibited books. In 1609 he was imprisoned briefly by the government of the duke of LERMA for his tract *Del cambio de la moneda* (On Monetary Exchange), which criticised the devaluation of the currency. His best-known work is the *De rege et regis institutione* (On Kingship) (1599), an analysis of the nature of the state and of monarchic power. It argued that kings were created by the will of the people, which remains sovereign at all times (through elected representatives); if a ruler becomes tyrannical the representatives may elect to have him deposed or even killed. Though he and other Jesuits became notorious for supporting tyrannicide, it was a doctrine commonly found among many political theorists. Mariana also wrote a fine and original *History of Spain* (in Latin 1592, in Spanish 1601–15).

Marie de Médicis (1573–1642) queen of France 1600–42. Daughter of the grand duke of Tuscany, in 1600 she was married to HENRY IV of France, whose many mistresses she had to tolerate, and in 1610 on Henry's assassination became regent for her son LOUIS XIII. She left public affairs in the hands of her Italian favourites, Leonora Galigai and her husband CONCINI, whom the young king removed in 1617 by assassination. After this, conflict between her and her son was constant. In 1620 the conflict took the form of military action, 'the wars of the mother and the son'. RICHELIEU, who was her close counsellor, attempted to reconcile the two, but then passed over to the side of the king. Marie and her advisers favoured a pro-Spanish policy at home and abroad, which Richelieu did not support. She tried to remove Richelieu in the course of the Day of Dupes (1630), but the king supported him and she was obliged (1631) to go into exile for the rest of her life, living mainly in Brussels and finally in Cologne.

Marillac A prominent noble family from the Auvergne.
Louis de Marillac (1573–1632) The marshal Louis de Marillac, brother of Michel, was commander of the French army in Italy. Arrested for treason, on no evidence at all, after an eighteen-month trial he was condemned, and beheaded on the Place de Grêve. The removal of the Marillacs was part of LOUIS XIII's policy to crush what he perceived as opposition to himself and Richelieu.
Louise de Marillac (Mademoiselle Le Gras) (1591–1660) French religious reformer. In 1613 she was married to Antoine Le Gras, secretary to the queen of France. Widowed in 1625, she turned to pious works and with the advice of VINCENT DE PAUL founded in 1633 the order of the Daughters of Charity, which was not

enclosed nor were its members nuns but dedicated themselves to work among the laity. The order rapidly grew to become the largest female religious foundation of modern France. Louise was canonised in 1934.

Michel de Marillac (1563–1632) French statesman. He became master of requests in Paris then a member of the council of state, in 1624 was superintendent of finance and finally in 1626 Keeper of the Seals. In 1629 he helped to draw up the famous code of administrative reform known after him as the Code Michau; and became a close collaborator of the queen mother MARIE DE MÉDICIS. After the triumph of RICHELIEU in the Day of Dupes (1630), he was removed from office and confined to his residence, where he died.

Marlborough, John Churchill, 1st duke of (1650–1722) most famous of English military commanders. He rose to prominence as a friend of the duke of York (later JAMES II) thanks to his sister Arabella, the duke's mistress. As a soldier he served in Flanders (from 1672) under TURENNE with troops supplied to the French by CHARLES II. Under James II he helped to crush the MONMOUTH rebellion, but in 1688 he joined the side of WILLIAM III of Orange and was rewarded with the title of earl of Marlborough (1689). His relations with the new government were uneasy, and he continued to retain contact with the exiled king; as a result in 1692 he spent a few weeks under arrest in the Tower, but was in favour again by 1698. When ANNE STUART succeeded to the throne (1702) he enjoyed her favour thanks to the influence of his wife Sarah (married 1678), Anne's lady-in-waiting since 1683. Already active in politics, he formed with GODOLPHIN and HARLEY the Whig group which governed Britain for the next decade. He was confirmed as supreme commander of the forces engaged in the war of the Spanish Succession (from 1702) and was created duke.

His brilliant campaigns during the war made him undoubtedly the most distinguished general of his time. He commanded the joint Allied forces that won the famous victories over the French at Blenheim (1704), Ramillies (1706), Oudenaarde (1708) and Malplaquet (1709); after Blenheim a grateful Parliament approved the gift to the general of the manor of Woodstock, where an immense palace (named 'Blenheim') soon rose. In the 1710 Parliamentary elections the victory of the Tory groupings, who sought an end to the war and blamed him for wishing to continue it, changed his situation. He was recalled to England after the peace overtures made by the new ministry in 1711 (his wife Sarah had continued to hold sway over queen Anne Stuart until supplanted in 1711 by the queen's new friend Mrs MASHAM). Bitter criticisms of his conduct of the war made him decide to emigrate and live in Germany (1712–14), and he returned only after Anne's death.

Marlowe, Christopher (1564–93) English dramatist and poet. Born in Canterbury, the son of a shoemaker, he became a member of the earl of Nottingham's theatrical company, 'The Admiral's Men'. His first play *Tamburlaine* was produced in 1587. Other plays include *Dr Faustus*, *The Jew of Malta* and *Edward II*; the latter is considered his finest and is compared favourably with SHAKESPEARE's version. He took the medium of blank verse and gave it grandeur and energy, 'Marlowe's mighty line' according to Ben JONSON. His lyric poems, *Hero and Leander* and *The Passionate Shepherd* are full of grace and sensuality. Marlowe led a double life working for Sir Francis WALSINGHAM as a secret agent. He was also reckless, freethinking and indiscreet. In 1593 he was on the point of being arrested for disseminating atheistic opinions; on May 30th he was fatally stabbed in a brawl in a tavern in Deptford. This was almost certainly a coldly arranged murder in order to prevent disclosures which would have endangered his masters in the espionage service.

[GG]

Marnix, Philippe de, seigneur de Sainte-Aldegonde (1538–98) Netherlands soldier and poet. Born in Brussels, second son of a leading noble of Savoyard origin, he inclined towards the Reformation and went to study at Geneva, where he met BEZA. To his theological studies he added the study of Greek and Hebrew, and also picked up several modern languages; he was thus formidably equipped to serve the cause of Calvinism in the Netherlands. On returning home, he made common cause with the lesser nobles, joining Brederode and LOUIS OF NASSAU in presenting the Compromise (1566) to MARGARET OF PARMA. After the repression that followed the image-breaking of 1566, he was sentenced in his absence to banishment (1568), and wrote in exile that year a famous attack on the Catholic Church, *Den Byenkorf der H. Roomsche Kercke.* He joined WILLIAM I of Orange in preparing military attacks on the ALBA regime, but an invading force headed by William of Orange was scattered by the duke. At this low point in fortune, Marnix composed the *Wilhelmuslied*, a moving affirmation of faith in the prince and of opposition to Spain, that later became the country's national anthem. On a military mission in 1573, he was captured by the Spaniards and released a year later. He subsequently acted in various diplomatic missions, to Germany, Poland and England. He was the main agent on the rebel side for the agreements leading to the Pacification of Ghent (1576). He took part thereafter in all the major negotiations of the conflict, but was disillusioned when the attempt to have ANJOU as ruler (1582–3) ended in débacle. In 1583 he was appointed by William of Orange as mayor of Antwerp, and led the town's unsuccessful resistance to the army of Parma (1585). He retired for four years

of isolation to his estates, and dedicated most of his remaining years to indefatigable published controversies with his opponents.

Marvell, Andrew (1621–78) English poet. Yorkshire-born, he was educated at Cambridge and travelled on the continent for four years as a tutor (1642–6). In 1650 he was appointed tutor to the daughter of the Parliamentary general, lord FAIRFAX, at Nunappleton (where his best poems were written, including 'Upon Appleton House'); later (1653) he tutored a ward of Oliver CROMWELL at Eton (1653–7) (where he wrote 'Bermudas'). In 1657 he was, on MILTON's recommendation, appointed a Latin secretary to the government, and from 1659 to his death was MP for Hull. At the Restoration he continued to serve as a member of Parliament, and went to Russia in an embassy 1663–5; he also wrote scathing attacks on the politics of the period and the intolerance of the state church. Accomplished as a scholar and satirist, he was a religious person but not a sectarian, and though active in politics was not a politician. His detachment may be seen in his love poems, which though beautiful seem abstract. He is remembered entirely for his verse, including the famous 'Coy Lover'. His *Horatian Ode* to Cromwell was tactfully removed from his works when they were printed in 1681, and only published in 1776.

Mary I Tudor (1516–58) queen of England 1553–8. Daughter of HENRY VIII and CATHERINE OF ARAGON, she was educated by humanist tutors, and fleetingly betrothed in 1518 to the dauphin of France and in 1522 to the emperor CHARLES V. She was treated with disdain by Anne BOLEYN, who persuaded Henry in 1533 to exclude her from the succession in favour of newborn ELIZABETH. She was partially restored to favour from 1536, and in 1544 was recognised as successor to the throne after her brother EDWARD VI.

Queen in 1553, her first challenge came from the rebellion led by Sir Thomas WYATT the Younger, with unfortunate consequences for the young Lady Jane GREY. Her marriage to PHILIP II of Spain (1554) provoked widespread opposition, but her restoration of the link with Rome, solemnly declared in Parliament in 1554 by the papal legate cardinal POLE, was received complacently. The policy of burning heretics (1555), for which she was blamed both then and later, marked her in the memory of the English Protestants as 'bloody Mary'. About 273 persons, mostly of humble origin but including some bishops, were executed; and many Protestant sympathisers fled to the continent. The alliance with Spain took the country into war with France, with the consequent loss of Calais (1558), England's last foothold on mainland Europe.

Mary II Stuart (1662–94) queen of England and Scotland 1689–94. Eldest daughter of James, duke of York (later king as JAMES II) by his first wife Anne Hyde, in 1677 she married WILLIAM III of Orange and went to live at The Hague. She was proclaimed joint ruler with him after the Revolution of 1688, because her blood established the continuity of the hereditary succession to the throne. Devoted to her husband, she had few friends; she remained childless, quarrelled with her sister ANNE STUART, and rejected both her father and his son born in 1688.

Mary of Burgundy (1457–82) duchess of Burgundy 1477–82. The only child of CHARLES THE BOLD of Burgundy and his second wife, Isabelle of Bourbon, she inherited his extensive realms after his death, and immediately faced a serious challenge from LOUIS XI of France, who invaded her territories. In search of a defender, she married in 1477 Maximilian of Habsburg (later emperor as MAXIMILIAN I), who took charge of the military effort and defeated the French forces at

Guinegatte (1479). Tragically, Mary died young, after falling off her horse. She left two children, PHILIP THE FAIR and MARGARET OF AUSTRIA.

Mary of Guise (1515–60) queen of Scotland 1538–60. Daughter of Claude of Lorraine, 1st duke de GUISE, she was married in 1534 to Louis d'Orléans, duke de Longueville, who died three years later. In 1538 she married JAMES V of Scotland and had a daughter, MARY STUART, later queen. After the death of James in 1542, she took on the difficult task of regent of Scotland at a time when both religion and nationalism made Scots politics turbulent. Supporter of the link with France, she faced strong noble opinion in favour of a dynastic link with England. After her death her body was taken to Reims.

Mary of Hungary (1505–58) queen of Hungary 1522–26 and governor of the Netherlands 1530–55. Daughter of PHILIP THE FAIR of Burgundy, and of JUANA THE MAD of Castile, she was born in Brussels and brought up in Mechelen in the household of MARGARET OF AUSTRIA, then taken in 1514 to live with her grandfather the emperor MAXIMILIAN I in Austria, where she was educated in Vienna and Innsbruck. She was married (1522) to the sixteen-year-old king Louis II of Hungary and lived in Buda, but aroused Magyar hostility (led by John ZÁPOLYA) and had to rely for support on a small group of German and Magyar nobles, many of them active sympathisers of the Reformation. In August 1526 the Hungarian army, led by the king and most of the Magyar élite, was wiped out by Turkish forces at the battle of Mohács. Mary successfully backed her brother (the future emperor FERDINAND I) to succeed to the vacant throne; three years later she left the country to become, at the invitation of her brother the emperor CHARLES V, governor of the Netherlands. She was sympathetic to the Reformation for some time, and was in touch with LUTHER in Augsburg in 1530. She was apparently willing to act as a Lutheran in private, but not in public. She was also an admirer of ERASMUS, and when regent tried to get him to return to the Netherlands. In the Netherlands she carried out most of Charles' repressive measures, which were in any case directed mostly against radicals. Shortly after leaving the government of the Netherlands she went to Spain with Charles V (in 1556) and died there.

Mary Stuart (1542–87) queen of Scots 1542–67 and queen of France 1559–60. Daughter of MARY OF GUISE and JAMES V, she was born a few days before her father's death and therefore started life as a queen, with her mother as effective regent. To strengthen her anti-English policy, Mary of Guise in 1548 betrothed her daughter to the dauphin of France (later FRANCIS II) and sent her to live in that country, where she was educated and got married (1558). Francis II reigned for barely a year (1559–60) before his death; his young widow then returned to Scotland (her mother died in June 1560), which she found in ferment as a result of the Reformation. She attempted to play a moderate role between the contending parties, and also married a native Catholic lord, her cousin Henry Stuart, lord DARNLEY (1565), by whom she later had a son, James. Darnley's jealousy of Mary led him in 1566 to murder her private secretary (and possible lover) the Italian David RIZZIO. Alienated by the crime, Mary deposited her affection in James Hepburn, earl of BOTHWELL and a Protestant, who did her the favour of arranging an explosion at Holyrood which in February 1567 killed Darnley. Bothwell was cleared of any blame by the investigating judges, but Mary flouted opinion on the matter by marrying him (May 1567), a mistake which aroused widespread hostility. Rebel forces defeated her army, imprisoned her in Lochleven castle and forced her to abdicate in favour of her infant son, who became king with the earl

of MORAY as regent. She escaped from Lochleven in 1568 but her forces were defeated by Moray and she fled to England, placing herself under the protection of her cousin queen ELIZABETH I. In England Mary, as nearest successor to the throne (she was granddaughter of HENRY VII) after Elizabeth, was a political embarrassment and various interests tried to involve her in plots against the throne. She was confined for safety in several castles and last of all in Fotheringay. The last of the plots involving her was that of BABINGTON (1586), which provoked her arrest and eventually her execution at Fotheringay. A lady of culture and political ability, she became victim to political interests, notably those of Spain, and to her own habitual lack of discretion.

Masaccio (Tommaso di Ser Giovanni di Mone Cassai) (1401–28) Italian painter. The first painter to make full use of a unified lighting scheme and of BRUNELLESCHI's linear perspective system was Brunelleschi's young friend Masaccio ('sloppy Tommaso'), who achieved unprecedented effects of the third dimension. The son of a notary from the village of San Giovanni val d'Arno, near Florence, he was enrolled in the Florentine painters' guild in 1422, and in the Compagnia di San Luca in 1424, but had apparently been active in the city since 1418. In the mid-1420s he became the assistant to Masolino ('little Tommaso') in frescoing the Brancacci family chapel in the Carmelite church, Santa Maria del Carmine, on the unfashionable side of the Arno in what was then a slum neighbourhood. The theme of the chapel is the life of St Peter – probably a quasi-political choice on the part of the donor, for the Brancaccis were active members of the Guelph (papal) party. Masaccio's contributions include the scenes of the *Tribute Money*, in which correct linear and aerial perspective and a new grace and individualism in the handling of figures are used, and *St Peter Healing by Means of His Shadow* – a theme which earlier artists would have found impossible to depict. A still more revolutionary painting – a totally nude Adam and Eve bewailing their expulsion from Eden – the Eve in the pose of a *Venus pudica* – was painted at the entrance to the chapel. He also painted an epitaph for the Lenzi family in the nave of Sta. Maria Novella which not only make uses of Brunelleschi's perspective system but pays tribute to his architecture as well, with its coffered ceiling and accurate adjustment to the eye level of the (fifteenth-century Italian) spectator. He left the chapel to work in Pisa in 1426 on an altarpiece (now dismembered) for the Carmelite church there. He died in Rome in the spring of 1428, 'at about the age of twenty-seven', as the fifteenth-century writer Antonio Manetti says, having apparently gone there to fulfil a commission for pope Martin V.

[JH]

Masaniello (Tommaso Aniello) (1620–47) A fisherman from the village of Amalfi, he emerged as the leader of the rising that broke out in Naples in June 1647, provoked by the fiscal policies of the Spanish viceroy the duke of Arcos. The centre of agitation was the monastery of the Carmine, where Masaniello was based, his chief adviser being the priest Genoino. Elected 'captain-general of the people', he soon appears to have acted tyranically, and six weeks later was murdered, apparently by his own followers. The revolt was then led by Genoino, who was shortly captured and taken to Spain. In October a new leader arose, Gennaro Annese, who attempted an alliance with French forces under the duke de Guise (December 1647), but soon broke with the French and was overthrown by a Spanish expeditionary force led by JUAN JOSÉ OF AUSTRIA. Masaniello passed into popular folklore as the hero of the rebellion.

Masham, Abigail Hill, Lady (d.1734) English court lady. Daughter of a ruined London trader, she was rescued from poverty and befriended by Sarah, duchess of Marlborough, who placed her in the household of queen ANNE STUART, where she gradually supplanted the duchess in the queen's favour. In 1707 she married Samuel Masham, who was created a peer in 1712. She had an important influence on political decisions at court; after the queen's death, she lived in retirement with her husband.

Matthias (1557–1619) emperor 1612–19. He was born in Vienna, the third son of the future emperor MAXIMILIAN II and of Maria, the sister of PHILIP II of Spain. In 1577 he accepted the invitation of the States General, then in revolt against Philip II, to become governor of the Netherlands, but his stay was short. Despite his efforts, the Netherlands split in 1579 into two separate states, and the successes of the Spanish army obliged him to leave the country in 1581. His brother the emperor RUDOLF II did not grant him any post of authority until 1593, when he became governor of Austria, where he helped to repress the great peasant rising of 1596. He thereafter devoted his attention to the war against the Hungarian rebels and the Turks. In 1606 a peace was signed with the Hungarian leader Stephen BOCSKAI in Vienna. An armistice was agreed with the Turks in 1615, and lasted to 1663. In 1608 he took over the effective rule of the main Habsburg territories from his brother the emperor Rudolf II, and in 1611 was also formally invested as ruler of Bohemia. In 1612 he became emperor, and chose as his chief adviser cardinal Khlesl of Vienna. His marriage to Anna of the Tyrol was childless; he therefore nominated as his heir his cousin Ferdinand of Styria (the future emperor FERDINAND II), who was crowned king of Bohemia 1617 and of Hungary 1618. The Bohemian estates refused to accept Ferdinand, and a group of nobles carried out the defenestration of Prague (1618) and defeated troops sent against them. Khlesl was seized by Ferdinand and removed to a castle in the Tyrol (1618–22). At Matthias' death, therefore, the government was in chaos.

Maupertuis, Pierre-Louis Moreau de (1698–1759) French scientist. Born in Saint-Malo, he became known for his work in geometry and was elected to the Académie des Sciences (1723) and the Royal Society (1728). He became a leading proponent of experimental method, and in 1736 led an expedition to Lapland to measure the inclination of the pole and helped finally to prove that the earth was an oblate spheroid. He was also invited to Berlin by Frederick II in 1744 to reform the Academy of Sciences, and became its president (1746–59). He formulated the principle of 'least action' in mechanics: 'Whenever any change occurs in nature, the quantity of action employed is always the smallest possible' (1746). He extended this principle into an explanation of the universe in *Essai de cosmologie* (1750), in which argued that God's participation in creation was minimal. He had other writings on biology and epistemology and ethics, but his writings were unsystematic and never attained popularity. They were therefore of limited significance, though his contribution to certain aspects of physical thought has been neglected.

Maurice (Moritz) (1521–53) duke of Albertine Saxony 1541–7 and later elector of Ernestine Saxony 1547–53. He was born in Freiburg and succeeded his pro-Lutheran father Henry (duke 1539–41) as head of the duchy. The territories of Saxony, ruled by the Wettin family since 1423, were in 1485 divided between two brothers, Ernest and Albert; the former took the title of elector and most of Thuringia, the latter ruled that part of the province with Leipzig as its capital. Maurice, a convert to the Reformation since 1539, later married the daughter of

PHILIP OF HESSE. Though a Lutheran and active supporter of the Reformed cause, he refused to enter the military league of Schmalkaden, and in 1546 at the Diet of Regensburg was persuaded by GRANVELLE to make an agreement of neutrality with CHARLES V. The reward he was offered were the title and lands of electoral Saxony, whose elector JOHN FREDERICK thereupon withdrew from the Schmalkadic alliance in order to defend his lands against Maurice. The split in the Lutheran forces enable Charles to win the decisive victory at Mühlberg (1547), when John Frederick and Philip of Hesse were captured and sent to honourable confinement in the Netherlands. Maurice's possession of the title of elector was confirmed by the Diet in 1548. Though regarded as a traitor to the Reformed cause, he in fact continued actively to support the spread of Lutheran discipline in the Saxon lands. He persuaded his theologians to issue a modified version of the emperor's Interim (1548), which became known as the Leipzig Interim (1549). By 1550, he found his half-way position politically insupportable. He entered into secret agreements with Lutheran leaders and France (to whom he arranged the transfer of the three strategic bishoprics of Metz, Toul and Verdun in 1551), and in 1552 led an army against Charles, then at Innsbruck. Taken by surprise, the emperor was forced to flee, and had to agree to the peace of Passau (1552). When the margrave of Brandenburg Albert Alcibiades refused to honour the peace, Maurice went to war against him but was mortally wounded in the battle of Sievershausen (July 1553), dying two days after. In 1554 most of the lands confiscated from Ernestine Saxony were returned to it, but the electorate remained in the Albertine line. Maurice's daughter Anna in 1561 married WILLIAM I of Orange.

Maurice of Nassau, prince of Orange (1567–1625) stadholder of Holland, Zeeland and the major provinces of the northern United Provinces. Second son of WILLIAM I and Anna of Saxony, he succeeded to leadership of the rebel Netherlands after the murder of his father (1584) and dedicated himself to the struggle against Spain, winning important victories that established him as the greatest general of his time. His reforms in military tactics and strategy converted the Dutch army into the most advanced in Europe. Thanks to his efforts, in 1609 the Provinces were able to sign the Twelve Years Truce with Spain; despite its name, the truce established Dutch independence. In internal politics, his rule was marked by a bitter rivalry between the strict Calvinists, who supported the house of Orange, and the liberal 'Remonstrants', supporters of the republican oligarchy. The conflict ended with the arrest and execution of the republican leader OLDENBARNEVELT (1619). Maurice did not marry, and was succeeded by his brother FREDERICK HENRY.

Maximilian I of Habsburg (1459–1519) emperor 1493–1519. Son of the emperor FREDERICK III OF HABSBURG, in 1477 he married MARY OF BURGUNDY, daughter and heir of CHARLES THE BOLD, through whom he joined the territories of Burgundy to the Habsburg succession, a union that immediately made the Habsburg family a world power. One consequence was continual war against France, which also claimed part of Burgundy. A settlement was reached with the treaty of Arras (1482), which conceded Picardy and the duchy of Burgundy to LOUIS XI of France, retaining Franche-Comté and the Netherlands for the Habsburgs. After the death of Mary (1482) he acted as regent of Burgundy (1482–93) but faced serious problems with the independent-minded Netherlands, which he handed over first to his son PHILIP THE FAIR then to his daughter (MARGARET OF AUSTRIA). In 1490 he left the Netherlands for Austria, where he acquired the Tirol and fixed his capital at Innsbruck. He then recovered

Vienna and Lower Austria from the Hungarians, and after the peace of Bratislava (1491) began to use the title of king of Hungary. Crowned king of the Romans in 1486, he succeeded to the imperial title after the death of his father in 1493. As emperor Maximilian pursued an active policy of marriage alliances: in 1496 he married his son Philip to JUANA THE MAD of Castile; and in 1515 married his grandchildren into the Jagiełło family (1506), thereby securing succession to the thrones of Bohemia and Hungary (1526). In 1493 he himself married, as second wife, Bianca Sforza of Milan, which, however, brought him into the Italian wars, from which he gained neither territory nor prestige. He carried out important reforms in the government of Germany, creating a supreme Imperial court (1495) and an Aulic council to manage finances; he also divided the empire into six administrative 'circles' (1500), and founded the universities of Vienna and Ingolstadt. An archetypal Renaissance prince, he had universal intellectual interests in every branch of the arts, enjoyed hunting and jousting, could speak seven languages, composed creative writings, and patronised architects, painters and musicians. He also planned a series of historical works to commemorate his reign: 'he who during his lifetime does not plan to be remembered', he said, 'will not be remembered'.

Maximilian I Wittelsbach (1573–1651) duke of Bavaria 1597–1651, and elector 1623–51. Born in Munich, the son of duke William V, he was educated with the Jesuits at Ingolstadt (1587–91), and became one of the most efficient rulers of his time. His new law code of 1616 reformed the administration and finances of the state and remained in force till the end of the eighteenth century. A fervent Catholic, he gave solid support to the extension in his domains of the Counter Reformation, which left a permanent impact on the religion and architecture of Bavaria. He headed in 1609 the Catholic

League of German princes who opposed Protestant advance, and became the principal leader on the Catholic side during the Thirty Years War, in which his armies, led by general TILLY, defeated the Bohemian rebels (1620). In 1623 the emperor FERDINAND II granted him by decree the Upper Palatinate formerly ruled by the king of Bohemia (FREDERICK V OF WITTELSBACH) and with it Frederick's title of elector; both acts were confirmed in the peace of Westphalia (1648). He supported the policies of the emperor, in particular the Edict of Restitution (1629). But he was also a strong defender of the rights of the German princes, and opposed Ferdinand's method of implementing the Edict, and the pretensions of the Imperial general, WALLENSTEIN. In search of a strong ally against the invading forces of GUSTAV II ADOLF VASA (which routed the Catholic armies at Breitenfeld 1631 and at the Lech 1632), he allied with France for part of the war, but in 1635 joined forces with Saxony and the emperor (Peace of Prague 1635) to call for an end to all foreign intervention. Thanks to him, Bavaria survived the Thirty Years War more powerful than it had entered it.

Maximilian II (1527–76) emperor 1564–76. Eldest son of the emperor FERDINAND I, he was born and educated in Innsbruck, where his uncle CHARLES V knew him and was impressed enough to take him on his travels and campaigns. From 1548 to 1551 he was regent of Spain in the absence of prince Philip, whose sister Maria he married upon arriving in Castile; in 1548 he was also elected king of Bohemia. As ruler after 1562 of Hungary, his constant concern was the war against the Turks, but neither then nor later did he achieve any military successes. In Vienna he showed clear tendencies from this period of his refusal to support entirely either the Catholic or the Lutheran position; he is said to have informed the papal nuncio that he was 'neither Catholic nor Protestant, but a Christian'. However he was conscious of his duties to his position, swore solemnly to his father in 1562 at Prague to live and die a Catholic, and was crowned emperor in 1564. A careful politician, he maintained good relations with the Habsburgs in Spain, where he sent four of his sons to study, but openly criticised Spanish policy towards the Netherlands. Fluent in seven languages, cultured and an active supporter of humanists and the arts, he opposed religious persecution and attempted where possible (as in Lower Austria in 1568 and 1571) to concede toleration to Lutherans in the Habsburg territories. On his deathbed he refused to accept the Catholic sacraments.

Maximilian II Emmanuel (1662–1726) elector of Bavaria 1679–1726. As a soldier, he played a prominent part in the capture of Belgrade (1688). Subsequently, he accepted the governorship of the Netherlands (1691–99) for Spain. On the outbreak of the war of Succession he was confirmed as governor by Spain and France, but the Imperialist forces overran his electorate after the victory of prince EUGÈNE OF SAVOY-CARIGNAN at Blenheim (1704) and his forces in the Netherlands were defeated at Ramillies (1706); his states were not returned to him until the treaty of Rastatt (1714).

Mayenne, Charles of Lorraine, duke de (1554–1611) Second son of Francis, duke de GUISE, he became head of the Catholic League after the assassination (1589) of his brother Henry, 3rd duke de GUISE, and took over effective command of France in the name of the Catholic forces, declaring himself 'lieutenant general of the realm'. Defeated by HENRY IV at Ivry (1590), he was unable to pull together the various Catholic factions and disliked collaborating with the Spanish. In 1596 he eventually made his submission to Henry IV, and was appointed governor of the Ile-de-France.

Mazarin, Jules (Mazarini, Giulio) (1602–61) cardinal and chief minister of France. From a Neapolitan family, he studied in Rome and in Spain, had a short military career in the papal forces and then settled for the career of diplomat. While on a mission to Paris he met RICHELIEU, who employed him in the service of France: his first great success was in securing the treaty of Cherasco (1631), by which France obtained Pinerolo. As a Church diplomat, he was appointed legate to Avignon then nuncio to France (1635–6), after which he entered definitively into French service, and in 1641 was created cardinal (though he never became a priest). When ANNE OF AUSTRIA became regent (1643) he became her closest adviser and (according to rumour) also her lover. He also acted directly as tutor to the young LOUIS XIV, whose ideas he influenced profoundly. Faced by continuous opposition from the higher nobility, first in the 'cabale des Importants' (1643) and then in the Frondes (1648–53), he displayed his great capacity for survival. Attacked bitterly in the propaganda leaflets known as Mazarinades, he made tactful retreats from the conflict (in 1651 he went to Brühl, in 1652 to Bouillon) but returned eventually in 1653, consolidated his position and helped to establish the monarchy of the young Louis XIV, to whom his greatest legacy was the body of administrators (including LE TELLIER, COLBERT and LIONNE) in his service. During his ministry France resolved its international position through the treaty of Westphalia (1648), which brought peace in the north and confirmed possession of important fortresses bordering Germany; and through the treaty of the Pyrenees (1659), which ended the long war with Spain and secured possession of Roussillon. An active patron of the arts, he built for public use the famous Bibliothèque Mazarine.

Mazepa, Ivan Stepanovich (c.1652–1709) Ukrainian leader. From a noble family of Podolia, he was brought up at the Polish court, and from 1669 held office under the *hetman* (chief) of the Ukraine, mainly in a military capacity. In 1687, as one of the largest landowners of the area, he was appointed *hetman* of the Ukrainian Cossacks. In the struggle between Russia and Sweden, he supported the latter and promised to support CHARLES XII VASA at Poltava, but the Swedes were soundly defeated (1709) by PETER THE GREAT. Mazepa fled with Charles XII and apparently died in Rumanian territory. A hero of Cossack folklore, his career also inspired poems by Byron (1818) and by Pushkin (1828), as well as a symphonic poem by Liszt (1851).

Medici, Cosimo de' (1389–1464) Florentine banker and first citizen, 1434–64. Son of the wealthy banker Giovanni di Bicci de' Medici, he learned the family business of finance and management and used his power and influence to establish himself and his family as uncrowned rulers and later a 300-year dynasty in Florence. The family fortunes were built directly upon the fortune of the Medici bank, which was established in 1397 and profited greatly from his management of the finances of the Council of Constance, from its international banking network, and from enterprises in commerce and manufacturing. After the death of his father in 1429, the clan consolidated its position against the powerful rival family of the Albizzi, whose banishment of him in 1433 was irreversibly overturned in the 1434 election of the Medici party. With Cosimo's return, he assumed covert control of the city as a private citizen. He manipulated the pool of prospective city officials and later established a Council of One Hundred to set the legislative agenda before measures reached the public council and commune. In 1439 he lured the ecumenical council attempting reconciliation with the Eastern Orthodox Church from Ferrara to Florence. In foreign affairs, he allied himself with Francesco SFORZA, duke of Milan, who assisted in putting down an attempted Florentine coup in 1458. He became the pope's banker and in 1462 contracted a profitable monopoly over the papal alum mines at Tolfa. His patronage of the arts fuelled the Florentine Renaissance with support of architects BRUNELLESCHI and Michelozzo, sculptors Ghiberti and DONATELLO, painters Andrea del Castagno, Frate ANGELICO, and Benozzo Gozzoli, and the humanists Poggio Bracciolini and Marsilio FICINO. His legacy is debated as that of *padrino* (Mafia-like godfather/ward boss) or *pater patriae* (father of his country), the title conferred on him by the Signoria the year after his death.

[JM]

Medici, Cosimo I de' (1519–74) duke of Florence (1537–69), grand duke of Tuscany (1569–74). Son of the mercenary leader Giovanni delle Bande Nere ('of the Black Bands') who was killed in battle in 1526, he was a descendent of the junior branch of the Medici line from Cosimo de' MEDICI's brother, Lorenzo. He was raised by his mother, Maria Salviati, a granddaughter of Lorenzo de' MEDICI, outside the Florentine political sphere and was called to rule at eighteen upon the assassination of Duke Alessandro in 1537 by Lorenzino. Conservative patricians such as GUICCIARDINI, intent on forestalling a drift to a republican regime, installed him as duke with the support of the Spanish garrisons of CHARLES V. His long thirty seven year reign forged a stable, centralised state noted for its consolidation of power and imagery into Medici hands. Although he married Eleonora of Toledo, daughter of the Spanish viceroy in Naples, in 1539, his foreign policy aimed at creating independence from the Spanish hegemony by playing off Valois and Habsburg. It resulted in the annexation of Siena and its territories in 1557 as part of his policy to create a Tuscan state, not a Florentine 'city-state', which was recognised in 1569 with papal investiture as grand duke of Tuscany. He consolidated

all public offices in a single building (VASARI's Uffizi) and was himself the undisputed central figure in decision making. He patronised the court painters Pontormo and Bronzino, opened up Etruscan excavations, commissioned CELLINI's *Perseus* and Ammanati's Neptune fountain, and founded the Florentine Academy, but reserved his greatest cultural energies in building projects for Medici glory. VASARI's Uffizi and Ammanati's Bridge of S. Trinita stand out, as do redecoration of the Palazzo Vecchio, expansion of the Pitti Palace, the long gallery connecting the two across the Ponte Vecchio, the plan for the Boboli gardens, and the avenues along the Arno.

[JM]

Medici, Lorenzo de' (1449–92) Florentine 'first citizen', 1469–92, called by the honorific title, 'the Magnificent'. Grandson of Cosimo de' MEDICI, he assumed the unofficial leadership of Florence in 1469 upon the death of his ineffectual father, Piero. He continued the ruse of constitutional rule by manipulation of offices and councils and through the largesse of patronage. Two years into his leadership, dissidents in the popular council caused it to lose its financial powers and the Council of One Hundred was purged in favour of more sympathetic Medici partisans. He sponsored festivals and pageantry to move the Florentine patriciate closer to the aristocratic culture of the northern Italian courts. In 1478, the Pazzi, a rival Florentine banking family in league with Pope Sixtus IV, killed his brother Giuliano but failed to assassinate him in the Pazzi Conspiracy. The people stood by the Medici and he was able personally to travel to Naples and work out an alliance with FERRANTE I. His reputation derives, above all, from patronage of the arts during the late fifteenth-century Florentine Renaissance. He supported and received counsel from the philosophers FICINO and PICO DELLA MIRANDOLA, patronised the writers

Poliziano and Pulci, commissioned the artists Filippino Lippi, Giuliano da San Gallo, BOTTICELLI, Verrochio, LEONARDO DA VINCI and the young MICHELANGELO, and was himself a poet-humanist. In 1489, he provided for the family's fortunes by securing a cardinalate for his thirteen-year-old son, Giovanni, the future LEO X. Despite GUICCIARDINI's claims of a precipitous calamity in 1494 two years after Lorenzo's death, the weakness in the system had built up over his lifetime. The Medici bank was near bankruptcy and his lavish patronage had taxed it to the limit. In 1490, he allowed SAVONAROLA to preach at San Marco as the illusory peace was soon to erupt into the more than thirty years of the Italian Wars.

[JM]

Medina Sidonia, dukes of The ducal title was created in 1445 for a member of the powerful Guzmán family from Andalucia. Alonso Pérez de Guzmán, the 7th duke (1550–1619), was entrusted by Philip II with command of the Armada against England (1588). After its resounding failure, he was not held culpable by the king, and continued to hold high office. The 9th duke, Gaspar Alonso (d.1664), became implicated in 1641 in a plot to set up an independent state in Andalucia, but was saved from serious punishment because of his family link with the count duke of OLIVARES.

Melanchthon, Philip (1497–1560) German religious reformer. Born in the Palatinate, son of an armourer, Georg Schwarzerd (a surname Philip later changed for its equivalent in Greek), he was great-nephew of the humanist REUCHLIN and soon showed promise in the same field. He was educated at the universities of Heidelberg and Tübingen, then gave classes in the latter and began publishing his first works, on Greek grammar (1518) and on rhetoric. In 1518 he became first holder of the chair of Greek at Wittenberg, and soon made common cause with

LUTHER. In the same period he began to publish (1521) sections of his main theological work, the *Loci communes*, published by him in German in 1555; it was the first systematic exposition of the main points of Lutheran theology. His vigorous activity brought him to the forefront of the reforming movement, but he differed somewhat from Luther's approach: at the diet of Augsburg (1530) he helped to formulate the Confession of Augsburg, which Luther refused to accept without modification. Melanchthon took part in several important discussions (diet of Regensburg 1541) aimed at finding a common ground for the reformers, whether Protestant or Catholic. After Luther's death he was increasingly suspect to the Lutherans, because of his support for the emperor's Interim (1548). A strong supporter of the idea of unity among Germans, he was willing to accept compromises that advanced the idea. In 1552 he was even preparing to go (a journey he did not complete) to the council of Trent to argue the Lutheran case. Despite his failure to achieve religious unity among reformers or with Catholics in Germany, he made a major contribution to the Reformation, drawing up programmes for the reorganisation of several universities, and editing ordinances for church discipline. A lifelong admirer of ERASMUS, whose views he scrupulously respected, he differed from Luther in theological emphasis.

Mendoza, Bernardino de (1540–1604) Spanish diplomat. From an illustrious grandee family, he studied at Alcalá university and from 1560 began his military career; he served in north Africa, Malta and Italy. In 1572–4 he was in the Netherlands with the Spanish troops. From 1574 he began his diplomatic career. From 1578 to 1584 he served as ambassador to ELIZABETH I of England, a sensitive post in which he felt it necessary to participate in plots against the throne; he was expelled in 1584 for implication in the Throckmorton Plot. PHILIP II appointed him ambassador to France (1584–91), where he allied with the Catholic League and had cognisance of plots against the French king, HENRY IV; at the same time, he continued plotting against the English. Withdrawn from France when Paris fell to Henry IV, he passed briefly through Flanders and Italy before returning to Madrid in 1592. He took part in few diplomatic negotiations after this, and withdrew to a monastery where, his sight failing, he devoted himself to writing. Author of a commentary on the Dutch revolt (1591) and of a successful treatise on war (1595), he also translated Justus LIPSIUS into Spanish (1599). The most notable Spanish ambassador of the century, his reputation has been compromised by his apparent belief that conspiracy was a necessary part of diplomatic activity.

Menno Simons (1496–1559) Dutch Anabaptist leader. Born in Witmarsum, Friesland, he took holy orders and from 1531 was parish priest of his home village. Sympathetic to the Anabaptists, he was opposed to the radicals who occupied Münster in 1534, and in 1536 joined the movement in order to win its members over to peaceful methods. Persecuted and in hiding, he moved to Germany, lived for a period (1544–6) near Cologne, and spent his last years on the Baltic coast of Germany. He died at Wustenfelde, near Hamburg. His followers, first called Mennists then Mennonites, continued to grow after his death, and emigrated from Europe to Canada and the United States in large numbers during the nineteenth century. Like other Anabaptists, he rejected infant baptism: 'we are not reborn because we have been baptised', he said, 'but baptised because we are reborn'. He taught a complete separation between the church (his followers) and the state, and even among themselves the Mennonites always remained separated communities.

Menshikov, Alexander Danilovich, prince (1672–1729) Russian noble and minister.

Son of a minor court official, he became a friend of the young PETER THE GREAT, accompanying him on his foreign tours (1697). He owed his subsequent rise to his efficiency as a soldier in the wars against Sweden; his services in the victory at Poltava (1709) earned him the titles of prince and field-marshal, and he continued with successful campaigns in Kurland and Pomerania (1713). During his campaigns he met his mistress Marta, whom he subsequently married to tsar Peter and who in her turn became empress as CATHERINE I. He remained in complete control of the government under her, until overthrown in 1727 by the Dolgoruki family and exiled to Siberia.

Mercator, Gerhard Kremer, known as (1512–94) Flemish geographer. Born in Rupelmonde (Flanders), he took his degree at the university of Louvain then studied geography and astronomy, and set himself up as an instrument-maker at Louvain, where he published his first map, of the Holy Land (1537), and also a world map (1538), the first to apply the name 'America' to both halves of the continent. In 1540 he settled in Duisburg, and from 1559 taught geography at the university. His most famous maps were produced here, including those of Europe (in fifteen sheets, 1572); the British Isles (eight sheets, 1564); and that of the world (eighteen sheets, 1569), drawn for the use of mariners, in which for the first time he used his 'projection' to illustrate global distances. Though it had some advantages, the projection did not become generally applied to nautical charts until a century later. His first atlas of the Europe of his day began to appear in 1585, with a second part in 1589. A full edition, including Britain and northern Europe, was published in 1595 by his son; the work totalled 105 maps. He based much of his work on Ptolemy, whom he revised and corrected, but was quickly recognised as the leading cartographer of his day. His sons carried on the enterprise.

Mercoeur, Philip Emmanuel of Lorraine, duke de (1558–1602) French noble and general. A leading member of the GUISE family, duke from 1577, in 1582 he was appointed governor of Brittany and became one of the leaders of the Catholic League. He rebelled against HENRY III after the assassination of the Guise leaders in 1588, and then refused to recognise the Protestant HENRY IV as king after the death of Henry III. He allied with Spain in the last years of the French civil wars, but finally submitted to the new king. He died of fever in Germany on his way back from serving in the wars against the Turks on behalf of the emperor.

Mersenne, Marin (1588–1648) French natural philosopher. Although he lived as a friar of the Minim order from 1611 until his death, he did not believe that theology should be allowed to dictate how knowledge of the natural world was pursued. Whilst opposing the 'atheistic' tendencies of some authors, he became a whole-hearted advocate of the new mechanical philosophy. From 1620 he travelled extensively through Europe. His own research was largely concerned with sound, which he produced through the vibration of long strings and was thus able to study and quantify pitch and aspects of harmony; he also offered mechanical explanations for the effect of music upon human emotions. Looking at language as a system of signs, he was one of several contemporary scholars who endeavoured to create a universal language. His most important contribution, however, lay in transmitting the ideas of others. From his Paris convent he sustained a vast network of correspondence embracing most of the leading scientists and philosophers of Europe.

[FW]

Michael (Mikhail) Fyodorovich Romanov (1596–1645) founder of the Romanov dynasty and tsar of Russia 1613–45. Son of the patriarch FILARET, after the chaos of the Time of Troubles and the expulsion of the Poles, he was chosen by the national assembly (*zemsky sobor*) to be tsar when only sixteen. Since the boy had little experience, he and his father were made joint rulers till 1633, when Filaret ceased to govern.

Michelangelo Buonarotti. (Michelangelo di Lcdovico di Leonardo di Buonarotti Simoni) (1475–1564) Florentine sculptor, painter, architect and poet. He elevated the social status of Italian sculptors to equal that of painters, and served four popes – JULIUS II, LEO X, PAUL III and JULIUS III. Born in Caprese, a small village in the Appenines, into an impoverished family of the lower nobility, he was apprenticed at thirteen to the Florentine fresco painter Ghirlandaio, but was soon discovered by Lorenzo de' MEDICI, who invited him into the Medici palace on the Via Larga to live, with access to the collection of ancient Roman sculpture, and individual instruction from one of DONATELLO's last assistants. After the expulsion of the Medici from Florence he travelled to Venice, Bologna and finally, aged twenty-one, to Rome, where at age twenty-three he received the first of his important commissions – the marble *Pietà* (1498; Rome, St Peter's,) commissioned by cardinal Jean Bilheres de Lagraulas of France. Returning to Florence, he was permitted to use a huge but flawed block of marble abandoned by another sculptor, creating his colossal (14 feet 3 inches) *David* (1501–4; Florence, Accademia), which was enthusiastically received by the Florentines for its republican political possibilities and placed in front of the city hall as a warning to tyrants. Called to Rome (1505) by the new Pope, JULIUS II, he was given the commission to design the papal tomb, which was to have been a vast structure with forty-four over-life-sized figures. However, Julius soon decided to raze the ancient basilica of St Peter, replacing it with an entirely new building to be designed by BRAMANTE in which to place the tomb. Consequently, Michelangelo was given a new contract – to fresco the ceiling of the Sistine Chapel. In the process of painting this colossal fresco, some 80 feet above the floor, he wrote a comic poem about the physical discomforts involved. The death of Julius II soon after the ceiling was unveiled, and the election of cardinal Giovanni de' MEDICI as the new pope (LEO X) brought to an end the grandiose plans for Julius' tomb, but brought new Medici commissions in Florence, including that for the architecture and the sculptural program for the Medici Chapel (S. Lorenzo, 1520–34). Returning to Rome, his late works there include the *Last Judgement* (Sistine Chapel; 1536–41), begun when he was sixty years old; the scaled-down tomb of Julius II (S. Pietro in Vincoli; completed 1545); the frescoes in the Capella Paolina (1545–50), finished at age seventy-five; the design of the group of civic buildings known as the *Campidoglio*, on the Capitoline Hill; and the design for the dome and apse alterations of New St Peter's. Still working only a few days before his death at eighty-nine, he left two unfinished *Pietà* groups: one originally intended for his own tomb (Florence, Cathedral, and the *Rondanini Pietà* (Milan, Castello Sforzesco).

[JH]

Milton, John (1608–74) English poet and prose writer. Highly educated and an exceptional scholar at Cambridge (1625), Milton began writing poetry in English and Latin while still a schoolboy. Between 1632 and 1637 he wrote *L'Allegro, Il Penseroso, Comus* and *Lycidas*. After two years travelling in Europe, he returned to London just before the outbreak of the civil war and concentrated on producing tracts and pamphlets in sup-port of the Puritan cause. However his pamphlets on divorce earned the wrath of his party and he was threatened with prosecution. He replied, in 1644, with *Areopagitica*, a plea for the freedom of the press and his most celebrated prose work. In 1649 he was appointed Latin Secretary to CROMWELL and official apologist for the Commonwealth; in this post he produced several powerful defences of the execution of CHARLES I. After the Restoration, old and blind, he returned to poetry. His epic masterpiece *Paradise Lost* (completed in 1665 and published in 1671), was followed by *Paradise Regained* (1671) and *Samson Agonistes* (1674). A true son of the Reformation, Milton had a hatred of religious intolerance, a firm belief in the freedom of speech, and an enduring hostility to tyranny. He married three times: his first wife died in 1652, his second in childbirth.

[BT]

Molière (pseudonym of Jean-Baptiste Poquelin) (1622–73) The classic French comic dramatist was the son of an upholsterer attached to the royal court. Like many of his contemporaries he was educated by the Jesuits. From childhood he evinced an irresistible passion for the theatre, which he first experienced at the Hôtel de Bourgogne. Tradition has it that Scaramouche, the famous Italian clown, gave him lessons. He began his apprenticeship with a company called the Illustre Théâtre, in which the Béjart family was prominent. After twelve years in the provinces he returned to Paris, to the Louvre and appeared before LOUIS XIV. Successful at last, he gained the managership of a troop of actors who were eventually based at the Palais-Royal (1661). They soon won the approval of the king. MOLIÈRE himself played all parts: manager, director, comedian, tragedian, author, courtier. Defeating all attempts by jealous competitors to unseat him, he ruled the stage and practically died on it in the role of *Le Malade imaginaire* (*The Malingerer*) (1673), one of his most famous pieces. He showed his genius early on with *Les Précieuses Ridicules* (*The Affectations of Ladies in Society*) (1659), a title which explains the object of his satire. He forged his own comic drama, moving away from earlier imitations of Terence and Plautus. He concentrated on the contemporary scene, and his main aim was to amuse. Rarely do we see the darker side of life as in *Le Misanthrope* (1666). His best known comedies are *Tartuffe* (1669), a study in hypocrisy; *Le Bourgeois Gentilhomme* (*The Social Upstart*) (1670); and *Les Femmes Savantes* (*The Bluestockings*) (1672). His targets were chosen from all ranks of society. He created such a reputation for himself and his troop that after his death many theatres disintegrated. But out of the disorganisation rose the famous Comédie Française.

[BT]

Molina, Luis de (1535–1600) Spanish Jesuit theologian, famous for elaborating the official doctrine of the Jesuit order on the problems of grace and free will. He studied and taught at Coimbra, Evora, Lisbon and Madrid. His principal works were *Concordia liberi arbitrii cum gratiae donis* (Free Will and Grace) (1588), and *De justitia et jure* (Justice and Right) (1592), which with special reference to France, affirmed that heretics should not succeed to the throne in a Christian state. Applying himself to the problem of how man's ability to choose freely (free will) can be assured if God foreknows and therefore predetermines everything, he proposed a doctrine of middle knowledge, *scientia media*, which was meant to preserve human free will but also the efficacy of divine grace. According to Molina, God foreknows what an individual will do under all circumstances, but also provides him with all the means wherewith he can decide, thereby preserving freedom of choice; this is God's 'middle

knowledge', whereby he knows all but does not determine all, allowing the individual 'grace' to make his own choice. Molina was opposed by Thomists (especially in the Dominican order) such as Bañez, who maintained the older view, propounded by Aquinas, on sufficient and efficient grace. The differing views led to serious clashes at many Spanish universities between Molinists and Thomists. The Molinist view also accentuated the debate about the different types of grace offered by God, which later embittered the Jansenist controversy.

Molina, Tirso de (pseudonym of Fray Gabriel Téllez) (?1581–1648) Spanish dramatist. About 1600 he entered the Mercedarian Order, whose main purpose was to ransom Christian captives from the Muslims. He studied theology, and travelled widely for the Order (including a trip to the Caribbean), eventually settling in Toledo where he began to publish prose stories, poems and plays, and creating something of a scandal because of his status. This did not discourage him, nor did the Order do much more than banish him from time to time. He was an excellent lyric poet, but he is known as one of LOPE DE VEGA's best disciples after CALDERÓN DE LA BARCA. His main claim to fame rests on two plays, one of them *El burlador de Sevilla* (*The Trickster from Seville*) (1630). This is a version of the Don Juan legend. Don Juan is not presented as an admirable figure; he is both despicable and a fool, but he succeeds by working on human gullibility. *El condenado por desconfiado* (*Damned Through Doubt*) (1635) shows how convictions can be eroded by doubt and the failure to trust. The authorship of both plays has been questioned, but most critics now believe them to be genuinely Tirso's.

[BT]

Molinos, Miguel de (1628–96) Spanish theologian. Born in Teruel (Aragon) of modest origins, he apparently studied in

Valencia, where he took holy orders (1652). In 1663 he was sent by his superiors on a mission to Rome, where he came into contact with Spanish clergy with Quietist beliefs. In 1675 he published in Rome in Italian and Spanish his principal work, *The Spiritual Guide*, which was approved by the highest theological authorities and attained immediate success; later it was translated into the major European languages. Shortly after, Quietism began to excite Church opinion, and suspicion fell on Molinos' ideas. He was arrested by the Roman Inquisition in 1685 together with a large number of sympathisers. After a lengthy examination of witnesses, sixty eight of Molinos' propositions (taken from letters and conversations, but not from his *Guide*) were condemned in 1687, he was made to recant his errors publicly and condemned to perpetual prison, where he died. The condemnation set in train further repressive measures against Quietism. In 1688 the Inquisition condemned similar writings by (the later cardinal) Petrucci, and in 1699 condemned the *Maxims of the Saints* of FÉNELON. With these moves the Church expressed its formal hostility to mysticism.

Monck, George, 1st duke of Albemarle (1608–70) English military commander. Born in Devon of a gentry family, he spent all his active career in the army. He spent the years 1629–40 serving in the Dutch army in the Netherlands, was given command of a regiment (1642–3) to help put down the Irish rebellion, served the royalists in the civil war and was taken prisoner and confined in the Tower (1644–6). On promising not to act against the Parliament, he was sent again to Ireland (1646–9) against the rebels. When CROMWELL invaded Scotland in 1650 he took Monck, for whom a special regiment was created (later known as the Coldstream Guards). In 1651 Cromwell returned to England, leaving Monck as commander-in-chief in Scotland. In 1652

Monck was appointed as one of the generals to command the fleet which engaged with the Dutch off Portland and scored a victory that cost admiral TROMP his life (1653); he then returned to Scotland as commander (1654–60). A faithful supporter of Cromwell, on the protector's death he was the only commander in Britain with a sizeable armed force at his disposal. After overtures from all sides, he decided to impose order, commenting of the current protector that 'Richard Cromwell forsook himself, else I had never failed my promise to his father'. In January 1660 he crossed into England, and recognised in London that a restoration of monarchy was inevitable. In May he received CHARLES II at Dover, and was subsequently showered with honours, including a dukedom.

Monmouth, James Scott, duke of (1649–85) English pretender to the throne. Son of CHARLES II and of Lucy Walter, he left England with his mother and spent his early years in Paris. After the Restoration he was allowed back and though never formally recognised by his father was showered with honours. In 1663 the king created him duke of Monmouth, made him a knight of the Garter, and married him to the heiress Anne Scott, countess of Buccleuch, whose surname he adopted; the couple were created duke and duchess of Buccleuch. James was made captain of the king's guard, admitted to the privy council, and in 1678 appointed captain general of the army of England. As a Protestant, during the Exclusion Crisis (1678–81) he was looked to by the Protestant interest as a possible successor to the throne in place of the Catholic duke of York; but after getting involved in the Rye House Plot (1683) he fled to Holland. When the duke of York became king as JAMES II, Monmouth and a small army landed in the west country (1685), but failed to raise adequate support and his forces were routed at Sedgemoor. He was later captured and beheaded.

Montagu, Lady Mary Wortley (1689–1762) Eldest daughter of the (later) duke of Kingston, she early showed her attachment to letters, an interest she shared with Edward Wortley Montagu, then MP for Huntingdon, whom she married in 1712 in defiance of her father's command to marry another. At the accession of GEORGE I, Edward briefly entered the administration and Mary participated in life at court. In 1716 he was appointed ambassador to Turkey, to which they and their infant son travelled, returning in 1718. In England she publicised – an act establishing her permanent fame – the practice of inoculation for small-pox, which she had seen used in Adrianople. She received the warm support of GEORGE II's wife queen Caroline, but inoculation was not commonly accepted by the medical profession for a generation. She also occupied a prominent place in the literary world, cultivating a close friendship with Alexander POPE, with whom she later quarrelled. A woman of independent mind, in 1739 she left home and husband and went abroad for twenty three years, drifting through Italy, settling at Avignon (1742–6) and eventually in Venice (1758–62). She died shortly after returning to England in 1762. Her letters were published in three volumes in 1763.

Montaigne, Michel Eyquem de (1533–92) French moralist and philosopher. He was born in Périgord and educated in Bordeaux. Well schooled in Latin, he was taught by the eminent Scots humanist George BUCHANAN, who introduced him to the works of Socrates and Cato. He is known best for his *Essais*. The first books appeared in 1580 and the final edition came out in 1595; they were subsequently translated into many European languages. It was he who was responsible for the popularity of the essay form, subsequently imitated by writers like Francis BACON. In his hands the essay became a personal instrument for reflections on human nature, its virtues and vices, and above all, human mortality. All his writing is informed by a sympathetic tolerance, a refusal to adopt a patronising or authoritative voice. The outcome of these prolonged meditations on the human condition can be phrased in the classic question '*Que sais-je?*' (What Can I Know?), a modest comment on the fallibility of human intelligence, including his own.

[BT]

Montchrétien, Antoine de (1576–1621) French writer. The son of an apothecary of Normandy, he branched out into literature, producing his first written tragedy for the public in Caen in 1596. A man of many skills, he was obliged to flee from his country in 1605 after killing his opponent in a duel. He went to England, where he turned his interests to political economy and finance. Returning to France in 1611, he married well and used the money to set up metallurgical centres at Châtillon-sur-Loire. In 1615 he published his most famous work, the *Traité de l'économie politique*, which earned him later fame as a mercantilist and protectionist but was unappreciated at the time. He subsequently seems to have joined Huguenot groupings (1621), and was killed in an obscure incident between Catholics and Protestants in Normandy.

Montecuccoli, Raimondo, count (1609–80) An Italian noble from near Modena, he became a professional soldier and made his reputation serving the emperor during the Thirty Years War in Germany, distinguishing himself at the battles of Breitenfeld and Nördlingen. Much later he fought against the Turks and achieved a notable victory over them at St Gotthard (1664). In the wars against LOUIS XIV, he commanded the Imperial troops on the Rhine, and in 1679 was made a prince of the Empire. In his leisure hours he composed some of the best known military treatises of the time.

Montesquieu, Charles de Secondat, baron de (1689–1755) French polymath and political commentator. From a family of robe nobility based near Bordeaux, he followed their traditions and rose to become a president of the parlement of Guyenne (1716). In his early years he became absorbed in physics and natural history, but he soon changed into an acute observer of his fellow humans. He is best known for the *Lettres persanes* (*Letters from a Persian Friend*) (1721) which eventually gained him a seat in the Académie Française (1727). This fictional correspondence, written from the standpoint of an exotic foreign tourist in France, highlighted the customs and foibles of social behaviour; this genre was much imitated in later centuries. Montesquieu himself was an enthusiastic traveller; from 1728 to 1731 he travelled through western Europe, studying institutions and customs, spending nearly two years in England. His admiration for the latter helped him to compose over a long period the greatest of his works, *L'esprit des lois* (*The Spirit of the Law*) (1748). This vast study was published in Geneva and became an instant success, being soon translated into all major languages. It is an elaborate survey of the variety of political constitutions by an enquiring mind equipped with an agile and precise style. His intention is to attempt to explain the relation of the body of law of a state to the physical and spiritual context of its evolution. He ends up, despite his criticism of French royalty, by favouring a liberal monarchy.

[BT]

Monteverdi, Claudio (1567–1643) Italian composer. He was the greatest seventeenth-century composer, who consolidated the musical style of the Baroque and left a long-lasting imprint on European music. His eight books of madrigals, four operas and numerous religious works crystallised the aesthetic concept of the 'modern style', which sought to express the deepest feelings through a novel compositional approach to the text. His remarkable originality began to emerge during his maturing years at the court of Mantua (*c.*1592–1612). His *Orfeo* (1607) is regarded as the first great European opera. *Arianna*, his second opera (1608), was lost, except for the famous scene of 'Lamento d'Arianna', a gem of early operatic writing. His collection of sacred works for the feasts of the Blessed Virgin (1610) displays a striking amalgam of styles, ranging from traditional polyphony to the most recent operatic idiom. From 1613 until his death he held the post of chapelmaster at St Mark's in Venice and composed his most innovative and moving works. They include numerous sacred works, the last books of madrigals, the cantata *Il combattimento di Tancredi e Clorinda* (based on excerpts from Tasso's *Gerusalemme liberata*), and the operas *Il ritorno d'Ulisse in patria* (1641) and *L'incoronazione di Poppea* (1642).

[JE]

Montluc (also, Monluc), Blaise de Lasseran-Massencôme, lord of (1501–77) French military commander. Of noble origin, he was brought up as a page at the court of Lorraine, then made his reputation as a soldier for the king of France in the Italian wars, where he served under BAYARD and defended Siena against CHARLES V's troops. After fighting for France on several fronts, he served for ten years in Piedmont as governor of Moncalieri (1548–58). An uncompromising Catholic, after the outbreak of the civil wars in France he was appointed governor of Guyenne (1564) and became the scourge of the Huguenots. At the siege of Rabastens (1570) he received a severe face wound which obliged him to wear a mask over part of his face for the rest of his life. In 1574 he was made a marshal of France. After the civil wars he retired to his estates and devoted his last years to writing his famous *Commentaires*, published at Bordeaux in 1592.

Montmorency, dukes of

1st duke, Anne (1493–1567) French grandee. Scion of one of the greatest noble lineages of medieval France, he made his military reputation in the Italian wars, distinguishing himself at Ravenna (1512) and Marignano (1515). Captured along with the king of France at the battle of Pavia (1525), he accompanied his close friend FRANCIS I in captivity. He was subsequently appointed governor of Languedoc (1526), and director of the king's household, in which role he played the principal part in the political and military policies of the monarch, organising in 1527 the League of Cognac against the emperor CHARLES V. Appointed constable of France in 1536, he retired from the court in 1541 but returned to political activity on the accession of HENRY II. Created duke in 1551, he was defeated and captured when leading the French forces against the army of PHILIP II at St Quentin (1557). When the civil wars broke out he allied with the Catholic nobles and defeated the Huguenots at Dreux (1562) where, however, he was also captured by them. Released a year later, he was mortally wounded in the battle of St Denis against the Huguenot forces of CONDÉ.

2nd duke, François (1530–79) Eldest son of Anne, he was duke from 1567, and became one of the principal leaders of the moderate Catholic party, known as the '*politiques*', during the French civil wars.

3rd duke, Henry I (1534–1614) Younger brother of François, he became duke from 1579 and took the title Montmorency-Damville, was governor of Languedoc from 1563 and was created marshal in 1566. He also led the '*politiques*' and in 1593, in reward for his support of HENRY IV as king, was granted the office of Constable of France.

4th duke, Henry II (1595–1632) Grandson of the 1st duke, he became admiral of France at the age of seventeen (1612) and governor of his home province of Langue-

doc shortly after (1614). He played a leading role in the wars against the Huguenots under LOUIS XIII, especially in the sieges of Montauban and Montpellier (1622), and after further campaigns in Piedmont against the Spaniards was created marshal (1630). However, he allied himself with the party of GASTON-JEAN-BAPTISTE, duke d'Orléans and MARIE DE MÉDICIS against the newly emergent RICHELIEU, and after the failure of the armed rebellion (1632) which he led in the south of France was arrested, condemned to death by the parlement of Toulouse and, despite appeals from the pope and other prominent persons, executed. The title became extinct with him. His beautiful sister Charlotte de Montmorency (1594–1650), with whom king HENRY IV fell madly in love when she was just fifteen, married the 3rd prince of CONDÉ, Henry II of Bourbon; she remained extremely active in politics, especially during the Fronde, and was the last great patron of the Jansenists of Port-Royal.

Montpensier, Anne Marie Louise d'Orléans, duchess de

Montpensier, Anne Marie Louise d'Orléans, duchess de (1627–93) known as 'la Grande Mademoiselle'. Daughter of GASTON-JEAN-BAPTISTE, duke d'Orléans, like him she was an intriguer, took active part in the Fronde against MAZARIN, and turned the guns of the Bastille on the royal troops when they threatened the forces of CONDÉ in Paris in 1652. Exiled to her estates after the Fronde, she returned to the court in 1657 and fell madly in love with the duke of Lauzun, an adventurer like her and six years younger. Despite the opposition of LOUIS XIV, they married secretly in 1681, but the relationship was not a success and they effectively separated in 1685. He went off to further wars; she turned to religious devotion and to writing her *Mémoires*.

Montrose, James Graham, 5th earl and

Montrose, James Graham, 5th earl and 1st marquis of (1612–50) Scots royalist general. Educated at St Andrews university, he travelled in Europe (1633–36) and in 1638 took a prominent part in support of the Covenant in Scotland. In 1640 he took part in the Scots invasion of England, but since he also opposed the predominance of the greater Scots lords, ARGYLL and HAMILTON, he soon moved to support the cause of CHARLES I. In 1644 (when Charles also created him marquis) he rallied royalist support in Scotland and won several battles against the Covenanters, but was unable to persuade the clans to make common cause. After the defeat of Charles I at Naseby, he went abroad (1646–9), to France and the Netherlands. He returned to Scotland after the execution of Charles (December 1649) and attempted to raise the highlands for CHARLES II, but was betrayed, and executed in Edinburgh.

Moray, James Stuart, 1st earl of (1531–70) regent of Scotland. Natural son of JAMES V of Scotland and half-brother to MARY STUART, he supported the Reformation from 1556 and became its principal leader, but continued advising his half-sister, who created him earl (1562). He opposed her marriage with DARNLEY, however, and subsequently fled the court and took refuge in England. After the murder of Darnley, in which he played a part, he was appointed regent of Scotland following the abdication of Mary (1567), and routed her followers in an engagement at Langside (1568). His pro-Protestant and pro-English policies failed to win support, and he was assassinated shortly after by James Hamilton.

More, Sir Thomas (1478–1535) English statesman. Son of the leading judge Sir John More, he was educated at Oxford and began studying law at the Inns in 1494. In 1505 he married Jane Colt, from whom he had four children; a month after her death in 1511 he married the widow Alice Middleton, mainly to help him care for the family. He entered Parliament in

1504 and then in 1523 when he was elected speaker; he was appointed under-sheriff of London 1510–19. He first met ERASMUS in London in 1499, initiating a lifelong friendship. A favourite of HENRY VIII, he was a member of the royal council from 1517, knighted 1521, appointed treasurer of the king's exchequer, then chancellor of the duchy of Lancaster 1525–9, and finally lord chancellor 1529–32. His differences with the king began when he opposed Henry over his divorce from CATHERINE OF ARAGON and resigned the chancellorship in 1532. In 1534 he refused to take the oath acknowledging the king as head of the English Church, and was imprisoned in the Tower, where he wrote his *Dialogue of Comfort* (published 1553). Fifteen months later a charge of treason was brought against him. He was beheaded in 1535. The most prominent English humanist of his day, he wrote extensively, and engaged in controversial writings with Protestants including William TYNDALE. His most famous work, *Utopia* (Louvain, 1516), was written in Latin and its title (meaning 'no place') brought a new word into the language; published widely on the continent, it appeared in English only in 1553. The first book is a dialogue with the commentator Hythloday; the second book, purporting to depict the imaginary isle of Utopia, is a commentary on the social problems of the day. More was canonised in 1935.

[HK & GG]

Morone, Giovanni (1509–80) Italian cardinal. Bishop of Modena in 1529, in 1536 he was sent to Germany by the pope to attempt reconciliation between Catholics and Protestants, and assisted at the principal Imperial Diets of the 1540s. Created cardinal (1542) when he returned to Rome, he was appointed papal delegate to the Council of Trent, then made bishop of Novara (1553). Unfortunately he fell foul of a new pope, PAUL IV, and was imprisoned in Rome for two years (1557–9) on charges of heresy. Released on the pope's death, he was declared innocent, and appointed in 1563 as president of the last session of the council of Trent, where he made important contributions to agreement between the factions. Made bishop of Ostia in 1570, he was also a patron of the English College in Rome.

Morozov, Boris (1590–1661) Russian noble. From an important boyar (upper noble) family, he was tutor to tsar ALEXEI I and became his chief minister in the years 1645–8. He was also the leading businessman of Muscovy, controlling vast estates, ironworks and mills, and was one of Russia's chief industrialists. As a member of the government, he controlled the important customs dues. His tax measures in 1648, which included an increase in the salt tax, were the direct cause of a major revolt in Moscow and several other cities in 1648, which overthrew his government. Exiled for a few months from Moscow, he was back in power the next year, when he prepared the great law code (*Ulozhenie*) of 1649. He continued into the 1650s as effective ruler of the state.

Morton, John (*c.*1420–1500) English cardinal. Educated at Oxford, where he studied law, he won the patronage of the archbishop of Canterbury and entered the privy council. A supporter of the house of Lancaster in the wars of the Roses, he submitted to the power of the Yorkists, and in 1479 became bishop of Ely. In disfavour with RICHARD III, he fled to Flanders (1483), returning after the victory of HENRY VII, under whom he was appointed archbishop of Canterbury and lord chancellor (1486–7).

Moura, Cristóbal de (1538–1613) Spanish minister of state. Portuguese by birth, he came to Spain in the household of the princess Juana, sister of PHILIP II, when she came to act as regent for her brother (1554). He served Juana faithfully, and on her deathbed (1573) she asked her brother

to favour Moura, who subsequently served the king in matters concerning Portugal, playing a major part in the diplomatic and political moves that prepared the way for the succession of Philip to the throne of Portugal (1580) after the vacancy created by the deaths of king SEBASTIAN and then of his successor the aged cardinal, HENRY I OF PORTUGAL. During Philip's stay in Portugal (1581–3) Moura was his effective chief minister, and was later created marquis of Castel-Rodrigo and grandee of Spain. From 1586 he served in the three-man committee that ran Spain's government, and during the last years of the king (1596–8) he directed all matters of the internal government. The government of the new king, PHILIP III, appointed him viceroy of Portugal in order to get him out of the way; he died in office in Lisbon.

Muggleton, Lodowicke (1609–98) English religious sectarian. Born in London, he became apprenticed to a tailor, discovered religion and moved in a radical direction, rejecting (1647) all existing creeds and disciplines. After reading a translation of BOEHME, he experienced inner revelations (1651–2); he and his cousin John Reeve proclaimed a new dispensation, with Muggleton as the 'mouth' of God. In 1652 they published their *Transcendent Spirituall Treatise*, and were imprisoned briefly (1653) for blasphemy. He was tried again in 1677, and imprisoned for a while, but lived the rest of his life in peace. His spiritual approach was firmly moral, rejecting all theology (his followers did not pray) and all coercion.

Mun, Thomas (1571–1641) English merchant. Son of a London mercer, from an early age he appears to have taken part in trading activities in the Mediterranean, and also lived in Italy a while. In 1615 he became a director of the East India Company, whose interests he thereafter promoted, publishing in 1621 his *A Discourse of Trade*, which defended the policies of the company. His most famous work, *England's Treasure by Forraign Trade*, was possibly written around 1630, but not published until 1664, after his death. In it he laid down the principle that 'the means to increase our wealth and treasure is to sell more to strangers than we consume of theirs in value'; Adam Smith later commented that this became 'a fundamental maxim in the political economy of all countries'.

Münster, Sebastian (1489–1552) German cosmographer. Born at Ingelheim, in the Palatinate, he entered the Franciscan order, taught 1524–7 at Heidelberg and became professor of Hebrew at Basel in 1527, where he also converted to the Reformation. He here produced an edition of the Hebrew Bible 1534–5 with an accompanying Latin translation, and numerous other works on astronomy and mathematics. Another notable work was his Latin edition of the geographer Ptolemy (1540) with forty eight woodcut maps. His most famous work was the *Cosmographia (Beschreibung aller Länder)* (1543), produced in six books with engravings and maps, the earliest European descriptive survey of the world and a landmark in geographical achievement. By 1650 it had been through twenty seven editions.

Müntzer, Thomas (1489–1525) German Anabaptist leader. Born in Saxony, he studied and became a priest in Leipzig, where in 1519 he met LUTHER, who found him a post as minister in Zwickau. Here he made common cause with a group of radical illuminists called 'the prophets of Zwickau', among them the weaver Nicolas Storch; and adopted more revolutionary views. Forced to leave Zwickau, he moved to Allstedt in Saxony where in 1523 he founded a radical community. He was now a convinced exponent of the doctrine of continuous and direct revelation, seeing himself as a prophet who would help to destroy the godless and usher in the Millennium. When the princes of Saxony visited the town in 1524, he preached before them a sermon claiming that 'the sword is necessary for the destruction of the godless; if the princes fail to use it, it will be taken from them'. That year he was obliged to leave, made contact with the Swiss Anabaptists and headed an Anabaptist community at Mühlhausen, where he preached the same doctrine and called upon the discontented peasants to take up the sword of the Lord. A leader of the Peasants Revolt of 1525 in Saxony and Thuringia, he called himself 'the servant of God against the godless', but was captured at the battle of Frankenhausen (May 1525), tortured and executed along with other rebel leaders.

Muratori, Ludovico (1672–1750) scholar and pioneering historian of the Italian Middle Ages. He studied in Modena with the Benedictines and learned the historical-cultural method of the French Maurists. Ordained in 1694, he found employment in Milan's Ambrosian library, which provided the texts for his first publication, *Anecdota* (2 vols, 1697–98; 2 new vols, 1713). In 1700 he became librarian to the duke of Modena and began research on the disputed lordship of Comacchio between the Este and the papacy. He came to see the Middle Ages, despite what he saw as its barbarisms, as the origin of the modern state and he began to collect its documentation. Through the collaboration of local correspondents, he published a definitive collection of medieval chronicles, diaries and other documents, *Rerum Italicarum Scriptores* (29 vols, 1723–51). He also published the conclusions from his own historical research on institutions, economy, religion and society in his *Antiquitates Italicae Medii Aevi* (6 vols, 1738–42), and a narrative of the Italian states as a unified whole in his *Annali d'Italia* (12 vols, 1744–9).

[JM]

Murillo, Bartolomé Esteban (1618–82) Spanish painter. Murillo was born and died in Seville. Both his father, a barber-surgeon, and his mother died when he was ten years old, and he became a ward of his uncle, who apprenticed him (1629) to another relative, the painter Juan del Castillo. By the time he was twenty one Murillo was able to support himself independently by painting small Madonnas and other religious works for export to the Spanish colonies in the Americas. In 1645 he married Beatriz de Cabrera de Sotomayor, with whom he had nine children. He was the founder (1660) and director of Seville's academy of fine arts. He is best known even today for his religious paintings, such as the images of the Immaculate Conception, or for his genre-like Holy Families and beggar urchins, all of which are a bit saccharine for modern taste. However, he was actually quite a capable painter of landscapes and portraiture. He decorated both the Dominican and Franciscan monasteries in Seville, and his works can be seen in nearly every major European museum, as well as in the cathedral of Seville. In 1681 he fell from the scaffolding of the Capuchin church in Cadiz where he had been working and sustained the injuries that led to his death several months later. His work was much admired in eighteenth-century England, especially by REYNOLDS and GAINSBOROUGH, as well as in France by Greuze.

[JH]

N

Nasi, Joseph (*c.*1504–79) Jewish leader. Born João Miguez, son of a Portuguese physician of New Christian (i.e. Jewish) origin, he left Lisbon to study at the university of Louvain (1537), began working for bankers in Antwerp, and in 1547 left for the east, passing through France and Venice. In 1554 he was in Istanbul, where he formally became a Jew and changed his name. Adopted as an adviser by the sultan Selim II because of his great knowledge of western Europe, he obtained important trading privileges. He was also created duke of the Greek island of Naxos, achieved great wealth, and was granted authority over lands in Palestine. One of the great figures of Jewish politics, he used his money to advance Jewish scholarship, and used his influence with the Turks to harass the Christian states, mainly Venice.

Nayler, James (?1617–60) English Quaker leader. A native of Wakefield, he served Parliament in the civil war, and after a visit to his town by George FOX became a Quaker (1651). He later became a travelling preacher, was gaoled at Exeter for provoking a disturbance, and in 1656 made a symbolic entrance into Bristol, riding a horse and accompanied by seven followers, mostly women, chanting 'Holy, holy'. Arrested for blasphemously claiming to be the Son of God, he was taken to London, where the Parliament voted that he be pilloried, whipped, his tongue bored and the letter B (for 'blasphemer') branded on his forehead. Released from prison in 1659, he died shortly after. His case, which illustrated an extreme trend in Quakerism that rapidly disappeared, provoked a sharp controversy over the use of the law against religious sectarians; CROMWELL and other members of his government insisted that the punishment was illegal because there were no laws in force against heresy.

Nebrija, Antonio de (1444–1522) Spanish classical and Biblical scholar and philologist. Born in Andalusia, he studied in Italy for about ten years, chiefly in the university of Bologna. and returned to Spain to denounce the manner in which the classics were taught in Salamanca University. He was also severely critical of the inadequate traditions of native scholarship in the larger context, and saw as his aim the reform of teaching so that he could wipe out the contempt that Italian scholars felt for their Spanish counterparts. He believed firmly that a study of the nature of language in itself lay at the heart of all learning, and that not only a proper study of Latin, but also of the vernacular was the key to academic, social and political advancement. To this end he wrote *Introductiones latine* (1481) to provide an up-to-date grammar for students. Using the model of Latin, with due modifications, he wrote the first grammar of a common tongue, *Gramática sobre la lengua castellana* in the significant year 1492. In the preface dedicated to ISABELLA THE CATHOLIC he stated that as in the case of Rome, language was the travelling companion of imperial expansion, a declaration that turned out to be prophetic. As a teacher in Salamanca he was involved in many academic disputes, but both Ferdinand and Isabella used his works and his Latin histories of contemporary Spain to promote their image abroad. He eventually moved out of Salamanca to the new university at Alcalá to dedicate his later years to biblical criticism, contributing eventually to the famous Polyglot Bible printed there from 1514–17, the first one of its kind. In his time, he was the major representative in Spain of humanist scholarship.

[BT]

Neri, Filippo (1515–95) Italian founder of the Oratory of Jesus. In 1533 in Rome he decided to give up his life in business and dedicate himself to religion. Affected by the state of the poor, he initiated charitable services and in 1548 founded a group to assist poor pilgrims to the city. Ordained priest in 1551, he became one of the most vocal advocates of reformed religious practice, especially frequent communion. He grouped round him a small community of priests who were in 1575 officially formed into the Congregation of the Oratory. The central figure of the Counter Reformation in Rome, he was canonised in 1622. The Oratory, which later took up education as one of its main activities (hence the Oratory schools), was introduced with great success into France (1611, patronised by BÉRULLE), and spread to all countries. Its dedication to sacred music led to the evolution of the *oratorio*.

Newcastle, Thomas Pelham-Holles, duke of (1693–1768) English minister of state. Son of the 1st lord PELHAM, and educated at Cambridge, he commanded high office from his early days, was lord-lieutenant of several counties as well as very wealthy, and was in 1715 created marquis and duke (of Newcastle-upon-Tyne) for his services against the troops of the Old Pretender. He married (1717) into the Churchill family, and became thereby related to the earl of SUNDERLAND, in whose ministry (1717) he entered the privy council. In 1724 he became a secretary of state in WALPOLE's administration; and subsequently held office in Carteret's government (1743–4) and in subsequent administrations. In 1754 he became first lord of the treasury, until 1756 when succeeded by PITT, under whom he served (1757–62). In 1756 he was created duke of Newcastle-under-Lyme. His years in office marked the high-tide of Pelham family influence.

Newton, Sir Isaac (1642–1727) English mathematician, physicist and natural philosopher. Coming to Cambridge (from Lincolnshire) as a student, he was appointed Lucasian Professor of the mathematical sciences in 1669. He had already formed the idea of a universal law of gravitation and developed new mathematical tools to explore and express it. What he termed 'fluxions' were essentially what later became known as differential calculus; his claim to priority of invention was later justifiably challenged by LEIBNIZ. Newton first achieved wider recognition, however, for constructing the first reflecting telescope and for innovatory work on the composition and nature of light, published in the *Philosophical Transactions* in 1672. The Royal Society elected him a Fellow, but HOOKE's criticisms made him wary of publishing anything further; it was only in 1685 that the young HALLEY persuaded him to begin preparing a major volume for publication. Whilst its full title is *Philosophiae naturalis principia mathematica* (1687), it is generally known simply as the *Principia*. Its approach was to set out laws of motion, to explore their implications in terms of terrestrial mechanics, and then to extend this understanding to the behaviour of the solar system's components under the influence of gravity. As it was not explained how gravitational forces might operate over huge distances, contemporary readers were at first slow to be convinced; but once the ideas had been taken up by younger scholars and interpreted for a wider public they became extremely influential, both in England and, more gradually, across Europe. That their originator also spent much of his time studying alchemy and Biblical chronology was less well known and has only recently come to the attention of historians. In 1696 he abandoned academic life and moved to London. Through a patron, Lord Halifax, he was appointed Warden and then Master of the Mint; he was knighted in 1705. His later publications included *Optics* (1704) and a revised second edition of the *Principia* (1713). As President of the Royal Society from 1703, he dominated London scientific circles until his death and achieved the kind of eminence that generates myth and legend.

[FW]

Nicholas V (Tommaso Parentucelli, 1397–1455) pope 1447–55. Florentine by birth, he studied at Bologna and was imbued with the new humanist learning. Serving as secretary to the cardinal archbishop of Bologna for twenty years, he was active in Church councils and diplomatic missions before succeeding his patron as bishop of Bologna in 1444. Upon election to the papacy in 1447, he worked at three goals: priest, governor and builder of the Church and of the city of Rome in order to restore the splendour of Rome and the authority of the papacy. He sponsored minimal reforms of abuses against simony and clerical concubinage, and promulgated the Jubilee Year of 1450 to encourage pilgrimage to Rome. His building plan, often seen as the beginning of town planning in Rome, included a new St

Peter's, reconstructing the Vatican Palace, repairing the city walls, and restoring the Capitoline Hill. On the international scene, he ended the schism, participated in the Peace of Lodi (1454), and made belated calls for an unheeded crusade against the Turks. The plot against him and the papacy in 1453 by Stefano Porcari, who had been previously exiled, failed. He was the first pope to espouse humanism – often seen as the first Renaissance pope, is credited as founding the Vatican Library, and surrounded himself with scholars, writers and artists such as cardinal Bessarion, George of Trebizond, Theodore of Gaza, Lorenzo VALLA, Francesco Filelfo, Gianozzo Manetti, Leon Battista Alberti, Frate ANGELICO, and Benozzo Gozzoli to make learning a part of the glory of the papal court.

[JM]

Nicholas of Cusa (1401–64) cardinal and scholar with wide-ranging knowledge of mathematics, philosophy and science. Born in the Rhineland, he studied mathematics, astronomy, Greek, Hebrew and civil law at Padua. In 1432 at the council of Basel, he opposed Eugenius IV's candidate for archbishop of Trier and in a 1433 treatise, 'On Catholic Concordance', used an astronomical metaphor to describe harmony in the Church in sustaining his conciliarist stance that a general council had authority over the pope. By 1437 he had changed his position and supported papal primacy. After ordination in 1440, he was made a cardinal, bishop of Brixen in 1450, and served as papal legate to Germany for two years under NICHOLAS V. He returned to Italy in his last years to continue study and writing. His most important work, *On Learned Ignorance* (1440), argues for the limits of human understanding of God and the universe. Using a characteristic geometrical metaphor – the impossibility of turning a circle into a square – he asserts the mind's inability to conceive of infinity or the absolute. As a corollary, since the universe is God-centred and as such the centre is everywhere, the earth cannot be the centre of the universe, but must move. He was a Neoplatonist who believed in universal forms – the universe being the central form; and he criticised Aristotelian and Ptolemaic cosmological views. His interests extended to diagnostic medicine and applied science, even to the conducting of formal experiments on plant growth. He discovered a dozen lost Roman comedies by Plautus. He is remembered as a man of learning and as a magus, who explored the limits of human knowledge.

[JM]

Nicole, Pierre (1625–95) French theologian. Educated at the university of Paris, he rose to prominence as a defender of the Jansenist group associated with the convent of Port-Royal, and was the author of much of the polemical literature written in their defence. His 1662 book, *The Logic of Port-Royal*, written jointly with Antoine ARNAULD, was his most important contribution. Apart from his works for the Jansenists, he was the author of a weighty *Essays on Morality* (4 vols, 1671).

Nikon (1605–81) patriarch of Russia 1652–66. Son of a peasant of Finnish origin, strongly inclined to religion, he married but then took holy orders and both he and his wife decided to separate and enter the religious life. He joined a monastery. During a visit to Moscow in 1646 he gained the confidence of the young tsar ALEXEI I, through whom he was named metropolitan of Novgorod in 1649 and then patriarch of Moscow (1652). This enabled him to begin a modernisation of the usages and ceremonies of the Church. The changes aroused bitter opposition on the part of the Old Believers, but he was supported by the tsar and in 1657 named regent. Differences with Alexei, however, provoked his disgrace in 1658: he was sent to a monastery, and then in 1666 formally tried and deposed and

exiled. Recalled to Moscow fourteen years later by tsar Fyodor, he died during his journey back. The Russian authorities supported the Church reforms, and dealt brutally with the sometimes fanatical opposition of the Old Believers, whose most outstanding leader at the time was the priest AVVAKUM.

Noailles A distinguished family that served in the highest diplomatic and military levels.

Louis Antoine de Noailles (1651–1729) French ecclesiastic. Bishop first of Cahors then of Châlons-sur-Marne, he became archbishop of Paris in 1695 and cardinal in 1700. A leading champion of the Gallican movement during the assemblies of the French clergy in 1681–2, he subsequently became involved with the Quietist controversy. In 1713 he led a group of clergy who refused to accept, on Gallican grounds, the papal bull *Unigenitus* which condemned Quietism, and maintained his opposition until 1728.

2nd duke de Noailles, Anne Jules, count d'Ayen (1650–1708) The elder brother of Louis Antoine de Noailles, he was governor of Languedoc (1682–9) and then commander of the French forces invading Catalonia (1689–96), a successful campaign during which (1693) he was created marshal of France.

3rd duke de Noailles, Adrien Maurice, count d'Ayen (1678–1766) Son of the 2nd duke, he served under his father in Catalonia, and was subsequently appointed by LOUIS XIV as tutor to the new French king of Spain, PHILIP V. He commanded the Franco-Spanish forces in Catalonia during the war of Succession. On returning to France, he was appointed president (1715–18) of the council of Finance under LOUIS XV, and opposed the fiscal schemes of John LAW. He resumed his military career (1733–43) and gained the rank of marshal (1734), but retired after his defeat at the battle of Dettingen (1743). He became foreign minister for a while (1744–5), then ambassador to Spain.

Norfolk, dukes of

2nd duke, Thomas I Howard, 1st earl of Surrey (1443–1524) Son of Sir John Howard (a prominent Yorkist supporter created 1st duke of Norfolk by RICHARD III and killed fighting at Bosworth), he was – after three years in the Tower – pardoned by the new Tudor regime and given important posts, rising to become treasurer (1501–22) and earl marshal (1510–24). His most notable achievement was to lead the English forces to victory over the Scots at Flodden (1513), which earned him his dukedom (1514).

3rd duke, Thomas II Howard, 2nd earl of Surrey (1473–1554) Eldest son of the 2nd duke, he was one of the principal military commanders of HENRY VIII. Appointed lord admiral (1513–25), he shared in his father's victory at Flodden (1513), crushed revolt as lord lieutenant of Ireland (1520–1), and was created earl marshal (1533). An enemy of cardinal WOLSEY and subservient to Henry VIII, he repressed with severity the Pilgrimage of Grace (1536), despite his own Catholic beliefs, and sat on the tribunal that condemned his own niece, Anne BOLEYN. After CROMWELL's fall, he dominated the king's council; but another niece, Catherine Howard (executed 1542), fared little better as wife of the king. He and his son the poet Henry Howard, earl of Surrey, were arrested in 1546, thanks to the political indiscretions of the latter, and accused of treason. Surrey was executed (1547); Norfolk escaped this fate by the opportune death of the king, but remained in prison until the reign of queen MARY I, when he led the forces that crushed Wyatt's rebellion.

4th duke, Thomas III Howard (1536–72) Son of the ill-fated earl of Surrey, he was brought up by the duchess of Richmond and had the martyrologist John FOXE as tutor, remaining thereafter a lifelong Protestant. He succeeded to the dukedom in 1554, and became earl marshal. By his marriage to the daughter of the earl of Arundel (1556) he joined Arundel castle

to his estates. After the flight of MARY STUART to England (1568), he was talked into supporting a plan to marry himself (now a widower) to Mary, who could then be restored to her throne and recognised as successor to ELIZABETH I. Arrested briefly for this indiscretion, he was released in 1570. However, when the RIDOLFI plot was exposed (1571) he was suspected of complicity, arrested (September 1571) and executed nine months later on Tower Hill.

Nostradamus, Michel de Nostradame, known as (1503–66) French astrologer. Born in Provence, from a family of converted Jews who had served as advisers in the court of the count of Provence, he studied in Avignon and gained a degree in medicine (1529) at Montpellier. He later settled in Salon de Provence. In 1555 and 1558 he published in Lyon two volumes of his famous prophecies, the *Centuries*, which had an immediate success and were reprinted in numerous editions. Summoned to court by CATHERINE DE MÉDICIS, he was appointed doctor (1564) to CHARLES IX. However, he normally resided in Salon, where he was visited by the famous. The *Centuries* consisted of texts in the form of quatrains, put together from various literary and astrological sources; each quatrain, couched in cryptic and ambiguous terms, purported to foretell significant future events. Nostradamus claimed that the prophecies extended to the year 3797. They were taken very seriously by contemporaries, both in France and elsewhere, who found that the texts often coincided with subsequent events. The predictions continue to be applicable to events of the twenty-first century.

Nottingham, Daniel Finch, 2nd earl of (1647–1730) Son of the 1st earl, Heneage Finch, he was educated at Oxford and the Temple, was elected to Parliament in 1672 but did not sit until 1679, when he was made lord of the admiralty and privy councillor; he entered the Lords in 1682. As a firm Tory he was faithful to JAMES II, but accepted the 1688 Revolution, serving as a secretary for war till 1693. Under queen ANNE STUART, he served as secretary of state (1702–4) but disagreed strongly with the Whigs, remained in opposition, and supported SACHEVERELL in 1710. In 1711 he succeeded in making law the Occasional Conformity Bill, which penalised nonconformist dissenters. Returned to office briefly under GEORGE I (1714–15), he was shunned by the court for supporting clemency to the Jacobites after the 1715 rebellion.

O

Oates, Titus (1649–1705) English perjurer. Educated at Cambridge, he took holy orders in 1673; accused of perjury in a court case in 1675, he was sent to prison, from which he escaped. Destitute in London in 1676, he met the clergyman Israel Tonge, who enlisted him into a campaign to expose Jesuit conspiracy. He became a Catholic in 1677, with the express purpose of getting information; then spent five months in Spain in the English college at Valladolid, and a short while in the college at St-Omer. Returning to England in 1678, he denounced the existence of a Popish Plot against the king's life. The story gained credibility at all levels, and was officially accepted by Parliament: several innocent people were arrested and executed, among them the archbishop of Armagh, Oliver Plunket. Eventually he was arrested on charges of perjury (1684), tried (1685) and sentenced to be whipped and imprisoned. Released at the Glorious Revolution, he continued with his disreputable career till his death.

Ochino, Bernardino (1487–1565) Italian religious leader. Born in Siena, he entered the Franciscan order, then moved to join the more austere Capuchins, a newly founded branch of the order, becoming their general in 1538. Famous for his preaching, he was won over to the Reformation by Peter Martyr VERMIGLI and fled from Italy in 1542. His defection created a sensation. In 1554 he settled down in Zürich as pastor of the Italian community, but fell foul of the authorities through the publication of his *Dialogues* (1563), which appeared to favour polygamy and Unitarianism. He was expelled by the city, then under the control of BULLINGER. Now an old man of seventy-six, he was forced to set out in a wintry December, with four small children whose mother had recently died. His wanderings took him through Germany to Poland and Moravia, where he died in the Anabaptist colony at Slavkov (Austerlitz), victim to an epidemic that had carried off three of his children.

Oecolampadius, Johannes (1482–1531) German religious reformer. Born in Swabia, he was educated at the university of Heidelberg, where he also tutored the elector's children, then became a priest (1509) and returned to take up a benefice in his home town. Briefly in Basel around 1518, he was appointed cathedral preacher in Augsburg shortly after, and made contact with LUTHER's writings. He left the area in 1522, and returned to Basel, where he was appointed preacher and one of the professors of theology at the university. From this period he headed the Reformation party in the city, but progress was slow and he took part meanwhile in helping reform movements in neighbouring cities. The reform triumphed in Basel in 1529 as the result of a popular riot which forced the city council to change its ordinances, and Oecolampadius was called in to supervise the new order.

Oldenbarnevelt, Jan van (1547–1619) Netherlands statesman. Born in the southern Netherlands, he studied law at Louvain, Bourges and then Heidelberg (where he may have picked up his sympathy for Reformed doctrines). Adviser to WILLIAM I of Orange, in 1576 he became pensionary (legal official) of Rotterdam, and later was one of the men responsible for forming the Union of Utrecht (1579), which joined together the seven northern Dutch provinces opposed to Spanish and Catholic rule. In 1584 he backed MAURICE OF NASSAU as successor to William. Elected grand pensionary (1586) of the province of Holland, he directed the politics and foreign policy of the United Provinces, and helped to found the East India Company. His great achievement as leader was the conclusion in 1609 of the Twelve Years Truce with Spain. He was less successful with two of the main problems that beset the United Provinces: the religious conflict between rigorous Calvinists (represented by the theologian GOMARUS) and liberals (represented by ARMINIUS), in which he and his supporters tended to the Arminians or Remonstrants; and the political conflict between a dominant province of Holland, and the remaining six provinces. Maurice of Nassau and his supporters were in sharp disagreement with Oldenbarnevelt on both matters, and also had doubts about the utility of a peace settlement when the war had appeared so favourable to Dutch interests. In 1618 he organised a coup, arrested Oldenbarnevelt and his colleagues, and had him tried by a special court and executed in 1619.

Olivares, Gaspar de Guzmán, count duke of (1587–1645) Spanish politician. Second son of Enrique de Guzmán, former Spanish ambassador to Rome, he studied for the priesthood at the university of Salamanca (1601–4) but on his elder brother's death assumed his role in the family, succeeding in 1607 to his father's title and estates in Andalusia. He entered the life of court, where his uncle Baltasar de Zúñiga was powerful, and in 1615 was appointed head of the household of prince Philip, who became king in 1621 as PHILIP IV. The death of Zúñiga in 1622 confirmed the preponderance of Olivares, who now became chief minister (or *valido*). Till then enjoying the title of count of Olivares, in 1625 he was made duke of Sanlucar la Mayor, and thereafter adopted the style of 'count duke'. His ascendancy over the king was total, but he had serious difficulties in attempting to convince the ruling Spanish élite to co-operate with him. He buttressed his own position by extensive use of clientage and patronage at all levels, and by recourse to committees (*juntas*) for specific administrative matters. His many projects for reform in government and finance were not original but rather derived from ideas shared by other men of state during the reign of PHILIP III. His genius lay in the capacity to visualise policies as integral parts of a general plan to strengthen the crown, consolidate Spain's imperial position, and unify the peninsula. The demands of foreign policy, aggravated by the expiry of the Twelve Years Truce with the Dutch rebels (1621) and the outbreak of the Thirty Years War in Germany, threatened to destroy financial stability; an unfortunate intervention in a dispute over the Mantuan succession (1628–31) made the situation worse. The declaration of war by France (1635) set off a chain reaction that brought about the revolts of Catalonia and Portugal in 1640, and instability both in the peninsula and Italy. In 1643 Olivares was dismissed from office by the king, and died mad two years later. A failure in every aspect of his political activity, he remains a symbol of Spain's efforts to conserve itself against collapse.

O'Neill, Hugh, 2nd earl of Tyrone (?1540–1616) Irish leader. Taken to England for his own protection when aged about twenty, he was sent back five years later in the hope that he would help to stabilise the situation among the Irish, and admitted to the title of earl of Tyrone. In 1595 he rebelled against his English masters, and made contact with PHILIP II of Spain, but also negotiated with the English. Pardoned by England in 1598, he returned to the struggle almost immediately, continuing to lead resistance to the English until 1603, when he again made his submission. Suspected of plotting, he fled from Ireland in 1607 with his family, going first to Louvain then to Rome, where he died.

Orléans, Philip duke d' (1674–1723) regent of France. Son of LOUIS XIV's only brother Philip duke d'ORLÉANS (1640–1701), his early career was a distinguished military one: he served brilliantly 1691–3 in Flanders, then during the war of Succession served first in Italy (1706) and then (1707–8) commanded the French forces in Spain, but was recalled by Louis XIV because it was feared that he had designs on the Spanish throne. Until Louis' death he lived in retirement and in disfavour. The king's testament gave him no more status than nominal president of the regency council, but he succeeded (1715) in having the parlement of Paris quash the testament and name him regent with full royal powers. He then introduced a virtual reaction against the system of the late king, in particular by restoring the traditional nobility to positions of importance. LOUIS XV was allotted a court in the Tuileries while the regent governed from the Palais-Royal. The period was notable for the financial schemes of LAW, and a military alliance with England against Spain, directed by cardinal Dubois, who was in charge of foreign policy. Though Louis XV came of age in 1723 he left Orléans at the head of affairs, but the regent died that year. The regency period in France became notorious for its cultural freedom and alleged sexual profligacy.

Ormonde, James Butler, 12th earl of and first duke of (1610–88) Anglo-Irish general. From the prominent Butler family in Ireland, which had allied with the English for generations, he was born in London, succeeded to the earldom in 1633, and served from that year in Ireland under Wentworth, later earl of STRAFFORD. Commander of the troops that put down the Irish rebellion of 1640, he was appointed lord lieutenant of Ireland in 1642 but left after the defeat of CHARLES I in the English civil war. He returned in 1648 and tried to put together a confederacy of Catholics and Protestants, but left after the arrival of Cromwell in Ireland. In exile during the Parliamentary period, he was one of the architects of the Restoration in 1660, and was later created duke in 1682. He was appointed lord lieutenant of Ireland again in 1662–9 and 1677–84.

Orobio de Castro, Isaac (1617–87) Jewish writer. Born in Bragança, Portugal, of New Christian ancestry, around mid-century he moved with his parents to Málaga, Spain, and studied medicine at the local university of Osuna. In 1654 he and his family were arrested by the Inquisition of Seville on a charge of practising the Jewish religion. They appeared in an *auto de fé* but were released in 1658, and left Spain a couple of years later. Orobio moved to Amsterdam in 1662, changed his name from Balthasar to Isaac and became a Jew, and began to write in defence of Judaism. His principal works were written as a response to writings by SPINOZA, and by LIMBORCH. Orobio met the latter in Amsterdam in the 1680s and may have been one of the principal direct sources for Limborch's studies on the Inquisition.

Orry, Jean (1652–1719) A obscure French official of finances, he was sent by LOUIS XIV to Spain to reform the financial system inherited by PHILIP V from his predecessors. During his stay in Madrid, from 1703 to 1714, he managed remarkably to make a survey of the entire Spanish fiscal system, reformed the system of accounting, and for the first time put the Spanish treasury into order, thereby enabling the government to finance the war of the Spanish Succession. On his return to France he was created marquis de Vignory. His son Philibert Orry (1689–1747) became controller general of finances under LOUIS XV, and (from 1736) minister of public works.

Ortelius (Ortels), Abraham (1527–98) Netherlands geographer. He was born in Antwerp, son of an antique dealer; his father died young and he was brought up by his uncle. He began his career as an illuminator of maps, often travelling to the Frankfurt book fair in order to purchase engraved maps which he brought back to illustrate and sell for profit. On a trip to Frankfurt in 1554 he met MERCATOR, whom he also put in touch with PLANTIN; the two became friends. Under Mercator's influence, he gave up mere illustration of maps for the drawing of maps, for which he began to study geometry. He also began to travel through Europe in search of material. He visited Italy, and with Mercator and other friends travelled through Lorraine and Poitou in 1559–60. As a friend of Plantin, it is likely that he also belonged to the spiritualising tendency known as the 'Family Of Love'. He and Mercator were the leading cartographers of the century. He produced several maps of distinct countries in the 1560s, then began preparation of a one-volume map of the world, published in 1570, titled *Theatrum orbis terrarum*, printed by Plantin; the seventy copperplate maps were mostly engraved by Frans Hoogenberg. The work was a great success, re-edited and produced in several languages (in English in 1603), and earned official Spanish favour from PHILIP II.

Osuna, Pedro Téllez y Girón, duke of (1579–1624) Spanish grandee. An active soldier in Flanders in his early years, he owed his political rise to the duke of LERMA, who appointed him viceroy of Sicily (1611–15) and then of Naples (1618). In Naples he actively defended Spanish interests against Turkish sea power and against other Italian states. But in 1618 the authorities in Venice accused him and the Spanish ambassador in Venice, the marquis of Bedmar, of backing a plot to overthrow their republic; a number of supposed spies were executed. No historical evidence for this 'plot' has emerged. Suspected of political ambitions in Italy, Osuna was subsequently recalled to Spain (1620), brought to trial, and imprisoned in the fortress of Almeida, where he died.

Oxenstierna, Axel Gustavsson, count of (1583–1654) Swedish statesman. From a distinguished family, he was educated at German universities, entered the Swedish administration in 1602 and soon rose, thanks to the favour of GUSTAV II ADOLF VASA, to the rank of Chancellor (1612), a post he occupied till his death. His contribution lay in creating a working alliance between the aristocracy and crown, and in directing the areas of administrative reform and diplomacy while the king dealt with the waging of war. He negotiated the peace of Knäred with Denmark (1613) and that of Altmark with Poland (1629). In 1631 he was summoned to accompany the king during the intervention in Germany, and after Gustav's death (1632) became supreme director of Swedish affairs. He attempted to secure peace while retaining the military advantages secured by Sweden, but failed to do the former and therefore had to continue the war in order to keep the latter. In 1643 he launched the war against Denmark that resulted in the favourable treaty of Brömsebro (1645). The gains made at the treaty of Westphalia (1648) seemed to justify his military strategy. He was one of the regents governing Sweden during the minority of queen CHRISTINA VASA, but after she attained her majority (1644) he disagreed with her on both foreign and domestic policy. Their relations improved after 1650 and when he died he was still firmly in control of the government.

Oxenstierna, Bengt Gabrielsson, count (1623–1702) Swedish man of state. A relative of Axel Oxenstierna, he began his career as a diplomat in Germany during the Thirty Years War, then served as an officer in the Polish campaigns of CHARLES X GUSTAV VASA (1655–8) and helped to negotiate the peace of Oliva (1660), which deprived Poland of its Baltic territories and gave Sweden supremacy over the Baltic. He continued in the diplomatic service, and took part in negotiating the treaty of Nijmegen (1678). From 1680 he was head of the Chancellery and in effective control of foreign affairs, but his influence declined after the accession of CHARLES XII VASA (1697).

P

Padilla, Juan de (1490–1521) Castilian rebel leader. From a noble Toledo family, he served as military commander in Saragossa, and supported the Comunero revolt which broke out in 1520. Captured at the battle of Villalar (23 April 1521), he and the other leading rebels were executed without trial the next day. His wife, the noble María Pacheco, from the grandee Mendoza family, continued to lead the defence of Toledo against the royal troops; she later fled to Portugal, where she died in 1531.

Palestrina, Giovanni Pierluigi da (*c*.1525–94) Italian composer. He spent his entire musical career in religious posts in Rome. His works (all religious) have been regarded as the consummate musical reflection of the Counter-Reformation and the perfect model of the *stile antico* (the 'old style' of the Renaissance). His reputation was one of the most durable in European music history and his compositional techniques have served as a basis for the study of counterpoint ever since. His style is characterised by well-balanced melodic contours, careful treatment of dissonances, and highly divergent yet transparent polyphonic textures. He composed over 100 masses, 250 motets and one volume of spiritual madrigals.

[JE]

Palladio, Andrea (Andrea di Pietro della Gondola) (1508–80) North Italian architect and theorist. Palladio, who succeeded in adapting classical Roman architecture for domestic use, was arguably the most influential of all Italian architects, influencing building styles in England and North America as well as in the Netherlands and Scandinavia. Born in Padua, he was apprenticed to a local mason at thirteen, moving to Vicenza at sixteen, where he was enrolled in the guild of masons, stone-cutters and stone carvers as an assistant in the workshop of Giovanni da Porlezza and Girolamo Pittoni, a position he maintained until 1540. In July of 1532, however, as he worked on stone carvings for the villa of the humanist Tressino at Cricoli, his patron took a personal interest in him, explaining the writings of Vitruvius to him and taking him to Rome on three occasions (1541; 1546; 1547). His many works include the Porto, Chiericati, Thiene and Valmarana palaces and the Villa Capra ('La Rotonda'), and the Teatro Olimpico in Vicenza; the Palazzo della Torre in Verona; the Palazzo Antonini in Udine; and the churches of the Redentore and San Giorgio Maggiore in Venice, where he became official architect to the Republic in 1570. Despite his popularity as an architect, and his lasting importance for posterity, he never became wealthy, and was forced to send the eldest of his four sons to a boarding school for poor children in Padua (1563). He was the author of a famous treatise on Roman antiquities (*L'antichità di Roma raccolta brevemente dagli autori antichi e moderni*, Rome, 1555), as well as of an important one on architecture (*I quattri libri dell'architettura*, Venice, 1570).

[JH]

Pappenheim, Gottfried Heinrich, count zu (1594–1632) Bavarian general. Of noble Swabian origin, he studied at the universities of Altdorf and Tübingen, then made the grand tour through the Netherlands, France and Italy, and in the process converted to Catholicism. He enlisted to serve in the wars in Poland, then joined the forces of the Catholic League under TILLY, rose to become colonel, and took part in the battle of the White Mountain (1620), during which he was seriously wounded. He next served with the French in Italy (1623–6) before returning to enter the service of emperor FERDINAND II with command of the famous 'Pappenheim regiment'. He helped to crush the great peasant rising of 1626 in Upper Austria, and then served in northern Germany as second in command under Tilly. He directed the siege of the city of Magdeburg, which was stormed and destroyed (1631) in one of the worst atrocities of the Thirty Years War. His precipitate entry into battle was one possible reason for the serious defeat of Tilly's army at Breitenfeld (1631). He was mortally wounded fighting against the Swedes at the battle of Lützen (1632).

Paracelsus, Theophrastus (*c.*1493–1541) Swiss physician. Born Theophrastus Bombastus von Hohenheim, from 1529 he took the surname by which he is commonly known. He was born at Einsiedeln in Switzerland, son of a doctor, who educated him and apparently sent him to study also in Italy. Thereafter, from 1507, he travelled very widely through Europe,

apparently studying at different universities but professing dissatisfaction with them all. He journeyed the length and breadth of Europe, including England, Scandinavia and Russia, then went further afield to the Middle East and Istanbul. He returned in 1524 and some time later in 1527 was appointed town physician of Basel and lecturer at the university, despite the disapproval of many learned men. He seems to have offended by lecturing in the vernacular rather than Latin, and by rejecting the established wisdom of Galen and Avicenna, whose books he burned before his cheering students. Dismissed in 1528, he resumed his pilgrim life, travelling widely through France and the German-speaking lands, changing his religious affiliation according to his place of residence. He died in mysterious circumstances at an inn in Salzburg. In 1536 one of his studies achieved success when published, but most of his highly original and iconoclastic works, which later attained wide popularity, were published only after his death. He is historically significant for his acute emphasis on experimental observation, as a result of which he devised interesting and sometimes successful cures (he suggested mercury compounds for treating syphilis). He used novel chemical methods to prepare drugs. He also offered a neo-mystical view of the relation between human health and the natural universe, which his followers and modern homeopaths have built upon. Unjustly derided then and later as a charlatan, he was a brilliant though erratic innovator.

Parker, Matthew (1504–75) English ecclesiastic. Of humble origin, he was educated at Cambridge, where he became a fellow (1527). In 1535 he became chaplain to Anne BOLEYN, then to king HENRY VIII (1537) and master of his college (1544) and vice-chancellor of the university. In retirement during the reign of MARY I, he was appointed by ELIZABETH I as archbishop of Canterbury (1559). He carved out for the Anglican church a middle way between Reformers and Catholics, sponsored a new edition of the Bible, and attempted through his 'Advertisements' (1565) to impose on his clergy the use of church vestments. Firm opponent of Puritan practices, he attempted to ban the unauthorised meetings called 'prophesyings'. He left his rich manuscript library to the university of Cambridge, and fostered historical scholarship.

Pascal, Blaise (1623–62) French mathematician and philosopher. He was born in Clermont-Ferrand, a precocious child, fascinated by mathematical theory. At sixteen he wrote an essay on conic sections. With his father he conducted experiments on air pressure which led to the development of the barometer. His further mathematical accomplishments included the invention of a calculating machine, patented in 1647, work on the theory of probability, and contributions towards the basis of differential calculus. He came early under the influence of Jansenism. As a result of a religious crisis he entered the abbey of Port-Royal (1654–62), the centre of Jansenist teaching. During his stay he published his polemic against the casuistry of the Jesuits, *Lettres Provinciales* (*Letters to a Provincial Director*), but his *Les Pensées* (*Reflections*) is unfinished. These are in effect fragments of an attack on the so-called *libres-penseurs* or free-thinkers, and a defence of the orthodox Christian religion. Many editors have tried to reconstitute the plan of these scattered observations, edited eventually after his death, in 1670. He argued that man's reason could not deal convincingly with spiritual matters, expressing his views in a series of remarkable images which have circulated widely in posterity: 'man is a reed, the weakest element in nature, but he is a thinking reed, if the universe crushes him, he is aware of his death'; 'the universe is ignorant'; 'there are two types of wager, if you wager your belief in God, you have won the lot; if

you lose, you have lost nothing'. For Pascal, the greatest proof of Christ's existence lies in the prophecies. He was a scientist who knew the limits of his mental powers, but whose imagination and intuition compel the reader to think seriously about the truth of Christ's mission.

[BT]

Patiño, José, marquis (1666–1736) Spanish minister of state. Born in Milan, he spent his active career serving the Spanish government in Spain, where he began as a military intendant in the provinces, then moved to the central administration in Madrid, becoming minister of Marine in 1726 and of War in 1730. Thanks to his efforts, Spain for the first time became a serious naval power in the Mediterranean, challenging the British presence there.

Patkul, Johann Reinhold von (1660–1707) A Livonian noble, he took up the cause of the lords against the economic policies applied by Sweden, overlords of the country. Condemned to death by the authorities (1694), he fled to the Poland of AUGUSTUS II for support. Transferring later to Russia, he was appointed by PETER THE GREAT as ambassador to Poland and from there organised the military alliance of the two countries against Sweden. After a disagreement with the Poles, he was handed over by Augustus to the Swedes, who executed him.

Paul III (Alessandro Farnese, 1468–1549) pope 1534–49. Descended from Roman nobility long in papal service, he had a humanist education in the Medici circle of Lorenzo de' MEDICI and at the university of Pisa. His sister's marriage to a relative of Cardinal Roderigo Borgia (the future ALEXANDER VI) and her alleged intimacy with Alexander himself was gossiped about as the cause of his ecclesiastical rise to apostolic protonotary in 1491 and cardinal in 1493. He lived the life of a Renaissance prince with a mistress who bore him four children and a vast fortune to maintain the largest household among the cardinals and to build the Farnese palace in Rome. Invested as bishop of Parma in 1509 (one of sixteen he held), he began a change of his private life that led to ordination in 1519, identification with the Catholic reform party, and faithful service to the two Medici popes, LEO X and CLEMENT VII (the latter recommending him as his successor). As pope, he immediately created a number of reform-minded cardinals, appointed a papal commission to investigate reform, began preparations for a reform council, and oversaw the foundation of new religious orders – Theatines, Somaschi, Barnabites, Ursulines and Jesuits. The long-delayed general council eventually met at Trent in 1545 largely as a result of his determination and diplomatic skills. In its first session, he directed the council of Trent toward doctrinal and disciplinary matters. Although the reforming spirit of his papacy determined the future of Catholic reform, his administrative reforms met local resistance and his continued nepotism was notorious. He made his son Pierluigi duke of Parma and Piacenza, which established a Farnese dynasty there from 1545 to 1731. Sympathetic to art and culture, he patronised scholars, writers and artists; most notably, Michelangelo completed *The Last Judgement*, the Pauline chapels, and provided an architectural design for the new St Peter's.

[JM]

Paul IV (Gian Pietro Carafa, 1476–1559) pope 1555–9. A Neapolitan nobleman, his ecclesiastical career was promoted by his uncle cardinal Olivero Carafa. As bishop of Chieti, he was one of the organisers of the Theatines (named after his episcopal see), a Catholic Reformation order that promoted clerical reform through asceticism and apostolic work modelled on the spiritual program of St CATHERINE OF GENOA's Oratory of Divine Love. He served on PAUL III's reform

commission and was made a cardinal in 1536. He became increasingly identified with a hardline, uncompromising Counter-Reformation and headed the reinstituted Roman Inquisition in 1547. His pontificate is considered politically disastrous and marked a shift to a more authoritarian and dogmatic conformity with papal teaching. His virulent anti-Spanish policies precipitated the Valois–Habsburg War that ended with the Spanish victory at Saint-Quentin in 1557 and further Spanish dominance in Italy. He refused to accept the Protestant settlement of the Peace of Augsburg and exacerbated the English situation by demanding that monastic lands be restored. He opposed conciliar reform and kept the council of Trent, which had recessed in 1552, suspended. He attacked reform from a self-righteous austerity and prosecuted heresy ferociously, even illegitimately persecuting Cardinals Giovanni MORONE and Reginald POLE. In 1559 he instituted the Index of Forbidden Books in an attempt to censor dissent. He formally established the Jewish ghetto in Rome in 1555 and promulgated laws separating and excluding Jews. On his death, a popular city uprising sacked and burned the Inquisition palace in hated reaction to his reign.

[JM]

Peiresc, Nicolas-Claude Fabri de (1580–1637) French scholar, antiquary, humanist, and influential patron of learning. Son of a noble member of the parlement of Aix-en-Provence, he was educated locally then travelled in Italy (1599–1602) and studied at Padua, before returning to study law at Montpellier. In 1604 he occupied the place vacated by his uncle in the parlement, went to Paris in 1605 and in 1606 accompanied an embassy to England. These travels, and his own links with Galileo GALILEI, whom he had met in Padua, stimulated his interest in all branches of learning, but particularly astronomy. In 1610, using the newly discovered telescope, he was among the first to observe the planets and was the first man to see the Orion nebula. In Paris he made contacts with many scholars, including MERSENNE. He left Paris for Provence in 1623 and spent the rest of his life there; in 1624 he became a priest. In Provence he began (1624) a close and enduring friendship with GASSENDI, with whom he developed several projects, including one to determine the length of the Mediterranean. He was among the first to emphasise the study of coins for historical research, and sponsored experiments in human surgery. His favourite leisure was his gardens, the third largest in France, in which he cultivated rare species. He was also fond of cats. He published no books, but his extensive humanist and scientific interests, and his substantial correspondence with scholars throughout Europe, including Grotius and Rubens, underline his unusual achievement. 'No one', Pierre BAYLE commented, 'did more for the republic of letters'.

Pelham, Henry (c.1695–1754) English politician. Originating in Sussex, the Pelhams were one of the powerful political families of the early eighteenth century. Younger brother of Thomas Pelham Holles, duke of NEWCASTLE, Henry was educated at Oxford and entered Parliament in 1717. A firm supporter of WALPOLE, he rapidly became one of the pillars of the Whig party. He became a lord of the treasury (1721), and secretary for war (1724) and member of the privy council (1725). In 1743 he became first lord of the treasury and chancellor of the exchequer, but his power as prime minister was balanced by the role of Newcastle and Carteret in the government, and by the influence exercised by the king and the prince of Wales. In 1746 he strengthened his administration by taking in PITT, and with the elections of 1747 established his full control of the political scene. In 1751 he sponsored the act to adopt the Gregorian calendar: from 1752 the year began on 1 January and ten days were omitted

from the month of September to bring the year up to date.

Penn, William (1644–1718) English religious leader. Son of admiral Sir William Penn (d.1670), he was educated at Oxford and toured France and Italy (1661–4), then returned to serve in the army in Ireland. From 1667 he became an active member of the Quaker sect, was arrested and detained six months in the Tower (1669), from which he was released by the intervention of the duke of York, then left to spend a year in Ireland visiting Quaker groups. Back again in England, he was twice arrested, fined for refusing to take off his hat in court and refusing to take the oath to the crown, and imprisoned for six months (1670). He went to the continent for a year; on his return, as his father's heir he was now a rich country gentleman, and used his influence to present a petition to Parliament on behalf of the Quakers. During this period he published tracts in favour of religious freedom, *The Great Case of Liberty of Conscience* (1670) and *England's Present Interest Discovered* (1675). From 1676 onwards he encouraged Quakers to emigrate to New Jersey in north America, where he purchased territory. Letters patent of 1681 granted him land to the west of the Delaware river, where in 1682 he founded a colony that took the name of Pennsylvania, and was intended expressly as a refuge for those persecuted for religion. He visited the colony (1682–4) and back in England used his friendship with JAMES II to secure the release from prison of numerous Quakers. After the Revolution of 1688 he was harassed by the new government, and for a while (1692–4) deprived of the control of Pennsylvania, to which he returned briefly (1699–1701). His last years were made difficult by disputes in the American lands, and by debts in England. His numerous pioneering writings advocated religious toleration, and the full participation of all citizens in government.

Pepys, Samuel (1633–1703) English administrator and diarist. He took his degree (1653) at Cambridge, married two years later, and thanks to family influence began work (1660) as a clerk in the naval administration, to which he later added other posts. From this year he also began writing his famous Diary. In 1673 he was appointed 'secretary for the affairs of the navy', entered Parliament that year, and became master of Trinity House (1676). As client of the duke of York, he was for a while deprived of office during the Popish Plot, but in 1684 was reappointed by the crown as head of the Admiralty, and became one of the most significant men in the country. Among his achievements, he reformed the system of appointments in the naval administration, and directed a programme of building warships. After the Revolution of 1688 he was forced into retirement, giving him time to devote to his collection of books and manuscripts. His Diary, written in shorthand and occupying six small volumes, was first deciphered and published in 1825. A full edition in ten volumes was published in 1893, omitting passages 'unfit for publication' which Pepys had left in French or in code. Apart from the uniquely valuable light it sheds on the public life of the time, the Diary is an astonishing window into the private life of an exceptionally human, honest and cultured Englishman.

Pérez, Antonio (1540–1611) Spanish royal secretary. Son of the royal secretary Gonzalo PÉREZ, on his father's death he succeeded to one of the posts of secretary to PHILIP II of Spain, and became both wealthy and powerful. His downfall was precipitated by his differences with Juan de Escobedo, secretary to Don JUAN OF AUSTRIA, with whose policies Pérez strongly disagreed. In 1578 Escobedo was assassinated in the streets of Madrid, and shortly after Pérez was formally accused of the murder and subjected to house arrest. Implicated with him was

Ana de Mendoza, princess of EBOLI, widow of Ruy Gómez, prince of Eboli; their close links may have been as conspirators rather than as lovers. The princess began a long confinement in castles. Pérez was interrogated and tortured in 1585; he then accused the king of having ordered him to carry out the murder, but the charge is both unproven and unlikely. In 1590 he escaped to the Aragonese capital, Saragossa. Philip sent in an army to seize him (1591) but Pérez escaped to France and then to England. He spent the rest of his life encouraging France and England to undertake expeditions against Spain. A man of erudition and culture, Pérez wrote extensively; his best-known work is the *Relaciones*, published in different versions after its first publication in Pau in 1592.

Pérez, Gonzalo (*c.*1500–66) Spanish royal secretary. The longest-serving of Philip II's personal secretaries. He was born in Segovia, studied at Salamanca, and acquired extensive experience in public affairs. From about 1527 to 1532 he was with CHARLES V in Germany, became in 1532 an assistant to the emperor's secretary Alfonso de VALDÉS, and from 1542 was private secretary to prince Philip, a post he retained all his life, playing a secondary but always efficient role in the direction of administration and the formulation of policy. Appointed archdeacon of Segovia in 1542, he never took holy orders. He was a distinguished humanist, corresponded with ARETINO and BEMBO, and translated the *Iliad* into Spanish from the Greek, publishing the first chapters in 1550 and then the whole work in Antwerp in 1556.

Pergolesi, Giovanni Battista (1710–36) Italian composer. He was one of the leading exponents of the Italian comic opera (*opera buffa*). Most of his short life was spent in Naples, first as a student at the conservatory and then in the service of various patrons. His best-known comic opera is *La serva padrona* (*The Maid as Mistress*, 1733). Its staging in Paris in 1752 provoked the 'Battle of the Buffoons', which divided the Parisian literati into the advocates of the 'modern' Italian style and defenders of the traditional French opera (as exemplified by those of LULLY and RAMEAU). He also composed numerous arias, vocal chamber pieces, instrumental works and church music. His last work, *Stabat Mater*, enjoyed a long-lasting popularity throughout Europe.

[JE]

Perrenot de Granvelle, Nicolas (*c.*1485–1550) Franche-Comtois statesman. Born in the Franche-Comté, he was educated at the university of Dôle, married in 1513, and made the acquaintance of GATTINARA, president of the parlement, thanks to whom he became a councillor of the Dôle parlement and then moved to the Netherlands as a legal councillor of MARGARET OF AUSTRIA. In 1524 he was appointed to the new emperor CHARLES V's council of state, and held the post till his death. In 1527 he acquired the estates and lordship of Granvelle. On Gattinara's death in 1530 he took over all the functions of the chancellor (but without the formal title; he was instead First Councillor and Keeper of the Seals). He was thereafter present in every great matter affecting the diplomacy, administration or religious policy of Charles V in Germany and the Netherlands; Spanish matters were left to COBOS. Perrenot was respected by the German Protestant leaders, and was instrumental in winning MAURICE of Saxony to the emperor's side. Poor health obliged him to retire to Besançon in Franche-Comté in 1550, where he died that August. His voluminous correspondence, most of it unpublished, is scattered through the state archives of various countries, and in Besançon. His son Antoine, later cardinal GRANVELLE, acted as his secretary from about 1538. Another son, Thomas Perrenot de Chantonnay,

served PHILIP II as ambassador in France from 1559 to 1563, and then as ambassador in Vienna.

Persons (or Parsons), Robert (1546–1610) English Jesuit. Educated at Oxford, where he became dean of Balliol (1574), he left for the continent and in Rome entered the Society of Jesus and became a priest (1578). In 1580 he and Edmund CAMPION returned secretly to England, where they ministered to Catholics and printed leaflets; when Campion was captured, Persons escaped to the continent and obtained Spanish help for projected invasions of England. Briefly rector of the English college in Rome in 1588, he spent the next nine years in Spain, where he continued to support projected invasions, before returning as rector (1597), a post he held till his death. During this later period he was involved in controversy with some Catholic clergy of England, who favoured co-operation with the Elizabethan government and opposed the policies of the Jesuits and their nominee the 'archpriest' George Blackwell.

Peter the Great (Peter I) (1672–1725) tsar of Russia 1682–1725. Son of tsar ALEXEI I, he succeeded the co-tsars Fyodor III and Ivan V (his half-brother), but because of his youth power was in fact exercised by his half-sister SOFIA. During this period he developed links with foreigners in Moscow (among them the Scotsman Gordon) and an interest in foreign technology, especially military and naval. In 1689 he displaced Sofia and asserted his position as tsar, initiating active military policies to extend Muscovite power southward against the Turks and northward against the Swedes, in each case with the objective of gaining a foothold on the sea (Azov was captured in 1696). In 1697–8 he made an incognito visit to western Europe, visiting in particular Holland, England and Germany and studying western technology. He broke off the visit in 1698 to return home to crush a revolt in

Moscow of the palace guard (the *streltsy*). The rest of his reign, without doubt the most innovative in all Russia's history, was spent in three major enterprises: fortifying the Russian state and eliminating foreign power (he founded the city of St Petersburg, defeated the Swedish forces at Poltava in 1709, and gained the Baltic provinces by the treaty of Nystad 1721); modernising the administration and the fiscal system; and reforming aspects of religion and culture (the alphabet was reformed). The changes, introduced by force, had limited success; but Peter established Russia as the dominant power in eastern Europe. His ruthless methods affected his own family: his son and heir, Alexei, was tortured to death (1718) for plotting against him.

Petty, Sir William (1623–87) English scholar and statistician. Son of a clothier, he went to sea when young, and studied with the Jesuits at Caen; he later studied medicine at Leiden (1644), and went to Paris where he became friendly with MERSENNE and HOBBES. He then studied medicine at Oxford, becoming a fellow of Brasenose. Sent to Ireland as physician-general to the army (1651), he directed a pioneering statistical survey of confiscated lands (some of which later passed into his ownership). At the Restoration he became one of the founding members of the Royal Society (1662), showing an active interest in technical inventions. He is remembered chiefly for writings on what he called 'political arithmetic'. He collaborated (1662) with John Graunt in studying mortality figures for London, and produced a similar work on Dublin (1682); more general studies were those on England, and on *The Political Economy of Ireland* (1672).

Philip II of Spain (1527–98) regent of Spain 1543–56, and king 1556–98. The only surviving son of Emperor CHARLES V and Isabel of Portugal, he began governing Spain as regent in his father's absence, from 1543. He was married four times: in 1543 to Maria of Portugal (d.1545), mother of Don CARLOS; in 1554 to MARY I of England; in 1560 to Elizabeth of Valois (d.1568), mother of his daughters ISABEL and Catalina; in 1570 to Anna of Austria (d.1580), mother of the next king. Inheriting the debts and wars of his father, he attempted to achieve peace, but was dragged further into war against the Turks, the Dutch rebels, England and France. The major problem, which he never solved, was adequate finance, for lack of which he mortgaged the revenues of Castile. His successes included the consolidation of the American empire, the naval victory against the Turks at Lepanto (1571), and the occupation of Portugal (1580) in support of his claim to the throne; the most famous of his failures was the Armada (1588) sent against England. In an effort to control his world-wide empire, he relied on his own bureaucratic application and the loyalty of ministers. A fervent Catholic, he strongly supported the Inquisition; but suffered the hostile propaganda of Protestants, who accused him of bloodthirsty excesses in his political activity and his private life. He was accused, even in his day, of the death of his son Don CARLOS. Admirer of European art and culture, and patron of the leading artists of his time (his favourite was TITIAN), he imported his tastes into Castile, where he built notable palaces and gardens, of which the most notable example was the gardens at the palace of Aranjuez. His most enduring monument was the construction of the palace-monastery of the Escorial, which took twenty years to complete.

Philip III (1578–1621) king of Spain 1598–1621. Son of the preceding and of Anna of Austria, in 1599 he married the archduchess Margaret of Austria (then aged thirteen), who gave him eight children. A timid successor to his father PHILIP II, he allowed his ministers, most notably Juan de Idiáquez and the duke of

LERMA, to dominate policy-making. This opened the way to major changes: the expression of liberal and reformist political ideas; moves towards ending discrimination against those of Jewish origin; and above all the ending of war, through peace treaties with England (1604) and above all with the rebel Dutch (the Twelve Years Truce, 1609). The arrival of peace also enabled ministers to implement at last the expulsion of the Morisco minority, some 250,000 people, from Spain (1609–14). This act merely aggravated the difficult economic situation in which the country found itself. Foreign policy under him was marked by a rapprochement with France through the marriages (1615) between the Spanish infanta Anna and LOUIS XIII, and the future PHILIP IV with the princess Isabel. Despite the general wish for peace in his government, marked by a remarkable phase of diplomatic activity, Spain became drawn into the complex events that led to the outbreak of the Thirty Years War.

Philip IV (1605–65) king of Spain 1621–65. The son of PHILIP III, he was married in 1615 to princess Isabel of France, a marriage not consummated until 1619; the queen, who gave Philip seven children, died in 1644. In 1649 he married again, Mariana of Austria, by whom he had five children, among them Charles, born in 1661. The king also had numerous lovers and illegitimate children. His reign was dominated by the ministry of OLIVARES, whose policies determined both external and internal events until his removal in 1643, and after him by Luis de HARO. For political guidance the king relied extensively on the mystic María de AGREDA, whom he met in 1643 and who encouraged him during his frequent moods of depression.

Philip V (1683–1746) king of Spain 1700–24, 1724–46. Grandson of LOUIS XIV, he could claim through his grandmother María Teresa, daughter of PHILIP

IV, a right to the throne of Spain, left without a ruler on the death of the childless CHARLES II HABSBURG in 1700. He was duke d'Anjou when Charles II's final testament bequeathed him the Spanish throne. After some hesitation because of opposition by other European powers, Louis XIV accepted the testament on his grandson's behalf, and installed Philip in Madrid with French advisers and officials. Philip thus became the first Spanish monarch of the Bourbon dynasty. Acceptance of the throne, which threatened to unite the resources of France and Spain, unleashed the war of the Spanish Succession (1701–14), fought on several fronts in western Europe and the Iberian peninsula. The duke of BERWICK won a decisive victory at Almansa in 1707. As a result of these victories the crown abolished the independent laws (fueros) of the eastern realms of the peninsula. After later reverses, Louis XIV in 1709 withdrew his troops and advisers from Spain in the hope of achieving peace. Philip however declared his intention to fight on, alone if necessary. French troops returned to the peninsula in 1710. The peace of Utrecht (1713) deprived Spain of most of its European territories. Philip's first wife (1701) was a French princess, Marie-Louise of Orléans; in 1714 he married the Italian Elizabeth FARNESE, who brought a more energetic spirit into decision-making (aided by ALBERONI), and gave him seven children. Philip had a tendency to depression; during one of these phases, in 1724, he decided to abdicate in favour of his son the infante Luis, who became king but died seven months later. Philip then became, for the second time, king of Spain. The second reign was a period of active participation in wars, motivated principally by a concern to confirm Bourbon influence (in the shape of Farnese's sons) in Italy. Philip's reign was one of notable Spanish resurgence in Europe; the king was also an outstanding patron of culture and established French tastes among the élite.

Philip the Fair (1478–1506) duke of Burgundy (1482–1506) and king of Castile (Philip I) (1504–6). Born in Bruges, only son of MARY OF BURGUNDY and the emperor MAXIMILIAN I, he inherited the Netherlands while an infant on the sudden death of his mother (1482). Invested formally as duke in 1494, in 1496 he was married to JUANA (THE MAD) (daughter of FERDINAND II and ISABELLA THE CATHOLIC of Spain), who came to the north for the wedding in Lille. They had six children, all of them destined to become queens (of France, Denmark, Hungary and Portugal) and emperors (CHARLES V and FERDINAND I). Successive deaths in the Spanish royal family made the crown of Castile devolve on Juana; the young couple made a short visit to Spain in 1502 to confirm their claim as heirs. When Isabella died in 1504 they were proclaimed as rulers of Castile, and in 1506 came to Spain, where Ferdinand met Philip and agreed to withdraw to his realms of Aragon and Italy; both also agreed that Juana was unfit to rule (the Cortes thought otherwise, and in her lifetime always recognised her as fully queen). Philip died suddenly in September 1506 of a mysterious illness.

Philip of Hesse (1504–67) landgrave of Hesse 1518–67. Born in Marburg, he succeeded to the government of Hesse at the age of five on the death of his father the landgrave William II, but was declared of age and therefore effective ruler in 1518. When he attended the Diet of Worms (1521) he visited LUTHER, and soon became sympathetic to the reformer. He declared himself a Lutheran in 1524, the first prince of the empire to do so; in 1523 he married the daughter of the duke of Saxony, thereby creating an alliance decisive for the survival of the Reformation in Germany. After putting down ruthlessly the forces of the peasant revolt in 1525, he began to introduce changes into the religion of Hesse. Despite his championship of Lutheranism, he was a notably tolerant ruler in purely religious matters. In 1529 he arranged the colloquy at his castle in Marburg between Luther and ZWINGLI over their religious differences. Over the next few years he skilfully steered his way between the conflicting pressures in the empire, overcoming the problems caused by his taking of a second wife in 1540, an action in which Luther loyally supported him. But he was finally unable to arrest the clash between the emperor CHARLES V and his own Schmalkaldic League, which broke out into war in 1546. After Charles' victory at Mühlberg (1547), Philip was persuaded to surrender, and remained in honourable confinement in the Netherlands until 1552. At the peace of Passau (1555) he intervened in favour of a peaceful accord between Catholics and Reformers. At his death, the territory of Hesse was divided among his sons into the states of Hesse-Kassel and Hesse-Darmstadt. He sired seventeen children by his two wives.

Piccolomini, Ottavio (1599–1656) Italian general. One of the leading noble families of sixteenth-century Siena, the Piccolomini produced two popes and several famous military men. Ottavio entered the service of Spain in 1616, first in Italy and then in Germany, where he took part in the battle of the White Mountain (1620). He later (1627) entered the service of WALLENSTEIN, went to serve in the Mantuan war (1629–30) and commanded the cavalry at Lützen (1632), after which he was promoted to major general. He was drawn by the emperor FERDINAND II to take part in the conspiracy against Wallenstein (he has a prominent role in Schiller's play on the theme). On the latter's murder, he was rewarded with a part of his lands and the rank of field-marshal. He played a leading part in subsequent campaigns of the Thirty Years War, notably in the victory at Nördlingen (1634). The climax of his career was the victory over the French at Diedenhofen (1639), for which he was named to the Imperial privy council and granted the duchy of Amalfi by Spain. After being defeated by the Swedes at Breitenfeld (1642), he was called to command the Spanish forces in the Netherlands 1644–7, then returned to the emperor's service as commander-in-chief of his armies in 1648, and in 1650 was created a prince of the Empire. He did not find time to marry until the end of his life (1651), and died in Vienna.

Pico della Mirandola, Giovanni (1463– 94) Renaissance Italian philosopher with eclectic influences and synthetic interests. Son of a prince of the small Lombard principality of Mirandola, he studied at Bologna, Padua and Florence. His interests in the Greek, Arabic and Hebrew traditions led to linguistic study and philosophical investigation of Plato, Neoplatonism, hermeticism, Averroes (Ibn-Rushd) and the Kabbala. His goal was a broad synthesis of Christian and non-Christian ideas. In 1486, he announced a public disputation in Rome on 900 theses, which proposed that all philosophies hold valuable truths. As an introduction, he composed his famous *Oratio de dignitate hominis astrologum* (Oration on the Dignity of Man), which argues that human beings are not fixed in a hierarchical chain of being, but that free will provides limitless possibilities for human development. A papal commission found a number of propositions heretical and his *Apologia* in response led him to seek refuge in France. Released from a short imprisonment, he returned to Florence where he remained close to the Platonic Academy of FICINO under the patronage of Lorenzo de' MEDICI. He continued to write philosophical-religious works until his early death at thirty one. The *Heptaplus* was a seven-part exegesis of Genesis; *De ente et uno* (On Being and the One) was part of a synthesis of Plato and Aristotle; and an incomplete *Disputationes adversus astrologum* (Disputation Against Astrology) attacked conventional astrology as an enemy of true religion. He

became a follower of SAVONAROLA's sermons at San Marco, but died before the French invasions and Savonarola's emergence in politics.

[JM]

Piero della Francesca (Pietro di Benedetto di Pietro) (*c.*1415–92) Italian painter and mathematician. The eldest son of a tanner and shoemaker who was also a woolmerchant, he was born in Borgo Sansepolcro, near Arezzo in the upper valley of the Tiber. He seems first to have been apprenticed to a minor local painter, Antonio da Anghiari, but was apparently precocious, and was recorded as assistant to Domenico Veneziano for the frescoes (destroyed) in Sant'Egidio, Florence, on his only visit to that city (1437). He was back in Sansepolcro in 1442, and was elected to the town council. The Confraternita della Misericordia commissioned him to paint a large polyptych (Palazzo Communale) representing the Madonna of Mercy, which was finished by assistants when he left town, presumably to work for Federigo da Montefeltro at the court in Urbino, since the *Flagellation of Christ* is said to have been done there about 1444. By 1448 he was in Ferrara, where he painted frescoes (now lost) in the Castello and in the church of S. Agostino; and by 1451 he was in Rimini, where he painted the large fresco of Sigismondo Malatesta kneeling before his patron saint, St Sigismund. His major works, however, are the portrait diptych of Federigo da Montefeltro and his wife Battista Sforza (*c.*1472; Uffizi), painted in Urbino; the cycle of frescoes depicting the *Legend of the True Cross* (1452–66; Arezzo, church of S. Francesco); and the *Resurrection* (after 1458; Sansepolcro, Museo Civico). His will, drawn on 5 July 1486, is preserved in the Archivio di Stato in Florence, leaving the *Nativity* (London, National Gallery) to his family, where it remained among his descendants until the nineteenth century. During his last six years of life Piero was blind, and it was shortly before this time that he wrote his important treatise on perspective (*De prospectiva pingendi*) which was presented to Federigo da Montefeltro in 1482. The notice of his death and burial in the Badia is reported in the necrology of the Confraternity of S. Bartolommeo in Sansepolcro on October 12, 1492.

[JH]

Piranesi, Giovanni Battista (1720–78) Italian engraver, etcher, architect, theorist and dealer in antiquities. He was the defender of Roman style against Winkelmann's rather overheated preference for things Greek, and was one of the printmakers whose creations best seemed to illustrate the ideal of 'the Sublime' in art (as opposed to the merely beautiful). Born in Mestre, the son of a master stonemason and builder, he was educated in Venice, largely by his father and a maternal uncle who was an engineer and architect. In 1740 he went to Rome, as draftsman for the Venetian ambassador, remaining there until 1744, with side trips to Naples, Herulaneum and Paestum, while he learned the technique of etching from Giuseppe Vasi and Felice Polanani. The first of his volumes in large format, the *Prima parte de architetture* (Rome, 1743) was published at this time. After a brief return visit to Venice he settled permanently in Rome in 1745. His series of large plates of the views of Rome (*Vedute de Roma*; 135 plates) was begun in the late 1740s and continued until his death. The imaginative *Carceri* (prisons) series was begun at about the same time, but completed largely between 1760–9, as was his book of designs for interior decoration (*Diverse maniere di adornare i cammini*, Rome, 1769). His chief work of architecture was the rebuilding of the church of Sta. Maria del Priorato, on the Aventine hill (1764–5). His prints were widely collected by English travellers as souvenirs of the Grand Tour, and were a major influence on French Romantic writers such as Victor Hugo, and such nine-teenth-century printmakers as Charles Meryon and Gustave Doré, while his book on ornament was utilised by the creators of the Empire style. His personal collection of antique sculpture was sold by his sons to the king of Sweden, and they remain in Stockholm to this day.

[JH]

Pitt, William, 1st earl of Chatham (1708–78) known as Pitt the Elder. Educated at Eton and Oxford, he entered Parliament in 1735 as member for Old Sarum, joined the 'patriot' Whigs and became a fierce opponent of WALPOLE. After Walpole's death, Pitt was taken into the PELHAM administration as paymaster-general of the forces and made a member of the privy council (1746); from 1751 he began to develop the famous rivalry with Henry Fox. Dismissed from office in 1755, he returned to power as prime minister in 1756, but was driven out by GEORGE II (1757). On the outbreak of the Seven Years War (1757) against France, he was called upon to lead a coalition government including Fox and NEWCASTLE. His successful leadership was shown notably in foreign policy, both in Europe and in the burgeoning Empire. He resigned in 1761, after facing the hostility of the new king, George III; but returned to head a ministry again in 1766, and was created earl. Bad health forced him to abandon power (1768).

Pius II (Aeneas Silvius Piccolomini, 1405–64) pope 1458–64. One of eighteen children of an impoverished branch of a leading family of Siena, he distinguished himself as a Latinist in the humanist curriculum as a youth. He served as secretary for a number of bishops and amassed extensive administrative and diplomatic experience with special expertise in German affairs. He served as secretary to cardinal Domenico Capranica at the council of Basel (1431–7), represented the bishops who refused obedience to Eugenius IV, and became secretary to the anti-pope Felix V in 1439. In 1442 he became secretary to emperor FREDERICK III OF HABSBURG, who crowned him poet laureate for his Latin poetry, a comedy, and novella (*The Tale of Two Lovers*). Serious illness led him to reform his life and he was ordained in 1446. He came to papal service as chief mediator between the German states (both princes and bishops) and the papacy. He advanced to bishop and cardinal under Eugenius IV, NICHOLAS V, and Calixtus III, whom he succeeded in 1458. During his pontificate he asserted papal authority against conciliarist claims, continued the recovery of the Papal States, opposed French monarchical claims over their local church, and worked ceaselessly but ineffectually to launch a crusade against the Ottoman Turks who had taken Constantinople in 1453. His rebuilding of his Sienese village hometown, Corsignano, into the ideal Renaissance town, Pienza, inspired by Alberti and executed by Bernardo Rossellino, is his greatest building project. He patronised humanist learning and was a prolific writer, with his autobiographical commentaries translated in English as *Memoirs of a Renaissance Pope*.

[JM]

Pius IV (Gian Angelo de' Medici, 1499–1565) pope 1559–65. From a Milan family unconnected with the Medici of Florence, he rose in the Church to become titular archbishop of Ragusa (1545) and cardinal (1549). Elected to succeed PAUL IV as pope, he immediately ordered the arrest and trial of the latter's notorious nephews, two of whom were executed. He took control of the Church at one of the most decisive moments in its history, and introduced crucial changes in favour of the movement for reform. He re-called the council of Trent, concluding its work (1562–3) and issuing its authoritative decrees (1564). He also supervised the new Index of prohibited books (1564), and reformed the college of cardinals. He was powerfully helped by the collabora-

tion of his nephew, Carlo BORROMEO, archbishop of Milan.

Pius V (Antonio Michele Ghislieri, 1504–72) pope 1566–72. An austere Dominican friar, cardinal in 1557, he succeeded PIUS IV and actively continued his work in favour of the Tridentine reform, publishing the Roman catechism (1566), and the new Tridentine breviary (1568) and missal (1570). An ardent champion of the faith, he issued the bull excommunicating Elizabeth of England (1570) and laboured to unite the Christian west against the Turks, a task that bore fruit in the Holy League, whose naval forces under the command of Don JUAN OF AUSTRIA defeated the Turks at Lepanto (7 October 1571). He was canonised in 1712.

Pizarro Family of humble origins from Trujillo in Extremadura. The Pizarro brothers played a leading part in the early Spanish conquests in Peru.
Francisco Pizarro (1475–1541) Travelling to the New World in 1507 to seek his fortune, he subsequently took part in the expedition by Balboa that came upon the Pacific. In Panama he, Diego Almagro and the priest Hernando de Luque entered into a partnership to send expeditions to discover the riches of Peru. After his first two voyages (1524–5 and 1526–7) he returned to Spain and received from the crown special authority over the territories he would discover. He returned to America with his half-brothers who took part in the expedition that left Panama in January 1531 and made landfall at Tumbez in the territory of the Incas. He found an empire divided by civil war, allied himself with Huascar against Atahualpa, and seized the capital Cajamarca (November 1532). Atahualpa was imprisoned and made to collect an enormous ransom, after which he was killed (August 1533). In 1535 Pizarro founded the coastal city of Lima as the new Spanish centre. The victorious Spaniards soon quarrelled over their gains: the wars between the Pizarros

and Almagro ended with the defeat and execution of the latter. In their turn the Almagrists plotted against Pizarro and assassinated him.

Gonzalo Pizarro (1502–48) Absent from Peru at the time of his brother Francisco's assassination, he returned to take part in the revolt of the Pizarrists against the crown's attempt to enforce the 1542 New Laws in Peru. He defeated and executed the viceroy (1546), but in his turn was defeated by royal forces, imprisoned and executed.

Hernando Pizarro (1508–60) The youngest and only legitimate one of the Pizarro brothers, he returned to Spain in 1540 to present their case to the crown, but was imprisoned for life in the fortress at Medina del Campo (1540–60). The Pizarros enriched their home town of Trujillo in Extremadura and succeeded in entering the Spanish nobility.

Plantin, Christophe (c.1520–89) French printer. Born in Normandy, he took up the profession of bookbinding at Caen, and in 1549 moved to Antwerp, thenceforward his home, where he began printing books, of a quality that soon made him famous. He was visited by PHILIP II, who was sufficiently impressed to grant him royal patronage and all his future commissions for printing. Of these the most famous was the king's Polyglot Bible, prepared under the direction of the scholar ARIAS MONTANO in eight volumes (1569–72). When Antwerp was sacked by troops during the Spanish Fury (1576), Plantin established an office in Paris and then moved to Leiden (1583), where he worked for the university authorities. His business in Antwerp was continued by his son-in-law Moretus, who continued to direct the firm after Plantin's death. Plantin himself returned to Antwerp in 1585, when the Spaniards recaptured the city. Always a Catholic by inclination, Plantin had a liberal attitude to religious allegiances, and was a supporter of the spiritual tendency known as the 'Family of Love'.

Platter, Felix (1536–1614) He was born in Basel, and sent to Montpellier to study medicine. He returned to Basel to take his doctorate (1557), taught at the university and was appointed chief physician of the city. Like his father, Thomas PLATTER, Felix wrote an important autobiography. His book on human pathology, *De corporis humani structura* (The Structure of the Human Body) (1583), made him famous. Among other works, he wrote the *Praxis medicae opus* (Practice of Medicine) (1603), describing symptoms of illnesses. He was among the first doctors to study the causes of insanity.

Platter, Thomas (c.1499–1582) Born into a poor peasant family in Grächen, southern Switzerland, he left home when young and travelled through Europe, supporting himself by working as a shoemaker and educating himself in the process. His travels took him as far as Silesia. He returned to Switzerland and lived in Zürich, where he played an important role as a humanist and printer, and helped establish Zwingli's Reformation. He then settled in Basel, where he became notable as a schoolteacher. He wrote one of the most remarkable autobiographies of the time (completed 1576), consisting in part of letters to his son Felix PLATTER.

Pole, Reginald (1500–58) English ecclesiastic. Of direct royal descent, he was destined by his mother Margaret countess of Salisbury for a church career. Educated at Oxford, he spent six years (1521–7) in Italy, mainly Padua and Rome, making contact with the leading European humanists, including ERASMUS. In England he was offered high office, but refused to support HENRY VIII's divorce plans, and returned to Italy during the early stages of the royal supremacy over the Church. He was summoned to Rome by pope PAUL III, who in 1536 made him a cardinal (though Pole was not a priest), appointed him to the committee 'de emendanda Ecclesia' (for the reform of the Church), and made him papal legate to England. Henry, enraged by the cardinalate, persecuted and arrested (1538) Pole's family; the elderly countess Margaret was executed in 1541. Pole was one of the papal legates who opened the council of Trent in 1545. On the accession of MARY I to the throne, he returned to England (1554) where he took charge of the measures to end the Henrician schism. In 1556 he was made priest and subsequently appointed archbishop of Canterbury. He died on the same day that Mary Tudor died.

Polignac, Melchior de (1661–1742) French diplomat. Of an old noble family from southern France, he made the Church his career, and worked in Rome from 1689, where he contributed to sealing the rift between France and Rome caused by the Gallican Articles of 1682. At the instance of LOUIS XIV he was given important diplomatic commissions, first in Poland (where in 1696 he succeeded in obtaining the election of the prince of CONTI as king) and then in the negotiations (1710–12) for the peace of Utrecht. Created cardinal in 1713, he remained out of politics during the Regency but became involved in the Cellamare conspiracy. In 1724 he was nominated French ambassador to the Holy See, and helped to resolve the long-standing problems raised by the bull *Unigenitus* of 1713.

Pompadour, Jeanne Antoinette Poisson, marquise de (1721–64) French court lady. Daughter of a financier who had to leave the country because of his deals, she was brought up by her mother's lover, also a rich financier, who in 1741 married her to his nephew the financier Charles Le Normant. In Paris she soon became known as one of the most beautiful society ladies, active in the salons of the day. Presented at the court of Versailles, she became from 1745 mistress of LOUIS XV, who

created her marquise. Though active lover of the king for only a few years (1745–51), she remained his close friend until her death, playing an active life at court and occupying positions of importance. She received generous gifts from the king, including money, lands and chateaux (her Paris residence the hôtel d'Évreux is today the presidential palace of L'Élysée). Her brother became superintendant of works in 1752. A close friend of the philosophers of the Enlightenment, she obtained for VOLTAIRE a place in the French Academy, entertained well-known intellectuals at home, and patronised the publication of the *Encyclopédie* in 1752. Though her role in politics has been exaggerated, she was a considerable influence on many aspects of public policy.

Pomponne, Simon Arnauld, marquis de (1618–99) French minister of state. Son of Arnauld d'Andilly and nephew of the Great Arnauld, he served as military intendant in Naples and Catalonia before becoming ambassador to Sweden (1666, and again in 1671) and The Hague (1669). As secretary of state for foreign affairs (1671–79) he directed policy during the war against Holland, and negotiated the peace of Nijmegen (1679). Displaced for a period from politics because of his links with the Jansenists, in 1691 he returned to power and became minister of posts (1697).

Pontchartrain, Louis Phélypeaux, count de (1643–1727) French minister of state. The family emerged as established members of the robe nobility through his grandfather. He became member of the parlement of Paris at the age of seventeen, and president of the parlement of Brittany in 1677. Thereafter he occupied major posts in government: as controller general of finance (1689–99), secretary of Marine (1690–9), and secretary of the royal household (1690–9). He crowned his career as chancellor of France (1699–1714), and thereafter retired to a contemplative life in the Oratory.

Pope, Alexander (1688–1744) English poet. Childhood illness left him with curvature of the spine, stunted growth and permanent ill health. Denied access to formal schooling because of his Catholicism, he was largely self-educated and already by the age of sixteen was displaying his metrical skills in *The Pastorals*. He enjoyed the patronage of established figures in the literary world. *An Essay on Criticism* was published when he was twenty-three. Written in heroic couplets, it dictated the rules of neoclassicism with intelligence and wit. It made him famous and, a year later in 1712, *The Rape of the Lock* confirmed him as an established poet. His translations of Homer brought him financial independence and recognition as the chief literary man of the age. He purchased a fine villa in Twickenham and proceeded to cultivate a miniature classical garden and the friendship of the nobility. From the outset of his career Pope was involved in bitter and spiteful controversies with other writers, notably with the Shakepearean scholar Lewis Theobald and the playwright and Poet Laureate, Colly Cibber. *The Dunciad*, a satire on dullness, mocked his enemies while at the same time deploring falling standards in literature and forcefully attacking scientific humanism. *Essay on Man* and four *Moral Essays* were published in the 1730s. In his last years he prepared his correspondence for publication, altering and editing it so as to present himself in the best possible light. He is the major writer of the English Augustan age.

[GG]

Postel, Guillaume (1510–81) French scholar. Born in Barenton (Avranches) and orphaned at the age of twelve, he later studied and worked in Paris. A brilliant student of languages, he mastered the three scholarly tongues (Hebrew, Latin and Greek), picked up other European languages, and learnt Arabic during a diplomatic mission to Istanbul (1535). In 1538 he became professor of Greek, Hebrew and Arabic in Paris at what later became the Collège de France, but in 1542 resigned after differences with the authorities, and went to Switzerland. In Basel he published his great work *De Orbis terrae Concordia* (Peace on Earth) (1544), a philosophical treatise demonstrating the truth of Christianity when compared with Islam, Judaism and paganism. The work had in mind the establishment of universal harmony among all men, and to that end set out a number of basic truths that could, on grounds of reason, be accepted by everybody, whatever their faith. But Postel also had visionary tendencies. He went to Rome in 1544 and was accepted into the new Society of Jesus by IGNATIUS OF LOYOLA, but was dismissed the following year. His subsequent writings became more unusual. In his *Panthenosia* (published in the late 1540s) he called for the unity of all believers in God, and the rejection of dogma and intolerance. He travelled again to the Ottoman empire in 1548–9, and published in 1560 his *De la République des Turcs*, in which he again emphasised the common ground shared by Muslims and Christians. He was twice arrested briefly on suspicion of heresy, and his books were subsequently placed on the Roman Index of prohibited works, but he died in tranquility in Paris.

Poussin, Nicolas (1594–1665) French painter, active largely in Rome. Born in Les Andelys (Normandy), he ran away from home, staying first in Rouen and later moving to Paris (1612–23), where he studied anatomy in one of the city's hospitals. At the age of thirty he left for Rome (1624), where he studied Raphael's frescos, antiquities and anatomy, before finally coming to the notice of cardinal Francesco Barberini and Cassiano dal Pozzo. After a life-threatening illness he was nursed back to health by a French pastry-cook, whose daughter he married in 1630. He sketched outdoors in the Campagna with her brother Gaspard

Dughet (whose works have often been sold as Poussins). Other sketching companions included CLAUDE LORRAIN. Poussin was inducted into the Academy of St Luke (1632), and his beautifully executed cabinet paintings on erudite subjects were popular with French tourists and *libertins*. He also received commissions from CLEMENT XI and RICHELIEU, who ordered a set of Bacchanals in 1636. He returned to Paris as First Painter to LOUIS XIII to decorate the Grand Galerie of the Louvre and the king's chapel at St Germain-en-Laye (1640–2), and was given his own pavilion in the Tuileries. Finally, however, he was unable to stand the constant backbiting of the Parisian painters who had been passed over for his royal appointment, and returned permanently to Rome in late 1642. His œuvre is both unusually well-preserved and well-documented. Of particular interest are his letters to the collector Chantelou (24 November 1647) and to Roland Fréart de Chambray (1665), in which he outlines his theoretical principles for choosing and depicting proper ('noble') subject matter in accordance with what he believed to be the various modes of ancient music – e.g. Dorian (for 'grave and severe' subjects, such as wars). He plotted his compositions by using shadow boxes filled with small wax figures. His rational, stoic art was to inspire the future 'Poussinistes' of the French Academy, who believed line to be the essential basis of art (as opposed to colour), and would also influence such artists of the eighteenth and nineteenth centuries as Jacques-Louis David, John Flaxman, and J.A.D. Ingres.

[JH]

Poynings, Sir Edward (1459–1521) English official. Appointed lord deputy of Ireland (1494–6) by HENRY VII, he is famous in history as the author of 'Poyning's Law', a set of resolutions of the Irish Parliament (December 1494) which subjected all Irish affairs and legislation to the jurisdiction of the Parliament of England, and re-

mained in force until 1782. After his return to England he served the government in various diplomatic and military missions, mainly in the Netherlands.

Prynne, William (1600–69) English radical controversialist. Educated at Oxford and Lincoln's Inn, he very early became a Puritan, publishing his first tract in 1627. In 1630 he published *Histriomastix*, a work of over a thousand pages attacking the theatre, which was seen as slanderous, and earned him imprisonment in the Tower, expulsion from Lincoln's Inn, and the pillory (with loss of both his ears). He continued to write from his cell, and was in 1637 sentenced to a similar punishment, including branding on his cheeks; he was also removed first to Wales then to Jersey. He was released by the Long Parliament (1640) and played a leading part in the prosecution of archbishop LAUD. Over the next few years he published a flood of energetic pamphlets against all opinions other than his own, and especially against the army-dominated Commonwealth government, which imprisoned him (1650–3). Unsurprisingly, he supported the Restoration of CHARLES II, sat in Parliament (where he continued to disagree with government policy), and after 1660 was appointed keeper of the records in the Tower of London. No doubt because he did not bide anyone else's opinions, he never married.

Pufendorf, Samuel (1632–94) German legal authority. Son of a Lutheran pastor, he was born in Chemnitz, and educated at the university of Leipzig (1650–6), where he abandoned theology in favour of studying law and history; he then went to study in Jena. He was accepted as tutor to the family of a Swedish nobleman who inopportunely visited Copenhagen in 1658 in the middle of the Swedish–Danish war; Pufendorf was captured by the Danes, and cooled his heels for eight months in prison reading HOBBES and GROTIUS. He then went to The Hague, and began to publish works on legal theory which came to the attention of the elector Palatine, who granted him a chair at Heidelberg (1661). It was there that he wrote his fundamental work on the constitution of the Holy Roman Empire. In 1668 he was appointed to the chair of natural law at the new university of Lund, Sweden, where he spent the next twenty years and was created baron. In 1688 he was invited to Brandenburg as official historian by the elector, and died in Berlin. His best known work, published in 1672, was the *De jure naturae et gentium* (The Laws of Nature and Peoples), in which he developed his theories on the nature of natural law. His interests were wide: he wrote a history of Sweden and a biography of the Great Elector; he also made important contributions to the theory of religious toleration, arguing (in his *De habitu religionis* of 1687) that 'compulsion can fill the church with none but hypocrites'.

Purcell, Henry (*c*.1659–95) English composer, keyboard player and singer. He was one of the greatest English composers. During his brief yet remarkably prolific career he held the posts of organist at Westminster Abbey and the Chapel Royal (where he started as a chorister), of composer to the king's violins (i.e. string orchestra), harpsichordist of the king's private music, and composer for the two principal theatres in London. His multiple duties occasioned the composing of numerous sacred choral works (particularly anthems), odes and welcome songs, solo songs, and keyboard and ensemble music. Concurrently, he provided incidental music for over forty plays by leading contemporary dramatists (e.g. CONGREVE, DRYDEN, D'Urfey, Southerne and Shadwell), as well as for adaptations of plays by SHAKESPEARE and MOLIÈRE. In the last six years of his life he composed five semi-operas (*Dioclesian, King Arthur, The Fairy Queen, The Indian Queen* and *The Tempest*) and the opera masterpiece, *Dido and Aeneas*. Although his style reveals unmistakable footprints of French and Italian music, it is equally rooted in the English tradition. He is distinguished for his extraordinary melodic and harmonic inventiveness. In his treatment of the English language, he had 'a peculiar Genius to express the energy of English Words, whereby he mov'd the Passions of all his Auditors' (Henry Playford's introduction to Purcell's *Orpheus Britannicus*, 1698). His frequent employment of the ground bass, in addition, is noted for its highly imaginative compositional mastery, as in the moving 'When I am laid in earth' from *Dido and Aeneas*. His viol fantasias and trio sonatas exhibit intricate, audacious contrapuntal skill coupled with expressive power unequalled by his English predecessors.

[JE]

Pym, John (1583–1643) English Parliamentary leader. Educated at Oxford and then a student of law in London, he entered Parliament in 1614 as a client of the Russell family, the earls of BEDFORD. In 1626 he was one of those who moved to impeach the duke of BUCKINGHAM, and supported the 1628 Petition of Right. During the eleven year personal rule of CHARLES I (1629–40) he took part in the colonising activities of the Providence Island Company. In the Long Parliament (November 1640) he led the moves to impeach STRAFFORD and LAUD, and under his moderate but firm control the various groups in Parliament combined to destroy (1641) the constitutional machinery of the Stuart government. He was one of the members of the Commons whom the king tried to arrest personally in January 1642. He directed the decisions of Parliament during the early months of the ensuing civil war, and managed the moves to make an alliance with the Scots (1643) based on acceptance of the Presbyterian church system.

Q

Quesnay, François (1694–1774) Famous as an economic theorist, his profession was in reality medicine: he began practice as a doctor in Mantes and then went to Paris in 1727, where he became secretary of the Academy of Surgeons and eventually in 1752 medical consultant to the king. A friend of the famous and powerful, he exposed his ideas on the economy first with his contributions to the *Encyclopédie*, then with the publication of his *Tableau économique* (1758) and his *Maximes générales du gouvernement économique* (Maxims of Economic Policy) (1760), which became the classic statement of the school of political economists known as the Physiocrats.

Quesnel, Pasquier (1634–1719) French theologian. He joined the order of the Oratory in 1657, was ordained two years later, and made himself well known for his studies on the Church fathers. He associated himself with the clergy of the Jansenist convent of Port-Royal, and in the 1660s signed the Formulary by which the Jansenists accepted a papal condemnation of statements contained in the *Augustinus* of JANSEN. In 1684, however, he was expelled from the Oratory for his persistent pro-Jansenist views, and left France for Brussels, where he had the company of another Jansenist exile, Antoine ARNAULD. In 1703 he was arrested and his papers seized, but he escaped to Amsterdam, where he published his *Moral Reflexions on the New Testament* (1703). A total of 101 propositions from the work were condemned as heretical by pope CLEMENT XI in the bull *Unigenitus* (1713), provoking a major conflict among the French clergy and the threat of a schism on the part of those defending the 'Gallican' rights of the French church.

Quevedo y Villegas, Francisco de (1580–1645) Spanish man of letters, Quevedo is one of the most brilliant, complex and contradictory writers in the Spanish language during the Golden Age. Born in Madrid, his father was secretary to the empress Maria of Austria, sister of PHILIP II. He studied at the universities of Alcalá de Henares and Madrid, where he led a stormy youth, ultimately abandoning his theological studies. He entered court life in Valladolid and Madrid and remained in its circles as a satirical wit, quarrelsome, tendentious, handling a barbed prose style bristling with conceits. Witness to this are his savage and often surrealist picaresque novel *El Buscón* (*The Swindler*) (1626), and his *Sueños* (*Dreams*) (1627–9), satirical fantasies showing men as they would wish to appear and as they really are – full of hypocrisy and deceit. He continued his tempestuous political life as secretary to the viceroy of Naples, was imprisoned when the viceroy fell from power, raised up by OLIVARES, then dashed down again by the same. This see-saw life was followed by a period of solitary confinement in the city of León. Broken in health he was released to spend the last few years of his life with his pen. Quevedo was one of the best educated writers of his day. He knew French, Greek, Latin and Hebrew. As a poet his versatility was unmatched. He could jump from a scabrous sonnet to a metaphysical conceit, from an amorous lyric of the highest quality to deeply religious composition. If there was a dominant question, it was whether love, in all its senses, was permanent, faced with death; a Petrarchan commonplace, perhaps, but expressed by him with astonishingly graphic power and remarkable modernity of tone.

[BT]

R

Rabelais, François (*c*.1494–1553) French humanist, satirist and doctor of medicine. Born in Chinon, son of a lawyer, he became first a Franciscan friar, then a Benedictine monk, and finally joined the secular clergy. He attended various universities and took his degree in medicine at Montpellier (1530–1), eventually gaining a post in Lyons at the Hôtel-Dieu. He visited Rome three times in the 1530s and 1540s, as doctor to cardinal Jean DU BELLAY, one of his powerful patrons. At the same time he loosened his previous contacts with the doctrines of CALVIN and of Etienne DOLET, obtaining absolution from pope PAUL III for his backsliding. Near the end of his life he was appointed to two livings, but he did not take up his duties, thus leaving him the freedom to write. His first books, *Gargantua* and *Pantagruel*, were published in Lyon. In 1535 he revised the former as Book I of his complete works, under a pseudonym. In the third book (1546) his proper name appeared for the first time. The whole sequence of five books was completed in 1552. The two giants, folkloric in origin, Gargantua and Pantagruel, father and son, wander through fantastic territories. The narrative has a loose weave, affording Rabelais the opportunity of embroidering a whole series of episodes and range of topics. They contain caricatures of contemporary figures and types, local gentry, doctors, philosophers etc. Above all what attracts is the irrepressible invention, the verbal ingenuity with which he endows his personalities – the strings of synonyms, the puns, the elaborate wordplay and the whole range of linguistic performance; this is what posterity remembers. His purpose, beneath this rumbustious manner, was not only to entertain, but to enlighten. He was an acerbic critic of pretentiousness and obscurantism in scholarship, and a determined reformer in matters of education.

[BT]

Racine, Jean (1639–99) French dramatist. He was born at La Ferté-Milon to a middle-class family. Orphaned early on, he was sent to Port-Royal to study with the Jansenists, where he acquired a passion for Greek literature. He then, surprisingly, entered the world of high society in Paris, making the acquaintance of BOILEAU, MOLIÈRE, LA FONTAINE and of the various popular cabarets of the time. To the despair of Port-Royal, he decided to write for the theatre. His first success was the tragedy *Andromaque* (1667), which, like CORNEILLE's *Cid*, provoked a long-running altercation amongst the critics. There followed from his pen a string of equally successful tragedies on classical subjects, of which the best known are *Britannicus* (1669), *Mithridate* (1673) and *Phèdre* (1677). Tired of controversy and easily wounded by criticism, RACINE renounced the theatre in 1677 and was reconciled with the Jansenists, thanks to the intervention of Boileau, official historian of the realm. The only dramatic works he wrote after that were for the young schoolgirls of Saint-Cyr, at the request of Madame de MAINTENON – *Esther* (1689) and *Athalie* (1691). Indeed, his dramatic career, covering over just ten years, seems an unusual interval in his life as a disciple of the Jansenists of Port-Royal. His drama can be contrasted sharply with that of Corneille. Where will and duty prevail in the latter, human passion boils over and destroys Racine's protagonists who, despite their antique dress, belong in the hearts of contemporary society. He left no independent work on dramatic art, except comments in the prefaces to his plays, where he criticised the (to him) implausibility and declamatory speech of Corneille's theatre.

[BT]

Rákóczi, count Francis (Ferenc II) (1676–1735) From an illustrious family that had governed the Hungarian people as princes of Transylvania since the sixteenth century, he conspired to make his nation independent of the Austrian Habsburgs, and in 1703 led an insurrection that liberated the eastern half of the country. The Hungarian diet confirmed him as prince of Transylvania (1704) and then as regent (1705); he sought to ally with France but failed to impede a settlement with the Habsburgs by other nobles (1711). After the peace of Utrecht (1713), which confirmed Habsburg rule, he went into exile, living mainly in France (1713–17) and Turkey. Long considered Hungary's chief national hero, a march – the Rákóczi march – was composed in his honour in 1809.

Raleigh, Sir Walter (*c*.1552–1618) English scholar and adventurer. Born of Devon gentry and educated at Oxford, but too restless to take any degree, he went to France to fight for the Huguenots (1569–

75) in the civil wars, then in 1578 went to sea with his half-brother Humphrey GILBERT, and in 1580–1 went to Ireland to help put down a rising. Presented at the court of ELIZABETH I through the protection of the earl of LEICESTER, his good looks quickly impressed the queen, who showered him with favours. Knighted in 1584, made lord lieutenant of Cornwall in 1585 and captain of the queen's guard in 1587, he was given vast estates in Ireland and England, and entered Parliament. He also chartered an expedition (1584) to Florida and other new lands, which on his return were named Virginia by the queen herself; attempts over the next few years to settle colonies here ended in failure. The voyages did result in the introduction into England of the new plants, potatoes and tobacco. In 1592 he fell into disfavour with Elizabeth because of his love affair with one of her ladies-in-waiting, and was sent to the Tower for three months. In 1595 he headed an expedition to search for 'Eldorado' in the area of the river Orinoco, where some gold was found; and in 1596 took part in the attack on Cadiz. When JAMES I came to the throne, Raleigh's enemies combined to discredit him; he was tried for treason and sent to the Tower (1603), where he began writing his famous *History of the World* (published 1614). In 1616 he was released by the government on condition he headed an expedition to seek new wealth in the Orinoco; its failure (1617) and the demand of the Spanish ambassador GONDOMAR that he be punished for his attacks on American territory, sealed his fate, and he was condemned to death. A universal man, gifted in all fields of intellectual and physical achievement, he was one of the luminaries of his time.

Rambouillet, Catherine de Vivonne, marquise de (1588–1665) Daughter of the French ambassador in Rome, where she was born, she married when young the marquis de Rambouillet and returned with him to France. In Paris she rebuilt a residence in the rue St Thomas du Louvre, where from then on she held a series of intellectual salons. This Hôtel de Rambouillet became, from 1620 to around 1660, one of the most lively intellectual and social centres of Paris, and was frequented by the great cultural figures of the time, including MALHERBE and Conrart. The main star of the Hôtel was the poet Vincent Voiture, who composed light verse for the entertainment of the nobles and revived French verse forms. The main aim of the Hôtel was to communicate culture and taste to an élite that still lacked it. One of the consequences of the revived interest in culture was the founding by Conrart of the French Academy (1634).

Rameau, Jean-Philippe (1683–1764) French composer and theorist. He was the leading musical figure in eighteenth-century France. After holding several posts as an organist, he entered the service of the prominent Parisian patron, Le Riche de la Pouplinière (1731–53). His best known works are the operas *Hyppolyte et Aricie* (1733), *Castor et Pollux* (1737), *Dardanus* (1739) and *Zoroastre* (1749), and the opera-ballets *Les Indes galantes* (1735) and *Les fêtes d'Hébé* (1739). Louis XV awarded him an annual pension and an honorary title of *compositeur du cabinet du Roy*. Although he essentially follows the dramatic approach of LULLY's stage works, he exhibits a much broader emotional range, flexible handling of traditional French forms, richer orchestration and greater harmonic inventiveness. His lasting influence however, lies in his theoretical treatises, *Traité de l'harmonie* (1722) and the *Nouveau système de musique* (1726). These exemplify his rigorous, scientific approach to the study of music theory and the articulation of the concept of tonal harmony.

[JE]

Ramus, Peter (Pierre de la Ramée) (1515–72) French humanist, logician, and educator. Educated in his hometown of Cuts and at the Collège de Navarre in Paris, where he received his Master of Arts in 1536, he had a long career teaching and criticising university education. His pedagogical ideas are similar to MONTAIGNE in their emphasis on making education applicable to life's decision-making demands. He taught logic and mathematics, and criticised Aristotle, with numerous Latin writings on logic, dialectics and against Aristotle. In 1544, his work in reforming logic was condemned and suppressed in Paris. In 1547 the ban was lifted, and in 1551 he received a royal appointment to the Collège de France as its first professor of mathematics through the influence of the Cardinal of Lorraine. In 1561 he converted to Protestantism and lost his academic chair, which he regained after the Peace of Amboise (1563). In 1568 he travelled to Germany where his ideas on logic were well received. Back in Paris after 1570, he was assassinated in 1572 in the midst of the St Bartholomew Day massacres.

[JM]

Raphael (Raffaello Santi, Sanzio) (1483–1521) Italian painter and architect. His development as an artist – an amalgam of impressions from ancient sculpture to the heroic style of his older contemporaries – seemed to embody the principle that art can be taught; consequently he became – for better or worse – the poster boy for art academies of the future. Born in Urbino the son of Giovanni Santi, a painter, poet and historian employed at the court of Guidobaldo Montefeltro, he was apprenticed to Pietro Perugino, in Perugia. Settling in Florence (1504) he sketched works of LEONARDO DA VINCI and MICHELANGELO. Late in 1508 he was summoned to Rome by JULIUS II on the recommendation of his architect, BRAMANTE (a distant relative), who named Raphael as his successor as architect of new St Peter's. He frescoed the Stanza della Segnatura (1509–12) with murals, including the *Disputà*; the *School of Athens*, and the *Parnassus*, while in the adjoining *Stanza d'Eliodoro*, he painted scenes from the Bible and from medieval chronicles (1511–14). In addition to Popes Julius II and his successor LEO X, during whose pontificate most of the late Madonna paintings were done, Raphael's other Roman clients included the papal banker, Agostino Chigi, whose mausoleum in Santa Maria del Popolo he designed (*c*.1513), and for whom he also painted the *Galatea* (Villa Farnesina) built by his patron to honour his favourite mistress. Cardinal Giulio de' Medici commissioned the *Transfiguration* (which, however, was hung above the artist's own tomb in the Pantheon when he died). During his last years he also produced his most memorable portraits, including those of Baldassare CASTIGLIONE; the mysterious *Dona Velata*; and *Leo X with Cardinals Giulio de' Medici and Luigi de' Rossi*. His close association with the Vatican lent a somewhat unrealistic odour of sanctity to the artist as well: when he obligingly died on Good Friday in 1520 it was widely rumoured that he had been in line for a cardinal's hat (others said a cardinal's niece), and various of his altarpieces were declared to have miraculous powers.

[JH]

Ravaillac, François (1578–1610) French regicide. Born in Angoulême of an impoverished family, he went to Paris to study law then returned to work in his home town as a clerk, earning extra money by teaching children. He went back to Paris and entered a religious order of the Benedictines, but left after a few weeks. He then asked to be admitted into the Jesuits, but was refused. He began to suffer religious hallucinations, together with the obsession that he must kill the king, HENRY IV. After several attempts to see the king in 1609, in May 1610 he caught up to the king's carriage near the

Louvre and stabbed him. He was arrested, interrogated and tortured, and eleven days later brutally done to death in the place de Grève. A brilliant study by Roland Mousnier, *L'Assassinat d'Henri IV* (1964), analyses the context of Ravaillac's act.

Razin, Stepan (Stenka) (*c*.1630–71) Cossack leader. Son of one of the leading Cossacks of the river Don, he continued the armed struggle to protect the Cossack areas against the Tatars and Turks; in 1662 he became *ataman* (chief) of the Don Cossacks. His people were also concerned to defend themselves against the Russians, against whom he commenced attacks in 1667. In 1670 he became the leader of a large uprising of Cossacks along the Volga, aiming to 'remove the traitor boyars and give freedom to the common people'. He succeeded in capturing the cities of Tsaritsyn and then Astrakhan (June), but his forces were defeated near Simbirsk (October). From a new base in Kagalnik he prepared a new campaign, but Cossack enemies betrayed him and handed him over to the Russians. He was tortured and quartered alive in Moscow, but the people believed that he had survived and would return to free them.

Réaumur, René-Antoine Ferchault de (1683–1757) French scientist. He became a member of the Académie des Sciences in 1708, and two years later was put in charge of a project to assess the natural and industrial resources of France. This led him to pursue a variety of topics with potential practical applications, such as metallurgy, mining, the composition of porcelain and glass manufacture; his attempts to improve techniques for making iron and steel included the construction of the first cupola furnace in 1720. In sharp contrast, he also investigated digestion, especially the role of gastric juice, studied marine animals and devoted much time to entomology; he planned a comprehensive survey of the insect world, and successfully produced the first five volumes between 1734 and 1742. He is best known, however, as the designer of a thermometer with its zero at the freezing-point of water and 80° at boiling-point; this scale was devised in 1730 and widely used for more than a century thereafter, especially in Germany.

[FW]

Rembrandt (Rembrandt Harmenszoon van Rijn) (1606–69) Dutch painter and etcher, one of very few attempting to support himself entirely by his art. Born in Leiden, he moved permanently in 1632 to Amsterdam, becoming a successful portraitist and painter of biblical 'history' pictures, including many scenes from the Old Testament inspired by his contact with the sephardic Jews, including the rabbinical scholar MANASSEH BEN ISRAEL who were his neighbours in the central city. Constantijn Huyghens, secretary to prince FREDERICK HENRY of Orange had previously visited him in Leiden, noting with pride that the young artist saw no need to visit Italy, alleging that the best of Italian painting could be seen on the market in the Dutch Republic. In Amsterdam Rembrandt attended auctions, amassing a large number of prints, drawings and small paintings that he used in lieu of travel as sources of inspiration. His self-portraits in all media would continue throughout his life, becoming more profound and less detailed, as did his narrative paintings. In 1656 Rembrandt was forced to declare a *cessio bonorum*, involving the sale of his house and art collection, after which he moved to a working-class neighbourhood on the opposite side of the city. His most famous works include three group portraits *The Anatomy Lesson of Dr Tulp* (1632), *The Night Watch* (1642) and the *Syndics of the Cloth Guild* (1662; Rijksmuseum), as well as portraits and costume pieces featuring his young wife Saskia (d.1642), their only surviving child Titus, and later his mis-

tress, Hendrickje Stoffels. The most inventive printmaker of his age, his etchings include the famous *100 Guilder Print*; the *Three Crosses*; and the composition erroneously known as *Dr Faustus*. During his last years he received a commission from Don Antonio Ruffo in Sicily for the *Aristotle Contemplating the Bust of Homer* (New York, Metropolitan Museum), as well as the commission for a large painting for the new City Hall, the *Oath of the Batavians* (*Conspiracy of Claudius Civilis*), (1662; Stockholm, now a fragment). The latter painting, at once a celebration of the freeing of the ancient Netherlands from Roman rule, as well as a pointed allusion to the freeing of the northern provinces from Spanish oppression by WILLIAM I, was returned to the artist for reasons unknown, and was trimmed down to its present size, but remains one of his most impressive works.

[JH]

Rémy, Nicolas (*c*.1530–1612) French demonologist. Born near the city of Toul in Lorraine, his father was a high judicial official and his uncle was lieutenant of the *bailliage* of the Vosges, a post to which he succeeded after his education at Toulouse in law. In 1575 he was appointed secretary to the duke de Lorraine at his capital, Nancy. Appointed a judge of the ducal court there in 1576, Rémy began his judicial career, and made himself famous as a persecutor of witches. Granted nobility in 1583, in 1591 he was appointed *procureur-général* of Lorraine, the highest legal office in the province. He held the post until 1606, when he resigned in favour of his son. In 1595 he published in French at Lyon his *Daemonolatreiae*, one of the most influential studies on witchcraft written in that period, and which had particular success in Germany. In his book, based on cases that had come before him, he claimed to offer an analysis of Satanic influences in the Lorraine countryside. He also claimed in the book to have condemned to death in the preceding twenty years (1575–95) about 900 persons for the crime of witchcraft. Though the incidence of prosecution of witches was very high in Lorraine in this period, the figures for capital punishment appear exaggerated, and the judicial records offer evidence for only about one-seventh of the numbers cited by Rémy.

Renaudot, Théophraste (1586–1653) father of French journalism. Born into a Protestant family in Loudun, he was educated at Montpellier, where he graduated as doctor in medicine (1606). After several years travelling, he settled in Loudun and by chance made the acquaintance of RICHELIEU. By 1626 he was in Paris, became a Catholic, and ran a flourishing information agency. In 1631 he founded a newspaper, the *Gazette*, and was employed by the government to produce other information sheets, notably the *Mercure français*. Enjoying Richelieu's favour, he became rich and successful, but after the cardinal's death fell into difficulties. During the Fronde he convinced MAZARIN of the utility of the *Gazette*, which continued in existence despite Renaudot's economic problems.

Renée de France (1510–75) The second daughter of LOUIS XII of France and Anne of Brittany, in 1528 she married Hercule d'ESTE, who succeeded to the dukedom of Ferrara in 1534. A lettered and intellectual lady, she showed her sympathies for the Reformation by welcoming its adherents in Ferrara (CALVIN went there in 1536) and holding discussions between Protestant thinkers. Though enjoying the favour of the pope (PAUL III) she had to contend with the hostility of her husband to her ideas. On her husband's death (1559) she returned to France and lived in Montargis, which became a centre for Protestant propaganda.

Requesens y Zúñiga, Luis de (1528–76) Spanish general. Born in Barcelona into a leading family of Catalan nobility, son of PHILIP II's childhood tutor, Juan de Zúñiga, he grew up with prince Philip and accompanied him on his tour of Germany and the Netherlands (1548–51). When Luis' father died in 1546, CHARLES V granted him Zúñiga's rank of Commander of Castile. He served as ambassador to Rome (from 1563), was one of the generals in charge of suppressing the revolt of the Moriscos of Granada (1568–70), and took part in the battle of Lepanto (1571). He was then appointed viceroy of Milan (1571–3), where one of his main problems was the attitude of the archbishop, Carlo BORROMEO. Now in poor health, he was obliged against his own will to accept the post of governor of the rebellious Netherlands (1573–6) in succession to Don JUAN OF AUSTRIA. He was given a free hand by the king to make the maximum of concessions, saving only the conservation of the Catholic faith, but the Dutch preferred a military solution and refused to compromise on religion. Deeply conscious of his failure, he died of ill-health. His brother Juan de Zúñiga y Requesens (1536–86) also played a prominent role in the service of Philip II, serving as ambassador to Rome (1568–81) and viceroy of Naples (1579–83). In 1583 he was called to Spain by the king to enter the ruling council of three and to act as governor to prince Philip, but died shortly after.

Retz, Jean François Paul de Gondi, cardinal de (1613–79) French ecclesiastic. His family came from Florence to France with CATHERINE DE MÉDICIS in the sixteenth century and rose to eminence in the royal service: his grandfather became a marshal of France and his father a general of the navy. His family designated him for the Church, and he became coadjutor bishop to his uncle the archbishop of Paris (1643). A brilliant but restless spirit, he shone as preacher and as writer, but did not see eye to eye with his fellow-Florentine MAZARIN; when the Fronde broke out in Paris, he assumed leadership of the revolutionary movement in the city. When Mazarin was exiled (1651) he succeeded in obtaining for himself the dignity of cardinal (February 1652); but after the return of Mazarin and the court he was imprisoned first in Vincennes (December 1652) then at Nantes. On his uncle's death (1654) his friends secured his succession to the see of Paris; he escaped from Nantes in August 1654, and for eight years led a wandering life in Spain, Italy, England and the Netherlands. After Mazarin's death (1661) he returned to Paris (1662), agreed not to occupy his see and in return was given other benefices, including the abbey of Saint-Denis. In subsequent years he was employed by LOUIS XIV on diplomatic missions to Rome, where he participated in several conclaves. He also began to write his *Mémoires* (published 1717), an entertaining first-hand account, of doubtful historical value, on the events of the Fronde.

Reuchlin, Johannes (1455–1522) German humanist, jurist, writer, and translator, most famous for his study of Hebrew and the Hebrew bible. Born in Pforzherm, he studied in the south German city of Freiburg im Breisgau from 1470, Basel from 1474, Paris in 1478, Orléans from 1479, and Poitiers from 1480 where he received his doctorate in law. His legal career as a professor and judge gave him the means to pursue humanist studies in Latin and Greek, and he published a Latin dictionary (1478) and a lost Greek *Micropedia*. In the 1480s and 1490s he began to study Jewish literature and Hebrew. He published a Hebrew grammar (1506) and several works on the Kabbala. In a 1510 report to the emperor MAXIMILIAN I on the Jewish question, he expressed a tolerant, yet ambivalent attitude towards the Jews – he pleaded for their Christianisation, but opposed forced baptism and their expulsion. His Jewish scholarship and moderation led to attacks from the fanatical Johannes Pfefferkorn, a Jewish

convert, and condemnation from the Dominicans of Cologne under their leader Jakob Hochstraten. Defended by Ulrich von HUTTEN and other humanists in the *Letters of Obscure Men*, he was associated with the reform movement in Germany, although he himself remained within the Old Church.

[JM]

Reynolds, Sir Joshua (1723–92) English painter and academician. Reynolds, eighteenth-century England's most fashionable portrait painter, was born in Devonshire, the son of a clergyman/schoolmaster. Utilising the experiences of his own travels on the continent, especially his sketches after MICHELANGELO, RAPHAEL and Giulio Romano, together with the more homegrown influence of Godfrey Kneller, he created an imposing and erudite new style of painting, replete with classical references, that he called 'the Grand Manner'. This new style, which glorified – and sometimes mythologised – the British ruling class, was to become inextricably associated with the Royal Academy of Arts, of which he was a founding member (1768) and president (1768–91). His fifteen annual presidential lectures for the Royal Academy, published as the *Discourses* (1797), contain some of the century's most valuable writing on the arts in any language, and are of particular interest for their revelations about painting practices on the Continent, gained during his 1771 trip to Paris, when he was horrified to observe François Boucher painting without a model; and his 1781 trip to the Dutch Republic, where he greatly admired VERMEER's *Milkmaid* (which he referred to as 'Hollandia'), remarking that this artist rendered nature 'just as it appears in the camera obscura'. In 1775 he was elected to the Florentine Academy, and in 1784 he was made principal painter to George III, who, however, was not unduly fond of him. His circle of friends included most of London's leading intellectuals, from Dr

JOHNSON, for whom he published three essays on art criticism in *The Idler* (1759), to Burke and Goldsmith. Portrait clients included Horace Walpole, Thomas Sterne, and David GARRICK. His allegorical portraits of women could be a bit much (e.g. *Lady Sarah Bunbury Sacrificing to the Graces; Miss Morris as Hope nursing Love; Kitty Fisher as Cleopatra*, etc.). Reynolds never married; his sister, and later his niece kept house for him. His private collection of paintings, drawings and sculpture was the largest in eighteenth-century England. He suffered strokes in 1771 and 1783, but was able to travel to Belgium in 1785, where he obtained a new respect for the work of RUBENS that infuses his late works. He continued to exhibit until 1790 and was given a state funeral when he died in 1792.

[JH]

Richard III (1452–85) last Yorkist king of England 1483–85. Youngest son of Richard duke of York, when his brother became king as EDWARD IV (1461) he was created duke of Gloucester and occupied important positions. Edward and Richard were driven from power by the earl of Warwick in 1470, but in 1471 Richard took part with Edward in the victories at Barnet and Tewkesbury over the Lancastrian forces. The then king, Henry VI, was put in the Tower and murdered there, probably at Richard's instigation. Edward died in 1483 (hostile chronicles insinuate that he was murdered by his brother). Gloucester became 'protector' of the realm for Edward's twelve-year-old heir EDWARD V, but faced the opposition of his brother's widow, Elizabeth Woodville, and her family. Gloucester eliminated the Woodville faction brutally, and took into custody the king and his younger brother the duke of York, who were lodged in the Tower. Gloucester then declared the children illegitimate, and had himself crowned king as Richard III (June 1483). Two months later the princes in the Tower perished mysteriously. Contemporaries, and posterity, blamed the king, who has traditionally been presented as a figure of evil, in part thanks to Shakespeare's drama *Richard III* (1592). Historians however have tended to take a more favourable view of Richard as administrator of the realm. There appears moreover to be no evidence that he was a hunchback, as portrayed in Shakespeare. Taking advantage of the growing opposition to the king, the earl of Richmond invaded from France in 1485 and defeated the army of the king at Bosworth. Richard died on the field, and the earl became the first ruler of the Tudor dynasty, HENRY VII.

Richardson, Samuel (1689–1761) English novelist. A carpenter's son, in 1706 he became apprenticed to a stationer and in 1719 set himself up as a printer in London. After several years of printing newspapers, and the *Journal* of the House of Commons, he broke into print himself. In 1739 he was asked to prepare a manual of letter writing and this inspired him to write a novel in the form of letters. *Pamela, or Virtue Rewarded* was hugely successful and he followed it with *Clarissa* (1747–8) and *The History of Sir Charles Grandison*. They are long and didactic and not much read today, but at the time they had an immense influence on the development of the novel in England and on the continent. He became master of the Stationers' Company (1754), and wealthy. Richardson explored the motives and characters of ordinary people in recognisable situations and thus expanded the scope of fiction and laid the foundation of the modern novel.

[GG]

Richelieu, Armand Jean du Plessis, cardinal and duke de (1585–1642) French statesman. From a family of soldiers, he began his career as one but was persuaded to take over the family-controlled see of Luçon, vacated by his elder brother, and was made its bishop (1606). Appointed delegate for Poitou to the Estates General of 1614, he attracted the attention of the regent MARIE DE MÉDICIS and was taken into the administration (1616). He intervened with success to reconcile Marie and her son LOUIS XIII during the conflicts between them (1619–20), was created cardinal thanks to Marie (1622) and in 1624 entered the council of state. From this time he participated in the formation of policy in the areas he outlined at the time in his *Political Testament* (*c*.1624): the reduction of Huguenot influence, the taming of the great nobility, and the strengthening of the crown in foreign affairs. His differences with Marie led to the famous Day of Dupes (1630), when Louis excluded her from his councils (she went into exile) and confirmed Richelieu as chief minister. Subsequent revolts against the change of regime, notably the MONTMORENCY rebellion (1632) in Languedoc, were dealt with severely. Richelieu's ministry, based on a broad network of power alliances between the cardinal, his followers or 'creatures', and provincial aristocrats, stabilised royal authority and began the emergence of a modern France. He is famous above all for his aggressive anti-Spanish foreign policy, pursued at first through foreign generals (such as GUSTAV II ADOLF VASA) willing to accept French money, and then later through a declaration of war against Spain (1635). Author of numerous early writings (1617–19) on religious matters, some of his state documents were published as *Papiers d'état* (8 vols, 1853), and further papers as his *Mémoires* (in 10 vols, 1907). He also left the brief *Political Testament*, intended for the guidance of the king, and put together for him by a secretary but first published only in 1688.

Ridley, Nicholas (*c*.1500–55) English ecclesiastic and martyr. Student then fellow at Cambridge, he was appointed a chaplain of CRANMER, then bishop of Rochester (1547), by which time he had

become a firm supporter of the Reformation. In 1550 he took over the see of London from bishop BONNER, but in 1553 made the mistake of supporting Lady Jane GREY and preaching publicly against the legitimacy of princesses Mary and Elizabeth. He was immediately arrested on the accession of MARY I, and invited in 1554 to debate his Protestant views in the divinity school at Oxford. Refusing to change his views, he was condemned under the new laws against heresy, and in October 1555 he and bishop LATIMER were burnt at the stake beside Balliol college. A memorial to the burning was erected in 1841.

Ridolfi, Roberto (1531–1612) Conspirator. A Florentine businessman who settled in London in the 1550s, he had personal links with government ministers and foreign envoys, and in 1568 discussed with the Spanish ambassador, Guerau de Spes, means of helping the persecuted English Catholics. In 1569 he was examined by Francis WALSINGHAM on suspicion of having acted as agent for the rebels in the rising of the northern earls, but continued to retain the trust of the ministers of ELIZABETH I. In 1570 he was in touch with agents of PHILIP II, MARY STUART and the pope over the possibility of a Catholic rising, and went to Brussels in April 1571 to discuss details with ALBA (who opposed the plans), and then to Spain in June. His letters to English sympathisers were intercepted, and several persons were arrested, including the duke of NORFOLK. Ridolfi did not return to England, and retired to Florence, where he became a senator. It is likely that his role in the alleged 'plot' was as agent provocateur of Walsingham.

Ripperda, Jan Willem, baron then duke of (1680–1737) minister of state in Spain. Born in Groningen, son of a Catholic noble who was governor of the fortress of Namur, he was educated by the Jesuits in Cologne and entered the army. After his father's death he became a Protestant, took part on behalf of the Dutch in the negotiations for the peace of Utrecht (1713), and was sent as ambassador of the United Provinces to Madrid (1715). He made Spain his home, converted to Catholicism and was appointed by ALBERONI as director of the textile factories in Guadalajara. In 1721 he married a Spanish court lady, was promoted to director of the textile industries in the kingdom, and became an adviser to the crown. After the fall of Alberoni (1719) he became influential in matters concerning commerce and diplomacy. He was made duke and grandee of Spain, and in effect chief minister of the government, with responsibility in finances and war. After his disgrace in 1726 because of the failure of diplomatic manœuvres involving an alliance with the Empire, he was imprisoned for fifteen months but escaped (1728). He went to England, then (after a brief stay in Holland when he converted back to Protestantism) in 1731 to Morocco, where he apparently converted to Islam and changed his name to Osman Pasha.

Rizzio (or Riccio), David (c.1533–66) secretary to Mary Stuart. A native of Piedmont, he went to Scotland in 1561 in the household of the ambassador of Savoy, impressed the Scots court by his good singing voice, and entered the royal household, becoming secretary to MARY STUART in 1564 and possibly also her lover. He thereafter became powerful as the queen's adviser, superseding her state secretary MAITLAND OF LETHINGTON, and attracting the hostility of the court nobility and of Mary's husband, DARNLEY. A group of nobles, led by the earl of Morton, burst into the queen's chambers in March 1566, stabbed Rizzio to death then threw his body out into the courtyard.

Rohan, Henri de, duke de (1579–1638) French grandee. From an ancient noble family of Brittany which rose to impor-

tance in the sixteenth century, he became after the end of the civil wars the most prominent supporter of the Huguenot party. In 1603 HENRY IV made him a duke and peer of France, and in 1605 he married the daughter of the chief minister SULLY. Despite this, after the death of Henry IV he took part in all the Huguenot rebellions against central authority (1620–2, 1625–6, 1627–9). After the last of these, at La Rochelle, he accepted the conditions of a pardon, which were that he serve the crown against the Spaniards in Italy. In the 1630s he took part in the Thirty Years War in the French-subsidised armies of BERNARD of Saxe-Weimar, and died in action. His brother Benjamin de Rohan, lord of Soubise, was one of his fellow-rebels, and from 1622 actively entered the service of England, participating in 1628 in the unsuccessful La Rochelle campaign against France.

Ronsard, Pierre de (1524–85) French poet. Born near Vendôme to a well-connected family, he had no difficulty in becoming a page to the duke d'Orléans and MARY OF GUISE amongst others; the latter he followed to Scotland where she married JAMES V. After several similar trips throughout Europe he was struck by deafness and so the page was transformed into poet. He returned to his youthful studies in 1543, concentrating on Greek and Latin and the humanist disciplines for seven years. His eclogues, elegies, hymns and above all his sonnets awoke the enthusiasm of princes like HENRY II, FRANCIS II, CHARLES IX and MARY STUART, daughter of James V; while the major genres, the *Odes* (1550–3), *Les Discours* (1562–3), and the unfinished epic poem *La Franciade* (1572), turned him into the leader of a literary movement dedicated to the renewal of poetic form and language. This movement in turn affected English sonneteers of the late seventeenth century. BOILEAU, however, regretted that his muse spoke Latin and Greek rather than French. Ronsard had, it is true, turned aside from traditional medieval genres. But he created a lyric of marked Petrarchan character and also provided France with a national epic which followed in the path of Virgil.

[BT]

Rubens, Sir Peter Paul (1577–1640) Flemish painter, author and diplomat. His art dominated Catholic Europe during the second quarter of the seventeenth century. The son of an attorney at the court of WILLIAM I, he was born in Siegen and christened a Lutheran, but was converted to Catholicism when his widowed mother returned to her native Antwerp with her children (1587). Trained in Antwerp, he spent eight years (1600–8) in Italy as court painter to Federigo Gonzaga in Mantua, also representing the Duke on diplomatic missions to the Medici court in Florence and to the court of PHILIP III of Spain (1603). In Rome he painted the high altar for the Chiesa Nuova. Returning to Antwerp he married Isabella Brant (1609), acquired the house and the Italianate studio of his own design that now constitute the 'Rubenshuis' museum, and was officially court painter to the archdukes ALBERT and ISABEL. Rubens and his workshop, which for a time included the young Anthony VAN DYCK, provided a dazzling array of devotional paintings in the new post-Tridentine mode stressing points of Catholic doctrine, as well as political allegories promoting divine right monarchy. In the late 1620s he represented the widowed archduchess Isabel at the courts of PHILIP IV and CHARLES I as an emissary of peace. Knighted by both kings, and granted honorary degrees from Oxford and Cambridge, he died a multimillionaire. Rubens was unusual in his ability to handle large commissions, inventing totally new subject matter as needed (e.g. the ceiling and altarpieces for the new Jesuit church in Antwerp, dedicated to IGNATIUS OF LOYOLA, who had not yet been canonised; the extensive cycle of enormous paintings illustrating the life of the tedious MARIE DE MÉDICIS;

or the ceiling for Inigo JONES' Banqueting House at Whitehall, celebrating the apotheosis of JAMES I and the union of England and Scotland). In the 1630s a second marriage (at fifty three) to teenager Helene Fourment and a second family inspired his most magnificent paintings on mythological themes – the great *Festival of Venus* (Vienna) and the life-sized *Three Graces* (Madrid) being the most notable.

[JH]

Rudolf II (1552–1612) emperor 1576–1612. Born in Vienna, eldest son of the emperor MAXIMILIAN II and of María the sister of PHILIP II of Spain, he spent his early years in Munich and in 1563 travelled to Spain with his brother Ernst, spending eight years in the Spanish court. Thanks to the rich artistic collections of Philip, the stay appears to have been decisive in fomenting his interest in exotic, intellectual and scientific matters; he also learnt to speak six languages. He returned to Vienna in 1571, was elected king of Hungary 1572 and king of Bohemia 1575, succeeding his father as emperor in 1576. He never married, though he had various love affairs. In 1583 he moved his court from Vienna to Prague, where he lived the rest of his life. The Bohemian capital experienced a rich cultural life under his rule: Rudolf invited to his court intellectuals and scientists from all over the continent, and built up a notable artistic collection. Among the scholars invited were Tycho BRAHE, John KEPLER and John DEE. The most notorious aspect of his interests was his dedication to the occult, which earned him the reputation of being mad. He seems to have had little interest in politics, and in Bohemia staved off rebellion by issuing the tolerant 'Letter of Majesty' (1609). His brother MATTHIAS replaced him as ruler in Austria and Hungary (1608) then finally in Bohemia (1611).

Rupert, prince, count palatine of the Rhine and duke of Cumberland (1619–82) The third son of FREDERICK V OF WITTELSBACH, elector of the Palatinate and king of Bohemia, and of ELIZABETH STUART, daughter of James I of England, he was born in Prague and grew up with his exiled family in Holland. In 1636 he went to England and was well received. From 1637 he served as a soldier in the Thirty Years War, was taken prisoner and confined at Linz for three years. On the outbreak of the English civil war he went to help his uncle CHARLES I, played a prominent part in the campaigns, was created duke (1644) and made commander of the royal armies but was defeated at Naseby (1645). After the war he left England, entered the service of France and later (1649) was appointed commander of the English royalist fleet, which he used to attack English Parliamentary vessels in a long three-year campaign in the Mediterranean, Azores and West Indies. In 1653–4 he was resident in France, then spent the next six years soldiering in Germany. After the Restoration in 1660 he was based mainly in England, where he served in various naval engagements, becoming commander of the navy in 1673 (after the duke of York was forced to resign because of his Catholic faith) and first lord of the admiralty. Tall, handsome and dashing, a gifted linguist and consummate soldier, he never married but left two daughters.

Russell, Lord William (1639–83) Third son of the 1st duke of BEDFORD, he sat as member for Tavistock from 1660, and from about 1672 identified himself with the Whig interest, opposing the earl of DANBY and leading the moves to exclude the duke of York from the succession; he also closely associated with SHAFTESBURY and the Protestant interest. After the Exclusion crisis, he was accused on flimsy evidence of being party to the alleged 'Rye House plot' (1682) to assassinate the king; he was tried in 1683, condemned and executed. His wife Rachel, a woman of exceptional literary and business talents, managed the family's fortunes with great success until her death at the age of eighty seven.

S

Sacheverell, Henry (*c*.1674–1724) English ecclesiastic. Educated at Oxford, where he became a fellow and obtained his doctorate, he became chaplain in Southwark in 1705. Noted for his High Church views and hostility to the Whigs, which he put forth in notable sermons in Oxford and London, he attracted special attention by a sermon in St Paul's in 1709, subsequently published, in which he declared that the Church of England was in danger from enemies within. The sermon was declared a 'seditious libel' by the House of Commons, which voted his arrest and impeachment. The case stirred passions both in Parliament and in the country. In March 1710 he was suspended from preaching for three years and the offending sermons were ordered burnt. This was seen as a victory for his cause; he was feasted everywhere like royalty, and in the subsequent (November) election the Tories were returned with a majority. He received preferment to a good living, and became rich.

Sadoleto, Jacopo (1477–1547) Italian scholar and cardinal. Born into the upper social stratum in Ferrara, he went to the university there and in *c*.1498 went to Rome, where he studied for twelve years under the supervision of the dean of the sacred college, mixed with other scholars, and took minor orders. In 1513 he (together with Pietro BEMBO) was appointed to the secretariat of the new pope, LEO X; the event determined his career, which thereafter was directed entirely towards Latin scholarship. He was financed by several benefices, and the bishopric in absentia of Carpentras in France. Shortly before the sack of Rome (1527), he fortunately left the Eternal City for Carpentras, which he thenceforward made his base as a dedicated and reforming prelate, while he also thought and wrote. He produced a work on pedagogy, *De pueris instituendis* (1530), and on philosophy. Summoned to Rome by PAUL III to help in preparing the council of Trent, he was named cardinal (1536) and appointed to the council *de emendanda Ecclesia*, where he stood out for his uncompromising reformist views. A faithful adherent of Catholic belief, he was also an outspoken partisan of ERASMUS; at the same time, he prepared the papal decrees against LUTHER. But he was willing to negotiate face to face with humanist Protestant leaders, and told them so in letters; he even wrote to the people of Geneva. His overtures were treated with suspicion on both sides. In Rome again in 1542 he drafted the summons to the council of Trent, and went off on missions to FRANCIS I and to the emperor to try and achieve unity among Christian princes. He returned again to Rome in 1545 to help with the opening of the council, which commenced that year.

Saint-Cyran, Jean Duvergier de Hauranne, abbé de (1581–1643) one of the founders of the Jansenist movement. Born in Bayonne, he studied theology at the university of Louvain, then settled in Paris where he took minor orders and met the Belgian Cornelis JANSEN, a supporter of Augustinian theology and opponent of the Jesuits, with whom he spent a period of reflection (1611–16) at Bayonne. After Jansen's return to Louvain (1617), Duvergier became secretary to the bishop of Poitiers. He was ordained priest in 1618 and appointed to the sinecure of Saint-Cyran in Poitou (1620), from which he took the name by which he is generally known. He emerged into prominence from about 1634, as spiritual adviser to the young abbess of Port-Royal, Angélique ARNAULD, a ready sympathiser of the doctrines that he now developed and which later came to be identified as 'Jansenism'. In 1637 he established at the associated but now abandoned convent of Port-Royal des Champs a community that became known as the 'solitaires' (hermits). Duvergier's political activities, however, attracted the attention of cardinal RICHELIEU; he was arrested in 1638 and imprisoned at Vincennes until the cardinal's death in 1642, but himself died of an apoplexy the year after.

Saint-Évremond, Charles de Saint-Denis, seigneur of (1613–1703) writer and sceptic. His early career was spent as a general in the French army, when he supported the crown during the Fronde (1648–53). In 1661, however, his criticism of MAZARIN's policy in the treaty of the Pyrenees (1659) earned him official disfavour, and he fled to England to avoid arrest. Apart from an interlude in Holland (1666–72), where he met SPINOZA, he spent the rest of his life in London, where CHARLES II befriended him and gave him the sinecure of keeper of the ducks in St James' Park. A man of great learning, he was fêted in England as a literary oracle. He published no books, but his short articles were received with respect and he gained a European reputation. It has been argued that during the 1680s he was virtually the intellectual leader of France. Famous as a philosophical Epicurean, he literally lived his philosophy. One of his epitaphs composed in his honour ran: 'Écrire, et bien manger, fut son double talent, Il nourrit pour la vie un amour violent' (Writing and good food were his two passions, his love of life was extreme). He was buried in Poets Corner in Westminster Abbey.

Saint-Pierre, Charles-Irénée Castel, abbé de (1658–1743) French publicist. A well-known writer, in 1693 he obtained a clerical post in the household of the duchess d'Orléans, who presented him to the post of abbé of Tiron. He entered the French Academy in 1695, but was expelled from it subsequently for criticising the aggressive foreign policy of LOUIS XIV. From 1712 to 1714 he acted as secretary to Melchior de POLIGNAC, French plenipotentiary at the congress of Utrecht. His writings are full of schemes for reforms in all branches of state administration, including government and taxation. He is most remembered for his work, *Le Projet de paix perpétuelle* (Project for Perpetual Peace) (1712), which was translated into English as early as 1714, and can be seen as a reaction against the wars of Louis XIV. 'I asked myself whether war was really an evil beyond all cure', he wrote, and proposed a union of European countries, with common institutions including a tribunal to which all disputes would be referred before hostilities could break out.

Saint-Simon, Louis de Rouvroy, duke de (1675–1755) French diplomat. Son of Claude de Rouvroy, who was created duke de Saint-Simon in 1635, he was brought up among the court élite at Versailles and became a lifelong devotee of the privileges of his class. In the 1690s he served in the French army in the Netherlands, and in 1699 married the daughter of marshal de Lorges. In the background of court politics during the last years of LOUIS XIV, he formed with members of the élite (FÉNE-LON, the duke de Chevreuse) a small group that discussed reforming the government and substituting for absolutism a system based on the traditional constitution and the rights of the nobility. When his friend the regent ORLÉANS came to power, he was appointed (1715) to the regency council, and in 1721 became ambassador to Spain. After the regent's death (1723) he lost influence, and retired to his estates at La Ferté-Vidame to write his celebrated *Mémoires*. Based on his own direct observations and on original government documentation, the *Mémoires* are a fundamental source for the history of the period; the definitive edition, in 43 volumes, is that of A. de Boislisle (1879–1928).

Santa Cruz, Alvaro de Bazán, marquis of (1526–88) Spanish naval commander. Born in Granada, the son of a Spanish naval commander, he entered the navy at eighteen and fought against the French off Galicia, and against the Turks and Muslims in the Mediterranean. His title of Santa Cruz derived from a property settled on him by his parents at his first marriage in 1549, which was later erected into a marquisate. He distinguished himself in several Mediterranean naval campaigns, and in the battle of Lepanto against the Turks (1571) as commander of the reserve fleet he displayed excellent seamanship and played a key role in the victory. He was appointed in 1576 captain-general of the galleys of Spain, and in 1580 led the naval force that backed up the occupation of Portugal by the duke of ALBA. After a successful engagement against the French off the Azores he was appointed Commander of León in the order of Santiago. He led the naval expedition that defeated the French intervention in 1583 in the island of Terceira in the Azores, thereby assuring PHILIP II's full control of Portuguese territory. When he returned the grateful king named him grandee of Spain

and captain-general of the Ocean Sea. Santa Cruz now suggested to the king that he use the navy to undertake an invasion of England. Philip eventually adopted the proposal, which was also being pressed on him by the pope, and appointed him commander of the projected Armada, which was ultimately smaller than the immense force initially suggested by Santa Cruz. He died inopportunely in Lisbon shortly before the Armada was due to put to sea, and his place was taken by the less fortunate duke of MEDINA SIDONIA.

Sarpi, Paolo (1552–1623) Venetian theologian and polemical opponent of papal absolutism. Reared in relative poverty in Venice, he became a Servite friar at fourteen and court theologian to the duke of Mantua at twenty. Provincial of his order at twenty seven, he knew the leading figures of Counter-Reformation Italy (from Robert BELLARMINE to GALILEI) and frequented learned patrician circles at home in Venice. He himself engaged in mathematical and scientific study, with special interest in anatomy, optics and magnetism. As consultant in theology and canon law to the Republic of Venice, he wrote against the papal interdict of 1606–7 and supported Venetian claims to restrict church building in the island-city and to try civil crimes of clerical defendants in civil courts. He specialised in historical/legal precedents and advised Venice to develop alliances with France and the Protestant states as a counterweight against papal and Spanish power in Italy. He wrote his major work, *The History of the Council of Trent*, between 1610 and 1618, and it was published in London in English translation in 1619 under the pseudonym of Pietro Soave Polano. It castigated the papacy for arrogating Church authority to itself (away from the clergy at large) and for manipulating Trent for its own advantage. He remained a loyal Catholic opposed to papal and curial power, although his private *Pensieri* reveal him to have been an extreme religious radical, sympathetic to the Protestants in their opposition to papal pretensions and sceptical of much traditional Christian doctrine.

[JM]

Savonarola, Girolamo (1452–98) Dominican friar and preacher who inspired the Florentine state, 1494–98. Born in Ferrara, he followed his father and grandfather in medical studies, but after taking an arts degree, he entered the Dominican order at Bologna in 1475. From 1482–85 he taught and preached at San Marco in Florence without great success until a sudden revelation led him to begin delivering prophetic sermons on the need for Church reform and how a scourge would come and renew the Church. Transferred from Florence, he returned to San Marco in 1490 through the influence of Lorenzo de' MEDICI. He preached more boldly about political events, more austerely against rampant materialism, and more dangerously in opposition to the Medici – although he did visit Lorenzo on his deathbed. With the French invasions and expulsion of the Medici in 1494, he supported a broadly based republican regime intent on establishing a theocratic state in fulfilment of a divine destiny for Florence. He continued to preach against ALEXANDER VI's immorality and led puritanical campaigns against gambling, sumptuous dress and pagan art in public bonfires of vanities. By 1498 his support in the Florentine government waned; and, backed by his enemies in the Church and among the great powers, his Florentine opponents seized him amid false charges of heresy, and had him hanged and burned. His preaching and 'martyrdom' had profound influence on the Florentine political generation that followed him.

[JM]

Saxe, Maurice count de, known as marshal de (1696–1750) Illegitimate son of AUGUSTUS II of Saxony and of the countess Aurora von KÖNIGSMARK, he spent his active life in the army, first under prince EUGÈNE OF SAVOY-CARIGNAN in the Netherlands against the French, then under PETER THE GREAT against the Swedes (participating in the capture of Stralsund 1712). In 1720 he entered French service, distinguishing himself in various campaigns throughout Europe; in the war of the Austrian Succession he directed the capture of Prague (1742). Created marshal of France in 1743, in 1745 he won the notable victory of Fontenoy over the English and was rewarded with the territory of Chambord. A man of enormous prowess both in war and in love, he had several notable mistresses, and found time for casual writing (*Mes rêveries* – My Dreams) as well as for writing his *Mémoires*.

Scaliger, Joseph Justus (1540–1609) Italian Protestant scholar most famous for his philological studies and research in comparative chronology. Son of Julius Caesar Scaliger, a natural philosopher, doctor and humanist who was originally named Bordone and claimed to be the last survivor of the della Scala of Verona, he studied for three years at the Collège de Guyenne before becoming his father's secretary until his death in 1558. He was self-educated without the help of a tutor in numerous languages, including Greek, Hebrew and Aramaic. In the 1560s he converted to Calvinism, frequented learned Protestant circles in Paris, and travelled with a nobleman in Italy. He studied Roman law, taught briefly in Geneva (1572–4), and his commentaries on Latin texts made his reputation as a textual critic. He is most famous for his work in establishing a unified chronology in his *Opus novum de emendatione temporum* (1583). He took a research position at the university of Leiden in 1593 where his method influenced the younger generation of scholars, especially Hugo GROTIUS and Daniël HEINSIUS, and he worked on his most ambitious project, *Thesaurus* *temporum*. He reconstructed Eusebius' history, contributed to the philological understanding of the New Testament, and studied the context of the early Christian era with his interest in Hellenised Jews. By the time of his death, he found himself attacked from all sides, Catholics and Protestants alike, and even had his esteemed family origins debunked.

[JM]

Scarlatti, (Gaspare) Alessandro (1660–1725) Italian composer. He was the founder of the Neapolitan school of opera and a prolific composer of operas, cantatas and sacred works. Supported by prestigious patrons in Rome and Naples, his works enjoyed tremendous popularity during his life time. He is noted for his extraordinary melodic inventiveness and novel harmonic progressions. His three-movement operatic overture (*sinfonia*) served eventually as one of the prototypes of the early classical symphony.

[JE]

Scarlatti, (Giuseppe) Domenico (1685–1757) Italian composer and keyboard virtuoso, the sixth child of Alessandro Scarlatti. After spending his initial career in Naples and Rome, he moved to Lisbon in 1719, as chapelmaster at the Patriarchal Seminary and a harpsichord teacher to infanta Maria Barbara. Following her marriage to the Spanish crown prince (later FERDINAND VI), he moved with her to the Spanish court (1728) and remained there until his death. His fame rests on some five hundred sonatas for the harpsichord, which exhibit striking originality, dazzling keyboard virtuosity, and an immense variety of styles, including Spanish popular music and guitar techniques.

[JE]

Schomberg, Friedrich Hermann (Frédéric Armand), duke of (1615–90) soldier and Protestant. Born in the Palatinate of an English mother and a German father in the family castle of Schönberg, he lived for a while in France (1625–30), then studied at Leiden (1631–2) and subsequently served as a soldier during the Thirty Years War against the Catholics. After the peace, he served with the Dutch, then in 1650 entered the service of France, when he made notable contributions to the victory of the Dunes (1658) against the Spaniards and CONDÉ. From 1660 he served the Portuguese as military commander, achieving the victory of Villaviciosa (1665), which finally secured the independence of their country from the Spaniards. From 1664 he settled in France, but continued his military career. In 1674 he was created duke, and in 1675 marshal of France, the last Protestant in old regime France to gain that honour. At the Revocation of the Edict of Nantes (1685) he chose exile rather than conversion to Catholicism, and returned to service first with Brandenburg then with the Dutch, accompanying WILLIAM III of Orange in the invasion of England in 1688. He died in action fighting against the forces of JAMES II at the battle of the Boyne. Created duke by William III in 1689, he is buried in Dublin.

Schomberg, Henri de, count de Nanteuil (1575–1632) French soldier. Son of Gaspard de Schomberg, from Saxony, who served HENRY IV, he in his turn occupied important posts under LOUIS XIII, as ambassador in London, and superintendant of finances and head of the artillery. Member of the royal council in 1621, he was also a distinguished soldier who helped to suppress the Huguenot rebellions of the 1620s, was created marshal in 1625 and in 1627 led the forces that drove back the English at the Ile de Ré. He helped to lead the royal forces against the MONTMORENCY rebellion of 1632, and supplanted the duke as governor of Languedoc. He was succeeded as governor by his son Charles (1601–56), who also became marshal and secured Roussillon for the crown in the 1640s.

Schütz, Heinrich (1585–1672) German composer and the foremost musical figure in seventeenth-century Germany. His ingenuity rests on a highly individual synthesis of the sixteenth-century German polyphonic tradition and the new stylistic features of Italian music. In addition to his solid musical education at the court of Kassel (1599–1609), his most significant years were under the guidance of Giovanni GABRIELI in Venice (1609–12). He subsequently revisited Venice (1628) to master the latest style of MONTEVERDI and his Italian contemporaries. From 1615 until his death he served at the court of Dresden, with some brief periods away, notably at the Danish royal court. His fame is owed to his twelve collections of sacred choral works, which exhibit immense stylistic variety and a remarkable musical treatment of the German language. The majority of their texts are adapted from the Old and New Testaments, and their musical settings range from simple, small-scale choral works to Venetian-like motets of multiple choruses, soloists and instruments. Among his dramatic vocal works, the *Resurrection History*, the *Christmas Oratorio* and *The Seven Last Words* (*c.*1645) served as important models for J.S. Bach.

[JE]

Schwenckfeld, Kaspar von (1489–1561) spiritual leader. Born into a noble family at Ossig in Lower Silesia, he studied in Cologne and Frankfurt an der Oder before entering service with the local lords. Already sympathetic to LUTHER, in 1521 he won over his lord, duke Frederick II of Liegnitz, to the new doctrines; he thus began to earn the reputation of being the soul of the Reformation in Silesia. But he was beginning to develop Lutheranism in the direction of a more mystical and inner-orientated religion, and disagreed with the reliance of Lutherans on the state. Banished from Silesia in 1529 by the emperor, he went to Strasbourg, where he took part (1535) in a debate

with BUCER, and then to Württemberg. A spiritual figure totally lacking in the violence or dogmatism of his time, he asserted the total separation of Church from state, and held that the universal Church was invisible, 'consisting of all saintly and faithful persons from the beginning of the world to the end'. He died, quietly, at Ulm. His doctrine of an inner spirituality had medieval predecessors, and was to return also in the case of another Silesian, BOEHME. After his death his many friends and followers organised themselves into the movement known as the Schwenckfeldians, especially in Swabia and Silesia. They were inevitably persecuted. In 1734 a large group emigrated to Pennsylvania, where they still flourish.

Scot, Reginald (*c.*1538–99) English authority on witchcraft. A native of Kent, where he lived all his life, in 1588 he entered Parliament and was probably a justice of the peace. He is noted for two books. One is his *Perfect Platform of a Hop Garden* (1574), the first practical and illustrated study on growing hops. The other is *The Discoverie of Witchcraft* (1584), the first profound analysis of this social phenomenon; it was based on extensive reading of classic and contemporary authors in Latin and English, including the leading European treatises on the subject, and on his own observations and experience. The work was influential in England: SHAKESPEARE used it as a source, and JAMES I ordered copies of it to be burnt. A Dutch edition appeared in Leiden in 1609.

Scudéry, Madeleine de (1607–1701) French writer. Younger sister of the dramatist Georges de Scudéry, she joined her brother in Paris and made her mark in the literary salons and as a writer. Her first novel, *Ibrahim ou l'illustre bassa* (1642) was published in four volumes. Her later novels *Artamène* (1649–53) and *Clélie* (1654–60) were even longer. She is most remembered for the gatherings which she held at her salon on Saturdays, known as the '*samedis de Sappho*' (a name used for her by friends, and under which she figured in her novel *Artamène*). The meetings began in 1653 and went on for nearly ten years. Her salon, like others of the time conducted by society ladies, was criticised for its 'preciosity', or the inclination to use refined and often artificial language in both speech and written prose; the tendency was later harshly satirised by MOLIÈRE in his *Précieuses ridicules*.

Sebastian (1554–78) king of Portugal 1557–78, and last ruler of the house of Avis. Posthumous son of prince João of Portugal and the infanta Juana, sister of PHILIP II of Spain, he succeeded his grandfather João as king. Obsessed from youth with war games, he dreamed of liberating north Africa from the Muslims, and made a secret visit there for four months in 1574 to reconnoitre the territory. Despite Spanish opposition to his plans, in 1578 he invaded Africa with a force that included most of the nobility and several bishops. The army was wiped out by Muslim forces in August 1578 at the battle of Alcazarquivir; the few who survived were ransomed by relatives in the peninsula. Among those who disappeared was the king. His remains, never definitively identified, were formally interred at the monastery of Belem in Lisbon in 1581, but many Portuguese, looking for a leader to liberate them from the Spanish crown, preferred to believe in the authenticity of several pseudo-Sebastians who made their appearance periodically in subsequent years.

Séguier, Pierre (1588–1672) French minister of state. From a noblesse de robe family that rose to prominence in Languedoc in the early sixteenth century and occupied important posts in the Paris government, he made his career as intendant of Guyenne (1621) and later (1624) became one of the presidents of the parlement of Paris. In 1633 he was appointed Keeper of the Seals and in 1635 chancellor of France, thus initiating a very long and distinguished career. As head of the legal system he was responsible for some of the most celebrated prosecutions of the time, including the Nu-Pieds rebels of Normandy (1639), the marquis de Cinq-Mars (1642), and the minister FOUQUET (1661). His correspondence on these matters with the intendants of France, has provided historians with some of their most valuable source material for the period. One of the founders of the French Academy, he became its principal patron after the death of RICHELIEU.

Seignelay, Jean-Baptiste Colbert, marquis de (1651–90) French minister of state. Eldest son of the great Colbert, at the age of eighteen he was granted the right to succeed his father as secretary for naval affairs (the Marine), and trained carefully for the post: he was sent to Rochefort to learn the sailor's trade, and to Holland and England to study the art of naval construction. From 1672 he took part in the naval administration, began to sign orders, and accompanied the king on some of his military campaigns. After his father's death (1683) he succeeded, despite opposition, in holding on to the post, and became an active and efficient administrator, taking personal charge of the naval campaigns against England and in the Mediterranean. He made French naval power supreme in Europe for a time.

Selden, John (1584–1654) English jurist. Educated at Oxford and the Inner Temple, he was called to the bar in 1612, but did not limit his interests to the law: he was friendly with Ben JONSON, and published a prefatory poem to his *Volpone* (1607). From early on, he began producing significant studies bearing on the legal system of England. His *Titles of Honour* (1614) analysed noble titles; in 1616 he edited the treatise of Fortescue on the laws of

England, in which he argued that England was a 'mixed monarchy'; and in 1617 he brought out a *History of Tythes*, a work that provoked considerable reaction. In 1624 he entered Parliament, where he played a prominent part in the attack against the duke of BUCKINGHAM, and in the preparation of the Petition of Right (1628); he and other members were imprisoned 1629–31 for their attitude. In the Long Parliament in 1641 he opposed the crown on significant matters, but also defended the state Church; he maintained this moderate stance throughout the years of crisis, and took no further part in politics. In the events leading up to the king's execution he kept his opinion: 'the wisest way for men in these times is to say nothing', was one of his later aphorisms. In 1636 he published, at the behest of the crown, *Mare Clausum*, a treatise directed against Dutch views expressed already in GROTIUS' *Mare Liberum* (1619); Selden argued that the adjacent seas were within the sovereignty of the state, namely England. Around 1650 he took up residence in a well-appointed house in the city. The bulk of his magnificent collection of books and manuscripts ended up in the Bodleian Library after his death. The book for which he is chiefly famous, *Table Talk*, was put together by a secretary from his sayings on a wide variety of subjects and published in 1689.

Sepúlveda, Juan Ginés de (1489–1573) Spanish scholar. A native of Córdoba, he studied theology at the university of Alcalá, took orders and went to Bologna to study for his doctorate at the Spanish college there (1515–23). In 1523 he went to Rome, where his protector CLEMENT VII appointed him as official translator of Aristotle (1526–36); he was present when CHARLES V's troops sacked the city in 1527. The emperor soon took note of Sepúlveda's learning, and in 1536 appointed him as chronicler and confessor, in which role he accompanied Charles on his travels, writing the famous *History* of

the emperor in Latin, the *De Orbe Novo* on the New World discoveries, and a history of the feats of Hernan CORTÉS in Mexico. In 1542 he was appointed tutor to the young prince Philip. His best-known role is as opponent of Las CASAS in the controversy over the Indians of America. He wrote his *Democrates Segundus* in 1544, but because of the opposition of Casas and others it was not published (until 1892). The ban was imposed because of the virulent way in which Sepúlveda presented his argument that the natives of America were (applying Aristotelian categories) natural slaves and therefore should be subdued. In 1550 he took part in a debate on the theme against Casas, before the royal council in Valladolid. But supporters of Casas enjoyed greater influence, and Sepúlveda's work remained unpublished.

Serlio, Sebastiano (1475–54) Renaissance architect known for his treatise on architecture. From Bologna, he was trained by his father as a painter. He went to Rome in 1514 as a follower of BRAMANTE and studied with Baldassare Peruzzi, whose literary estate he inherited and incorporated into his work. After the 1527 Sack of Rome, he went to Venice until moving to France to work for FRANCIS I at Fontainebleau. His architectural treatise, *Tutte l'opere d'architettura e prospettiva*, was published in eight books beginning in 1537 with the last book published posthumously in 1575. The work emphasises practical rather than theoretical architecture, models itself on Vitruvius, and is the first printed architectural treatise to employ illustrations as an integral part of the text. Book IV on the five orders is one of his most important contributions. In addition to its influence on architects, it also had notable significance in the development of scenography for the theatre.

[JM]

Servet, Miguel (*c*.1511–53) Spanish doctor and martyr. Son of a notary of Aragon, he went in 1528 to study at the university of Toulouse, before travelling through Italy and Germany, where he met some of the leaders of the Reformation. Radical in his ideas, in 1531 he published in Germany his *On the Errors of the Trinity* (*De Trinitatis erroribus libri septem*), which maintained that there was no foundation in the Bible for the doctrine of the Trinity. The scandal forced him to go underground; under the assumed name of Michel de Villenueve he moved to France, where he lived for twenty years, practising various professions and always behaving as an orthodox Catholic. At Vienne, where he became physician to the archbishop, he published in 1553 his *Christianismi restitutio*, arguing among other ideas that Christ was not God, but only man. He also began corresponding with CALVIN, who was outraged at his ideas and helped to denounce him to the Inquisition in France. Servet escaped and made his way to Geneva, where he was arrested by the authorities and, at Calvin's instigation, burnt alive as a heretic. His execution sparked off an active debate, instigated by CASTELLION, about whether heretics should be persecuted. A man of remarkable erudition, and competent in various disciplines, Servet has also been credited with discovering the principle of the circulation of blood in the human body, mentioned in the *Christianismi restitutio*.

Sévigné, Marie de Rabutin-Chanal, marquise de (1626–96) French writer. Born in Paris to a noble family, she was well-educated, married a Breton noble Henri de Sévigné in 1644, and entered court society and the cultured world of the salons, notably that of Madame du Plessis-Guénégaud. Her husband was killed in a duel in 1651, but she continued living in Paris, where she brought up her two children. Her daughter Françoise in 1669 married the Comte de Grignan, who later moved to Provence to take up the post of lieutenant general there. Separation from

her daughter and consequent loneliness, gave birth to Madame de Sévigné's most important literary achievement, her letters to Madame de Grignan, written without literary intentions. The majority of the 1,700 letters were composed in the first seven years after their separation in 1670. They give a direct report of events in fashionable society, and about leading personages and topics, but also provide personal details about her own daily life and habits. Unaffected and natural, reflecting both creativity and humour, the letters set a new standard for the genre of epistolary composition. But they are also of considerable value to historians, and offer an excellent source for understanding what France under LOUIS XIV was really like. Madame de Sévigné's earlier letters reflect the enthusiasm for the brilliant court society of the Sun King, but her later correspondence shows awareness of the misery of the peasants and the complaints of the provincial nobility.

Seyssel, Claude de (1450–1520) French lawyer. From 1494 to 1498 he was legal adviser to the house of Savoy, before entering the service of LOUIS XII of France. He served as a judge in the parlement of Toulouse, then in that of Paris; he was also appointed bishop of Marseille. He is known principally for his work *Le Grant monarchie de France*, written in 1519 as a political guide for the young FRANCIS I. The book is considered the first clear expression of French 'absolutism'; it defines the nature of royal power and its limits, concluding that 'absolute' power is the least harmful form of government. At the same time, his work analysed the nature of society in France.

Sforza, Francesco (1401–66) duke of Milan 1450–66. The SFORZA family were descended from Muzio Attendolo of the Romagna (1369–1424), whose successful career as a *condottiere* (mercenary leader) led him to assume the name Sforza ('Force'). Francesco, the illegitimate son of Muzio Attendolo, assumed his father's *condottiere* command and nickname in 1424. Filippo Maria Visconti, duke of Milan, became his main employer over the following two decades as he fought for and against Milan in its rivalry with Venice to dominate the Po Valley. His ties to the Visconti were strengthened with his betrothal (1433) and marriage (1441) to the duke's only child, Bianca Maria. In 1434 Cosimo de' MEDICI hired him as *condottiere* of Florence and his military force bolstered the Medici dominance, even defeating the Milanese at Anghiari in 1440 (commemorated in LEONARDO DA VINCI's lost Palazzo Vecchio fresco). He used his army to seize Milan upon Visconti's death in 1447 by defeating the self-styled Ambrosian Republic of Milan (1447–50). With Medici support he consolidated his Milanese power base and participated in the 1454 defensive alliance among the Italian states, the Peace of Lodi. As ruler of Milan, he patronised humanists such as his secretary Cicco Simonetta and the mercurial Greek scholar Francesco Filelfo, whose *Sforziad* memorialised his military career. He commissioned the architect Filarete to design the Ospedale Maggiore and restored the damaged Visconti fortress of Porta Giovia in Milan.

[JM]

Sforza, Ludovico (1452–1508) usurped regency of Milan in 1480 and was its duke 1494–1500. Second son of Francesco SFORZA, he was called 'il Moro' (the Moor) for his dark hair and complexion. After his elder brother Duke Galeazzo Maria was murdered in 1476, he began his notorious machinations for power. Initially failing to secure the regency over his seven-year old nephew, he succeeded four years later in 1480 in becoming the virtual duke and assumed the title in 1494 on his nephew's death. He played a ruthless and deceitful role in relations with the other Italian states and foreign powers in his attempts to promote

Milanese interests. He encouraged the French king CHARLES VIII to invade Italy in 1494 and relied on alliances with the emperor MAXIMILIAN I. After he switched sides and joined the Italian league to expel Charles, he enjoyed a short-term advantage that soon dissolved when LOUIS XII invaded Italy anew with Orleanist claims to Milan itself. He lost Milan to the French in 1499 and attempted to return from exile in 1500, but was captured and died a French prisoner in 1508. His court was one of Renaissance Italy's most renowned, with patronage of music, art and literature that included LEONARDO DA VINCI and BRAMANTE.

[JM]

Shaftesbury, Anthony Ashley-Cooper, 1st earl of (1621–83) English politician. Born of Dorset gentry, endowed with exceptional intellectual gifts and heir to extensive estates, he entered politics at the early age of eighteen as a member of the Short Parliament (1640). During the civil war he took up arms first for the king and then in 1644 for Parliament, for whom he was active in Dorset. In 1650 he married (his second wife) the sister of the earl of Exeter, and in 1654 was appointed to the council of state under CROMWELL. In 1655 he married again, this time the daughter of the royalist earl of Southampton. In 1660, at the Restoration, he was appointed to the privy council. He was created lord Ashley in 1661 and earl in 1672, the year that he was also appointed as lord chancellor. His support for CHARLES II's Declaration of Indulgence in 1672 reflected his continuous concern to secure toleration for Dissenters. But from 1673, when he supported the Test Act, and from 1678, when he backed Titus OATES and then those wishing to exclude the duke of York from the succession (the Exclusion crisis 1679–81), he placed himself firmly out of favour with the government. From the 1670s too he began to suffer severely from the liver cyst that afflicted his small, bent body. During this period he brought into existence the beginnings of a broad-based opposition that became known as the Country party, and as the Whigs. He was also derided in DRYDEN's satirical *Absalom and Achitophel*. Arrested for treason in 1681, he was acquitted but fled the country the following year, and settled in Holland, where he died shortly after. Shaftesbury was a man of great culture and extensive interests. He took a direct part in the colonisation of the colony of Carolina in North America. He was also known as a philosopher, and originated the 'moral sense theory', according to which human beings distinguish between right and wrong because of perceptions they develop rather than because they have an instinct instilled in them by God.

Shakespeare, William (1564–1616) English poet and dramatist. The son of a glovemaker and leather craftsman, he was born in Stratford-upon-Avon and probably educated at Stratford grammar school. At the age of eighteen he married Anne Hathaway, eight years his senior. Little is known about his life until about 1592 when he appears as an established actor and playwright in London. Between 1592 and 1594, the plague forced the closure of the theatres and he published his two erotic poems, *Venus and Adonis* and *The Rape of Lucrece*. He became a member of the Lord Chamberlain's Company, later The King's Men, and was part of a syndicate formed to build and operate the Globe Theatre. By 1596 he was successful and wealthy enough to buy a fine house in Stratford. There is much conjecture about the dates and order of his early plays and even some dispute about authorship. The comedies *Love's Labour's Lost* and *The Taming of the Shrew* and the historical dramas *Henry VI* and *Richard III* belong to the period before 1595. By 1597 he had written *Romeo and Juliet*, *Richard II*, *Henry IV*, *Much Ado About Nothing*, *The Merchant of Venice*, *A Midsummer Night's Dream*

and *The Merry Wives of Windsor*. The turn of the century saw the production of *As You Like It* and *Twelfth Night*, his finest comedies; *Hamlet* the most discussed work ever written for the theatre; and *Measure for Measure*. 1604–8 was the period of some of the greatest plays: *Othello*, *King Lear*, *Macbeth* and *Antony and Cleopatra*. In 1608 The King's Men acquired the Blackfriar's Theatre and Shakespeare entered his last phase with *Cymbeline*, *Henry VIII*, *The Winter's Tale* and *The Tempest*. The 154 *Sonnets*, composed over a number of years, were published in 1609. Arguably the best love poems ever written, they divide into two groups. Sonnets 1–126 are addressed to and are inspired by affection for the mysterious Mr W.H. The latter poems are concerned with a dark beauty. Shakespeare retired to Stratford in 1613 where, three years later, he died and was buried. Universally regarded as the greatest poet in the English language, Ben JONSON said of him 'he was not of an age, but for all time'.

[GG]

Shuisky, Vasilii Ivanovich (1552–1612) tsar of Russia 1606–10 as Vasilii IV. From an old noble family, he became boyar in 1584, and in 1587 was part of a plot to oppose Boris GODUNOV, but was pardoned. He took a leading part in military preparations against the first pseudo-DMITRI, but after the death of Godunov collaborated with the pseudo-Dmitri (1605) for a while, then was exiled after plotting against him. In 1606 he was involved in another broad-based plot against him, in which Dmitri was assassinated. Shuisky was then proclaimed tsar as Vasilii IV. He faced, however, major problems with the BOLOTNIKOV uprising (1607), then with the military intervention of the second Dmitri (1607–8), who was helped by Poland. In the latter struggle he was worsted and had to seek the aid of Sweden (1609). But his army was defeated at Klushino by the Swedes, and an uprising in Moscow put an end to his control there. He was taken prisoner to Poland, where he died in captivity.

Sickingen, Franz von (1481–1523) German noble. Only son of an Imperial knight and chief steward to the elector Palatine, he was born in castle Ebernburg near Kreuznach. After his wife died he became restless and devoted his energies to direct action against those he felt were responsible for the declining fortunes of his class: the towns and the princes. With his mercenaries he began bandit-like attacks on the city of Worms (1514), and later took the struggle further with attacks on Metz (1518) and other cities. His military activity served to give him prestige, and he was sought after as a captain by the French and then by CHARLES V, who appointed him field commander. Persuaded by von HUTTEN to support the Lutheran cause, he extended the protection of his castle to Hutten, BUCER and OECOLAMPADIUS. Inadequately rewarded for his services to the emperor in a war against France (1521), in 1522 he formed a union of the Imperial knights, with the aim of seizing the riches of the archbishopric of Trier. Trier allied with PHILIP OF HESSE and the elector Palatine, and Sickingen and his knights were driven back. Cornered in his castle of Landstuhl, he died during the siege.

Sidney, Algernon (1622–83) English noble and republican. Second surviving son of the 2nd earl of Leicester and brother of the 3rd earl, he served for a while in Ireland where his father was lord deputy, and in the civil war briefly commanded a regiment on the Parliamentary side. Elected to the Long Parliament in 1646, he expressed scruples over the trial and execution of the king in 1649. He returned when the Long Parliament resumed in 1659, but as a presumed regicide went to live on the continent at the Restoration. He obtained royal permission to return in 1677 to England, where he could not resist the pull of politics, and became associated with others of a republican persuasion. In 1683 when the Rye House plot to murder the king was exposed, he was arrested, sentenced on flimsy evidence by judge JEFFREYS, and executed three weeks later, the last English aristocrat to die for his opinions. A convinced non-believer and republican, his *Discourses Concerning Government* (written 1680–3) were published posthumously in 1698.

Sidney, Sir Philip (1554–86) English poet and courtier. Born into a noble family, his father was three times lord deputy of Ireland and his mother the sister of the earl of LEICESTER. He married the daughter of Sir Francis WALSINGHAM. A favourite of ELIZABETH I, he was sent in 1577 as ambassador to the emperor RUDOLF II and later to the prince of Orange. In 1579 after a quarrel with the earl of Oxford he fell out of favour with the court. He retired to the country where he wrote his pastoral romance, *Arcadia*, and *The Apologie for Poetrie*. His graceful, metrically skilful *Astrophel and Stella* was the first sonnet sequence in English and it had many imitators. In 1585 he was sent as governor to Flushing and the following year he was fatally wounded during an attack on a Spanish convoy for the relief of Zutphen. The early heroic death of this cultured, courteous man inspired many elegies including *Astrophel* written by his friend Edmund SPENSER.

[GG]

Sigismund I 'the Old' (Zygmunt I Stary) (1467–1548) king of Poland and grand duke of Lithuania 1506–48. Fifth son of Casimir IV Jagiełło, his reign is noted for continuous wars during Poland's most formative phase. Elected king in 1506 he was crowned the year after. His territory was under constant threat from the Russians, to whom he lost Smolensk in 1514 but whom he defeated in 1535; he was faced likewise by military threats from the Vlachs and the Tatars. Through his brother Vladislav II, king of Bohemia and Hungary, he negotiated (Vienna 1515) a peaceful succession for those realms by guaranteeing that they passed to the Habsburg family as a result of marriage between Vladislav's son Louis II and a Habsburg. He also supported the election of Charles of Burgundy as emperor in 1519. He went to war against the Teutonic Knights (1519–25) and in 1525 (treaty of Cracow) forced them to accept the suzerainty of Poland over Prussia. By marrying Bona Sforza of Milan in 1518 he helped to make the west aware of Poland as a power. Advised by his wife, he passed some administrative duties to their son during his lifetime. Hostile to the Reformation (in 1525 he put down a Lutheran rising in Gdańsk) and a correspondent of ERASMUS, he accepted the Reformation where he could not control it. He was a patron of Renaissance art and a great builder of castles.

Sigismund II Augustus (Zygmunt II August) (1520–72) king of Poland and grand duke of Lithuania 1548–72. Only son of the preceding, he was proclaimed grand duke of Lithuania in 1529 and elected king of Poland by the Polish Diet that year, being crowned the year after, but did not act as king until after his father's death. On succeeding to the throne he made public his secret marriage to the Protestant noble Barbara Radziwiłł, who died in mysterious circumstances in 1551. He married as his next wife the daughter of the emperor FERDINAND I, but remained childless. He fought to secure Polish rights over the port of Gdańsk, and also incorporated Livonia into Poland. The most notable event of his reign was the union of Lublin (1569), by which the duchy of Lithuania and the kingdom of Poland were united as a single state. A humanist and supporter of religious toleration, he allowed the entry of Reformation movements but also (1565) invited the Jesuits into Poland. He left no heir,

and with him the Jagiełło dynasty was extinguished.

Sigismund III Vasa (Zygmunt III Waza) (1566–1632) king of Sweden 1592–9, king of Poland 1587–1632. Son of the Swedish king John III and of a Jagiełło princess, and nephew of SIGISMUND II AUGUSTUS, he was elected king of Poland in 1587 and succeeded in 1592 to the throne of Sweden on his father's death. His pro-Catholic policies in the latter realm led to him being deposed in 1599 and replaced by his uncle CHARLES IX. Even in Poland, his hostility to the Reformation minorities provoked conflicts in the diet from some nobles, who provoked a rebellion in 1606. He was more fortunate in his conflicts with Russia, now in the weak period of the Time of Troubles; his forces occupied Moscow and he had his son Władysław elected tsar by the boyars. In later years he was occupied with defending Poland against the attacks of his nephew GUSTAV II ADOLF VASA of Sweden, who wrested most of Livonia from Poland and forced it to accept the peace of Altmark (1629). Sigismund was succeeded in turn by his sons WŁADYSŁAW IV and JOHN CASIMIR.

Silesius, Angelus (Johannes Scheffler) (1624–77) German mystical poet. Born in a Lutheran family in Breslau, Silesia, he grew up experiencing some of the calamities of the Thirty Years War, studied medicine and philosophy at Strasbourg and Leiden, and increasingly began to immerse himself in the mystical writings of Meister Eckhart and Jakob BOEHME. He was in Padua in 1647–8, and obtained his doctorate in medicine there; he returned to Silesia in 1649 and took up a post as doctor. Disillusioned with the Lutherans and with his previous mystical pantheism, in 1653 he converted to Catholicism, gave up his desirable position as physician to the duke of Württemberg, and began to write polemics in favour of the Catholic position. He changed his name to signify his mystical rebirth, became a priest in 1661, and eventually became physician to the emperor Ferdinand III. He is remembered principally for his work *Cherubinischer Wandersmann* (The Angelic Pilgrim), first published under another title in 1657 and then, with this title, in 1674. Consisting of mystical reflections, the work is a bridge between his pantheistic and his Catholic period, and consequently appeals to a wide range of readership.

Simnel, Lambert (*c*.1475–*c*.1535) English impostor and pretender to the throne. A native of Oxford, he was groomed by opponents of HENRY VII to impersonate Edward, earl of Warwick, last Yorkist pretender to the throne who was imprisoned in the Tower after Henry's victory at the battle of Bosworth (1485). Supported by the Yorkist John de la Pole, earl of Lincoln, Simnel claimed to have escaped the clutches of Henry and was crowned king in Dublin (1487). With the help of foreign mercenaries, the pretender invaded Lancashire and Yorkshire but was defeated by Henry at Stoke (June 1487). It was the last battle of the Wars of the Roses. Simnel was put to work in the kitchens of the royal household.

Simon, Richard (1638–1712) founder of Biblical criticism in France. He studied at the college of the religious order of the Oratory in Dieppe, then decided to enter the order, which he did in Paris. He chose to study Hebrew, and while doing so turned himself into an expert philologist; in 1670 he took orders. Convinced that the basis of correct knowledge was an exact understanding of texts, he made it his life's work to establish the philological basis of the Bible, and in 1678 published in French his *Critical History of the Old Testament*. Immediately, the authorities reacted. He was expelled from the Oratory, his book was banned by the state, and in 1683 Rome placed it on the Index of forbidden works. He continued to publish further studies in criticism, but in Amsterdam. Finally in 1702 he issued his great dream, the *New Testament* in French, published at Trévoux. Technically translated from the Latin, it had notes commenting on the Greek and Hebrew texts. It too was condemned. He retired to Normandy, where he burnt his papers, and died tranquilly as a faithful Catholic.

Sixtus V (Felice Peretti, 1525–90) pope 1585–90. Entering the Franciscans at an early age, he was ordained in 1547, served as Inquisitor General in Venice between 1557–60, became Franciscan vicar general and bishop in 1566, and a cardinal in 1570. The reputation of his strong papacy rests upon his reforms as a theological hardliner promoting the Counter-Reformation policies, as an administrator reorganising the papal bureaucracy, and as a builder whose projects remade the face of the city of Rome. Regarding faith and morals, he promoted the reform of religious orders and in 1586 issued a papal bull condemning prediction, prophecy and astrology as diabolic not learned ways to knowledge, especially as they were linked to social and political unrest. For Church administration, he reformed the College of Cardinals by fixing its number at seventy, reorganised the secretariat of state, and revamped the curia by establishing fifteen departments or congregations which effectively executed the canons and decrees of the council of Trent. In the Papal States, he launched an offensive against bandits and pirates, encouraged the textile industries, and imposed financial reforms. In Rome itself, his city plan established the city's characteristic trident street structure, placed four great obelisks in public squares, and remade the city into its modern form. He was a great builder of streets, fountains and buildings from the Lateran palace to the completion of St Peter's dome, the enlargement of the Quirinal, and the building of aqueducts.

[JM]

Slavata of Chlum, Vilém (1572–1652) Czech minister of state. A member of the upper Czech nobility and by religion a member of the Utraquist Bohemian Brethren, in the early 1600s he found it profitable to convert to Catholicism and advanced his career in Prague as a supporter of the Habsburg interest. In 1617 he was appointed leader of the regency council, but in 1618 was one of the two ministers (the other was Martinic) defenestrated from the Hradčany palace in Prague. Restored to power after the battle of the White Mountain (1620) he was appointed chancellor of Bohemia.

Smith, captain John (1580–1631) English explorer. Born in Lincolnshire, his search for adventure took him at the age of twenty to the wars in Hungary, where he was captured by the Turks but escaped to England (1604). In 1606 he set sail with the first expedition of the Virginia Company of London, which arrived in April 1607 in Chesapeake Bay and subsequently founded Jamestown, the first permanent English settlement in north America. Smith soon became the leader of the community. During an exploration in December 1607 he was ambushed by Indians and taken to their chief, Powhatan, who spared his life after pleas by his young daughter Pocahontas. Smith went back to England in 1609 and returned in 1614, this time making a careful reconnaissance of the coast of what he called New England. He was in England again in 1615, but a trip he planned for 1617 never set sail, and he never returned to the New World. His writings include *A Description of New England* (1625); *The Generall Historie of Virginia, New England, and the Summer Isles* (1624); and *The True Travels, Adventures and Observations of Captaine John Smith in Europe, Asia, Africa and America* (1630).

Smith, Sir Thomas (1513–77) English statesman. Son of a wealthy Essex gentleman, he was educated at Cambridge, where he became a fellow. In 1540 he travelled to France and Italy, obtaining a doctorate in laws at Padua. In 1543 he became professor of civil law at Cambridge, and vice-chancellor; then in 1546 he took orders, and the following year was appointed provost of Eton and secretary of state. In 1548 he was knighted. A firm Protestant, he supported the regime of Protector SOMERSET, but survived his fall and managed to live in retirement during the reign of MARY I. He resumed his public role under ELIZABETH I, entered the privy council and served as ambassador to France. One of the great humanists and scholars of his time, he analysed social problems of the country in his *Discourse of the Common Weal* (1549). During his period as ambassador in Paris (1562–6) he wrote the first draft of his famous *De Republica Anglorum*, published 1583. It is the principal statement of the view that England is a mixed monarchy, with sovereignty residing in people, Parliament and crown.

Sobieski, John (Jan) III (1624–96) king of Poland 1674–96. Of gentry origin (his father was castellan of Cracow), he was sent to be educated in western Europe and became an admirer of France. In 1648 he entered the Polish army and made his name in wars against the Swedes, Cossacks and Tatars. In 1655 he established a relationship with a lady-in-waiting of the queen, and later (1665) married her; the court connection greatly enhanced his position. Between 1665 and 1668 he was conceded the highest military posts in the realm, and in 1667 was made governor (*voivod*) of Cracow. After a significant victory over the Turks in 1673 he was elected king in 1674, in succession to Michael Wisnowiecki (king 1669–73). His most notable achievement was his march to relieve Vienna, besieged in 1683, and his subsequent victory over the Turks at Kahlenberg, which forced them to raise the siege of Vienna. Further campaigns against the Turks were less fruitful. Moreover, at home he began to suffer conflicts within his family and with a section of the nobles. A great patron of the arts, he built impressive residences, in particular the Baroque palace at Wilanów (that is, Villa Nova) near Warsaw (1677).

Socinus (Sozzini), Fausto (1539–1604) Italian Unitarian leader. He was born in Siena of a noble family, which produced in Lelio Sozzini (1525–62) its first important recruit to Protestantism. Lelio travelled through Europe, knew many leaders of the Reformation, and died in Zürich, leaving his papers to his nephew Fausto. Fausto became a sympathizer of the Reformation rather late in life. Apart from a stay in France and Switzerland (1559–62), he lived in Italy until 1574, at the court of the sister of the grand duke of Tuscany. On her death, he left Italy and settled in Basel, where he wrote his principal study, *De Jesu Christo Servatore* (Jesus Christ the Saviour), not published until 1594, and then in Poland. In 1578 he left Switzerland and settled in Poland at Cracow, where he lived comfortably till his death. During his stay in Poland, he helped to give the various sectarian groups, who had in common a rejection of the doctrine of the Trinity, some semblance of a shared identity. After his death they grouped together, adopted a common catechism (1605) and confession of faith, and began to call themselves Socinians. Those who share the tradition are now termed Unitarians.

Sofia (1657–1704) regent and ruler of Muscovy 1682–9. Daughter of tsar ALEXEI I, after the death of her brother the tsar Fyodor Alexeevich in 1682, she opposed the placing of her 10-year-old half-brother Peter I (PETER THE GREAT) on the throne, and supported the coup which made her retarded brother Ivan V joint tsar with him. Brought to power by the palace guard (*streltsy*), she imposed her authority on them with the help of the chief boyars led by Vasilii Golitsyn. No-

velties in her foreign policy were the peace of 1686 with Poland and one of 1689 with China. In 1689 the boyar supporters of Peter removed her and put her in a convent. The failure of an attempt by the *streltsy* to restore her in 1698, led to her permanent reclusion in the convent.

Somerset, Edward Seymour, 1st duke of (1506–52) English statesman. Son of Sir John Seymour and elder brother of HENRY VIII's third wife Jane Seymour, his fortunes rose with those of his sister: in 1537 he was created earl of Hertford. He played a significant military role as commander of the English forces that invaded Scotland by sea in 1544, wasted the country and burnt Edinburgh. Appointed a member of the regency council (1547) to control government during the minority of Edward VI, he adopted the title of Protector of the realm and became duke of Somerset; in effect he governed as virtual king and made himself rich. Facing trouble from Scotland, he invaded the north with a huge army and crushed the Scots at the battle of Pinkie (September 1547). A convinced supporter of the Reformation, he followed a policy of freedom of religion for all faiths, and supported the abolition (1547) of penal laws against heresy. The consequence was a rapid advance of the Protestant cause in England and the issue of a wholly Protestant Book of Common Prayer (1549) for the Church. In the face of social unrest, from 1548 he supported new laws against enclosures (the turning of arable land to pasture), but faced opposition from landowners. In the early summer of 1549 agrarian disturbances broke out all over southern England. Somerset's main rival in the council, the earl of Warwick (John DUDLEY), crushed the rebels under KET in Norfolk. Discontent with Somerset's policies led to his removal by the other members of the council, and his imprisonment in the Tower (October 1549). Released shortly after, he was re-arrested under Warwick's regime in October 1551, convicted of felony and executed. Traditionally viewed as a 'progressive' figure, recent research has tended to be more critical of him.

Somerset, Robert Carr, earl of (c.1585–1645) A Scots noble who began his career as page to the earl of Dunbar, he became a favourite of JAMES I, was created viscount Rochester, member of the privy council, and in 1613 earl. His career was complicated by the scheming of his mistress, Frances Howard, countess of Essex, who after various pressures on the Church courts succeeded in annulling her marriage to the earl of Essex and marrying Carr (December 1613). However, she objected violently to a friend of Carr, the poet Sir Thomas Overbury, who had advised against the marriage. She persuaded the king to imprison him in the Tower, then arranged to have him poisoned (September 1613). The murderers were discovered and executed (1615), but Carr remained untouched until the rise of his protégé the duke of BUCKINGHAM supplanted him in the favours of the homosexual king. The enemies of the Howards then combined to bring about Carr's disgrace, and he and his wife were convicted of murder and imprisoned in the Tower (1616–21) but pardoned three years later. He died in obscurity.

Sophia (1630–1714) electress of Hanover. Youngest of the children of ELIZABETH STUART of Bohemia, who was daughter of JAMES I of England, she became after the exclusion of the Jacobite line of succession the most direct heir to the throne of England. In 1658 she married ERNST AUGUSTUS of Brunswick, who subsequently acquired the title of elector of Hanover. Her son Georg Ludwig became GEORGE I of Great Britain; her daughter Sophie Charlotte subsequently became queen of Prussia by her marriage (1684) to FREDERICK I, and mother to FREDERICK WILLIAM I, the 'soldier king' of Prussia.

Southwell, Robert S.J. (c.1561–95) English Jesuit poet. Born in England, he had his early education with the Jesuits in Douai, an order he entered in 1580. He went to teach at the English college in Rome, and was ordained priest 1584. In 1586 he returned to England secretly in company with other Jesuits, ministering to the Catholic population and acting (1589) as chaplain to the Howard family, earls of Arundel. In 1592 he was tracked down and arrested by the government's anti-Catholic officer, Topcliffe. He was tortured, and imprisoned in filthy conditions for three years, but managed to write his poetry in the cell. In 1595 the king's bench condemned him to death as a traitor, and he was hanged and decapitated. His verse began to be published, at first in anonymous editions, after his death.

Spanheim, Ezekiel (1629–1710) diplomat. Born in Geneva, son of a theology professor, he did his studies in Leiden, and returned to take up his father's chair when only twenty. In 1656 he was appointed tutor to the son of the Calvinist elector Palatine, for whom he also undertook several diplomatic missions. In 1665 he was appointed roving envoy of the Palatinate, and in 1675 went as resident ambassador to London, where he also represented Brandenburg. In 1680 he was appointed to the privy council of the Great Elector and served from 1680 to 1689 and then from 1698 to 1701 as ambassador of Brandenburg in France, where he helped to organise emigration of expelled Huguenots to Brandenburg, and wrote a perceptive account of the French court (*Relation de la cour de France*). In 1697 he was plenipotentiary for Brandenburg in the negotiations for the peace of Rijswijk, and was sent to London as ambassador in 1701, the year he was created a baron of the empire. He died in London. One of the most cultured and accomplished diplomats of his day, he built up during his travels a remarkable library that the emperor acquired at his death.

Spee von Langenfeld, Friedrich (1591–1635) German Jesuit poet. Born in Kaiserswerth of an élite family, he entered the Jesuit order (1610), and from 1613 to 1621 taught in Cologne. In 1625–6 he was a preacher in Paderborn. In 1627–8 he was appointed by the bishop of Würzburg to minister to those condemned for witchcraft, and accompanied 200 persons to the scaffold. Severely wounded in an attempt on his life during a mission in Hildesheim, he began to write the poems which were published only after his death. In 1631 he published anonymously his *Cautio Criminalis*, one of the most important attacks of its time on the witchcraft beliefs and trials of the period. From 1633 he was teaching in Trier, where he died in a plague epidemic. Though known for his mystical-religious poetical work, he is remembered chiefly for the impact of his study on witchcraft.

Spener, Philipp Jakob (1635–1705) Founder of German Pietism. A pastor in Frankfurt am Main, he wished to raise the devotional level of his congregation and of all Christians. He began by having meetings at his home, known as '*collegia pietatis*', in which relevant themes on the Bible and religious life were discussed. In his *Pia Desiderata* (1675), he called for a reformation of religious practice with a view to improving the personal religion of Christians, by emphasising inner piety rather than intellectual sophistication. His other writings, all published in Frankfurt, followed the same theme. Invited later to Berlin by elector FREDERICK I of Brandenburg, he disseminated Pietist views through the newly founded (1694) university of Halle. An active Pietist at the university was August Francke, one of whose pupils was count Nicolas von ZINZENDORF. A reaction against the theological excesses of the Reformation period, Pietism aimed to restore simple faith,

and became very influential in eighteenth-century Germany. It began a new trend that had parallels in English Methodism, and has remained as a fundamental component of Protestant Christianity both in Europe and in north America.

Spenser, Edmund (1552–99) English poet. Acknowledged as the first major poet in English since Chaucer, he was educated at the Merchant Taylor's school and at Cambridge where he met Gabriel Harvey, through whose influence he was found a place in the household of the earl of LEICESTER. There he became a friend of Philip SIDNEY to whom he dedicated his first major work, *The Shepheardes Calender*. The same year, 1579, Spenser, Sidney, Dyer, Harvey, Greville and others formed a literary club, the Areopagus. In 1580 he went as secretary to Lord Grey of Wilton, the lord deputy of Ireland, and he was to spend most of the next eighteen years at Kilcoman castle in county Cork. He wrote a number of shorter poems and *Astrophel*, an elegy on the death of Sidney. His epic allegory, *The Faerie Queene*, was planned in twelve books and was intended both to be a celebration of England and ELIZABETH I, and a portrayal of the virtues of a true gentleman. In 1589, with the help of his friend Sir Walter RALEIGH, the first three books were presented to the queen, who was impressed enough to bestow on Spenser a pension of £50 but not enough to give him the preferment he desired. Reluctantly he returned to Ireland. His autobiographical pastoral poem *Colin Clouts Come Againe* reflects on his mood at this time. His second wife, Elizabeth Boyle, is regarded as the source of inspiration for the sonnet sequence *Amoretti* (1595) and for his finest lyrical achievement, the marriage poem *Epithalamion*. Three more books of *The Faerie Queene*, four *Hymnes to Love and Beauty* and the betrothal poem, *Prothalamion* appeared in 1596. He became sheriff of Cork in 1598, but in the rebellion of that year Kilcoman castle was attacked and burned, probably destroying most of the last books of his great poem, and he fled with his family to Cork and thence to London, where he died the following year in reduced circumstances. He is buried near Chaucer in Westminster Abbey.

[GG]

Spinola, Ambrogio, marquis of Los Balbases (1569–1630) general and financier. From one of the great patrician families of Genoa that had periodically given financial and political support to Spain, he advanced money and raised troops for the Spanish campaigns in the Netherlands. In 1602 he led his forces personally to the Netherlands and raised the siege of Ostend (1604). After the Twelve Years Truce (1609–21) he was given full powers as commander-in-chief of the army of Flanders. The army was used to occupy the Palatinate (1620–1) after the defeat of the elector (FREDERICK V OF WITTELSBACH) in Bohemia. Spinola's forces thus secured Spanish communications along the Rhine, and were in a position to renew the war in the Netherlands, where his most notable feat was the capture of Breda (1625) after a year's siege. He also served in Italy, where he helped in 1630 to capture Casale and Monferrato.

Spinoza, Baruch (1632–77) Dutch philosopher. Born and educated in the Jewish community of Amsterdam, at twenty two he gave up his born name of Baruch for that of Benedict. From 1652 to 1656 he studied the philosophy of DESCARTES, but his views caused his excommunication by the Jewish community in 1656. Despite incurring hostility, he lived tranquilly first in Amsterdam then in The Hague, dying at an early age of consumption. The only work published under his name during his lifetime was his Latin work *Principles of Descartes' Philosophy* (1663). His *Tractatus Theologico-Politicus*, an analysis of Church–state relations, was published anonymously in 1670. Then his major remaining works were published in 1677

as the *Opera Postuma*, among which the towering achievement was the *Ethics*, a work that spans metaphysics and psychology. In it he frequently uses the term '*Deus, sive Natura*', which has led many to see his philosophy as pantheistic naturalism, and some contemporaries viewed him as an atheist. The *Ethics*, however, is centred closely on experience; Bertrand Russell has pointed out that 'Spinoza is concerned to show how it is possible to live nobly even when we recognise the limits of human power'. His naturalistic philosophy had a great influence on subsequent imaginative writers and poets, such as Novalis and Wordsworth.

Sprenger, Jakob (1436–95) Born in Rheinfelden, he entered the Dominican order and from 1472 to 1488 was prior of the order in Cologne. Appointed in 1481 inquisitor for the bishoprics of Mainz, Cologne and Trier, he is remembered for his co-authorship with Heinrich Institoris of the *Malleus Maleficarum* (The Hammer of Witches) (1487), a compendium of theology and folklore about so-called witches that served for nearly two centuries as the basis upon which clergy and judges drew conclusions about the reality of witchcraft.

Stair, James Dalrymple, 1st viscount of (1619–95) Scots statesman. From an Ayrshire family, he studied at Glasgow university, where he became a professor from 1641. In 1647 he was admitted to the bar at Edinburgh, and became a leading judge. A prominent supporter of CHARLES II, he played an important role in the government of Scotland after the 1660 Restoration, and firmly supported Scots interests against the measures of the English privy council and in particular, from 1677, the policy of LAUDERDALE. In 1682 he left the country, fearing for his safety, and lived in Leiden, returning only with WILLIAM III of Orange at the Revolution of 1688. He was created a viscount and peer in 1690. In the middle of his legal and political activity, he found time to write the first great treatise on Scots law, *Institutions of the Law of Scotland* (1681). His wife Margaret, whom he married in 1643, was unjustly maligned by contemporaries as a witch; he himself was directly involved in the infamous massacre of Glencoe (1692).

Stanhope, James, 1st earl (1673–1721) English general and politician. Born in Paris to a diplomat father, educated at Eton and Oxford, he accompanied his father to Madrid for a year (where he learned the language), then served as a soldier in Italy and Flanders. In 1701 he entered Parliament as a Whig, but also continued with his military career. In 1705 he accompanied the earl of Peterborough to the peninsula during the war of the Spanish Succession, then served as minister in Madrid (1706) and was appointed general and commander of the English troops (1708), capturing Menorca in this year. At the battle of Brihuega (1710) he was taken prisoner by the French under Vendôme and remained a year and a half in captivity. Returning to England in 1712, he resumed his Parliamentary role, becoming chief minister under GEORGE I. As secretary of state (1714–17 and 1718–21) he negotiated the Triple and Quadruple alliances with France. He became 1st lord of the treasury in 1717. Created viscount Stanhope of Mahon in 1717, he became earl the year after. His correspondence, largely unpublished, is an important source for the events of the time.

Stanislas (Stanisław) Leszczynski (1677–1766) king of Poland 1704–9, 1733–35. One of the magnates of Greater Poland, he was placed on the throne by the invading CHARLES XII VASA of Sweden, but was forced to flee the country after Charles' defeat at Poltava (1709). He joined him in exile in Bessarabia and was like him imprisoned by the Turks (1713–14). After Charles' death in Sweden he

moved to France, where his daughter Marie Lesczynska married LOUIS XV (1725). This gave him the opportunity to use French support for his claims to the Polish throne, to which he was re-elected in 1733 by his supporters there, even though the throne was effectively in the hands of the Russian candidate, Augustus III. Escaping from Poland through Gdańsk, he was compensated by the treaty of Vienna (1738) with the duchies of Lorraine and of Bar, which at his death were integrated into France. He proved to be a brilliant ruler of Lorraine, and made Nancy into a great cultural centre; his own writings, mainly on philosophical themes, were significant.

Steele, Sir Richard (1672–1729) English dramatist and essayist. Born in Dublin, he was a schoolfellow of ADDISON at Charterhouse. After Oxford he joined the Life Guards, became secretary to the colonel of the Coldstream Guards and obtained the rank of captain. Although something of a rake himself, Steele had a strong sense of guilt and a reforming zeal. In 1701 he published *The Christian Hero: an Argument proving that no Principles but those of Religion are Sufficient to Make a Great Man*. He also wrote a number of successful comedies for the theatre. In 1706 he was appointed gentleman waiter to prince George, queen ANNE STUART's consort, and in 1707 he became gazetteer, an official government writer. However, journalism was to be his true métier and in 1709 he founded *The Tatler*, with help from SWIFT, which he edited under the pseudonym of 'Isaac Bickerstaff'. He invented a lady editor 'Jenny Distaff' to deal with women's interests. He and Addison founded *The Spectator* in 1711. Both periodicals covered a wide range of subjects while gently satirising the affectations and vices of the time and they appealed to a very wide readership. When the Tories came to power in 1710 Steele lost his government post. He became a member of Parliament in 1713 but was expelled from the Commons the following year after the publication of his pamphlet *The Crisis* which was written in support of the house of Hanover. On the succession of GEORGE I his fortunes were restored and he was given a number of posts including supervisor of Drury Lane theatre and was knighted. His denunciation of the Peerage Bill in 1718 led to a break with Addison, who was in the ministry, and to loss of office. He continued his work as a journalist and was one of those who warned against the investment mania of the South Sea Bubble. His last, and best, play *The Conscious Lovers* (1722) held the stage for a number of years. He died, soon after suffering a stroke, in Carmarthen, Wales.

[GG]

Stradivari, Antonio (1644–1737) Italian violin-maker. He is regarded as the greatest of all violin makers. He learned his *métier* from Niccolò Amati in Cremona and eventually passed his art to his own two sons (historically the family has been called Stradivarius in connection with the violin). He also produced other string instruments of remarkable quality, notably cellos and guitars. Although the instruments are not uniform in design and quality, they share a powerful sound projection and unusually warm tone. This is due to his particular workmanship, special treatment of the wood (usually maple) and the 'secret', inimitable varnish. Over 600 authentic instruments have survived (and thousands of imitations of inferior quality). For nearly three centuries they have remained the most valued instruments among celebrated violinists.

[JE]

Strafford, Thomas Wentworth, 1st earl of (1593–1641) Of a Yorkshire gentry family, he was educated at Cambridge and the Inner Temple. Elected to the Parliament of 1614, he joined the opposition to the policies of BUCKINGHAM; in return, he was deliberately excluded from the 1626

Parliament by being selected as sheriff for Yorkshire. Here he stood out for his opposition to the forced loan, and was even arrested. He was returned to Parliament in 1628, where he resumed his attacks on crown policy, and supported the Petition of Right. After this, considering that opposition had overreached itself, he gave his support to the crown, was appointed by CHARLES I as president of the council of the North (1628), and in 1632 made lord deputy of Ireland, where for seven years (till 1639) he put into effect with considerable success the policy of authority and moderation to which he gave the name 'Thorough'. When the Bishops' Wars broke out in 1639, he returned to help LAUD and Charles in the government, and was created earl (January 1640). But he was accused by the opposition of intending to bring the Irish (Catholic) army into England to help the king. When the Long Parliament met (November 1640) he was impeached by PYM and the king was unable to save him being sent to the Tower. When it appeared that impeachment would not succeed, Pym changed the procedure and secured a bill of attainder, which the king under pressure agreed to sign. Strafford was executed on Tower Hill.

Stuart, Charles Edward, the Young Pretender (1720–88) Eldest son of James STUART, the Old Pretender and princess Clementina Sobieska, he took up his father's claims to the British throne. Handsome and irresponsible, he landed in Scotland in August 1745, without informing either his father or his political supporters, and backed directly only by French promises and the aid of a handful of Irish adventurers and French privateers. He was at first remarkably successful. He rallied the support of most of the clans, was welcomed in Edinburgh then marched into England, defeated the English forces at Prestonpans and advanced as far as Derby, after which he was obliged to retire because of the lack of guaranteed support. Once more in Scotland, he scored a victory at Falkirk but was routed at Culloden (April 1746) by the army of the duke of CUMBERLAND. Apart from the savage repression in Scotland, several prisoners were taken to England: about 120 leading supporters, including four peers, were executed. In hiding for six months in the highlands, Charles eventually escaped to France, from were he was expelled by the stipulations of the peace of Aix-la-Chapelle (1748). He then moved about, living for a while in London but also in Paris and Basel, and eventually in Italy, where he married a German princess but ended his days as a drunkard. His position as pretender was taken over by his younger brother Henry, duke and cardinal of York (1725–1807), also resident in Italy, who assumed the title of Henry IX.

Stuart, James Francis Edward, the Old Pretender (1688–1766) Son of JAMES II of England and Mary of Modena, his birth was the event that precipitated the Revolution of 1688, since it ensured the succession and made the opponents of James fear a permanent Catholic dynasty. Though excluded from the British throne, he was recognised as king by LOUIS XIV, an act that helped to provoke the war of the Spanish Succession. Counting on strong sentimental support for the Stuarts, he returned to back a rising in Scotland in 1715, but his forces were decisively defeated. The peace of Utrecht (1713) prohibited further support from France, so he went to Italy, where he was fortunate enough to achieve in 1719 marriage with Clementina Sobieska, granddaughter of John SOBIESKI, a marriage that later turned sour. He was unaware of the plans for the invasion of Scotland made by his son Charles STUART in 1745.

Sturm, Jakob (1489–1553) German Reformation leader. Born into the ruling circles of Strasbourg, he was educated at Heidelberg (1501–3) for a Church career, then studied theology at Freiburg (1504–11), and later law. In Strasbourg in 1517 he took up an administrative post in the cathedral. From the 1520s he became a supporter of the Reformation, and entered the political administration of the city, ending as member of the senate and of the ruling committee of Thirteen. As a politician, he undertook diplomatic missions for the city, aware that the changing alliances in the empire were now being dictated by religious affiliation. He made it his aim, therefore, to unite the Reformation cities, not only politically but also in theology, in order to combat the superior forces of Catholicism. In 1530 at the Diet of Augsburg, he and BUCER worked to build a united front, which later took shape in the Schmalkaldic League.

Suárez, Francisco (1548–1617) Spanish theologian. Born in Granada, he entered the Society of Jesus in 1564, then studied at Salamanca (1564–70) and taught in various Castilian colleges. Throughout his career he had problems with clergy who denounced him for views deemed to be novel. Eventually PHILIP II obtained his appointment to the chair of theology at Coimbra, which he filled for many years (1599–1615). His major work was the *Tractatus de legibus* (Treatise on Laws) (1612), but the book for which he became notorious was his *Defensio Fidei* (Defence of the Faith) (1613), which was ordered burned by the parlement of Paris for its presumed defence of tyrannicide. One of the most influential thinkers of his day, Suárez argued that political society is created by the people, who can determine the form of government they wish, and can change it if the ruler does not promote the common good. He also clearly separated political power from spiritual power: the state is a human institution, whereas the Church (that is, the pope) is of divine origin.

Sully, Maximilien de Béthune, baron Rosny and duke de (1560–1641) Of a staunchly Protestant noble family, from the age of eleven he was attached to the entourage of Henry of Navarre (later HENRY IV) and remained one of his closest companions and confidants throughout the civil wars. He married in 1584 the wealthy heiress Anne de Courtenay. At the end of the wars he advised Henry to turn Catholic, but himself remained always a Calvinist. Appointed superintendant of finances to the king in 1598, he succeeded in carrying out a remarkable reform of state income, and directed all aspects of policy. He accumulated posts of authority, was made head of the artillery (1599), governor of the Bastille (1602), and governor of Poitou (1604); in 1606 he was also created duke. After Henry's assassination he served briefly on the regency council but gave up his posts and withdrew from active politics, though he helped the troubled government by attempting to mediate with Huguenot rebels (among them his son-in-law ROHAN) during the 1620s. In 1634 he was created marshal of France. His voluminous memoirs, generally known as the *Oeconomies royales*, occupied much of his time during his retirement, and remain a major source for the politics of the period.

Sunderland, Robert Spencer, 2nd earl of (1640–1702) After studying at Oxford he spent two years on the continent doing the Grand Tour, which served him in his first political employment, as diplomatic envoy (1671–3) to France and other states. In 1679 he entered government as secretary of state, and formed a cabinet that included GODOLPHIN, but when the Exclusion crisis broke he voted for the Bill against the duke of York, and was excluded from government. When the duke came to power as JAMES II, Sunderland, always an opportunist, supported him, became lord president of the council (1685), and even converted to Catholicism. But he also made contact with WILLIAM III of Orange, and after the latter became king converted back to

Anglicanism, and from 1692 until his death exercised some influence on the crown.

Sunderland, Charles Spencer, the 3rd earl of (1674–1722) The second son of Robert Spencer, he displayed the same agility in politics as his father. He entered Parliament in 1695 as an active Whig, later forming part of the '*junto*' of five which included lords HALIFAX and Somers. His marriage in 1700 to the daughter of MARLBOROUGH helped his entry into government, and in 1706 he became secretary of state; in 1708 the rest of the '*junto*' entered government and replaced the Tories. Out of office in 1710, he cultivated his influence with the new dynasty and GEORGE I and became secretary for the northern department in 1717 and in 1718 first lord of the treasury. The collapse in 1720 of the South Sea Company, which he had promoted, obliged him to resign.

Süss Oppenheimer, Joseph (1698–1738) Known as 'the Jew Süss' and often viewed as the prototype court Jew, he rendered financial services to the elector Palatine and the elector of Cologne, becoming in 1732 financial adviser to the duke of Württemberg, whose fiscal system he overhauled. Widely hated for his activities, after the duke's death he was arrested and executed.

Swift, Jonathan (1667–1754) English satirist. Swift was born, shortly after his father's death, in Dublin, but his parents were English. At Trinity College he was censured for misbehaviour and only graduated by 'special grace'. Through family connections he became secretary to the diplomat Sir William TEMPLE of Moor Park, where he acted as tutor to the eight-year-old Esther Johnson who was to become the most lasting attachment of his life. She is immortalised in his verse and in his affectionate *Journal to Stella*. There is much conjecture, but no proof that they were ever married. By 1691 Swift had decided that the only way he could achieve preferment was by entering the Church; in 1694 he was ordained and went to a living in Ireland. He returned to Moor Park in 1696 where he wrote his mock epic and savage attack on pedantry, *The Battle of the Books*. It was published alongside *The Tale of a Tub*, a satire on 'corruptions in religion', in 1704. After Temple's death in 1669, Swift returned to Dublin where he became friends with STEELE, POPE and CONGREVE and where he also met Esther Vanhomrigh who fell in love with him and followed him to Ireland. She is the Vanessa of his mock-classical poem *Cadenus and Vanessa*. In 1713 he was appointed Dean of St Patrick's Cathedral in Dublin, a position he held until his last illness. He published pamphlets in support of the Tory government, including his plan for peace, *The Conduct of the Allies* (1711). While professing to hate Ireland, Swift wrote many notable works on behalf of the Irish including *Proposal for the Universal Use of Irish Manufactures* and *The Drapier's Letters*. Swift's most famous work, *Gulliver's Travels*, published anonymously in 1726, is a powerful satire on the folly of man and his institutions. By the time of Stella's death in 1728 Swift was already suffering from what was probably Meniere's Disease; after a brain tumour he became insane and spent the last years of his life in an asylum. Swift has been accused of cynicism and misanthropy but his indignation at injustice and oppression were genuine. He gave one-third of his income as Dean to charities and another third towards founding St Patrick's Hospital. When he died 'a hush fell on Dublin' where he was greatly loved. He is buried next to Stella in St Patrick's cathedral.

[GG]

T

Talavera, Hernando de (c.1430–1507) Spanish ecclesiastic. Born in Talavera de la Reina (Toledo, Spain), he studied at the university of Salamanca, where he became a priest (c.1460) and went on to teach philosophy (1463–6). In 1466 he entered the Jeronimite order, was appointed prior of his order in Valladolid (c.1470), and came to the attention of queen ISABELLA THE CATHOLIC, who made him her confessor. In 1485 he was appointed to the see of Avila, and in 1493 became the first archbishop of the newly conquered territory of Granada. From the late 1470s onwards, he formed part of the royal Council, and played an important role in the military and fiscal decisions of the government. In Granada he attempted conversion of the Muslim population by moderate means, but clashed with cardinal CISNEROS, who preferred more rapid methods. In 1506, as a result of enquiries by the fanatical inquisitor Lucero of Córdoba, he and his family were accused of secretly practising Jewish rites. He was imprisoned for a while, and released shortly before his death. No evidence has been found for the presumption that he was of Jewish origin.

Talbot, Elizabeth, countess of Shrewsbury (Bess of Hardwick) (1518–1608) English aristocrat. Born in Hardwick, Derbyshire, of gentry stock, she married at fourteen, but her husband died within the year, leaving her as a wealthy widow. In 1549 she married Sir William Cavendish, by whom she had six surviving children (two of whom became dukes); then married a gentleman from Gloucestershire; and finally in 1568 as fourth husband married George Talbot, 6th earl of Shrewsbury. From 1569 to 1584 the earl was entrusted with the care of MARY STUART. Bess devoted her now vast fortune to the building of houses: among others, she built a mansion at Chatsworth (later replaced by the present edifice), and in 1590, after the death of the earl (she had conjugal differences with him in his later years) she began Hardwick Hall, her principal home, where she died at a great age.

Tallis, Thomas (c.1505–85) English composer and organist. During his early career he held various posts in Dover, London, Waltham Abbey (Essex) and Canterbury Cathedral. In 1543 he was appointed Gentleman of the Royal Chapel and acted there as organist until his death. To a great extent his religious works were contingent upon the shifting religious policies during the reigns of HENRY VIII, EDWARD VI, MARY I and ELIZABETH I. Brought up as a Catholic, his early compositions comprise mainly Latin works. Among the finest are the votive antiphon *Gaude gloriosa Dei mater*, the mass *Puer natus est nobis*, and the sumptuous forty-voice motet *Spem in alium* (probably presented to queen Elizabeth on her fortieth birthday). His numerous anthems for the Anglican church generally exhibit greater polyphonic simplicity, yet are among his most expressive works (e.g. the *Lamentations*). He was also known as a very gifted organist, but a relatively small number of his keyboard works has survived.

[JE]

Tasso, Torquato (1544–95) late Renaissance Italian poet, prose stylist, and literary theorist, author of the epic *Jerusalem Liberated* (1581). Born in Sorrento to his exiled courtier father, his education in court society and literature at Urbino and in law and literary theory at the universities of Bologna and Padua prepared him for a brilliant, yet troubled career as a writer and courtier. In 1565 he became associated with the Este court in Ferrara where he wrote lyrics and the greatest Renaissance pastoral drama, *Aminta* (1573), which embodies the arcadian world of rustic simplicity and unrequited love. He worked continually on his masterpiece *Jerusalem Liberated*, which he completed in 1575 and published in 1581, but remained obsessed that it was never completely satisfactory. The epic tells the story of the Christian capture of Jerusalem in the First Crusade under Godfrey of Bouillon with romantic subplots and chivalric romance tied to an orthodox Counter-Reformation religiosity and a neo-Aristotelian poetics. It became the centrepiece of a late sixteenth-century critical debate on the nature of epic poetry and a comparison with ARIOSTO's *Orlando furioso*. In the course of his revisions, he began to exhibit bouts of violence and madness, a kind of persecution complex that led the duke of Ferrara to confine him in the hospital of S. Anna (1579–86). The Gonzaga prince of Mantua secured his release, but the final ten years of his life were spent in constant wandering throughout Italy, especially

between Rome and Naples, as he reworked and rewrote his epic (a new version, *Jerusalem Conquered*, appeared in 1593), composed religious poetry, and defended his literary revisions in his *Discorsi del poema eroico* (1594). Late Renaissance literary debates, Counter-Reformation austerity, his persona as the peripatetic poet racked by mental illness, romantic loves and persecutions contributed to the legend of a misunderstood genius.

[JM]

Tavera, Juan Pardo de, cardinal (1472–1545) Spanish cardinal and minister of state. Born at Toro (Zamora), a nephew of Diego de Deza, archbishop of Seville and Inquisitor General, he studied locally and at Salamanca. His career, thanks to his family connections, was meteoric. In 1504 he became rector of Salamanca university, later member of the supreme council of the Inquisition, and vicar general of the diocese of Seville, in 1514 bishop of Ciudad Rodrigo, then of Osma and then was translated (1524) to the archbishopric of Santiago. By the same period he was president of the high court of Valladolid, created cardinal 1531, and in 1534 became archbishop of Toledo. He was one of the principal ministers of CHARLES V, became Inquisitor General (1539), was president of the royal council, and one of the regents of the realm during the absences of the emperor from Spain. Enormously wealthy, he left much of his money to maintain the large hospital for the poor he founded in Toledo in 1541.

Telemann, Georg Philipp (1681–1767) German composer. He was the most famous German composer during his lifetime and one of the most prolific composers in European history. As a law student at the university of Leipzig (1701–5), he already stood out as a gifted composer, organist and music director. Subsequently he was employed in Soray (in Poland), Eisenach and Frankfurt am Main. From

1721 until his death he lived in Hamburg as Kantor, music director of the city's main churches, director of the collegium musicum and director of the Hamburg opera. Throughout his career he composed numerous operas, hundreds of sacred dramatic works (cantatas, passions and oratorios), and thousands of works for diverse instrumental ensembles. His intensive activities as director of public concerts and multifarious publications of relatively undemanding works contributed enormously to the cultivation of music among middle-class amateurs. Although his melodious, light-hearted *style galant* was greatly admired by leading musical figures of the period, his reputation declined in the nineteenth century, for he came to be regarded as too superficial in comparison with J.S. Bach.

[JE]

Temple, Sir William (1628–99) diplomat. Of Anglo-Irish origin, he was born in London and travelled widely on the continent during the years of civil war and instability in England. In 1655 he married and went to live in Ireland, returning to England in 1663. In 1665 he received the first of his diplomatic assignments on the continent, being posted to Brussels, where he took his family; at the same time he received a baronetcy. He successfully negotiated the Triple Alliance (1668) with the United Provinces and Sweden against France, and from 1668–70 served as ambassador to the Hague. He spent 1671–4 in retirement at home in England, and dedicated himself to writing some of his most important essays. In 1674 he returned to the Hague, and played a part in the negotiations of the peace of Nijmegen (1678), with which he disagreed. He retired in 1681 to his estate at Moor Park, Surrey, devoting himself to gardening and writing; among his visitors was the young SWIFT, whom he befriended and who acted as his secretary. His most memorable work is the *Observations upon the United Provinces of the Netherlands*

(1672), a brilliant analysis of the politics and society of the country that he knew intimately from his long stay there.

Teresa of Avila (de Cepeda) (1515–82) Spanish mystic and writer. Born in Avila of a rich peasant family of Jewish origin, she entered the Carmelite Order at the age of nineteen. She did not have much of a formal education, devoting all of a very active life to the reform of the order. She founded her first convent at the same time as she completed her spiritual autobiography. This reveals that in her youth she was an assiduous reader of the romances of chivalry. The same theme of the quest, but this time of spiritual perfection, couched in familiar rather than exotic terms, forms the basis of *Camino de perfección* (*The Path to Perfection*), begun 1562, written for the education of her nuns at the request of her confessors. *Las moradas* (*The Mansions*) (1570) is the most fascinating of her visions of the spiritual journey by which the soul, in search of mystic union, travels through seven mansions, each set one within another. The narrative is infused with a wealth of illustrative metaphor drawn, as was her practice, from everyday experience. Hers is a wholly personal prose style, impulsive, sometimes illogical, the train of thought broken by digression, the spelling inconsequential, all driven towards illuminating the inexpressible. The writings of Teresa, to a greater extent than those of Luis de LEÓN, show how individual religious initiatives could escape the control of the Counter-Reformation. Canonised in 1621, in 1627 she was declared by PHILIP IV patroness of Spain.

[BT]

Tetzel, Johann (*c.*1465–1519) German ecclesiastic. Son of a goldsmith from Pirna (Saxony), he studied at Leipzig and entered the Dominican order (1488). He is remembered in history for being director of the campaign 1516–17 to raise funds in Germany for the building of St Peter's in

Rome, through the preaching of indulgences, a campaign that provoked LUTHER to draw up his 95 theses against indulgences. Tetzel retorted with 122 theses, for which the pope rewarded him with a doctorate. From the Catholic point of view it was the vulgarised popular view of indulgences – the belief that cash payment assured salvation – that Luther was correct to attack. Implicit in Luther's criticism, as Tetzel saw, was a questioning of other Catholic tenets.

Thomasius, Christian (1655–1728) German lawyer and philosopher. Born in Leipzig, he was educated at the universities of Leipzig and of Frankfurt an der Oder, where he received (1679) his doctorate. He began lecturing at Leipzig in 1682, then in 1690 moved to Halle, where he helped to found the university and became professor of law (1694), later becoming rector there. Rejecting the orthodox emphasis on revelation as the basis of truth, and the church as the basis of conduct, he sought to base conduct on natural reason and ethics; in this respect he was a sceptic. Rejecting any pretension of founding a system, he presented his ideas as a mere guide or 'introduction', a word which appears in the titles of various works published between 1688 and 1696. However, in about 1694 he had a deep religious crisis, disavowed his previous writings, and maintained that only God's grace gives access to truth. In works of 1696–7, dealing with Church–state relations, he also affirmed the necessity for religious toleration. The period 1694–1705 is generally seen as his Pietist phase, and these views quickly became both popular and dominant in German universities of the mid-eighteenth century.

Thou, Jacques-Auguste de (1553–1617) French historian. Of noble origin, son of a president of the parlement of Paris, he did his studies in law and became councillor of the parlement (1577), then councillor of state, playing an important part in the legislation of the period, notably the preparation of the Edict of Nantes (1598). From 1604 he began publishing his *Historia sui temporis* (History of My Times), an ambitious work, written in Latin, that covered events in all Europe from about 1543 and established itself as the major historical work of its time; in 1734 it was translated into French. He also wrote his *Memoirs*, translated in 1711.

Tiepolo, Giovanni Battista (1696–1770) Italian painter and etcher, the most brilliant painter of decorative fresco cycles. His father was a Venetian merchant; his wife's brothers were the view painters Francesco and Giovanni Antonio Guardi. Two of his nine children, Giovanni Domenico and Lorenzo also became artists, and were his workshop assistants. Joining the Venetian painters' confraternity in 1717, at twenty one, his patrons soon included the doge Giovanni II Cornaro; archbishop Dionisio Dolfin of Udine; the Swedish ambassador, count Carl Gustav de Tessin; the prince-bishop Karl Philipp von Greiffenklau, for whom he frescoed the *Kaisersaal* of the Würzburg Residenz (1750–3); and CHARLES III of Spain, in whose service he was working when he died in Madrid. His work went rapidly out of style after his death, due largely to the neo-classic manner advocated by Anton Raphael Mengs, but he began to be reappreciated about 1900, and particularly after 1945, when the brilliance of his prints and drawings began increasingly to be recognised.

[JH]

Tilly, Albert-Octave de T'serclaes (1646–1715) A military commander in Flanders before being invited to Spain (1703) to serve the new king, PHILIP V. Appointed commander of the royal guards, he was created grandee of Spain (1705), viceroy of Navarre (1706), and second in command of the royal armies in Aragon and Catalonia (1709). He died in Barcelona shortly after it was recovered for the Bourbons.

Tilly, Johann T'serclaes, count of (1559–1632) professional soldier. From an illustrious Brabant family, he intended to make his career in the Jesuit order, then entered the army instead (1574) and served in the Spanish forces in the Netherlands under Alessandro FARNESE. After serving in other areas, including France, he entered the service of the emperor, distinguished himself in Hungary against the Turks and was made a field-marshal (1605). In 1610 he was appointed by MAXIMILIAN I WITTELSBACH of Bavaria as head of the army of the newly created Catholic League, in which role he commanded the forces that defeated the Bohemians at the White Mountain (1620). He pursued the defeated forces into the Palatinate, and in 1622 stormed Heidelberg. As reward for his services, the emperor created him a count of the empire (1622). The principal Catholic general in Germany prior to WALLENSTEIN, he defeated the Protestant princes then crushed the Danes at Lutter (1626); but he was also in part responsible for the brutal sacking of Magdeburg (1631), and was defeated by GUSTAV II ADOLF VASA at Breitenfeld (1631). He was killed in a subsequent skirmish at the river Lech. His family continued to produce notable soldiers, among them Albert-Octave de T'serclaes TILLY.

Tintoretto (Jacopo Robusti) (1519–94) Italian painter Jacopo Robusti, the only major Venetian painter of the sixteenth century who was actually born in Venice, was the leading painter of Venetian Mannerism. He became an independent master by 1539, leaving Venice only once or twice in his life, for brief visits to Mantua (September, 1580) and possibly to Rome (1547?). Nicknamed 'Tintoretto' because his father was a silk-dyer, he married the daughter of the Dean of the Scuola San Marco (c.1555), by whom he had eight children, three of whom – including a daughter, Marietta – became painters. Praised by Pietro ARETINO (in letters to TITIAN, dated 1545 and 1548), but reviled by VASARI, he was known for his ability to work with unusual speed (some thought this an admirable trait; others not). Other distinguishing traits were his low prices, and his dramatic use of foreshortening and of unusual or simply irrational angles of vision, as seen in such works as the *St Mark Rescuing a Slave* (1548) the *Finding of the Body of St Mark* (after 1562) (both Venice, Accademia). He also made frequent use of novel effects of lighting, particularly in his many paintings of *The Last Supper* (e.g. the one in the church of San Giorgio Maggiore, in which lamplight and divine light are both at work). His most notable painting are on panels of walls and ceilings in the Scuola di San Rocco, the Doges' Palace, and in a large number of the churches of Venice. His art was to exert a strong influence on El GRECO, who emulated both his dematerialised figures and his experimental uses of space and light.

[JH]

Titian (Tiziano Vecellio da Cadore) (c.1488/90–1576) Italian painter active in Venice. Born in Pieve di Cadore, in his approximately seventy years of professional activity Titian became the most sought-after painter of portraits, mythologies and religious works in Europe – his fame enhanced by the press-agentry of his close friend ARETINO and the political power of his patrons. In 1513 he refused Pietro BEMBO's invitation to come to Rome to serve as court painter to pope LEO X, petitioning instead to serve the Venetian Republic, and was named official painter to the Venetian state three years later. His Venetian works include the enormous (nearly 21 feet tall) *Assumption of the Virgin* in the Church of S. Maria Gloriosa dei Frari (completed 1518), and the altar of the Immaculate Conception in same church – the city's largest. Other patrons included Alfonso d'ESTE of Ferrara; the duke of Mantua, Federigo Gonzaga and the duke of Urbino, Francesco delle Rovere (his brother-in-law); and most importantly the emperor CHARLES V, who made him a knight of the Golden Spur, count Palatine, count of the Lateran Palace, of the Consiglio Aulico and of the Consistoro, conceding to his sons the title of noble of the empire. Charles' sister MARY OF HUNGARY; his brother FERDINAND I, and his son PHILIP II of Spain provided further splendid commissions. His earliest works for Gonzaga and Charles V were largely portraits, which brought him to the attention of pope PAUL III, for whom he worked in the 1540s. The emperor's invitation to his painter 'primero' to attend the Diet at Augsburg resulted both in the splendid equestrian portrait of Charles at the Battle of Mühlberg (1548; Madrid), and a lifetime of Habsburg commissions. Among his most glorious works are the twenty-five large canvases painted for Philip, among them the *Venus and Adonis* and *Danae* (Madrid); the *Diana and Actaeon* (London); *Diana and Callisto* (Edinburgh); and the *Rape of Europa* (Boston, Gardner Museum). These late mythologies are characterised by an ever greater freedom of brushwork and richness of colour, as well as by the knowledge of Roman and Hellenistic antiquities which he had gained on a brief visit to Rome (October 1545–March 1546), when his guide was the aged MICHELANGELO and the latter's disciple VASARI. His ability as portraitist was, and is, unrivalled, and his compositions and his brushwork were to be imitated throughout the century to come by such painters as RUBENS, REMBRANDT and VAN DYCK, none of whom was old enough to have known him in life, but all of whom envied him his status as 'Prince of Painters'.

[JH]

Toland, John (1670–1722) Irish writer and deist. Born in Derry and a Catholic,

he became a Protestant at sixteen, and went to be educated in Scotland, then in Leiden, where he spent two years. He then spent a year (1694–5) studying on his own account in libraries at Oxford, where he wrote his *Christianity Not Mysterious*, published in 1696. The essay raised a storm of controversy, and was ordered burnt by the House of Commons in 1697. However, he obtained support from freethinking Whigs: in 1699 the duke of NEWCASTLE employed him to edit the memoirs of Denzil Holles, and in 1700 HARLEY (later earl of Oxford) encouraged him to edit HARRINGTON'S *Oceana*. He also obtained help from the earl of SHAFTESBURY. In 1701 he may have modified his views, for he referred to his essay of 1696 as a youthful 'indiscretion'. In 1707–10 he made a visit to Germany, Bohemia and Holland. After returning to England he wrote political tracts which helped him to make a living, but he died poor. Remembered chiefly as a freethinker, he was a man of considerable intellectual ability.

Torcy, Jean-Baptiste Colbert, marquis de (1665–1746) French statesman. Son of Colbert de CROISSY and nephew of the great COLBERT, he studied law and was trained by his father to succeed him. In the 1680s he was sent on diplomatic missions all over Europe, to Spain, Scandinavia and Vienna; he also visited Germany and England, and made a lengthy stay in Italy, with the intention of learning foreign languages and studying the condition of other nations. From 1691 he participated in government, and followed his father as secretary of state for foreign affairs (1696), a post he exercised for three years under the care of his father-in-law POMPONNE, before assuming full authority. He played a leading role in the events leading to the acceptance of the crown of Spain for LOUIS XIV's grandson PHILIP V, and directed the diplomacy of the war of the Spanish Succession with great ability. He also signed the peace treaties which ended the war. During the regency after Louis XIV's death he played a diminishing part in affairs, retiring in 1721. He was the first to create an archive for the papers of the ministry of foreign affairs, now housed in the Quai d'Orsay. His valuable *Mémoires* were published posthumously, in 1756.

Torquemada, Tomás de (1420–98) Spanish Inquisitor General. He entered the Dominican order in Valladolid, and was later appointed prior of the friary of Santa Cruz in Segovia (1452–74), as well as confessor to FERDINAND II OF TRASTÁMARA and ISABELLA THE CATHOLIC. In 1482 he was chosen as one of the seven new inquisitors to continue the work of the recently founded (1480) Inquisition. In 1483 he was chosen to head it as Inquisitor General, playing a key role in introducing it into the realms of the crown of Aragon. There is no evidence that he was responsible for the markedly anti-semitic character of the new tribunal, but it is certain that his advice was instrumental in bringing about the expulsion of the Jews (1492). He drew up a comprehensive code of Instructions (1484 onwards) that gave the tribunal its administrative structure for the next century.

Torricelli, Evangelista (1608–47) Italian mathematician and physicist. A pupil of and secretary to Benedetto Castelli, he served briefly as assistant to the elderly Galileo GALILEI and succeeded him as mathematician to the Duke of Tuscany in 1642. His principal mathematical publication was the influential *Opera geometrica* (1644), which spread knowledge of Cavalieri's new geometry of 'indivisibles' whilst combining it with classical methods. Meanwhile, in conducting experiments on air-pressure he found the use of water impractical, employed mercury instead and discovered the principle of the mercury barometer (1643), which was thus commonly known as the 'Torricellian tube'. Unlike some of his contemporaries,

he believed that a vacuum was created above the mercury in the inverted tube. He was also responsible for the law explaining the flow of liquid through small holes, now known by his name.

[FW]

Torstensson, Lennart, count (1603–51) Swedish general. Trained as an artillery commander under GUSTAV II ADOLF VASA, he succeeded BANÉR in 1641 as head of the Swedish forces in Germany (1641–6) during the Thirty Years War. Victor at the battle of Breitenfeld (1642), he led the Swedish army against the Danes in the war (1643–4) that led to the treaty of Brömsebro. He was created field-marshal in 1641 and member of the royal council, and count in 1647.

Tourville, Anne Hilarion de Cotentin, count de (1642–1701) French admiral. From the age of eleven he spent all his active life in the navy, mainly in the Mediterranean fighting the Barbary corsairs. After a career as officer, in 1689 he was made vice-admiral of the Levant and then head of the naval forces fighting England and Holland. He defeated admiral Herbert's fleet off Beachy Head (1690), but was himself defeated in the decisive battle of La Hougue (1692). Created marshal despite the reverses, he won another victory at Cape St Vincent (1693).

Townshend, Charles, 2nd viscount (1674–1738) English politician. Active in politics from the time he entered the Lords in 1697, he supported the Whigs and in 1707 entered the privy council. As ambassador to the United Provinces 1709–11 he secured the Barrier Treaty (1709) by which English troops helped garrison the frontier against France. Throughout his career he was particularly active in matters concerning foreign policy. Appointed secretary of state for the north 1714–16, he was in charge of the suppression of the Jacobite rising of 1715. Member of the government led by WALPOLE in 1721, he was subsequently pushed out in 1730. In retirement on his estate in Norfolk, he dedicated himself to agriculture, his particular claim to fame being the introduction of large-scale turnip culture as a fodder crop for animals, for which he became known as 'Turnip' Townshend.

Trauttmansdorf, Maximilian von (1584–1650) Austrian diplomat. Son of a leading minister of state of the Habsburg court at Linz, Inner Austria, his early career was in the army in Hungary and in the Spanish Netherlands. Appointed to the Imperial Aulic council in 1612, he was later appointed to the Imperial household, and from 1637 till his death was head of the privy council. He was employed mainly as a diplomat to deal with the political affairs of the Habsburg dynasty, and was their single most important minister during the Thirty Years War. He gained for FERDINAND II the alliance with the Catholic League and Bavaria; concluded peace (1622) with BETHLEN GÁBOR of Transylvania; arranged the question of the Palatinate after the White Mountain; and after WALLENSTEIN's assassination in 1634 (in which he had no part) emerged as chief minister in Vienna. He negotiated the peace of Prague (1635) with Saxony. His most outstanding role was as Imperial plenipotentiary in the negotiations for the peace of Westphalia, in which he participated from 1645 to 1647.

Tromp, Maarten Harpertszoon (1597–1653) Dutch admiral. He went to sea as a child, and rose through the ranks of the navy, receiving his first commission as captain in 1624. In 1636 he was appointed lieutenant admiral of Holland, ranking second only to the stadholder. His most famous victory was that over the Spanish fleet of Antonio de Oquendo in the battle of the Downs (1639) in the Channel. The event is normally taken to mark the end of Spain's naval power in the narrow seas, and Tromp was knighted

by both LOUIS XIII of France and CHARLES I of England. He rendered further services to France by helping them to take Dunkirk, the centre of intensive pirate activity backed by Spain, in 1646. In the Anglo–Dutch naval wars, he defeated BLAKE in an incident in December 1652 off Dover, but was defeated off Portland (March 1653), and died in a naval engagement against ships commanded by MONCK.

Tull, Jethro (1674–1741) English farming innovator. Born in Berkshire, and educated at Oxford and the Inns, where he was called to the bar in 1699, he did not take up the practice of law but turned to farming on his estates in the Midlands. Around 1701 he perfected his sowing drill, to which he owes his fame. In 1711–14 he travelled extensively in France and Italy to improve his health, while taking note of agricultural practice on the continent, and some years later published several essays dealing with agricultural improvement. After his death his writings were published in French, and influenced VOLTAIRE's gardening methods at Ferney.

Turenne, Henri de la Tour d'Auvergne, viscount (1611–75) French marshal. Second son of Henri de la Tour d'Auvergne, duke de BOUILLON and prince de Sedan, and grandson of WILLIAM I of Orange through his mother, he came from a firmly Protestant background and served when young in the Dutch army of MAURICE OF NASSAU. From 1630 he continued his service against Spain as an officer in the French armies, both on the Rhine and in Italy, winning the rank of marshal of France in 1643. In the last stages of the Thirty Years War, he won a victory at Nördlingen (1645) (the second great battle at this city during the war) against the Imperial army. After the peace of Westphalia (1648), he supported the rebellious noble party in the Fronde, forcing the royal court to flee Paris; but in 1651 was reconciled with LOUIS XIV and became the king's chief general against the Frondeurs of CONDÉ. He then took up the war against Spain, winning the decisive victory of the Dunes (1658) in the Netherlands. He was France's chief general in the subsequent war of Devolution. Killed in action during the wars on the Rhine, he was buried beside the kings of France in the church at St Denis, and later moved at Napoleon's behest to the Invalides. His conversion in 1668 to the Catholic faith, brought about by BOSSUET, was a major loss to the Protestant cause in France.

Tyndale, William (*c.*1494–1536) English translator of the Bible. Born of a gentry family on the Welsh borders, he was educated at Oxford (where the humanist John COLET was teaching) and then subsequently at Cambridge (where ERASMUS was lecturing in 1511). He took holy orders, and became employed as tutor in Gloucestershire, where he became convinced of the need to communicate the Scriptures to ordinary readers. In 1523 he moved to London, where he first encountered Lutheran opinions. Seeking a freer environment for his proposed translation of the Bible, he went in 1524 to Germany, where he personally met LUTHER and subsequently published his uncompleted work in 1526. Copies of the translation reached England, where they were denounced by the bishops and ordered burnt. The English authorities tried to arrest him, but he moved to Marburg, where he had the protection of PHILIP OF HESSE. By this time his views were developing in a radical direction, towards those of ZWINGLI. In 1528 he published in Marburg his most important original work, *The Obedience of a Christian Man*, which stressed the authority of Scripture over that of the Church, and emphasised the duty of obedience to the state, two of the basic principles that made the Reformation possible. The work invited a refutation by Thomas MORE in 1529, to which Tyndale replied in 1531 with his *An Answere unto Sir Thomas Mores Dialoge*; the controversy between the two continued with further writings down to 1533. Meanwhile, HENRY VIII had also found reason to disapprove of Tyndale, who was opposed to the king's divorce. Attempts to kidnap him ended in Tyndale being betrayed in 1535 and taken prisoner to the Netherlands, where he was sentenced as a heretic by the authorities in 1536 and burnt at the stake. According to the martyrologist John FOXE, his last words were, 'Lord, open the king of England's eyes!'

Tyrconnel, Richard Talbot, earl of (1630–91) From the leading Anglo-Irish Catholic family of Talbot, he served the royalist cause in the civil war and after CROMWELL's invasion of Ireland left for Spain and Flanders, where he met James, duke of York. After the Restoration, he became a confidant of the duke, served under him in naval campaigns and enjoyed social life in London; he also married, and lived for several years in Dublin, where he acquired estates. When York became king as JAMES II, Talbot was appointed lord deputy of Ireland (1685–8) and created earl. He actively pursued the Catholic cause in Ireland, welcomed James to the country when the king was dethroned in England, and led the subsequent unsuccessful military campaigns to preserve the Stuart throne. He died of illness during the campaign around Limerick.

U

Uceda, Cristóbal de Sandoval y Rojas, duke of (d.1624) Spanish minister of state. Eldest son of the duke of LERMA, chief minister of PHILIP III of Spain, he was groomed by his father as his successor in power, and given the title of duke. But relations between father and son were poor, and the young duke allied with other nobles to displace his father (1619), becoming for a while chief minister to the king, at whose death (1621) he lost power and went into exile on his estates. In the subsequent ministry of OLIVARES, he was recalled to office briefly as viceroy of Catalonia, but was subsequently arrested and imprisoned in Alcalá, where he died.

Ulrike Leonora (1688–1741) queen of Sweden 1719–20. Youngest daughter of CHARLES XI VASA, she acted as regent during the absence of CHARLES XII VASA (1713–14). In 1715 she married Frederick of Hesse-Kassel, and took possession of the crown after the death of Charles XII. She ceded the crown to Frederick in 1720.

Urban VIII (Maffeo Barberini, 1568–1644) pope 1623–44. Of noble birth, he was educated by the Jesuits in Florence. Sponsored by his uncle, an apostolic protonotary, he studied at the Jesuit Collegio Romano in Rome before receiving his doctorate in law at Pisa in 1589. He entered papal service with numerous diplomatic offices and rose to become bishop of Spoleto. In his long papal reign during the Thirty Years War (1618–48), he tried to remain neutral, although pro-French sympathies surfaced as a way to gain independence from Habsburg dominance in Italy. In Italy he consolidated the Papal States with the acquisition of the duchy of Urbino. In the Church, he established the Collegium Urbanum for training missionaries and opened China and Japan once again to missionary activity. He condemned Jansenism in France and prohibited slavery in the New World, but he also condemned Galileo GALILEI. In the arts, he patronised BERNINI above all others. He continued the practice of ruling through a cardinal nephew and promoted his family in open nepotism, which met with the opprobrium of the people of Rome.

[JM]

Ursins, Marie Anne de la Trémoille, princess of (1642–1722) French court lady. Married to the prince of Chalais (1657), and after his demise to Flavio Orsini, duke of Bracciano (1675), on the latter's death in 1698 she returned to live in France, using the name Ursins (Orsini). Appointed head of the household of the new queen of Spain in 1701, Marie Louise of Savoy, she dominated the king and queen, and influenced most aspects of government policy in the years of French influence during the war of the Spanish

Succession. On the death of Marie Louise she was appointed head of the household of the new queen (1714), Elizabeth FARNESE, whom she attempted to dominate, which led to her immediate dismissal. She retired to live in Rome. Her extensive correspondence has been published.

V

Valdés, Alfonso de (1500–32) Spanish humanist. With his brother Juan de VALDÉS he was the best known of six children of a noble of Cuenca; though it is usually affirmed that they were twins, this seems unlikely. Alfonso first emerged when he went to Germany in 1520 with the secretarial team supporting CHARLES V, and in 1526 was appointed imperial secretary for Latin to the emperor. He was an enthusiastic supporter of ERASMUS, with whom he made contact in the mid-1520s, when he sent him information on matters in Spain. In 1527, after the troops of the emperor horrified Europe by sacking the city of Rome, he wrote his well-known *Dialogue on the Events in Rome*, which circulated in manuscript and was not published until 1529. He went to Italy and Germany with Charles V (1529–32), and played a role as negotiator with the Protestants at the Diet of Augsburg. He died of the plague in Vienna.

Valdés, Fernando de (1483–1568) Inquisitor General. A native of Asturias, he studied canon law at Salamanca, then entered the service of cardinal CISNEROS and from the 1520s enjoyed the confidence of CHARLES V. He was made bishop of Oviedo (1532) and president of the high court (chancellery) of Valladolid (1535), then in 1539 was moved to the bishopric of Sigüenza and made president of the royal council, a post he held till

1546. In that year he was created archbishop of Seville and later Inquisitor General (1547). He was thus one of the most powerful men in the country, and one of those appointed to advise prince Philip when he became regent of Spain in 1544. Valdés helped to introduce fundamental changes in the financing and organisation of the Inquisition, and was also directly responsible for the first Spanish Index of prohibited books (1559). Faced by a decline in his position at court, he made use of the discovery of groups of Protestants in Castile (1558) in order to reaffirm his role. He instituted a rapid repression of heresy, and brought about the arrest of the archbishop of Toledo, CARRANZA (1559). An uncompromising conservative, he did more than anyone to establish an administrative structure for the Inquisition.

Valdés, Juan de (1509–41) Spanish humanist. Son of a noble of Cuenca, Juan was brought up in Spain, and in the 1520s was a member of the household of the marquis de Villena, where he had links with the illuminists (*alumbrados*). He studied at Alcalá 1526–31, and corresponded with Erasmus. In 1529 he published his important *Dialogue of Christian Doctrine*, a spiritual work closely influenced by Erasmus and to some extent also by Luther. When the Inquisition began to take an interest in his writings, he went to Rome, where from 1531 he acted as imperial agent at the papal court. He finally settled in Naples (1535), where he was in contact with and inspired a radical aristocratic group centring round Giulia Gonzaga, and including other prominent religious figures such as OCHINO. He never broke formally with the Catholic Church, but the evidence suggests that he ceased to share its teaching, especially on the question of justification by faith.

Valenzuela, Fernando de (1636–92) Spanish political figure. Born in Naples, son of a Spanish noble officer, he returned to Spain with his widowed mother in 1640 and after various adventures and a fortunate marriage (1661), entered the service (1671) of the queen mother and regent, Mariana of Austria, during the minority of CHARLES II HABSBURG. He rose quickly in her favour, became known as the 'palace ghost' (*duende de palacio*) because of his ubiquity, and received important offices. When the king attained his majority, various nobles, led by don JUAN JOSÉ OF AUSTRIA, engineered plots to get rid of him. The favourite continued to flourish, and in 1676 was created by the king grandee of Spain and given control of the government. Juan José led a coup d'état in December that year; the favourite was arrested, stripped of his titles and his property confiscated. In 1678 he was exiled for ten years to the Philippines, which he reached a year later. After don Juan's death he returned to Mexico and prepared to return to Spain, but was killed accidentally by the kick of a horse.

Valla, Lorenzo (1407–57) Roman humanist, polemicist, and controversialist. Son of a lawyer in papal employ, he was educated in Latin grammar and rhetoric in Rome for a humanist career in secretarial service. Embittered by his inability to secure a position as a papal secretary, he left Rome in 1530 and taught rhetoric at the university of Pavia where he wrote *On Pleasure*, a dialogue against Stoicism and in favour of epicureanism. After further sojourns in Milan and Genoa, in 1435 he became royal secretary and historian to Alfonso the Magnanimous, king of Naples. He wrote *The Treatise on the Forgery of the Alleged Donation of Constantine*, his best known work today, in 1440 as political propaganda against Pope Eugenius IV, then at war with Alfonso. He used humanist source criticism to prove that this purported papal claim to temporal power was an eighth-century forgery, not a fourth-century original document. During his thirteen years at the Neapolitan court, his other works included: *On Free Will* against the attempt of Boethius to reconcile man's free will and God's foreknowledge; *Dialectical Disputations* against Aristotelian categories and scholastic vocabulary; *Elegancies on the Latin Language* on good Latin style; *Recriminations Against Bartolomeo Facio* on the writing of history; and *Annotations on the New Testament*, which applied humanist philology to scripture. In 1448 he accepted a position as papal secretary to NICHOLAS V and spent his remaining years in papal service. His work on the New Testament, grammar, and anti-scholasticism influenced ERASMUS, and his anti-papal *Donation*, the Protestant movement.

[JM]

Van Dyck, Sir Anthony (1599–1641) Flemish painter and etcher, also active in Italy and finally in England as court painter to CHARLES I. Van Dyck had the misfortune to be overshadowed by RUBENS, whose studio assistant he had been, and whom he survived by only one year. A precocious talent, Rubens himself described Van Dyck as his most gifted pupil and named him as principal assistant in the contract for the decoration of the Jesuit church in Antwerp. In the autumn of 1620 Van Dyck was salaried briefly in London by JAMES I. He next left for Italy, where he stayed for six years, painting portraits as requested – among them the likenesses of Sir Robert and Lady Shirley, and cardinal Guido Bentivoglio, done in Rome; the viceroy Emmanuel Filiberto in Palermo; and numerous portraits of the Genoese aristocracy. He also visited the aged court painter Sofonisba ANGUISCIOLA, whom he consulted about portrait painting while drawing her own likeness in his sketchbook. Returning to Antwerp in 1627 he joined a Jesuit sodality, the Brotherhood of Bachelors, for whom he painted an altarpiece, and began the *Iconography* series of intaglio portraits of famous men. He was given a court appointment for his portrait of the archduchess ISABEL. At the Dutch court in The Hague that winter he did portraits at the court of FREDERICK HENRY and his wife. In 1632 he was in England again, and on 5 July was knighted by CHARLES I and made 'principal painter in ordinary' to the court. He was also permitted to share the royal summer residence at Eltham, Kent, where he made the landscape drawings and watercolours that were to influence the English watercolourists of the following century. Van Dyck totally redesigned the royals according to a sleek and languid new standard of dress and posture, managing to make a beauty of even the buck-toothed queen HENRIETTA MARIA and an elegant figure out of the diminutive and bandy-legged Charles, the first British monarch to be portrayed on horseback. In 1639 he married Mary Ruthven, one of the queen's ladies-in-waiting. In December 1641 he died, after a lingering illness, and was buried in the choir of Old St Paul's.

Vanbrugh, Sir John (1664–1726) English architect and playwright; with Nicholas Hawksmoor, one of the creators of the socalled 'heroic baroque' style of architecture of the early eighteenth century. The grandson of a Flemish refugee from Ghent, his father was a financier and his mother a niece of Sir Dudley Carleton – social connections that were to stand him

in good stead. During the Anglo-French War he was captured at Calais (1690) and imprisoned in the Bastille for eighteen months as a spy; in 1696 he became a captain of marines, serving until 1698 when his regiment was disbanded. However, in 1696 and 1697 the first two of his ten comedies were produced on the London stage: *The Relapse*, and *The Provok'd Wife*. He was apparently self-taught as an architect, and his career as a builder began most auspiciously with Castle Howard (1700–12) for the earl of Carlisle and, for MARLBOROUGH, Blenheim Palace (1705–16), the latter's reward for his victory over the forces of LOUIS XIV. Carlisle engineered his appointment as Comptroller of the Queen's Works (May 1702), a post that he would hold for life, with the exception of the years 1713–15. In 1715 he received the additional title of Surveyor of Gardens and Waters, and in 1716 he succeeded Christopher WREN as Surveyor of the Royal Hospital, Greenwich. He was knighted by GEORGE II in 1714, having been sent to Hanover previously (1706) to confer the Order of the Garter on the future king.

[JH]

Vane, Sir Henry, the Elder (1589–1655) English Parliamentary figure. From a family of Kentish gentry, he was educated at Oxford and Gray's Inn, knighted in 1611, entered the service of the court and became treasurer of the household of CHARLES I in 1639. He entered Parliament in 1614, and went on diplomatic missions to Holland and Germany in 1629–31. During these years he built up his fortune and accumulated posts of influence, entering the privy council in 1630, and obtaining the rank of secretary of state in 1640. A close supporter of the king, he was usually opposed by STRAFFORD. At Strafford's trial, Vane's evidence that the former in a meeting of the privy council had advised bringing his army over to help the king, proved to be fatal to the earl. Vane was dismissed from his posts, and in

Parliament moved to join the opposition. He held posts of authority with the Long Parliament, and was also returned for CROMWELL's first Parliament, but played no active role in politics.

Vane, Sir Henry, the Younger (1613–62) Eldest son of the preceding, he became a convinced Puritan when young, studied at Oxford and then went to Geneva. In 1635 he went to New England in search of liberty of conscience, and the next year was elected as governor of Massachusetts, but became embroiled in controversies and in 1637 returned to England. Knighted in 1640, he entered Parliament, and became one of the chief opponents of CHARLES I, voting for the execution of STRAFFORD and for the league with Scotland in 1643. His support for toleration and constitutional government earned him hostility from both radicals and royalists; he refused to support the trial and execution of the king. Member of the council of state of the Commonwealth (1649–53), he left the government after the rise of CROMWELL, and was briefly imprisoned (1656). At the Restoration he was excepted from the general amnesty, imprisoned in the Tower and finally executed. One of the great statesmen of his time, supporter of democratic government and religious freedom, he did not attach himself to any party, and consequently found little support when events turned against him.

Vasari, Giorgio (1511–74) Florentine painter, architect, and author of *The Lives of the Artists* (1550; revised 1568). Born of artisanal stock in Arezzo, his talent was recognised at an early age and he was brought to Florence to be educated within the Medici circle. He produced a large body of work and Cosimo I de' MEDICI was his most consistent patron and supporter. His paintings include fresco cycles in the Palazzo Vecchio in Florence (the Room of the 500) and scenes from the life of PAUL III in the Cancellaria in Rome

(the Room of the 100 Days). Architectural works include the Uffizi in Florence and the palace of the Knights of St Stephen in Pisa. He was a great admirer and heavily influence by MICHELANGELO. Overshadowing his own work is his monumental history of art, *Lives of the Most Excellent Architects, Painters, and Sculptors*. Each of its three books opens with a theoretical treatise on the development of periods and styles and follows in the manner of ancient and Renaissance *vite* with critical portraits of the lives and works of Italian artists from Giotto to Michelangelo. The revised edition of 1568 enlarges the number of portraits to include living artists and even himself, but maintains the same didactic goal of shaping and criticising art practices. The key concept is the controlling role of design that unites all three of the visual arts. In keeping with his principles, he was one of the founding members of the Florentine Accademia del Disegno in 1562.

[JM]

Vauban, Sébastien le Prestre, marquis de (1633–1707) French military engineer. His family were lesser nobility. He served in the army of CONDÉ during the Fronde, then entered the royal service and trained as an engineer. In 1658 he directed the sieges of fortresses in the Netherlands, and was later entrusted with reconstruction of French fortresses, notably Dunkirk. During the Dutch War (1672–8) he personally directed, with the king at his side, all the major sieges, and was created field-marshal (1676). In 1678 he was put in charge of all French fortifications, and commenced the building of a protective line of fortresses on France's new borders; among his reformed forts were Strasbourg (1681) and New Breisach (1698). The most outstanding and innovative military engineer of early modern times, his abilities were also employed in the construction of ports and canals; among weaponry reforms he promoted was the use of the socket bayonet. His chief successes were in the war of the League of Augsburg (1688–97), against the Spanish Netherlands. In 1703 he was created marshal of France. His constant travels through France and his untiring interest in all aspects of public policy, led him to oppose the revocation of the Edict of Nantes (1685), and to draw up proposals for tax reform, notably the *Projet de dîme royale* (written 1698, published 1707), which proposed abolishing most existing taxes and imposing instead a 10 per cent general duty on all land and trade from which nobody would be exempt. He also wrote several treatises on fortification. In 1808 his remains were deposited by Napoleon in the Invalides.

Velázquez, Diego Rodriguez de Silva y (1599–1660) Spanish court painter. Although both parents claimed descent from the lower nobility, they allowed him to be apprenticed to the painter Francisco Pacheco. Licensed in 1617, he worked at first (*Old Woman Cooking*, Edinburgh; and *Water Seller*, London, Wellington Museum; both 1618) in the dark Caravaggist manner. In Madrid (1622) he painted the portrait of the poet Gongora. Later, living in the house of Juan de Fonseca, chamberlain to PHILIP IV, he was appointed court painter. By 1627 he had been named Usher of the Chamber, and was RUBENS's escort during the latter's diplomatic mission in Madrid (September 1628–April 1629). Probably at Rubens' urging, he travelled to Italy, remaining for two years. On returning to Madrid his style was totally changed – his palette had become brilliant and his brushwork detached, effects that centuries later would be much admired by the French Impressionists. His status in the royal household rose, first to Constable of the Royal Household (1633), then Assistant of the Wardrobe. On a military campaign in Aragon with Philip (1644) he produced the dazzling *Portrait of Philip IV at Fraga* (New York, Frick Collection). In 1648 he returned to Italy

as Philip's agent, to buy art works for the royal collections. While in Rome he painted the portrait of his Moorish assistant, *Juan de Pareja* (New York, Metropolitan Museum), which was exhibited in the Pantheon to great acclaim, and then was commissioned to portray Innocent X (Rome, Galleria Doria-Pamphili). In 1658 Philip wished to invest him with the Order of Santiago. When repeated applications were denied on grounds of unproven nobility, and two successive papal dispensations from ALEXANDER VII were presented to the Council without result, Philip ennobled him and Velázquez was grudgingly admitted to the Order on November 28, 1659. He wears the red cross of Santiago triumphantly in the *Maids of Honour* (*Las Meninas*, Madrid, Prado), which is both an artful portrait of the royal family and of himself as an intimate functionary of the royal household.

[JH]

Vendôme, dukes de
César de Bourbon (1594–1665) Eldest son of HENRY IV by GABRIELLE D'ESTRÉES, he was legitimised in 1595 and given the title of duke in 1598. In 1609 he married the daughter of the duke de MERCOEUR and later succeeded his father-in-law as governor of Brittany. In the reign of LOUIS XIII he participated in noble conspiracies, and was arrested and imprisoned (1626–30) for plotting with the prince of Chalais. After LOUIS XIII's death, he also took part, together with his son Francis, duke de Beaufort, in the Cabale des Importants (1643) against MAZARIN, with whom he later became reconciled. After the Fronde he was appointed governor of Burgundy (1651).
Louis de Bourbon (1612–69) Son of César de Bourbon, he was duke Mercoeur and then of Vendôme. He was commander of the French forces in Catalonia in 1649; in 1651 he married Laura MANCINI, Mazarin's daughter, and at her death entered holy orders (1657), and became cardinal (1667).

Louis Joseph de Bourbon (1654–1712) Eldest son of Louis de Bourbon, he was governor of Provence (1681) then commanded the French troops in Catalonia (1695-7) and captured Barcelona. During the war of the Spanish Succession he commanded French forces in Italy, but made little headway against the troops of prince EUGÈNE OF SAVOY-CARIGNAN. Serving next in Flanders, he was defeated by the Allies at Oudenarde (1708). Placed at the head of the French forces in Spain from 1710, he won decisive victories at Brihuega and above all Villaviciosa (1710).

Vermeer, Johannes (1632–75) Dutch painter and art dealer. Born in Delft, and baptised in the Reformed church, he was the son of the innkeeper and art dealer Reynier Vos. In 1653 he married Catharina Bolnes (1631–87), a practising Roman Catholic, and was admitted to the Delft Guild of St Luke as a master painter. He was mentioned as successor to Carel Fabritius as Delft's major artist in the eulogy published by Arnold Bon (1668). The Vermeers and their eleven children lived in her mother's home in the 'Papist's Corner' of the city, next door to one of Delft's two hidden Jesuit churches. Vermeer painted fewer than thirty works, and died heavily in debt; however he was elected head of the St Luke's Guild twice (1662-4; 1670-2), and was called to The Hague to give expert testimony regarding twelve Italian paintings that had been placed on the market (his notarised statement declares them to be 'great pieces of rubbish'). He was only forty three years old when he died in December of 1675 and was buried in the (Reformed) Oude Kerk. Anthony van LEEUWENHOEK, inventor of the microscope, was appointed by the court to be executor of his estate. Leeuwenhoek may have ground the lenses for the camera obscura that Vermeer almost certainly used as an aid to perspective construction for such works as the *View of Delft* (The Hague, Maurit-

shuis). Catherina was forced to file a *cessio bonorum* after her husband's death, explaining that, due to the war with France he had been unable to sell the stock of paintings acquired in his capacity as an art dealer. She had been forced to give up twenty six of Vermeer's own paintings to one of his many creditors, and had sold two others to the baker in exchange for a debt of 617 guilders. Leeuwenhoek was able to repossess the twenty-six paintings for the estate and to arrange a public sale. Over Catharina's strenuous objections, *The Art of Painting* (or *Artist in His Studio*; Vienna) was included in the sale, which took place in the Guild Hall of St Luke on March 15, 1677.

[JH]

Vermigli, Peter Martyr (1500–62) Italian religious reformer who joined the Protestants. Florentine born, he became an Augustinian canon and studied at Padua. He was ordained in 1525, taught philosophy and scripture, and studied Hebrew. In 1537 he became abbot of S. Pietro ad Aram, a city monastery in Naples, and frequented the circle of the Spanish mystic exile Juan de VALDÉS. Suspected of heretical views in his preaching, he was allowed to return to Tuscany as abbot of S. Frediano in Lucca. Rather than appear before an inquiry by his order for the introduction of reform doctrine and worship, he fled to Switzerland in 1542. He was a professor of theology at Strasbourg (1542-7), moved to England where he became professor of divinity (1547–53), before returning to his Strasbourg professorship (1553–6). In 1556, he went to Zürich, where he lived as professor of Hebrew and Old Testament until his death in 1562. He propounded ideas contrary to the Old Church on the papacy and the Eucharist, and maintained a commitment to biblical theology and humanism.

[JM]

Vesalius, Andreas (1514–64) Flemish anatomist. He studied at Paris, Louvain and Padua, at the last of which he was promptly appointed professor of surgery. In his publications he used dissections as a source of evidence for criticising some of the beliefs of Galen. His lavishly produced *De humani corporis fabrica* (The Structure of the Human Body) (1543) incorporated unprecedentedly accurate and detailed engravings based upon dissections, which set a pattern for views of the human body for generations thereafter. His approach caused much controversy in its time, and he consequently left academic life to become court physician to the emperor CHARLES V and to his son PHILIP II of Spain. He died whilst returning from a pilgrimage to Jerusalem.

[FW]

Vespucci, Amerigo (1454–1512) Italian banker. A native of Florence, his profession was banking and he was sent by the Medici to direct their operations in Seville. He later claimed that during his years there he participated in several voyages to the New World. It was his narrative of these that inspired the German cartographer Waldseemüller to give the name 'America' to the new continent. Vespucci in 1505 was appointed navigation officer of the House of Trade in Seville.

Vico, Giambattista (1668–1744) Neapolitan lawyer, philosopher, historian and rhetorician. One of eight children of an impoverished bookseller, he attended various schools in Naples, but was largely self-taught and remained tangential to the fashionable Cartesian learning dominant at the time. He found meagre employment as a tutor to noble children, married, and won the poorly paid chair of Latin eloquence at the university of Naples in 1699. His early writing, mostly in Latin, consisted of occasional or commissioned pieces – lectures, inaugural orations, epitaphs, panegyrics, funeral orations and inscriptions, and most important *The Most Ancient Wisdom of the Italians*. His failure to win the chair of civil law (vacated in 1717) in the academic competition of 1723 proved to be the most decisive event in his life. In preparation for the competition, he applied his learning in linguistics, philology, literature, law and history in a Latin treatise on *Universal Law* (1720–2), which contained the seedbed of his pathbreaking thought. Passed over in the competition, he dedicated himself to his new ideas and published in Italian his first edition of *The New Science* in 1525. A second revised edition appeared in 1732 and a definitive third edition was published posthumously in 1744. Vico's *Principi di Scienza Nuova* originally attempted to replace natural law theory. It grew into a completely new system that explains the common nature of nations, the origins of religious and secular institutions including languages and literature, and the principles underlying change – his characteristic idea of *corsi* and *ricorsi*, 'flux' and 'reflux'.

[JM]

Victor Amadeus II (Vittorio Amedeo II) (1666–1732) duke of Savoy 1675–1730, king of Sicily 1713–20 and then of Sardinia 1720–30. Son and successor of Carlo Emanuele II of Savoy, he married (1684) a niece of LOUIS XIV but persisted in an anti-French military policy which merited several defeats, until in 1696 (treaty of Turin) he rallied to France. He defected during the war of the Spanish Succession to the Imperial cause, whose armies under prince EUGÈNE OF SAVOY-CARIGNAN confirmed him in his states, after the victory at the battle of Turin (1706). At the peace of Utrecht he retained Savoy, was granted the duchy of Montferrat and also given the crown of Sicily (exchanged in 1720, at Austrian insistence, for Sardinia) and part of Milan. From this date, because of their lands in the Mediterranean, the rulers of Savoy used the title of king.

Victoria, Tomás Luis de (*c*.1548–1611) Spanish composer. He was the greatest and last composer of the sixteenth-century 'Golden Age' of Spanish sacred polyphony. Born in Ávila and educated in Segovia, he was sent by PHILIP II to further his music studies in Rome (1567). There he was ordained a priest, held several musical posts and was profoundly influenced by PALESTRINA's style. Returning to Spain (*c*.1585), he spent the rest of his life at the service of empress Maria, at the royal convent in Madrid (*Descalzas Reales*). He composed some 200 sacred works (masses, offices for the dead, motets, magnificats, lamentations, hymns and others), which represent the pinnacle of religious fervour in Spanish polyphony of the Counter-Reformation.

[JE]

Vieira, António de (1608–97) Portuguese preacher and defender of the Indian. Born in Lisbon, at the age of six he went with his parents to live in Brazil, in Bahia, where he later joined the Jesuits (1625) and took orders (1634). He rose to fame as a preacher, stirring up his fellow-citizens to defend the country against the invading Dutch (1638). When Portugal rebelled against Spain, he was one of those sent by Brazil to congratulate the new Braganza king, JOHN IV (1641), whose friend and adviser he became. He was appointed tutor to the prince, court preacher, member of the royal council, and employed on diplomatic missions (1646–50) throughout Europe, to France, Holland and Italy. His fiery, apocalyptic sermons, and his brilliant written prose, established him as the leading Portuguese eminence of his day. Suddenly in 1652 he decided to give up this dazzling career, and go back to Brazil as a missionary, because of his deep concern for the fate of the Indians. In Bahia he had already learnt native languages, the Tupi-Guaraní of the Indians and the Kimbundu of the blacks, which he now put to use. With Jesuit colleagues, he went 700 miles up

the Amazon and began a hectic and heroic period of missionary activity, interrupted by a short return to Lisbon (1654–5) when he persuaded the king to grant more liberty to Indians and give the Jesuits a completely monopoly over the missions in Brazil. His work in the Amazon delta had limited success, for he faced the resistance of both Indians and settlers; in 1661 the Jesuits were expelled to Portugal by the authorities. Vieira in 1662 preached his resounding sermon on 'The Missions' before the court, but his influence was now on the wane. Condemned by the Inquisition for his messianic sermons, he was confined to his college for two years (1665–7). He then went to Rome, where he spent six years (1668–73), championed the cause of Portuguese citizens of Jewish origin ('New Christians'), and became confessor to queen CHRISTINA VASA of Sweden. He returned to Bahia in 1681, spent his years writing and still fighting, and died in the Jesuit college.

Villars, Claude-Louis-Hector, duke and marshal of (1653–1734) French soldier. Son of a soldier-diplomat, he made his own military reputation rapidly as a cavalry commander in the war against the Dutch (1672–8) and the war of the League of Augsburg (1689–97). His greatest services were in the war of the Spanish Succession: his campaigns in Germany earned him the title of marshal of France (1702). He subsequently commanded some of the forces fighting the rebel Camisards in southern France, but distinguished himself above all by his defensive campaigns against the victorious MARLBOROUGH. Though defeated at the battle of Blenheim (1704), he was created a duke (1705), and successfully prevented the enemy from crossing the Rhine (1707) into French territory. Despite the severe defeat inflicted on French forces at Malplaquet (1709), he was able to score the last convincing French victory of the war by defeating prince EUGÈNE OF SAVOY-

CARIGNAN at the battle of Denain (1712). This placed France in a more favourable position for the peace negotiations that led to the treaty of Utrecht. He was appointed a member of the regency council in the early years of the reign of LOUIS XV, and during the war of the Polish Succession was sent to command the French forces in northern Italy, where he died of ill-health.

Villon, François (1431–?63) French poet. Originally François de Montcorbier, he adopted the name of his protector. The greatest French poet of the Later Middle Ages, he was born in Paris, became a poor scholar at the university, graduating in 1452. After being accused of murdering a priest, he was banished from the capital and drifted into a vagabond life with a roaming gang of petty criminals. He was arrested and pardoned several times but eventually was condemned to hang in 1463; at this point all traces are lost. He left two collections of verse, the *Petit Testament* (*My Brief Last Will*) (1456) and the *Grand Testament* (*My Longer Last Will*) (1461). Hardly a professional criminal, he allowed circumstance and temptation to waylay him, or so he says in his verse. His poems are not self-pitying; a touch of melancholy, yes, but for the most part graced with wit and lightheartedness. They are set in the traditional modes of ballads and *rondeaux*, treating with striking imagery the commonplaces of love and death. But however commonplace the topic, the language is never banal. As one can well imagine he had no following, and translations into English had to wait for Rossetti and Swinburne in the nineteenth century. And then his reputation grows.

[BT]

Vincent de Paul, St (1581–1660) French religious reformer. Born in Gascony, he was educated by the Franciscans at Dax in the Pyrenees, took holy orders in 1600 and studied at the university of Toulouse.

He went to Rome (1605), and during a trip back to Marseille was captured by Barbary pirates, from whom he escaped after a year (1607). He spent a year in Rome, and went to Paris, where he was befriended by cardinal BÉRULLE, who secured him the post of chaplain to the former queen MARGUERITE OF VALOIS (1609). Considering that Vincent's mission really lay elsewhere, the cardinal advised him to leave the court and work in the country parish of Châtillon-les-Dombes, in the Bresse. Here Vincent developed the main lines of his future activity, among the people. He founded in 1624 the Congregation of the Mission, dedicated to preaching; in 1632 it moved its centre to Saint-Lazare, in Paris. In 1633, together with Louise de MARILLAC, he founded the Daughters of Charity, associations of gentlewomen who undertook charitable work. In recognition of his own experience as a prisoner in the galleys, Vincent established visits to galley prisoners and to imprisoned criminals, as part of the programme of charity (1619). During the destructive years of the Fronde (1648–51) in the Paris region, he and his helpers were outstanding in their ministry to the poor and homeless. Known generally as 'Monsieur Vincent', he was perhaps the most popular saint in French history. He was canonised in 1737.

Vitoria, Francisco de (1486–1546) Spanish theologian, known as the founder of international law. He was born in Vitoria, moved to Burgos where he entered the Dominican order when very young; then went for several years to Paris, where he became a priest, studied philosophy and theology (1509–16) and obtained his doctorate (1522). He returned to Spain to teach at the college of St Gregory in Valladolid (1523–6), and from 1526 till his death he occupied the principal chair of theology at Salamanca. Famed as the founder of the theory of international law, during his lifetime he wrote little and published no book; his fame was entirely posthumous. The work by which he is principally known, the *Relectiones theologicae*, texts of some of his university lectures, was first published in Lyon in 1557. It includes his lecture on the Indians of America (*De indis*), and on the laws of war (*De iure belli*), both given in the same year 1539. It was mainly in the latter work that he defined the rights of nations (*jus gentium*). He headed a group of professors and students who emphasised the role of natural law in the formation both of society and of relations between societies. The sum of relations between societies is the *jus gentium*, giving each nation inherent rights (independence, trade, defence), including the right to wage war when rights are violated.

Vivaldi, Antonio (1678–1741) Italian composer and violinist. One of the foremost composers of the concerto solo and concerto grosso of the late Baroque. From 1703 to 1740 he was employed at the Venetian *conservatorio* of the Pietà (a shelter and school for girls). There he composed numerous vocal and instrumental works for the girls, whose exceptional proficiency drew admiring audiences to their concerts. Concurrently he composed operas for the Venetian stage, as well as instrumental works for various patrons. He also took frequent leaves to stage his operas and conduct concerts in Italy and abroad. His fame as a composer of concertos began to spread especially after the publication of *L'Estro armonico* (opus 3, 1712). He composed about 450 concertos, principally for violin(s) but also for many other solo instruments. Their catchy themes, rhythmic drive, brilliant instrumental techniques, and contrasting colouring are indeed extraordinary, despite occasional criticism of their conventional formulas. The best known are *The Four Seasons* (opus 8, nos 1–4, 1725), which introduce, in addition, programmatic elements. His concertos became the most fashionable instrumental repertoire in Europe during the first half of the eight-

eenth century and left a strong imprint on the works of numerous composers, including J.S. Bach.

[JE]

Vives, Juan Luis (1492–1540) Spanish humanist. He spent most of his life outside Spain, and was regarded by many contemporary European thinkers as the equal of ERASMUS. Born in Valencia, he went to study in Paris (1509–12) then left for Bruges, his permanent home. In Valencia his father, a convert from Judaism, was accused by the Inquisition of relapsing and burnt in 1524; Vives never returned to Spain. In 1517 he was appointed tutor to young Guillaume de CROY, archbishop of Toledo; and seems to have first met Erasmus this year. After the death of Croy in 1517, he had difficulty in finding a sponsor, and one finds him at the Sorbonne, Oxford, Bruges and Louvain, like a sort of wandering scholar. Invited to occupy a chair in Spain in 1522, he went instead in 1523 to England, which he made his base for five years, teaching at Oxford. He cultivated friendships with English humanists and the royal family, but left finally in 1528 when the matter of HENRY VIII's divorce became problematic; he was also in contact with Spanish Erasmians in these years. He was in turn philosopher, philologist, sociologist and pedagogue. His treatise on *De disciplinis* (1531) deals with contemporary learning and the adverse effects of the popular romances of chivalry. He is well-known for his *De institutione foeminae christianae* (*On the Education of a Christian Woman*) (1524, translated into Spanish in 1528). This contained little of traditional anti-feminist prejudice and took women out of their subject role as procreators. Ahead of his time in his sympathetic attitude to the poor and the aged, he rejected the accepted view that madmen were objects of mirth. His *De subventione pauperum* (*On the Relief of the Poor*) (1525) was a pioneering essay which guided several European cities in their policy of distributing charity; and his *De concordia* (1529) echoes Erasmus' writings about war and peace. On human behaviour in general he claimed that man's will, properly guided by reason, could make choices between different courses of action. This set him aside from reformers such as LUTHER. As a citizen of Europe, rather like Erasmus, he wrote all his works in Latin.

[BT]

Voltaire (pseudonym of François Marie Arouet) (1694–1778) French poet, historian, philosopher and pamphleteer. Son of a solicitor, Voltaire was born in Paris. His education was liberal, far removed from the doctrines of the Jesuits or the Jansenists. He occupied briefly a few official posts, but his combative temperament and satiric wit brought about his exile to England (1726–9), which event profitably introduced him to a distinct political and literary climate, including the works of Shakespeare. In England he composed his *Lettres philosophiques*, published 1734. On returning to France he dabbled in history and the theatre before the aforementioned letters obliged him to seek refuge in Lorraine at the residence of Mme de Châtelet. Here he worked incessantly on his history of the reign of LOUIS XIV and his essay on customs and habits (*Le siècle de Louis XIV*, 1751; *Essai sur les moeurs*, 1753). After reconciliation with the crown through the intervention of the duke de Richelieu and Madame de POMPADOUR he was appointed official historian of the realm (1745) and gained a seat in the Académie Française a year later. In 1750 Frederick II of Prussia brought him to Potsdam, but Voltaire soon tired, as he said, of washing the emperor's dirty linen. So he fled to Switzerland and settled in Verney on the shores of Lake Geneva, to 'cultivate his garden' (1759–78). He returned to Paris

in his old age and died shortly after. His published works cover a vast range, covering seventy volumes or more, not to mention his voluminous correspondence which is still being edited today. He provoked anger and admiration in equal measure, and showed merit in everything he attempted: for instance tragedy (*Zaire* 1732, *Mérope* 1743, all in the Racinian mode), the short story (of which *Candide* is the best remembered), and philosophy (in the *Dictionnaire philosophique* 1764). In belief he was a sceptic, a deist rather than an atheist; he hated above all superstition and intolerance. He had enough wit to avoid serious clashes with authority, and enough energy to turn his so-called 'garden' at Verney into a literary empire of which he was the benign designer.

[BT]

Vondel, Joost van den (1587–1679) Dutch poet and dramatist, he was born in Cologne, but spent all his life in Amsterdam. Considered to be the major poet of the Low Countries, he derived his experience of life from the religious debates which raged in that city between Catholics and reformers of all kinds. This experience was soon converted into drama – *Palamedes* (1625). Some ten years later he became the central force in the formation of the national Dutch theatre with the drama *Gysbrecht van Amstel* (1637), which continues to be played every year on the feast of St Sylvester in Amsterdam. He was also a competent translator of the Graeco-Roman classics, and his own poetry covered lyric, didactic and epic genres. It was, however, his Biblical dramas which brought him fame, on themes like Solomon, Jephtha, Adam and Eve, Noah and above all *Lucifer* (1654). Most of his work has been translated into German.

[BT]

W

Wallenstein (Waldstein, Valdšteyn), Albert (Albrecht) von (1583–1634) Czech military commander. Son of minor Czech nobility of Lutheran persuasion, born in eastern Bohemia and orphaned when young, he was educated at the university of Altdorf and later did the grand tour (1600–2) through France and Italy, a journey that may have helped him to convert to Catholicism (1606). His marriage in 1609 to an older and wealthy widow benefited him decisively when she died five years later, leaving him immense estates in Moravia. Through diligent management, he began to turn the estates into a source of income. The proceeds were used by him in 1617 to raise troops for the future emperor FERDINAND II in a campaign against Venice. His breakthrough came after the battle of the White Mountain (1620) in Bohemia. Ferdinand II appointed him governor of Bohemia and provisioner of the army, and later granted him the title of duke of Friedland (1625). Wallenstein also improved his social position by marrying (1623) a daughter of the influential Harrach family. From this time he dominated the military scene in Germany. His forces were used to stave off Danish intervention, he defeated the troops of MANSFELD at the bridge of Dessau (1626), and after he had overrun the entire north of Germany he was rewarded with the title (1629) of the deposed duke of Mecklen-burg. Appointed also 'general of the Ocean Sea' (1628), he had plans to establish himself on the Baltic coast. His critics and enemies feared he was getting too powerful, particularly when it seemed his armies might be used to implement the emperor's Edict of Restitution (1629), and persuaded Ferdinand in the Diet at Regensburg (1630) to revoke his commission. He was recalled, however, from his Bohemian retirement in 1631 to counter the threat from GUSTAV II ADOLF VASA. After the battle of Lützen (1632), doubts were again raised about his role. Aware that the emperor was planning to remove him, he obtained a pledge of loyalty from his generals. The plot against him proceeded, and at Eger (Bohemia) he and his companions were murdered by a group of mainly Irish and English mercenaries in the pay of the emperor. His dramatic military career, his meteoric rise and fall, and his impenetrable personality (he believed in the forces of destiny), have inspired playwrights (notably Schiller in *Wallensteins Ende*, 1798) and historians alike. He must also be seen within his local context as a supporter of Czech national aspirations.

Wallis, John (1616–1703) English cleric and mathematician. During the 1640s he was secretary of the Westminster Assembly and demonstrated mathematical abilities by deciphering coded royalist despatches intercepted by the parliamentarians. He was consequently appointed Savilian Professor of Geometry at Oxford in 1649, and held the post until his death in 1703. As an early member of the Royal Society, he attempted to establish a comparable Oxford Philosophical Society; but it proved short-lived. His many publications included: *Arithmetica infinitorum* (Oxford, 1655), which is regarded as marking an important stage in the pre-history of the calculus; a series of tracts in a protracted dispute with Thomas Hobbes; and *A Treatise of Algebra* (London, 1685), which gave the subject a strictly English historical pedigree. Most of his mathematical works were reprinted in the collected *Opera mathematica* (Oxford, 1693–9).

[FW]

Walpole, Sir Robert, 1st earl of Orford (1676–1745) English statesman. Son of a Norfolk squire, he studied at Eton and Cambridge, succeeded to his father's estates in 1700 and entered the Commons in 1701 as member for the family seat of Castle Rising. In 1702 he was member for King's Lynn, which he represented for the rest of his career in the Commons. He became secretary for war in the Whig ministry of 1708 and treasurer of the navy (1711–12), a post from which he was dismissed by the incoming Tory ministry on accusations of misconduct (he was impeached and sent briefly to the Tower). He returned to power with the new Hanoverian dynasty, became paymaster general of the army, then rose to be first lord of the treasury and chancellor of the Exchequer (1715). As chief minister, he collaborated closely with his brother-in-law Charles TOWNSHEND, but had to contend with a strong opposition, which identified itself with the prince of Wales. Through his friendship with the princess of Wales, Caroline of Ansbach, he managed to secure his survival in power when the prince succeeded to the throne as GEORGE II in 1727. Walpole overcame all the political crises of his

time, from the South Sea Bubble in the 1720s to the Jacobite conspiracies of the 1740s, by his great managerial ability in the House of Commons, where he skilfully maintained political alliances. He also used royal patronage to consolidate his regime. His policies have been summarised as: tranquillity at home (with low taxes), and the French alliance abroad. He kept England out of wars (such as that of the Polish Succession) that did not serve its interests. The opposition directed an effective campaign of political literature, notably in the weekly *The Craftsman*, in which writers such as POPE and FIELDING participated. The war of Jenkyn's Ear (1739), which he did not favour, weakened Walpole's position in Parliament. After losing a Commons vote in 1742, he resigned, and was created earl (he received his knighthood in 1725). Though he did not use the title, he is generally considered as being the first British 'prime minister'. Creator of the Whig supremacy in the country, and the first great manager of party politics, he was described by Dr JOHNSON as 'the best minister this country ever had'.

Walsingham, Sir Francis (*c*.1530–90) English minister of state. Born in Kent, educated at Cambridge and Gray's Inn, he was a firm Protestant, and during the reign of MARY I left for the continent, where he made acquaintances that he later put to good purpose. He entered Parliament in 1563 and soon after was working for William CECIL in building up a network of intelligence agents. He uncovered (or provoked) the RIDOLFI conspiracy in 1569, became ambassador to France (1570–3), and was in Paris during the massacre of St Bartholomew's. In 1573 he entered the privy council and became secretary of state, a post he retained till his death; he was knighted in 1577. He took part in subsequent diplomatic missions, but his chief contribution lay in the development of an active pro-Protestant foreign policy, against the interests of Spain and the papacy. He diligently directed the espionage system both in England and abroad, uncovering in 1586 the BABINGTON plot that fatally implicated MARY STUART, and securing reliable information about Spain's preparation of the great Armada of 1588. He had an active interest in colonial expansion to America, and was patron to the arts; his daughter married Sir Philip SIDNEY.

Warbeck, Perkin (1474–99) pretender to the English throne. A native of Flanders (he was born in Tournai), he went in 1491 to Ireland, where opponents of the regime in England trained him in the role of Richard duke of York, one of the princes assassinated in the Tower under RICHARD III. He quickly received support on all sides, and in 1492 went to Flanders, where he was recognised as her nephew by Margaret of Burgundy, sister of EDWARD IV. Supported by the Yorkist opponents of HENRY VII, he took the title of Richard IV, tried without success in 1495 to invade England and then went to Scotland (1495–7), where the king supported him. At the end of 1497 he invaded the west of England but was taken prisoner and paraded through the streets of London. After an attempt at escape, he was put in the Tower, where he continued plotting; he was tried with his accomplices, and hanged at Tyburn.

Ward, Mary (1585–1645) English Catholic educationist. Born into a leading Catholic family from near Ripon, she joined the order of Poor Clares at St Omer in 1606, but felt her future was in England, where she returned and with a small group of supporters began her ministry, visiting the country several times before 1618. In St Omer she found colleges for English girls and for the poor, with other similar colleges founded by 1621 in Liège and Cologne. From 1621–5 she was in Rome, vainly seeking official backing for her foundations. From 1625

she set up colleges in Germany and Austria, but had problems with the authorities, and eventually Rome pressurised her to change the religious nature of her order (which she had modelled directly on the Jesuits) into one based on personal vows only. In 1639 she returned to England and gained the support of the queen, HENRIETTA MARIA, for her work; but the political situation blocked success and she died of illness at York. Her aims were to give women an intelligent and religious grounding equivalent to that offered to men at that period.

Warham, William (*c*.1450–1532) English ecclesiastic. Educated at Oxford, he pursued a career in civil law and took part in diplomatic missions before taking up in 1495 a rectorate in Hertfordshire. Further diplomatic duties to Scotland, Burgundy and the Baltic ensued. In 1502 he was consecrated bishop of London, became keeper of the great seal and eventually in 1504 lord chancellor, at the same time as he was appointed archbishop of Canterbury. Prominent in all matters concerning Church and state, in 1515 he gave up his post of chancellor to cardinal WOLSEY. He was reluctant to be dragged into the matter of the projected divorce of HENRY VIII from CATHERINE OF ARAGON, and had even greater problems when after Wolsey's fall the clergy of England were prosecuted by the king's courts (1530) for having recognised the cardinal's status as papal legate. In 1531 he led the clergy in accepting the king's headship of the Church in England, but appended the clause 'in so far as the law of Christ allows'. In 1532 he protested energetically against the measures being taken by Parliament against the pope's authority, but died before the split with Rome was completed.

Watteau, Jean-Antoine (1684–1721) French painter. Inventor of the *fête galante* style featuring well-dressed couples or theatrical characters in park-like settings. He was born in Valenciennes the son of a roofer and came to Paris in 1702, studying with Claude Gillot and Claude Audran III, curator of the Palais Luxembourg. His delicate work, some of it featuring stock characters from the Commedia dell'Arte, was extremely popular and he was accepted into the Academy in 1712, but did not complete his diploma piece – the *Pilgrimage to Cythera* – until 1717. His patrons included the Swedish collector Carl Gustaf Tessin; the wealthy banker and collector Pierre Crozat, and the Duc d'Arenberg. He travelled to England in 1720 where he was treated for tuberculosis by Dr. Richard Mead (1673–1754). Returning to Paris he met Rosalba Carriera, who later drew his portrait in pastels (Treviso, Museo Civico). Watteau was now living with another friend, the art dealer Gersaint, for whose shop he painted one of his best works, *The Sign of Gersaint* – a casual view of the dealer's shop. In spring he moved to Nogent-sur-Marne, where he died of tuberculosis on July 18, aged thirty-six. His style was imitated by both Pater and Lancret, and was posthumously praised by the Goncourts. One version of the *Embarkation for Cythera* was acquired by Frederick the Great (Berlin, Charlottenburg).

[JH]

Wentworth, Peter (*c.*1530–96) English Parliamentarian. He was the eldest son of a family of prominent Buckinghamshire gentry; in the 1550s he married, as his second wife, the sister of Francis WAL-SINGHAM. He entered the House of Commons in 1571, devoting the rest of his life to a Parliamentary career, during which he defended the interests of Puritanism. In 1576 he was committed to the Tower for a few weeks for contempt of the House. In 1587 he actively supported Cope's Puritan bill to reform the Church, and was again sent to the Tower, with four other members. In 1593 he raised in the House the question of the succession to

the throne, a theme on which the queen had prohibited discussion, and was sent by royal command to the Tower, where he died. In his campaigns in the House Peter was seconded by his younger brother Paul (1533–93), who had entered Parliament in 1563 but did not have problems with the administration.

Wesley, John (1703–91) English religious leader. Fifteenth of the nineteen children of the rector of Epworth (Lincolnshire), he was educated at Oxford, where he became a fellow and lecturer, and then entered the Church, receiving orders in 1728. At Oxford he, his younger brother Charles (then studying at the university), and a small group became known as 'Methodists' for their religious practices. In 1735 he and Charles accepted an invitation to preach a mission in Savannah, Georgia; during this journey he made contact with members of the Moravian Brethren. He returned to England in 1738, in which year he had a spiritual experience that changed his life; thereafter he devoted himself to preaching, and in Bristol in 1739 opened the first 'Methodist' chapel. The movement spread rapidly, with Wesley making extensive journeys (over twenty to Ireland) throughout the British Isles. He was said to have preached 40,000 sermons and travelled 250,000 miles during his life. By the 1750s the movement was ready for separation from the Anglican church, but no formal organisation was given to the movement until a deed of declaration in 1784, which sanctioned the creation of their own ministers. Like Wesley himself, the early movement was anti-intellectual and indifferent to social problems; it appealed instead to the emotionally dissatisfied, and grew rapidly. John left remarkable *Journals* covering the years 1735 to 1790, and composed several hymns, many translated from German. His brother Charles (1707–88), who aided him throughout in the development of the movement, is notable as author of some of the most memorable hymns ever written in English.

West, Benjamin (1738–1820) American painter active in England. Largely self-taught, West became the first American-born painter to win international recognition. He was sent to Italy by a group of local Philadelphia merchants in 1760, and studied with Anton Raphael Mengs at the Capitoline Academy in Rome. He was inducted into the artists' academies of Bologna, Florence and Parma, and finally settled in England in 1763, where his studio became a mecca for young American artists abroad, including Gilbert Stuart and John Trumbull. He was one of the founders of the Royal Academy of Arts, and at thirty four he was appointed history painter to George III. In 1792 he succeeded Sir Joshua REYNOLDS as president of the Academy, a post he held until 1805. Major works include a cycle on *The History of Revealed Religion* for the Royal Chapel at Windsor, as well as paintings for the Audience Chamber. He served as the king's purchasing agent at auctions, and was one of the first to paint neo-classical works, also breaking new ground by portraying *The Death of General Wolfe* (1771) in contemporary dress.

[JH]

Weyden, Rogier van der (*c.*1399/1400–64) Flemish painter, praised by both Nicolas of Cusa and RAPHAEL's father, and by the Genoese humanist Bartolommeo Fazio (*c.*1456). He was appointed official painter to the city of Brussels in 1435, an office which he held for life. He is thought to have been trained in Tournai in the workshop of Robert Campin and was declared a master painter there in 1432. He married (1426) Elisabeth Goffaert of Brussels, a woman who had the same family name as Campin's wife, by whom he had four children, all apparently born in Brussels: Peter (1437–68), a painter; Jan (1438–68), a goldsmith; and two older children – Corneille, who became a

Carthusian monk after studying at the University of Louvain, and a daughter Marguerite who died young. He is known to have travelled to Rome in the Holy Year 1450, though neither the length of his stay nor the route of his travel outside Italy is recorded. He died in Brussels in June of 1464 and was interred in the Cathedral of St Gudule. Memorial masses were also held in Tournai under the sponsorship of the painters' guild. He neither signed nor dated his work, and most of the paintings praised by his contemporaries, including the set of Justice pictures for the City Hall in Brussels, have disappeared. Unlike Jan van Eyck, his surviving religious works do not betray knowledge of complex theological issues but are centred on the familiar Christian liturgies of Christmas and Easter. His most notable surviving works include the *Descent from the Cross* (*c.*1435; Madrid); the *Last Judgement* polyptych (*c.*1444–8; 7 feet 4 inches high by nearly 18 inches wide) commissioned by chancellor Nicholas Rolin for the chapel of the hospital he endowed in Beaune; the Bladelin Altarpiece, a Nativity triptych commissioned by the founder of the new town of Middelburg (*c.*1452; Berlin); and the Columba Altarpiece (*c.*1460–2; Munich, Alte Pinakothek) painted for the Wasservass family chapel in Cologne's church of St Columba. His portrait sitters included several members of the immediate family of Philip the Good, including both CHARLES THE BOLD and Antoine the 'Grand Bastard' of Burgundy. He also fulfilled commissions for Juan II of Castile, and for the MEDICI, SFORZA and ESTE families.

[JH]

Weyer, Johann (1550–88) German physician. A disciple of the Renaissance physician Cornelius Agrippa, and a Lutheran, he spent most of his professional life as court doctor to the humanist duke William of Cleves. He is famous as the author of *De Praestigiis Daemonum* (1563), the first substantial attack on the current spate of witch prosecutions. He claimed to show that natural reason disproved the reality of witchcraft, a phenomenon he attributed to the physical illnesses and mental delusions of old, ignorant and poor women. His book achieved great success; within the next five years it went through four Latin editions and came out in French and German. Another book on the same theme was published by him in 1582. However, his views did not gain general acceptance, and were firmly rejected by writers who believed in the reality of witchcraft, such as Jean BODIN.

Whitgift, John (c.1530–1604) Son of a Grimsby merchant, he was educated at Cambridge, where he gained a fellowship. He took holy orders in 1560, and in 1563 became Lady Margaret professor of divinity, and then regius professor (1567–9); in 1571 he used his position of vice-chancellor to secure the deprivation and expulsion of CARTWRIGHT from his posts at Cambridge. From this time he became an uncompromising opponent of dissidents in the Church, engaging in a sharp controversy with Cartwright in the 1570s. In 1577 he was nominated to the see of Worcester, and in 1583 succeeded GRINDAL as archbishop of Canterbury. He immediately set about imposing disciplinary measures on his clergy, including an 'ex-officio' oath obliging them to own up to offences, and in 1586 he backed a severe Star Chamber decree controlling printing. In 1588–9 the secretly printed Marprelate Tracts attacked him; those responsible were arrested and executed. Under JAMES I, he attended the Hampton Court conference (1604) between bishops and the Puritan leaders.

William I (1533–84) ('the Silent') prince of Orange-Nassau and stadholder of Holland 1573–84. He was born at Dillenburg to William, count of Nassau, one of LUTHER's strongest supporters. In 1544 the inheritance of his cousin René of

Nassau devolved upon him, propelling him into eminence as lord of the extensive estates, in the Netherlands and the south of France, of the principality of Orange. A close confidant of CHARLES V, he was invited to the court of Brussels, where he was drawn into a traditional Catholic environment. After the emperor's abdication he fell out with the Habsburg ministers in Brussels, in part because of his marriage in 1561 to a Lutheran princess, Anna of Saxony. Later he began to oppose aspects of PHILIP II's policies. When the duke of ALBA was sent to Brussels with an army to put down opposition (1567), Orange took refuge abroad, and assumed leadership of resistance to Spain after the execution of EGMONT and HORNES, relying for help mainly on France and on the Sea Beggars, who began a concerted uprising against Spain in 1572. Though converting officially to Calvinism in 1573, Orange constantly attempted to unite all groups and faiths into a common national struggle, insisting that 'freedom of conscience is essential to commercial prosperity'. Despite him, the Netherlands split along religious lines; he succeeded in drawing the rebellious northern provinces into a Union of Utrecht (1579), which formally revoked their allegiance to Philip II in 1581. The Spaniards outlawed him and sponsored plans to assassinate him; in response, he published a propagandist Apology (1580), which justified the national struggle and bitterly attacked the person of Philip II. An unsuccessful attempt on his life was made in 1583; a successful one was made by Balthasar GÉRARD the year after.

William II (1626–50) prince of Orange-Nassau and stadholder of Holland 1647–50. Son of the stadholder FREDERICK HENRY and grandson of WILLIAM I, he married (1641) Mary Stuart, daughter of CHARLES I of England, and succeeded on his father's death to his offices and titles. An opponent of the treaty of Münster concluded with Spain in 1648, he came into conflict with the powerful province of Holland, which favoured peace. Relying on the support of the other provinces, he staged a coup in 1650, arrested the leading members of the States of Holland and attempted to occupy Amsterdam. He died suddenly of smallpox before the consequences of the coup could be felt, and was succeeded by his infant son, born eight days after his death.

William III (1650–1702) prince of Orange-Nassau, stadholder of the United Provinces 1672–1702, king of Great Britain 1689–1702. Son of WILLIAM II of Orange, he grew up during the republican regime of the de WITT brothers, and was installed in power when they were overthrown in 1672. Although a mediocre military commander in the fight against the French army which invaded that year, he was a talented negotiator, secured the help of England (one consequence was his marriage in 1677 to CHARLES I's niece, MARY STUART, daughter of the future JAMES II) and eventually obtained from France the peace of Nijmegen (1678). Thereafter he became the chief opponent of LOUIS XIV's expansionist policies, and in 1686 brought about the anti-French alliance known as the League of Augsburg. In 1688 he was invited by the opponents of James II to invade England and seize the crown; he landed at Torbay at the head of an army, and secured a relatively bloodless 'Glorious Revolution'. Appointed joint ruler with his wife Mary in February 1689, he accepted the settlement set out for him (including the Declaration of Rights 1689). In 1690 he crossed over to Ireland to defeat the forces of James II (battle of the Boyne); and then returned to the Netherlands to lead, with scant success, the struggle against Louis XIV. In the following years he was active in his duties both in England and in Holland, where in 1697 he secured the peace of Rijswijk (1697). He was preparing a further military alliance against France over the succession to

the crown of Spain, when he died from injuries after falling off his horse at Hampton Court. During his reign he paid little attention to English politics, devoting himself to his main preoccupation of protecting the United Provinces against the aggression of Louis XIV.

Williams, Roger (c.1604–83) English coloniser of America and protagonist of liberty. Born in London, he was educated at Cambridge, and took orders shortly after though he was unsympathetic to Anglicanism. In 1631 he went to New England with his wife but disagreed with the colonists in Boston, and at the instigation of John Cotton was expelled from Massachusetts in 1635. In 1636 he and his companions founded the settlement of Providence, which they later purchased formally from the native Indians. He returned to England in 1643–4 and obtained an official charter for his colony. Meanwhile he engaged in printed controversy with John Cotton, and on this visit published in London his *The Bloudy Tenent of Persecution for cause of Conscience* (1644), the first major defence of religious toleration written in the western world, appealing for universal toleration of all beliefs; it was ordered burnt by the House of Commons. On a subsequent visit to England (1651–4) to protect the colony's charter, he published (1652) a rejoinder to an attack that Cotton had made on his *Bloudy Tenent*, and made contact with the new rulers of the country. Notable among his writings is his dictionary (1643) of the language of the natives of New England.

Winstanley, Gerrard (1609–?76) English radical agitator. A native of Lancashire, he went to London as a clothing apprentice in 1630, and set up business; but this failed by 1643 and in 1649 he was working as a hired labourer, writing religious pamphlets in his spare time. He emerged into prominence that year as one of a group of 'diggers' who began digging up common land at St George's Hill, Walton-on-Thames, Surrey, with the claim that the land was the common birthright of all. Though the Diggers (who called themselves True Levellers) were scattered, Winstanley continued producing pamphlets to publicise the cause of the underprivileged and poor. In his *The Law of Freedom* (1652) he argued for a redistribution of land to the people: 'true freedom lies in the free enjoyment of the earth'. He also rejected established religion as a deception perpetrated on the people, and desired that men should labour to better their condition on earth. He ended his life as a Quaker.

Witt, Johan de (1625–72) Dutch statesman. Son of a leading patrician family of Dordrecht, he was educated at Leiden and did the Grand Tour through France and England. He became a lawyer at The Hague, pensionary of Dordrecht (1650) and in 1653 grand pensionary of Holland, a post he retained till his death. An enemy of the house of Orange, which was backed by the provinces as a whole and by the strict Calvinist clergy, he dedicated himself to maintaining the dominance of the province of Holland and its regent class. Despite his wish for peace, which guaranteed trade, he was forced into the wars of 1652–4 and 1665–7 with England. The advent of LOUIS XIV's aggressive policies made him turn to an alliance with England (Triple Alliance 1668, including Sweden). Eventually he was overthrown by the popular coup which in 1572, in the wake of Louis XIV's invasion of the United Provinces, brought WILLIAM III of Orange to power. His brother Cornelis (1623–72) was arrested on a charge of conspiring against William, and imprisoned. In August 1572, when Johan was on his way to visit his brother in gaol, he and Cornelis were lynched by an Orangist mob. Despite the shortcomings of de Witt's policies, the years he ruled marked the high point of Dutch cultural, economic and imperial success.

Witte, Hans de (c.1585–1630) Dutch entrepreneur. Born in Amsterdam, where he appears to have made his beginnings as a trader, he first appeared in Prague in 1603 as a factor of the Dutch Calvinist firm of Nikolaus Snoukkaert, in the service of the emperors RUDOLF II and MATTHIAS. After the battle of the White Mountain (1620), he emerged as the most active financier in the country, risking his capital in the political chaos and buying up properties. Ennobled by the emperor FERDINAND II in 1624, he married the daughter of the treasurer of Bohemia. Having built up a powerful consortium that traded to Genoa, Venice and Antwerp, in 1625 he signed contracts that made him director of the financial and industrial operations on the estates of the imperial commander WALLENSTEIN. By 1627 he was one of the richest and most powerful men in Bohemia. But in 1630 the vast apparatus crumbled, he had to sell his own house, and he shot himself.

Władisław IV Vasa (1595–1648) king of Poland 1632–48. Son and successor of SIGISMUND III VASA, he was for a brief while during the Russian Time of Troubles elected tsar (1610) by the boyars, but the election was not generally accepted and there was strong opposition to the presence of the Poles, who made territorial gains in the treaty of Deulino (1618). As king, he waged a successful war against Russia, from whom he captured Smolensk (1634), in return for which he abandoned his claim to the tsardom of Muscovy. He also managed to end years of Swedish intervention by a peace treaty (1635). Recognising the confessional diversity of Poland, he granted toleration to Lutheran areas of the country, and accepted the Orthodoxy of the Ukraine. He was unable, however, to control the resistance of the Cossacks, who at the end of his reign banded together under the leadership of KHMELNITSKY.

Wolff, Christian (1679–1754) German philosopher. Born in Breslau, he went to the university of Jena to study theology then mathematics (his principal interest) and philosophy, then did further studies at Leipzig. By 1707 he was teaching mathematics in Halle, and on the recommendation of LEIBNIZ was elected to the Berlin Academy. Appointed to the Calvinist university in Marburg as professor of mathematics and philosophy, he returned to Halle in 1740 as professor of law and vice-chancellor. In 1743 he became chancellor of the university and in 1745 was made a baron of the empire. A highly influential philosopher who was one of the luminaries of the early Enlightenment, he corresponded for many years with Leibniz and founded his earlier work on the method of teaching mathematics, being the first to distinguish clearly between pure and applied sciences. His system of philosophy was meant to evolve mathematically from the simple to the complex. For him, facts derive from two principles: that of identity, the basis of all axioms; and that of sufficient reason, based on demonstration. His system was first expounded in German works published between 1713 and 1725, and then in Latin works, which sought a wider public, between 1728 and 1754. His writings covered logic, physics and ethics. By founding ethics entirely on 'reason' (i.e. as a speculative science) rather than theology, he created an influential school of rationalist philosophers.

Wolsey, Thomas (c.1473–1530) English cardinal and statesman. Son of an Ipswich butcher, he studied at Oxford, took orders, became a rector in Somerset then after other posts became parish priest in Suffolk (1506) and a chaplain to the king (1507), for whom he undertook diplomatic missions. Under HENRY VIII he continued to accumulate Church posts, and accompanied the king on his campaign in France in 1513. Henry made him bishop of Lincoln then archbishop of York (1514), and gave him other sees and benefices, secured him a cardinalate (1515) and made him lord chancellor (1515). Appointed *legatus a latere* in 1518, Wolsey's position as the pope's direct representative made him superior to all other bishops. He became wealthy, and had imposing residences (Hampton Court). As the most powerful man in England after the king, he dominated the ruling council and increased the authority of the crown. He augmented the functions of the courts of Chancery and Star Chamber, but his overriding dedication to matters of foreign policy pushed domestic concerns into second place, and his active reforms were uncompleted. Despite his international standing, he was never seriously interested in securing election as pope. He was ruined by the king's wish to divorce CATHERINE OF ARAGON. His inability to secure approval for it from Rome led to his fall from royal favour. In 1529 he was deprived of his posts and accused of treason; the disgrace hastened his death.

Wotton, Sir Henry (1568–1639) English diplomat and poet. Born in Kent, and educated at Oxford (where he became a friend of DONNE), he spent seven years (1588–94) on a grand tour of the continent, particularly Austria, Italy and France. In 1595 he entered the service of the earl of ESSEX, but left England when the earl's conspiracy was exposed and went to live in Venice and Florence. During this time he made a visit to Scotland (1602) to warn JAMES VI of a plot against him. On the succession of James to the English throne, Wotton returned home, and was knighted and appointed ambassador to Venice, where he served (with intervals) for nearly twenty years. In 1614 he entered Parliament. In these years he undertook minor diplomatic missions in Germany. On finally returning to England in 1624 he was made provost of Eton college, where he spent his leisure writing and communicating with scientists and intellectuals. He also spent much time fishing, in the company of Izaak Walton, later famous as author of *The Compleat Angler* (1653). Wotton's letters and diplomatic despatches are of great historical interest. Of the poems he wrote in his moments of leisure, the most famous is that (1619) 'On his Mistress the Queen of Bohemia'.

Wrangel, Karl Gustaf, count of Salmis (1613–76) Swedish general. His father Herman came from German-Estonian stock, and rose in the Swedish armies to become field-marshal (1621) and member of the royal council (1630). Karl was born in Sweden, also made the Swedish army his career, won his first successes against the Danes (1644) and took over command from TORSTENSSON of the Swedish armies (1646) in Germany in the Thirty Years War. He led the army that won the victory of Zusmarshausen (1648), then after the German peace took part in CHARLES X GUSTAV VASA's wars against Poland, Brandenburg and Denmark (1655–8), serving as grand admiral of the navy from 1657. Created count in 1651, he took the name of Salmis from his estates in Karelia. Field marshal (1664) and member of the regency council (1660–72) during the minority of CHARLES XI VASA, he led the forces against Brandenburg in the war of 1674–5 but was decisively defeated at Fehrbellin.

Wren, Sir Christopher (1632–1723) English architect. Son of a Wiltshire rector, educated at Oxford, he held university professorships in astronomy in Gresham College, London (1657) and later in Oxford. One of the founders of the Royal Society (president after 1680), his experiments were praised by NEWTON as important contributions to knowledge of the laws of motion. His first major architectural commission came from the bishop of London, Gilbert Sheldon, for the design and construction of the Sheldonian Theatre at Oxford (1663–8), for which he used

Sebastiano SERLIO's depiction of the ancient Roman Theatre of Marcellus as archetype. Although the general effect from the exterior is quite odd, the interior is both original and highly successful: he was able to roof the 70-foot wide auditorium without the use of interior supports. Two years after its completion he was given the commission – probably through Sheldon – to renovate Old St Paul's, which had become unsafe. In preparation he made his only visit to the Continent (1665), meeting BERNINI in Paris where he studied the rebuilding of the Louvre as well as Le Mercier's tall dome for the church of the Sorbonne. In September 1666 however, the Great Fire of London broke out, destroying Old St Paul's as well as eighty-seven churches and public buildings in the central city. This great tragedy gave Wren an unparalleled opportunity to change the face of the city. He was appointed one of three Royal Commissioners charged to supervise the rebuilding, also being named Surveyor General of the King's Works (1669), and was knighted for his efforts (1673). He reconstructed fifty-two of the churches, crowning many with new steeples of his own design. (Many, unfortunately, were destroyed during the air raids of the Second World War.) Most important was the building of New St Paul's (1668–1711), with an elevation inspired by Inigo JONES's Whitehall Banqueting House, and its famous three-layered dome with its high stone lantern.

[JH]

Wyatt, Sir Thomas, the Elder (*c*.1503–42) English diplomat and poet. Son of a leading Kentish gentleman, he was educated at Cambridge, entered the royal service and in 1527–8 joined a diplomatic mission to Italy; on his return he resumed his posts at court, and in 1533 was admitted to the privy council. A love-affair with Anne BOLEYN threatened to ruin him; he was sent to the Tower (1536) but only so that he might testify against the queen, executed that year. Knighted in 1537, he became sheriff in Kent, then ambassador to CHARLES V (1537–40), mostly in Spain and Flanders. He was sent again briefly to the Tower (1540) after the fall of Thomas CROMWELL, his protector, but justified himself, and retired to his extensive estates in Kent. One of the best minor poets of his day, he introduced the Petrarchian sonnet from Italy.

Wyatt, Sir Thomas, the Younger (1520–54) A Catholic like his father (Sir Thomas WYATT the Elder), and the only surviving son, he became prominent as a member of the conspiracy to prevent the marriage of MARY I to PHILIP II of Spain. He tried to raise Kent, and marched on London in January 1544 with 4,000 men. The attempt failed, he was arrested, tried and beheaded.

Z

Zamoyski, Jan (1542–1605) Polish statesman. From a family of great magnates dating from the fifteenth century, he was educated outside Poland, in Paris and Padua, as a humanist. In 1565 he was appointed secretary to king SIGISMUND II AUGUSTUS. During the interregnum after the death of the childless king, he first supported the election of the duke d'Anjou as king, then backed the election of his cousin Stephen I BÁTHORY, who appointed him chancellor (1578) and commander-in-chief of the army (1581). After Báthory's death, he supported SIGISMUND III VASA as king (1587), and led several military expeditions against the Turks and Swedes. He opposed some of the king's policies, particularly Polish involvement in the Time of Troubles in Muscovy. During his mandate he amassed a large fortune; his estates included eleven towns and over 200 villages.

Zápolyai, John (János) (1487–1540) king of Hungary 1526–40. Son of one of the leading noble families of Hungary, where the monarchy was by election, already when young he established himself as the leader of the most powerful noble faction, with ambitions to succeed to the throne. By leading the troops that suppressed the great peasant rising of 1514, he enhanced his claim. The advance of Turkish armies under Suleiman the Magnificent changed the political scene completely, by their defeat of the Hungarian army under king Louis II at the battle of Mohács (1526). Zápolyai was opportunely not present, and as the most prominent surviving magnate was elected next king in November that same year by the Diet at Székesfehérvár. His title, however, was questioned by Ferdinand of Habsburg (the future emperor FERDINAND I), who had himself elected king at Bratislava by a dissident noble faction in December, and invaded Hungary with superior forces the next year. Zápolyai fled to Poland and then to the Turks, whose help he obtained in recovering the throne; further struggles ended with an agreement in 1538 by which Hungary was partitioned into two kingdoms with Ferdinand as overlord and the right to resume control over the whole realm if Zápolyai died childless.

Zevi, Sabbatai (1626–76) Jewish messianic leader. Born in Smyrna into a wealthy family of Ashkenazi origin, he was destined by his family for a rabbinic career and educated accordingly, picking up also some Kabbalistic learning. From his late teens he began to draw apart from others and spend his time in mystical contemplation, and in the late 1640s began to claim that he was the Messiah, for which he was duly expelled by the Jewish community; he moved to Salonika and Istanbul, returning to Smyrna in 1662. He then undertook a more extensive journey, to

Jerusalem and Cairo, in which city he married a girl of Polish origin. In Gaza in 1665 he had a fateful meeting with a holy man, Nathan, who announced that Sabbatai was the true Messiah. The latter accepted the identification, which only confirmed his own visions, and duly announced the news, which took the Jewish communities of Palestine by storm. Despite some opposition, the movement spread, and the news filtered through western Europe. Returning to Smyrna, Sabbatai managed to excite a movement of popular enthusiasm among the Jews; scenes of wild hysteria were recorded. He promised the fulfilment of the prophecies, an end to Turkish rule, and freedom for women. In western Europe many Jews, especially in Amsterdam, knowing that the new movement had originated in the Holy Land, gave it their fervent support. Though Sabbatai was arrested by the Turkish authorities in 1666, the movement continued its triumph throughout the Jewish communities of Europe, with few dissenting voices. In September 1666 the Turks offered Sabbatai a choice between death or conversion to Islam, whereupon he surprisingly accepted the latter. The news of the apostasy began the collapse of the prophetic movement. Sabbatai lived as a Muslim until 1672 in Istanbul, then in 1673 was deported to Albania, where he died. The biggest apocalyptic movement in Jewish history, Sabbatianism continued to linger on as a live belief well into the eighteenth century, especially in the Mediterranean and central Europe.

Zinzendorf, Nikolaus Ludwig, count von (1700–60) Moravian leader. Born in Dresden, son of a noble state official whose family originated in Lower Austria, he was brought up in a deeply religious family, studied law at Wittenberg and did the grand tour through Europe. He took up a post at the Saxon court (1721), then turned his attention to lands he inherited from his family and in 1722 founded a

religious community on his estate at Bethelsdorf in Saxony. Here he received Christians fleeing from persecution elsewhere, in particular a group of refugees from Moravia. He befriended the Moravian Brethren and created for them the colony of Herrnhut (1727); in so doing he became convinced of the value of small communities as the true form of brotherly Christianity. He became a Lutheran pastor in 1734, but three years later accepted the status of Moravian bishop and thereafter dedicated his life to promoting the beliefs of the Brethren. He travelled widely, set up further communities in Germany, the Baltic and the Netherlands, explored the possibility of settlements in the West Indies, and visited England, where he made contact with John WESLEY. From 1741 to 1743 he was in Pennsylvania and New York, creating new congregations. He returned to Saxony in 1747, and died at Herrnhut. His ecumenical spirit and tolerance, and the emphasis on personal fulfilment in small communities, breathed a new spirit into Protestant religion on both sides of the Atlantic.

Zurbarán, Francisco de (1598–1664) Spanish painter. Born in Fuente de Cantos (Badajoz), and active in Llerena (1617–29), Seville, where he settled at the invitation of the city council, refusing to take the examination ordered by the Painters' Guild; and Madrid (1634 and 1659–64), where he was living when he died. Considered somewhat primitive by his contemporaries, his major works include those in Seville for the church of the Trinidad Calzada, the Mercedarian Library, the Colegio Mayor Universitario, the city hall and the Charterhouse; the monastery church of San Jerónimo in Guadalupe; and twelve canvases for the Buen Retiro palace in Madrid. He also produced a large amount of work for export to South America (1640–58), particularly to Lima, Peru.

[JH]

Zwingli, Huldrych (1484–1531) Swiss religious reformer. Born in Wildhaus (St Gall), son of a local official, he was educated locally, then in Vienna and at the university of Basel (1502–6). He took orders and became parish priest at Glarus (1506–16), a fruitful period in which he studied the Church fathers and improved his knowledge of the classical languages, but also witnessed the carnage at the battle of Marignano (1515). In 1516 he transferred to Einsiedeln and in 1518 was appointed a priest in the cathedral at Zürich. His early sympathy for ERASMUS had now become more radical, and with the support of the city council in 1523 he began to introduce the Reformation. In 1525 the mass was abolished in Zürich. He faced, however, disagreement not only from the Catholics but also from LUTHER and from the locally active Anabaptists. He met Luther and others at the Marburg colloquy (1529), but failed to resolve differences over the doctrine of the Eucharist. The Anabaptists were invited to public disputations, but later treated with violence. Defence against the Catholic cantons was the biggest problem. Unable to win the military alliance of neighbouring Bern, which he had helped to win for the Reformation (1528), he felt that attack was the surest safety, and after an initial conflict which ended in a truce took the field alone against the Catholic cantons. His forces were overwhelmed on the field at Kappel, and Zwingli, armed and fighting, died in the battle.